C0-ARC-530

IMPORTANT

HERE IS YOUR REGISTRATION CODE TO ACCESS MCGRAW-HILL
PREMIUM CONTENT AND MCGRAW-HILL ONLINE RESOURCES

For key premium online resources you need THIS CODE to
gain access. Once the code is entered, you will be able to
use the web resources for the length of your course.

Access is provided only if you have purchased a new book.

If the registration code is missing from this book, the registration screen on our
website, and within your WebCT or Blackboard course will tell you how to obtain
your new code. Your registration code can be used only once to establish access.
It is not transferable.

To gain access to these online resources

1. USE your web browser to go to: **www.mhhe.com/chambers9**

2. CLICK on "First Time User"

3. ENTER the Registration Code printed on the tear-off bookmark on the right

4. After you have entered your registration code, click on "Register"

5. FOLLOW the instructions to setup your personal UserID and Password

6. WRITE your UserID and Password down for future reference. Keep it in a safe place.

If your course is using WebCT or Blackboard, you'll be able to use this code to
access the McGraw-Hill content within your instructor's online course.

To gain access to the McGraw-Hill content in your instructor's WebCT or
Blackboard course simply log into the course with the user ID and Password
provided by your instructor. Enter the registration code exactly as it appears to
the right when prompted by the system. You will only need to use this code the
first time you click on McGraw-Hill content.

These instructions are specifically for student access. Instructors are not required
to register via the above instructions.

The McGraw-Hill Companies

Higher Education

ISBN 13: 978-0-07-325089-2
ISBN 10: 0-07-325089-9

Thank you, and welcome to your
McGraw-Hill Online Resources.

3NHC-QJ6N-MT64-MNE4-BQ6J

REGISTRATION CODE
REGISTRATION CODE

The McGraw-Hill Companies

Higher Education

Mc Graw Hill

THE WESTERN EXPERIENCE

VOLUME B:
THE EARLY MODERN ERA

THE WESTERN EXPERIENCE

Ninth Edition

MORTIMER CHAMBERS
University of California, Los Angeles

BARBARA HANAWALT
The Ohio State University

THEODORE K. RABB
Princeton University

ISSER WOLOCH
Columbia University

RAYMOND GREW
University of Michigan

LISA TIERSTEN
Barnard College

Boston   Burr Ridge, IL   Dubuque, IA   Madison, WI   New York   San Francisco   St. Louis
Bangkok   Bogotá   Caracas   Kuala Lumpur   Lisbon   London   Madrid   Mexico City
Milan   Montreal   New Delhi   Santiago   Seoul   Singapore   Sydney   Taipei   Toronto

Higher Education

THE WESTERN EXPERIENCE, VOLUME B: THE EARLY MODERN ERA
Published by McGraw-Hill, a business unit of The McGraw-Hill Companies, Inc., 1221 Avenue of the Americas, New York, NY, 10020. Copyright © 2007, 2003, 1999, 1995, 1991, 1987, 1983, 1979, 1974 by The McGraw-Hill Companies, Inc. All rights reserved. No part of this publication may be reproduced or distributed in any form or by any means, or stored in a database or retrieval system, without the prior written consent of The McGraw-Hill Companies, Inc., including, but not limited to, in any network or other electronic storage or transmission, or broadcast for distance learning.

Some ancillaries, including electronic and print components, may not be available to customers outside the United States.

This book is printed on acid-free paper.

1 2 3 4 5 6 7 8 9 0 DOW/DOW 0 9 8 7 6

ISBN-13: 978-0-07-325084-7
ISBN-10: 0-07-325084-8

Vice President and Editor-in-Chief: *Emily Barrosse*
Publisher: *Lyn Uhl*
Senior Sponsoring Editor: *Monica Eckman*
Director of Development: *Lisa Pinto*
Developmental Editor: *Angela W. Kao*
Permissions Coordinator: *The Permissions Group*
Marketing Manager: *Katherine Bates*
Managing Editor: *Jean Dal Porto*
Project Manager: *Emily Hatteberg*
Art Director: *Jeanne Schreiber*
Art Editor: *Ayelet Arbel*
Lead Designer: *Gino Cieslik*
Cover and Interior Designer: *Ellen Pettengell*
Cover credit: *Paul Delaroche,* The Conquerors of the Bastille before the Hotel de Ville, *1839 Musée du Petit Palais, Paris, France. Erich Lessing/Art Resource, NY*
Senior Photo Research Coordinator: *Alexandra Ambrose*
Photo Research: *Photosearch, Inc., New York*
Senior Production Supervisor: *Carol A. Bielski*
Lead Media Producer: *Sean Crowley*
Media Project Manager: *Kate Boylan*
Composition: *9.5/12 Trump, by Carlisle Publishing Services*
Printing: *45 # Pub Matte Plus, R.R. Donnelley & Sons*

Credits: The credits section for this book begins on page C-1 and is considered an extension of the copyright page.

Library of Congress Cataloging-in-Publication Data

The Western experience / Mortimer Chambers ... [et al,].—9th ed. [main text]
    6 v. cm.
    Includes bibliographical references and index.
    ISBN-13: 978-0-07-288369-5 (alk. paper)
    ISBN-10: 0-07-288369-3 (alk. paper)
    1. Civilization—History. 2. Civilization, Western—History. I. Chambers, Mortimer.
  CB59.W38 2007
  909'.09821—dc22

                                          2006041940

The Internet addresses listed in the text were accurate at the time of publication. The inclusion of a Web site does not indicate an endorsement by the authors or McGraw-Hill, and McGraw-Hill does not guarantee the accuracy of the information presented at these sites.

www.mhhe.com

About the Authors

Mortimer Chambers is Professor of History at the University of California at Los Angeles. He was a Rhodes Scholar from 1949 to 1952 and received an M.A. from Wadham College, Oxford, in 1955 after obtaining his doctorate from Harvard University in 1954. He has taught at Harvard University (1954–1955) and the University of Chicago (1955–1958). He was Visiting Professor at the University of British Columbia in 1958, the State University of New York at Buffalo in 1971, the University of Freiburg (Germany) in 1974, and Vassar College in 1988. A specialist in Greek and Roman history, he is coauthor of *Aristotle's History of Athenian Democracy* (1962), editor of a series of essays entitled *The Fall of Rome* (1963), and author of *Georg Busolt: His Career in His Letters* (1990) and of *Staat der Athener*, a German translation and commentary to Aristotle's *Constitution of the Athenians* (1990). He has edited Greek texts of the latter work (1986) and of the *Hellenica Oxyrhynchia* (1993). He has contributed articles to the *American Historical Review* and *Classical Philology* as well as to other journals, both in America and in Europe. He is also an editor of *Historia*, the international journal of ancient history.

Barbara Hanawalt holds the King George III Chair of British History at The Ohio State University and is the author of numerous books and articles on the social and cultural history of the Middle Ages. Her publications include *The Middle Ages: An Illustrated History* (1999), *'Of Good and Ill Repute': Gender and Social Control in Medieval England* (1998), *Growing Up in Medieval London: The Experience of Childhood in History* (1993), *The Ties That Bound: Peasant Life in Medieval England* (1986), and *Crime and Conflict in English Communities, 1300–1348* (1979). She received her M.A. in 1964 and her Ph.D. in 1970, both from the University of Michigan. She has served as president of the Social Science History Association and the Medieval Academy of America and has been on the Council of the American Historical Association and the Medieval Academy of America. She was a fellow of the Netherlands Institute for Advanced Study (2005–2006), a fellow of the Guggenheim Foundation (1998–1999), an ACLS Fellow in 1975–1976, a fellow at the National Humanities Center (1997–1998), a fellow at the Wissenschaftskolleg in Berlin (1990–1991), a member of the School of Historical Research at the Institute for Advanced Study, and a senior research fellow at the Newberry Library in 1979–1980.

Theodore K. Rabb is Professor of History at Princeton University. He received his Ph.D. from Princeton in 1961 and subsequently taught at Stanford, Northwestern, Harvard, and Johns Hopkins universities. He is the author of numerous articles and reviews in journals such as *The New York Times* and the *Times Literary Supplement*, and he has been editor of *The Journal of Interdisciplinary History* since its foundation. Among his books are *The Struggle for Stability in Early Modern Europe* (1975), *Renaissance Lives* (1993), and *Jacobean Gentleman* (1999). He has won awards from the Guggenheim Foundation, the National Endowment for the Humanities, the American Historical Association, and the National Council for History Education. He was the principal historian for the PBS series *Renaissance*, which was nominated for an Emmy.

Isser Woloch is Moore Collegiate Professor of History at Columbia University. He received his Ph.D. (1965) from Princeton University in the field of eighteenth- and nineteenth-century European history. He has taught at Indiana University and at the University of California at Los Angeles, where, in 1967, he received a Distinguished Teaching Citation. He has been a fellow of the ACLS, the National Endowment for the Humanities, the Guggenheim Foundation, and the Institute for Advanced Study at Princeton. His publications include *Jacobin Legacy: The Democratic Movement under the Directory* (1970), *The Peasantry in the Old Regime: Conditions and Protests* (1970), *The French Veteran from the Revolution to the Restoration* (1979), *Eighteenth-Century Europe: Tradition and Progress, 1715–1789* (1982), *The New Regime: Transformations of the French Civic Order, 1789–1820s* (1994), *Revolution and the Meanings of Freedom in the Nineteenth Century* (1996), and *Napoleon and His Collaborators: The Making of a Dictatorship* (2001).

Raymond Grew is Professor of History Emeritus at the University of Michigan. He has also taught at Brandeis University, Princeton University, and at the Écoles des Hautes Études en Sciences Sociales in Paris. He earned both his M.A. and Ph.D. from Harvard University in the field of modern European history. He has been a Fulbright Fellow to Italy and a Fulbright Travelling Fellow to Italy and to France, a Guggenheim Fellow, and a Fellow of the National Endowment for the Humanities. In 1962 he received the Chester Higby Prize from the American Historical Association, and in 1963 the Italian government awarded him the Unità d'Italia Prize; in 1992 he received the David Pinkney Prize of the Society for French Historical Studies and in 2000 a citation for career achievement from the Society for Italian Historical Studies. He has twice served as national chair of the Council for European Studies, was for many years the editor of the international quarterly *Comparative Studies in Society and History*, and is one of the directors of the Global History Group. His recent publications include essays on historical comparison, global history, Catholicism in the nineteenth century, fundamentalism, and Italian culture and politics. His books include *A Sterner Plan for Italian Unity* (1963), *Crises of Development in Europe and the United States* (1978), *School, State, and Society: The Growth of Elementary Schooling in Nineteenth-Century France* (1991), with Patrick J. Harrigan, and two edited volumes: *Food in Global History* (1999) and *The Construction of Minorities* (2001).

Lisa Tiersten is Associate Professor of History at Barnard College, Columbia University. She received her Ph.D. (1991) at Yale University and has taught at Wellesley College and Barnard College. She has been the recipient of a Chateaubriand Fellowship, a French Historical Studies Society Fellowship, and a Getty Fellowship. She also received the Emily Gregory Teaching Award at Barnard College in 1996. Her publications include *Marianne in the Market: Envisioning Consumer Society in Fin-de-Siècle France* (2001). She is currently at work on a history of bankruptcy and the culture of credit in modern France, entitled *Terms of Trade: The Capitalist Imagination in Modern France*, and on an edited volume on the comparative history of children's rights in twentieth-century Europe. Her research interests include modern France, gender, consumer culture, empire, and the comparative culture of capitalism.

This book is dedicated to the memory of David Herlihy, whose erudition and judgment were central to its creation and whose friendship and example continue to inspire his coauthors.

Brief Contents

Contents

Chapter 16

CULTURE AND SOCIETY IN THE AGE OF THE SCIENTIFIC REVOLUTION 459

Chapter 17

THE EMERGENCE OF THE EUROPEAN STATE SYSTEM 491

Chapter 21

THE AGE OF NAPOLEON 615

Maps

Boxes

Primary Source Boxes

Historical Issues Boxes

Chronological Boxes

Global Moment Boxes

Preface

When *The Western Experience* was originally conceived, we sought to write a textbook that would introduce students to the growing field of social history and exciting new ways of thinking about history. We wanted the textbook not merely to set forth information but to serve as an example of historical writing. That means we cared a lot about the quality of the writing itself and also that we wanted the chapters to be examples of a historical essay that set up a historical problem and developed arguments about that problem using historical evidence. We also recognized that for American students the Western Civilization textbook needed to provide an overview of that civilization, giving students an introduction to the major achievements in Western thought, art, and science as well as the social, political, and economic context for understanding them. And lastly, we were determined that our book would treat all these various aspects of history in an integrated way. Too many books, we felt, dealt with cultural or social change entirely separately, even in separate chapters, and we sought to demonstrate and exemplify the connections. To that end, *The Western Experience* is designed to provide an analytical and reasonably comprehensive account of the contexts within which, and the processes by which, European society and civilization evolved.

Now in the ninth edition, this book has evolved with the strength of prior revisions, including Barbara Hanawalt's impressive rewriting and reordering of the six chapters that cover the Middle Ages for the seventh edition. To continue that evolution, we are proud to welcome another distinguished scholar, Lisa Tiersten of Barnard College, to our author team. She has written a new chapter on nineteenth-century empires (chapter 26), one of the first among western civilization textbooks, and she has undertaken the substantial revision and reorganization of chapters 25 and 27. With a fresh voice and lucid approach, Dr. Tiersten has greatly enriched the coverage in these chapters by incorporating recent research on gender, bourgeois and consumer culture, imperialism, technology, and globalization.

EXPERIENCING HISTORY

Everyone uses history. We use it to define who we are and to connect our personal experience to the collective memory of the groups to which we belong, including a particular region, nation, and culture. We invoke the past to explain our hopes and ambitions and to justify our fears and conflicts. The Charter of the United Nations, like the American Declaration of Independence, is based on a view of history. When workers strike or armies march, they cite the lessons of their history. Because history is so important to us psychologically and intellectually, historical understanding is always shifting and often controversial.

Historical knowledge is cumulative. Historians may ask many of the same questions about different periods of history or raise new questions or issues; they integrate the answers, and historical knowledge grows. The study of history cannot be a subjective exercise in which all opinions are equally valid. Regardless of the impetus for a particular historical question, the answer to it stands until overturned by better evidence. We now know more about the past than ever before, and we understand it as the people we study could not. Unlike them, we know the outcome of their history; we can apply methods they did not have, and often we have evidence they never saw.

Humans have always found pleasure in the reciting and reading of history. The poems about the fall of Troy or the histories of Herodotus and Thucydides entertained the ancient Greeks. The biographies of great men and women, dramatic accounts of important events, colorful tales of earlier times can be fascinating in themselves. Through these encounters with history we experience the common concerns of all people; and through the study of European history, we come to appreciate the ideals and conflicts, the failures and accidents, the social needs and human choices that formed the Western world in which we live. Knowing the historical context also enriches our appreciation for the achievements of European culture, enabling us to see its art, science, ideas, and politics in relationship to real people, specific interests, and burning issues.

We think of Europe's history as the history of Western civilization because the Greeks gave the names east and west to the points on the horizon at which the sun rises and sets. Because the Persian Empire and India lay to their east, the Greeks labeled their own continent, which they called Europe, the west. However, we need to be cautious about the view that Western civilization is a united whole, entirely distinct from other civilizations, except perhaps in its cultural development. We will see many occasions when a larger context is appropriate.

The Western Experience thus gives primary attention to a small part of the world and honors a particular cultural tradition. Yet the concentration on Europe does allow us to explore contrasts of worldwide significance; between city and rural life; among empires and monarchies and republics; in life before and after industrialization; among societies that organized labor through markets, serfdom, and slavery; between cultures little concerned with science and those that used changing scientific knowledge; among different ways of creating and experiencing forms of literature and the arts; and among Christian and non-Christian religions and all the major forms of Christianity.

A college course alone cannot create an educated citizen. Moreover, Western history is not the only history a person should know, and an introductory survey is not necessarily the best way to learn it. Yet, as readers consider and then challenge interpretations offered in this text, they will exercise critical and analytical skills. They can begin to overcome the parochialism that attributes importance only to the present. To learn to think critically about historical evidence and know how to formulate an argument on the bases of this evidence is to experience the study of history as one of the vital intellectual activities by which we come to know who and where we are.

A BALANCED, INTERPRETIVE, AND FLEXIBLE APPROACH

At the same time, we recognize that the professional scholar's preference for new perspectives over familiar ones makes a distinction that students may not share. For them, the latest interpretations need to be integrated with established understandings and controversies, with the history of people and events that are part of our cultural lore. We recognize that a textbook should provide a coherent presentation of the basic information from which students can begin to form their historical understanding. We believe this information must be part of an interpretive history but also that its readers—teachers, students, and general readers—should be free to use it in many different ways and in conjunction with their own areas of special knowledge and their own interests and curiosity.

USE OF THEMES

Throughout this book, from the treatment of the earliest civilizations to the discussion of the present, we pursue certain key themes. These seven themes constitute a set of categories by which societies and historical change can be analyzed.

Social Structure   In early chapters, social structure involves how the land was settled, divided among its inhabitants, and put to use. Later discussions of how property is held must include corporate, communal, and individual ownership, then investment banking and companies that sell shares. Similarly, in each era we treat the division of labor, noting whether workers are slave or free, male or female, and when there are recognized specialists in fighting or crafts or trade. The chapters covering the ancient world, the Middle Ages, and the early modern period explore social hierarchies that include nobles, clergy, commoners, and slaves or serfs; the treatments of the French Revolution, the Industrial Revolution, and twentieth-century societies analyze modern social classes.

The Body Politic   Another theme we analyze throughout this book is what used to be called the body politic. Each era contains discussions of how political power is acquired and used and of the political structures that result. Students learn about the role of law from ancient codes to the present, as well as problems of order, and the formation of governments, including why government functions have increased and political participation of the population has changed.

Technology   From cultivation in the plains of the Tigris and Euphrates to the global economy, we follow changes in the organization of production and in the impact of technology. We note how goods are distributed, and we observe patterns of trade as avenues of cultural exchange in addition to wealth. We look at the changing economic role of governments and the impact of economic theories.

Gender Roles and Family The evolution of the family and changing gender roles are topics fundamental to every historical period. Families give form to daily life and kinship structures. The history of demography, migration, and work is also a history of the family. The family has always been a central focus of social organization and religion, as well as the principal instrument by which societies assign specific practices, roles, and values to women and men. Gender roles have changed from era to era, differing according to social class and between rural and urban societies. Observing gender roles across time, the student discovers that social, political, economic, and cultural history are always interrelated; that the present is related to the past; and that social change brings gains and losses rather than evolution in a straight line—three lessons all history courses teach.

War No history of Europe could fail to pay attention to war, which, for most polities, has been their most demanding activity. Warfare has strained whatever resources were available from ancient times to the present, leading governments to invent new ways to extract wealth and mobilize support. War has built and undermined states, stimulated science and consumed technology, made heroes, and restructured nobility, schooling, and social services. Glorified in European culture and often condemned, war in every era has affected the lives of all its peoples. This historical significance, more than specific battles, is one of the themes of *The Western Experience*.

Religion Religion has been basic to the human experience, and our textbook explores the different religious institutions and experiences that societies developed. Religion affects and is affected by all the themes we address, creating community and causing conflict, shaping intellectual and daily life, providing the experiences that bind individual lives and society within a common system of meaning.

Cultural Expression For authors of a general history, no decision is more difficult than the space devoted to cultural expression. In this respect, as elsewhere, we have striven for a balance between high and popular culture. We present as clearly and concisely as possible the most important formal ideas, philosophies, and ideologies of each era. We emphasize concepts of recognized importance in the general history of ideas and those concepts that illuminate behavior and discourse in a given period. We pay particular attention to developments in science that we believe are related to important intellectual, economic, and social trends. Popular culture appears both in specific sections and throughout the book. We want to place popular culture within its social and historical con-

text but not make the gulf too wide between popular and high or formal culture. Finally, we write about many of the great works of literature, art, architecture, and music. Because of the difficulties of selection, we have tried to emphasize works that are cultural expressions of their time but that also have been influential over the ages and around the globe.

Attention to these seven themes occasions problems of organization and selection. We could have structured this book around a series of topical essays, perhaps repeating the series of themes for each of the standard chronological divisions of European history. Instead, we chose to preserve a narrative flow that emphasizes interrelationships and historical context. We wanted each chapter to stand as an interpretive historical essay, with a beginning and conclusion. As a result, the themes emerge repeatedly within discussions of a significant event, an influential institution, an individual life, or a whole period of time. Or they may intersect in a single institution or historical trend. Nevertheless, readers can follow any one of these themes across time and use that theme as a measure of change and a way to assess the differences and similarities between societies.

CHANGES TO THE NINTH EDITION

For us the greatest pleasure in a revision lies in the challenge of absorbing and then incorporating the latest developments in historical understanding. From its first edition, this book included more of the results of quantitative and social history than most general textbooks of European history, an obvious reflection of our own research. Each subsequent edition provided an occasion to incorporate current methods and new knowledge, such as the rise of gender studies: a challenge that required reconsidering paragraphs, sections, and whole chapters in the light of new theories and new research, sometimes literally reconceptualizing part of the past.

Newly Revised Chapter 25: "Progress and Its Discontents"

From the last edition, chapters 25 and 26, "European Power: Wealth, Knowledge, and Imperialism" and "The Age of Progress," have been combined into a new chapter 25, "Progress and Its Discontents." Relevant material on imperial Europe has been moved to chapter 26. This new chapter 25 treats late-nineteenth-century economic transformations that brought the bourgeoisie to power along with the intellectual developments that both reinforced that power and raised doubts about its bases and its legitimacy. It also explores the class identity of the new ruling elite and examines both the pleasures and anxieties evoked by the mass commercial culture it created.

New Chapter 26: "Nineteenth-Century Empires"

In the past fifteen years, European historians increasingly have acknowledged the centrality of imperial experience to European history. Spanning a long nineteenth century from 1780 to 1914, this chapter not only explores the impact of major European economic, cultural, and political developments on imperial practice and attitudes, but also explores the profound impact of imperialism on Europe itself (making use of new scholarship on gender and popular culture, for example, to show how empire increasingly touched upon the lives of everyday Europeans). The chapter thus argues that empire did not happen "out there," but at the center of nineteenth-century European society and culture. This chapter includes fresh new illustrations and photographs, primary source boxes, and a Global Moment box on the Indian Rebellion of 1857.

Newly Revised Chapter 27: "World War I and the World It Created"

The revised chapter 27 brings to bear new scholarship on the war, including research on gender relations and the home front and on the imperial dimension of war. It emphasizes in particular how the military mobilization of the colonies—combined with the postwar rhetoric of national self-determination—raised expectations of colonial reform and gradual self-government. When these hopes were disappointed in the postwar period, the chapter shows, colonial reform movements were transformed into militant movements for colonial independence.

Streamlined Narrative throughout the Book

All of the chapters in the ninth edition have been substantially shortened and streamlined. We have worked to make difficult concepts more understandable and to remove material that interfered with the general flow of the text.

New Global Moment Features

The process whereby worldwide connections have intensified in the past two centuries, usually referred to as globalization, has caused a revision in the way we think about the histories of individual states and regions. Although revolutions in communications and transport have made the interconnections inescapable since the 1800s, it is important to see them in perspective and to pay attention to early signs of cross-cultural activity. Five Global Moment boxed essays highlight significant occasions when Europeans had to come to terms with neighbors in other continents. And we have tried, throughout, to keep students aware of the larger context within which European history has developed.

PEDAGOGICAL FEATURES

Each generation of students brings different experiences, interests, and training into the classroom—changes that are important to the teaching-learning process. The students we teach have taught us what engages or confuses them, what impression of European history they bring to college, and what they can be expected to take from a survey course. Current political, social, and cultural events also shape what we teach and how we teach. Our experience as teachers and the helpful comments of scores of other teachers have led to revisions and new additions throughout the book as we have sought to make it clearer and more accessible without sacrificing our initial goal of writing a reasonably sophisticated, interpretive, and analytic history.

Primary Source Boxes

These excerpts from primary sources are designed to illustrate or supplement points made in the text, to provide some flavor of the issues under discussion, and to allow beginning students some of that independence of judgment that comes from a careful reading of historical sources.

"THEY HAVE A MASTER CALLED LAW"

As King Xerxes leads his army into Greece in 480 B.C., he asks a former king of Sparta, who is accompanying him, whether the Greeks will really fight against the Persians.

"Now, Demaratus, I will ask you what I want to know. You are a Greek and one from no minor or weak city. So now tell me, will the Greeks stand and fight me?" Demaratus replied, "Your Majesty, shall I tell you the truth, or say what you want to hear?" The king ordered him to tell the truth, saying that he would respect him no less for doing so.

"Your Majesty," he said, "I am not speaking about all of them, only about the Spartans. First, I say they will never accept conditions from you that would enslave Greece; second, that they will fight you in battle even if all the other Greeks join your side."

Xerxes said, "Demaratus, let's look at it in all logic: why should a thousand, or ten thousand, or fifty thousand men, if they are all free and not ruled by a single master, stand up against such an army as mine? If they were ruled by one man, like my subjects, I suppose they might, out of fear, show more bravery than usual and, driven into battle by the lash, go up against a bigger force; but if allowed their freedom, they wouldn't do either one."

Demaratus said, "Your Majesty, I knew from the beginning that if I spoke the truth you wouldn't like my message, but, since you ordered me to do so, I told you about the Spartans. They are free men, but not wholly free: They have a master called Law, whom they fear far more than your soldiers fear you. And his orders are always the same—they must not run away from any army no matter how big, but must stand in their formation and either conquer or die. But, your Majesty, may your wishes be fulfilled."

From *Herodotus*, book VII, M. H. Chambers (tr.).

Historical Issues Boxes

These boxes explain major controversies over historical interpretations so that students can see how historical understanding is constructed. They encourage students to participate in these debates and formulate their own positions.

New *Global Moment Boxes*

These boxes focus on particularly vivid occasions when Europeans encountered other world civilizations, in order to suggest the broader context within which Western history unfolded.

HISTORICAL ISSUES: TWO VIEWS OF LOUIS XIV

Implicit in any assessment of the reign of Louis XIV in France is a judgment about the nature of absolutism and the kind of government the continental European monarchies created in the late seventeenth and eighteenth centuries. From the perspective of Frenchman Albert Sorel, a historian of the French Revolution writing at the end of the nineteenth century, the Revolution had been necessary to save France from Louis' heritage. For the American John Rule, a historian who concerned himself primarily with the development of political institutions during the seventeenth century, the marks of Louis XIV's rule were caution, bureaucracy, and order.

Sorel: "The edifice of the state enjoyed incomparable brilliance and splendor, but it resembled a Gothic cathedral in which the height of the nave and the arches had been pushed beyond all reason, weakening the walls as they were raised ever higher. Louis XIV carried the principle of monarchy to its utmost limit, and abused it in all respects to the point of excess. He left the nation crushed by war, mutilated by banishments, and impatient of the yoke which it felt to be ruinous. Men were worn-out, the treasury empty, all relationships strained by the violence of tension, and in the immense framework of the state there remained no institution except the accidental appearance of genius. Things had reached a point where, if a great king did not appear, there would be a great revolution."

From Albert Sorel, *L'Europe et la rèvolution française,* 3rd ed., Vol. 1, Paris, 1893, p. 199, as translated in William F. Church (ed.), *The Greatness of Louis XIV: Myth or Reality?,* Boston: D. C. Heath, 1959, p. 63.

Rule: "As Louis XIV himself said of the tasks of kingship, they were at once great, noble, and delightful. Yet Louis' enjoyment of his craft was tempered by political prudence. At an early age he learned to listen attentively to his advisers, to speak when spoken to, to ponder evidence, to avoid confrontations, to dissemble, to wait. He believed that time and tact would conquer. Despite all the evidence provided him by his ministers and his servants, Louis often hesitated before making a decision; he brooded, and in some instances put off decisions altogether. As he grew older, the king tended to hide his person and his office. Even his officials seldom saw the king for more than a brief interview. And as decision-making became centralized in the hands of the ministers, [so] the municipalities, the judges, the local estates, the guilds and at times the peasantry contested royal encroachments on their rights. Yet to many in the kingdom, Louis represented a modern king, an agent of stability whose struggle was their struggle and whose goal was to contain the crises of the age."

From John C. Rule, "Louis XIV, *Roi-Bureaucrate,*" in Rule (ed.), *Louis XIV and the Craft of Kingship,* Columbus: Ohio State University Press, 1969, pp. 91–92.

Global Moment

THREE EMPIRES AND AN ELEPHANT

Although trade and diplomatic ties between the West and the East diminished in the period of the seventh through the tenth centuries, merchants, pilgrims, envoys, and religious officials still traveled extensively and spread news. If we look at events surrounding the year 800, we find that diplomatic missions among the Franks (a Germanic kingdom), the Byzantines (the Eastern Roman Empire), and the Abbasid caliphate (an Arabic-speaking Muslim empire) continued. The main actors in these negotiations and contacts were Charles the Great or Charlemagne (r. 768–814), king of the Franks and, as of Christmas Day 800, Roman emperor in the West; Irene (r. 796–802), who became empress of Roman Empire in the East after she blinded her son, who subsequently died; and the Caliph Harun al-Rashid (786–809), heir to the Abbasid Dynasty, centered in Baghdad in Persia.

These three rulers dominated the area around the Mediterranean, but their empires were vastly different in terms of economic sophistication, religion, and in-

the scholars were the world's leaders in medicine and science. A great hospital flourished in this period. Harun al-Rashid was said to have sponsored the "golden age" for the Arabic world. It took centuries for Arab learning in geography, astronomy, and medicine to reach the West. Charlemagne's court in Aachen was a long way from this intellectual achievement and cultural splendor.

The three empires had a history of clashes. The Arabic expansions had left the Eastern Roman Empire with far less territory. The Franks and other Germanic tribes had taken over the Western Empire and established independent kingdoms, with the Franks conquering most of them. Charlemagne, as King of the Franks, wanted the title of emperor. But before 800, no other Germanic ruler had had the audacity to take the title of emperor of the Romans, and he had some trepidation over assuming the title without permission or blessings of the real successor to the title in Constantinople. The Franks and the Arabs also had considerable conflicts. After all, Charlemagne's grandfather, Charles Martel, had defeated the Arabs 70 years before (732) and he,

Among the many exotic gifts that Harun al-Rashid gave to Charlemagne was, perhaps, this crystal pitcher. It is certainly a piece of late eighth or early ninth century craftsmanship from Persia. It has long been assumed that this pitcher was among the gifts.
To come

was a rash hope, if he ever had it. He could not, as a Christian, make a real alliance with Arabs. The Church forbade such treaties with non-Christians. What did Charlemagne hope to gain with such a diplomatic overture?

Although the Arabic sources are silent about the exchange, Carolingian sources speak of diplomatic mis-

and the governor of Egypt back with a white elephant named Abu l'-Abbas from India. The elephant and Isaac took four years to travel from Baghdad to Jerusalem and then on to Carthage. From there they went by ship to Italy. It is not clear what ship would have been large enough to hold an elephant in 800. Waiting until spring to cross the Alps, Isaac and the Abu l'-Abbas arrived in

New *Chapter-Opening Timelines*

Each chapter now opens with a new timeline. These timelines are meant to offer students a visual aid with which to track simultaneous developments and important dates to remember. Ultimately, we hope that they will help give readers a grounded sense of chronology.

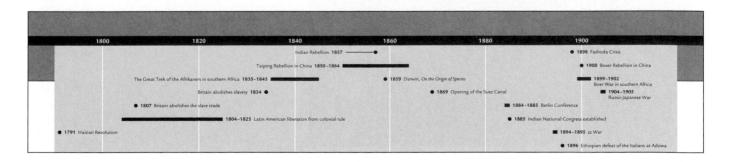

Chapter Twenty

THE FRENCH REVOLUTION

REFORM AND POLITICAL CRISIS • 1789: THE FRENCH REVOLUTION •
THE RECONSTRUCTION OF FRANCE • THE SECOND REVOLUTION

Well into the eighteenth century, the long-standing social structures and political institutions of Europe were securely entrenched. Most monarchs still claimed to hold their authority directly from God. In cooperation with their aristocracies, they presided over realms composed of distinct orders of citizens, or *estates* as they were sometimes known. Each order had its particular rights, privileges, and obligations. But pressures for change were building during the century. In France, the force of public opinion grew increasingly potent by the 1780s. A financial or political crisis that could normally be managed by the monarchy threatened to snowball in this new environment. Such vulnerability was less evident in Austria, Prussia, and Russia, however, where strong monarchs instituted reforms to streamline their governments. Similarly, in Britain the political system proved resilient despite explosions of discontent at home and across the Atlantic.

Unquestionably, then, the French Revolution constituted the pivotal event of European history in the late eighteenth century. From its outbreak in 1789, the Revolution transformed the nature of sovereignty and law in France. Under its impetus, civic and social institutions were renewed, from local government and schooling to family relations and assistance for the poor. Soon its ideals of liberty, equality, and fraternity resonated across the borders of other European states, especially after war broke out in 1792 and French armies took the offensive.

The French Revolution's innovations defined the foundations of a liberal society and polity. Both at home and abroad, however, the new regime faced formidable opposition, and its struggle for survival propelled it in unanticipated directions. Some unforeseen turns, such as democracy and republicanism, became precedents for the future even if they soon aborted. Other developments, such as the Reign of Terror, seemed to nullify the original liberal values of 1789. The bloody struggles of the Revolution thus cast a shadow over this transformative event as they dramatized the brutal dilemma of means versus ends.

New *Chapter-Opening Outlines*

Each chapter now opens with a short outline to give students a sense of what's to come in each chapter.

New *Glossary and Key Terms*

Reviewers of the last edition requested this new feature. Glossary words are bolded in each chapter and compiled in the end-of-book glossary.

Cahiers and Elections   For the moment, however, patriot spokesmen stood far in advance of their grass roots. The king had invited all citizens their local parishes to elect delegates to toral assemblies and to draft grievan (*cahiers*) setting forth their views. The gre rural cahiers were highly traditional in to plained only of particular local ills or h pressing confidence that the king would

Anabaptists Individuals who, citing that the Bible nowhere mentions infant baptism, argued that the sacrament was effective only if the believer understood what was happening and that therefore adults ought to be rebaptized. Opponents argued that infant baptism was necessary so that a baby would not be denied salvation if it died young.

anarchists Radical activists who called for the abolition of the state, sometimes by violent means.

The Art

The ninth edition of *The Western Experience* continues the precedent of earlier editions, with more than four hundred full-color reproductions of paintings and photographs and over one hundred clearly focused maps.

The Maps

The maps in *The Western Experience* are already much admired by instructors. Each carries an explanatory caption that enhances the text coverage to help students tackle the content without sacrificing subtlety of interpretation or trying to escape the fact that history is complex. In the ninth edition, each caption has been further improved with a thought question.

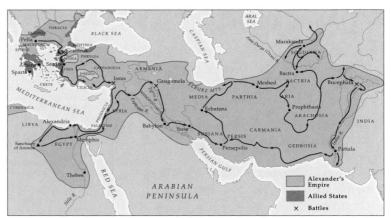

MAP 3.2 THE EMPIRE OF ALEXANDER THE GREAT AND THE ROUTE OF HIS CONQUESTS
Alexander formed the largest empire known down to his own time. He even conquered some territory across the Indus River in India. What were the two major Persian cities near the Persian Gulf?
◆ For an online version, go to www.mhhe.com/chambers9 > chapter 3 > book maps

---

QUESTIONS FOR FURTHER THOUGHT

1. The Greeks invented historical writing. In looking at the past, what are the most important questions a historian should ask?

2. The Greek city-states and their system of alliances gave way to the rising power of Macedonia. How might the Greek states have preserved their strength and political power?

Questions for Further Thought

To encourage students to move beyond rote learning of historical "facts" and to think broadly about history, the authors have added "Questions for Further Thought" at the end of each chapter. These are too broad to be exam questions; instead, they are meant to be questions that stimulate the students to think about history and social, political, and economic forces. Some are comparative, some require students to draw on knowledge of a previous chapter, some ask about the role of great leaders in politics, and some ask about how the less famous people living at the time perceived the events surrounding them.

More Heading Levels

We have given particular attention to adding more descriptive content guides, such as the consistent use of three levels of headings. We believe these will help students identify specific topics for purposes of study and review as well as give a clear outline of a chapter's argument.

Chronological Charts

Nearly every chapter employs charts and chronological tables that outline the unfolding of major events and social processes and serve as a convenient reference for students.

CHRONOLOGY
The Persian Wars
(All dates B.C.)

499, autumn	Greek cities of Ionia in Asia Minor revolt from Persian Empire.
498	Athens and Eretria (on island of Euboea) take part in burning Sardis in Persian Empire.
496	Persians besiege Miletus, the leading city in the revolt.
494	Fall of Miletus.
493	End of Ionian revolt.
492, spring	Persian expedition to northern Greece suffers heavy losses in storms.
490, mid-August	Battle of Marathon near Athens; Persians defeated.
486, November	Death of King Darius of Persia; accession of Xerxes.
484, spring–480, spring	Xerxes prepares for new invasion of Greece.
480, spring	Persian army sets out from Sardis.
480, late August	Battles of Thermopylae and Artemisium.
480, late September	Battle of Salamis.
479, early August	Battle of Plataea.

AVAILABLE FORMATS

To provide an alternative to the full-length hardcover edition, *The Western Experience* Ninth Edition, is available in two-volume and three-volume paperbound editions.

- Volume I includes chapters 1–17 and covers material through the eighteenth century.
- Volume II includes chapters 15–30 and covers material since the sixteenth century.
- Volume A includes chapters 1–12, Antiquity and the Middle Ages.
- Volume B includes chapters 11–21, The Early Modern Era.
- Volume C includes chapters 19–30, The Modern Era.

SUPPLEMENTARY INSTRUCTIONAL MATERIALS

McGraw-Hill offers instructors and students a wide variety of ancillary materials to accompany *The Western Experience.* Please contact your local McGraw-Hill representative for details concerning policies, prices, and availability.

For the Instructor

Instructor's Resource CD-ROM   The Instructor's Resource CD-ROM (IRCD) contains several instructor tools on one easy CD-ROM. For lecture preparation, teachers will find an Instructor's Manual with Power-Point samples by chapter. For quizzes and tests, the IRCD contains a test bank and *EZ Test,* McGraw-Hill's flexible and easy-to-use electronic testing program. Extras on the IRCD also include map images from the book as well as extra photographs and art images.

Online Learning Center for Instructors   At www.mhhe.com/chambers9. At this home page for the text-specific website, instructors will find a series of online tools to meet a wide range of classroom needs. The Instructor's Manual, PowerPoint presentations, and blank maps can be downloaded by instructors, but are password protected to prevent tampering. Instructors can also create an interactive course syllabus using McGraw-Hill's *PageOut* (www.mhhe.com/pageout).

Overhead Transparency Acetates   This expanded full-color transparency package includes all the maps and chronological charts in the text.

For the Student

McGraw-Hill's Primary Source Investigator (PSI) CD-ROM   This CD-ROM, bound into each copy of *The Western Experience,* provides students with instant access to hundreds of world history documents, images, artifacts, audio recordings, and videos. PSI helps students practice the art of "doing history" on a real archive of historical sources. Students follow the three basic steps of *Ask, Research,* and *Present* to examine sources, take notes on them, and then save or print copies of the sources as evidence for their papers or presentations. After researching a particular theme, individual, or time period, students can use PSI's writing guide to walk them through the steps of developing a thesis, organizing their evidence, and supporting their conclusion.

More than just a history or writing tool, the PSI is also a student study tool that contains interactive maps, quiz questions, and an interactive glossary with audio pronunciation guide.

Student Study Guide/Workbook with Map Exercises, Volumes I and II   Includes the following features for each chapter: chapter outlines, chronological diagrams, four kinds of exercises—map exercises, exercises in document analysis, exercises that reinforce the book's important overarching themes, exercises in matching important terms with significant individuals—and essay topics requiring analysis and speculation.

The Online Learning Center   At www.mhhe.com/chambers9. The Online Learning Center is a fully interactive, book-specific website featuring numerous student study tools such as multiple-choice and true-false practice quizzes; interactive, drag-and-drop games about significant individuals and chronologies; key

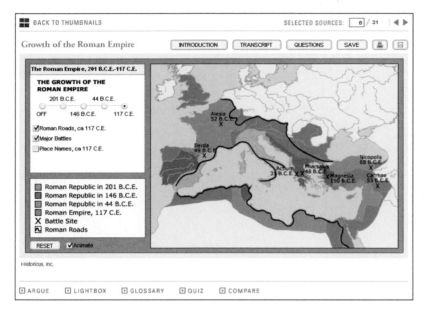

terms with correct identifications; an audio function to help students pronounce difficult terms; and drag-and-drop map exercises. Animated maps from the book are also available through the site. These maps carry a specific URL in their caption.

ACKNOWLEDGMENTS

Manuscript Reviewers, Ninth Edition

Robert Bast, University of Tennessee; Stephen Blumm, Montgomery County Community College; Nathan Brooks, New Mexico State University; Susan Carrafiello, Wright State University; Steven Fanning, University of Illinois at Chicago; Betsy Hertzler, Mesa Community College; Paul Hughes, Sussex County Community College; Mary Kelly, Franklin Pierce College; Paul Lockhart, Wright State University; Eileen Moore, University of Alabama at Birmingham; Penne Prigge, Rockingham Community College; William Roberts, Fairleigh Dickinson University; Steven Ross, Louisiana State University; Charles Sullivan, University of Dallas; Robert Thurston, Miami University.

Manuscript Reviewers, Eighth Edition

Tyler Blethen, West Carolina University; Owen Bradley, University of Tennessee; Dan Brown, Moorpark College; Richard Cole, Luther College; Vickie Cook, Pima Community College; Mary DeCredico, U.S. Naval Academy; Gunar Freibergs, Los Angeles Valley College; Ron Goldberg, Thomas Nelson Community College; Neil Heyman, San Diego State University; Elizabeth McCrank, Boston University; Edrene Stephens McKay, Northwest Arkansas Community College; George Monahan, Suf-

folk Community College; Fred Murphy, Western Kentucky University; Laura Pintar, Loyola University; Anne Quartararo, U.S. Naval Academy; Thomas Rowland, University of Wisconsin–Oshkosh; Charles Steen, University of New Mexico; Sig Sutterlin, Indian Hills Community College; John Tanner, Palomar College; Valentina Tikoff, DePaul University; Guangquin Xu, Northwest Arkansas Community College.

Manuscript Reviewers, Seventh Edition

Frank Baglione, Tallahassee Community College; Paul Goodwin, University of Connecticut; Robert Herzstein, University of South Carolina; Carla M. Joy, Red Rocks Community College; Kathleen Kamerick, University of Iowa; Carol Bresnahan Menning, University of Toledo; Eileen Moore, University of Alabama at Birmingham; Frederick Murphy, Western Kentucky University; Michael Myers, University of Notre Dame; Robert B. Patterson, University of South Carolina at Columbia; Peter Pierson, Santa Clara University; Alan Schaffer, Clemson University; Marc Schwarz, University of New Hampshire; Charles R. Sullivan, University of Dallas; Jack Thacker, Western Kentucky University; Bruce L. Venarde, University of Pittsburgh.

Manuscript Reviewers, Sixth Edition

S. Scott Bartchy, University of California, Los Angeles; Thomas Blomquist, Northern Illinois University; Nancy Ellenberger, U.S. Naval Academy; Steven Epstein, University of Colorado at Boulder; Laura Gellott, University of Wisconsin at Parkside; Drew Harrington, Western Kentucky University; Lisa Lane, Mira Costa College; William Matthews, S.U.N.Y. at Potsdam; Carol Bresnahan Menning, University of Toledo; Sandra Norman, Florida Atlantic University; Peter Pierson, Santa Clara University; Linda Piper, University of Georgia; Philip Racine, Wofford College; Eileen Soldwedel, Edmonds Community College; John Sweets, University of Kansas; Richard Wagner, Des Moines Area Community College.

Focus Group Reviewers from Spring 1992

Michael DeMichele, University of Scranton; Nancy Ellenberger, U.S. Naval Academy; Drew Harrington, Western Kentucky University; William Matthews, S.U.N.Y. at Potsdam.

We would like to thank Lyn Uhl, Monica Eckman, Angela Kao, and Emily Hatteberg of McGraw-Hill for their considerable efforts in bringing this edition to fruition.

THE WESTERN EXPERIENCE

THE HUNDRED YEARS WAR: THE BATTLE OF AGINCOURT
The war between England and France started in 1340 and continued off and on for over 100 years. Only three pitched battles were fought; most of the warfare consisted of plunder, minor skirmishes, and sieges of towns. In the skirmish shown here, Henry V of England crosses the Somme River. The English army is represented by the banner with the fleur-de-lis quartered with the lions of England, meant to illustrate the English claim to the French throne. The French banner is shown with the fleur-de-lis. The English use of the long bow and the French preference for the cross bow are apparent. The culmination of this encounter was the last major battle of the war fought at Agincourt in 1415.
Bibliothèque Nationale de France, Paris/The Art Archive

Chapter Eleven

BREAKDOWN AND RENEWAL IN AN AGE OF PLAGUE

POPULATION CATASTROPHES • ECONOMIC DEPRESSION AND RECOVERY •
POPULAR UNREST • CHALLENGES TO THE GOVERNMENTS OF EUROPE •
THE FALL OF BYZANTIUM AND THE OTTOMAN EMPIRE

In the fourteenth century, plague, famine, and recurrent wars decimated populations and snuffed out former prosperity. At the same time, feudal governments as well as the papacy struggled against mounting institutional chaos. But despite all the signs of crisis, the fourteenth and fifteenth centuries were not merely an age of breakdown. The failures of the medieval economy and its governments drove the Western peoples to repair their institutions. By the late fifteenth century the outlines of a new equilibrium were emerging. In 1500 Europeans were fewer in number than they had been in 1300, but they had developed a more productive economy and a more powerful technology than they had possessed two hundred years before. These achievements were to equip them for their great expansion throughout the world in the early modern period.

Some historians refer to the fourteenth and fifteenth centuries as the "autumn of the Middle Ages," emphasizing the decline and death of a formerly great civilization. People living at the time tended to think in terms of the Biblical passage in Revelation referring to the Four Horsemen of the Apocalypse—famine, disease, war, and the white horse of salvation. Constantinople, the last remnant of the Byzantine Empire, fell to the Ottoman Turks, providing a powerful symbol of decay. But the study of any past epoch requires an effort to balance the work of death and renewal. In few periods of history do death and renewal confront each other so dramatically as in the years between 1300 and 1500.

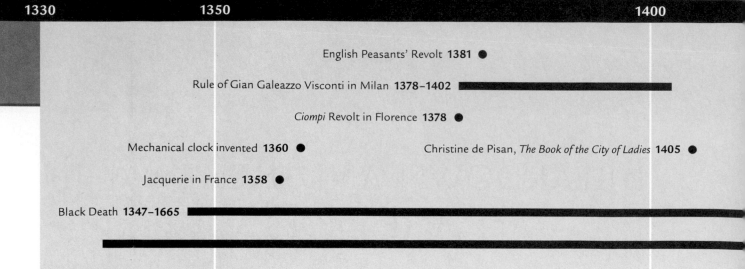

English Peasants' Revolt **1381** ●

Rule of Gian Galeazzo Visconti in Milan **1378–1402** ▮▬▬▬▬▬▬

Ciompi Revolt in Florence **1378** ●

Mechanical clock invented **1360** ●   Christine de Pisan, *The Book of the City of Ladies* **1405** ●

Jacquerie in France **1358** ●

Black Death **1347–1665** ▬▬▬▬▬▬▬▬▬▬

POPULATION CATASTROPHES

The famines and plagues that struck European society in the fourteenth and fifteenth centuries profoundly affected economic life. While the disasters disrupted the economy, Europeans recovered and reorganized to greatly changed demographic conditions. They significantly increased the efficiency of economic production.

Demographic Decline

A few censuses and other statistical records give us an insight into the size and structure of the European population in the 1300s. While incomplete, the figures show how population was changing.

Population Losses Almost every region of Europe shows an appalling decline of population between approximately 1300 and 1450. In Provence in southern France, the population seems to have shrunk after 1310 from between 350,000 and 400,000 to roughly one-third, or at most one-half, of its earlier size; only after 1470 did it again begin to increase. In Italy the decline of population was more severe.

For the larger kingdoms of Europe, the figures are less reliable, but they show a similar pattern. England had a population of about 3.7 million in 1347 and 2.2 million by 1377. France by 1328 may have reached 15 million; it was not again to attain this size for two hundred years. It can safely be estimated that all of Europe in 1450 had no more than one-half, and probably only one-third, of the population it had had around 1300. Population did not begin to recover until the end of the fifteenth century.

Famine and Hunger The first demographic catastrophe in late medieval Europe was **famine** and general food scarcities. In 1315, 1316, and 1317 a severe famine swept the north of Europe. Chroniclers described the incessant rainfall that rotted crops in the fields and prevented harvests; they spoke of people dying in the city streets and country lanes; cannibalism is another theme. In 1339 and 1340 a famine struck southern Europe. During famines, the starving people ate not only their reserves of grain but also most of the seed they had set aside for planting. Medieval Europe lacked a welfare system that could handle such massive crop failures.

Why was hunger so widespread in the early fourteenth century? Some historians see the root of trouble in the sheer number of people the lands had to support by 1300. The medieval population had been growing rapidly since about 1000, and by 1300 Europe, so this analysis suggests, was becoming the victim of its own success. Parts of the continent were crowded, even glutted, with people. Some areas of Normandy, for example, had a population in the early fourteenth century not much below what they supported six hundred years later. Thousands, millions even, had to be fed without chemical fertilizers, power tools, and fast transport. Masses of people had come to depend for their livelihood on infertile soils, and even in good years they were surviving on the margins of existence.

Although hunger did not always result in starvation, malnutrition raised the death rate from respiratory infections and intestinal ailments. While some parts of Europe returned to prosperity and good diets before the next disaster—plague—the experience of others demonstrated the dual impact of famine and

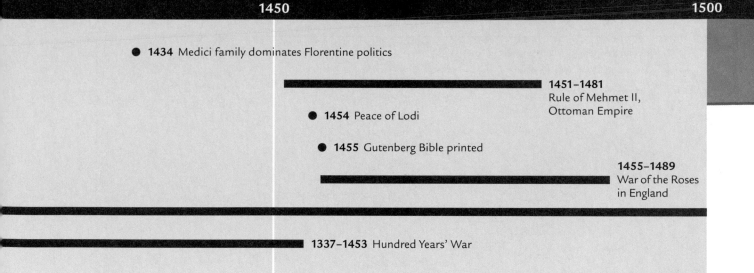

● **1434** Medici family dominates Florentine politics

1451–1481
Rule of Mehmet II,
Ottoman Empire

● **1454** Peace of Lodi

● **1455** Gutenberg Bible printed

1455–1489
War of the Roses
in England

1337–1453 Hundred Years' War

plague. Barceleona and its province of Catalonia experienced famine in 1333; plague in 1347–1351; famine in 1358–1359; and plague in 1362–1363, 1371, and 1397.

Plague

The great plague of the fourteenth century, known as the **Black Death,** provides a dramatic, but not a complete, explanation for the huge human losses. Plague is endemic (always present) in several parts of the world, including the southwestern United States, and occasionally spreads to become a pandemic. In the mid-fourteenth century it spread along caravan routes of central Asia and arrived at the Black Sea ports. Europe's active trade in luxury items from the East gave plague a route to Europe. In 1347 a merchant ship sailing from Caffa in the Crimea to Messina in Sicily seems to have carried rats infected with the plague. A plague broke out at Messina, and from there it spread rapidly throughout Europe (see map 11.1).

Nature of the Disease　　The plague took several forms in Europe. The most identifiable one—the one that contemporary sources describe (see "Boccaccio on the Black Death," p. 309)—is the bubonic form. The pathogenic agent (not discovered until the late nineteenth century) is *Bacillus pestis*. While normally a disease of rodents, particularly house rats, it can spread to humans by fleas that carry the infection from rodents to humans through a flea bite. Bubonic plague has an incubation period of about two to ten days; its symptoms are chills, high fever, headache, and vomiting. The next symptoms are swellings (bubos) in lymph nodes of the groin and clotting blood under the skin, hence the

name "Black Death." Death is likely in 90 percent of the cases. Plague also spreads through a pneumonic variety in which the droplets containing the infection can spread directly from human to human. Infection is rapid and bubos may not form before the bacillus travels through the bloodstream to the lungs, causing pneumonia and death within three or four days. The real killer in the 1300s seems to have been pneumonic plague; it probably was spread through coughing and was almost always fatal.

What made plague so much more terrifying than famine was that it struck rich and poor, young and old, women and men, urban dwellers and villagers, nobles, peasants, monks, and clergy. Not knowing the cause of plague, physicians could do no more than lance the bubos to bring comfort, and many refused to treat plague patients at all. Those members of the clergy who went among the dying usually became infected themselves. Not knowing the true cause of the disease, people blamed the Jews for poisoning the wells; others (the Flagelants) thought it was the wrath of God and walked in procession beating themselves. Eventually, cities formed a contagion theory of the disease and refused admittance within their walls of anyone who came from a city in which the plague was prevalent.

Pandemic　　The Black Death was not so much an epidemic as a pandemic (universal disease), striking an entire continent. The plague was the same one that had visited the Mediterranean and Western Europe in 542, during the reign of Justinian (see chapter 7). It struck not just once but repeatedly, until the last great outbreak in 1665, the Great Plague in London. Plague revisited every generation, and other diseases came into

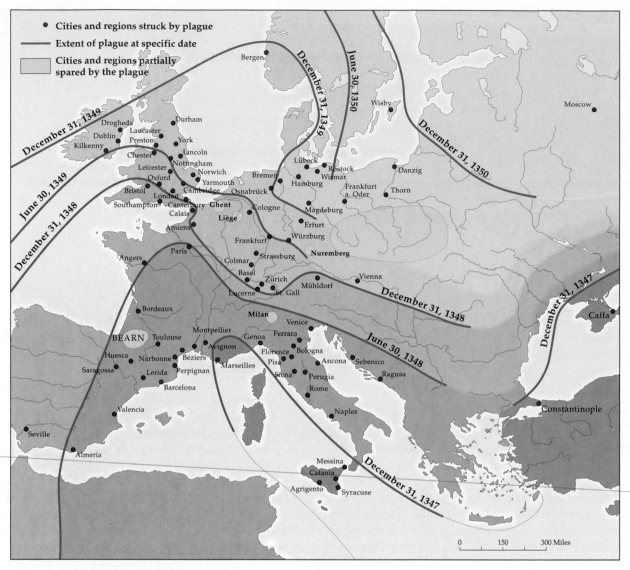

MAP 11.1 THE BLACK DEATH
The plague, as this map shows, took three years to move from Sicily to Sweden. Europe's poor travel conditions contributed to the gradual spread of plague. Where did plague appear first in Europe? Which cities and regions of Europe were partially spared by the plague?
◆ For an online version, go to www.mhhe.com/chambers9 > chapter 11 > book maps

Europe. Population did not begin to recover until the late fifteenth century.

Some of the horror of the plague can be glimpsed in this account by an anonymous cleric who visited the French city of Avignon in 1348: "To put the matter shortly, one-half, or more than a half, of the people at Avignon are already dead. Within the walls of the city there are now more than 7,000 houses shut up; in these no one is living, and all who have inhabited them are departed. . . . On account of this great mortality there is such a fear of death that people do not dare even to speak with anyone whose relative has died, because it

is frequently remarked that in a family where one dies nearly all the relations follow him."[1]

ECONOMIC DEPRESSION AND RECOVERY

A continent does not lose a third to a half of its population without feeling the effects immediately. After

[1] *Breve Chronicon clerici anonymi,* quoted in Francis Aidan Gasquet, *The Black Death of 1348 and 1349,* 1908, p. 46.

BOCCACCIO ON THE BLACK DEATH

The following eyewitness description of the ravages of the Black Death in Florence was written by one of its most famous citizens, the writer Giovanni Boccaccio. This passage comes from his masterpiece, The Decameron, *written during the three years following the plague.*

"In the year of our Lord 1348, there happened at Florence a most terrible plague, which had broken out some years before in the Levant, and after making incredible havoc all the way, had now reached the west. There, in spite of all the means that art and human foresight could suggest, such as keeping the city clear from filth and the publication of copious instructions for preservation of health, it began to show itself in the spring. Unlike what had been seen in the east, where bleeding from the nose is the fatal prognostic, here there appeared certain tumors in the groin or under the arm-pits, some as big as a small apple, others as an egg, and afterwards purple spots in most parts of the body—messengers of death. To the cure of this malady neither medical knowledge nor the power of drugs was of any effect; whether because the disease was in its own nature mortal, or that the physicians (the number of whom, tak-

ing quacks and women pretenders into account, was grown very great) could form no just idea of the cause. Whichever was the reason, few escaped; but nearly all died the third day from the first appearance of the symptoms, some sooner, some later, without any fever or other symptoms. What gave the more virulence to this plague was that it spread daily, like fire when it comes in contact with combustibles. Nor was it caught only by coming near the sick, but even by touching their clothes. One instance of this kind I took particular notice of: the rags of a poor man just dead had been thrown into the street. Two hogs came up, and after rooting amongst the rags, in less than an hour they both turned around and died on the spot."

From C. Warren Hollister et al., *Medieval Europe: A Short Sourcebook,* McGraw-Hill Companies, 1992, pp. 248–249.

burying the dead, often in mass graves outside city walls, the survivors took stock of their economic position. According to contemporaries, survivors of the plague often gave up toiling in the fields or looking after their shops; presumably, they saw no point in working for the future when it was so uncertain. But in the long run Europeans adapted to the new conditions and prospered.

Agricultural Specialization

Perhaps the best indication of the changes in the European economy comes from the history of prices. The cost of most agricultural products—cereals, wine, beer, oil, and meat—shot up immediately after the Black Death and stayed high until approximately 1375 in the north and 1395 in Italy. High food prices in a time of declining population suggests that production was falling even more rapidly than the number of consumers. But high food prices mask the shift in agricultural production that led to greater specialization and, ultimately, improved diets.

Impact on the Peasantry   Some historians have called the period following the depletion of population a golden age for peasantry. Conditions did change for the peasants, but these changes were not uni-

formly for the better across Europe. The peasantry quickly realized that with labor in short supply they could demand higher wages for their labor, and that they could even break the bonds of their serfdom and move around the countryside to follow higher wages. The nobles and landlords were swift in their reaction to such gains.

In England, as elsewhere in Europe, the peasants had enjoyed a period of relative freedom from the labor demands of serfdom, but in the late thirteenth century landlords reimposed serfdom to take advantage of the money they could make from their crops in the period of high population and high demand for grain. With the sudden drop in population and demand for higher wages, Parliament passed the Statute of Laborers in 1351, which fixed prices and wages at what they were in 1347, the year before the plague. Like any law against supply and demand, the statute was hard to enforce, and during the course of the fifteenth century serfdom gradually disappeared in England, as the population moved away from the old manors or simply refused to pay any dues other than their rent.

Agricultural Specialization   One branch of agriculture that enjoyed a remarkable period of growth in the fifteenth century was sheep raising. Since the prices

TRIUMPH OF DEATH
The great social disaster of the Black Death left few traces in the visual arts; perhaps people did not wish to be reminded of its horrors. One exception was the *Triumph of Death*, a mural painted shortly after 1348 in the Camposanto (cemetery) of Pisa in Italy. In this detail of the mural, an elegant party of hunters happens upon corpses prepared for burial. Note the rider who holds a handkerchief—scented, undoubtedly—to his nose, to ward off the foul odors.
Art Resource, NY

for wool, skins, mutton, and cheese remained high, English landlords sought to take advantage of the market by fencing large fields and converting them from plowland into sheep pastures and expelling the peasants or small herders who had formerly lived there. This process, called enclosure, continued for centuries and played an important role in English economic and social history. Other countries as well began to have agricultural specialization. The Netherlands did cheese and dairy while Spain developed Merino wool.

By the middle of the fifteenth century, agricultural prices stabilized, suggesting that production had become more dependable. Farms enjoyed the advantages of larger size, better location on more profitable soil, and increased capital investments in tools and animals. Agriculture was now more diversified, which benefited the soil, lowered the risk of famine from the failure of a single staple crop, and provided more nourishment for the people.

Gentry   The specialized agriculture brought prosperity to the land-owning nobility, but also to a new rural middle class. The middle-class urban dwellers, lawyers, bureaucrats, and wealthy peasants began to invest in land in the countryside. With capital to invest in either the purchase or lease of land, these people made considerable profits. New fortunes gave rise to a country middle class called the **gentry.**

Protectionism

The population decline caused wages to rise. The price of goods also increased, but not fast enough to offset

wages. Between 1349 and 1351, England, France, Aragon, Castile, and other governments tried to fix prices and wages at levels favorable to employers. Such early experiments in a controlled economy failed.

Guilds on the Defensive   A related problem for businesses was that competition grew as population fell and markets contracted. Traders tried to protect themselves by creating restricted markets and establishing monopolies. Guilds limited their membership, and some admitted only the sons of established masters. To keep prices high, some guilds prohibited their members from hiring any women as workers, because their wages were low. Only wives and daughters of the household could work in the shops.

The Hanseatic League   Probably the best example of the monopolizing trend is the association of northern European trading cities, the **Hanseatic League.** Formed in the late thirteenth century as a defensive association, by the early fourteenth century it imposed a monopoly on cities trading in the Baltic and North seas. It excluded foreigners from the Baltic trade and could expel member cities who broke trade agreements. At its height, the Hanseatic League included seventy or eighty cities, stretching from Bruges to Novgorod and led by Bremen, Cologne, Hamburg, and especially Lübeck (see map 11.2). Maintaining its own treasury and fleet, the league supervised commercial exchange, policed the waters of the Baltic Sea, and negotiated with foreign princes. By the late fifteenth century, however, it began to decline and was unable to meet growing competition from the Dutch in northern commerce. Never formally

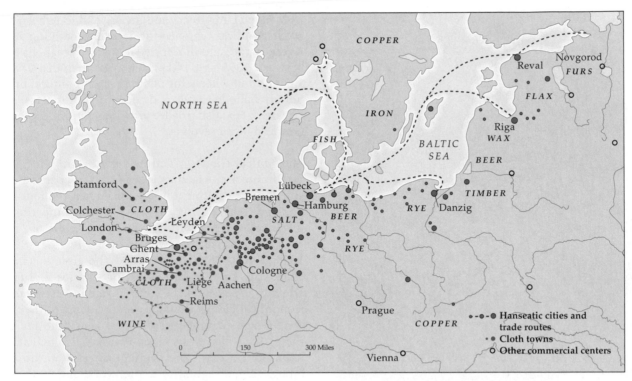

MAP 11.2 THE HANSEATIC LEAGUE AND THE GOODS IT TRADED IN THE FOURTEENTH CENTURY
Northern Europe developed a vigorous trade, mostly centered in cities around the Baltic Sea and along the rivers of
Europe. The cities involved in the trade formed an association called the Hanseatic League, with its own
regulations and requirements for membership. What would be the benefit of joining such a trade association? What
types of goods did the Hanseatic League trade? Of these, which commodities seem to have been most in demand?
Which cities predominated in the trade?
◆ For an online version, go to www.mhhe.com/chambers9 > chapter 11 > book maps

abolished, the Hanseatic League continued to meet—at lengthening intervals—until 1669.

Technological Advances

Attempts to raise the efficiency of workers proved to be far more effective than wage and price regulation in laying the basis for economic recovery. Employers were able to counteract high wages by adopting more rational methods of production and substituting capital for labor—that is, providing workers with better tools. Although hard times and labor shortages inspired most technical advances of the 1300s and 1400s, increased efficiency helped to make Europe a richer community.

Metallurgy Mining and metallurgy benefited from a series of inventions after 1460 that lowered the cost of metals and extended their use. Better techniques of digging, shoring, ventilating, and draining allowed mine shafts to be sunk several hundred feet into the earth, permitting the large-scale exploitation of the deep, rich mineral de-

posits of central Europe. During this period, miners in Saxony discovered a method for extracting pure silver from the lead alloy in which it was often found—an invention that was of major importance for the later massive development of silver mines in America.

By the late fifteenth century, European mines were providing an abundance of silver bullion for coinage. Money became more plentiful, which stimulated the economy. Exploitation also began in the rich coal deposits of northern Europe. Expanding iron production meant more and stronger pumps, gears and machine parts, tools, and iron wares.

Firearms and Weapons Europeans were constantly trying to improve the arts of war in the Middle Ages. The crossbow was cranked up and shot with a trigger; it was so powerful that it could penetrate conventional armor. The long bow came into widespread use during the Welsh wars of Edward I. It was light, accurate, and could be shot rapidly. In response to these two weapons, armor became more elaborate,

MINING, 1389
**One does not normally associate miners with elegant
decoration, but in this fourteenth-century manuscript, a
miner provides the subject for the ornamentation of the
capital *M* that starts the word *metalla* (metals). That the
artist even considered such a subject is an indication of the
growing importance of the industry in this period.**
© Giancarlo Costa/Index

Medieval architects and artists had long been interested in military engineering as well as building. Konrad Kyeser wrote and illustrated a book of weapons of war between 1395 and 1405. His work included cannons, siphons and wheels for raising water, pontoon bridges, hot-air balloons, and a device to pull horses across streams. He also made drawings of multiple guns arranged like a revolver.

Mechanical Clocks   Telling time in the Middle Ages was imprecise, based as it was on the position of the sun and the canonical hours for prayer at about three-hour intervals during the day. Times of meetings, for instance, were set within vague parameters of "at vesper," "at sunrise," or even within a few days. But in 1360 Henry De Vick designed the first mechanical clock with an hour hand for King Charles V of France, which was placed in the royal palace in Paris. Large astronomical clocks that showed the signs of the zodiac were the precursors of clocks that kept time and tolled the hours. Milan had a clock that struck a bell at every hour of the day. The regular ringing of the hours brought a new regularity to life, work, and markets and gave time itself a new value. Pocket watches, although cumbersome, had appeared by 1550 with the invention of the spring for running clocks.

Printing   The extension of literacy among laypeople and the greater reliance of governments and businesses on records created a demand for a cheap method of reproducing the written word. The introduction of paper from the East was a major step in reducing costs, for paper is far cheaper than parchment to produce. A substitute for the time-consuming labor of writing by hand was also necessary: Scribes and copiers were skilled artisans who commanded high salaries. To cut costs, printers first tried to press woodcuts—inked blocks with letters or designs carved on them—onto paper or parchment.

By the middle of the fifteenth century several masters were on the verge of perfecting the technique of printing with movable metal type. The first to prove this practicable was Johannes Gutenberg of Mainz, a former jeweler and stonecutter. Gutenberg devised an alloy of lead, tin, and antimony that would melt at a low temperature, cast well in the die, and be durable in the press; this alloy is still the basis of the printer's art. His Bible, printed in 1455, is the first major work reproduced through printing. The technique spread rapidly. By 1500 some 250 European cities had presses.

The Information Revolution   The immediate effect of the printing press was to multiply the output and cut

with exaggerated convex surfaces designed to deflect arrows from the chest, arms, and knees.

Siege weapons that hurled projectiles with great force and accuracy were also important. Adapting a Chinese invention for fireworks—consisting of an explosive mixture of carbon, sulfur, and saltpeter—the Europeans developed gunpowder and cannons to hurl boulders at an enemy. Firearms are first mentioned in 1328, and cannons were used in the early battles of the Hundred Years' War. With firearms, fewer soldiers could fight more effectively; capital, in the form of an efficient though expensive tool, was being substituted for labor.

ENGLISH SIEGE OF ORLÉANS (1428–1429)
This piece shows the English soldiers behind a siege wall (left) firing cannons across the Loire River. The cannons at this stage were more frightening for their noise than for their destructive power because of design problems. The siege of Orléans was brought to an end by a French relief force led by Joan of Arc.
Bibliothèque Nationale de France, Paris

the costs of books (see map 11.3). It made information available to a much broader segment of the population, and libraries could store more information at lower cost. Printing helped disseminate and preserve knowledge in standardized form—a major contribution to the advance of technology and scholarship. Printing produced a revolution in what we would call information technology, and indeed it resembles in many ways the profound changes that computers are making in our own lives. Finally, printing could spread new ideas with unprecedented speed.

The Standard of Living

For those who survived the famine, plagues, and wars, the standard of living became better as the economy began to grow again in the late fifteenth century; but the pall of death and disease hung over the survivors.

Reduced Life Expectancy   The average life expectancy in the fifteenth century was thirty years of age. The principal victims of plague, other diseases, and famine were the very young. In many periods, between a half and a third of the babies born never reached age fifteen. Society swarmed with little children, but their deaths were common occurrences in almost every family.

The plague took a greater toll among young adults than among the aged. In effect, a person who survived one or more major epidemics had a good chance of living through the next onslaught. A mild attack of plague brought immunity rather than death as the population built up resistance to the disease; a favored few thus did reach extreme old age. The death toll of people in their child-bearing years slowed the demographic recovery.

Female Survival   Women seemed to be more robust than men in resisting or recovering from plague and the other diseases, and they became a disproportionately

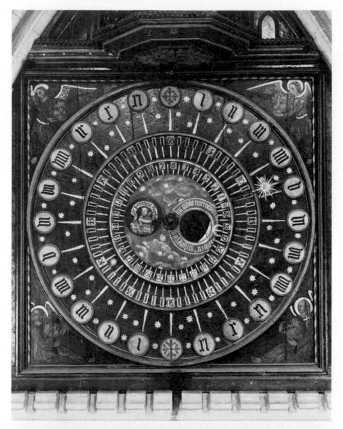

The mechanical clock, a medieval invention, was installed in major buildings. The Wells Cathedral clock was built in England. The face was decorated with the four winds and angels. The clock told the hours twenty-four hours a day and told the days in the lunar month. Bells tolled the hours.
(Top) Derek Bayes/Aspect Picture Library Ltd.
(Bottom) The Science Museum, London

larger part of the population. Historians have interpreted this fact in a number of ways. Some have argued that women took a greater role in urban and rural life and that this was a golden age for women. As historians find more evidence about women during this period, however, it appears that while more women found employment in urban centers, their roles were limited to household servants and unskilled labor. Women did not move into positions of power in government or guilds. Indeed, female guilds that had women as guild officers were forced to elect men.

Misogyny and the Debate over Women's Nature

Witchcraft charges against women were rare in the Middle Ages, but some historians have argued that the greater preponderance of women in the population contributed to the witch hunts of the sixteenth centuries. By the Late Middle Ages the intellectual debate about women's nature had become more pointed (see chapter 16). Both the ancient and the medieval world had relegated women to inferior positions, and some of the ancient and Christian authors had added strong negative invectives against women. The Church offered two images of women—Eve, the sinner who led Adam astray in the Garden of Eden, and the Virgin Mary, mother of Jesus. Neither image fit ordinary women's lives very well. As we saw in the last chapter, some very pious women commanded the respect of the Church through their asceticism.

Women were not without champions, however. Christine de Pisan, a widow with young children, turned to writing and translating to make a living. Among her books was *The Book of the City of Ladies.* She pointed to all the heroic women in history as examples of women's superior qualities, describing virtue in the most trying circumstances, heroism, self-sacrifice, wisdom, and leadership (see "The Status of Women in the Middle Ages," p. 317).

Knowledge of the Human Body

During the Late Middle Ages, some modest advances were made in medicine. Eyeglasses, invented in the thirteenth century, were perfected in the fourteenth century. For the most part they were designed for reading rather than distance vision.

Until the later part of the Middle Ages, religious prohibitions against dissecting the human cadaver meant that medicine had not advanced much beyond the Hellenistic and Arabic contributions. By the end of the thirteenth century, a teacher of medicine at the University of Bologna wrote a textbook on dissections with illustrations of human anatomy. With a superior knowledge of the human body, physicians' ability to diagnose illnesses advanced, but their knowledge of cures did not. Surgery remained the practice of barber-surgeons, guildsmen whose sharp knives could shave beards and perform surgery and whose supply of leeches could draw blood.

Housing and Diets   The revitalized economy brought improvements in housing, dress, and diet and increased spending on art and decorative objects. Housing was generally improving for most people in the Late Middle Ages. The increasing use of brick and tile meant that buildings were more substantial and more spacious. The nobility, gentry, and wealthy urban dwellers built large town houses and country houses with gardens and large windows rather than defensive walls. The fireplace on the wall replaced the hearth in the center of the room even in peasant houses.

The European diet had been largely based on cereal products, and when population was dense, all land had to be devoted to raising grain, even if the land was not particularly well suited for it. Reduced population meant that land could be devoted to other crops or to

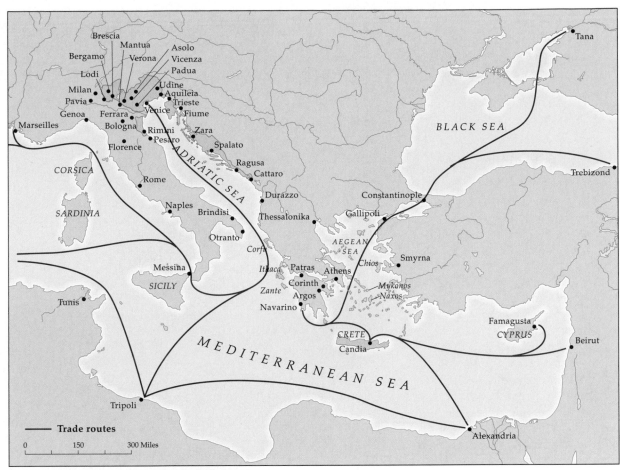

MAP 11.5 THE VENETIAN EMPIRE IN THE 1400s
The Venetian trade routes, as this map shows, moved Venice to a position of major power. How far did Venice's rule extend? Which cities did it control? Who were its trading partners in the eastern Mediterranean?
◆ For an online version, go to www.mhhe.com/chambers9 > chapter 11 > book maps

ranean the strengthening of central governments that took place elsewhere in Europe in the 1400s. The court he created at Naples was one of the most brilliant centers of art and literature of the age.

Balance of Power Relations between the city-states on the Italian peninsula were tense as they clashed over trade and the acquisition of surrounding territory. The Peace of Lodi in 1454 ended a war among Milan, Florence, and Venice. Cosimo de Medici sought to make the peace a lasting one by creating an alliance system between Milan, Naples, and Florence on one side and Venice and the Papal States on the other (see map 11.6). During the next forty years, until the French invaded the peninsula in 1494, the balance was occasionally rocked but never overturned. This system represents one of the earliest appearances in European history of a diplomatic **balance of power** for maintaining peace.

THE FALL OF BYZANTIUM AND THE OTTOMAN EMPIRE

Although the Byzantine Empire revived under Michael VIII Palaeologus, by the mid-fifteenth century the empire's control was effective only in Greece, the Aegean, and the area around Constantinople. The Ottoman Turks eventually fell heir to Byzantium's former power and influence, and by the early sixteenth century they were the unquestioned masters of southeast Europe and the Middle East.

The Fall of Constantinople

The Rising Threat Turkish peoples had been assuming a large military and political role in the Middle East since the late tenth century. The Seljuk Turks dominated western Asia Minor since the late 1000s.

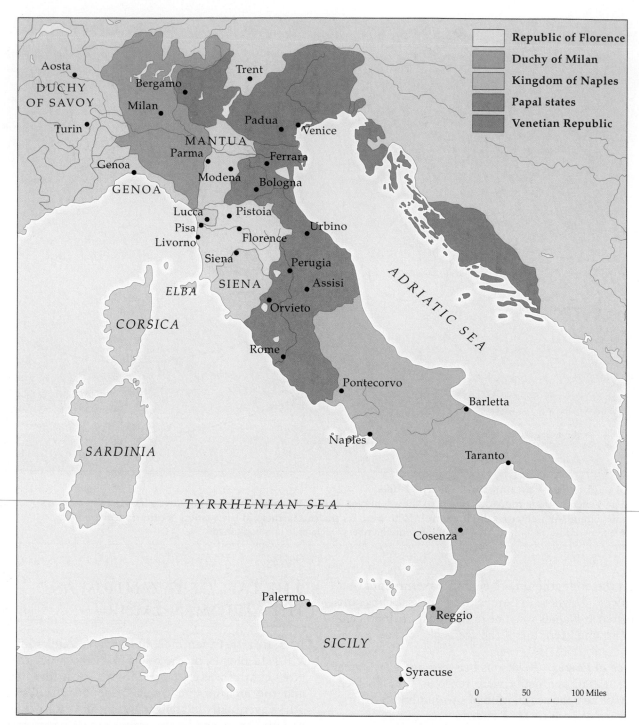

MAP 11.6 THE ITALIAN STATES IN 1454
As this map shows, after the Peace of Lodi in 1454, five major states dominated Italy. For forty years they maintained a balance of power among themselves. What were the five major states of Italy? What forms of government did these states represent?

◆ For an online version, go to www.mhhe.com/chambers9 > chapter 11 > book maps

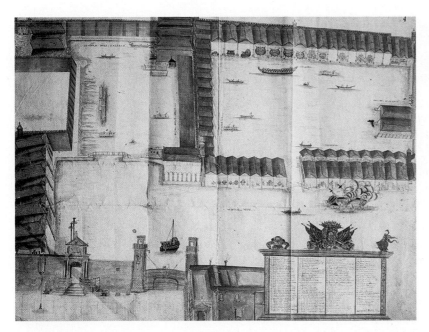

Antonio Natale
VENICE ARSENAL
This eighteenth-century depiction of the huge complex that made up the Arsenal in Venice indicates some of the specialized buildings that formed the production line around the pools in which the ships were built. At the back, hulls are being laid, and in the foreground, a ship is being scuttled. At the very front are the two towers that flanked the entrance gate to the Arsenal.
© Giancarlo Costa/Index

Although Turks survived the attacks of Western crusaders, they were defeated by the Mongols in the thirteenth century. The Ottoman Turks, who had converted to Islam, followed the Mongol invasions and took over Asia Minor. They took their name from Osman, or Othman (r. 1290–1326), who founded a dynasty of sultans that survived for six centuries.

Establishing themselves at Gallipoli on the European-side of the Straits in 1354, the Ottomans completely surrounded the Byzantine territory. The Byzantine emperors, fearing the worst for their small and isolated realm, tried desperately but unsuccessfully to persuade the West to send military help. At the council of Florence in 1439, Emperor John VII even accepted reunion with Rome, largely on Roman terms, in return for aid, but he had no power to impose the reunion of the churches on his people; in fact, many Eastern Christians preferred Turkish rule to submission to the hated Westerners.

The Capture of the City

The Ottomans were unable to mount a major campaign against Constantinople until 1453, when Sultan Mehmet II, the Conqueror, finally attacked by land and water. The city fell after a heroic resistance, and Emperor Constantine XI Palaeologus, whose imperial lineage stretched back more than 1,400 years to Augustus Caesar, died in this final agony of the Byzantine Empire.

The fall of Constantinople had little military or economic effect on Europe and the Middle East. The Byzantine Empire had not been an effective barrier to Ottoman expansion for years, and Constantinople had dwindled commercially as well as politically. The shift to Turkish dominion did not, as historians once believed, substantially affect the flow of trade between the East and West. Nor did the Turkish conquest of the city provoke an exodus of Byzantine scholars and manuscripts to Italy. Scholars from the East, recognizing the decline and seemingly inevitable fall of the Byzantine Empire, had been emigrating to Italy since the late fourteenth century; the revival of Greek letters was well under way in the West by 1453.

The End of an Era

The impact of the fall was largely psychological; although hardly unexpected, it shocked the Christian world. The end of the Byzantine Empire and the rise of the **Ottoman Empire** had great symbolic importance for contemporaries and, perhaps even more, for later historians. In selecting Byzantium as his capital in 324, Constantine had founded a Christian Roman empire that could be considered the first authentically medieval state. For more than 1,000 years this Christian Roman empire played a major political and cultural role in the history of both Eastern and Western peoples. In some respects, the years of its existence mark the span of the Middle Ages, and its passing symbolizes the end of an era.

The Ottoman Empire

Under Mehmet II (r. 1451–1481), who from the start of his reign committed his government to a policy of conquest, the Ottomans began a century of expansion (see

THE SULTAN MEHMET II

One of the first histories of the Ottomans by a Westerner was written by an English schoolmaster named Richard Knolles and published in 1603. It is obvious that a great deal of research went into his work, which is marked by vivid portraits such as this one of the Sultan Mehmet II, known as the Conqueror because of his capture of Constantinople, who had lived a century before Knolles wrote.

"He was of stature but low, square set, and strongly limbed; his complexion sallow and melancholy; his look and countenance stern, with his eyes piercing, and his nose so high and crooked that it almost touched his upper lip. He was of a very sharp and apprehending wit, learned especially in astronomy, and could speak the Greek, Latin, Arabic, Chaldee, and Persian tongues. He delighted much in reading of histories, and the lives of worthy men, especially the lives of Alexander the Great and Julius Caesar, whom he proposed to himself as examples to follow. He was of an exceeding courage, and a severe punisher of injustice. Men that excelled in any quality, he greatly favored and honorably entertained, as he did Gentile Bellini, a painter of Venice, whom he purposely caused to come from thence to Constantinople, to draw the lively counterfeit of himself for which he most bountifully rewarded him. He so severely punished theft, as that in his time all the ways were safe. He was altogether irreligious, and most perfidious, ambitious above measure, and in nothing more delighted than in blood: insomuch that he was responsible for the death of 800,000 men; craft, covetousness and dissimulation were in him accounted tolerable, in comparison of his greater vices. In his love was no assurance, and his least displeasure was death; so that he lived feared of all men, and died lamented of none."

From Richard Knolles, in John J. Saunders (ed.), *The Muslim World on the Eve of Europe's Expansion*, Prentice Hall, 1966, adapted by T. K. Rabb.

Gentile Bellini
MEHMET II
Mehmet II, here shown in a painting attributed to the Venetian artist Gentile Bellini, was the conqueror of Constantinople in 1453.
The Granger Collection, New York

"The Sultan Mehmet II," above). After the fall of Constantinople, which became his capital under the name of Istanbul (though the name was not officially adopted until 1930), Mehmet subjugated Morea, Serbia, Bosnia, and parts of Herzegovina. He drove the Genoese from their Black Sea colonies, forced the khan of the Crimea to become his vassal, and fought a lengthy naval war with the Venetians. At his death the Ottomans were a power on land and sea, and the Black Sea had become a Turkish lake (see map 11.7).

Early in the following century, under the leadership of Suleiman II, the Magnificent (r. 1520–1566), the Ottoman Empire came to the height of its power. Turkish domination was extended over the heart of the Arab lands through the conquest of Syria, Egypt, and the western coast of the Arabian peninsula. (The Arabs did not again enjoy autonomy until the twentieth century.) With the conquest of the sacred cities of Mecca and Medina, the sultan assumed the title of caliph, "successor of the Prophet," claiming to be Islam's supreme religious head as well as its mightiest sword. Suleiman II also extended Turkish conquests into the Balkan peninsula and Hungary. His attempts to conquer Austria failed when Vienna withstood the onslaught of the Ottomans in 1529. (For more on Suleiman II and the Ottomans see chapter 14.)

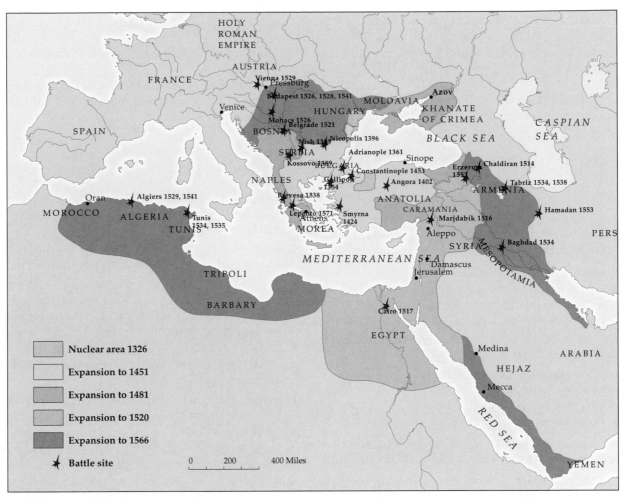

MAP 11.7 THE OTTOMAN EMPIRE, 1300–1566
This map shows the gradual expansion of the Ottoman Empire from 1300 to 1566. What areas of Europe did the Ottoman Empire include? What was the decisive battle that stopped further advances into Europe?

◆ For an online version, go to www.mhhe.com/chambers9 > chapter 11 > book maps

Summary

While the fall of Constantinople had a strong psychological effect on Europe, the threat of the Ottoman invasion initially meant little except to the Austrians, Hungarians, Balkan states, and the Knights Hospitalers. The West was preoccupied with the reality of the Four Horsemen of the Apocalypse. Early fourteenth-century famines, recurrent plague, and wars, including the Hundred Years' War, diverted their attention. By the end of the fifteenth century, peace was generally restored. England emerged as a government that would come to be described as a constitutional monarchy, the French king was on his way to a control over his subjects that would be called absolutism, and Italy had established a balance-of-power politics. The economy was strengthened by new inventions, such as the printing press, that would change the way people spread and received information to the present day. Europe was on the verge of new expansions. The explorations of the late fifteenth century introduced new concepts of power and wealth to the competing countries; the problems of the Church intensified with major splits; and the economy, although plagued with problems of overpopulation once again, was expanding in new directions and with new products from the conquests in America.

QUESTIONS FOR FURTHER THOUGHT

1. What made the Hundred Years' War different from the other wars that you have studied in the Middle Ages?
2. Compare Europe in 800 to Europe in 1450. What new political boundaries had been established?

How had society changed? How was the economy different?
3. What influence has epidemic disease and famine had on the history of Europe and the world in general?

RECOMMENDED READING

Sources

*Brucker, Gene A. (ed.) *The Society of Renaissance Florence: A Documentary Study.* 1971. Collection of primary sources.

Byrne, Joseph P. *The Black Death.* 2004.

*Dobson, R. B. (ed.). *The Peasant's Revolt of 1381.* 1983. Primary sources related to the revolt.

*Froissart, Jean. *The Chronicles of England, France, Spain and Other Places Adjoining.* 1961. Chronicles of the Hundred Years' War.

*Horrox, Rosemary. *The Black Death.* 1994. Primary sources on the Black Death.

The Pastons: The Letters of a Family in the War of the Roses. Richard Barber (ed.). 1981.

Pernoud, Regine (ed.). *Joan of Arc: By Herself and Her Witnesses.* 1966. Documents relating to Joan's life and trial.

*Pisan, Christine de. *The Book of the City of Ladies.* Earl Jeffrey Richards (tr.). 1982. The author was a court writer who wrote this book on women's virtues in response to the debate of the time on women.

Studies

*Allmand, Christopher. *The Hundred Years' War: England and France at War, c. 1300–1450.* 1988. An account of the military aspects.

*Bennett, Judith M. *Women in the Medieval English Countryside.* 1987. An assessment of peasant women's status.

*Brucker, Gene A. *Giovanni and Lusanna: Love and Marriage in Renaissance Florence.* 1986.

Cohn, Samuel K. *The Black Death Transformed: Disease and Culture in Early Renaissance Europe.* 2002. Cohn has provided a new interpretation of possible diseases that may not be the plague described by previous historians.

Eisenstein, Elizabeth L. *The Printing Press as an Agent of Change in Early-Modern Europe.* 2 vols. 1979. Provocative interpretation of the place of printing in European history.

Gillingham, John. *The Wars of the Roses: Peace and Conflict in Fifteenth-Century England.* 1981. Readable political and military history.

Gimpel, Jean. *The Medieval Machine.* Penguin, 1976. Useful analysis of mechanical innovations in the Middle Ages.

*Hanawalt, Barbara. *The Ties That Bound: Peasant Families in Medieval England.* 1986. Peasant life in England sympathetically viewed.

*—— (ed.). *Women and Work in Preindustrial Europe.* 1986. Collection of essays covering the issues of working women in Europe.

Harvey, L. P. *Islamic Spain 1250–1500.* 1990. A survey of the one non-Christian territory in Western Europe and its steady decline.

*Hilton, Rodney. *Bond Men Made Free.* 1979. A study of peasant unrest in the Late Middle Ages.

Jordan, William Chester. *The Great Famine: Northern Europe in the Early Fourteenth Century,* 1996. An overview of the famines and their climatic causes and effects in northern Europe.

Kaeuper, Richard W. *War, Justice, and Public Order: England and France in the Late Middle Ages.* 1988. Assessment of the intersection of war and justice in two countries.

Oakley, Francis. *The Western Church in the Later Middle Ages.* 1979.

*Perroy, Edouard. *The Hundred Years' War.* 1965. Classic; excellent survey.

Unger, Richard W. *The Ship in the Medieval Economy.* 1980. The evolution of medieval ship design.

Warner, Marina. *Joan of Arc: The Image of Female Heroism.* 1981. Examination of Joan's life and legend.

Wittek, Paul. *The Rise of the Ottoman Empire.* 1971.

*Ziegler, Philip. *The Black Death.* 1970. Synthesis of plague studies.

*Available in paperback.

Jan Van Eyck
PORTRAIT OF GIOVANNI ARNOLFINI AND HIS WIFE, 1434
The symbolism that permeates this depiction of a husband and wife has led to the suggestion that it is a wedding picture. The bed and seeming pregnancy are symbols of marriage, and the husband blesses his wife as he bestows the sacrament of marriage (for which the Church did not yet require a priest). On the back wall, the mirror reflects the witnesses attending the wedding. Van Eyck's use of the new medium of oil paint allowed him to reproduce vividly the texture of the fur-edged robe and the glimmer of the mirror's glass.

Chapter Twelve

Tradition and Change in European Culture, 1300–1500

THE NEW LEARNING • ART AND ARTISTS IN THE ITALIAN RENAISSANCE •
THE CULTURE OF THE NORTH • SCHOLASTIC PHILOSOPHY AND RELIGIOUS THOUGHT
• THE STATE OF CHRISTENDOM

By 1300 the civilization of Europe appeared to have settled into stable and self-assured patterns. Society as a whole shared assumptions about religious beliefs, about the appropriate way to integrate faith with the heritage of the ancient world, about the purposes of scholarship, and about the forms of literature and art. These shared assumptions have led historians to describe the outlook of the age as "the medieval synthesis." But such moments of apparent stability rarely last long. Within a few generations, profound doubts had arisen on such fundamental questions as the nature of religious faith, the authority of the Church, the aims of scholarship, the source of moral ideals, and the standards of beauty in the arts. As challenges to old ideas arose, especially in the worlds of religion and cultural expression, there was an outpouring of cre-

ativity: a "golden age" comparable to those which, five hundred years earlier, had transformed the cultures of China and the Tang Dynasty or the Muslim world under the Abbassids. Like those flowerings, it has dazzled us ever since. Because those seeking new answers in Europe tended to look for guidance to what they considered to be a better past—in this case classical antiquity or the early days of Christianity—and sought to revive long-lost values, their efforts, and the times in which they lived, have been called an age of rebirth, or **Renaissance.**[1]

---

[1] The creator of the modern view of the Renaissance as one of the formative periods of Western history, and the single most influential historian of the subject, was Jacob Burckhardt (see Recommended Reading).

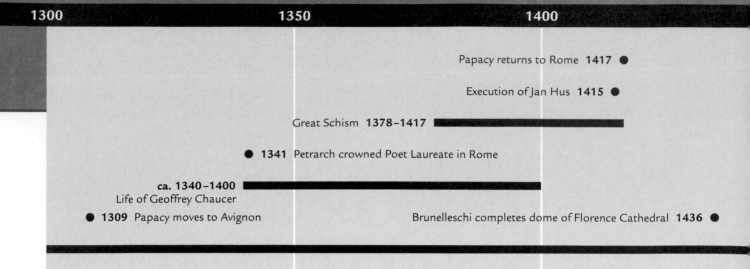

Papacy returns to Rome **1417** ●

Execution of Jan Hus **1415** ●

Great Schism **1378–1417**

● **1341** Petrarch crowned Poet Laureate in Rome

ca. 1340–1400
Life of Geoffrey Chaucer

● **1309** Papacy moves to Avignon

Brunelleschi completes dome of Florence Cathedral **1436** ●

THE NEW LEARNING

Although traditional forms of learning remained vital in the fourteenth and fifteenth centuries, medieval Scholasticism, with its highly refined forms of reasoning, had little to offer Europe's small but important literate lay population. The curriculum was designed mainly to train teachers and theologians, whereas the demand was increasingly for practical and useful training, especially in the arts of persuasion and communication: good speaking and good writing. For many, the Scholastics also failed to offer moral guidance. As Petrarch emphasized, education was meant to help people lead a wise, pious, and happy life. A central aim of the Renaissance was to develop new models of virtue and a system of education that would do exactly that.

The Founding of Humanism

One minor branch of the medieval educational curriculum, rhetoric, was concerned with the art of good speaking and writing. More and more, its practitioners in Italy began to turn to the Latin classics for models of good writing. Their interest in the Classical authors was helped by the close relationship between the Italian language and Latin, by the availability of manuscripts, and by the presence in Italy of countless Classical monuments. It was rhetoricians who first began to argue, in the late thirteenth century, that education should be reformed to give more attention to the classics and to help people lead more moral lives.

These rhetoricians were to found an intellectual movement known as **Humanism.** The term *Humanism* was not coined until the nineteenth century. In fifteenth-century Italy, *humanista* signified a professor of humane studies or a Classical scholar, but eventually Humanism came to mean Classical scholarship—the ability to read, understand, and appreciate the writings of the ancient world. Humanists wanted to master the classics so as to learn both the right way to conduct their lives and the eloquence to persuade others to follow that same way. The modern use of the word *humanism* to denote a secular philosophy that denies an afterlife has no basis in the Renaissance. Most Renaissance humanists read the Church fathers as avidly as they read pagan authors and believed that the highest virtues were rooted in piety. Humanism sought far more to enrich than to undermine traditional religious attitudes.

Petrarch The most influential early advocate of Humanism was Francesco Petrarca, known as Petrarch (1304–1374). He was a lawyer and cleric who practiced neither of those professions but rather devoted his life to writing poetry, scholarly and moral treatises, and letters. He became famous for his Italian verse—his sonnets inspired poets for centuries—but he sought above all to emulate Virgil by writing a Latin epic poem. A master of self-promotion, he used that work as the occasion for reviving the ancient title of "poet laureate" and having himself crowned in Rome in 1341. But he was also capable of profound self-examination. In a remarkable work, which he called *My Secret*—a dialogue with one of his heroes, St. Augustine—he laid bare his struggles to achieve spiritual peace despite the temptations of fame and love. Increasingly, he became concerned that nowhere in the world around him could he find a model of virtuous behavior that he could respect. The leaders of the Church he considered poor examples, for they seemed worldly and materialistic. Convinced that no guide from his own times or the immediate past would serve, Petrarch concluded that he had to turn to the Church fathers and the ancient

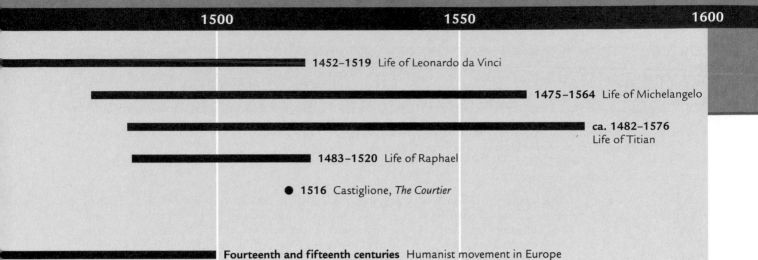

1452–1519 Life of Leonardo da Vinci

1475–1564 Life of Michelangelo

ca. 1482–1576 Life of Titian

1483–1520 Life of Raphael

● **1516** Castiglione, *The Courtier*

Fourteenth and fifteenth centuries Humanist movement in Europe

Romans to find worthy examples of the moral life (see "Petrarch on Ancient Rome," p. 340).

How could one be a good person? By imitating figures from antiquity, such as Cicero and Augustine, who knew what proper values were and pursued them in their own lives, despite temptations and the distractions of public affairs. The period between their time and his own—which Petrarch regarded as the "middle" ages—he considered contemptible. His own world, he felt, would improve only if it tried to emulate the ancients, and he believed that education ought to teach what they had done and said. In particular, like the good rhetorician he was, he believed that only by restoring the mastery of the written and spoken word that had distinguished the great Romans—an imitation of their style, of the way they had conveyed their ideas—could his contemporaries learn to behave like the ancients.

Boccaccio   The program Petrarch laid out soon caught fire in Florence, the city from which his family had come and in which he found influential friends and disciples. The most important was the poet and writer Giovanni Boccaccio (1313–1375), famous for a collection of short stories known as *The Decameron*. The first prose masterpiece in Italian, *The Decameron* created new aims in Western Literature with its frank treatment of sex and vivid creation of ordinary characters. But in his later years Boccaccio grew increasingly concerned with the teaching of moral values, and he became a powerful supporter of Petrarch's ideas.

The Spread of Humanism   In the generation after Petrarch and Boccaccio, Humanism became a rallying cry for the intellectual leaders of Florence. They argued that, by associating their city with the revival of antiquity, Florentines would be identified with a distinctive

vision that would become the envy of their rivals elsewhere in Italy. And that was indeed what happened. The campaign for a return to the classics started a revolution in education that soon took hold throughout Italy; the writing and speaking skills the humanists emphasized came to be in demand at every princely court (including that of the papacy); and the crusade to study and imitate the ancients transformed art, literature, and even political and social values.

Led by the chancellor of Florence, Coluccio Salutati (whose position, as the official who prepared the city's official communications, required training in rhetoric), a group of humanists began to collect ancient manuscripts and form libraries, so as to make accessible virtually all the surviving writings of Classical Latin authors. These Florentines also wanted to regain command of the Greek language, and in 1396 they invited a Byzantine scholar to lecture at the University of Florence. In the following decades—troubled years for the Byzantine Empire—other Eastern scholars joined the exodus to the West, and they and Western visitors returning from the East brought with them hundreds of Greek manuscripts. By the middle of the fifteenth century, Western scholars had both the philological skill and the manuscripts to establish direct contact with the most original minds of the Classical world, and they were making numerous Latin and Italian translations of Greek works. Histories, tragedies, lyric poetry, the dialogues of Plato, many mathematical treatises, and the most important works of the Greek fathers of the Church fully entered Western culture for the first time.

Civic Humanism   Salutati and his contemporaries and successors in Florence are often called civic humanists because they stressed that participation in public affairs is essential for full human development.

PETRARCH ON ANCIENT ROME

Petrarch was so determined to relive the experience of antiquity that he wrote letters to famous Roman authors as if they were acquaintances. In one letter, he even described Cicero coming to visit him. While he was passing through Padua in February 1350, he recalled that the city was the birthplace of the Roman historian Livy, and he promptly wrote to him.

"I only wish, either that I had been born in your time or you in ours. If the latter, our age would have benefited; if the former, I myself would have been the better for it. I would surely have visited you. As it is, I can merely see you reflected in your works. It is over those works that I labor whenever I want to forget the places, times, and customs around me. I am often filled with anger at today's morals, when people value only gold and silver, and want nothing but physical pleasures.

"I have to thank you for many things, but especially because you have so often helped me forget the evils of today, and have transported me to happier times. As I read you, I seem to be living with Scipio, Brutus, Cato, and many others. It is with them that I live, and not with the ruffians of today, among whom an evil star had me born. Oh, the great names that comfort me in my wretchedness, and make me forget this wicked age! Please greet for me those older historians like Polybius, and those younger than you like Pliny.

"Farewell forever, you unequalled historian!

"Written in the land of the living, in that part of Italy where you were born and buried, in sight of your own tombstone, on the 22nd of February in the 1350th year after the birth of Him whom you would have seen had you lived longer."

Petrarch, *Epistolae Familiares*, 24.8. Passages selected and translated by Theodore K. Rabb.

Petrarch had wondered whether individuals should cut themselves off from the larger world, with its corruptions and compromises, and focus only on what he called the contemplative life, or try to improve that world through an active life. Petrarch's models had offered no clear answer. Cicero had suggested the need for both lives, but Augustine had been fearful of outside temptations. In the generations following Petrarch, however, the doubts declined, and the humanists argued that only by participating in public life, seeking higher ends for one's society as well as oneself, could an individual be truly virtuous. Republican government was the best form, they argued, because unless educated citizens made use of their wisdom for the benefit of all, their moral understanding would not benefit their societies. These were lessons exemplified by the ancient classics, and thus in one connected argument the civic humanists defended the necessity of studying the ancients, the superiority of the active life, and the value of Florentine republican institutions.

Humanism in the Fifteenth Century

As the humanist movement gained in prestige, it captured all of Italy. Pope Nicholas V (1447–1455), for example, founded a library in the Vatican that was to become the greatest repository of ancient manuscripts in Italy. And princely courts, such as those of the Gonzaga family at Mantua and the Montefeltro family at Urbino, gained fame because of their patronage of humanists. Moreover, the influence of antiquity was felt in all areas of learning and writing. Literature was profoundly influenced by the ancients, as a new interest in Classical models reshaped the form and content of both poetry and drama, from the epic to the bawdy comedy. Purely secular themes, without religious purpose, became more common. And works of history grew increasingly analytic, openly acknowledging inspiration from ancient writers such as Livy.

Education Perhaps the most direct effect was on education itself. Two scholars from the north of Italy, Guarino da Verona and Vittorino da Feltre, succeeded in turning the diffuse educational ideas of the humanists into a practical curriculum. Guarino argued for a reform of traditional methods of education, and Vittorino brought the new methods to their fullest development in the various schools he founded, especially his Casa Giocosa ("Happy House") at Mantua. The pupils included boys and girls, both rich and poor (the latter on scholarships). All the students learned Latin and Greek, mathematics, music, and philosophy; in addition—because Vittorino believed that education should aid physical, moral, and social development—they were taught social graces, such as dancing and courteous manners, and received instruction in physical exercises like riding and fencing. Vittorino's school attracted pupils from all over Italy, and his methods were widely imitated.

Raphael
Portrait of Baldassare Castiglione, ca. 1514
**Raphael painted this portrait of his friend, the count
Baldassare Castiglione, around 1514. Castiglione's solemn
pose and thoughtful expression exude the dignity and
cultivation that were described as essential attributes of the
courtier in Castiglione's famous book on courtly behavior.**
Giraudon/Art Resource, NY

Ultimately, a humanist education was to give the elite throughout Europe a new way of measuring social distinction. It soon became apparent that the ability to quote Virgil or some other ancient writer was not so much a sign of moral seriousness as a badge of superiority. What differentiated people was whether they could use or recognize the quotations, and that was why the new curriculum was so popular—even though it seemed to consist, more and more, of endless memorizations and repetitions of Latin texts.

New Standards of Behavior   The growing admiration for the humanists and their teachings also gave an important boost to the patronage of arts and letters. In the age of gunpowder, it was no longer easy to claim that physical bravery was the supreme quality of noblemen. Instead, nobles began to set themselves apart not just by seeking a humanist education but also by patronizing artists and writers whose praise made them famous.

Thus, a new image of fine behavior, which included the qualities that Guarino fostered—a commitment to taste and elegance as well as to courage—became widely accepted. This new lifestyle was promoted in a book, *The Courtier*, written in 1516 by Baldassare Castiglione, which took the form of a conversation among the sophisticated men and women at the court of Duke Federigo Montefeltro of Urbino, Castiglione's patron. *The Courtier* became a manual of proper behavior for gentlemen and ladies for centuries.

Humanism Triumphant   By the mid-1400s Humanism dominated intellectual life in much of Italy, and by 1500 it was sweeping all of Europe, transmitted by its devotees and also by a recent invention, printing, which made the texts of both humanists and ancients far more easily available. Dozens of new schools and universities were founded, and no court of any significance was without its roster of artists and writers familiar with the latest ideas. Even legal systems were affected, as the principles of Roman law (which tended to endorse the power of the ruler) were adopted in many countries. But in the late fifteenth century the revival of antiquity took a direction that modified the commitment to the active life that had been the mark of the civic humanists. A new movement, **Neoplatonism,** emphasized the interest in spiritual values that was the heart of the contemplative life.

The Florentine Neoplatonists

The turn away from the practical concerns of the civic humanists toward a renewed exploration of grand ideals of truth and perfection was a result of the growing interest in Greek as well as Roman antiquity—especially the works of Plato. A group of Florentine philosophers, active in the last decades of the fifteenth century and equally at home in Greek and Latin, led the way. They were known as "Neoplatonists," or "new" followers of Plato.

Ficino   The most gifted of these Neoplatonists was the physician Marsilio Ficino. His career is a tribute to the cultural patronage of the Medici family, which spotted his talents as a child and gave him the use of a villa and library near Florence. In this lovely setting, a group of scholars and statesmen met frequently to discuss philosophical questions. Drawn to the idealism of Plato, Ficino and his colleagues argued that Platonic ideas demonstrated the dignity and immortality of the human soul. To spread these views among a larger audience, Ficino translated into Latin all of Plato's dialogues and the writings of Plato's chief followers. Another member of the group, Giovanni Pico della Mirandola, tried to reconcile all philosophies, including

MAP 12.1 THE SPREAD OF UNIVERSITIES IN THE RENAISSANCE
This map charts the growing importance of education and the emergence of new universities throughout Europe during the Renaissance. Even where earlier universities existed, as at Oxford, many new colleges were founded, and the number of graduates increased rapidly in the fifteenth and sixteenth centuries. How do you suppose that Humanism is related to the growing number of universities?
◆ For an online version, go to www.mhhe.com/chambers9 > chapter 12 > book maps

those of Asia, in order to show that there was a single truth that lay behind every quest for the ideal.

Both Ficino and Pico started from two essential assumptions. First, the entire universe is arranged in a hierarchy of excellence, with God at the summit. Second, each being in the universe, with the exception only of God, is impelled by "natural appetite" to seek perfection; to try to achieve—or at least contemplate—the beautiful. As Pico expressed it, humans are placed in the middle of the universe, linked with both the spiri-

tual world above and the material world below. Their free will enables them to seek perfection in either direction; they are free to become all things. The good life should thus be an effort to achieve personal perfection, and the highest human value is the contemplation of the beautiful.

These writers believed that Plato had been divinely illumined and, therefore, that Platonic philosophy and Christian belief were two wholly reconcilable faces of a single truth. Because of this synthesis, and also its passionate idealism, Neoplatonic philosophy was to be a major influence on artists and thinkers for the next two centuries.

The Heritage of the New Learning

Although its scholarship was often arid and difficult, fifteenth-century Italian Humanism left a deep imprint on European thought and education. The humanists greatly improved the command of Latin; they restored a large part of the Greek cultural inheritance to Western civilization; their investigations led to a mastery of other languages associated with great cultural traditions, most notably Hebrew; and they laid the basis of modern textual criticism. They also developed new ways of examining the ancient world—through archaeology, numismatics (the study of coins), and epigraphy (the study of inscriptions on buildings, statues, and the like), as well as through the study of literary texts. As for the study of history, while medieval chroniclers had looked to the past for evidence of God's providence, the humanists used the past to illustrate human behavior and provide moral examples. They also helped standardize spelling and grammar in vernacular languages; and the Classical ideals of simplicity, restraint, and elegance of style that they promoted helped reshape Western literature.

No less important was the role of the humanists as educational reformers. The curriculum they devised spread throughout Europe in the sixteenth century, and until the twentieth century it continued to define the standards by which the lay leaders of Western society were trained. The fact that men and women throughout Europe came to be steeped in the same classics meant that they thought and communicated in similar ways. Despite Europe's divisions and conflicts, this common humanistic education helped preserve the fundamental cultural unity of the West.

ART AND ARTISTS IN THE ITALIAN RENAISSANCE

The most visible effect of Humanism and its admiration for the ancients was on the arts. Because the movement first took hold in Florence, it is not surprising that its first artistic disciples appeared among the Florentines. They had other advantages. First, the city was already famous throughout Italy for its art, because the greatest painters of the late 1200s and 1300s, Cimabue (1240–1302) and his pupil Giotto (1276–1336), were identified with Florence. Giotto, in particular, had decorated buildings from Padua to Naples and thus gained a wide audience for the sense of realism, power-

Giotto di Bondone
PIETÀ (LAMENTATION)
The Florentine Giotto di Bondone (ca. 1267–1337) was the most celebrated painter of his age. He painted fresco cycles in a number of Italian cities, and this segment from one of them indicates the qualities that made him famous: the solid bodies, the expression of human emotion, and the suggestion of landscape, all of which created an impact that was without precedent in medieval art.
Scrovegni Chapel, Padua, Italy. Alinari/Art Resource, NY

ful emotion, and immediacy that he created (in contrast to the formal, restrained styles of earlier artists). Second, Florence's newly wealthy citizens were ready to patronize art; and third, the city had a tradition of excellence in the design of luxury goods such as silks and gold objects. Many leading artists of the 1400s and 1500s started their careers as apprentices to goldsmiths, in whose workshops they mastered creative techniques as well as aesthetic principles that informed their painting, sculpture, and architecture.

Three Friends

The revolution in these three disciplines was started by three friends, who were united by a determination to apply the humanists' lessons to art. They wanted to break with the styles of the immediate past and create paintings, statues, and buildings that would not merely imitate the glories of Rome but actually bring them back to life. All three went to Rome in the 1420s, hoping by direct observation and study of ancient masterpieces to re-create their qualities and thus fulfill the

Masaccio
THE EXPULSION OF ADAM AND EVE, **1425–1428**
**Masaccio shows Adam and Eve expelled from paradise
through a rounded archway that recalls ancient architecture.
Also indicative of the influence of Roman art is the attempt
to create what we would consider realistic (rather than
stylized) human beings and to portray them nude, displaying
powerful, recognizable emotions. This was one of the
paintings that made the Brancacci Chapel an inspiration to
generations of artists.**
Brancacci Chapel, S. Maria del Carmine, Florence, Italy. Erich
Lessing/Art Resource, NY

humanists' goal of reviving the spirit of Classical
times. The locals thought the three very strange, for
they went around measuring, taking notes, and calculating sizes and proportions. But the lessons they
learned enabled them to transform the styles and purposes of art.

Masaccio   Among the three friends, the painter Masaccio (1401–1428) used the inspiration of the ancients to
put a new emphasis on nature, on three-dimensional
human bodies, and on perspective. In showing Adam
and Eve, he not only depicted the first nudes since
antiquity but showed them coming through a rounded
arch that was the mark of Roman architecture, as opposed to the pointed arch of the Middle Ages. The
chapel he decorated in a Florentine church, the
Carmine, became a place of pilgrimage for painters,
because here the values of ancient art—especially
its emphasis on the individual human figure—were
reborn.

Donatello   Masaccio's friend Donatello (1386–1466)
was primarily a sculptor, and his three-dimensional figures had the same qualities as Masaccio's in paint.
Once again the focus was on the beauty of the body itself, because that had been a notable and distinctive
concern of the ancients. The interest in the nude, accurately displayed, transformed the very purpose of art,
for it led to an idealized representation of the human
form that had not been seen in centuries. Because the
biblical David—shown by Donatello in contemplation
after his triumph over Goliath—symbolized vigor,
youth, and the weak defeating the strong, he became a
favorite hero for the Florentines.

Brunelleschi   The most spectacular of these three pioneers was the architect Brunelleschi (ca. 1377–1446).
For decades, his fellow citizens had been building a
new cathedral, which, as a sign of their artistic superiority, was going to be the largest in Italy. Seen from
above, it was shaped—as was traditional—like a cross.
The basic structure was in place, but the huge space at
which the horizontal and vertical met, the crossing,
had not yet been covered. In response to a competition
for a design to complete the building, Brunelleschi, inspired by what he had learned in Rome, proposed covering the crossing with the largest dome built in
Europe since antiquity. Although the first reaction was
that it was impossible, eventually he got the commission. In an extraordinary feat of engineering, which required that he build the dome in rings, without using
scaffolding, he erected a structure that became not only
a fitting climax to the cathedral but also the hallmark
of Renaissance Florence and an inspiration for all archi-

Brunelleschi
DOME OF FLORENCE CATHEDRAL, 1420–1436
Brunelleschi's famous dome—the first built in Italy since the fall of the Roman Empire—embodied the revival of Classical forms in architecture. The contrast with the bell tower designed a century earlier by Giotto, with its suggestion of pointed Gothic arches, is unmistakable. The dome was a feat of engineering as well as design: Its 135-foot diameter was spanned without scaffolding, and Brunelleschi himself invented the machines that made the construction possible.
© David Ball/Corbis Stock Market

Donatello
***DAVID*, CA. 1430–1432**
Like Masaccio, Donatello imitated the Romans by creating idealized nude bodies. His David has just killed and decapitated Goliath, whose head lies at his feet. Goliath's helmet recalls those worn by Florence's enemies, which makes this sculpture a work of patriotism as well as art. It happens also to have been the first life-size bronze figure cast since antiquity.
Alinari/Art Resource, NY

tects. The symmetrical simplicity of his other buildings shaped a new aesthetic of harmony and balance that matched what Masaccio and Donatello accomplished in painting and sculpture. In all three, the imitation of ancient Rome inspired subjects and styles that broke decisively with their immediate medieval past.

New Creativity During the remaining years of the 1400s, a succession of artists, not just in Florence but increasingly in other parts of Italy as well, built on the achievements of the pioneer generation. They experimented with perspective and the modeling of bodies and drapery, so as to recapture the ancients' mastery of depth, and they made close observations of nature. Sculptors created monumental figures, some on horseback, in imitation of Roman models. And architects perfected the use of the rounded arches and symmetrical forms they saw in antique buildings. Subject matter also changed, as artists produced increasing numbers of portraits of their contemporaries and depicted stories out of Roman and Greek myths as well as traditional religious scenes. By the end of the 1400s, the leading Florentine painter of the day, Botticelli (ca. 1444–1510), was presenting ancient subjects like the *Birth of Venus*, goddess of love, in exactly the way a Roman might have fashioned them.

The High Renaissance

The artists at work in the early years of the 1500s are often referred to as the generation of the High Renaissance. Four in particular—Leonardo, Raphael, Michelangelo, and Titian—are thought of as bringing the new movement that had begun a hundred years before to a climax.

Leonardo The oldest, Leonardo (1452–1519), was the epitome of the experimental tradition. Always seeking new ways of doing things, whether in observing

Leonardo da Vinci
MONA LISA, CA. 1503–1505
This is probably the most celebrated image in Renaissance art. The famous hint of a smile and the calm and solid pose are so familiar that we all too easily forget how striking it seemed at the time and how often it inspired later portraits. As in his *Last Supper*, however, Leonardo was experimenting with his materials, and the picture has therefore faded over the years.
Louvre, Paris, France. Réunion des Musées Nationaux/Art Resource, NY

CHRONOLOGY
A Century and a Half of Renaissance Art

1420s	Masaccio, Donatello, and Brunelleschi visit Rome and begin transforming painting, sculpture, and architecture
1430s	Donatello's *David*; completion of Brunelleschi's dome; Van Eyck's *Arnolfini Marriage*
1440s	Botticelli born; death of Brunelleschi
1450s	Leonardo da Vinci born
1460s	Death of Donatello
1470s	Dürer, Michelangelo, and Titian born
1480s	Raphael born; Botticelli's *Birth of Venus*
1490s	Dürer's *Apocalypse*
1500s	Leonardo's *Mona Lisa*; Michelangelo's *David*; Cellini born
1510s	Raphael and Michelangelo decorate the Vatican; Titian's *Bacchanal*
1520s	Deaths of Raphael and Dürer
1530s	Michelangelo's *Last Judgement* in the Sistine Chapel
1540s	Cellini's *Salt Cellar*; Titian's *Charles V at Mülberg*
1550s	Giorgio Vasari begins publishing *Lives of the Artists*, the first study of the achievements of Renaissance art
1560s	Death of Michelangelo
1570s	Deaths of Cellini and Titian

anatomy or designing fortifications, he was unable to resist the challenge of solving practical problems, even in his paintings. They are marvels of technical virtuosity, which make difficult angles, tricks of perspective, and bizarre geological formations look easy. His portrait of the Mona Lisa, for example, is famous not only for her mysterious smile but for the incredible rocky landscape in the background. Unfortunately, Leonardo also experimented with methods of painting; as a result, one of his masterpieces, the *Last Supper*, has almost completely disintegrated.

Raphael By contrast, Raphael (1483–1520) used the mastery of perspective and ancient styles that had been achieved in the 1400s to produce works of perfect harmony, beauty, and serenity. His paintings give an impression of utter relaxation, of an artist in complete command of his materials and therefore able to create sunny scenes that are balanced and at peace. His tribute to the ancient world, *The School of Athens*, places

in a Classical architectural setting the great philosophers of Greece, many of whom are portraits of the artists of the day: Plato, for instance, has Leonardo's face. If the philosophers were the chief glory of Athens, Raphael seems to be saying, then the artists are the crowning glory of the Renaissance.

Michelangelo For Michelangelo (1475–1564), painting was but one means of expression. Equally at home in poetry, architecture, and sculpture, he often seems the ultimate embodiment of the achievements of his age. Constantly seeking new effects, he once said that no two of the thousands of figures he depicted were the same, and one might add that just about every one of them conveys the sense of latent strength, of striving, that was Michelangelo's signature. In *The Creation of*

Raphael
SCHOOL OF ATHENS
Painted in 1510 and 1511, this fresco celebrating the glories of Greek philosophy represents the triumph of the Renaissance campaign to revive antiquity. That the classical setting and theme could have been accepted as appropriate for a wall of the Vatican suggests how completely Humanism had captured intellectual life. A number of the figures are portraits of artists whom Raphael knew: Plato, pointing to heaven at the back, has the face of Leonardo, and the notoriously moody Michelangelo broods, with his head on his arm, at the front.
Scala/Art Resource, NY

Man Adam, shown at the moment of his creation, has not yet received the gift of life from God, but he already displays the vigor that Michelangelo gave to every human body. The same is true of Michelangelo's version of David, seemingly tranquil but showing his potential power in his massive, oversized hand. The human being is shown in full majesty, as an independent and potent individual.

Titian   In Venice, developments in art took a slightly different form. This was also a rich trading city, sophisticated, with broad international connections. But here Humanism was not so central, and the art—as befitted this most down-to-earth and cosmopolitan of Europe's cities—was more sensuous. The most famous Venetian painter, Titian (ca. 1482–1576), depicted rich velvets, lush nudes, stormy skies, and dogs with wagging tails

with a directness and immediacy that enable the viewer almost to feel them. His friend Aretino said of one of his pictures: "I can say nothing of the crimson of the garment nor of its lynx lining, for in comparison real crimson and real lynx seem painted, and these seem real." Titian was Europe's most sought-after portraitist, and to this day we can recognize the leading figures of his time, and sense their character, because of the mastery of his depictions.

Status and Perception

Art as Craft   To the generation of Masaccio, a painter was merely one of the many people engaged in a craft, not inherently more admired than a skilled clothworker or mason. Like them, he was a member of a guild, he had to pass a carefully regulated apprenticeship, and he was

◀ **Michelangelo**
THE CREATION OF MAN
Michelangelo worked on the ceiling of the Sistine Chapel in the Vatican from 1508 to 1512 and painted hundreds of figures. None has come to symbolize the rebirth associated with the Renaissance and the power of creative genius so forcefully as the portrayal of God extending a finger to bring the vigorous body of Adam to life. Tucked under God's other arm is the figure of Eve, ready to join Adam in giving birth to humankind.
Detail of the Sistine ceiling. Scala/Art Resource, NY

◀ **Titian**
BACCHANAL (THE ANDRIANS), 1518–1519
The earthy realism of Venice contrasted sharply with the idealization common in Florentine art. The setting and even the sky seem more tangible, and Titian's lush nude in the foreground (who was to be much copied) is the essence of sensuality. It has been suggested that the painting represents the different stages of life, from the incontinent child through the vigorous youths and adults to the old man who has collapsed in the back.
Museo del Prado, Madrid, Spain. Scala/Art Resource, NY

Joos van Wassenhove and Pedro Berruguete
FEDERICO DA MONTEFELTRO WITH HIS SON GUIDOBALDO
This remarkable painting embodies the new ideal of the gentleman that emerged in the Renaissance. Federico da Montefeltro was both one of the most notable warriors and one of the most distinguished patrons of learning of the age, and this portrait captures both sides of his princely image. Sitting in his study with his richly clothed son, Guidobaldo, Duke Federico is reading a book but is also dressed in armor.
Galleria Nazionale delle Marche, Urbino, Italy. Scala/Art Resource, NY

subject to the rules that controlled his trade. Both Donatello and Brunelleschi were trained as goldsmiths, and the latter was even briefly imprisoned by his guild for not paying his dues while he was working on the cathedral dome—as an independent person, so he thought, and thus outside the guild structure. Given the Florentines' interest in gaining fame by beautifying their city, it was not surprising that the work of these artists should have attracted considerable attention. But it rarely occurred to anyone in the early 1400s—as Brunelleschi discovered from his guild—that they might deserve special respect or be considered more elevated than tradesmen. It was true that some of them were becoming famous throughout Italy, but would that lead to a change in their social status?

Humanism and the Change in Status   The answer was that it did, and again the impetus came from the humanist movement. Three consequences of the revival of antiquity, in particular, began to alter the position of the artist. First was the recognition that the most vivid and convincing re-creations of the achieve-

ments of the ancient world were being produced in the visual arts. No letter written like Cicero's could compare with a painting, a statue, or a building as a means of bringing Rome back to life for all to see.

A second influence was the humanists' new interest in personal fame. This had been an acceptable aspiration in antiquity, but during the Middle Ages spiritual

ISABELLA D'ESTE'S QUEST FOR ART

As the passion for art took hold, the great patrons of the Renaissance became relentless in their search for new works. None was more avid than Isabella d'Este (1474–1539), who became the wife of the Gonzaga prince of Mantua at the age of sixteen and made her private suite of rooms (which she called her studio) a gathering place for artists, musicians, and poets for nearly fifty years. Her passion for art shines through her letters; in these extracts, she is pursuing both the Venetian painter Bellini and Leonardo da Vinci.

"To an agent, 1502: 'You may remember that many months ago we gave Giovanni Bellini a commission to paint a picture for the decoration of our studio, and when it ought to have been finished we found it was not yet begun. We told him to abandon the work, and give you back the 25 ducats, but now he begs us to leave him the work and promises to finish it soon. As till now he has given us nothing but words, tell him that we no longer care to have the picture, but if instead he would paint a Nativity, we should be well content, as long as he does not keep us waiting any longer.'

"Two months later: 'As Bellini is resolved on doing a picture of the Madonna and Child and St. John the Baptist in place of the Nativity scene, I should be glad if he would also include a St. Jerome; and about the price of 50 ducats we are content, but above all urge him to serve us quickly and well.'

"Three years later, to Bellini himself: 'You will remember very well how great our desire was for a picture painted by your hand, to put in our studio. We appealed to you for this in the past, but you could not do it on account of your many other commitments. (We recently heard you might be free,) but we have been ill with fever and unable to attend to such things. Now that we are feeling better it has occurred to us to write begging you to consent to painting a picture, and we will leave the poetic invention for you to make up if you do not want us to give it to you. As well as the proper payment, we shall be under an eter-nal obligation to you. When we hear of your agreement, we will send you the measurements of the canvas and an initial payment.'

"In the meantime, in May 1504, she wrote to Leonardo da Vinci: 'Hearing that you are staying in Florence, we have conceived the hope that something we have long desired might come true: to have something by your hand. When you were here and drew our portrait in charcoal, you promised one day to do it in color. Since it would be inconvenient for you to move here, we beg you to keep your good faith with us by substituting for our portrait a youthful Christ of about twelve years old, executed with that sweetness and soft ethereal charm which is the peculiar excellence of your art.'

"Five months later she wrote again: 'Some months ago we wrote to you that we wanted to have a young Christ, about twelve years old, by your hand. You replied that you would do this gladly, but owing to the many commissioned works you have on your hands, we doubt whether you remembered ours. Wherefore it has occurred to us to send you these few lines, begging you that you will turn to doing this little figure for us by way of recreation, which will be doing us a very gracious service and of benefit to yourself.'"

From D. S. Chambers (ed.), *Patrons and Artists in the Italian Renaissance*, London: Macmillan, 1970, pp. 128–130 and 147–148.

---

concerns encouraged a disdain for worldly matters. It was still a problem for Petrarch to admit that, like the ancients he admired, he wanted to be famous. Among later humanists, the doubts receded, and the princes who valued their ideas eagerly accepted the notion that they should devote their lives to attaining fame. That was what nobles previously had won as warriors, but now there was a more reliable way to ensure that one's name lived forever.

The New Patrons That way was provided by the third of the humanists' lessons: that the truly moral person had to combine the contemplative with the active life. A prince, therefore, ought to cultivate the fine as well as the martial arts. No aristocratic court could be complete without its poets and painters, who sang their pa-tron's praises while fashioning the masterpieces that not only brought prestige but also endured forever. As a result, if an aristocrat wanted immortality, it was no longer enough to be a famous warrior; now it became essential to build a splendid new palace or have one's portrait done by a famous painter. To be most like the virtuous heroes of Rome who were the society's ideal, vigorous leadership had to be linked to patronage of culture, and this outlook was not confined to noblemen. Noblewomen, whose chief role had long been to offer an idealized object of chivalric devotion and who continued to struggle to gain access to education, occasionally won that struggle, and the result was a refined patronage that could be crucial in fashioning a princely image. Without Isabella d'Este, for example, the court in Mantua would not have achieved its fame as a center of

Sandro Botticelli
THE BIRTH OF VENUS
Sandro Botticelli was a member of the intellectual circle of Lorenzo de Medici, and this painting is evidence of the growing interest in Neoplatonism at the Medici court. The wistful, ethereal look on Venus' face reflects the otherworldliness that was emphasized by the Neoplatonists; moreover, their belief in the analogies that link all ideas suggests that Botticelli may have been implying that Venus resembled the Virgin Mary as a source of divine love. In depicting an ancient myth as ancient painters would have shown it, Botticelli represents the triumph of Renaissance ambitions, and the idealized beauty of his work helped shape an aesthetic standard that has been admired ever since.
Erich Lessing/Art Resource, NY

painting, architecture, and music. That both Leonardo and Titian did her portrait was a reflection not of her husband's importance but of her own independent contribution to the arts. Her rooms, surrounding a lovely garden, remain one of the wonders of the palace at Mantua and a worthy testimony to her fame as a patroness (see "Isabella d'Este's Quest for Art," p. 350).

The effect of this new attitude was to transform the status of artists. They became highly prized at the courts of aristocrats, who saw them as extraordinarily effective image makers. Perhaps the most famous family of patrons in Italy, the Medici of Florence, were envied throughout Europe mainly because, for generations, they seemed always to be surrounded by the finest painters, sculptors, and architects of the age. And soon the richest princes in Italy, the popes, followed suit. The Church had been the main sponsor of art in the Middle Ages, but now it was the papacy in particular that promoted and inspired artistic production. In their determination to rebuild and beautify Rome as a worthy capital of Christendom, the popes gave such artists as Raphael and Michelangelo their most famous commissions—notably Michelangelo's Sistine Chapel within the Vatican. It was thus as a result of shifting patterns in the commissioning and buying of art that, as honored members of papal as well as princely courts, Renaissance artists created both a new aesthetic and a new social identity.

THE CULTURE OF THE NORTH

North of the Alps the transformations of the 1300s and 1400s were not as dramatic as in Italy, but they had consequences after 1500 that were no less dramatic than the effects of Humanism, Neoplatonism, and the other changes in the south. This area of Europe did not have the many large cities and the high percentages of

Benozzo Gozzoli
Procession of the Three Kings to Bethlehem (detail), 1459
This enormous fresco in the Medici palace in Florence, completed in 1459, gives place of honor in the biblical scene of the procession of the Magi to the future ruler of Florence, the ten-year-old Lorenzo de Medici, riding a white horse, and to his grandfather Cosimo de Medici, the founder of the dynasty's power, who is behind Lorenzo, also on a white horse.
Palazzo Medici Riccardi, Florence, Italy. Erich Lessing/Art Resource, NY

urban dwellers that were crucial to the humanist movement in Italy. Nor did the physical monuments and languages of northern Europe offer ready reminders of the Classical heritage. Humanism and the revival of classical learning—with its literate, trained laity—did not come to the north until the last decade of the fifteenth century. But in these territories, where cultural life was dominated by the princely court rather than the city, and by the knight rather than the merchant, there were other vital shifts in outlook.

Chivalry and Decay

In 1919 a Dutch historian, Johan Huizinga, described northern European culture in the 1400s and 1500s not as a renaissance but as the decline of medieval civiliza-

tion. His stimulating book, *The Waning of the Middle Ages*, focused primarily on the court of the dukes of Burgundy, who were among the wealthiest and most powerful princes of the north. Huizinga found tension and frequent violence in this society, with little of the serenity that had marked the thirteenth century.

Its uneasiness and inclination to escape from reality was reflected in its extravagant cultivation of the notion of chivalry. Militarily, the knight was becoming less important than the foot soldier armed with longbow, pike, or firearms. But the noble classes of the north continued to pretend that knightly virtues governed all questions of state and society; they discounted such lowly considerations as money, arms, recruitment, and supplies in deciding the outcome of wars. For example, before the Battle of Agincourt, one knight told the French king

Benvenuto Cellini
SALT CELLAR FOR FRANCIS I
Benvenuto Cellini, a Florentine goldsmith who challenged
the common distinction between artisan and artist in his
lively *Autobiography* (1562), executed this work for the
French king Francis I in 1543. Juxtaposing allegorical images
of the Earth and the Sea, which he presented as opposing
forces, Cellini created figures as elegant as any sculpture and
set them on a fantastic base of gold and enamel. His
extraordinary skills indicate why so many Renaissance
artists began their careers in goldsmiths' workshops.
Erich Lessing/Art Resource, NY

Charles that he should not use contingents from the
Parisian townsfolk because that would give his army an
unfair numerical advantage; the battle should be decided strictly on the basis of chivalrous valor.

Bravery and Display

This was the age of the perfect
knight and the "grand gesture." King John of Bohemia
insisted that his soldiers lead him to the front rank of
battle, so that he could strike at the enemy even
though he was blind. The feats of renowned knights
won the admiration of chroniclers but hardly affected
the outcome of battle. And the reason for the foundation of new orders of chivalry—notably the Knights of
the Garter in England and the Burgundian Knights of
the Golden Fleece—was that these orders would reform
the world by cultivating knightly virtues.

Princes rivaled one another in the sheer glitter of
their arms and the splendor of their tournaments.
They waged wars of dazzlement, seeking to confound
rivals with spectacular displays of gold, silks, and tap-
estries. Court ceremony was marked by excess, as
were the chivalric arts of love. A special order was
founded for the defense of women, and knights frequently took lunatic oaths to honor their ladies, such
as keeping one eye closed for weeks. Obviously, people
rarely made love or war in this artificial way. But they
still found satisfaction in dreaming about the possibilities for love and war if this sad world were only a
perfect place.

The Cult of Decay

Huizinga called the extravagant
lifestyle of the northern courts the "cult of the sublime," or the impossibly beautiful. But he also noted
that both knights and commoners showed a morbid
fascination with death and its ravages. Reminders of
the ultimate victory of death and treatments of decay
are frequent in both literature and art. One popular
artistic motif was the **danse macabre,** or dance of
death, depicting people from all walks of life—rich and
poor, clergy and laity, good and bad—dancing with a
skeleton. Another melancholy theme favored by artists
across Europe was the *Pietà*—the Virgin weeping over
her dead son.

This morbid interest in death and decay in an age of
plague was not the result of lofty religious sentiment.
The obsession with the fleetingness of material beauty
in fact indicated how attached people were to earthly
pleasures; it was a kind of inverse materialism. Above
all, the gloom reflected a growing religious dissatisfaction. In the 1200s Francis of Assisi addressed death as a
sister; in the fourteenth and fifteenth centuries people
apparently regarded it as a ravaging, indomitable fiend.
Clearly (as Petrarch, too, had noted) the Church was
failing to provide consolation to many of its members,
and a religion that fails to console is a religion in crisis.

Devils and Witches

Still another sign of the unsettled
religious spirit of the age was a fascination with the
devil, demonology, and witchcraft. The most enlightened scholars of the day wondered whether witches
could ride through the air on sticks. One of the more
notable witch trials of Western history was held at Ar-
ras in 1460, when scores of people were accused of participating in a witches' sabbath, giving homage to the
devil, and having sexual intercourse with him. In 1486
two inquisitors who had been authorized by the pope to
prosecute witches published the *Malleus Maleficarum*
("hammer of witches"), which defined witchcraft as
heresy and became the standard handbook for prosecu-
tors. Linked to the fear of the devil was a fear of women.
They were the most frequent victims of witchcraft accusations, easy scapegoats in an age of social upheaval.
Any hint of change in their traditional subordination to
men, such as learning to read, combined with their vulnerability to make them targets of denunciation.

Relics

There was also a growing fascination with
concrete religious images. The need to have immediate, physical contact with the objects of religious devotion added to the popularity of pilgrimages and
stimulated the obsession with the relics of saints.
These were usually fake, but they became a major commodity in international trade. Some princes accumulated collections of relics numbering in the tens of
thousands.

Huizinga saw these aspects of northern culture as signaling the disintegration of the cultural synthesis of the Middle Ages. Without a disciplined and unified view of the world, attitudes toward war, love, and religion lost balance, and disordered behavior followed. The culture was not young and vigorous but old and dying. Yet the concept of decadence must be used with caution. Certainly this was a disturbed world that had lost the self-confidence of the thirteenth century; but these supposedly decadent people, though dissatisfied, were also passionately anxious to find solutions to the tensions that unsettled them. We need to recall that passion when trying to understand the appeal and the power behind other cultural movements—lay piety and efforts of religious reform.

Literature, Art, and Music

Literature In addition to the fascination with the chivalric and the supernatural, there was also a fascination with the everyday, the equivalent in the North of the down-to-earth work of Boccaccio. His most famous disciple was an Englishman, Geoffrey Chaucer (ca. 1340–1400), who was a soldier, diplomat, and government official. His *Canterbury Tales*, written in the 1390s, recounts the pilgrimage of some thirty men and women to the tomb of St. Thomas Becket at Canterbury. For entertainment on the road, each pilgrim agrees to tell two stories. Chaucer's lively portraits are a rich tapestry of English society, especially in its middle ranges. The stories also sum up the moral and social ills of the day. His robust monk, for example, ignores the Benedictine rule; his friar is more interested in donations than in the cure of souls; his pardoner knowingly hawks fraudulent relics; and the wife of Bath complains of prejudice against women. Apart from the grace of his poetry, Chaucer had the ability to delineate character and spin a lively narrative. The *Canterbury Tales* is a masterly portrayal of human personalities and human behavior that can delight readers in any age.

Art The leaders of the transformation in both the style and the status of artists in the 1400s were mainly Italians. But there were also major advances in northern Europe. Indeed, oil painting—on wood or canvas—was invented in the Netherlands, and its first great exponent, Jan Van Eyck, a contemporary of Donatello, revealed both the similarities and the differences between North and South. Van Eyck was less interested in idealization than were the Florentines and more fascinated with the details of the physical world. One sees almost every thread in a carpet. But his portrait of an Italian couple, the Arnolfinis, is shot through with religious symbolism as well as a sly sense of humor about

Albrecht Dürer
THE RIDERS ON THE FOUR HORSES FROM THE APOCALYPSE, **CA. 1496**
The bestseller that Dürer published in 1498, *The Apocalypse*, has the text of the biblical account of the apocalypse on one side and full-page woodcuts on the other. The four horsemen who will wreak vengeance on the damned during the final Day of Judgment are Conquest holding a bow, War holding a sword, Famine, or Justice, holding scales, and Death, or Plague, riding a pale horse and trampling a bishop.
Woodcut. The Metropolitan Museum of Art, Gift of Junius S. Morgan, 1919. (19.73.209). Photograph © 2002 The Metropolitan Museum of Art, New York

sex and marriage. The dog is a sign of fidelity, and the carving on the bedpost is of St. Margaret, the patron saint of childbirth; but the single candle is what newlyweds are supposed to keep burning on their wedding night, and the grinning carved figures behind their clasped hands are a wry comment on their marriage. The picture displays a combination of earthiness and piety that places it in a tradition unlike any in the Italy of this time (see p. 336).

The leading northern artist of the period of the High Renaissance was a German, Albrecht Dürer, who deliberately sought to blend southern and northern styles. He made two trips to Venice, and the results were clear in a self-portrait that shows him as a fine gentleman, painted in the Italian style. But he continued, especially in the engravings that made him famous, to emphasize the detailed depiction of nature and the religious purposes that were characteristic of northern art.

Dürer refused to break completely with the craft origins of his vocation. He knew, from his visits to Venice, that Italian painters could live like lords, and he was invited by the Holy Roman Emperor to join his court. But he preferred to remain in his home city of Nuremberg, earning his living more through the sale of his prints than from the stipends he was offered by patrons. Eventually he became a highly successful **entrepreneur,** creating different kinds of prints for different markets—the elite liked elegant and expensive copper engravings, while others preferred cruder but cheaper woodcuts—and producing a best seller in a book of illustrations of the Apocalypse. His wife was a highly effective seller of his prints, and she preferred running her stall in the marketplace to fine entertainments by city fathers. Indeed, the couple can be seen as pioneers in the business of art.

Developments in Music

The process that was at work in the visual arts had similar effects in music, which again had developed primarily for liturgical purposes in the Middle Ages. In the Renaissance, musicians became as prized as artists at princely courts, and their growing professionalism was demonstrated by the organists and choir singers hired by churches, the trumpeters employed by cities for official occasions, and the composers and performers who joined the households of the wealthy. Musical notation became standardized, and instruments became more diverse as old ones were improved and new ones—such as the viol, the oboe, and the clavichord—were invented. Moreover, unlike the practice of art, which usually required apprenticeship to guilds that were closed to women, musical performance, whose patron saint was St. Cecilia, relied on the talents of both men and women.

Unlike the visual arts, the chief musical center of Europe around 1500 was in the Low Countries, not Italy. The choirmasters of cathedral towns like Bruges employed professional singers who brought to new levels the traditional choral form of four-part polyphony (that is, four different lines playing against one another). This complex vocal harmony had no need of instrumental accompaniment; as a result, freed from their usual subservience to the voice, instruments could be developed in new ways. The greatest masters of the time, Guillaume Dufay and Josquin des Prez, excelled in secular as well as religious music, and theirs was one field of creativity in which new techniques and ideas flowed mainly from the north to Italy, not the other way around.

SCHOLASTIC PHILOSOPHY AND RELIGIOUS THOUGHT

In theology, Scholasticism retained its hold even as Humanism swept the literary world. But it was not the thirteenth-century Scholasticism of Thomas Aquinas, which asserted that human reason could fashion a universal philosophy that embraced all truths and reconciled all apparent conflicts. Nor did the traditional acceptance of ecclesiastical law continue, with its definition of the Christian life in terms of precise rules of behavior rather than interior spirit. The style of thinking changed as the Scholastics of the 1400s and 1500s were drawn to analysis (breaking apart) rather than synthesis (putting together) as they examined philosophical and theological statements. Many of them no longer shared Aquinas' confidence in human reason, and they hoped to repair his synthesis or to replace it with new systems that, though less comprehensive, could at least be more easily defended in an age growing doubtful about reason. Discussions of faith changed too, as more and more Christian leaders sought ways to deepen the interior, sometimes mystical, experience of God.

The "Modern Way"

The followers of Aquinas remained active in the schools, but the most original of the Scholastics in the fourteenth century took a different approach to their studies. They were known as **nominalists,** because they focused on the way we describe the world—the names (in Latin, *nomina*) that we give to things—rather than on its reality. The nominalists denied the existence, or at least the knowability, of the universal forms that supposedly make up the world—"manness," "dogness," and the like. The greatest among them was the English Franciscan William of Ockham (ca. 1300–ca. 1349), and his fundamental principle came to be called Ockham's razor. It states essentially that, between alternative explanations for the same phenomenon, the simpler is always to be preferred.

Ockham

On the basis of this "principle of parsimony," Ockham attacked the traditional focus of philosophy on universal, ideal forms. These concepts had led Aquinas to argue, for instance, that all individual beings must be understood as reflections of their universal forms. By contrast, Ockham argued that the simplest way to explain the existence of any specific object is just to say it exists. The mind can find resemblances among objects and make generalizations about them, which can then be examined in coherent and logical ways. But these offer no certainty of the actual existence of Aquinas' ideal forms—the universal principles like "manness" that all beings and objects reflect.

The area of reality that the mind can grasp is thus severely limited. The universe, as far as human reason can detect, is a collection of separate beings and objects, not a hierarchy of ideal forms. The proper way to deal with this universe is by direct experience, not by speculating about abstract natures. Such a philosophy, based on observation and reason, sought limited, not universal, truths. Ockham believed that one could still prove the existence of some general principles, but he thought human beings could know very little about the ultimate necessary principle, God.

Nominalist Theology   Ockham and many of his contemporaries insisted on the total power of God and humanity's absolute dependence on him. If he chose, God could reward vice, punish virtue, and act erratically; which raised the question, how could there be a stable system of theology or ethics? The nominalists' answer was that, instead of using his absolute power, God relied on his ordained power: through a covenant, or agreement, God assures people that he will act in consistent and predictable ways. Thus, theology becomes the study not of metaphysics but of God's will and covenant with the human race.

Nominalists rejected Aquinas' high assessment of human powers and his confident belief in the ordered and knowable structure of the natural world. Living in a disturbed, pessimistic age, they reflected the crisis of confidence in natural reason and human capability that is a major feature of the cultural history of the North in these years. Nominalists were popular in the universities, and Ockhamite philosophy, in particular, came to be known as the *via moderna* ("modern way"). Although nominalists and humanists were frequently at odds, they did share a dissatisfaction with aspects of the medieval intellectual tradition, especially the speculative abstractions of medieval thought; and both advocated approaches to reality that concentrated on the concrete and the present and demanded a strict awareness of method.

Social and Scientific Thought

Marsilius   The belief of the nominalists that reality was to be found not in abstract forms but in concrete objects had important implications for social thought. The most remarkable of these social thinkers was Marsilius of Padua, an Italian lawyer who served at the French royal court. In 1324 he wrote a book, *Defender of Peace*, which attacked papal authority and supported lay sovereignty within the Church. His purpose was obviously to endorse the independent authority of his patron, the king of France, who pursued a running battle with the pope. But his work had wider implications. Using nominalist principles, Marsilius argued that the reality of the Christian community, like the reality of the universe, consists of the sum of all its parts. The sovereignty of the Church thus belongs to its members, who alone can define the collective will of the community.

Marsilius was one of the first theorists of the modern concept of sovereignty. Emphasizing secular authority, he maintained that only regulations supported by force are true law and that, therefore, the enactments of the Church do not bind because they are not supported by coercive force. The Church has no right to power or to property and is entirely subject to the sovereign will of the state, which is indivisible, absolute, and unlimited. *Defender of Peace* is noteworthy not only for its radical ideas but also for its reflection of deep dissatisfactions. Marsilius and others revealed a hostile impatience with the papal and clerical domination of Western political life. They wanted laypersons to guide the Church and the Christian community. In this respect at least, the book was a prophecy of things to come.

New Explanations of Nature   In studies of nature, a few nominalists at Paris and Oxford in the fourteenth century took the first hesitant steps toward a criticism of the Aristotelian world system that had dominated European studies of physics ever since they had been recovered through translations by Muslim scholars. At the University of Paris, for example, Jean Buridan proposed an important revision in Aristotle's theory of motion. If, as Aristotle had said, all objects are at rest in their natural state, what keeps an arrow flying after it leaves the bow? Aristotle had reasoned rather lamely that the arrow disturbs the air through which it passes and that it is this disturbance that keeps pushing the arrow forward. Buridan suggested, instead, that the movement of the bow lends the arrow a special quality of motion, an "impetus," that stays with it permanently unless removed by the resistance of the air. In addition, Buridan and other fourteenth-century nominalists theorized about the acceleration of falling objects and made some attempt to describe this phenomenon in mathematical terms. Although they were often inadequate or inaccurate, these attempts at new explanations started the shift away from an unquestioned acceptance of ancient systems (such as Aristotle's) that was to climax, three hundred years later, in the scientific revolution.

Humanism and Science   Humanists also helped prepare the way for scientific advance. They rediscovered important ancient writers whose works had been forgotten, and their skills in textual and literary criticism taught people to look with greater precision at works inherited from the past. As more of the classics became available, it became apparent that ancient authors did not always agree. Could they, therefore, always be correct? Furthermore, the idealism of Plato and the number mysticism of Pythagoras suggested that unifying forms and harmonies lay behind the disparate data of experience and observation. Once this assumption took hold, it was soon being argued that perhaps the cosmic harmonies might be described in mathematical terms.

THE STATE OF CHRISTENDOM

The Church as an institution also experienced major transformations in the 1300s and 1400s. It continued to seek a peaceful Christendom united in faith and obedience to Rome. But the international Christian community was in fact beset by powerful forces (reflected by Marsilius) that undermined its cohesiveness and weakened papal authority and influence. Although the culmination of these disruptions did not come until the Reformation in the 1500s, the history of the previous two centuries made it clear that the institution was profoundly troubled.

The Avignon Exile   The humiliation of Pope Boniface VIII by the agents of Philip IV of France at Anagni in 1303 opened the doors to French influence at the curia. In 1305 the College of Cardinals elected a French pope, Clement V, who because of the political disorders in the Papal States eventually settled at Avignon (1309). Though technically a part of the Holy Roman Empire, Avignon was in language and culture a French city. The popes who followed Clement hoped to return to Rome but remained at Avignon, claiming that the continuing turmoil of central Italy would not permit papal government to function effectively. These popes were skilled administrators who expanded the papal bureaucracy enormously—especially its fiscal machinery—but the long absence from Rome clearly harmed papal prestige.

Fiscal Crisis   Like many secular governments, the papacy at Avignon faced an acute fiscal crisis. But unlike the major powers of Europe, its territorial base could not supply it with the funds it needed, because controlling the Papal States usually cost more money than they produced. As a result, the papacy was drawn into the unfortunate practice of exploiting its ecclesiastical powers for financial gain. Thus, the popes insisted that candidates appointed to high ecclesiastical offices pay a special tax, which usually amounted to a third or a half of the first year's revenues. The popes also claimed the income from vacant offices and even sold future appointments to office when the incumbents were still alive. Dispensations, which were also sold, released a petitioner from the normal requirements of canon law.

A monastery or religious house, for example, might purchase an exemption from visitation and inspection by the local bishop. The pope received in tithes one-tenth of the revenues of ecclesiastical benefices or offices throughout Christendom. And the Church offered indulgences, remissions of the temporal punishment for sin, in return for monetary contributions to the papacy.

These fiscal practices enlarged the popes' revenues, but they had deplorable results. Prelates who paid huge sums to Avignon tended to pass on the costs to the lower clergy. Parish priests, hardly able to live from their incomes, were more easily tempted to lower their moral standards. The flow of money to Avignon angered rulers and prompted demands for a halt to such payments and even for the confiscation of Church property. Dispensations gravely injured the authority of the bishops, since an exempt person or house all but escaped their supervision. The bishops were frequently too weak, and the pope too distant, to deal effectively with abuses on the local level. The fiscal measures thus helped sow chaos in many parts of the Western Church.

The Great Schism   The end of the seventy-year Avignon exile led to a controversy that almost split the Western Church. In 1377 Pope Gregory XI returned reluctantly to Rome and died there a short time later. The Roman people, fearing that Gregory's successor would once more remove the court to Avignon and thereby deprive Rome of desperately needed revenues, agitated for the election of an Italian pope. Responding to this pressure, the College of Cardinals found a compromise candidate who satisfied both French and Italian interests, but the new pope, Urban VI (1378–1389), soon antagonized the French cardinals by trying to limit their privileges and by threatening to pack the College with his own appointments. Seven months after choosing Urban, a majority of the cardinals declared that his election had taken place under duress and was invalid; they then named a new pope, who returned to Avignon. Thus began the **Great Schism** of the West (1378–1417), the period when two, and later three, popes fought over the rule of the Church.

Christendom now had two pretenders to the throne of Peter, one in Rome and one in Avignon. Princes and peoples quickly took sides (see map 12.2), and the troubles of the papacy multiplied. Each pope had his own court and needed yet more funds, both to meet ordinary expenses and to pay for policies that he hoped would defeat his rival. And since each pope excommunicated the other and those who supported him, everyone in Christendom was at least technically excommunicated.

The Conciliar Movement   Theologians and jurists had long speculated on who should rule the Church if

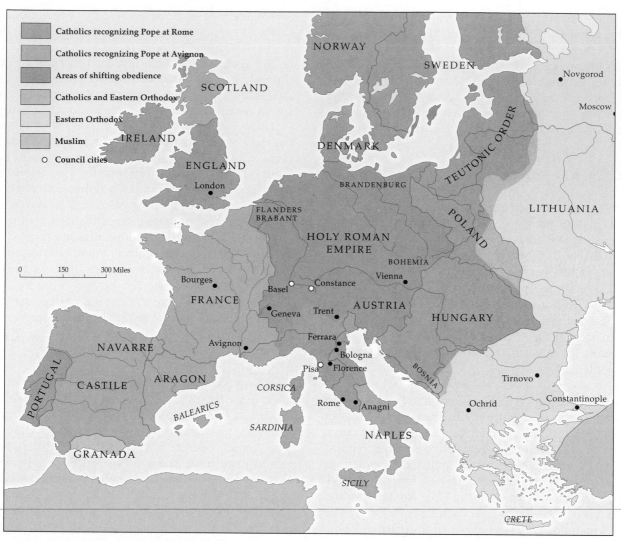

MAP 12.2 THE GREAT SCHISM, 1378–1417
The antagonisms in Europe during the Great Schism set neighboring regions against one another and created divisions from which the Church never fully recovered. One of the problems that made the Great Schism particularly acute was the presence of different papal candidates in different cities. Avignon was a long way from Rome, and it easy for the "pope" in one city to ignore his rival in the other. Which countries and regions recognized the pope at Rome? Which recognized the pope at Avignon? What were the areas of shifting obedience? What do you notice about the location of the councils that tried to end the schism? Where were they in relation to Avignon and Rome?

◆ For an online version, go to www.mhhe.com/chambers9 > chapter 12 > book maps

the pope were to become heretical or incompetent; some concluded that it should be the College of Cardinals or a general council of Church officials. Since the College of Cardinals had split into two factions, each backing one of the rival popes, many prominent thinkers supported the theory that a general council should rule the Church. These **conciliarists,** as they were called, went further. They wanted the Church to have a new constitution to confirm the supremacy of a general council. Such a step would have reduced the pope's role to that of a limited monarch, but the need to correct numerous abuses strengthened the

idea that a general council should rule and reform the Church.

Pisa and Constance　The first test of the conciliarists' position was the Council of Pisa (1409), convened by cardinals of both Rome and Avignon. This council asserted its supremacy within the Church by deposing the two popes and electing another. But this act merely added to the confusion, for it left Christendom with three rivals claiming to be the lawful pope. A second council finally resolved the situation. Some four hundred ecclesiastics assembled at the Council of Constance (1414–1418), the greatest international gathering of the Middle Ages. The council was organized in a new way, with the delegates voting as nations to offset the power of the Italians, who made up nearly half the attendance. This procedure reflected the new importance of national and territorial churches. It enabled the delegates to depose both the Pisan pope and the Avignon pope and persuade the Roman pope to resign. In his stead they elected a Roman cardinal, who took the name Martin V. Thus, the Great Schism was ended, and the Western Church was once again united under a single pope.

As the meetings continued, the views of the conciliarists prevailed. The delegates formally declared that a general council was supreme within the Church. To ensure continuity in Church government, they also directed that new councils be summoned periodically.

The Revival of the Papacy

In spite of this assertion of supremacy, the council made little headway in reforming the Church. The delegates, mostly great prelates, were the chief beneficiaries of the fiscal system and were reluctant to touch their own privileges and advantages. The real victims of the fiscal abuses, the lower clergy, were poorly represented. As a result, the council could not agree on a general program of reform, because it was too large, too cumbersome, and too divided to maintain effective ecclesiastical government. The restored papacy soon reclaimed its position as supreme head of the Western Church.

The practical weaknesses of the conciliar movement were revealed at the Council of Basel (1431–1449). Because disputes broke out almost at once with the pope, the council deposed him and elected another, Felix V. The conciliar movement, designed to heal the schism, now seemed responsible for renewing it. Recognizing the futility of its actions, the council tried to rescue its dignity when Felix died by endorsing the cardinals' election of a new pope, Nicholas V, in 1449 and then disbanding. This action ended efforts to give supreme authority to councils. But the idea of government by representation that they advanced was to have an important influence on later political developments in Europe.

Territorial Independence Although the popes remained suspicious of councils, they had much more serious rivals to their authority in the powerful lay princes, who were exerting ever tighter control over territorial churches. Both England and France issued decrees that limited papal powers within their kingdoms, and this policy was soon imitated in Spain and the stronger principalities of the Holy Roman Empire. Although such decrees did not establish national or territorial churches, they do document the decline of papal control over the international Christian community.

The Revival of Rome When Martin V returned to Rome in 1417, the popes faced the monumental task of rebuilding their office and their prestige as both political and cultural leaders of Europe. They wanted Rome to be a major capital, a worthy home for the papacy, and not dependent on French rulers or culture, as they had been for the past century. To this end, they adopted the new literary and artistic ideas of the Renaissance, and the result was a huge rebuilding program that symbolized the restored authority of the popes. They sought, as one contemporary put it, "by the construction of grand and lasting buildings to increase the honor of the Roman Church and the glory of the Apostolic see, and widen and strengthen the devotion of all Christian people." One of the popes even proclaimed that if any city "ought to shine by its cleanliness and beauty, it is above all that which bears the title of capital of the universe." The building of a new St. Peter's Church in the 1400s was but the climax of this campaign of beautification, designed to assert a cultural supremacy that went along with the supremacy of the pope's authority. At the same time, vigorous military campaigns in the Papal States subdued that difficult territory and established the papacy as a major Italian power.

It could be argued, however, that in identifying itself so closely with Rome and with Italian politics, the papacy became less universal. For all its splendor and its renewed control over the institution of the Church, it was failing to retain the spiritual allegiance of Europe, especially in the North. The popes may have succeeded in reshaping the Church into a powerful and centralized body, and in making Rome once again a cultural capital of the Western world, but the new cultural and intellectual forces that were at work in the 1400s ultimately undermined the centrality of the papacy to the life of Europe.

Styles of Piety

Partly in response to the disorder of the Church as an institution, new forms of piety and religious practice began to appear. Whereas praying for the salvation of the community had once been considered the clergy's responsibility, many now felt that it was up to each individual to seek the favor of God.

Lay Mysticism and Piety One consequence was that mysticism—an interior sense of the direct presence and love of God—which previously had been seen only in monastic life, began to move out of the monasteries in the thirteenth century. The prime mission of the Franciscans and the Dominicans was preaching to the laity, and they were now communicating some of the satisfactions of mystical religion. Laypersons wishing to remain in the outside world could join special branches of the Franciscans or Dominicans known as third orders. **Confraternities,** which were religious guilds founded largely for laypersons, grew up in the cities and, through common religious services and programs of charitable activities, tried to deepen the spiritual lives of their members. Humanism had strong overtones of a movement for lay piety. And hundreds of devotional and mystical works were written to teach laypersons how to feel repentance, not just how to define it. Translations of the Scriptures into vernacular languages also appeared, though the Church disapproved of such efforts, and the high cost of manuscripts before the age of printing severely limited their circulation.

This growth of lay piety was, in essence, an effort to give everyone access to forms of faith that hitherto had been restricted to a spiritual elite. Frightened by the disasters of the age, people hungered for emotional reassurance, for evidence of God's love and redeeming grace within themselves. Also, the spread of education among the laity, at least in the cities, made people discontented with empty forms of religious ritual.

Female Piety The commitment to personal piety among the laity was particularly apparent among women. It is significant that in the years between 1000 and 1150 male saints outnumbered females by 12 to 1, but in the years 1348 to 1500 the ratio dropped to 2.74 to 1. Moreover, the typical female saints of the later Middle Ages were no longer queens, princesses, and abbesses. They were mystics and visionaries, ordinary yet charismatic people who gained the attention of the Church and the world by the power of their message and the force of their own personalities. Catherine of Siena (1347–1380), for example, was the youngest of the twenty-five children of a humble Italian dyer. Her reputation for holiness attracted a company of followers from as far away as England, and she wrote (or dictated, for she probably couldn't write) devotional tracts that are monuments of Italian literature. Similar charismatic qualities made a simple Englishwoman, Margery Kempe, famous for her visions and her piety.

Women who out of poverty or preference lived a religious life outside convents became numerous, especially in towns. Some lived with their families, and others eked out a living on the margins of society. Still others lived in spontaneously organized religious houses—called *Beguines* in northern Europe—where they shared all tasks and property. The Church was suspicious of these women professing a religious life outside convents, without an approved rule. But the movement was too large for the Church to suppress or control. And many of them came to be particularly identified with one of the most powerful forms of lay piety in this period, mysticism.

Pisan Artist of XIV Century
THE MYSTIC MARRIAGE OF CATHERINE OF SIENA
Catherine of Siena was a nun who was known for her efforts to return the papacy to Rome. Part of the reason for her sainthood was that, like Joan of Arc, she experienced visions from an early age. She is shown here with her symbol, the lily, in a scene from one of her visions. About to enter into a mystic marriage with Christ, she is accepting the wedding ring directly from him. Note that in the Renaissance, wedding rings were often placed on the middle finger of the right hand.
Soprintendenza B.A.A.A.S., Pisa. Museo Nazionale di S. Matteo

The Mystics Among the most active centers of the new lay piety was the Rhine valley, a region that was especially noted for its remarkable mystics. The most famous was the Dominican Meister Eckhart (ca. 1260–ca. 1327), a spellbinding preacher who sought to bring his largely lay listeners into a mystical confrontation with God. Believers, he maintained, should cultivate the "divine spark" that is in every soul by banishing all thought and seeking to attain a state of pure passivity. If they succeeded, the divine presence would dwell within them. God is too great for dogma, he taught, and cannot be moved by conventional piety.

Brethren of the Common Life Just as the nominalists argued for philosophical reasons that God is unknowable, so the mystics dismissed the value of formal knowledge and stressed the need for love and an emotional commitment to God. Perhaps the most influential of the mystics was Gerhard Groote of Holland.

Groote wrote sparingly, exerting his influence over his followers largely through his personality. After his death in 1384, his disciples formed a religious congregation known as the Brethren of the Common Life. The Brethren founded schools in Germany and the Low Countries that imported a style of lay piety known as the *devotio moderna* ("modern devotion). This emphasized interior experience as essential to faith. The believer needed no fasting, pilgrimages, or other acts of piety, but only imitation of the life of Jesus. Later reformers, such as Erasmus of Rotterdam and Martin Luther, were to be among the pupils of the Brethren.

Features of Lay Piety

The new lay piety was by no means a revolutionary break with the medieval Church, but it implicitly discounted the importance of many traditional institutions and practices. In this personal approach to God, there was no special value in the monastic vocation. As Erasmus would later argue, what was good in monasticism should be practiced by every Christian. Stressing simplicity and humility, the new lay piety reacted against the pomp and splendor that surrounded popes, prelates, and religious ceremonies. Likewise, the detailed rules for fasts, abstinences, and devotional exercises; the cult of the saints and their relics; and the traffic in indulgences and pardons all seemed peripheral to true religious needs. Without the proper state of the soul, these traditional acts of piety were meaningless; with the proper state, every act was worship. This new lay piety, emerging as it did out of medieval religious traditions, was clearly a preparation for the reformations of faith that took place in the sixteenth century among both Protestants and Catholics. It helped produce a more penetrating faith at a time when the formal beliefs of the Middle Ages, for all their grandeur and logical intricacies, no longer fully satisfied the religious spirit and were leaving hollows in the human heart.

Although the *devotio moderna* was a religious movement with little regard for humanist learning, it shared the humanists' distaste for the abstractions and intellectual arrogance of Scholasticism, and their belief that a wise and good person will cultivate humility and will maintain a "learned ignorance" toward the profound questions of religion. Moreover, both movements directed their message primarily to laypersons, in order to help them lead a higher moral life. The humanists, of course, drew their chief inspiration from the works of pagan and Christian antiquity, whereas the advocates of the new lay piety looked almost exclusively to Scripture. But the resemblances were close enough for scholars like Erasmus and Thomas More, writing in the early 1500s, to combine elements from both in the movement known as Christian Humanism.

Movements of Doctrinal Reform

The effort to reform the traditions of medieval Christianity also led to open attacks on the religious establishment—fueled, of course, by antagonism toward the papacy and Church corruption and by the larger tensions of this troubled epoch. Above all, these attacks gained support because the Church remained reluctant to adapt its organization and teachings to the demands of a changing world. In two prominent cases, moreover, the critiques arose at a university, where the basic method of instruction, the disputation, encouraged the discussion of unorthodox ideas. At disputations, students learned by listening to arguments for and against standard views. It was not impossible for someone taking the "wrong" side in such a debate to be carried away and cross the line between a theoretical discussion and open dissent.

Wycliffe

Whatever its origins, the most prominent of the assaults of the 1300s was launched by an Englishman, John Wycliffe (ca. 1320–1384), who taught at Oxford University. Wycliffe argued that the Church had become too remote from the people, and he wanted its doctrines simplified. To this end, he sought less power for priests and a more direct reliance on the Bible, which he hoped would be translated into English to make it easier to understand. Beyond his unease over the Church's remoteness from ordinary believers, he may have had political reasons (and thus support) for his stand. He was close to members of the royal court, who were increasingly resistant to papal demands and who were troubled that, in the midst of England's war with France, the papacy should have come under French influence when it moved from Rome to Avignon. In 1365 Wycliffe denounced the payment of Peter's pence, the annual tax given by English people to the papacy, and shortly thereafter he publicly denounced the papal curia, monks, and friars for their vices.

Wycliffe argued that the Scriptures alone declared the will of God and that neither the pope and the cardinals nor the Scholastic theologians could tell Christians what they should believe. In particular, he questioned one of the central dogmas of the Church that emphasized the special power of the priest: **transubstantiation,** which asserts that priests at the Mass work a miracle when they change the substance of bread and wine into the substance of Christ's body and blood. Besides attacking the exalted position and privileges of the priesthood in such rites as transubstantiation, Wycliffe denied the authority of the pope and the hierarchy to exercise jurisdiction or to hold property. He claimed that the true Church was that of the predestined—that is, those whom God would save and

HUS AT CONSTANCE

A few weeks before he was executed, Jan Hus wrote to his Czech followers to tell them how he had responded to his accusers at the Council of Constance:

"Master Jan Hus, in hope a servant of God, to all faithful Czechs who love God: I call to your attention that the proud and avaricious Council, full of all abomination, condemned my Czech books having neither heard nor seen them; even if it had heard them, it would not have understood them. O, had you seen that Council which calls itself the most holy, and that cannot err, you would have seen the greatest abomination! I have heard it commonly said that Constance would not for thirty years rid itself of the sins which that Council has committed. That Council has done more harm than good.

"Therefore, faithful Christians, do not allow yourselves to be terrified by their decrees, which will profit them nothing. They will fly away like butterflies, and their decrees will turn into a spiderweb. They wanted to frighten me, but could not overcome God's power in me. They did not dare to oppose me with Scripture.

"I am writing this to you that you may know that they did not defeat me by any Scripture or any proof, but that they sought to seduce me by deceits and threats to recant and abjure. But the merciful Lord God, whose law I have extolled, has been and is with me, and I hope that He will be with me to the end and will preserve me in His grace until death.

"This letter was written in chains, in the expectation of death."

From Matthew Spinka (ed.), *The Letters of John Hus*, Manchester: University Press, 1972, pp. 195–197.

---

were thus in a state of grace. Only these elect could rule the elect; therefore, popes and bishops who had no grace could have their properties removed and had no right to rule. Responsibility for ecclesiastical reform rested with the prince, and the pope could exercise only as much authority as the prince allowed.

The Lollards Many of Wycliffe's views were branded heretical, but even though he was forced to leave Oxford when he offended his protectors at the royal court, they did keep him unharmed until he died. His followers, mostly ordinary people known as **Lollards**—a name apparently derived from lollar ("idler")—were not so lucky. They managed to survive as an underground movement in the countryside until the Protestant Reformation exploded more than a century later, but they were constantly hounded, and in 1428 the Church had Wycliffe's remains dug up, burned, and thrown into a river.

Hus An even harsher fate awaited Wycliffe's most famous admirer, a Bohemian priest named Jan Hus (1369–1415), who started a broad and even more defiant movement in his homeland. Hus was a distinguished churchman and scholar. He served as rector (the equivalent of president) of the Charles University in Prague, one of Europe's best-known institutions, and he was the main preacher at a fashionable chapel in Prague. Like Wycliffe, whose ideas he had first heard expounded at a disputation, he argued that priests were not a holy and privileged group, set apart from laypersons, but that the Church was made up of all the faithful. To emphasize this equality, he rejected the division that allowed the congregation at a Mass to consume the wafer that symbolized Christ's body but not the wine that symbolized his blood, which only the priest could drink. In a dramatic gesture, Hus shared the cup of wine with all worshipers, thus reducing the distinctiveness of the priest. His followers adopted a chalice, or cup, as the symbol of their movement.

Hus did not hesitate to defy the leadership of the Church. Denounced for the positions he had taken, he replied by questioning the authority of the pope himself: "If a Pope is wicked, then like Judas he is a devil and a son of perdition and not the head of the Church militant. If he lives in a manner contrary to Christ, he has entered the papacy by another way than through Christ." In 1415 Hus was summoned to defend his views before the Church Council at Constance. Although he had been guaranteed safe passage if he came to answer accusations of heresy, the promise was broken. He was condemned, handed over to the secular authorities, and executed (see "Hus at Constance," above). But his followers, unlike the Lollards who stayed out of sight in England, refused to retreat in the face of persecution.

The Hussites A new leader, Jan Žižka, known as John of the Chalice, raised an army and led a successful campaign against the emperor, who was also king of Bohemia and the head of the crusade that was now mounted against the **Hussites.** The resistance lasted twenty years, outliving Žižka, but sustained by Bohemian nobles, and eventually the Hussites were allowed to establish a special church, the Utraquist Church, in which both cup and wafer were shared by all worshipers at Mass. But Hus's other demands, such as the surrender of all personal possessions by the clergy (an echo of St. Francis), were rejected. Those who tried to fight on for these causes were defeated in battle, and after a long struggle the resistance came to an end, having made only a minor dent in the unity of the Church.

Summary

The popular appeal of Wycliffe and Hus reflected widespread dissatisfaction with official teachings in the late 1300s and 1400s—a dissatisfaction that Petrarch, too, had shared, though he did not challenge traditional doctrine but simply looked elsewhere for moral guidance. The movement that he launched, Humanism, transformed education and the arts, but others were determined to bring change to Europe's spiritual leadership as well. When, in pursuit of this ideal, Wycliffe and Hus chose to risk open confrontation, they demonstrated that reform ideas, advanced by charismatic leaders, could find a following among those who resented the authoritarian and materialistic outlook of the Church. At the same time, however, it became clear that such dissent could not survive without support from nobles, princes, or other leaders of society. Even with such help, the Hussites had to limit their demands; without it, they would have gained nothing. It was one hundred years after Hus's death before a new reformer arose who had learned these lessons, and he was to transform Western Christianity beyond recognition.

QUESTIONS FOR FURTHER THOUGHT

1. Why is it, when we think of the "golden ages" of history, that it is not just new ideas, but great art, that makes them seem such special times?

2. How do dominant cultural institutions like the medieval Church lose their hold over people's loyalty and respect?

RECOMMENDED READING

Sources

*Brucker, Gene A. (ed.). *The Society of Renaissance Florence: A Documentary Study.* 1971.

*Cassirer, Ernst, P. O. Kristeller, and J. H. Randall, Jr. (eds.). *The Renaissance Philosophy of Man.* 1953. Selections from Petrarch, Ficino, Pico, and others.

*Chambers, David, and Brian Pullan (eds.). *Venice: A Documentary History,* 1450–1630. 1992.

Kempe, Margery. *The Book of Margery Kempe* (1436). B. A. Windeatt (tr.). 1985. The autobiography of an extraordinary woman.

*Kohl, Benjamin G., and Ronald G. Witt (eds.). *The Earthly Republic: Italian Humanists on Government and Society.* 1978.

*Marsilius of Padua. *Defender of Peace.* Alan Gerwith (tr.). 1986.

Studies

*Berenson, Bernard. *The Italian Painters of the Renaissance.* 1968. Classic essays on the history of art.

Brown, Judith, and Robert Davis (eds.). *Gender and Society in Renaissance Italy.* 1998.

*Burckhardt, Jacob. *The Civilization of the Renaissance in Italy.* 1958. One of the pioneering works of European history, first published in 1860.

Campbell, Gordon (ed.). *The Oxford Dictionary of the Renaissance.* 2003.

*Hale, John. *The Civilization of Europe in the Renaissance.* 1993. The best overview.

*Hollingsworth, Mary. *Patronage in Renaissance Italy from 1400 to the Early Sixteenth Century.* 1994.

*Huizinga, Johan. *The Waning of the Middle Ages.* 1954.

Klapisch-Zuber, Christiane. *Women, Family, and Ritual in Renaissance Italy.* 1985. Collected essays.

Martin, John, J. *The Renaissance: Italy and Abroad.* 2003.

*Rabb, Theodore K. *Renaissance Lives.* 1993.

*Available in paperback.

Pieter Brueghel the Elder
THE PEASANT DANCE, 1568
The most vivid images of life in the village during the sixteenth century were created by the Flemish artist Pieter Brueghel. The different human types, and the earthiness of country life, are captured in scenes that show the villagers both at work and, as here, at ease and relaxed. But the world of these ordinary Europeans was transformed during these very years by massive campaigns of religious reform: the Reformation and the Counter-Reformation. Even a villager unable to read would have been aware of the competing claim of these two movements, which swept through Europe from the 1520s onward.
Erich Lessing/Art Resource, NY

Chapter Thirteen

REFORMATIONS IN RELIGION

PIETY AND DISSENT • THE LUTHERAN REFORMATION •
THE SPREAD OF PROTESTANTISM • THE CATHOLIC REVIVAL

Although it may have seemed monolithic and all-powerful, the Roman Church in the fifteenth century was neither a unified nor an unchallenged institution. It had long permitted considerable variety in individual beliefs, from the analytic investigations of canon lawyers to the emotional outpourings of mystics. There were local saints, some of whom were recognized as holy only by a few villages; and for many Europeans the papacy remained a distant and barely comprehensible authority. To assume that its theological pronouncements were understood by the average illiterate Christian is to misrepresent the loose, fragmentary nature of the medieval Church. Moreover, the political disputes and reform movements of the fourteenth and fifteenth centuries had raised doubts about the central structure and doctrines of the Church. That the papacy had weathered these storms by 1500 indicated both how flexible and how powerful it was. What was to be remarkable in the years that followed was the sudden revelation of the Church's fragility, as a protest by a single monk snowballed into a movement that shattered the thousand-year unity of Western Christendom.

Execution of Savonarola, Florentine religious reformer **1498**—

Invention of printing **1450s**

PIETY AND DISSENT

The Roman Church may have held sway throughout Western Europe in 1500, but it was proving less and less able to meet the increasingly varied needs of the faithful. Different ideas about the ways an individual might achieve salvation were spreading, and some were turning into criticisms that the Church hierarchy could neither refute nor silence.

Doctrine and Reform

Two Traditions　A fundamental question that all Christians face is: How can sinful human beings gain salvation? In 1500, the standard official answer was that the Church was an essential intermediary. Only through participation in its rituals, and particularly through the seven **sacraments** its priests administered—baptism, confirmation, matrimony, the **Eucharist**, ordination, penance, and extreme unction—did the believer have access to the grace that God offered as an antidote to sin. But there was another answer, identified with distinguished Church fathers such as St. Augustine: People can be saved by their faith in God and love of him. This view emphasized inward and personal belief and focused on God as the source of grace.

The two traditions were not incompatible; for centuries they had coexisted without difficulty. Yet the absence of precise definition in many areas of doctrine was a major problem for theologians, because it was often difficult to tell where orthodoxy ended and heresy began. The position taken by the papacy, however, had grown less inclusive and adaptable over the years; by 1500 it seemed to be stressing the outward and institutional far more than the inward and personal route to salvation. Reformers for over a century had tried to reverse this trend, and it was unclear whether change

would come from within or would require a revolution and split in the Church.

The Quest for Reform　The root of the demand for change, as Hus had known, was the need of many laypersons for a way to express their piety that was more personal than official practices allowed. Church rituals meant little, they felt, unless believers could cultivate a sense of the love and presence of God. Rejecting the theological subtleties of Scholasticism, they sought divine guidance in the Bible and the writings of the early Church fathers, especially St. Augustine. Lay religious fraternities dedicated to private forms of worship and charitable works proliferated in the cities, especially in Germany and Italy. The most widespread in Germany, the Brotherhood of the Eleven Thousand Virgins, consisted of laypersons who gathered together, usually in a church, to sing hymns. In the mid-fifteenth century, more than one hundred such groups had been established in Hamburg, a city of slightly more than ten thousand inhabitants. Church leaders, unhappy about a development over which they had no control, had tried to suppress them, to no avail.

Savonarola　The most spectacular outburst of popular piety around 1500 occurred in seemingly materialist Florence, which embraced Girolamo Savonarola, a zealous friar who wanted to banish the irreligion and materialism he saw everywhere about him. The climax of his influence came in 1496, when he arranged a tremendous bonfire in which the Florentines burned cosmetics, light literature, dice, and other such frivolities. Savonarola embodied the desire for personal renewal that had long been a part of Western Christianity but seemed to be gaining intensity in the 1400s. His attempts at reform eventually brought him into conflict with the papacy, which rightly saw him as a threat to

- **1509** Erasmus, *The Praise of Folly*

- **1516** More, *Utopia*

- **1517** Luther's ninety-five theses; start of Reformation

■ **1524–1525** Peasants' Revolt in Germany

- **1534** King Henry VIII has himself proclaimed head of the Church of England

1534–1549 Pope Paul III launches Counter-Reformation

1545–1563 Council of Trent

Anonymous
THE MARTYRDOM OF SAVONAROLA, CA. 1500
This painting still hangs in the monastery of San Marco where Savonarola lived during his years of power. It shows the city's central square—a setting that remains recognizable to anyone who visits Florence today—where the bonfire of the "vanities" had been held in 1496, and where Savonarola was executed in 1498. The execution is depicted here as an event that the ordinary citizens of Florence virtually ignore as they go about their daily routines.
Erich Lessing/Art Resource, NY

its authority. The Church therefore denounced him and gave its support to those who resented his power in Florence. His opponents had him arrested in 1498 and then executed on a trumped-up charge of treason.

Reform in Spain The widespread search for a more intense devotional life was a sign of spiritual vitality. But Church leaders in the age of Savonarola gave little encouragement to ecclesiastical reform and the evangelization of the laity. Only in Spain were serious efforts launched to eradicate abuses and encourage religious fervor, and they were led not by Rome but by Queen Isabella herself and by the head of the Spanish Church, Cardinal Ximenes de Cisneros. In other countries the hierarchy reacted harshly when such movements threatened its authority.

Causes of Discontent

Although its power over the Church had been restored by 1500, the papacy was still struggling to assert spiritual authority in the wake of the blows it had received in the previous two centuries. The move to Avignon, the Great Schism, and the conciliar movement had challenged its aura of moral and doctrinal superiority, and now its troubles multiplied.

Secular Interests Of major concern to many Christians were the papacy's secular interests. Increasingly, popes conducted themselves like princes. With skillful diplomacy and military action, they had consolidated their control over the papal lands in the Italian peninsula; Julius II (1503–1513) was even known as the Warrior Pope. An elaborate court arose in Rome, famous for its lavish patronage of the arts and symptomatic of a commitment to political power and grandeur that seemed to eclipse religious duties. Matters had reached such a point that some popes used their spiritual powers to raise funds for their secular activities. The fiscal measures developed at Avignon had expanded the papacy's income, but the enlarged revenues led to widespread abuses. High ecclesiastical offices were bought and sold, and men (usually sons of nobles) were attracted to these positions by the opportunities they provided for wealth and power, not by a religious vocation.

Abuse was widespread at lower levels in the Church as well. Some prelates held several offices at a time and could not give adequate attention to any of them. The ignorance and moral laxity of the parish and monastic clergy also aroused antagonism. Even more damaging was the widespread impression that the Church was failing to meet individual spiritual needs because of its remoteness from the day-to-day concerns of the average believer, its elaborate and incomprehensible system of canon law and theology, and its formal

Hans Baldung Grien
The Three Ages of Woman and Death, 1510
The preoccupation with the transitoriness of life and the vanity of earthly things took many forms in the sixteenth century. Here the point is hammered home unmistakably, as the central figure—a young woman at the height of her beauty between infancy and old age—is reminded of the passage of time (the hourglass) and the omnipresence of death even as she admires herself in a convex mirror.
Kunsthistorisches Museum, Vienna, Austria. Erich Lessing/Art Resource, NY

ceremonials. Above all, there was a general perception that priests, monks, and nuns were profiting from their positions, exploiting the people, and offering minimal moral leadership or religious guidance in return.

Anticlericalism These concerns provoked anticlericalism (hostility to the clergy) and calls for reform, which went unheeded except in the Spain of Cardinal Ximenes. For increasing numbers of deeply pious people, the growing emphasis on ritual and standardized practices seemed irrelevant to their personal quest for salvation.

Hans Sebald Beham
LARGE PEASANT HOLIDAY, WOODCUT, **1535**
The celebration of the anniversary of a church's consecration was one of the most important holidays in a village. Not everyone, however, used this opportunity for spiritual ends, like the couple getting married in front of the church. Some overindulged at the tavern (lower right); some had a tooth extracted (center left); and some, as the chickens in the center and various couples in the scene suggest, used the occasion for pleasure alone.
Photograph © 1998. The Art Institute of Chicago. Potter Palmer Collection, 1967. 491. All rights reserved

And their reaction was symptomatic of the broad commitment to genuine piety that was apparent not only in the followers of Wycliffe, Hus, and Savonarola but in many segments of European society in the early 1500s.

Popular Religion

The Spread of Ideas It was not only the educated elite and the city dwellers (a minority of Europe's inhabitants) who sought to express their faith in personal terms. The yearning for religious devotion among ordinary villagers, the majority of the population, was apparent even when the local priest—who was often hardly better educated than his parishioners—did little to inspire spiritual commitments. People would listen avidly to news of distant places brought by travelers who stopped at taverns and inns (a major source of information and ideas), and increasingly the tales they told were of religious upheaval. In addition, itinerant preachers roamed some regions, notably Central Europe, in considerable numbers, and they drew crowds when they started speaking—on street corners in towns or out in the fields—and described the power of faith. They usually urged direct communication between believers and God, free from ritual and complex doctrine. To the vast crowds they often drew, many of them seemed to echo the words of St. Augustine: "God and the soul I want to recognize, nothing else."

Equally important as a means of learning about the latest religious issues were the gatherings that regularly brought villagers together. Throughout the year, they would assemble to celebrate holidays—not only the landmarks of the Christian calendar like Christmas and Easter but also local festivals. Religion was always essential to these occasions. When, for example, the planting season arrived, the local priest would lead a procession into the countryside to bless the fields and pray for good crops. Family events, too, from birth to death, had important religious elements.

The Veillée The most common occasion when the community's traditional beliefs and assumptions were aired, however, was the evening gathering—generally referred to by its French name, *veillée,* which means staying up in the evening. Between spring and autumn, when the weather was not too cold, a good part of the village came together at a central location after each day's work was done. There was little point in staying in one's own home after dark, because making a light with candles or oil was too expensive. Instead, sitting around a communal fire, people could sew clothes, repair tools, feed babies, resolve (or start) disputes, and discuss news. It was one of the few times when women were of no lesser status than men; the views they expressed were as important as any in shaping the common outlook of the villagers.

A favorite occupation at the *veillée* was listening to stories. Every village had its storytellers, who recounted wondrous tales of local history, of magical adventures, or of moral dilemmas, as the mood required. Biblical tales and the exploits of Christian heroes like the Crusaders had always drawn an attentive audience. Now, however, in addition to entertainment and general moral uplift, peddlers and travelers who attended the *veillée* brought news of challenges to religious traditions. They told of attacks on the pope and Church practices and of arguments for a simpler and more easily understood faith. In this way the ideas of religious reformers spread, and those with unorthodox views, such as the Lollards, kept their ideas alive. In some cases, the beliefs that were described made converts of those who heard them. Traveling preachers came to regard the *veillée* as a ready-made congregation; they were usually far more knowledgeable, better trained, and more effective than local priests.

The Role of the Priest   The response of the traditional Church to this challenge, after decades of indifference, was to insist that the local priest be better educated and more aware of what was at stake in the religious struggles of the day. As long as he had the support of the local authorities, he could make sure that his views dominated the *veillée.* Whichever way the discussions at these communal gatherings went, however, they demonstrated the power of popular piety in the tens of thousands of villages that dotted the European countryside.

The Impact of Printing   The expression of this piety received unexpected assistance from technology: the invention of a printing press with movable type in the mid-1400s. At least a hundred years earlier, Europeans had known that by carving words and pictures into a wood block, inking them, and pressing the block onto paper, they could make an image that could be repeated on many sheets of paper. We do not know exactly when they discovered that they could speed up this cumber-

Jost Amman
"THE PRINTER" FROM *DAS STÄNDEBUCH (THE BOOK OF TRADES),* 1568
This illustration is the first detailed depiction of a printer's shop, showing assistants taking type from large wooden holders in the back, the press on the right, the pages of type being prepared and inked in the foreground, and the sheets of paper before and after they are printed.

some process and change the text from page to page if they used individual letters and put them together within a frame. We do know, however, that a printer named Johannes Gutenberg, who lived in the city of Mainz on the Rhine, was producing books this way by the 1450s. The technique spread rapidly (see table on next page) and made reading material available to a much broader segment of the population.

It has been estimated that some nine million books had been printed by 1500. As a result, new ideas could travel with unprecedented speed. Perhaps a third of the men (and half that percentage of women) among the trading and upper classes—townspeople, the educated, and the nobility—could read, but books could reach a much wider audience, because peddlers began to sell printed materials throughout Europe. They were bought everywhere and became favorite material for reading out loud at *veillées.* Thus, people who had had

THE SPREAD OF PRINTING THROUGH 1500
Number of towns in which a printing press was established for the first time, by period and country

Period	German- Speaking Areas	Italian- Speaking Areas	French- Speaking Areas	Spain	England*	Netherlands	Other	Total
Before 1471	18	4	1	1	—	—	—	14
1471–1480	22	36	9	6	3	12	5	93
1481–1490	17	13	21	12	—	5	4	72
1491–1500	9	5	11	6	—	2	8	41
Total by 1500	56	58	42	25	3	19	17	220

*In an attempt to try to control the printers, the English government ordered that they work only in London and at Oxford and Cambridge universities.

Adapted from Lucien Febvre and Henri-Jean Martin, *The Coming of the Book: The Impact of Printing 1450–1800*, David Gerald (tr.), London: NLB, 1976, pp. 178–179, 184–185.

little contact with written literature in the days of manuscripts now gained access to the latest ideas of the time.

Printing and Religion   Printers quickly took advantage of the popular interest in books by publishing almanacs filled with home-spun advice about the weather and nature that were written specifically for simple rural folk. Even the almanacs, however, carried religious advice. More importantly, translations of the Bible made it available to ordinary people in a language that, for the first time, they could understand. Books thus became powerful weapons in the religious conflicts of the day. Devotional tracts, lives of the saints, and the Bible were the most popular titles—often running to editions of around one thousand copies. They became means of spreading new ideas, and the ready markets they found reflected the general interest of the age in spiritual matters.

Printing lessened the dependence of ordinary people on the clergy; whereas traditionally the priest had read and interpreted the Scriptures for his congregation, now people could consult their own copies. By 1522, eighteen translations of the Bible had been published. Some fourteen thousand copies had been printed in German alone, enough to make it easy to buy in most German-speaking regions. The Church frowned on these efforts, and governments tried to regulate the numbers and locations of presses; but in the end it proved impossible to control the effects of printing.

Piety and Protest in Literature and Art

Literature   The printing press broke the Church's monopoly over the dissemination of religious teachings. The most gifted satirist of the sixteenth century, for

Matthias Grünewald
THE TEMPTATION OF ST. ANTHONY, CA. 1515
This detail from a series of scenes Grünewald painted for the Isenheim Altar suggests the power that the devil held over the imagination of sixteenth-century Europeans. The gentle, bearded St. Anthony is not seated in contemplation, as in Dürer's portrayal (see plate on p. 372). Instead, he is surrounded by the monsters the devil has sent to frighten him out of his faith. This fear was a favorite subject of the period and provided artists like Bosch and Grünewald the opportunity to make vivid and terrifying the ordinary Christian's fear of sin.
A panel from the Isenheim Altar. Musée d'Unterlinden, Colmar, France. Erich Lessing/Art Resource, NY

Albrecht Dürer
Engraving of St. Anthony,
CA. **1600**
The ease and mastery that Dürer brought to the art of engraving made it as powerful and flexible a form as painting. Here the massive figure of the saint, deep in study, is placed in front of a marvelously observed city. The buildings display Dürer's virtuosity—their shapes echo the bulk and solidity of the figure— and they may have symbolized the temptations of city life for a saint who was revered for his solitary piety in the desert.
Victoria & Albert Museum,
London/Art Resource, NY

instance, the French humanist François Rabelais, was able to ridicule openly the clergy and the morality of his day.

But the attacks came from many directions. Scurrilous **broadsides**, usually anonymous, became very popular during the religious disputes of the 1500s. These single sheets often contained vicious assaults on religious opponents and were usually illustrated by cartoons with obscene imagery. The broadsides were examples of partisan hostility, but their broader significance should not be ignored. Even the most lowly of hack writers could share with a serious author like Rabelais a sense of outrage at indifference in high places and find an audience for attacks on the inadequate spiritual leadership of the time.

Piety in Art   The emphasis on religious belief, so evident in European literature, also permeated the work of northern artists (see plates on p. 354 and p. 371). The gruesome paintings of Hieronymus Bosch, for example, depicted the fears of devils and hell that troubled his contemporaries at all times. He put on canvas the demons, the temptations, the terrible punishments for sin that people considered as real as their tangible surroundings. His paintings explored the darker side of faith, taking inspiration from the fear of damnation and the hope for salvation—the first seen in the demons, the second in the redeeming Christ.

The depth of piety, conveyed by an artist such as Bosch, reflected the temper of Europe. In art and literature, as in lay organizations and the continuing popularity of itinerant preachers, people showed their concern for individual spiritual values and their dissatisfaction with a Church that was not meeting their needs.

Christian Humanism

No segment of society expressed the strivings and yearnings of the age more eloquently than the northern humanists. The salient features of the Humanist movement in Italy—its theory of education, its emphasis on eloquence, its reverence for the ancients, and its endorsement of active participation in affairs of state— began to win wide acceptance north of the Alps in the late 1400s. But the northerners added a significant religious dimension to the movement by devoting considerable attention to early Christian literature: the Bible and the writings of the Church fathers. As a result, they have been called *Christian humanists.*

The Northern Humanists   By the end of the fifteenth century the influence of Humanism, carried by the printing press, was Europe-wide. The northern Humanists were particularly determined to probe early Christianity for the light it could throw on the origins and accuracy of current religious teachings. Indeed, northern Humanism's broad examination of religious issues in the early 1500s helped create an atmosphere in which much more serious criticism of the Church could flourish.

The Christian humanists did not abandon the interest in classical authors or the methods for analyzing ancient texts, language, and style that had been developed by Italian Humanism. But they put these methods to a new use: analysis of the Bible in order to explain more clearly the message of Jesus and his apostles, and thus to provide a better guide to true piety and morality. This deeply religious undertaking dominated the writings of the two most famous Christian humanists, one English and one Dutch.

More Sir Thomas More (1478–1535), a lawyer and statesman, was the central figure of English Humanism. His reputation as a writer rests primarily on a short work, *Utopia*, published in Latin in 1516, which describes an ideal society on an imaginary island. In it, More condemned war, poverty, intolerance, and other evils of his day and defined the general principles of morality that he felt should underlie human society. The first book of *Utopia* addresses the conflict between the active and the contemplative life that Petrarch had emphasized and asks whether a learned person should withdraw from the world to avoid the corruptions of politics or participate in affairs of state so as to guide policy. In his own career, More chose the latter path, with fatal results. The second, more famous, book of *Utopia* leaves such practical issues aside and describes what an ideal commonwealth might be like. Utopia's politics and society are carefully regulated, an almost monastic community that has succeeded in abolishing private property, greed, and pride—and thus has freed its inhabitants from some of the worst sins of More's day. Well-designed institutions, education, and discipline are his answer to human failings: Weak human nature can be led to virtuousness only if severely curbed.

Deeply devout and firmly attached to the traditional Church, More entered public life as a member of Parliament in 1504. He rose high in government service, but eventually he gave his life for remaining loyal to the pope and refusing to recognize the decision of his king, Henry VIII, to reject papal authority and become head of the English Church. When Henry had him beheaded for treason, More's last words revealed his unflinching adherence to the Christian principles he pursued throughout his life: "I die the King's good servant, but God's first."

Erasmus The supreme representative of Christian Humanism was the Dutchman Desiderius Erasmus (ca. 1466–1536). Erasmus early acquired a taste for ancient writers, and he determined to devote himself to classical studies. For the greater part of his life, he wandered through Europe, writing, visiting friends, and occasionally working for important patrons. He always retained his independence, however, for unlike More, he answered the question of whether a scholar should enter public life by avoiding the compromises a ruler might demand.

Erasmus was so famous for his learning that he dominated the intellectual world of letters of his time. Con-

Hans Holbein the Younger
PORTRAIT OF ERASMUS OF ROTTERDAM, 1523
The leading portraitist of the age, Hans Holbein, painted his friend Erasmus a number of times. Here he shows the great scholar at work, possibly writing one of the many elegantly constructed letters that he sent to colleagues throughout Europe. The richness of the scene bears noting: the gold ring, the fine coat with a fur collar, and the splendid tapestry hanging over the paneled wall.
Louvre, Paris, France. Scala/Art Resource, NY

stantly consulted by scholars and admirers, he wrote magnificently composed letters that reflected every aspect of the culture of his age. He became known throughout Europe, however, as a result of a little book, *The Praise of Folly* (1509), which was one of the first best-sellers created by the printing press. Some of it is lighthearted banter that pokes fun at the author himself, his friends, and the follies of everyday life and suggests that a little folly is essential to human existence. The book also points out that Christianity itself is a kind of folly, a belief in "things not seen." In many passages, though, Erasmus launches sharply satirical attacks against monks, the pope, meaningless ceremonies, and the many lapses from what he perceived to be the true Christian spirit.

The Philosophy of Christ At the heart of Erasmus' work was the message that he called the "philosophy of Christ." He believed that the life of Jesus and especially his teachings in the Sermon on the Mount should be models for Christian piety and morality. For the Church's ceremonies and for rigid discipline, he had only censure: Too often, he said, they served as substitutes for genuine spiritual concerns. People lit candles, for instance, but forgot that true devotion, meant far more than such practices. By simply following the precepts of Jesus, he argued, a Christian could lead a life guided by sincere faith. Because of his insistence on ethical behavior, Erasmus could admire truly moral people even if they were pagans. "I could almost say, 'Pray for me, St. Socrates!'" he once wrote.

Erasmus believed that the Church had lost sight of its original mission. In the course of fifteen centuries, traditions and practices had developed that obscured the intentions of its founder, and purity could be restored only by studying the Scriptures and the writings of the early Church fathers. Here, the literary and analytic tools of the humanists became vitally important because they enabled scholars to understand the meaning and intention of ancient manuscripts. Practicing what he preached, Erasmus spent ten years preparing a new edition of the Greek text of the New Testament so as to correct errors in the Latin **Vulgate,** which was the standard version, and he revised it repeatedly for another twenty years. But the calm, scholarly, and tolerant moderation Erasmus prized was soon left behind by events. The rising intensity of religious reformers and their opponents destroyed the effort he had led to cure the ills of the Church quietly, from within. Erasmus wanted a revival of purer faith, but he would never have dreamed of rejecting the traditional authority of the Church. As Europe entered an age of confrontation, he found it impossible to preserve a middle course between the two sides, and he was swept aside by revolutionary forces that he himself had helped build but that Martin Luther was to unleash.

THE LUTHERAN REFORMATION

The disputes over doctrine and the yearning for piety helped undermine the authority of the Roman Church. But it took a charismatic individual of extraordinary determination to break apart an institution that had survived for a thousand years. And without political support, even he could not have succeeded.

The Conditions for Change

That a major religious conflict should have erupted in the Holy Roman Empire is not surprising. In this territory of fragmented government, with hundreds of independent local princes, popular piety was noticeably strong. Yet anyone who was unhappy with Church leadership had all the more reason to resent the power of bishops, because in the empire they were often also princes—such as the aristocratic bishop who ruled the important city of Cologne on the Rhine. There were few strong secular princes who could protect the people from the fiscal demands of the Church, and the popes therefore regarded the empire as their surest source of revenue.

This situation was made more volatile by the ambitions of the secular princes. Their ostensible overlord, the emperor, had no real power over them, and they worked tirelessly to strengthen their control over their subjects and to assert their independence from all outside authority. A number of them were, in fact, to see the religious upheavals of the 1500s as a means of advancing their own political purposes. Their ambitions help explain why a determined reformer, Martin Luther, won such swift and widespread support.

Martin Luther

Martin Luther (1483–1546) was born into a miner's family in Saxony in central Germany. The household was dominated by the father, whose powerful presence some modern commentators have seen reflected in his son's vision of an omnipotent God. The boy received a good education and decided to become a lawyer, a profession that would have given him many opportunities for advancement. But in his early twenties, shortly after starting his legal studies, he had an experience that changed his life. Crossing a field during a thunderstorm, he was thrown to the ground by a bolt of lightning, and in his terror he cried out to St. Anne that he would enter a monastery.

Luther in the Monastery Although the decision may well have been that sudden, it is clear that there was more to Luther's change of direction than this one incident, however traumatic. A highly sensitive, energetic, and troubled young man, he had become obsessed with his own sinfulness, and he joined a monastery as an Augustinian friar in the hope that a penitential life would help him overcome his sense of guilt. Once in the monastery, he pursued every possible opportunity to earn worthiness in the sight of God. He overlooked no means of discipline or act of contrition or self-denial, and for added merit he endured austerities, such as self-flagellation, that went far beyond normal requirements. But it was all useless: When officiating at his first Mass after his ordination in 1507, he was so terrified at the idea of a sinner like himself administering the sacrament of the Eucharist—that is, transforming

LUTHER'S "EXPERIENCE IN THE TOWER"

The following passage was written by Luther in 1545, at least twenty-five years after the experience it describes. As a result, scholars have been unable to decide (a) whether the breakthrough was in fact as sudden as Luther suggests; (b) when it took place—possibly as early as 1512, five years before the indulgence dispute, or as late as 1519, when Luther was already under attack for his views; or (c) how it should be interpreted—as a scholar's insight, as a revelation from God, or as Luther's later crystallization into a single event of a process that had taken many years.

"I wanted very much to understand Paul's Epistle to the Romans, but despite my determination to do so I kept being stopped by the one word, 'the righteousness of God.' I hated that word, because I had been taught to understand it as the active righteousness by which a just God punishes unjust sinners. The trouble was that, although I may have been an impeccable monk, I felt myself to be a sinner before God. As a result, not only was I unable to love, but I actually hated this just God, who punishes all sinners. And so I raged, yet I still longed to understand St. Paul.

"At last, as I grappled with the words day and night, God had mercy on me, and I saw the connection between the words 'the righteousness of God' and 'The righteous shall live by faith' (Romans 1:17). I understood that the righteousness of God refers to the gift by which God enables the just to live—that is, by faith. A merciful God justifies us by faith, as it is written: 'The righteous shall live by faith.' At that point, I felt as if I had been reborn and had passed through open doors into paradise. The whole of Scripture took on new meaning. As I had previously hated the phrase, 'the righteousness of God,' so now I lovingly praised it."

Translation from the Latin by Theodore K. Rabb of Luther's preface to the 1545 edition of his writings, in Otto Scheel (ed.), *Dokumente zu Luthers Entwicklung*, Tübingen: Mohr, 1929, pp. 191–192.

---

the wafer and wine into the body and blood of Christ—that he almost failed to complete the ritual.

Fortunately for Luther, his superiors took more notice of his intellectual gifts than his self-doubts, and in 1508 they assigned him to the faculty of a new university in Wittenberg, the capital of Saxony. It was from his scholarship, which was excellent, and especially from his study of the Bible, that he was able at last to draw comfort and spiritual peace.

Justification by Faith   This second crucial change in Luther's life, as important as the entry into the monastery, happened while he was preparing his university lectures. Until this event, which is known as "the experience in the tower," Luther could see no way that he, a despicable mortal, could receive anything but the fiercest punishments from a God of absolute justice. Now, however, he had an insight that led him to understand that he needed only to rely on God's mercy, a quality as great as divine justice (see "Luther's 'Experience in the Tower,'" above). The many advances in Luther's thinking thereafter came from this insight: that justification—which removes sin and bestows righteousness through a gift of grace—is achieved by faith alone.

The Break with Rome

In 1517 an event occurred that was ultimately to lead Luther to an irrevocable break with the Church. In the spring, a friar, Johann Tetzel, began to peddle **indulgences** a few miles from Wittenberg as part of a huge fund-raising effort to pay for the new Church of St. Peter in Rome. Originally, an indulgence had been granted to anyone going on a crusade. It was then extended to those who, though unable to join a crusade, gave enough money for a poor crusader to be able to reach the Holy Land. Indulgences released sinners from a certain period of punishment in purgatory before they went on to heaven; the theory was that they drew on a sort of credit from the treasury of merit built up by Jesus and the saints. But neither the theory nor the connection with money had been fully defined, and clerics had taken advantage of this vagueness simply to sell indulgences. Tetzel, an expert peddler, was offering complete releases from purgatory without bothering to mention the repentance that, according to Church teachings, was essential if a sinner was to be forgiven or absolved.

The Ninety-Five Theses   The people of Wittenberg were soon flocking to Tetzel to buy this easy guarantee of salvation. For Luther, a man groping toward an evangelical solution of his own doubts, it was unforgivable that people should be deprived of their hard-earned money for worthless promises. On October 31, 1517, he published in Wittenberg ninety-five theses, or statements, on indulgences that he offered to debate with experts in Christian doctrine.

Jörg Breu
ENGRAVING DEPICTING THE SALE OF INDULGENCES, CA. 1530
This scene would have been a familiar one in Europe until Luther's attacks brought it to an end. The clerics on their fine horses on the right bring a cross and the papal bull, which is authenticated by the elaborate seals and ribbons that hang from it. The faithful put money in the barrel in the middle or hand it to the dispenser of certificates on the left, who sits near the large locked chest that will hold the revenues from the sales.
Bildarchiv Preussischer Kulturbesitz, Berlin/Art Resource, NY

This was no revolutionary document. It merely described, in Latin, what Luther believed to be correct teachings on indulgences: that the pope could remit only the penalties that he himself or canon law imposed; that, therefore, the promise of a general pardon was damnable; and that every true believer shared in the treasury of merit left by Jesus and the saints, whether or not he or she obtained an indulgence. Within a few weeks, the story was all over the empire that a monk had challenged the sale of indulgences. The proceeds of Tetzel's mission began to drop off; and other members of his order, the Dominicans, rallied to their brother by attacking his presumptuous critic, Luther, of the rival order of the Augustinians.

Luther Elaborates The controversy soon drew attention in Rome. At first, Pope Leo X regarded the affair as merely a monks' quarrel. But, in time, Luther's responses to the Dominicans' attacks began to deviate radically from Church doctrine, and by 1520 he had gone so far as to challenge the authority of the papacy itself.

In three pamphlets published that year, he outlined where he stood. He asked Emperor Charles V to call a council to end the abuses of the Church. He attacked the belief that the seven sacraments, the basis of the Church's authority, were the only means of attaining grace and thus salvation By accepting only two, baptism and the Eucharist, he asserted that justification was by faith alone. And, though he did not reject good works, he insisted that only the individual believer's faith could bring salvation from an all-powerful, just, and merciful God. These views had an overwhelming impact on Luther's fellow Germans. His appeal to their resentment of Church power and their wish for a more personal faith made him, almost overnight, the embodiment of a widespread yearning for religious reform.

The Diet of Worms There could no longer be any doubt that Luther was breaking with the Church, and in 1520 Pope Leo X issued a bull excommunicating him. Luther publicly tossed the document into a bonfire, defending his action by calling the pope an Antichrist. In 1521 Emperor Charles V, who was officially the papacy's secular representative, summoned the celebrated monk to offer his defense against the papal decree at a **Diet** of the empire (a meeting of princes, city leaders, and churchmen) at Worms, a city on the Rhine.

The journey across Germany was a triumphant progress for Luther, who now seemed a heroic figure. Appearing before the magnificent assembly dressed in his simple friar's robe, he offered a striking contrast to the display of imperial and princely grandeur. First in German and then in Latin, he made the famous declaration that closed the last door behind him: "I cannot and will not recant anything, since it is unsafe and wrong to go against my conscience. Here I stand. I cannot do otherwise. God help me. Amen." On the following day the emperor gave his reply: "A single friar who goes counter to all Christianity for a thousand years must be wrong."

Luther Protected Charles added legality to the papal bull by issuing an imperial edict calling for Luther's arrest and the burning of his works. At this point, however, the independent power of the German princes and their resentment of foreign ecclesiastical interference came to the reformer's aid. The Elector Frederick III of Saxony, who had never met Luther and who was never to break with the traditional Church, nonetheless determined to protect the rebel, who lived in his territory. A fake kidnapping brought Luther to the Wartburg castle, one of Frederick's strongholds, and here Luther remained for almost a year, safe from his enemies.

Lutheran Doctrine and Practice

While at the Wartburg castle, Luther, together with his friend Philipp Melanchthon, developed his ideas and shaped them into a formal set of beliefs that influenced most of the subsequent variations of Protestant Christianity. Codified in 1530 in a document known as the Augsburg Confession, these doctrines have remained the basis of Lutheranism ever since.

Faith and the Bible The two fundamental assertions of Luther's teachings derive from the emphasis on God's power and mystery that Luther learned in his nominalist monastery. First, faith alone—not good works or the receiving of the sacraments—justifies the believer in the eyes of God and wins redemption. People themselves are helpless and unworthy sinners who can do nothing to cooperate in their own salvation; God bestows faith on those he chooses to save. Second, the Bible is the sole source of religious authority. It alone carries the word of God, and Christians must reject all other authorities: Church tradition, commentaries on the Bible, or the pronouncements of popes and Church councils.

These two doctrines had far-reaching implications. According to Luther, all people are equally capable of understanding God's word as expressed in the Bible and can gain salvation without the help of intermediaries; they do not need a priest endowed with special powers or an interceding church. Luther thus saw God's faithful as a "priesthood of all believers," a concept totally foreign to the traditional Church, which insisted on the distinction between clergy and laity. The distinction disappeared in Luther's doctrines, because all the faithful shared the responsibilities formerly reserved for priests.

Sacraments and the Mass True to his reliance on biblical authority, Luther retained only two sacraments—baptism and the Eucharist—as means by which God distributes grace. Moreover, the ceremony of the Eucharist was now called *communion* (literally, "sharing") to emphasize that all worshipers, including the officiating clergy, were equal; all shared both wafer and wine. Luther also reduced the distinctiveness of priests by giving them the right to marry.

Luther's teachings on the sacraments transformed the Mass, the ceremony that surrounds the Eucharist. According to traditional dogma, when the priest raises

Lucas Cranach the Elder
Portrait of Martin Luther, **1529**
One of the first faces made familiar by portraits, but not belonging to a nobleman, was Luther's. Cranach painted the reformer a number of times, so we can see what he looked like at various periods of his life. Luther here is in his early forties, a determined figure who four years earlier had made his stand at the Diet of Worms.
Uffizi, Florence, Italy. Scala/Art Resource, NY

the wafer, the host, during the Mass and recites the words *Hoc est corpus meum* ("This is my body"), the sacrifice of Jesus on the cross is reenacted. The wafer and the wine retain their outward appearance, their "accidents," but their substance is transformed into the body and blood of Christ—in other words, transubstantiation takes place.

Luther asserted that the wafer and wine retain their substance as well as their accidents at the moment the priest says, "This is my body." The real presence of Christ and the natural substance coexist within the wafer and wine. Nothing suddenly happens; there is no miraculous moment. Instead, the believer is simply

CARTOON FROM LUTHERAN WOODCUT BROADSIDE
Vicious cartoons were a favorite device of religious propaganda during the Age of Religious Reformation. They were especially popular for an illiterate audience, which had to get the message from pictures. The more vivid the image, the easier it was to understand. Here the Protestants show the enemies of Luther as vicious animals. One theologian is a cat eating a mouse; another is a dog holding a bone. The pope is in the middle, reaching out to Eck.
Germanisches Nationalmuseum, Nürnberg

made aware of the real presence of God, who is everywhere at all times. Again, it is the faith of the individual, not the ceremony itself, that counts. Moreover, by allowing the congregation to drink the wine—as Hus had demanded—Luther further reduced the mystery of the Lord's Supper and undermined the position of the priest. And by abolishing the use of Latin, processions, incense, and votive candles, he simplified services and gave ordinary people a greater role in worship.

Translation of the Bible With the priest reduced in stature, it was vital to make God's word more readily available to the faithful, so that they could read or hear the Bible for themselves. To this end, Luther began the long task of translating the Bible. He completed the work in 1534, creating a text that is a milestone in the history of the German language. Families were encouraged to read Scripture on their own, and the reformed faith stimulated rising literacy among women as well as men. This was Luther's last major contribution to the religious changes of the sixteenth century. Although he lived until 1546, henceforth the progress of the revolution he had launched would rely on outside forces: its popular appeal and the actions of political leaders.

The Spread of Lutheranism

It is usually said that Lutheranism spread from above, advancing only when princes and rulers helped it along. Although this view has some merit, it does not adequately explain the growth of the movement. The response to Luther's stand was immediate and widespread. Even before the Diet of Worms, preachers critical of the Church were drawing audiences in many parts of the Holy Roman Empire, and in 1521 there were waves of image smashing, reports of priests marrying, and efforts to reform and simplify the sacraments.

Soon there were congregations following Luther's teachings throughout the empire and neighboring countries. Broadsides and pamphlets fresh from the printing presses rapidly disseminated the reformer's message, and they stimulated an immediate response from thousands who welcomed the opportunity to renew their faith.

Radical Preachers As long as his own doctrines remained unaltered, Luther was naturally delighted to see his teachings spread. But from the start, people drew inferences that he could not tolerate. Early in 1522, for example, three men from the nearby town of Zwickau appeared in Wittenberg claiming to be prophets who enjoyed direct communication with God. Their ideas were, in Luther's eyes, damnable. When he returned from Wartburg castle, therefore, he preached eight sermons to expose their errors—a futile effort, because the movement to reform the Church was now too dispersed to control. Capitalizing on mass discontent, radical preachers incited disturbances in the name of faith, and soon social as well as religious protest exploded, posing a new challenge for Luther as he struggled to keep his reform movement under control.

Social and Religious Protest The first trouble arose in the summer of 1522, started by the weakest independent group in the empire, the imperial knights. The knights occupied a precarious social position, because they rarely owned more than a single castle. They accepted no authority but the emperor himself, and they resented the growing power of cities and princes (rulers of large territories) in the empire. Calling themselves true representatives of the imperial system—that is, loyal supporters of the emperor, unlike the cities and princes who wanted to be more independent—and using Lutheranism as further justification, the knights launched an attack on one of the leading ecclesiastical rulers, the archbishop of Trier. They were crushed within a year, but the Lutherans' opponents could now suggest that the new religious teachings undermined law and order.

Peasant Revolt   The banner of the new faith rose over popular revolts as well. A peasant uprising began in Swabia in 1524 and quickly engulfed the southern and central parts of the empire. Citing Luther's inspiration, and especially his teaching that faith was all the individual needed, the peasants published a list of twelve demands in 1525. Admittedly, ten of their grievances concerned social, not religious, injustices: They wanted an end to the restrictions and burdens imposed by their overlords, including prohibitions on hunting and fishing, excessive rents and services, and unlawful punishments. But they also had two religious aims: They wanted the right to choose their own pastors, and they refused to accept any authority other than Scripture to determine whether their demands were justified.

Luther sympathized with the last two claims, and at first he considered the peasants' demands reasonable. But when it became apparent that they were challenging all authority, he ignored the oppressions they had suffered and wrote a vicious pamphlet, *Against the Rapacious and Murdering Peasants,* calling on the nobility to cut them down without mercy so as to restore peace. A few months later the rebels were defeated in battle, and thereafter Luther threw his support unreservedly on the side of the princes and the established political and social order. He also grew more virulent in his attacks on Catholics and Jews and became as insistent as the Roman Church he was defying that his doctrines were not to be questioned.

Lutheranism Established

The advance of Lutheranism thus far had depended largely on its appeal to the ordinary believer, and it continued to enjoy wide support. But when Luther was forced to choose between the demands of his humblest followers and the authority of the princes who had protected him, he opted for the princes. It was a decision that enabled his movement to survive and may well have saved him from the fate of Hus a century before. Had Luther not condemned the disorders, he would doubtless have been abandoned by the princes, and without their backing he and his followers could not have stood up to the traditional Church or been safe from the power of Charles V.

Luther's Conservatism   One of the reasons the new set of beliefs attracted these princes was its conservatism. Any person who adopted the basic doctrines of justification by faith alone and Scripture as the sole authority could be accepted as a Lutheran. Consequently, the new congregations could retain much from the old religion: most of the liturgy, the sacred music, and, particularly important, a structured church that, though less hierarchical than before, was still organized to provide order and authority.

The Lutheran Princes   Some rulers were swept up by the same emotions that moved their subjects, but others were moved by more material interests. Since the Church lost all its property when reform was introduced, princes could confiscate the rich and extensive ecclesiastical holdings in their domains. Furthermore, they now had added reason for flaunting their independence from Emperor Charles V, an unwavering upholder of orthodoxy. It was risky to adopt this policy, for Charles could strip a prince of his title. And if a prince promised to remain loyal to the Church, he could blackmail the pope into offering him almost as many riches as he could win by confiscation.

Nevertheless, the appeal of the new faith eventually tipped the balance for enough princes to create a formidable party capable of resisting Charles's power. While they were attending an imperial Diet at Speyer in 1529, they signed a declaration "protesting" the Diet's decree that no religious innovations were to be introduced in the empire. Thereafter, all who accepted religious reform, including the Lutherans, were known as Protestants; and adherents of the traditional Church, led from Rome, which continued to claim that it was universal (or catholic), came to be known as Roman Catholics.

The following year, at another imperial Diet, the Lutheran princes announced their support of the Augsburg Confession, the official statement of Lutheran doctrines that had been prepared by Melanchthon and Luther. Charles V now threatened to use military force to crush the heresy, and in the face of this danger, the Lutherans formed a defensive league in 1531 at the small Saxon town of Schmalkalden. Throughout the 1530s this alliance consolidated Protestant gains, brought new princes into the cause, and, in general, amassed sufficient strength to deter Charles, who was repeatedly distracted by foreign wars, from decisive military action.

War over Religion   The reform party became so solidly established that it negotiated with the Catholics on equal terms about the possibility of reconciliation in 1541, but the talks collapsed, and the chances for a reunification of Christendom evaporated. Not until 1546, the year of Luther's death, however, did

ENGRAVING OF THE DIET OF AUGSBURG, 1530
At the Diet—the meeting of the princes and cities of the Holy Roman Empire—in Augsburg in 1530, the Lutherans presented to the emperor, Charles V, a statement, or "confession," of their faith. This "Confession of Augsburg" became the founding doctrine of the Lutheran Church. It was rejected as heretical by Charles, but he could not suppress it. One of the Lutheran princes told him in 1530 that he would rather have his head cut off than attend a Catholic mass. Charles was unable to crush such defiance.
Bibliothèque Nationale de France, Paris

open war begin. Then, after a brief campaign, Charles won a crushing victory over the Lutherans in 1547. But matters had advanced too far for their movement to collapse merely because of a single defeat on the battlefield. The new faith had won the devotion of a large part of the German people, particularly in the north and the east, farthest away from the center of imperial power. Some of the great cities of the south, such as Nuremberg, which had been centers of Humanism, had also come over to the Lutheran side. By the 1550s Lutheranism had captured about half the population of the empire.

The Catholic princes also played a part in ensuring the survival of the new faith. Fearful of Charles V's new power, they refused to cooperate in his attempt to establish his authority throughout the empire, and he had to rely on Spanish troops, who further alienated him from his subjects. The Lutherans regrouped after their 1547 defeat, and in 1555 the imperial Diet at Augsburg drew up a compromise settlement that exposed the decline of the emperor's power. Henceforth,

each prince was allowed to determine the religion of his own territory, Lutheran or Catholic, and his subjects could leave (a major concession) if they were of the other faith. Religious uniformity was at an end, and the future of Lutheranism was secure.

The Heritage of Lutheranism The influence that this first Protestant Church was to exert on all of European life was immense. The idea that all believers were equal in the eyes of God inspired revolutionary changes in thought and society. It justified antimonarchical constitutional theories, it allowed people to feel that all occupations were equally worthy and that there was nothing wrong with the life of the merchant or even the moneylender, and it undermined the hierarchic view of the universe. One can easily overstate the notion that Lutheranism made people more self-reliant, because independent and pioneering behavior was far from new. Nevertheless, there is no question that, by condemning the traditional reliance on priests and the Church and by making individuals responsible for their own salvation, Luther did encourage his followers to act on their own. Yet the new faith had its most immediate effect on religious life itself: Before the century was out, the dissent started by Luther inspired a multitude of sects and a ferment of ideas without precedent in the history of Europe.

THE SPREAD OF PROTESTANTISM

Hardly had Luther made his protest in 1517 when religious dissent in many different forms suddenly appeared. It was as if no more was needed than one opening shot before a volley of discontent broke out—testimony to the deep and widespread desire for individual piety of the times.

Zwingli and the Radicals

Zwingli's Reforms   The most influential of the new initiatives began in the Swiss city of Zurich, where reform was led by Ulrich Zwingli (1484–1531), a priest, humanist, and disciple of Erasmus. The doctrines he began to develop between 1519 and 1522 were similar to Luther's in that Zwingli based his ideas entirely on Scripture and emphasized faith alone. Suspicious of any reliance on Church rituals, Zwingli, even more than Luther, wanted to simplify religious belief and practice. In his view, none of the sacraments bestowed grace; they were merely signs of grace already given. Thus, baptism is symbolic, not a ceremony that regenerates the recipient; and communion is no more than a memorial and thanksgiving for the grace given by God, who is present only symbolically—not in actuality, as Luther believed.

Despite his obvious debt to Luther, Zwingli diverged significantly from the German. His new form of Protestantism was more thoroughly dependent on the individual believer and more devoid of mystery and ritual than anything Luther could accept. Zwingli saw a need for constant correction if people were to lead godly lives, and he established a tribunal of clergy and secular officials to enforce discipline among the faithful. They supervised all moral issues, from compulsory church attendance to the public behavior of amorous couples. They could excommunicate flagrant transgressors, and they maintained constant surveillance—through a network of informers—to keep the faithful moral and godly. Because Zwingli considered education vital for discipline, he founded a theological school and authorized a new translation of the Bible. He also insisted on lengthy sermons at each service. Worship was stripped bare, as were the churches, and preaching began to assume tremendous importance as a means of instructing believers and strengthening their faith. Zwingli also revived the ancient Christian practice of public confession of sin—yet another reinforcement of discipline.

Zwingli's Church   Zwingli's ideas spread rapidly in the Swiss Confederation, helped by the virtual autonomy of each canton, or region. By 1529 a number of cantons had accepted Zwinglianism. As a result, two camps formed in the country, and a war broke out in 1531 in which Zwingli himself was killed. Thereafter, the Swiss Confederation remained split between Catholics and reformers. Zwinglianism never grew into a major religion, but it had a considerable effect on later forms of Protestantism, particularly Calvinism.

The Anabaptists   Both Luther and Zwingli wanted to retain Church authority, and both therefore insisted that infant baptism was the moment of entry into the Church, even though this belief had no scriptural sanction. Some radical reformers, however, insisted on taking the Bible literally and argued that, as in biblical times, baptism should be administered only to mature adults who could make a conscious choice to receive grace, not to infants who could not understand what was happening. Soon these reformers were being called **Anabaptists** ("rebaptizers") by their enemies. The term is often applied to all radicals, though in fact it described only one conspicuous group.

Radical Sects   Diversity was inevitable among the radical reformers, most of whom refused to recognize church organization, rejected priests, and gave individual belief free rein, sometimes to the point of recognizing only personal communication with God and disregarding Scripture. Many groups of like-minded radicals formed small sects—voluntary associations that rarely included more than one hundred or so adults—in an effort to achieve complete separation from the world and avoid compromising their ideals. They wanted to set an example for others by adhering fervently to the truth as they saw it, regardless of the consequences. Some sects established little **utopian** communities, holding everything in common, including property and spouses. Others disdained all worldly things and lived only for the supreme ecstasy of a trance in which they made direct contact with God himself. Many, believing in the imminent coming of the Messiah, prepared themselves for the end of the world and the Day of Judgment.

Persecution of the Radicals

Such variety in the name of a personal search for God was intolerable to major reformers like Luther and Zwingli, who believed that their own doctrines were the only means of salvation. Once these branches of Protestantism were firmly entrenched, they, like the

Catholic Church, became deeply committed to the status quo and to their own hierarchies and traditions.
The established reformers thus regarded the radicals'
refusal to conform as an unmistakable sign of damnation, and they were just as ready as Catholics to perse-
cute those who rejected their particular brand of
salvation.

Münster and the Melchiorites   The assault on the radicals began in the mid-1520s and soon spread through
most of Europe. The imperial Diet in 1529, for instance, called for the death penalty against all Anabaptists. Finally, in the northwest German city of
Münster, a particularly fiery sect, inspired by a
"prophet" named Melchior and known as Melchiorites,
provoked a reaction that signaled doom even for less
radical dissenters.

The Melchiorites had managed to gain considerable
influence over the ordinary workers of Münster and
over the craft guilds to which many belonged. They
gained political control of the city early in 1534 and began to establish their "heavenly Jerusalem" on earth.
They burned all books except the Bible, abolished private property, introduced polygamy, and in an atmosphere of abandon and chaos, dug in to await the
coming of the Messiah. Here was a threat to society
sufficient to force Protestants and Catholics into an alliance, and they captured the city and brutally massacred the Melchiorites. Thereafter, the radicals were
savagely persecuted throughout the empire. To survive,
many fled, first to Poland, then to the Low Countries
and England, and eventually to the New World.

John Calvin

During the 1530s, Protestantism began to fragment.
Neither Lutherans nor Zwinglians expanded much beyond the areas in which their reforms had begun; sects
multiplied but gained few followers; and it might have
seemed that the original energy had left the movement.
In the early 1540s, however, a new dynamism and also
a more elaborate and systematic body of doctrine were
brought to Protestantism by a second-generation reformer, John Calvin (1509–1564). Born in Noyon, a
small town in northern France, Calvin studied both
law and the humanities at the University of Paris. In
his early twenties he apparently had a shattering spiritual experience that he later called his "sudden conver-
sion," an event about which he would say almost
nothing else. Yet from that moment on, all his energy
was devoted to religious reform.

In November 1533 Calvin was indicted by French
Church authorities for holding heretical views, and after
more than a year in hiding, he took refuge in the Swiss
city of Basel. There, in 1536, he published a little treatise, *Institutes of the Christian Religion*, outlining the
principles of a new system of belief. He would revise and
expand the *Institutes* for the remainder of his life, and it
was to become the basis of Calvinism, the most vigorous
branch of Protestantism in the sixteenth century.

Geneva   Later in 1536, Calvin settled in Geneva, where, except for a brief period, he was to remain until his death and where he was to create a new church in the 1540s. The citizens of this prosperous market center had just overthrown their prince, a Catholic bishop. In achieving their independence, they had allied with other Swiss cities, notably Bern, a recent convert to Zwinglianism. Rebels who, with the help of Protestants, had just freed themselves from an ecclesiastical overlord were understandably receptive to new religious teachings, though Calvin's beliefs were also supported by persecution and intolerance.

Calvinism

Outwardly, Calvinism seemed to have much in common with Lutheranism. Both emphasized people's sinfulness, lack of free will, and helplessness; both rejected good works as a means of salvation; both accepted only two sacraments, baptism and communion; both regarded all occupations as equally worthy in the sight of God; both strongly upheld established political and social authority; and both had similar views of faith, people's weaknesses, and God's omnipotence. But the emphases in Calvinism were very different.

Predestination   In arguing for justification by faith alone, Luther assumed that God can predestine a person to be saved but rejected the idea that damnation can also be preordained. Calvin's faith was much sterner. He recognized no such distinction: If people are damned, they should praise God's justice, because their sins certainly merit such a judgment; if people are saved, they should praise God's mercy, because their salvation is not a result of their own merits. Either way, the outcome is predestined, and nothing can be done to affect an individual's fate. It is up to God to save a person; he then perseveres in his mercy despite the person's sins; and finally, he alone decides whether to receive the sinner into the small band of saints, or elect, whom he brings into heaven. Calvin's was a grim but powerful answer to the age-old Christian question: How can sinful human beings gain salvation?

Calvin believed that our behavior here on earth, whether good or bad, is no indication of our fate. He did suggest that someone who is to be saved by God is likely to be upright and moral, but such conduct is not necessarily a sign of salvation. However, because we should try to please God at all times, and because our communities ought to be fitting places for the elect to live, we must make every effort to lead lives worthy of one of the elect.

Morality and Discipline   Calvin therefore developed a strict moral code for the true believer that banned frivolous activities, like dancing, in favor of constant self-examination, austerity, and sober study of the Bible. To help the faithful observe such regulation, he reestablished public confessions, as Zwingli had, and required daily preaching. He made services starkly simple: Stripped of ornaments, worship concentrated on uplifting sermons and the celebration of communion. His doctrine of communion occupied a middle ground between Luther's and Zwingli's. He rejected Zwingli's interpretation, saying instead that Christ's body and blood were actually and not just symbolically present. But unlike Luther, he held that they were present only in spirit and were consumed only spiritually, by faith.

To supervise the morals of the faithful and ensure that the community was worthy of the elect, Calvin gave his church a strict hierarchical structure. It was controlled by church officials called deacons and by lay elders, who were able to function even in the hostile territories where many Calvinists found themselves. A body of lay elders called the *consistory* served as the chief ecclesiastical authority. These elders enforced discipline and had the power of excommunication, though local officials imposed the actual punishments—most notoriously in 1553, when a radical who denied the Trinity, Michael Servetus, was invited to Geneva and then executed for heresy.

Church Organization   Calvin's system produced a cohesiveness and organization achieved by no other Protestant church. The *Institutes* spelled out every point of faith and practice in detail—an enormous advantage for Calvin's followers at a time when new religious doctrines were still fluid. The believer's duties and obligations were absolutely clear, as was his or her position in the carefully organized hierarchy of the church. In France, for example, there was a small community (or cell) in each town, a governing synod (or council) in each local area, a provincial synod in each province, and a national synod at the top of the pyramid. Tight discipline controlled the entire system, with the result that Calvinists believed they were setting a moral and religious example that the entire world would eventually have to follow. They were part of a privileged community from whom the elect would be drawn. Thus, they could be oppressive when they had power, yet holy rebels when they were a minority. After all, since they were freed of responsibility for their own salvation, they were acting selflessly at all times. Like the children of Israel, they had a mission to live for God, and this sense of destiny was to be one of Calvinism's greatest strengths.

Preachers from Geneva traveled through Europe to win adherents and organize the faithful wherever they could. In 1559 the city opened a university for the purpose of training preachers, because Calvin regarded education as an essential means of instilling faith. From Geneva flowed a stream of pamphlets and books, which strengthened the faith of all believers and made sure that none who wished to learn would lack the opportunity. A special target was Calvin's homeland, France, where his preachers had their first successes, especially in the cities. Calvinism also won important support in the nobility, notably among women aristocrats, who often influenced their families to adopt the new beliefs.

By 1564, when Calvin died, his church was well established: more than a million adherents in France, where they were called Huguenots; the Palatinate converted; Scotland won by his fiery disciple, John Knox; and considerable groups of followers in England, the Low Countries, and Hungary. Despite its severity, Calvin's coherent and comprehensive body of doctrine proved to have wide appeal in an age of piety that yearned for clear religious answers.

The Appeal of Calvinism Certain groups seemed especially open to Protestant, and particularly Calvinist, teachings. All the reformed faiths did particularly well in cities, and it has been suggested that the long history of independence among townspeople made them more inclined to challenge traditional authorities. In addition, they tended to be more literate, and thus were drawn to beliefs that emphasized reading the Bible for oneself. Moreover, Calvinism put an emphasis on sobriety, discipline, and communal responsibility that appealed strongly to the increasingly self-confident merchants and artisans of the cities. That the Calvinists were also successful in the areas of southern France farthest away from central authority in Paris only reinforces the connection with an inclination toward independence and self-reliance. Geneva itself became a determinedly independent place—morals were strictly supervised, and there was an aura of public discipline that all visitors noted. Gradually in the seventeenth century the atmosphere of austerity softened, but the city continued to be seen as a model community for all Calvinists.

Women and Reform Cities were not the only centers of religious reform. In some parts of Europe, such as Scotland, new beliefs flourished outside towns because they won political support. But in all areas, the importance of women to the spread of Protestantism was unmistakable. Calvin's earliest significant converts were aristocratic women, whose patronage helped his faith take root at the highest levels of society. Like the literate women of the cities, they saw in its message an opportunity to express themselves and to work for others in ways that had not been possible before. They were often the main readers of the Bible in family gatherings; they took the lead in demanding broader access to education, especially for girls; and they were regularly prominent in radical movements.

One theologian who despaired at the results of Luther's translation of the New Testament reserved his most bitter complaints for the women who were studying the Bible for themselves. And the results were apparent not only among the literate. The records of the **Inquisition**, the Catholic tribunal charged with rooting out heresy, are full of the trials and executions of women who were martyrs for their beliefs and who died defending doctrines they had learned from preachers or other women. Again and again, they rejected the authority of priests and asserted their right to individual faith. It was determination like this that enabled the **Reformation** to establish itself and to spread until it posed a major challenge to the traditional Church (see "The Trial of Elizabeth Dirks," p. 385). Yet the encouragement of female piety by the major reformers should not be overdrawn, for (unlike the radicals) they insisted that women remain silent in services. Moreover, the abolition of nunneries, of the veneration of the Virgin, and of prayers to female saints narrowed the opportunities for spiritual expression among all Protestant women and reduced their roles in their faiths.

The Anglican Church

In England, which created its own version of the Protestant Church, the role of the prince was crucial. There was a local tradition of dissent, represented by the Lollards, but it was severely repressed in the early days of the Reformation. King Henry VIII even wrote an attack on Luther that persuaded the pope to grant him the title "Defender of the Faith" that British monarchs still use. But by the late 1520s this loyalty was in peril because Henry's wife was clearly not going to produce the male heir he needed to continue his dynasty, and the traditional solution—to have the pope annul the marriage—was unavailable. The result was another advance for the Reformation.

The King's Divorce The case Henry made to the pope was that he had married his brother's widow, Catherine of Aragon, under a special papal dispensation from the biblical law that prohibited a union between such close relatives. He argued that the lack of an heir proved the dispensation to have been sinful, and the marriage no marriage. Henry did not mention that he had become infatuated with a young lady at court, Anne Boleyn, but under normal circumstances the papacy would not have hesitated to comply. At this very moment, however, the pope was in the power of the Emperor Charles V, who had invaded Italy. Charles, it happened, was

THE TRIAL OF ELIZABETH DIRKS

In radical groups, women often occupied central roles they never achieved in the larger churches. Since the most important attributes of a believer in these groups were faith, commitment, and the presence of the Holy Spirit, there was frequently an egalitarianism not found elsewhere in sixteenth-century society. Thus it was that the radical "teacher" (or leader) whom the Inquisition in the Netherlands interrogated in January 1549 was a woman named Elizabeth Dirks. Her replies give us a vivid sense of the beliefs the Reformation was stimulating among ordinary people—though in this case they were put forward with a clarity and a conviction that would lead to Elizabeth's execution two months later.

"Examiner: We understand you are a teacher and have led many astray. Who are your friends?

"Elizabeth: Do not press me on this point. Ask me about my faith and I will answer you gladly.

"Examiner: Do you not consider our Church to be the house of the Lord?

"Elizabeth: I do not. For it is written that God said 'I will dwell with you.'

"Examiner: What do you think of our mass?

"Elizabeth: I have no faith in your mass, but only in the word of God.

"Examiner: What do you believe about the Holy Sacrament of the Eucharist?

"Elizabeth: I never in my life read in Scripture about a Holy Sacrament, but only of the Supper of the Lord.

"Examiner: You speak with a haughty tongue.

"Elizabeth: No. I speak with a free tongue.

"Examiner: Do you not believe that you are saved by baptism?

"Elizabeth: No: all the water in the sea cannot save me. My salvation is in Christ, who commanded me to love my God and my neighbor as myself.

"Examiner: Do priests have the power to forgive sins?

"Elizabeth: How should I believe that? Christ is the only priest through whom sins are forgiven.

"As torture was applied:

"Examiner: You can recant everything you have said.

"Elizabeth: No, I will not, but I will seal it with my blood."

Adapted from Thieleman von Bracht, *The Bloody Theater or Martyr's Mirror*, Daniel Rupp (tr.), Lancaster, PA: David Miller, 1837, pp. 409–410.

Catherine's nephew, and he refused to allow this blot on her honor.

Stymied by Rome, Henry summoned England's Parliament in 1529 and gave it free rein to express bitter anticlerical sentiments. He sought opinions in European universities in favor of the divorce, and he even extracted a vague recognition from England's clergy of his position as "supreme lord" of the Church. Finally, one of his ministers, Thomas Cromwell, suggested a radical but simple solution: that Henry break with the pope, declare himself head of the Church, and divorce Catherine on his own authority. The king agreed, and in 1534 Parliament declared him supreme head of the newly independent Church of England. By joining Europe's Protestants in opposition to Rome, Henry gave his subjects a cause that was increasingly to stimulate their patriotic pride.

The English Church The Reformation gave the monarchy a huge financial boost. Henry took over the ecclesiastical fees that the pope had collected, and he confiscated the immensely valuable property of all monasteries. When a revolt erupted against the Reformation in 1536, he crushed it easily. But in doctrine and the structure of the Church, Henry was deeply conservative; he allowed few changes in dogma or liturgy and seems to have hoped that he could continue the old ways, changing only the person at the head of the institution. He even tried to restrain the spread of Reformation beliefs, brought to England from the Continent by travelers and books, and he persecuted heresy.

But it proved impossible to stop the momentum. Although many English men and women clung to tradition, others were drawn to the new religious ideas, and they pressured Henry to accept Protestant doctrines. Lollards had kept Wycliffe's ideas alive, and they now joined forces with Protestants inspired by continental reformers to demand services in English and easier access to Scripture. New translations of the Bible appeared in the 1530s, as did echoes of the opposition to clerical privilege that had swept Protestant areas on the Continent. Perhaps realizing that the pressure would only grow, Henry had his son, Edward, tutored by a committed reformer. Edward VI ruled for only six years (1547–1553). He was followed by a committed Catholic, Mary, the daughter of Catherine of Aragon, but her attempt to turn back the clock failed. When her five-year reign ended, the English Church became firmly Protestant under the rule of Elizabeth I, the child Henry had with Anne Boleyn after the divorce (see chapter 15).

THE CATHOLIC REVIVAL

Those with Protestant sympathies usually refer to the Catholic revival that started in the 1530s as the **Counter-Reformation**, implying that the Roman Church acted only as a result of criticisms by Luther and others. Catholic historians call it the Catholic Reformation, implying that the movement began within the Church and was not merely a reaction to Protestantism. There is justification for both views. Certainly the papacy was aware of its loss of control over millions of Christians, but a great deal of the effort to put the Church's house in order was a result of strong faith and a long-standing determination to purify belief and practice.

Strengths and Weaknesses

Although the institution faced serious problems of doctrine and organization, and a major reform effort was certainly needed, it is important to remember that the Church had a vast reserve of loyalty and affection. In the long run, many more Europeans remained Catholic than converted to Protestantism. They took comfort from tradition and from priests who, rather than demanding that believers achieve salvation on their own, offered the Church's mediation, beautiful ceremonies, and rituals to help people overcome their sins. Catholicism had a long history of charity for the poor, which it strengthened during the sixteenth century. For ordinary Christians, the familiarity, support, and grandeur they found in the Church were often reason enough to resist the reformers.

Losses and Difficulties   There was no doubt, however, that the first half of the sixteenth century was the lowest point in the history of the Catholic Church and that few could have expected the recovery that followed. By 1550 many areas of Europe had been lost to the Protestants, and even in regions that were still loyal the papacy was able to exercise little control. The French Church, for example, had a well-established tradition of autonomy, exemplified by the right France's kings had held since 1516 to make ecclesiastical appointments. In Spain, too, the monarchy retained its independence and even had its own Inquisition. In the Holy Roman Empire, those states that had rejected Protestantism gave the pope no more than token allegiance.

Moreover, there was still no comprehensive definition of Catholic doctrine on justification, salvation,

Titian
POPE PAUL III FARNESE WITH HIS NEPHEWS OTTAVIO FARNESE, DUKE OF PARMA, AND CARDINAL ALESSANDRO FARNESE, **1546**
The psychological tension Titian created in this family portrait is extraordinary. The shrewd seventy-seven-year-old pope who had launched the Church's vigorous response to Protestantism looks benignly on Ottavio, whose seemingly calculated gesture of deference hints at the aggressiveness that was soon to cause a major family quarrel over land and money. And Cardinal Alessandro, standing apart, was already a famous patron of art with little concern for Church affairs. Perhaps because of its revelation of character, the painting was never finished.
Museo Nazionale di Capodimonte, Naples, Italy. Erich Lessing/ Art Resource, NY

and the sacraments. Worse yet, the Church's leadership was far from effective. Although one pope, Leo X, had attempted to correct notorious abuses such as simony (the sale of church offices) in the early sixteenth century, Rome simply did not have the spiritual authority to make reform a vital force in the Catholic Church.

Paul III   The situation changed with the pope elected in 1534: Paul III, a man not renowned for saintliness but a genius at making the right decisions for the Church. By the end of his reign, in 1549, the Catholic revival was under way.

The heart of Paul's strategy was his determination to assert papal responsibility throughout the Church. Re-

Titian
THE COUNCIL OF TRENT, CA. 1564
The splendor of the gathering of representatives of the Catholic Church from all of Europe is conveyed by this scene, attributed to Titian. The ranks of bishops in their miters, listening to one of their number address the assembly from the pulpit on the right, visibly embodied a Church putting itself in order as it faced the challenge of Protestantism.
Giraudon/Art Resource, NY

alizing that uncertainties in Catholic doctrine could be resolved only by reexamining traditional theology, he decided within a few months of taking office to call a Church council for that purpose, despite the danger of rekindling the conciliar movement. It took ten years to overcome resistance to the idea, but in the meantime Paul attacked abuses throughout the Church, disregarding both vested interests and tradition. He aimed his campaign at all levels of the hierarchy, undeterred by powerful bishops and cardinals long used to a lax and corrupt regime. In addition, he founded a Roman Inquisition, a decision that reflected the era's growing reliance on persecution as a means of destroying dissent.

Paul realized that, in the long run, the revival of Catholicism would depend on whether his successors maintained his efforts. During his fifteen-year reign, therefore, he made a series of superb appointments to the College of Cardinals (the body that elects the popes); the result was the creation of possibly the most illustrious College in history. Many of its members were famous for their piety, others for their learning.

They came from all over Europe, united by their devotion to the Church and their resolve to see it once again command admiration and reverence. The result of Paul's farsighted policy was to be a succession of popes through the early seventeenth century who would fully restore the atmosphere of spirituality and morality that had long been missing from the papacy.

The Council of Trent

The ecumenical, or general, council of Church leaders called by Paul finally assembled at Trent, a northern Italian city, in 1545, and met irregularly until the delegates managed to complete their work in 1563. The council's history was one of stormy battles between various national factions. The non-Italians pressed for decentralization of religious authority; the Italians, closely tied to the papacy, advocated a consolidation of power. For both sides, the divisions were political as well as ecclesiastical, because at issue was the independence not only of bishops but also of local princes and kings. A large majority of the delegates were Italians, however, and their conclusions almost always reinforced the dominance of the pope. The threat of a revival of conciliarism never materialized.

Defining Doctrine   In keeping with Paul's instructions, the Council of Trent gave more of its time to the basic issue of Church doctrine than to the problem of reform. Nearly all its decisions were intended to establish clear definitions of practice and belief and to end long-standing theological uncertainties or differences of opinion. The main sources for these decisions were the interpretations put forward by Thomas Aquinas, who now became the central theologian of the Catholic Church. At the same time, Trent's decrees were designed to affirm precisely those teachings that the Protestants had rejected. Catholicism from then on would be committed primarily to the outward, sacramental heritage of Christianity. In this view, the Bible is not the exclusive authority for the believer: Church tradition holds an equal place in establishing religious truth. Human will is free, good works as well as faith are a means of salvation, all seven sacraments are channels of grace, and Christ's sacrifice is reenacted in every Mass. The Council of Trent endorsed the special position of the priest and insisted that God be worshiped with appropriately elaborate ceremonies and rites.

These were the main decisions at Trent, but many minor matters were also settled: For the first time, the priest's presence became essential at the sacrament of marriage, a further reinforcement of his importance; the Vulgate, the Latin translation of the Bible prepared chiefly by St. Jerome, was decreed to be a holy text, a decision which rebutted humanists and other scholars who had found mistranslations of Greek and Hebrew in Jerome's work; and in direct contrast to the Protestants, gorgeous ritual was heavily stressed, which encouraged artists to beautify church buildings and ceremonies.

Restoring the Church   The achievement of the council was to adjust the Church to the world. Many ordinary people, troubled by the stern self-denial and predestination taught by most Protestant churches and sects, preferred the traditional comfort, ceremony, and support Catholicism had long offered. They were ready to champion their old faith as soon as its leadership restored its sense of purpose by removing abuses and defining doctrines. And the new discipline of the Church was apparent in the council's effort to deal with morality as thoroughly as with belief. When it gave its approval to the Inquisition and to the "Index of Forbidden Books," which informed all Catholics of the heretical works they were not allowed to read, the council signaled the determination of the Church to recover the ground it had lost.

The Aftermath of Trent

The new atmosphere of dedication swept through the Catholic Church, inspiring thinkers and artists throughout Europe to lend their talents to the cause. Painters, architects, and musicians caught up by the new moral fervor in Catholicism expressed their faith in brilliant and dramatic portrayals of religious subjects and in churches that were designed to dazzle the observer in a way that most Protestants could not allow. This artistic outpouring was, of course, far more than a reflection of the decisions of a few hundred prelates assembled in a council. It was also one of many indicators of the new vigor of Catholicism. In France, for example, a new generation of Church leaders appeared in the late sixteenth century who were distinguished for their austerity, learning, and observance of duties.

Women in the Church   Moreover, the crucial contribution of women to Protestantism was echoed in the revival of Catholicism. There was a remarkable flowering of new religious orders for women in the sixteenth and seventeenth centuries, many of which became identified with charitable works. Since one of the most important ways the Church set about winning back the faithful was by expanding its philanthropic activities—through new hospitals and expanded assistance to the poor, to orphans, and to other unfortunates—its female orders played an essential role in the Counter-Reformation. And nowhere was their devout spirituality more apparent than in Spain, the most fiercely Catholic of all European countries.

The Spaniards expressed their religious passion in many ways—by insisting on converting the native peoples they conquered overseas, by giving great power to the Inquisition that guarded orthodoxy from large Muslim and Jewish communities at home, by encouraging lay as well as clerical piety, and by founding the most famous new order of the age, the Jesuits (see below). But no indication of their devotion was as distinctive as the great flowering of mysticism, which was most famously represented by St. Teresa (1515–1582).

St. Teresa   The mystic seeks to worship God directly and immediately, in an encounter that usually takes place in a trance and without the intervention of a priest. Because this religious experience is entirely personal and does not require the mediation of the Church, it has always been looked on with suspicion by the authorities. St. Teresa was no exception. As a rich and spoiled young girl, she had led a rather loose life, and her concerned father had sent her to a convent to instill some discipline. Perhaps because the family had only recently converted from Judaism, considerable attention was also given to Teresa's religious edu-

St. Teresa's Visions

These two passages are among the most famous from the autobiography that St. Teresa began writing in 1562, when she was forty-seven years old. The book is essentially the story of a spiritual journey, as a restless young woman gains purpose and strength through mystical visions and unwavering faith. Her account of a mystical transport in the second passage quoted here was the inspiration for a famous sculpture by Gian Lorenzo Bernini, The Ecstasy of St. Teresa, in the seventeenth century.

"I: One day, when I was at prayer, the Lord was pleased to reveal to me nothing but His hands, whose beauty was so great as to be indescribable. This made me very fearful. A few days later I also saw the Divine face. On St. Paul's Day, I saw a complete representation of his sacred Humanity. If there were nothing else in Heaven to delight the eyes but the extreme beauty of the glorified bodies there, that alone would be the greatest bliss. If I were to spend years and years imagining how to invent anything so beautiful, I could not do it. In its whiteness and radiance, it exceeds all we can imagine. It is a soft whiteness which, without wearying the eyes, causes them the greatest delight. By comparison with it, the brightness of our sun seems quite dim."

"II: It pleased the Lord that I sometimes saw beside me an angel in bodily form. He was not tall, but short, and very beautiful, his face aflame. In his hands I saw a long golden spear, and at the end of the iron tip I seemed to see a point of fire. With this he seemed to pierce my heart several times. When he drew it out, he left me completely afire with a great love for God. During the days when this continued, I went about as if in a stupor."

From E. Allison Peers, *The Life of Teresa of Jesus*, London: Sheed & Ward, 1944; New York: Doubleday, 1960, pp. 258–260, 273–274.

---

cation. Soon she began to experience visions of God, which gradually convinced her that she had a special religious mission (see "St. Teresa's Visions," above).

Church authorities became worried when, after becoming a nun, Teresa began to attract a following as a spiritual adviser to a number of women in her native city of Avila. Some churchmen suggested that her visions were the work of the devil, not God. After many examinations, however—and finally an interview with the king of Spain himself, who was deeply impressed by her holiness—the doubts evaporated. Teresa founded a strict new order of nuns and traveled all over Spain establishing convents. She soon became a legendary figure and was made a saint only forty years after her death.

The Revitalized Papacy The most conspicuous embodiments of the new energy of the Church, however, were the popes themselves. Paul III's successors used their personal authority and pontifical resources not to adorn their palaces but to continue the enormous cleansing operation within the Church and to lead the counterattack against Protestantism. If a king or prince refused to help, the popes would try to persuade one of his leading subjects (for example, the Guise family in France or the dukes of Bavaria in the empire) to organize the struggle. Their diplomats and agents (often friars) were everywhere, urging Catholics to stamp out Protestantism. And the pontiffs insisted on strict per-

sonal morality so as to restore their reputation for piety and set a proper example to the faithful.

With the leaders of the Church thus bent on reform, the restoration of the faith and the reconquest of lost souls could proceed with maximum effect. And the popes had at their disposal a religious order established by Ignatius Loyola in 1540 specifically for these purposes: the Society of Jesus.

Ignatius Loyola

The third of the great religious innovators of the sixteenth century, after Luther and Calvin, was Ignatius Loyola (1491–1556); unlike his predecessors, however, he sought to reform the Catholic Church from within. Loyola was the son of a Basque nobleman, raised in the chivalric and intensely religious atmosphere of Spain, and he was often at the royal court. In his teens he entered the army, but when he was thirty, a leg wound ended his military career. While convalescing, he was deeply impressed by a number of popular lives of the saints he read, and soon his religious interests began to take shape in chivalric and military terms. He visualized Mary as his lady, the inspiration of a Christian quest in which the forces of God and the devil fight in mighty battle. This was a faith seen from the perspective of the knight, and though the direct parallel lessened as Loyola's thought developed, it left an unmistakable stamp on his future work.

Peter Paul Rubens
THE MIRACLE OF ST. IGNATIUS, **1617–1618**
**Loyola quickly became one of the major heroes of the
Catholic revival. Within less than sixty years of his death
(1556), he was to become a saint of the Church. He was one
of the heroes of Baroque art, as is apparent in this painting
by Peter Paul Rubens, which creates a powerful image of
Loyola at the moment when he cures a man and a woman
who have been possessed by the devil.**
Kunsthistorisches Museum, Vienna, Austria. Erich Lessing/Art
Resource, NY

In 1522 Loyola gave up his knightly garb and swore
to go on a pilgrimage to Jerusalem. He retired to a
monastery for ten months to absolve himself of the
guilt of a sinful life and to prepare spiritually for the
journey to the Holy Land. At the monastery he had a
momentous experience that, like Luther's and Calvin's,
dominated the rest of his life. According to tradition,
he had a vision lasting eight days, during which he saw
in detail the outline of a book, the *Spiritual Exercises*,
and a new religious order, the Society of Jesus.

The Spiritual Exercises   The first version of the *Spiritual Exercises* certainly dated from this period, but like
Calvin's *Institutes*, it was to be thoroughly revised
many times. The book deals not with doctrines or theology but with the discipline and training necessary for

a God-fearing life. Believers must undertake four weeks
of contemplation and self-examination that culminate
in a feeling of union with God, when they surrender
their minds and wills to Christ. If successful, they are
then ready to submit completely to the call of God and
to pursue the Church's commands without question.

The manual was the heart of the organization of the
Society of Jesus, and it gave those who followed its precepts (known as Jesuits) a dedication and determination
that made them seem the Church's answer to the
Calvinists. But while the end might be similar to
Luther's and Calvin's—the personal attainment of
grace—the method, with its emphasis on individual effort and concentration, could not have been more different. For the *Spiritual Exercises* emphasize that believers
can act for themselves; they do not have to depend on
faith alone to gain salvation, as Protestants assert. One
can prepare for grace through a tremendous act of will
and not rely solely on a gift from God. Loyola makes
immense demands precisely because he insists that the
will is free and that good works are efficacious.

Loyola's Followers   During the sixteen years after he
left the monastery, Loyola led a life of poverty and
study. Though lame, he traveled to Jerusalem and back
barefoot in 1523–1524, and two years later, at the University of Alcala, he attracted his first disciples, three
fellow students. Suspected by the Inquisition of being
rather too independent in their beliefs, the little band
walked to Paris, where six more disciples joined them.
In 1537 Loyola and his followers became ordained as
priests. With their activities beginning to take definite
shape, they decided to seek the pope's blessing for their
work. They saw Paul III in 1538, and two years later,
despite opposition from those who saw it as a threat to
the authority of local bishops, the pope approved a plan
Loyola submitted for a new religious order that would
be supervised directly by the papacy.

The Jesuits

Jesuit Activities   The Society, or Company, of Jesus
had four principal functions: preaching, hearing confessions, teaching, and missionary work. The first two
were the Jesuits' means of strengthening the beliefs of
individual Catholics or converting Protestants. The
third became one of their most effective weapons. The
Christian humanists he encountered convinced Loyola
of the tremendous power of education. The Jesuits
therefore set about organizing the best schools in Europe and were so successful that some Protestants sent
their children to the Society's schools despite the certainty that the pupils would become committed
Catholics. The instructors followed humanist principles and taught the latest ideas, including the most re-

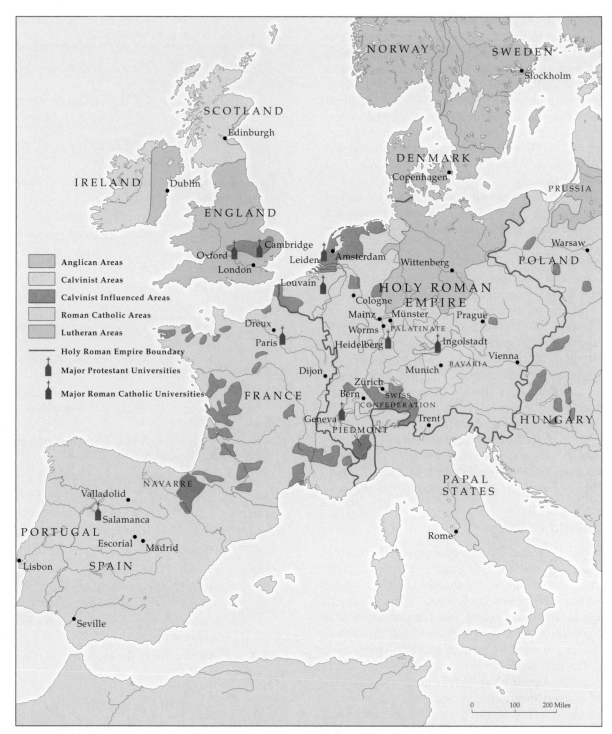

MAP 13.1 **RELIGIOUS DIVISIONS IN EUROPE AT THE END OF THE SIXTEENTH CENTURY**
By the late sixteenth century, the division of Europe into distinct areas, each committed primarily to one church, was virtually complete. Now that they were solidly established, the major faiths became associated with universities that elaborated and promoted their beliefs. Where were the major Roman Catholic universities? Where were the major Protestant universities?
◆ For an online version, go to www.mhhe.com/chambers9 > chapter 13 > book maps

cent advances in science. The Jesuits' final activity, missionary work, brought them their most spectacular successes among both non-Christians and Protestants.

Jesuit Campaigns A number of qualities combined to make the Jesuits extraordinarily effective in winning converts and turning Catholics into militant activists.

First, the order demanded high intellectual abilities. It selected recruits carefully (rejecting many applicants) and gave them a superb education. Jesuits were famous for their knowledge of Scripture and traditional teachings and their ability to out-argue opponents. In addition, they were highly effective preachers and excellent educators. Their discipline, determination, and awareness of the contemporary world soon won them a fearsome reputation. They had no equal in the forcefulness with which they advanced the aims of the Council of Trent and the papacy.

The Jesuits can be regarded as the striking arm of the Counter-Reformation; indeed, their organization was to some extent modeled on the medieval military orders. A Jesuit at a royal court was often the chief inspiration for a ruler's militant support of the faith, and in many areas the Society was the main conqueror of rival beliefs—for example in Poland, where Jesuits in the late sixteenth century led a campaign that eradicated widespread Protestantism and created a devoted Catholic country. Yet it must be noted that in an age that took persecution for granted, the Jesuits always opposed execution for heresy; they far preferred to win a convert than to kill a heretic. Their presence was soon felt all over the world: As early as the 1540s, one of Loyola's first disciples, Francis Xavier, conducted a mission to Japan. Despite the many enmities they aroused by their single-mindedness and their self-assurance, their unswerving devotion was a major reason for the revival of the Roman Church.

Religion and Politics

As a revived Catholic Church confronted the Protestants, religious warfare of unprecedented ferocity erupted throughout Europe (see chapter 15). More people seemed to feel more passionately about faith than at any other time in Western history. But the conflict would not have continued as long as it did without the armies and resources provided by princes and monarchs. Both sides drew crucial support from rulers who were determined either to suppress any sign of heresy in their territories or to overthrow heretical regimes in neighboring lands. For these rulers, the struggle over religion was a means of establishing their authority in their own realms and a justification for aggression abroad.

CHRONOLOGY
The Reformation and Counter-Reformation

1517	Luther's protest begins: the ninety-five theses on indulgences.
1521	Diet of Worms: Luther condemned by Emperor Charles V.
1524–1525	Peasants' Revolt in Germany.
	Zürich adopts Zwingli's Reformation.
1531	Protestant League of Schmalkalden formed in Germany.
	Death of Zwingli.
1534	Paul III becomes pope.
	Anabaptists take over the city of Münster in Germany.
	King Henry VIII is proclaimed head of the Church of England.
1535	Thomas More executed for not accepting Henry VIII as head of the Church of England.
1536	Calvin comes to Geneva; first edition of his *Institutes*.
	Death of Erasmus.
1540	Pope Paul III approves the Jesuit Order.
1541	Calvin settles in Geneva permanently.
1545	Council of Trent begins.
1546	Death of Luther.
1556	Death of Loyola.
1559	First "Index of Forbidden Books" published.
	Execution of Protestants after Inquisition trials in Spain.
1564	Publication of the Decrees of the Council of Trent.
	Death of Calvin.

Summary

The strong connection between politics and belief, and its dire consequences, was the result of a transformation that was almost as far-reaching as the Reformation itself. Just as Western Christianity was changed forever in the sixteenth century, so too were the power and the ambition of the ter-

ritorial state. At the same time as a handful of reformers, building on powerful social and intellectual forces, reshaped religious structures and practices, a handful of political leaders—building on
no less powerful military, social, and economic forces—created armies, systems of taxation, and bureaucratic organizations that reshaped the structures and practices of central governments
throughout Europe.

QUESTIONS FOR FURTHER THOUGHT

1. If spiritual yearning has often changed individuals, why are outside forces such as politics necessary before large-scale changes in faith can take hold?

2. Is religious belief best understood as personal or as communal?

RECOMMENDED READING

Sources

*Calvin, John. *On God and Political Duty.* J. T. McNeill (ed.). 1950.

*Erasmus, Desiderius. *Essential Works of Erasmus.* W. T. H. Jackson (ed.). 1965.

Loyola, Ignatius. *The Spiritual Exercises of St. Ignatius.* R. W. Gleason (ed.). 1964.

*Luther, Martin. *Martin Luther: Selections from His Writings.* John Dillenberger (ed.). 1961.

Studies

*Bossy, John. *Christianity in the West, 1400–1700.* 1985. An overview of the religious history of Europe by one of the leading historians of Catholic thought and practice.

*Bouwsma, William J. *John Calvin: A Sixteenth-Century Portrait.* 1988. The standard biography.

*Davis, Natalie Zemon. *Society and Culture in Early Modern France.* 1975. A collection of essays about popular beliefs and attitudes, particularly on religious matters, during the sixteenth century.

*Huizinga, Johan. *Erasmus and the Age of Reformation.* 1957. A warm and sympathetic biography, beautifully written.

Jones, M. D. W. *The Counter Reformation.* 1995.

*Kenny, Anthony. *Thomas More.* 1983. An excellent brief introduction to More's life and work.

Kittelson, James M. *Luther the Reformer: The Story of the Man and His Career.* 1986. The best introduction to Luther's life and thought.

*Mullett, Michael A. *The Catholic Reformation.* 1999.

O'Malley, John. *The First Jesuits.* 1993.

Scribner, Robert. *For the Sake of Simple Folk: Popular Propaganda for the German Reformation.* 1981. A pathbreaking analysis of how the Reformation was spread.

Tracy, James. *Europe's Reformations, 1450–1650.* 1999. A recent overview.

Wiesner, Merry. *Women and Gender in Early Modern Europe.* 1993.

Williams, George H. *The Radical Reformation.* 1962. The most comprehensive account of the sects and their founders.

*Available in paperback.

Hans Holbein the Younger
THE AMBASSADORS, 1533
**Hans Holbein the Younger's *The Ambassadors* shows the worldliness that was expected of
diplomats (many of whom were also soldiers) in the sixteenth century. The two men are
surrounded by symbols of the skills, knowledge, and refinement their job required—geography,
mathematics, literature, and music. But despite this emphasis on material concerns, Holbein
reminds us (in the optically distorted skull across the bottom of the painting) that death and
spiritual needs cannot be forgotten.**

Chapter Fourteen

ECONOMIC EXPANSION AND A NEW POLITICS

EXPANSION AT HOME • EXPANSION OVERSEAS • THE CENTRALIZATION OF POLITICAL
POWER • THE SPLINTERED STATES • THE NEW STATECRAFT

Europe in 1400 was a poor, technologically backward, and politically disorganized area compared to the realms of the Indian moguls or Chinese emperors. And yet within little more than a century, Europeans were expanding aggressively into Asia and the Americas. Their numbers were growing, their economy was booming, their technological advances were making possible the creation of new markets and new empires, and their political leaders were developing structures of government and authority more elaborate than any that had been seen since the fall of the Roman Empire.

The emergence of this new world power was one of the most astonishing transformations in Western history, and historians have long debated its causes. Their suggestions have ranged from the initiatives of specific kings or explorers to such forces as demographic change or climatic warming. Like the fall of the Roman Empire, however, this was so profound a reshaping of Europe's economy and politics that no definitive explanation seems possible. Yet a survey of the main individual changes can help explain how far the reordering had progressed by the late sixteenth century.

Cortès lands in Mexico; Magellan's voyage around the world (to 1522); Charles V Holy Roman Emperor (to 1556) **1519** ●

Machiavelli, *The Prince* **1513** ●

Vasco da Gama sails to India **1497** ●

Treaty of Tordesillas; Italian wars begin (to 1559) **1494** ●

1492 ●
Columbus' first voyage; capture of Muslim
Granada by Spanish; expulsion of Jews from Spain

Dias rounds the Cape of Good Hope **1488** ●

● **1469** Marriage of Ferdinand of Aragon and Isabella of Castile

EXPANSION AT HOME

During the last third of the fifteenth century, signs of change appeared in the demographic, economic, and political history of Europe. Some argue that the causes were political: that trade quickened and populations grew because of rising confidence as assertive regimes restored order and authority in a number of states. Others regard either economic or demographic advance as the source of change. In fact, though, all three were connected and all three reinforced one another. What is unmistakable is the increase in the number of Europeans after more than one hundred years of decline and the social and economic consequences of that increase.

Population Increase

Exact measurements are not possible, but it seems likely that the loss of population that began with the Black Death in the 1340s had run its course by the 1460s. Plagues, though recurrent, began to take less of a toll (perhaps because immunities developed); bad harvests became less frequent (perhaps because of a warming climate); and families were thus able to produce more surviving children. As a result, Europe's population rose by some 50 percent between 1470 and 1620. And cities expanded even faster: London had fewer than 50,000 inhabitants in the early sixteenth century but over 200,000 a hundred years later. There was also extensive reoccupation of marginal farmland, which had been abandoned in the fourteenth and fifteenth centuries because of a shrinking population. Now there were more mouths to feed, and the extra acres again became profitable.

Consequences of the Increase The rise in population was followed by a staggering jump in food prices. By the early 1600s wheat cost approximately five times

more than in the late 1400s, an increase that far outpaced the movement of prices in general. It is not surprising, therefore, that this period witnessed the first wave of enclosures in England: Major landowners put up fences around common tilling or grazing ground, traditionally open to all the animals of the locality, and reserved it for their own crops or their sheep, whose wool was also in increasing demand. By 1600 about one-eighth of England's arable land had been enclosed. The only answer, when changes like these made a village incapable of supporting its growing population, was for people to move to towns and cities.

Economic Growth

As markets began to grow in response to population pressures, the volume of trade also shot upward; commercial profits thus kept pace with those of agriculture. Customs receipts rose steadily, as did the yield of tolls from ships entering the Baltic Sea, one of the main routes of European trade. In many areas, too, shipbuilding boomed. This was the heyday of the English cloth trade and the great Spanish sheep farms, of the central German linen industry and the northern Italian silk industry. Printing became a widespread occupation, and gun making and glassmaking also expanded rapidly. Glassmaking had a major effect on European society because the increasing use of windows allowed builders to divide houses into small rooms, thus giving many people a little privacy for the first time.

The Growth of Banking Leading financiers who invested in the growing volume of trade accumulated large fortunes. For centuries the Italians had led economic advance, but in the sixteenth century firms of other nations were achieving international prominence. The most successful of the new enterprises was

1520–1566 Suleiman the Great expands the Ottoman Empire

● **1529** Reformation Parliament assembles

● **1545** Silver discovered in South America

run by a family descended from a fourteenth-century weaver, Johannes Fugger of Augsburg. The sixteenth-century Fuggers financed the Spanish King Charles I's quest for the throne of the Holy Roman Empire and his later wars after he became the Emperor Charles V. Great bankers were thus often closely allied with monarchs, and like all merchants, they gained from the growing power of central governments. Rulers encouraged commerce in the hope of larger revenues from customs duties and taxes, and they gave leading entrepreneurs valuable privileges. Such alliances were eventually the undoing of some firms, which were ruined when kings went bankrupt, but until the late sixteenth century, Italian and German bankers controlled Europe's finances.

New Kinds of Businesses Almost every level of commercial activity offered opportunities for advancement. The guild system expanded in the sixteenth century to incorporate many new trades, and the structure of merchant enterprises became more elaborate. The idea took hold that a business firm was an impersonal entity—larger than the person who owned it—with an identity, legal status, permanence, and even profits that were not the same as those of its members. Here was yet another indication of major economic change.

Inflation The surest sign of growth, however, was the slow inflation of prices, which began around 1500 after some one hundred fifty years of either stagnant or falling prices. By modern standards, the increase was tiny—1 or 2 percent a year, totaling 75 percent in Spain by 1600 and slightly less elsewhere in Europe—but it prompted bitter protests from those who thought a loaf of bread had a "just" price and that any increase was mere exploitation by the baker. In general, however, the modest inflation was an indication that demand

was rising, and it not only boosted profits but also reduced people's debts (because the amount that had been borrowed was worth less each year).

Silver Imports A major reason for the inflation was the growth of the population, but it was also propelled by the huge quantities of silver the Spaniards imported from the New World, which made money more readily available (see accompanying table). Most of the silver passed from Spain to the Italian and German merchants who financed Spanish wars and controlled the American trade, and thus it affected all of Europe. The flow of New World silver was the main reason for the end of the crippling shortage of precious metals and coins that had plagued Europe for centuries. By the middle of the seventeenth century, the continent's holdings in gold had increased by one-fifth and, more important, its stock of silver had tripled.

IMPORTS OF TREASURE TO SPAIN FROM THE NEW WORLD, 1511–1600

Decade	Total Value*
1511–1520	2,626,000
1521–1530	1,407,000
1531–1540	6,706,000
1541–1550	12,555,000
1551–1560	21,437,000
1561–1570	30,418,000
1571–1580	34,990,000
1581–1590	63,849,000
1591–1600	85,536,000

*In ducats.

Adapted from J. H. Elliott, *Imperial Spain, 1469–1716*, New York, 1964, p. 175.

Anonymous
MERCHANTS CLEARING ACCOUNTS, FRENCH MINIATURE
This sixteenth-century depiction of a group of people in a fine house calculating accounts gives a sense of the increasingly complicated exchanges that became necessary as commerce expanded. Books had to be checked and money counted. It is noteworthy that the transactions involve the monk on the left and the woman holding her purse on the right.
Bettmann/Corbis

With money circulating more freely and markets growing, the profits of traders and financiers improved dramatically. They could invest more widely (for example, in overseas ventures) and thus achieve new levels of wealth.

The Commercial Revolution   As the volume of trade rose, new mechanisms for organizing large-scale economic activity were put in place—a process that has been called Europe's commercial revolution. Bookkeepers devised new, standardized principles for keeping track of a firm's accounts, bankers created elaborate systems of agents and letters of credit to transfer funds across large distances, merchants developed more effective means of forming broad partnerships that were capable of major investments and of ensuring against losses, and governments gave increased support to new

ventures and to the financial community in general. Essential to these activities was an attitude and a way of conducting business that is known as *capitalism*.

Capitalism   Capitalism was both a product of economic change and a stimulus to further change. It is often thought of as a system, but it refers primarily to the distinct outlook and kinds of behavior displayed by certain people as they make, buy, and sell goods. At its root, capitalism means the accumulation of capital—that is, tangible wealth—for its own sake. In practice, this requires taking risks and also reinvesting whatever one earns so as to enlarge one's profits. Those who undertook long-distance trade had many capitalist traits: They took great risks, and they were prepared to wait months and even years in order to make as large a financial gain as possible. Similarly, bankers were prepared to lend their capital, despite the danger that the loan might not be repaid, in the hope of profit; and if they succeeded, they continually plowed their earnings back into their businesses to make them ever larger. The fortunes that these capitalists accumulated, and the desire for worldly riches that they displayed, became an essential stimulus to economic growth. Far from the rural world where food was grown primarily for survival, not for profit, they were forging a new way of thinking about money and wealth. Although their outlook had existed before, only in the sixteenth century did it come to dominate Europe's economy. As a result, traditional religious prohibitions on the charging of interest began to weaken, and materialist ambitions became more open and accepted.

Unease over this new outlook did not disappear. Shakespeare's play *The Merchant of Venice*, written in the 1590s, attacked the values that capitalism was coming to represent. He contrasted unfavorably the quest for profit with more traditional commitments, such as charity and mercy. But criticism had no effect on the relentless spread of capitalism.

Social Change

Unequal Impacts in the Countryside   Not everyone shared in the new prosperity of the sixteenth century. Landowners, food producers, artisans, and merchants benefited most from the rising population and could amass fortunes. Tenants who were able to harvest a surplus beyond their own needs did well, because for a while rents did not keep pace with food prices. But the wages of ordinary laborers lagged miserably. By the early 1600s, a laborer's annual income had about half the purchasing power it had had at the end of the 1400s, a decline that had its most drastic impact in Eastern Europe, where serfdom reappeared.

In the West, the large numbers of peasants who were forced off the land as the population rose turned to beg-

Jost Amman
ALLEGORY OF TRADE, Woodcut
This late-sixteenth-century celebration of the world of the merchant shows, around the sides, the shipping of goods, the keeping of accounts, and the exchange of money that were transforming economic life. In the center, the virtues of the merchant are symbolized: integrity (a man looking over his shoulder), taciturnity (two men on his right), and a knowledge of languages (two men in turbans) in front of judiciousness on a throne and a book representing invention.

ging and wandering across country, often ending up in towns, where crime became a serious problem. Peasant uprisings directed at tax collectors, nobles, or food suppliers were almost annual affairs in one region or another of France after the mid-sixteenth century, and in England the unending stream of vagrants gave rise to a belief that the country was overpopulated. The extreme poverty was universally deplored, particularly as it promoted crime and disorder.

Relief of Distress Nobody could understand, much less control, the forces that were transforming society. Some governments tried to relieve the economic distress, but their efforts were not always consistent. English legislation in the sixteenth century, for example, treated beggars sometimes as shirkers who should be punished and at other times as unfortunates who needed to be helped. Not until the enactment of the English Poor Law of 1601, which provided work for the poor, did the less severe view begin to prevail. In the years that followed, governments in a number of countries began to create institutions that offered basic welfare benefits.

The traditional source of food for the hungry and care for the ill, the monastery, had lost its importance because of the Reformation and because governments were now considered responsible for the needy. Among the remedies governments offered were the work-houses established by the English Poor Law where, although conditions could be horrible, the destitute could at least find work, food, and shelter. Other governments founded hospitals, often staffed by nuns, which were especially important as places that looked after abandoned women or children. But these institutions were few and far between, and it was exceptional for a poor person to find such relief. The conditions were especially harsh for women forced off the land, because few trades were open to them even if they got to a town; their choice might be either continued vagrancy or prostitution.

The Hazards of Life in the Town Vagrancy was only one of the signs that Europeans were witnessing the beginnings of modern urbanization with all its dislocations. Major differences also developed between life in the country and life in the town. Rural workers may have led a strenuous existence, but they escaped the worst hazards of their urban counterparts. Whole sections of most large cities were controlled by the sixteenth-century equivalent of the underworld, which offered sanctuary to criminals and danger to most citizens. Plagues were much more serious in towns— the upper classes soon learned to flee to the country at

Petrus Christus
St. Eligius as a Goldsmith, **1449**
**Goldsmiths played a vital financial role in the
early days of capitalism. Because of the value of
the merchandise they made and sold, their
shops—like the one here, with customers
looking in the window, reflected in the convex
mirror on the right—were sources of capital as
well as goods. In addition to providing such
items as the ring he is handing to the young
woman, the goldsmith might well have provided
investments for the traders in his city.**
The Metropolitan Museum of Art, Robert Lehman
Collection, 1975. (1975.1.110) Photography © 1993
The Metropolitan Museum of Art, New York

Quentin Metsys
The Money Changer and His Wife, **1514**
**That people engaged in this business could be the subject of
a respectful portrait by a leading artist is an indication that
money lending and currency dealing had come to be taken
for granted in European cities. It was a family enterprise,
with the wife helping her husband, and it is worth noting
that in business circles a literate woman—she has here
interrupted the reading of a book—was not that unusual.**
Erich Lessing/Art Resource, NY

the first sign of disease—and famines more devastating
because of the far poorer sanitation in urban areas and
their remoteness from food supplies.

New Opportunities   Nevertheless, it was in towns
and cities that the economic advances of the age were
most visible. As cities grew, they stimulated construction, not only of houses but also of public buildings and
city walls. Anyone skilled in bricklaying, in carpentry,
or even in carrying heavy loads found ready employment. Townsfolk needed endless services, from sign
painting to transportation, which created jobs at all levels. Given the demand for skills, guilds increasingly

allowed the widows of members to take over their husbands' trades, and women shopkeepers were not un-
common. Nobody would have been taken aback, for
example, to see an artisan's daughter or wife (like

Pieter Brueghel the Elder
FIGHT BETWEEN CARNIVAL AND LENT, **1559**
This detail from a huge scene shows one of the customary practices during the season of Lent: giving alms to the poor. Beggars were a common subject for Brueghel, who used them to convey a vivid sense of the appearance and behavior of the unfortunate as well as the more comfortable members of his society.
Erich Lessing/Art Resource, NY

Agnes Dürer, the wife of the famous German artist) take charge of a market stall or a shop. In some trades, such as oil making and baking, women were often essential to production as well as sales, and there is also evidence of their growing importance as the keepers of the paperwork and the accounts in family businesses. The expansion of opportunity in the cities, in other words, had social as well as economic consequences.

At the top levels of society—at princely courts and in royal administrations, in the law, among the leaders of the burgeoning cities, and in growing empires overseas— the economic expansion enabled ambitious families to win fortunes and titles and to found new aristocratic dynasties. The means of advancement varied. Once a family had become rich through commerce, it could buy the lands that, in Protestant countries, rulers had confiscated from the Church, or the offices that many governments sold to raise revenue and build bureaucracies. In addition, the New World offered the possibility of acquiring vast estates. Since the possession of land or high office was the key to noble status, the newly rich were soon able to enter the ranks of the nobility. The long boom in commerce thus encouraged broad social change. By the 1620s, when the growth in the economy came to an end, a new aristocracy had been born that was destined to dominate Europe for centuries.

Daily Life   The expanding resources changed many aspects of daily life. The availability (and affordability) of books, for example, helped promote literacy. Evidence is scarce, but the ability to sign documents, for example, tripled in many areas during the two centuries following the early 1500s. And many more could read than could write, though on both counts women lagged far behind. In Molière's play *The School for Wives* (1661), the lead character hopes his new wife can read, so that she can study the "Rules for Marriage" that he has written, but he is mortified when he discovers she can also write. With money, too, came broadening access to such consumer goods as household utensils, which transformed behavior at the table: by the late seventeenth century, meals in polite society required individual place settings, with plates, napkins, knives, and forks.

At the same time, an enormous boom in house building, and the dividing off of rooms within these houses, created new atmospheres in the homes of the well-to-do. Private spaces were created whose names reflected their purposes: thus, the place where one studied became the study; in French, the word *cuisine* still refers both to the kitchen and to the food that is cooked there. People began to collect souvenirs for decoration, to spend significant sums on furnishings and art, and to make the bedroom a special place. By the mid-1600s the dressing-gown was a popular item of clothing, and the room in which it might be worn could have suggestive overtones.

EXPANSION OVERSEAS

Long before Europe's demographic and economic recovery began in the late 1400s, pioneer explorers had taken the first steps toward creating huge empires overseas. Extending the voyages beyond Europe of the crusaders and such travelers as Marco Polo, sailors had been

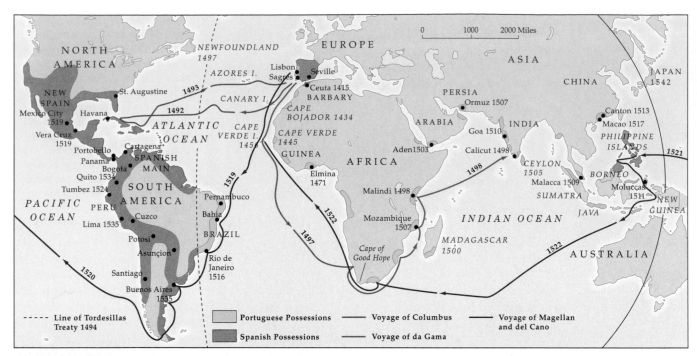

MAP 14.1 EXPLORATION AND CONQUEST IN THE FIFTEENTH AND SIXTEENTH CENTURIES
The division of the world between the Portuguese and the Spaniards led to distinct areas of exploration and settlement, demarcated by the line that both sides accepted at the Treaty of Tordesillas. Notice the extraordinary range of voyages and discoveries that were made in just a few decades after 1492. Which nation dominated exploration and settlement in the New World? What were other key areas of exploration and settlement?
◆ For an online version, go to www.mhhe.com/chambers9 > chapter 14 > book maps

inching around Africa seeking a route to the Far East. As they moved farther afield, they began conquering territory and peoples. The riches in goods and lands they eventually found would help fuel the boom of the sixteenth century.

The Portuguese

Henry the Navigator Among the Portuguese, who began these voyages in the 1410s, there was little expectation of world-shattering consequences. The Portuguese lived in an inhospitable land whose seafarers had always been essential to the country's economy. The need for better agricultural opportunities had long drawn them to Atlantic islands like the Canaries and to territories held by the Muslims (Moors) in North Africa. But this ambition had to be organized into a sustained effort if it was to achieve results. In the early fifteenth century, Prince Henry the Navigator, a younger son of the king, undertook that task.

Henry participated in the capture of the North African port of Ceuta from the Muslims in 1415, a crusading expedition that only whetted his appetite for more such victories. At Ceuta he probably heard stories about lost Christians and mines of gold somewhere in the interior of Africa. A mixture of motives—profit, re-

ligion, and curiosity—spurred him on, and in 1419 he began patronizing sailors, mapmakers, astronomers (for their help in celestial navigation), shipbuilders, and instrument makers who were interested in discovery. They were mainly Italians, and their aim was not merely to make contact with Africans but to find an alternative route to India and the Far East around Africa (in order to avoid the Ottoman Empire, which was coming to dominate the eastern Mediterranean). The early adventurers did not succeed, but during their gradual advance down the West African coast, they opened a rich new trade in ivory, gold, and slaves.

To India and Beyond Then, in 1488, a Portuguese captain, Bartholomeu Dias, returned to Lisbon after making a landfall on the east coast of Africa, beyond the Cape of Good Hope, which previously no one had been able to pass. The way to India now seemed open, but before the Portuguese sent out their first expedition, the news arrived that a sailor employed by the Spaniards, one Christopher Columbus, had apparently reached India by sailing west. To avoid conflicting claims that might interfere with their trade, Portugal and Spain signed the **Treaty of Tordesillas** in 1494. This gave Portugal possession of all the lands to the east of an imaginary line about 300 miles west of the Azores and Spain a monopoly of everything to the west. Portugal thus kept the only practical route to India (as well as the rights to Brazil, which one of its sailors may already have discovered). Three years later Vasco da Gama took the first Portuguese fleet across the Indian Ocean.

At first, he found it hard to trade, because the Arabs, who had controlled these waters for centuries, tried to keep out all rivals. Within fourteen years, however, the Portuguese merchants had established themselves. The key to their success was naval power. In addition to improving the design of sails to increase speed and maneuverability, the Portuguese were the first to emphasize firepower, realizing that cannon, not soldiers, won battles at sea. In addition, they deployed their ships in squadrons rather than individually, a tactic that further increased their superiority. The result was overwhelming military success. A series of victories reduced Arab naval strength, and bombardments quieted stubborn cities. By 1513 Portugal's trading posts extended beyond India to the rich Spice Islands, the Moluccas.

The Portuguese Empire   The empire Portugal created remained dependent on sea power, not overseas colonies. Except in Brazil, which was virtually unpopulated and where the settlers were able to establish huge estates worked by slave labor, the Portuguese relied on a chain of small trading bases that stretched from West Africa to China. They supplied and defended these bases, which usually consisted of little more than a few warehouses and a fort, by sea; and they tended to keep contacts with the local people to a minimum, so as to maintain friendly relations and missionary and trading rights. The one exception to the isolation was caused by the small numbers of Portuguese women who traveled to the settlements: In these early years there were more marriages with local women than there were in other European empires. But even though their effort remained relatively small-scale, the Portuguese soon profited from their explorations. Between 1442 and 1446 the Portuguese brought almost one thousand slaves from Africa. In the 1500s their wealth grew as they became major importers of luxuries from the East, such as spices, which were in great demand as medicines, preservatives, and tasty delicacies.

By dominating commerce with Eastern civilizations, which were not only richer but also more sophisticated than their own, Portugal's merchants controlled Europe's most valuable trade. But their dominance was to last less than a century, for their success spurred a competition for empire that was to stimulate new waves of overseas expansion. First, Spain determined to emulate its neighbor; and later, the Dutch, English, and French sought to outdo their predecessors and one another. This competition gave the Europeans the crucial stimulus that other peoples lacked, and it projected them into a dominance over the rest of the globe that would last for more than 450 years.

The Spaniards

Inspired by the same centuries-old crusading ambitions as the Portuguese, the Spaniards rode the second wave of expansion overseas. Because Spain was much larger than Portugal and directed its attention toward a more sparsely populated continent, the Spaniards founded their empire on conquest and colonization, not trade. But they got their start from a stroke of luck.

Columbus   Christopher Columbus—an experienced Genoese sailor who was widely read, well-versed in Atlantic sailing, and familiar with the leading geographers of his day—seems to have believed (we do not know for certain, because he was a secretive man) that Asia lay only 3,500 miles beyond the Canary Islands. Thus, convinced that sailing west across the Atlantic to the Far East was perfectly feasible, Columbus sought support from the Portuguese government. It refused, but he persisted and eventually gained the financial backing of Ferdinand V and Isabella I of Spain that enabled him to set sail in 1492. He was an excellent navigator (one of his discoveries on the voyage was the difference between true and magnetic north), and he kept his men going despite their horror of being so long at sea without sight of land. After thirty-three days, he reached the Bahamas. He was disappointed that he found no

Columbus Landing, Woodcut
This picture, by a contemporary, shows King Ferdinand, back in Spain, pointing to Columbus' three ships and the natives greeting the explorer in the New World.
New York Public Library

HISTORICAL ISSUES: TWO VIEWS OF COLUMBUS

The following two passages suggest the enormous differences that have arisen in interpretations of the career of Christopher Columbus. The first, by Samuel Eliot Morison, a historian and a noted sailor, represents the traditional view of the explorer's achievements that held sway until recent years. The second, by Kirkpatrick Sale, a writer and environmentalist, indicates how radically the understanding of the effects of exploration has changed in recent years.

1. "Columbus had a Hellenic sense of wonder at the new and strange, combined with an artist's appreciation of natural beauty. Moreover, Columbus had a deep conviction of the sovereignty and the infinite wisdom of God, which enhanced all his triumphs. One only wishes that the Admiral might have been afforded the sense of fulfillment that would have come from foreseeing all that flowed from his discoveries. The whole history of the Americas stems from the Four Voyages of Columbus, and as the Greek city-states looked back to the deathless gods as their founders, so today a score of independent nations unite in homage to Christopher the stout-hearted son of Genoa, who carried Christian civilization across the Ocean Sea."

From S. E. Morison, *Admiral of the Ocean Sea: A Life of Christopher Columbus*, Boston: Little, Brown, 1942, pp. 670–671.

2. "For all his navigational skill, about which the salty types make such a fuss, and all his fortuitous headings, Admiral Colón [Christopher Columbus] could be a

wretched mariner. The four voyages, properly seen, quite apart from bravery, are replete with lubberly mistakes, misconceived sailing plans, foolish disregard of elementary maintenance, and stubborn neglect of basic safety— all characterized by the assertion of human superiority over the natural realm. Almost every time Colón went wrong, it was because he had refused to bend to the inevitabilities of tide and wind and reef or, more arrogantly still, had not bothered to learn about them.

"Many of those who know well the cultures that once existed in the New World have reason to be less than enthusiastic about [the 1992 celebrations of] the event that led to the destruction of much of that heritage and the greater part of the people who produced it; others are planning to protest the entire goings-on as a wrongful commemoration of an act steeped in bloodshed, slavery, and genocide."

From Kirkpatrick Sale, *The Conquest of Paradise: Christopher Columbus and the Columbian Legacy*, New York: Knopf, 1990, pp. 209–210, 362.

Chinese or Japanese as he investigated Cuba and the west coast of Hispaniola (today's Haiti), but he was certain that he had reached Asia, even though the few natives he saw did not resemble those whom travelers such as Marco Polo had described.

Columbus crossed the Atlantic Ocean three more times, but he made no other significant discoveries. Yet he did also start the tradition of violence against local people that was to characterize the European conquest of the New World. During his first stay in the Caribbean, his men killed some of the natives they encountered. From the very beginning, therefore, it became clear that the building of empires in the Americas would be a process of destruction as well as creation, of cruelty as well as achievement (see "Two Views of Columbus," above). For the victims, the effect of the brutality, soon intensified by the devastating diseases that accompanied the Europeans, was to undermine their ancient civilizations.

The Limits of Westward Voyages By the end of Columbus' life in 1506, it was becoming apparent that he had found islands close by a new continent, not

Asia. The last hope of a quick journey to the riches of East Asia was dashed in 1522, when the one surviving ship from a fleet of five that had set out under Ferdinand Magellan three years before returned to Spain after the ordeal of having sailed around the world.

Magellan's 98-day crossing of the Pacific was the supreme accomplishment of seamanship in the age of discovery. But the voyage persuaded the Spaniards that Portugal had the fastest route to the East, and in 1529 they renounced all attempts to trade with the Spice Islands. Spain could now concentrate on the Americas, those unexpected continents that were to become not an obstacle on the way to the Spice Islands but possessions of unbelievable richness.

The Conquistador Volunteers for empire building were amply available. When the last Muslim kingdom in southern Spain was conquered by the Castilians in 1492, soldiers with long experience of military service found themselves at loose ends. Many were the younger sons of noble families, who were often kept from inheriting land because Spanish law usually allowed only the eldest son to inherit. The prospect of unlimited land

and military adventure across the Atlantic appealed to them, as it did to ambitious members of Castile's lower classes, and thus the **conquistador,** or conqueror, was born. There were not many of them—fewer than one thousand—but they overran much of the Americas in search of wealth and glory.

The first and most dramatic was Hernando Cortès, who in 1519 landed on the Mexican coast and set out to overcome the rich Aztec civilization in the high plateau of central Mexico. His army consisted of only six hundred troops, but in two years, with a few reinforcements, he had won a complete victory. Guns alone made no important difference, because Cortès had only thirteen muskets and some unwieldy cannons. More effective were his horses, his manipulation of the Aztecs' beliefs (especially after he murdered their ruler) to make them regard him as invincible, and the unshakable determination of his followers. The conquest of the Mexican Mayas also began under Cortès, while the Incas of Peru fell to Francisco Pizzaro. Other conquistadors repeated these successes throughout Central and South America. By 1550 the conquest was over, and the military leaders gave way to administrators who began organizing the huge empire they had won.

The First Colonial Empires

The Spanish government established in the New World the same pattern of political administration that it was setting up in its European territories. Representatives of the throne, viceroys, were sent to administer each territory and to impose centralized control. They were advised by the local *audiencia,* a kind of miniature council that also acted as a court of law, but the ultimate authority remained in Spain.

Real growth did not begin, however, until women pioneers came out to the settlements. In this empire, unlike Portugal's, intermarriage was strongly discouraged. Indeed, the indigenous peoples were treated with a brutality and disdain that set a dismal model for overseas empires. Their labor was cruelly exploited on farms and especially in silver mines that the Spaniards discovered, where working conditions were dreadful. Families were split apart so that men could be put to work, and local beliefs and traditions were actively suppressed (though many survived despite the oppression). Over the years, intermarriage between Europeans and natives increased, and a more united society evolved, but this transformation took centuries to achieve. In the meantime, Spain's colonies were an object of envy because of their mineral wealth. In 1545 Spaniards discovered a major vein of silver at Potosì, in Bolivia, and from those mines came the treasure that made fortunes for the colonists, sustained Spain's many wars, and ultimately enriched much of Europe.

For the balance of the sixteenth century, however, despite the efforts of other countries, Portugal and Spain remained the only conspicuous participants in Europe's overseas expansion.

The Perilous Life of the Settlers   It took a great deal of determination to board one of the ships that set off across the oceans from Europe. Life at sea offered discomfort and peril: horrible overcrowding, inadequate and often rotting food, disease, dangerous storms, poor navigation, and threats from enemy ships. One cannot determine numbers precisely, but it has been estimated that in some decades of the sixteenth and seventeenth centuries, fewer than two-thirds of those who embarked reached their destination. And their troubles did not end when they came off the ships. Unfamiliar countries, famine, illness, and attacks by natives and European rivals made life precarious at best. Although five thousand people sailed for Virginia between 1619 and 1624, for instance, disease and massacre kept the colony the same size at the end of that period—about one thousand inhabitants—as it had been at the beginning. And yet, despite the difficulties and dangers, people found reasons to keep coming.

The Aims of the Colonists   For a few leaders, like the Spanish minor nobles known as *hidalgos* who commanded most of Spain's first missions, the attraction was partly adventure, partly the chance to command a military expedition of conquest, and partly the hope of making a fortune that seemed unlikely at home. For another fairly small group, the clergy, the aim was to bring the word of God to people who had never encountered Christianity before. And government officials and traders hoped they might advance more rapidly than in their native lands. For these middle and upper levels of society, however, survival was rarely an issue: They might die in battle or from illness, and life may not have been as comfortable as it would have been at home, but the opportunities to exercise power or to make a fortune were far greater. The outlook was very different for the vast majority of the new settlers.

Finding Ordinary Settlers   For most of them, leaving Europe was a fairly desperate act, an indication that almost any alternative seemed preferable to the bleak prospects in their homeland. If it had not been for the growth of population in the sixteenth century—and the many thousands it made homeless, unable to remain in their villages or make a living in towns—it is unlikely that enough emigrants would have been found to do the work in ports and on the land that was crucial to building empires in Asia and America. It is significant that fewer people moved from a rich country like France than from the less prosperous Spain and Portugal. Despite the pressures that persuaded thousands of

SLAVE SHIP
This picture, made aboard a slave ship, shows the dangerously crowded conditions in which Africans were brought to the New World. It is small wonder that so many died of disease even before the end of this miserable voyage.
National Maritime Museum, Greenwich, London

people to leave their homelands, therefore, additional means had to be found to populate the empires.

Long before the English colonized Australia with convicts in the eighteenth century, for example, they were taking people out of prison to send overseas to places desperate for settlers. Another tactic was to offer land to anyone who was willing to work for others for seven years. The English, and to a lesser extent the French, permitted religious minorities who feared persecution at home to start a new and more independent existence in America. In general, powerful inducements like poverty or persecution were needed to drive Europeans to accept the hazards of the journey and the subsequent struggles of the pioneer. Some, such as the religious refugees, set out as families, but usually many more men than women made the voyage. In pioneer communities all labor was essential and difficult, but there is no question that women, not only more vulnerable to violence but also regarded as subordinate to males, had far more to risk by emigrating; the chronic imbalance between sexes thus became yet another hardship of life overseas.

Exploitation of Settlers and Natives When even distress at home provided too few volunteers, the coloniz-

ers relied on force to obtain the workers they needed. Just as captains often kidnapped men for a ship's crew, so, too, did the suppliers of settlers. Many persons woke up at sea surprised to find where they were. And once in the colonies, wage earners could expect their employment to be harsh.

Indigenous populations, however, faced the most ruthless treatment: In Central and South America millions died (estimates vary between 25 and 90 percent of the native peoples, with the worst devastations in Mexico) as a result mainly of the new diseases the Europeans brought, though their susceptibility may have been heightened by the terrible forced labor to which they were subjected. Even exploitation, however, was not enough to feed the insatiable need for miners, laborers, servants, and farmhands.

The Commerce in Slaves The solution the colonizers found was slavery, familiar since ancient times but virtually nonexistent among Europeans by 1500. To find the slaves, ships began visiting the west coast of Africa, where the local inhabitants were either captured or purchased from local rulers and then transported to the New World under the most ghastly conditions. They were thrown together in cramped, filthy quarters, often bound, barely fed, and beaten at the slightest provocation. Nor was there much improvement for those—often fewer than half—who survived the crossing. The slaves sustained the empires and made it possible for their white masters to profit from the silver, tobacco, cotton, and other goods they produced; but the grim conditions of their lives, and their high rates of mortality, would have wiped them out if there had not been a constant stream of slaves from Africa to replenish their numbers.

Long-Term Effects   For those settlers who reaped rewards from the mines and the agricultural products of America, or from the trade with Europe that enriched all the colonies, the hardships did not last long. They created flourishing cities and universities and made huge fortunes. Their commercial networks began to link the entire world together for the first time in history. But for the many who struggled to expand these empires, life on the frontier, despite the promise of new opportunities, remained hard and dangerous for centuries. And for the slaves, there was not the slightest improvement in conditions or even hope of improvement, until revolts and civil wars finally abolished slavery in the nineteenth century. This was the context in which European institutions and culture came to dominate the rest of the world, though the encounter was by no means a one-way process.

One historian has described the interaction that followed Columbus as the Columbian Exchange, because ideas, people, microbes, plants, and animals flowed in both directions between the Old and New Worlds. Although the Spaniards saw themselves as converting natives from paganism to Catholicism, local cultures often tailored Western ideas to their own needs and managed to retain ancient practices and attitudes. In India, both the Portuguese and the English adopted customs and language from the local population, thus confirming what the Frenchman Michel de Montaigne had said as early as the 1580s, when he had compared the greed and violence of the Europeans unfavorably with the simplicity and harmonious lives of those whom they had conquered. For all that they learned, however, there is no question that the Europeans saw themselves mainly as teachers: their military and technological might entitled them, so they believed, to bring their "civilization" to the rest of the world.

THE CENTRALIZATION OF POLITICAL POWER

The economic and social transformations that began around 1500 gained important support from the actions of central governments. Especially in England, France, and Spain, rulers gave vital encouragement to the growth of trade, overseas expansion, and attempts to relieve social distress. At the same time, the growing prosperity of the age enhanced the tax revenues that were essential to their power. Both of these mutually reinforcing developments had long-term effects, but it could be argued that the creation of well-organized states, built around strong central governments, was even more decisive than the economic boom in shaping the future of Western Europe.

The rulers of England, France, and Spain in the late fifteenth and early sixteenth centuries were especially successful in accumulating and centralizing power, and historians have therefore called them "new monarchs." The reigns of Henry VII, Louis XI, and Ferdinand and Isabella, in particular, have come to be regarded as marking the end of more than a century of political fragmentation. They set in motion a revival of royal authority that eventually weakened all rivals to the crown and created the bureaucracies characteristic of the modern state.

Tudor England

The English monarchs had relied for centuries on local cooperation to run their kingdom. Unlike other European countries, England contained only fifty or sixty families who were legally nobles out of a population of perhaps 2.5 million. But many other families, though not technically members of the nobility, had large estates and were dominant figures at the parish, county, and even national levels. They were known as gentry, and it was from their ranks that the crown appointed the local officers who administered the realm—notably the justices of the peace (usually referred to as JPs). These voluntary unpaid officials served as the principal public servants in the more than forty counties of the land.

For reasons of status as well as a feeling of responsibility, the gentry had always sought such appointments. From the crown's point of view, the great advantage of the system was its efficiency: Enforcement was in the hands of those who could enforce. As a "great man" in his neighborhood, the JP rarely had trouble exerting his authority. Thus, the king had at his disposal an administrative structure without rival in Europe because, unlike other rulers, he could count on the cooperation of the leaders of each locality. Since the gentry had so much responsibility, they developed a strong sense of duty over the centuries, and the king increasingly sought their advice.

Parliament and Common Law   In the sixteenth century an institution that had developed from this relationship, the consultative assembly known as **Parliament,** began to take on a general importance as the chief representative of the country's wishes; it was increasingly considered the only body that could give a

HENRY VIII CLAIMS INDEPENDENCE FROM THE POPE

One of the crucial acts of Parliament through which Henry VIII made the Church of England independent of Rome was the so-called Act in Restraint of Appeals, which became law in 1533. This law forbade English subjects from appealing court decisions to Rome, which they had been allowed to do when the pope was accepted as the supreme authority. To justify this action, the preamble of the act made a claim for the independence of England and the authority of the king that was typical of the new monarchs of the age.

"Where by divers sundry old authentic histories and chronicles it is manifestly declared that this realm of England is an empire, governed by one supreme head and king, having the dignity and royal estate of the imperial crown of the same, unto whom a body politic be bound and owe next to God a natural and humble obedience; he being also furnished by the goodness of Almighty God with whole and entire power, preeminence, authority, prerogative and jurisdiction to render justice and final determination in all causes, debates and contentions, without restraint to any foreign princes, [and] without the intermeddling of any exterior person, to declare and determine all such doubts. In consideration whereof the King's Highness, his Nobles and Commons, enact, establish and ordain that all causes, already commenced or hereafter coming into contention within this realm or within any of the King's dominions, whether they concern the King our sovereign lord or any other subject, shall be from henceforth heard, examined, discussed, finally and definitely adjudged and determined within the King's jurisdiction and authority and not elsewhere."

From 24 Henry VIII, c. 12, as printed in *Statutes of the Realm,* Vol. 3, London, 1810–1828, pp. 427–429.

ruler's actions a broad stamp of approval. Although Parliament remained subordinate to the crown for a long time, England's kings already realized that without parliamentary consent they could not take measures such as raising extraordinary taxes.

Just as Parliament served to unify the country, so too did another ancient institution: the common law. This was a system of justice based on precedent and tradition that was the same, or "common," throughout England. In contrast to the Roman law that prevailed on the Continent, common law grew out of the interpretations of precedent made by individual judges and the decisions of juries. A court could be dominated by local leaders, but in general this was a system of justice, administered by judges who traveled from area to area, that helped bind England together. Like Parliament, the common law would eventually be regarded by opponents of royal power as an independent source of authority with which the crown could not interfere. In the late 1400s, however, it was an important help to a king who was trying to overcome England's political fragmentation and forge a more unified realm.

Henry VII and the Revival of Royal Power
Henry VII (1485–1509), who founded the Tudor Dynasty, came to the throne as a usurper in the aftermath of more than thirty years of civil conflict, the Wars of the Roses. England's nobles had caused chaos in these wars, and they had consistently ignored the wishes of the monarchy. The situation hardly looked promising for a reassertion of royal power. Yet Henry both extended the authority of the crown and restored order with extraordinary speed.

With a combination of fiscal caution and the determined collection of revenues, he put royal finances on a sound footing. At the same time, by relying on JPs and exerting his own authority in both political and legal matters, he began to tame England's nobles. He increased the authority of the royal Council, and had his councillors serve on a new, powerful court (known as Star Chamber from the decorations on the ceiling of the room where they met). Here there was no jury, local lords had no influence, and decisions were quick and fair. Eventually, Star Chamber and other royal courts came to be seen as threats to England's traditional common law. Under the Tudors, however, they were accepted as highly effective means of restoring order and asserting the power of the central government.

Henry's son and successor, Henry VIII (1509–1547), was an arrogant, dazzling figure, a strong contrast to his careful father. In 1513 he removed a long-standing threat from England's north by inflicting a shattering defeat on an invading Scots army at Flodden. With his prestige thus enhanced, he spent the next fifteen years consolidating royal power.

The Transformation of Parliament
The turning point in the reign came when Henry decided to break with the Roman Church (see chapter 13). The creation of an independent English Church had major political consequences, notably its strengthening of the institution of Parliament. The Reformation Parliament, summoned in 1529, remained in existence for seven years and acted on more matters of importance than a Parliament had ever considered before. The laws it passed gave it

Anonymous
EDWARD VI AND THE POPE
The anti-Catholic feelings that began to grow in England during the reign of Edward VI are expressed in this painting. The young king sits on his throne. His father, Henry VIII, who started the Reformation in England, points to him as the victor over Catholicism. The crushing of the old faith is symbolized by Christ's conquering of the pope and monks (below) and the destruction of Roman churches and images (through the window).
By courtesy of The National Portrait Gallery, London (NPG4165)

new responsibilities, and the length of its sessions also enhanced its stature.

Previously, election to Parliament had been considered a chore by the townsmen and landed gentry in the House of Commons, who found the expense of unpaid attendance and the time it took more irksome than did the wealthy nobles in the House of Lords. But this attitude changed in the 1530s as members of the Commons met again and again; they came to know one another and to regard themselves as guardians of Parliament's traditions and privileges. Eventually, they were to make the Commons the dominant house in Parliament.

Royal Power   After guiding Henry through the break with Rome, Thomas Cromwell became the king's chief minister. He was a tireless bureaucrat who reorganized the administration of the country and used the newly created Privy Council, consisting of the king's principal advisers, to coordinate and direct royal government. The principal beneficiary of these events was the crown. Royal income rose markedly with the appropriation of Church fees and possessions, many of which were sold, making fortunes for speculators and new families of landowners. For all the stimulus he gave to parliamentary power and the landed class, Henry now had a much larger, wealthier, and more sophisticated administration at his disposal; and no one doubted where ultimate authority lay. He did not establish a standing army, as some of the continental kings did, because he could crush all opposition without it. And this strong central administration even survived the eleven years of uncertainty that followed Henry's death in 1547.

Edward VI and Mary I   During the reign of Edward VI (1547–1553), who died while still a minor, the nobility attempted to regain control of the government. There was a relaxation of central authority, and the Reformation advanced rapidly. But even when Edward's half-sister, Mary I (1553–1558), briefly reestablished Roman Catholicism, forced many of her subjects into exile, and provoked two major revolts, royal power was strong enough to survive. The next monarch, Henry VIII's last surviving child, Elizabeth, demonstrated that the growth of the monarchy's authority had hardly been interrupted under Edward and Mary.

Valois France

The rulers of France in the fifteenth century, members of the Valois family, were unlike the English kings in that they lacked a well-formed organization for local government. Aristocrats dominated many regions, particularly those farthest from Paris, and great nobles had become virtually independent rulers. With their own administrations and often their own courts and taxation, they left the crown little say in their affairs. The size of the kingdom also limited royal power; it took more than a week to travel from Paris to the remoter parts of the realm—almost double the time for the equivalent English journey. The monarchy had tried to resolve the problem of ruling distant provinces by granting to close relatives large blocs of territory that the crown seized or inherited. Theoretically, these relatives would execute royal wishes more effectively than the king could from Paris. In practice, however, an ambitious family member often became just as difficult to handle as any powerful noble. After 1469 the crown kept control over such acquisitions—an indication that it now had the resources to exercise authority even in areas far from the capital.

Royal Administration   The administrative center of the government was the royal council in Paris. The greatest court of law in the land was the Parlement of Paris, which had remained a judicial body, unlike the English Parliament, and whose members were appointed by the crown. As the central administration grew in the fifteenth and early sixteenth centuries, various provinces received their own **parlements,** a recognition of the continuing strength of the demand for local autonomy. But there was a countervailing force: the dominance of Roman law, which (unlike England's common law) was based on royal decree and which allowed the monarch to govern by issuing ordinances and edicts. These had to be registered by the parlements in order to take effect, but usually that was a formality.

Estates and Finance   Representative assemblies, known as **Estates,** also limited the power of the throne. A number of provinces had such Estates, and they had to approve the level of taxation and other royal policies. Negotiations with these bodies were essential for the support of the king's income and his army. But France's chief representative body, the Estates General—consisting of clergy, nobles, and townsmen from every region—never attained the prestige of the English Parliament and was never able to bind the country together or function as a vital organ of government. The French kings thus had a degree of independence that English monarchs did not achieve, particularly in the area of finance. For centuries they had supplemented their main sources of income, from lands and customs duties, with a sales tax (*aide*), a hearth tax (*taille*), and a salt tax (*gabelle*). In earlier days the consent of the localities had been required for such levies, but after 1451 the taxes could be collected on the king's authority alone, though he still had to negotiate the exact rate with provincial Estates and be careful not to go beyond what would seem reasonable to his subjects.

The Standing Army   The most decisive source of power available to the French king (unlike the English king) was his standing army. The upkeep of the troops accounted for more than half the royal expenditures in Louis XI's reign, mainly because their numbers grew as revenues increased. In the 1480s a force of at least fifteen thousand men, chiefly professional mercenaries and military-minded nobles, was kept in readiness every campaigning season from spring to fall. Because of the rising costs associated with the development of gunpowder weapons, only the central government could afford to maintain such an army. And the troops had to be billeted in various provinces, with support from the local Estates. As a result, the entire French population eventually bore the indirect burden of heavier taxation, while many regions of France had direct contact with royal soldiers. Although frequently short of pay, the troops were firmly under royal control and hence a vital device—rarely used, but always a threat—in the strengthening of royal authority.

Louis XI   When Louis XI (1461–1483) began his reign, he faced a situation as unpromising as that of Henry VII at his succession, for the country had just emerged from the Hundred Years' War and royal authority was generally ignored. English troops, which had been in France for most of the war, had finally departed in the 1450s; but a new and equally dangerous menace had arisen in the east: the dukedom of Burgundy.

Extending Control   By the 1460s the duke of Burgundy was among the most powerful lords in Western Europe. He ruled a loosely organized dominion that stretched from the Low Countries to the Swiss Confederation, and his capital, Dijon, had become a major cultural and political center. In 1474 Louis XI put together a coalition against Charles the Bold, Duke of Burgundy, who had been at war with him for some seven years, and in 1477 Charles was killed in battle. Louis then annexed the duchy of Burgundy itself, though Mary, the duke's daughter, retained the Low Countries, which would later form part of the inheritance of her grandson, the Holy Roman Emperor Charles V.

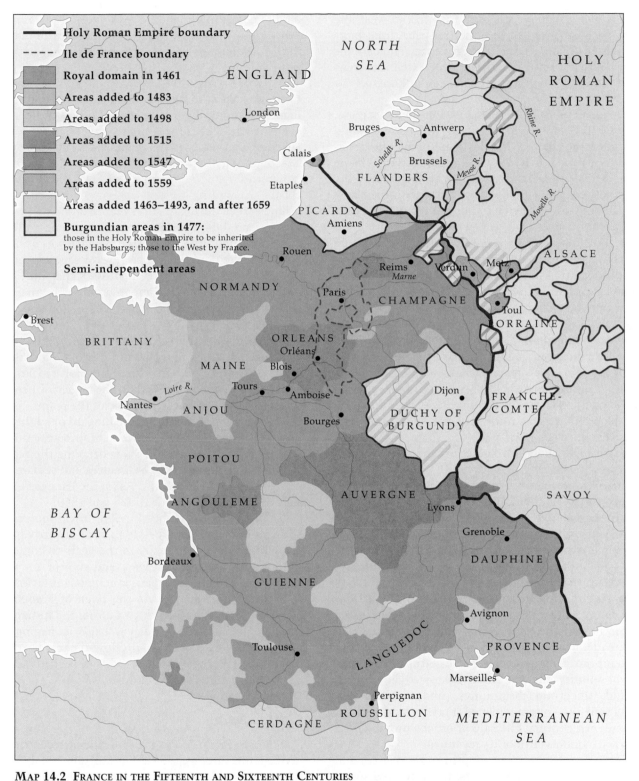

MAP 14.2 FRANCE IN THE FIFTEENTH AND SIXTEENTH CENTURIES
This map shows in detail the successive stages whereby the monarchy extended its control throughout France.
Note the territory that the king controlled directly in 1461. What were the largest new areas added after 1461?
Which Burgundian areas did France acquire?

◆ For an online version, go to www.mhhe.com/chambers9 > chapter 14 > book maps

Louis also expanded his authority to the west and south, because in 1481 he inherited the three large provinces of Anjou, Maine, and Provence. Thus, by the end of his reign, royal power had penetrated into massive areas where previously it had been unknown.

The Invasion of Italy Louis XI's son and successor, Charles VIII (1483–1498), was only thirteen years old when his father died. When he came of age, he determined to expand his dynasty's territory, and in 1494 he led an army into Italy. After some successes, the French settled into a prolonged struggle with the Habsburgs for control of the rich Italian peninsula. The conflicts lasted for sixty-five years, ending in defeat for the French. Although the Italian wars failed to satisfy the monarchy's territorial ambitions, they provided an outlet and distraction for the restless French nobility and gave the kings, as commanders in time of war, an opportunity to consolidate royal power at home.

Increasing Revenues After Charles VIII's reign, France's financial and administrative machinery grew in both size and effectiveness, largely because of the demands of the Italian wars. There was rarely enough money to support the adventure; the kings, therefore, relied heavily on loans from bankers, who sometimes shaped France's financial policies. At the same time, the crown made a determined effort to increase traditional royal revenues.

France was a rich country of 15 million people with the most fertile land in Europe; yet the financial needs of the monarch always outstripped his subjects' ability to pay. With exemptions from the *taille* and the *gabelle* for nobles, many towns, royal officeholders, and the clergy, the bulk of the taxes had to be raised from the very classes that had the least to give. Other means of raising revenue were therefore needed, and one solution was the sale of offices. Positions were sold in the administration, the parlements, and every branch of the bureaucracy to purchasers eager to obtain both the tax exemption and the considerable status (sometimes a title of nobility) that the offices bestowed. From modest and uncertain beginnings under Louis XII (1498–1515), the system widened steadily; by the end of the sixteenth century, the sale of offices provided the crown with one-twelfth of its revenues.

Many other rulers were adopting this device, and everywhere it had similar effects: It stimulated social mobility, creating dynasties of noble officeholders and a new administrative class; it caused a dramatic expansion of bureaucracies; and it encouraged corruption. The system spread most rapidly and the effects were most noticeable in France, where the reign of Francis I (1515–1547) witnessed a major increase in the government's power as its servants multiplied. Francis tried hard to continue expanding royal control by launching expeditions into Italy, but in fact, he contributed more to the development of the crown's authority by his actions at home.

Control of the Church One of the most remarkable of Francis' accomplishments was the power he gained over the Church. He was highly successful in his Italian campaigns early in his reign, and he used the power he won in Italy to persuade the pope in 1516 to give the crown the right to appoint all of France's bishops and abbots. According to this agreement, the income a bishop earned during his first year in office still went to the Vatican, but, in effect, Francis now controlled the French Church. Its enormous patronage was at his disposal, and he could use it to reward servants or raise money. By making an agreement with the pope, he did not need to break with Rome in order to obtain authority over the clergy, as did Henry VIII in England.

The Advance of Centralization In the 1520s Francis also began a major reorganization of the government. He legalized the sale of offices and formed an inner council, more manageable than the large royal council, to act as the chief executive body of the realm. Against the parlements, meanwhile, the king invoked the *lit de justice*, a prerogative that allowed him to appear in person before an assembly that was delaying the registration of any of his edicts or ordinances and declare them registered and therefore law. As for the Estates General, they did not meet between 1484 and 1560.

By the end of Francis' reign, royal power was stronger than ever before; but signs of disunity had appeared that would intensify in the years to come. The Reformation was under way, and one of its movements, Calvinism, soon caused religious divisions and social unrest in France. As the reign of Francis' son Henry II (1547–1559) came to a close, the Italian wars finally ended in a French defeat, badly damaging royal prestige. The civil wars that followed came perilously close to destroying all that France's kings had achieved during the previous one hundred years.

United Spain

The Iberian Peninsula in the mid-fifteenth century was divided into three very different kingdoms. Portugal on the west, with some 1.5 million inhabitants, looked overseas. Castile, in the center, with a population of more than 8 million, was the largest and richest area. Sheep farming was the basis of its prosperity, and its countryside was dominated by powerful nobles. Castile was the last kingdom still fighting Muslims on its southern frontier, and in this ceaseless crusade the nobles played a leading part. They had built up both a

union, precipitating a ten-year civil war. But the two monarchs emerged victorious, and they created a new political entity: the Kingdom of Spain. They and their successors were to be as effective as the kings of England and France in centralizing power and establishing royal control over their realms.

Ferdinand and Isabella   When Ferdinand and Isabella jointly assumed the thrones of Castile in 1474 and Aragon five years later, they made no attempt to create a monolithic state. Aragon remained a federation of territories, administered by viceroys who were appointed by the king but who allowed local customs to remain virtually intact. The traditions of governing by consent and preserving the subjects' rights were particularly strong in this kingdom, where each province had its own representative assembly, known as the **Cortes.** In Castile, however, the two monarchs were determined to assert their superiority over all possible rivals to their authority. Their immediate aims were to restore the order in the countryside that had been destroyed by civil war, much as it had been in England and France, and to reduce the power of the nobility.

The first objective was accomplished with the help of the Cortes of Castile, an assembly dominated by urban representatives who shared the wish for order because peace benefited trade. The Cortes established special tribunals to pursue and try criminals, and by the 1490s it had succeeded in ending the widespread lawlessness in the kingdom.

The Centralization of Power   To reinforce their authority, Ferdinand and Isabella sharply reduced the number of great nobles in the royal council and overhauled the entire administration, particularly the financial agencies, applying the principle that ability, rather than social status, should determine appointments. As the bureaucracy spread, the *hidalgo*, a lesser aristocrat who depended heavily on royal favor, became increasingly important in government. Unlike the great nobles, whose enormous wealth was little affected by reforms that reduced their political role, the hidalgos were hurt when they lost their tax exemptions. The new livelihood they found was in serving the crown, and they became essential figures in the centralization of power in Castile as well as in the overseas territories.

The monarchs achieved greater leverage over their nobles in the 1480s and 1490s, when they gained control of the aristocracy's rich and powerful military orders. These wealthy organizations, run by Castile's most important aristocratic families, gave allegiance primarily to their own elected leaders. To take over their leadership required assertiveness and determination, especially by Isabella, Castile's ruler. At one point

Anonymous
FRANCIS I AND HIS COURT
The splendor and the patronage of learning for which the new monarchs were known are evoked by this tiny painting of the French king. He sits at a table with his three sons, surrounded by his courtiers and listening to the author reading the very manuscript (a translation of an ancient Greek historian) that this picture illustrates.
From Les Trois Premiers Livres de Diodore de Sicile, translated by A. Macault, 1534. Parchment, Ms. 721, f. lv, frontispiece. Musée Condé, Chantilly, France. Réunion des Musées Nationaux/ Art Resource, NY

great chivalric tradition and considerable political strength as a result of their exploits, and their status was enhanced by the religious fervor that the long struggle had inspired. To the east, Aragon, slightly larger than Portugal, consisted of three areas: Catalonia, the heart of the kingdom and a great commercial region centered on the city of Barcelona; Aragon itself, which was little more than a barren hinterland to Catalonia; and Valencia, a farming and fishing region south of Catalonia along the Mediterranean coast.

In October 1469, Isabella, future queen of Castile, married Ferdinand, future king of Sicily and heir to the throne of Aragon. Realizing that the marriage would strengthen the crown, the Castilian nobles opposed the

414 Chapter Fourteen Economic Expansion and a New Politics

she rode on horseback for three straight days in order to get to one of the order's elections and control the outcome. The great nobles could not be subdued completely; nor did the monarchs seek to destroy their power, for they were essential servants of the crown in the army and the higher levels of government. But like the kings of England and France, Ferdinand and Isabella wanted to reduce the nobles' autonomy to a level that did not threaten central authority, and it was thus crucial that they overcame the independence of the military orders by 1500.

Independence of the Church   They also succeeded in weakening Spain's bishops and abbots, who were as strong and wealthy as leading nobles. When Ferdinand and Isabella finally destroyed the power of the Muslims in southern Castile in 1492, the pope granted the monarchy the right to make major ecclesiastical appointments in the newly won territory, and this right was extended to the **New World** shortly thereafter. During the reign of Ferdinand and Isabella's successor, Charles I, the monarchy gained complete control over Church appointments, making Spain more independent of Rome than any other Catholic state.

Royal Administration   Mastery over the towns and the Cortes of Castile proved easy to achieve. Where local rule was concerned, a minor royal official, the *corregidor*, was given new powers and a position of responsibility within the administrative hierarchy. He was usually a hidalgo, and he became the chief executive and judicial officer in his region, rather like the justice of the peace in England; he also supervised town affairs. The Cortes did not seriously restrict the crown, because Spanish taxes, like French, could be raised without consent. The Castilian assembly met frequently and even provided additional funds for foreign wars, but it never challenged royal supremacy during this reign.

The justice system the monarchs supervised directly, hearing cases personally once a week. As in most Roman law systems, all law was considered to come from the throne, and the monarchs had full power to overrule the decisions of local courts, often run by nobles. Centralized judicial machinery began to appear, and in a few decades Castilian law was organized into a uniform code—always a landmark in the stabilization of a state. The code remained in effect for centuries and was a tribute to the determination and effectiveness with which the crown had centralized its dominions.

The Increase in Revenues   Considering the anarchy at the start of their reign and the absence of central institutions, Ferdinand and Isabella performed greater wonders in establishing royal power than any of the other new monarchs. Thanks to their takeover of the military orders and their growing bureaucracy, their finances soon improved. After the main administrative reforms were completed in the 1490s, the yield of the sales tax (the *alcabala*), the mainstay of royal income, rose dramatically. Total annual revenue is estimated to have soared from 80,000 ducats in 1474 to 2.3 million by 1504, the year Isabella died.

Religious Zeal   Religious affairs, too, helped the consolidation of royal authority. After the civil wars in Castile ended in 1479, the two monarchs sought to drive the Muslims from southern Castile. The reasons for the aggressive policy were clear: First, it complemented the drive for centralized power; second, war was a traditional interest for ambitious rulers, and it helped keep restless nobles occupied; and finally, the crusade stimulated the country's religious fervor, which in turn promoted enthusiasm for its rulers.

The religious zeal aroused by the fight with the Muslims intensified Spaniards' loyalty toward their rulers, and it is not surprising that the monarchy sought religious uniformity as a means of strengthening political uniformity. Nor did the campaign come to an end when the last Muslim stronghold in the south, Granada, capitulated in 1492. Later that year, all Jews were expelled from Spain. Some 150,000 of the country's most enterprising people—including prominent physicians, government officials, and other leaders of economic and cultural life—were given four months to leave. Targeting a visible and often persecuted minority was a popular move, and it also fed a religious passion that indirectly enhanced the crown's authority.

The Inquisition   The same drive to consolidate their strength prompted Ferdinand and Isabella to obtain permission from the pope in 1478 to establish their own Inquisition. Beginning in 1483 this body was run by a royal council and given a mandate to root out those *Conversos* and *Moriscos*—converted Jews and former Muslims—who were suspected of practicing their old beliefs in secret. After the fall of Granada, the Church tried to convert the conquered Muslims, and in 1502 those who had not accepted Christianity were expelled from the country. Eventually, in 1609, the Moriscos too were exiled from Spain. The persecution helped foster a religious unity that only enhanced the political centralization that the monarchy had achieved.

Military and Diplomatic Achievements   Ferdinand focused heavily on foreign affairs during the twelve years he ruled on his own after Isabella's death in 1504. He regained two provinces on the French border, and then, worried by France's Italian invasion, Ferdinand entered the war in Italy.

His achievements in the next two decades were due to a combination of military and diplomatic skills unusual even among the highly capable rulers of the age. A reorganization of Spain's standing army made it the most effective in Europe, and it soon dominated Italy. Ferdinand also founded the finest diplomatic service of the sixteenth century, centered on five permanent embassies: at Rome, Venice, London, Brussels, and the Habsburg court. The ambassadors' reports and activities made him the best-informed and most effective maneuverer in the international politics of his reign. By the time of his death in 1516, the united Spain that he and Isabella created had gained both territory and authority at home and international power abroad.

Charles V, Holy Roman Emperor

To bolster their dynasty, Ferdinand and Isabella had married their children to members of the leading families of Europe. Their daughter Joanna became the wife of the Habsburg Archduke Philip of Austria, and her son Charles became heir to the royal throne of Spain as well as the Habsburg dukedom.

The Revolt of the Communes   Early in his reign as King of Spain, however, Charles (1516–1556) had to withstand a major onslaught on the crown's position. Educated in Flanders, he spoke no Castilian, and when he arrived in Spain late in 1517, he soon aroused the resentment of the local nobility, particularly when members of the large Flemish entourage he brought with him were given positions in the government. The young king stayed for two and a half years, during which time he was elected emperor of the Holy Roman Empire (1519). This enhanced his prestige, but it also intensified his subjects' fears that he would become an absentee ruler with little interest in their affairs. As he left for Germany in 1520, revolts began to break out in Spain's towns, and the risings of these communes racked the country for two years. The troubles Charles now endured were among the first of many major clashes during the next 150 years between the traditional dynastic aims of the leading European monarchs and the jealous sense of distinctiveness felt by their subjects.

Fortunately for the crown, the communes lacked clear aims; their resentments and hopes were deep but vague. They wanted to reverse the growth of royal power and restore their traditional autonomy—a grievance central governments were bound to encounter as they extended their authority. At first they had the strong sympathy of the Spanish nobles, who particularly disliked the foreign ruler. But the movement soon revealed other aims, with social overtones: The communes launched attacks on the privileged orders of society, especially the nobility, and this lost the revolt its only chance for success. For the nobles then turned against the communes and defeated them in battle even before Charles returned to Spain.

Imperial Ambitions   The king took warning from the uprisings and made sure that his administration was now kept entirely Spanish. As calm returned, his subjects could channel their energies into imperial missions overseas, where the conquest of Mexico was under way, and against the Ottoman Turks in the Mediterranean. The large empire the Spaniards established in Central and South America was the most notable extension of royal power during Charles's reign. Closer to home, however, there was little that pleased his Spanish subjects. As Holy Roman Emperor, Charles was the official ruler of almost all of continental Europe west of Poland and the Balkans, with the major exception of France; and although his real power in the Empire was limited, he was almost ceaselessly at war defending his territories. In the Spaniards' view, most of the wars helped Charles's ambitions as emperor and were thus irrelevant to Spain. As far as they were concerned, aside from the widening acquisitions in the New World, Charles did little to further the expansion started by Ferdinand and Isabella.

Royal Government   The recurrent crises and wars kept Charles away from Spain for more than two-thirds of his forty-year reign. In his absence, his representatives confirmed the supremacy of the crown by enlarging the bureaucracy and elaborating a system of councils that Ferdinand and Isabella had begun. In the 1520s this structure, which was to survive for centuries, received its final form. There were two types of council, one for each department of government—finance, war, the Inquisition, and so on—the other for each territory the crown ruled: Aragon, Castile, Italy, the Indies, and (later in the century) the Low Countries. At the head of this system was the Council of State, the principal advisory group, consisting of leading officials from the lower councils. All councils reported to the king or to his chief ministers, but since they all controlled their own bureaucracies, they were perfectly capable of running the empire in the monarch's absence.

What emerged was a vast federation, with Castile at its heart but with the parts, though directed from the center, allowed considerable autonomy. A viceroy in every major area (there were nine altogether, from Naples to Peru) ran the administration under the supervision of an *audiencia*, a territorial council, and while on the whole these officials were left to do as they wished, they had to report to Castile in minute detail at regular intervals and refer major decisions to the central government.

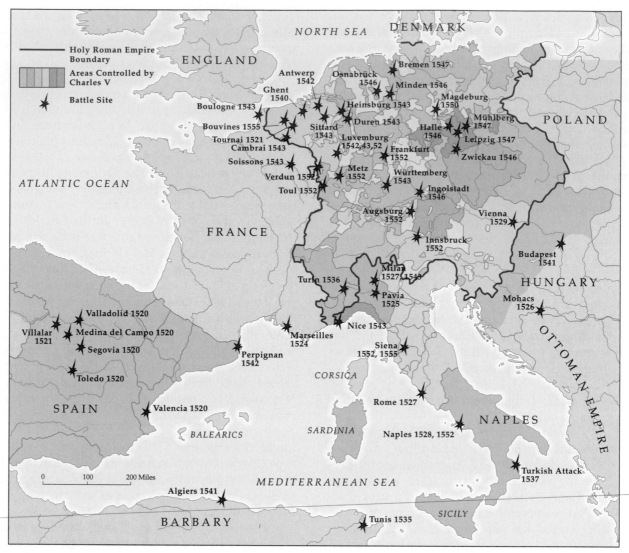

MAP 14.3 THE EMPIRE OF CHARLES V
This map indicates both the vastness of Charles's empire and the extent of the fighting in which he became involved. Almost every battle his troops fought—against Spanish communes, German Protestants, the Turks, and the French—is included here to show the full measure of the emperor's never-ending ordeal. When he abdicated in 1556, Charles decided to divide his realm between his brother and his son. What characteristics of his empire seem to have shaped his decision to divide his territories?
◆ For an online version, go to www.mhhe.com/chambers9 > chapter 14 > book maps

Control through the Bureaucracy Although corruption was widespread and communications slow (it took over eight months to send a message from Castile to Peru), the centralization gave the monarch considerable power. Spain's administrative machine was one of the most remarkably detailed (if not always efficient) structures ever devised for ruling so vast an empire.

The Financial Toll of War The only serious strain on Charles's monarchy was financial, the result of the Habsburgs' constant wars. Much of the money for the

fighting came from Italy and the Low Countries, but Spain had to pay a growing share of the costs, and Spaniards increasingly resented the siphoning away of their funds into foreign wars. It was the tragedy of their century of glory that so much of the wealth they discovered in South America was exported for hostilities that brought them little benefit.

The burden was by no means equally distributed. The more independent Cortes of Aragon was able to prevent substantial increases in taxation, which meant that Castile had to assume the brunt of the payments.

Pieter Brueghel the Elder
CENSUS AT BETHLEHEM
Although ostensibly a religious scene, the *Census at Bethlehem* gives us a glimpse of the growing intrusion into daily life of expanding governments. In their hardest season, winter, the people of this Flemish village have to line up in front of the bureaucrat at the table, who takes his fee even as he records the names of the villagers.
Art Resource, NY

To some extent this was balanced by a monopoly of trade with the New World that was granted to the inhabitants of Castile, but in the next century the basic inequality among different Spanish regions would lead to civil war.

New World Trade Charles's finances were saved from disaster only by the influx of treasure—mainly silver—from America. Approximately 40 percent of the bullion went into the royal coffers, while the rest was taken by merchants (mainly Genoese) in the Castilian port of Seville, which was the only city where ships carrying goods to and from America were permitted to load and unload. Charles was receiving some 800,000 ducats' worth of treasure each year by the end of his reign. Unfortunately, it was always mortgaged in ad-

vance to the Italian and German bankers whose loans sustained his armies.

The difficulties mounted as the wars continued for over a century and a half. Seville's monopoly on shipping prevented the rest of the nation from gaining a share of the new wealth, and foreigners—notably Italian and German financiers—came to dominate its economy and its commerce. Spain was squeezed dry by the king's financial demands, yet he only just kept his head above water. In 1557, early in the reign of Charles's successor, Philip II, the monarchy had to declare itself bankrupt, a self-defeating evasion of its mammoth debts that it had to repeat seven times in the next 125 years. There has never been a better example of the way that ceaseless war can sap the strength of even the most formidable nation.

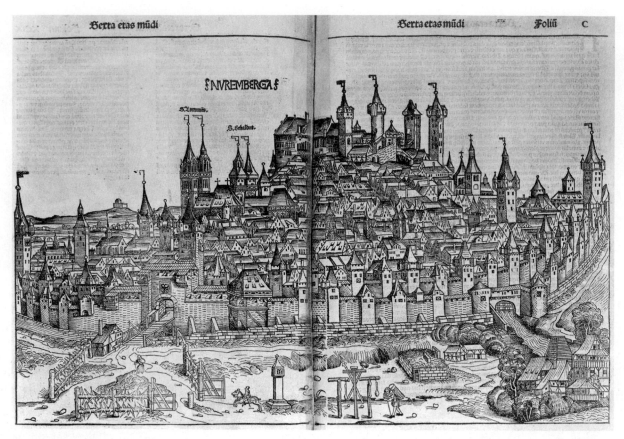

Hartmann Schedel
THE NUREMBERG CHRONICLE, 1493
This lavishly illustrated book, a history of the world since the creation, is one of the earliest masterpieces of the printer's art. It took about four years to produce and contains dozens of elaborate woodcuts, most of which are recognizable views of European cities. This one depicts the proud and independent German city in which the book was printed, Nuremberg, a major center of art and craft work.
Rare Books and Manuscripts Division, New York Public Library, Astor, Lenox, and Tilden Foundations

THE SPLINTERED STATES

Whereas in England, France, and Spain the authority of kings had begun to replace that of the local lord, to the east of these three kingdoms such centralization advanced fitfully and only within small states.

The Holy Roman Empire   In the largest of these territories, the Holy Roman Empire, weak institutions prevented the emergence of a strong central government. Members of the leading family of Central Europe, the Habsburgs, had been elected to the imperial throne since the thirteenth century, but they lacked the authority and machinery to halt the fragmentation of this large territory; indeed, except for their own personal domain in the southeast of the empire, they ruled most areas and princes in name only. In addition to about two thousand imperial knights, some of whom owned no more than four or five acres, there were fifty ecclesiastical and thirty secular princes, more than one hundred counts, some seventy prelates, and sixty-six cities—all virtually independent politically, though officially subordinate to the emperor.

Local Independence   The princes, whose territories comprised most of the area of the Holy Roman Empire, rarely had any trouble resisting the emperor's claims; their main concern was to increase their own power at the expense of their subjects, other princes, and the cities. The cities themselves also refused to remain subordinate to a central government. In 1500, fifty of them contained more than two thousand inhabitants—a sizable number for this time—and twenty had over ten thousand. Their wealth was substantial because many were situated along a densely traveled trade artery, the Rhine River, and many were also political powers. But their fierce independence meant that the emperor could rarely tap their wealth or the services of

Titian
EMPEROR CHARLES V AT THE BATTLE OF MÜHLBERG, **1547**
Because a statue of an ancient Roman emperor showed him in this pose, it was thought in the sixteenth century that a ruler appeared at his most magnificent on a horse and in full armor. Remarkable equestrian sculptures appeared in the fifteenth century, but this is the most famous such painting.
Museo del Prado, Madrid, Spain. Erich Lessing/Art Resource, NY

among local powers. Controlled and financed by the princes, the chief beneficiaries of its work, it made considerable headway toward ending the lawlessness that had marked the fifteenth century—an achievement similar to the restoration of order in France, Spain, and England at the same time. The tribunal's use of Roman law had a wide influence on legislation and justice throughout the empire, but again only to the advantage of the princes, who interpreted its endorsement of a leader's authority as referring only to themselves.

Other attempts at administrative reform had little effect, as ecclesiastical and secular princes tightened their hold on the many individual territories within the empire. The religious dissensions of the Reformation worsened the rivalries, dividing the princes and making Charles V no more than the leader of one party, incapable of asserting his authority over his opponents. The sheer number of Charles's commitments repeatedly diverted him, but even when he won decisive military victories, he could not break the long tradition of local independence. His dream had been to revive the imperial grandeur of an Augustus or a Charlemagne, and his failure brought to an end the thousand-year ambition to restore in Europe the power of ancient Rome.

Power and Decline in Hungary   In the late fifteenth century, the dominant force in Eastern and Central Europe was the Kingdom of Hungary, ruled by Matthias Corvinus (1458–1490). He was in the mold of the other new monarchs of the day: He restrained the great nobles, expanded and centralized his administration, dramatically increased the yield of taxation, and established a standing army. The king's power grew spectacularly both at home and abroad: He gained Bohemia and German and Austrian lands, and he made Vienna his capital in 1485.

Immediately after Matthias' death, however, royal authority collapsed. To gain Habsburg recognition of his right to the throne, his successor, Ladislas II (1490–1516), gave up the conquests of Austrian and German lands and married his children to Habsburgs. This retreat provided the nobles of Hungary with the excuse to reassert their position. They refused the king essential financial support and forced him to dissolve the standing army. Then, after a major peasant revolt against increasing repression by landowners, the nobles imposed serfdom on all peasants in 1514 at a meeting of the Hungarian Diet, which they controlled. Finally, they became the major beneficiaries of the conquest of Hungary by the Ottoman Empire over the next thirty years. That empire always supported leaders who promised allegiance to Constantinople; declaring loyalty to their new masters, the nobles were able to strengthen their power at the expense of both the

their inhabitants. The only central institution alongside the emperor was the Diet, which consisted of three assemblies: representatives of the cities, the princes, and the seven electors who elected each new emperor. Given this makeup, the Diet became in effect the instrument of the princes; with its legislation, they secured their position against the cities and the lesser nobility within their domains.

By the late fifteenth century, most princes had gained considerable control over their own territories. Their success paralleled the achievements of monarchs in England, France, and Spain except that the units were much smaller. Although the Habsburgs tried to develop strong central authority, they exercised significant control only over their personal domain, which in 1500 consisted of Austria, the Low Countries, and Franche-Comtè.

Attempts at Centralization   Nevertheless, the need for effective central institutions was recognized. In 1495 the emperor created a tribunal to settle disputes

Christoph Paudiss
PEASANTS IN A HUT
**The sadness in the eyes of these two figures, even in a
relaxed moment—the old man smoking a pipe, the boy
playing the bagpipes—reflects the hardships of the peasants
who were at the lowest level of European society and in
Eastern Europe were bound to the land as serfs.**
Kunsthistorisches Museum, Vienna

old monarchy and the peasantry. By the mid-sixteenth
century, a revival of central authority had become impossible.

The Fragmentation of Poland   Royal power in Poland
began to decline in the 1490s, when the king was
forced to rely on the lesser nobles to help him against
the greater nobility. In return, he issued a statute in
1496 that strengthened the lower aristocrats against
those below them, the townsmen and the peasants.
The latter became virtual serfs, forbidden to buy land
and deprived of freedom of movement. Once that was
accomplished, the nobles united against the king. In
1505 the national Diet, consisting only of nobles, was
made the supreme body of the land, and shortly thereafter it established serfdom officially. Since no law
could now be passed without the Diet's consent, the
crown's central authority was severely limited.

Royal and noble patronage produced a great cultural
flowering around 1500 in Poland, which became an active center of Renaissance humanism and scholarship,
most famously represented by the astronomer Nicolaus
Copernicus. Yet the monarchy was losing influence
steadily, as was apparent from the failure of its attempts to found a standing army. At the end of Sigis-
mund II's reign (1548–1572), his kingdom was the
largest in Europe; but his death ended the Jagellon
Dynasty, which had ruled for centuries. The Diet then
made sure that succession to the crown, which had always been elective and controlled by nobles, would depend entirely on their approval—thus confirming the
aristocracy's dominance and the ineffectiveness of
royal authority.

Aristocracies   The political and social processes at
work in Eastern and Central Europe thus contrasted
starkly with developments in England, France, and
Spain in this period. Nevertheless, although the trend
was toward fragmentation in the East, one class, the
aristocracy, did share the vigor and organizational ability that in the West was displayed by kings and queens.
To that extent, therefore, the sense of renewed vitality
in Europe during these years, spurred by economic and
demographic growth, was also visible outside the borders of the new monarchies. But where nobles dominated, countries lost ground in the fierce competition
of international affairs.

The Ottoman Empire   Only in one state in Eastern
Europe was strong central authority maintained in the
sixteenth century: the Ottoman Empire. From his capital in Constantinople, the sultan exercised unparal-
leled powers throughout the eastern Mediterranean
and North Africa, and the Ottomans prevented any serious challenges to their empire until they began to
lose ground to the Habsburgs in the eighteenth century.

The first signs of weakening at the center began to
appear after the death in 1566 of the sultan whose conquests brought the empire to its largest size, Suleiman
II. Suleiman had gained control of the Balkans with a
victory at Mohacs in 1526, and he had even briefly laid
siege to Vienna in 1529 (see "Suleiman the Magnificent
Invades Europe," pp. 422–424). Under his successors,
the determined exercise of authority that had marked
his rule began to decline; harem intrigues, corruption
at court, and the loosening of military discipline became increasingly serious. Yet the Ottomans remained
an object of fear and hostility throughout the West—
a constant threat to Central Europe from the Balkans
and, despite naval setbacks, a formidable force in the
eastern Mediterranean.

Republics in Italy   Italy, the cultural and economic
leader of Europe, had developed a unique political struc-

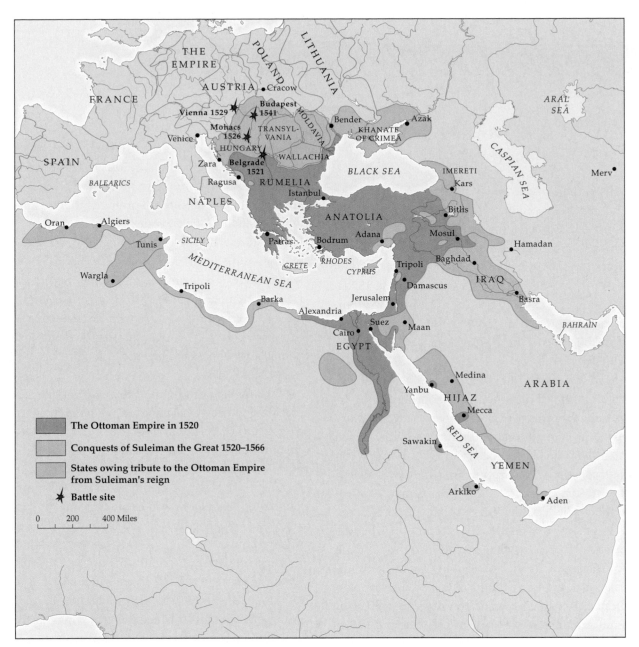

MAP 14.4 THE GROWTH OF THE OTTOMAN EMPIRE UNDER SULEIMAN THE GREAT, 1520–1566
The Ottoman Empire had expanded greatly during the fifteenth and sixteenth centuries (see map 11.7, p. 333). Note the area of Ottoman control in 1520. What were the key areas the Ottomans conquered under Suleiman the Great? Why would rulers of Central and Eastern Europe be alarmed at these advances? What key battle halted the Ottoman advance into Europe?
◆ For an online version, go to www.mhhe.com/chambers9 > chapter 14 > book maps

ture during the Renaissance. In the fifteenth century the five major states—Naples, the Papal States, Milan, Florence, and Venice—established a balance among themselves that was preserved without serious disruption from the 1450s to the 1490s. This long period of peace was broken in 1494, when Milan, abandoning a long tradition of the Italians settling problems among themselves, asked Charles VIII of France to help protect it against Florence and Naples. Thus began the Italian

wars, which soon revealed that these relatively small territories were totally incapable of resisting the force that newly assertive monarchies could bring to bear.

Venice and Florence had long been regarded by Europeans as model republics—reincarnations of Classical city-states and centers of freedom governed with the consent of their citizens. In truth, Venice was controlled by a small oligarchy and Florence by the Medici family, but the image of republican virtue was still

SULEIMAN THE MAGNIFICENT INVADES EUROPE

In the age of the Crusades and the Christian reconquest of Spain, Europeans seemed to be on the march against their Muslim neighbors. But there was widespread fear that the tables might be turned after Constantinople, the capital of the Byzantine Empire, fell to the Ottoman Turks in 1453. A crucial decade was the 1520s, when it looked as though the Ottoman Sultan, Suleiman II (known to his people as "The Lawgiver" but to the West as "The Magnificent") might sweep through Europe.

Ambitious, and the ruler of a rich and powerful empire that surrounded the eastern and southern Mediterranean, Suleiman was determined to earn eternal glory both for himself and for his faith at the expense of the Christians who ruled the lands to his west. He drew on Islamic traditions of governmental authority, particularly the notion that the Sultan was the successor of Muhammad, the legitimate ruler of all true believers. Like every member of the Islamic community, he was subject to the sacred law. But he was also the supreme judge of that law. Also influenced by Byzantine traditions that gave total control of society to the emperor, the Sultan united in his own person supreme civil, military, and religious power, and used elaborate Court ceremonies (as in Byzantium) to emphasize the aura of sanctity that surrounded him.

The chief source of his power was a superbly trained army, divided into two major sections: unpaid holders of lands that were granted by the Sultan in exchange for military service; and paid soldiers, technically considered slaves, who were permanently in the Sultan's service. As in the West, the landholder had to provide the military with armed men. The number was determined by the revenues raised from his lands, but it was always in his interest to expand his holdings, and thus for the Ottoman Empire to keep growing. Among the paid soldiers, the most important were the Janissaries, an elite corps of troops dedicated to Islam, who were feared by all who encountered the Ottomans. The Janissaries became an influential force in Ottoman politics and a major source of the Sultan's power. These were well-disciplined and thoroughly professional soldiers, but legally they were slaves—often captives from conquered peoples. Slave armies had been common in Islamic states, but the Ottomans did not adopt the practice until the 1430s, when they began converting war captives to Islam, teaching them Turkish, and training them as a tough, military contingent. Thereafter, the tribute the Ottomans demanded from the Christian parts of their empire was the handing over of young boys who would be trained to join this elite military corps.

With this superb fighting force at his disposal, and presiding over a government in which he held unquestioned authority, Suleiman drove to expand Ottoman rule into Europe. In 1521 he captured the citadel of Belgrade in the Balkan Peninsula, and the next year he conquered the island of Rhodes, home of an order of Christian knights who had been harassing his shipping. He was now in complete command of the eastern Mediterranean.

Then came the Ottomans' major overland advance. After the death of the Hungarian ruler Matthias Corvinus in 1490, domestic rivalries had drained the European kingdom of its former strength. When landowners and the Janissaries sought new lands to conquer after the fall of Rhodes, Suleiman decided to invade vulnerable Hungary. In April 1526 he left Constantinople and headed west. Four months later, on August 29, he met the Hungarian army in the plain of Mohacs. What followed was one of the decisive battles of world history. An opening charge by the Hungarian cavalry seemed to sweep all before them, but it was a trap. The Janissaries halted the charge and their artillery shattered the cavalry. As a contemporary Ottoman historian put it:

> At the order of the sultan the fusiliers of the Janissaries, directing their blows at the cruel panthers who opposed us, caused thousands of them, in the space of a moment, to descend into hell.

SULEIMAN AND OTTOMAN FORCES AT BATTLE OF MOHACS, 1526
Topkapi Palace Museum, Istanbul, Turkey. Giraudon/Art Resource

It has been estimated that some 30,000 men—three-quarters of the Hungarian army—not to mention their king, the leaders of their church, and their most prominent aristocrats, were all killed.

By September 10 the Ottomans were in the Hungarian capital, Buda, which they burned to the ground. Suleiman was now master of the Balkans, and he took the next three years to consolidate his position. When, finally, he decided to advance again, toward the Habsburg capital of Vienna, his communications were becoming stretched, and he had given his enemy time to prepare. The summer of 1529 happened to be extremely rainy, which meant that Suleiman was unable to bring his heavy artillery to the siege of Vienna, and his army had to move slowly. As a result, the garrison had time to assemble heavy reinforcements, and was ready to hold out against light artillery. After a few months of indecisive skirmishing, therefore, the Ottomans decided to withdraw. Their advance into Europe had been halted. The Balkans would be prize enough.

For the rest of his reign Suleiman turned his attention toward the East, where his armies overran Mesopotamia and southern Arabia. But the long-term effect of his conquest of the Balkans can be seen in the religious divisions that continue to trouble the area to this day. This came to be a major fault line in the boundary between Europe and the rest of the world, a perennial source of upheaval and discontent for centuries to come.

continued

What was remarkable about Suleiman's rule, however, was that he was able to hold together his huge empire in a way that avoided the local challenges to his power that were common in the West. The Sultan gained the loyalty of subject populations by allowing them to live by their own laws under their own officials, requiring them only to pay taxes and supply men for the Ottoman army and administration. Trade, for example, which remained vigorous in the Black Sea and the eastern Mediterranean, was still largely in the hands of Greeks, Armenians, and Jews. The Ottomans themselves remained aloof from commercial undertakings and confined their careers to government service and the army.

Although Ottoman power was to wane over the centuries that followed, hastened by corruption at court and the loosening of military discipline, the expansive days of Suleiman's reign were never forgotten. To this day, the mosque that he built, which houses his elegantly decorated tomb, dominates the Istanbul skyline.

widely accepted. Indeed, the political stability Venice had maintained for centuries was the envy of Europe. Tourists came not only to enjoy its many relaxations and entertainments but also to marvel at the institutions that kept the city calm, powerful, and rich. Venice's leaders were thought of as the heirs of Roman senators, and throughout Europe, the Italians were regarded as masters not only of politics but also of culture and manners.

The Italian Wars It was a considerable shock, therefore, when the Italian states crumbled before the onslaught of French and then Spanish and Habsburg armies. Charles VIII's invasion led to the expulsion of the Medici from Florence in 1494 and the establishment of a new Florentine republic. In 1512 the family engineered a return to power with the help of Ferdinand of Aragon, and eventually the Habsburgs set up the Medici as hereditary dukes of Tuscany. Ferdinand annexed Naples in 1504, and Emperor Charles V took over Milan in 1535. When the fighting ended in 1559, the Habsburgs controlled Italy and would do so for the next century. Only Venice, Tuscany under the Medici, and the Papal States remained relatively independent—though Venice was no longer a force in European affairs. The one major local beneficiary of the Italian wars was the papacy, whose army carved out a new papal territory in central and eastern Italy.

The critical lesson of these disastrous events was that small political units could not survive in an age when governments were consolidating their authority in large kingdoms. No matter how brilliant and sophisticated, a compact city-state could not withstand such superior force. Italy's cultural and economic prominence faded only slowly, but by the mid-sixteenth century, except for the papacy, the international standing of its states was fading.

THE NEW STATECRAFT

The Italian states of the fifteenth century, in their intense political struggles and competition with one another, developed various new ways of pursuing foreign policy. During the Italian wars, these techniques spread throughout Europe and caused a revolution in diplomacy. Any state hoping to play a prominent role in international affairs worked under a serious disadvantage if it did not conform. And an Italian observer, Machiavelli, suggested radically new ways of understanding the nature of politics and diplomacy.

New International Relations

The Italians' essential innovation was the resident ambassador. Previously, rulers had dispatched ambassadors to other states only for specific missions, such as to arrange an alliance, declare war, or deliver a message; but from the sixteenth century on, important states maintained representatives in every major capital or court at all times. The permanent ambassador could keep the home government informed of the latest local and international developments and could also move without delay to protect his country's interests.

Titian
THE VENDRAMIN FAMILY, 1547
The magnificence of the patrician families who ruled Venice is celebrated in this group portrait. Ostensibly, they are worshiping a relic of the true cross, but in fact they are displaying the hierarchy that rules their lives. Only men appear, dominated by the head of the family and his aged father, followed by his eldest son and heir, all of whom convey an image of wealth and power.
Reproduced by courtesy of the Trustees, © The National Gallery, London (NG4452)

The New Diplomacy As states established embassies, procedures and organization became more sophisticated. A primitive system of diplomatic immunities (including freedom from prosecution for ambassadors and their households) evolved, and formal protocol developed. Many advances were still to come, but by 1550 the outlines of the new diplomacy were already visible—yet another reflection of the growing powers and ambitions of central governments.

The new diplomacy took hold in the Italian wars, a Europe-wide crisis that involved rulers as distant as the English King Henry VIII and the Ottoman Sultan Suleiman the Great. Gradually, all states recognized that it was in everybody's interest not to allow one power to dominate the rest. In later years this prevention of excessive aggression was to be known as the balance of power, but by the mid-sixteenth century the idea was already affecting alliances and peace treaties.

Machiavelli

As the Italian wars unfolded, political commentators began to seek explanations for the new authority and aggressiveness of rulers and the collapse of the Italian city-states. Turning from arguments based on divine will or contractual law, they treated effective government as an end in itself. The most disturbing assessment came from an experienced Florentine diplomat, Niccolò Machiavelli, who was exiled when the Medici took control of Florence in 1512. Barred from politics and bitter over the collapse of Italy, he set about analyzing exactly how power is won, exercised, and lost.

The result, *The Prince*, is one of the few radically original books in history. To move from his predecessors to Machiavelli is to see legal and moral thought transformed. Machiavelli swept away conventions as he attempted, in an age of collapsing regimes, to understand how states function and how they affect their subjects. If he came out of any tradition, it was the Renaissance fascination with method that had produced manuals on cooking, dancing, fencing, and manners. But he wrote about method in an area that had never previously been analyzed in this way: power. Machiavelli showed not why power does or should exist, but how it works. Without reference to divine, legal, or natural justification, the book explains what a ruler needs to do to win and maintain complete control over his subjects. Machiavelli did not deny the force of religion or law; what concerned him was how they ought to be used in the tactics of governing—religion for molding unity and contentment, and devotion to law for building the ruler's reputation as a fair-minded person. *The Prince* outlines the methods to be used to deal with insurrection and the many other problems that rulers encounter. Fear and respect are the bases of their authority, and they must exercise care at all times not to relax their control over potential troublemakers or over their image among the people.

Few contemporaries of Machiavelli dared openly to accept so harsh a view of politics, but he did not hesitate to expand his analysis in his other masterpiece, the *Discourses*. This book developed a cyclical theory of every government moving inexorably from tyranny to democracy and back again. His conclusion, drawn mainly from a study of Roman history, is that healthy government can be preserved only by the active participation of all citizens in the life of the state. He also suggested that the state is the force that keeps people civilized—a notable testimony to the new importance of effective government.

Summary

It was appropriate that theorists emphasized the obsession with power that dominated this age. The relentless pragmatism and ambition of kings and princes as they extended their authority both at home and abroad reshaped institutions and governments throughout Europe. Given the assertiveness of these rulers and the rising fanaticism generated by religious dispute, it is not surprising that there should have begun in the mid-sixteenth century a series of wars of a ferocity and destructiveness that Europe had never before seen.

QUESTIONS FOR FURTHER THOUGHT

1. Is there some reason that major economic changes and major political changes always seem to go hand in hand?

2. Is it inevitable that rapid economic advance will have both favorable and unfavorable effects on ordinary people?

RECOMMENDED READING

Sources

*Guicciardini, Francesco. *The History of Italy and Other Selected Writings.* Cecil Grayson (tr.). 1964.

*Machiavelli, Niccolò. *The Prince and the Discourses.* Luigi Ricci (tr.). 1950.

*Parry, J. H. (ed.). *The European Reconnaissance: Selected Documents.* 1968.

Studies

*Anderson, M. S. *The Origins of the Modern European State System, 1494–1618.* 1998.

*Bonney, Richard. *The European Dynastic States, 1494–1660.* 1991. An excellent overview.

*Crosby, Alfred W. *The Columbian Exchange: Biological and Cultural Consequences of 1492.* 1972. A fascinating study of plants, diseases, and other exchanges between the Old World and the New World.

Dewald, Jonathan. *The European Nobility, 1400–1800.* 1996.

*Elliott, J. H. *The Old World and the New, 1492–1650.* 1970. A survey of the impact on Europe of the overseas discoveries.

*Femia, Joseph V. *Machiavelli Revisited.* 2004.

*Mattingly, Garrett. *Renaissance Diplomacy.* 1971. An elegant account of the changes that began in international relations during the fifteenth century.

*Rady, Martin. *The Emperor Charles V.* 1988. An excellent overview, with illustrative documents, of the reign of the most powerful ruler in Europe.

*Richardson, Glenn. *Renaissance Monarchy: The Reigns of Henry VIII, Francis I and Charles V.* 2002.

Scammell, G. V. *The First Imperial Age: European Overseas Expansion c. 1400–1715.* 1989. An excellent survey.

*Skinner, Quentin. *Machiavelli.* 1981. An excellent brief introduction to the man and his thought.

Wilford, John Noble. *The Mysterious History of Columbus: An Exploration of the Man, the Myth, the Legacy.* 1991. A judicious account, both of Columbus' career and of the ways it has been interpreted.

*Wrigley, E. A. *Population and History.* 1969. An introduction to the methods and findings of historical demography by one of the pioneers of the field.

*Available in paperback.

Francois Dubois
THE MASSACRE OF ST. BARTHOLOMEW'S DAY
Although it makes no attempt to depict the massacre realistically, this painting by a Protestant
does convey the horrors of religious war. As the victims are hanged, disemboweled, decapitated,
tossed from windows, bludgeoned, shot, or drowned, their bodies and homes are looted. Dubois
may have intended the figure dressed in widow's black and pointing at a pile of corpses near the
river at the back to be a portrait of Catherine de Medici, who many thought inspired the
massacre.
Musée Cantonal des Beaux-Arts, Lausanne

Chapter Fifteen

WAR AND CRISIS

RIVALRY AND WAR IN THE AGE OF PHILIP II • FROM UNBOUNDED WAR TO
INTERNATIONAL CRISIS • THE MILITARY REVOLUTION • REVOLUTION IN ENGLAND •
REVOLTS IN FRANCE AND SPAIN • POLITICAL CHANGE IN AN AGE OF CRISIS

In the wake of the rapid and bewildering changes of the early sixteenth century—the Reformation, the rises in population and prices, the overseas discoveries, and the dislocations caused by the activities of the new monarchs—Europe entered a period of fierce upheaval. So many radical alterations were taking place that conflict became inevitable. There were revolts against monarchs, often led by nobles who saw their power dwindling. The poor launched hopeless rebellions against their social superiors. And the two religious camps struggled relentlessly to destroy each other. From Scotland to Russia, the century following the Reformation, from about 1560 to 1660, was dominated by warfare; and the constant military activity had widespread effects on politics, economics, society, and thought. The fighting, in fact, helped bring to an end the long process

whereby Europe came to terms with the revolutions that had begun about 1500. As we will see, two distinct periods of ever more destructive warfare—the age of Philip II from the 1550s to the 1590s, and the age of the Thirty Years' War from the 1610s to the 1640s, with a decade of uneasy peace in between—led to a vast crisis of authority throughout Europe in the mid-1600s. From the struggles of that crisis there emerged fundamental economic, political, social, and religious changes, as troubled Europeans at last found ways to accept their altered circumstances. Interestingly, there were peasant revolts in Russia and China at the same time as those in Western Europe in the mid-seventeenth century, and they, too, reflected unease with state power, which was growing in Russia, but declining in China as the Ming Dynasty came to an end.

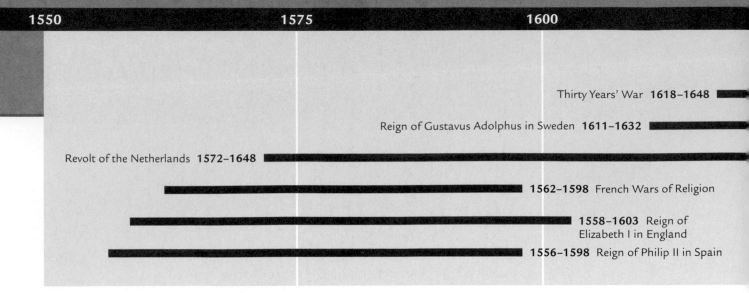

Thirty Years' War **1618–1648**

Reign of Gustavus Adolphus in Sweden **1611–1632**

Revolt of the Netherlands **1572–1648**

1562–1598 French Wars of Religion

1558–1603 Reign of Elizabeth I in England

1556–1598 Reign of Philip II in Spain

RIVALRY AND WAR IN THE AGE OF PHILIP II

The wars that plagued Europe from the 1560s to the 1650s involved many issues, but religion was the burning motivation, the one that inspired fanatical devotion and the most vicious hatred. A deep conviction that heresy was dangerous to society and hateful to God made Protestants and Catholics treat one another brutally. Even the dead were not spared: Corpses were sometimes mutilated to emphasize how dreadful their sins had been. These emotions, which shaped politics in this period, especially the decades dominated by Philip II, gave the fighting a brutality unprecedented in European history.

Philip II of Spain

During the second half of the sixteenth century, international warfare was ignited by the leader of the Catholics, Philip II of Spain (r. 1556–1598), the most powerful monarch in Europe. A stern defender of the Catholic faith, who is looked back on by Spaniards as a model of prudence, self-discipline, and devotion, he was also a tireless administrator, building up and supervising a vast and complex bureaucracy. It was needed, he felt, because of the far-spreading territories he ruled: the Iberian Peninsula, much of Italy, the Netherlands, and a huge overseas empire. Yet his main concern was to overcome the two enemies of his church, the Muslims and the Protestants.

Against the Muslims in the Mediterranean area, Philip's campaigns seemed to justify the financial strains they caused. In particular, his naval victory over the Ottomans at Lepanto, off the Greek coast, in 1571 made him a Christian hero at the same time that it re-

duced Muslim power. Although the Ottomans remained a considerable force in the eastern half of the Mediterranean, and indeed were able to besiege Vienna again in 1683, Philip was unchallenged in the west. He dominated the rich Italian peninsula; in 1580 he inherited the kingdom of Portugal; and his overseas wealth, passing through Seville, made this the fastest-growing city in Europe. The sixteenth century was the last age in which the Mediterranean was the heart of the European economy, but its prosperity was still the chief pillar of Philip's power.

Further north, Philip fared less well. He tried to prevent a Protestant, Henry IV, from inheriting the French crown and continued to back the losing side in France's civil wars even though Henry converted to Catholicism. Philip's policy toward England and the Netherlands was similarly ineffective. After the Protestant Queen Elizabeth I came to the English throne in 1558, Philip remained uneasily cordial toward her for about ten years. But relations deteriorated as England's sailors and explorers threatened Philip's wealthy New World possessions. Worse, in 1585 Elizabeth began to help the Protestant Dutch, who were rebelling against Spanish rule. Though their countries were smaller than Spain, the English and Dutch were able to inflict on Philip the two chief setbacks of his reign; and in the years after his death they were to wrest the leadership of Europe's economy away from the Mediterranean.

Elizabeth I of England

In a struggle with Spain, England may have seemed an unlikely victor: a relatively poor kingdom that had lost its continental possessions and for some time had played a secondary role in European affairs. Yet its people were united by such common bonds as the institution of Parliament and a commitment to the international Protes-

1640–1668
Revolts by Catalonia, Portugal, Sicily, and Naples against Spain

1642–1660 Revolution in England

1648–1653 *Fronde* revolt in France

tant cause that was carefully promoted by Queen Elizabeth I (r. 1558–1603).

Elizabeth is an appealing figure because she combined shrewd hardheadedness with a disarming appearance of frailty. Her qualities were many: her dedication to the task of government; her astute choice of advisers; her civilizing influence at court, where she encouraged elegant manners and the arts; her tolerance of religious dissent as long as it posed no political threat; and her ability to feel the mood of her people, to catch their spirit, to inspire their enthusiasm. Although social, legal, and economic practices usually subordinated women to men in this age, inheritance was respected; thus, a determined woman with a recognized claim to authority could win complete acceptance. Elizabeth was the most widely admired and most successful queen of her time, but she was by no means alone; female rulers also shaped the histories of France, Sweden, and the southern Netherlands in the sixteenth and seventeenth centuries.

Royal Policy Elizabeth could be indecisive, notably where the succession was concerned. Her refusal to marry caused serious uncertainties, and it was only the shrewd planning of her chief minister, Robert Cecil, that enabled the king of Scotland, James Stuart, to succeed her without incident in 1603. Similar dangers arose from her indecisive treatment of England's remaining Catholics. They hoped that Mary Queen of Scots, a Catholic, would inherit the throne; and since she was next in line, they were not above plotting against Elizabeth's life. Eventually, in 1587, Elizabeth had Mary executed and the plots died away. Despite her reluctance to take firm positions, Elizabeth showed great skill in balancing policy alternatives, and her adroit maneuvering assured her of her ministers' loyalty at all times. She also inspired the devotion of her subjects by traveling

throughout England to make public appearances; by delivering brilliant speeches (see "Queen Elizabeth's Armada Speech," p. 433); and by shaping her own image, even regulating how she was to be depicted in portraits. She thus retained her subjects' allegiance despite the profound social changes that were eroding traditional patterns of deference and order. England's nobility, for instance, no longer dominated the military and the government; nearly all Elizabeth's ministers were new in national life; and the House of Commons was beginning to exert more political influence within Parliament than the House of Lords. All groups in English society, however, shared a resentment of Spanish power, and Elizabeth cultivated this sentiment astutely as a patriotic and Protestant cause.

The Dutch Revolt

The same cause united the people living in the provinces in the Netherlands that Philip inherited from his father, the Emperor Charles V. Here his single-minded promotion of Catholicism and royal power provoked a fierce reaction that grew into a successful struggle for independence: the first major victory in Western Europe by subjects resisting royal authority.

Causes of Revolt The original focus of opposition was Philip's reorganization of the ecclesiastical structure so as to gain control over the country's Catholic Church, a change that deprived the aristocracy of important patronage. At the same time, the **billeting** of troops aroused the resentment of ordinary citizens. In this situation, the local nobles, led by William of Orange, warned of mass disorder, but Philip kept up the pressure: He put the Inquisition to work against the Calvinists, who had begun to appear in the Netherlands, and also summoned the Jesuits to combat the

El Greco
THE DREAM OF PHILIP II, **1578**
Characteristic of the mystical vision of El Greco is this
portrayal of the devout, black-clad figure of Philip II.
Kneeling alongside the doge of Venice and the pope, his
allies in the victory of Lepanto over the Turks, Philip adores
the blazing name of Jesus that is surrounded by angels in
heaven, and he turns his back on the gaping mouth to hell.
Reproduced by courtesy of the Trustees, © The National
Gallery, London (NG6260)

William Segar (attrib.)
PORTRAIT OF ELIZABETH I, **1585**
Elizabeth I was strongly aware of the power of propaganda,
and she used it to foster a dazzling public image. Legends
about her arose in literature. And in art she had herself
portrayed in the most elaborate finery imaginable. Here, she
is every inch the queen, with her magnificent dress, the
trappings of monarchy, and the symbol of virginity, the
ermine.
By courtesy of The Marquess of Salisbury

heretics. These moves were disastrous because they
further undermined local autonomy and made the
Protestants bitter enemies of the king.

Philip's aggressiveness provoked violence in 1566.
Although the Protestants were still a tiny minority,
they formed mobs in a number of cities, assaulted
Catholics, and sacked churches. In response, Philip
tightened the pressure, appointing as governor the
ruthless duke of Alba, who used his Spanish troops to
suppress opposition. Protestants were hanged in public,
rebel groups were hunted down, and two nobles who
had been guilty of nothing worse than demanding that
Philip change his policy were executed.

Full-Scale Rebellion Organized revolt broke out in
1572, when a small group of Dutch sailors flying the
flag of William of Orange seized the fishing village of
Brill, on the North Sea. The success of these "sea beggars," as the Spaniards called them, stimulated uprisings in towns throughout the Low Countries. The
banner of William of Orange became the symbol of resistance, and under his leadership full-scale rebellion
erupted. By 1576, when Philip's troops mutinied and rioted in Antwerp, sixteen of the seventeen provinces in
the Netherlands had united behind William. The next

Queen Elizabeth's Armada Speech

Elizabeth's ability to move her subjects was exemplified by the speech she gave to her troops as they awaited the fight with the Spanish Armada. She understood that they might have doubts about a woman leading them in war, but she turned that issue to her own advantage in a stirring cry to battle that enhanced her popularity at the time and her legendary image thereafter.

"My loving People: We have been persuaded by some that are careful of our safety, to take heed how we commit ourselves to armed multitudes, for fear of treachery; but I assure you, I do not desire to live to distrust my faithful and loving people.

"Let tyrants fear; I have always so behaved myself, that, under God, I have placed my chiefest strength and safeguard in the loyal hearts and good will of my subjects, and therefore I am come amongst you, as you see, at this time, not for my recreation . . . but being resolved in the midst and heat of the battle, to live or die amongst you all, to lay down for my God, and for my kingdoms, and for my people, my honour and my blood, even in the dust.

"I know I have the body of a weak and feeble woman; but I have the heart and stomach of a king, and of a king of England too; and think foul scorn that . . . Spain, or any prince of Europe should dare to invade the borders of my realm; to which rather than any dishonour shall grow by me, I myself will take up arms, I myself will be your general, judge, and rewarder of every one of your virtues in the field. . . . By your concord in the camp, and your valour in the field, we shall shortly have a famous victory over those enemies of my God, of my kingdoms, and of my people."

Walter Scott (ed.), *A Collection of Scarce and Valuable Tracts, on the Most Interesting and Entertaining Subjects: But Chiefly Such as Relate to the History and Constitution of These Kingdoms*, Vol. 1, London, 1809, pp. 429–430.

Anonymous
Engraving of the Spaniards in Haarlem
This engraving was published to arouse horror at Spanish atrocities during the Dutch revolt. As the caption indicates, after the Spanish troops (on the right) captured the city of Haarlem, there was a great bloodbath (*ein gross bluit batt*). Blessed by priests, the Haarlemites were decapitated or hung, and then tossed in a river so that the city would be cleansed of them. The caption states that even women and children were not spared.
New York Public Library

Pieter Brueghel the Elder
THE MASSACRE OF THE INNOCENTS, **1565**
Probably to avoid trouble, Brueghel hid his critique of the Spanish rulers of the Netherlands in this supposed portrayal of a biblical event. It would have been clear to anyone who saw it, however, that this was a scene of Spanish cruelty toward the local inhabitants in the harsh days of winter, as soldiers tear babies from their mothers and kill them.
Erich Lessing/Art Resource, NY

year, however, Philip offered a compromise to the Catholic nobles, and the ten southern provinces returned to Spanish rule.

The United Provinces In 1579 the remaining seven provinces formed the independent United Provinces. Despite the assassination of William in 1584, they managed to resist Spain's army for decades, mainly because they could open dikes, flood their country, and thus drive the invaders back. Moreover, Philip was often diverted by other wars and, in any case, never placed total confidence in his commanders. The Calvinists formed the heart of the resistance; though still a minority, they had the most to lose, because they sought freedom for their religion as well as their country. William never showed strong religious commitments, but his son, Maurice of Nassau, a brilliant military commander who

won a series of victories in the 1590s, embraced Calvinism and helped make it the country's official religion. Unable to make any progress, the Spaniards agreed to a twelve-year truce in 1609, but they did not recognize the independence of the United Provinces until the Peace of Westphalia in 1648.

The Armada In 1588 Philip tried to end his troubles in northern Europe with one mighty blow. Furious that the English were interfering with his New World empire (their traders and raiders had been intruding into Spain's American colonies for decades) and that Elizabeth was helping Dutch Protestants, he sent a mammoth fleet— the Armada—to the Low Countries. Its task was to pick up a Spanish army, invade England, and thus undermine Protestant resistance. By this time, however, English mariners were among the best in the world, and their

MAP 15.1 THE NETHERLANDS, 1579–1609
The seventeen provinces making up the Netherlands, or the Low Countries, were detached from the Holy Roman Empire when Charles V abdicated in 1556. As the map indicates, their subsequent division into two states was determined not by the linguistic differences between French-speaking people of the south and Dutch-speaking people of the north but rather by geography. The great river systems at the mouth of the Rhine eventually proved to be the barrier beyond which the Spaniards could not penetrate. Notice the shifting boundaries. Did the United Provinces gain more between 1590 and 1648 than they lost after 1579?
◆ For an online version, go to www.mhhe.com/chambers9 > chapter 15 > book maps

ships had greater maneuverability and firepower than did the Spaniards'. After several skirmishes in the Channel, the English set fire to a few of their own vessels with loaded cannons aboard and sent them drifting toward the Spanish ships, anchored off Calais. The Spaniards had to raise anchor in a hurry, and some of the fleet was lost. The next day the remaining Spanish ships retreated up the North Sea. The only way home was around Ireland; and wind, storms, and the pursuing English ensured that less than half the fleet returned safely to Spain. This shattering reversal was comparable in scale and unexpectedness only to Xerxes' disaster at Salamis more than two thousand years earlier. More than any other single event, it doomed Philip's ambitions in England, the Netherlands, and France and signaled a northward shift in power in Europe.

Civil War in France

The other major power of Western Europe, France, was rent apart by religious war in this period, but it too felt the effects of the Armada's defeat. By the 1550s Calvinism was gaining strength among French peasants and in the towns of the south and southwest, and its leaders had virtually created a small semi-independent state. To meet this threat, a great noble family, the Guises, assumed the leadership of the Catholics; in response, the Bourbons, another noble family, championed the Calvinists, about a twelfth of the population. Their struggle split the country apart.

It was ominous that in 1559—the year that Henry II, France's last strong king for a generation, died—the Calvinists (known in France as Huguenots) organized their first national synod, an indication of impressive strength. During the next thirty years, the throne was occupied by Henry's three ineffectual sons. The power behind the crown was Henry's widow, Catherine de Medici (see "The Kings of France in the Sixteenth Century," p. 436), who tried desperately to preserve royal authority. But she was often helpless because the religious conflict intensified the factional struggle for power between the Guises and the Bourbons, both of whom were closely related to the monarchy and hoped one day to inherit the throne.

The Wars Fighting started in 1562 and lasted for thirty-six years, interrupted only by short-lived peace agreements. Catherine switched sides whenever one party became too powerful; and she may have approved the notorious massacre of St. Bartholomew's Day—August 24, 1572—which started in Paris, spread through France, and destroyed the Huguenots' leadership. Henry of Navarre, a Bourbon, was the only major figure who escaped. When Catherine switched sides again and made peace with the Huguenots in 1576, the Guises formed the Catholic League, which for several years dominated the eastern half of the country. In 1584 the league allied with Spain's Philip II to attack heresy in France and deny the Bourbon Henry's legal right to inherit the throne.

The defeat of the Armada in 1588 proved to be the turning point in the French civil wars, for Spain could not continue helping the duke of Guise, who was soon assassinated, and within a few months Henry of Navarre inherited the throne as Henry IV (r. 1589–1610). He had few advantages as he began to reassert royal authority, because the Huguenots and Catholics ran almost independent governments in large sections of France. In addition, the royal administration was in a sorry state because the crown's oldest rivals, the great nobles, could now resist all outside interference in their domains.

Anonymous
The Armada
This depiction suggests the sheer splendor of the scene as Philip II's fleet sailed through the Channel on its way to invading England. The opposing ships were never this close, but the colorful flags (red cross English, yellow cross Spanish) and the elaborate coats of arms must have been dazzling. The firing cannon and the sinking ship remind us that, amidst the display, there was also death and destruction.
National Maritime Museum, Greenwich, London

THE KINGS OF FRANCE IN THE SIXTEENTH CENTURY

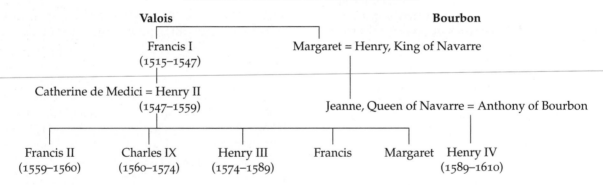

Valois   **Bourbon**

Francis I (1515–1547) ———— Margaret = Henry, King of Navarre

Catherine de Medici = Henry II (1547–1559)

Jeanne, Queen of Navarre = Anthony of Bourbon

| Francis II (1559–1560) | Charles IX (1560–1574) | Henry III (1574–1589) | Francis | Margaret | Henry IV (1589–1610) |

Peace Restored Yet largely because of the assassination of the duke of Guise, Henry IV was able to restore order. The duke had been a forceful leader and a serious contender for the throne. His replacement was a Spanish candidate for the crown who had little chance of success. The distaste for a possible foreign ruler, combined with war weariness, destroyed much of the support for the Catholic League, which finally collapsed as a result of revolts against it in eastern France in the 1590s. These up-risings, founded on a demand for peace, increased in frequency and intensity after Henry IV renounced Protestantism in 1593 in order to win acceptance by his Catholic subjects. The following year Henry had himself officially crowned, and all of France rallied to the king as he beat back a Spanish invasion—Spain's final, rather weak, attempt to put its own candidate on the throne.

When Spain finally withdrew and signed a peace treaty in 1598, the fighting came to an end. To complete

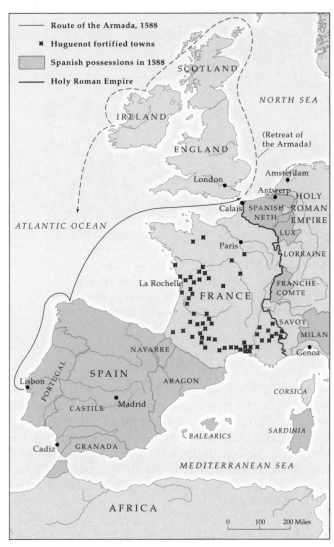

Route of the Armada, 1588
Huguenot fortified towns
Spanish possessions in 1588
Holy Roman Empire

SCOTLAND
IRELAND
NORTH SEA
ENGLAND
(Retreat of the Armada)
London
Amsterdam
Antwerp
Calais
SPANISH NETH.
HOLY ROMAN EMPIRE
LUX.
ATLANTIC OCEAN
Paris
LORRAINE
La Rochelle
FRANCE
FRANCHE-COMTE
SAVOY
MILAN
NAVARRE
Genoa
PORTUGAL
Lisbon
SPAIN
ARAGON
CORSICA
CASTILE
Madrid
Cadiz
GRANADA
BALEARICS
SARDINIA
MEDITERRANEAN SEA
AFRICA
0   100   200 Miles

MAP 15.2 CATHOLIC AND PROTESTANT POWERS IN THE LATE SIXTEENTH CENTURY.
The heart of the Catholic cause in the wars of religion was the Spain of Philip II. Spanish territories surrounded France and provided the route to the Netherlands, where the Protestant Dutch had rebelled against the Spaniards (see map 15.1). The Armada was launched to help that cause by crushing the ally of the Dutch, Protestant England. In the meantime, the surrounded French had problems of their own with the Huguenots, who protected their Protestantism in a network of fortified towns. Why did the Armada follow the route shown on the map?
◆ For an online version, go to www.mhhe.com/chambers9 > chapter 15 > book maps

the reconciliation, Henry issued (also in 1598) the Edict of Nantes, which granted limited toleration to the Huguenots. Although it did not create complete religious liberty, the edict made Calvinist worship legal, protected the rights of the minority, and opened public office to Huguenots.

FROM UNBOUNDED WAR TO INTERNATIONAL CRISIS

During the half century after Philip II's death, warfare spread throughout Europe. There was a brief lull in the early 1600s, but then the slaughter and the devastations began to multiply. For a while it seemed that nothing could bring the fighting to an end, and a feeling of irresolvable crisis descended on international affairs. Not until an entirely new form of peacemaking was devised, in the 1640s, was the fighting brought under control.

The Thirty Years' War

The new arena in which the warfare erupted was the Holy Roman Empire. Here religious hatreds were especially disruptive because the empire lacked a central authority and unifying institutions. Small-scale fighting broke out repeatedly after the 1550s, always inspired by religion. Although elsewhere the first years of the seventeenth century were a time of relative peace that seemed to signal a decline of conflict over faith, in the empire the stage was being set for the bloodiest of all the wars fired by religion.

Known as the Thirty Years' War, this ferocious struggle began in the Kingdom of Bohemia in 1618 and continued until 1648. The principal battleground, the empire, was ravaged by the fighting, which eventually involved every major ruler in Europe. At first it was a renewed struggle between local Protestants and Catholics, but eventually it became a fight among political rivals who were eager to take advantage of the fragmentation of the empire to advance their own ambitions. As the devastation spread, international relations seemed to be sinking into total chaos; but the chief victims were the Germans, who, like the Italians in the sixteenth century, found themselves at the mercy of well-organized states that used another country as a place to settle their quarrels.

The First Phase, 1618–1621   The immediate problem was typical of the situation in the empire. In 1609 the Habsburg Emperor Rudolf II promised toleration for Protestants in Bohemia. When his cousin Ferdinand, a pious Catholic, succeeded to the Bohemian throne in 1617, he refused to honor Rudolf's promise, and the Bohemians rebelled in 1618. They declared Ferdinand deposed, replacing him with the leading Calvinist of the empire, Frederick II of the Palatinate. Frederick accepted the crown, an act of defiance whose only possible outcome was war.

The first decade or so of the war was a time of victories for the Catholics. When Ferdinand became emperor (r. 1619–1637), the powerful Catholic Maximilian

"The Hanging Tree," Engraving from Jacques Callot's *Miseries of War*, 1633
An indication of the growing dismay over the brutality of the Thirty Years' War was the collection of sixteen prints produced by the French engraver Callot depicting the life of the soldier and the effects of armies on civilian populations. His soldiers destroy, loot, and rape, and only a few of them receive the punishments they deserve, like this mass hanging.
Anne S. K. Brown Military Collection, Brown University Library

"Heads of the Bohemian Rebels," Engraving from Mathaus Merian, *Theatrum Europaeum*, ca. 1630
Since the scene had not changed when the engraving was made, this illustration is probably a fairly accurate representation of the punishment in 1621 of the leaders of the Bohemian rebellion. Twenty-four rebels were executed, and the heads of twelve of them were displayed on long poles at the top of the tower (still standing today) on the bridge over Prague's river. The heads were kept there for ten years.

of Bavaria put an army at his disposal. Within a year, the imperial troops won a stunning victory over the Bohemians. Ferdinand II confiscated all of Frederick's lands. Maximilian received half as a reward for his army, and the remainder went to the Spaniards, who occupied it as a valuable base for their struggle with the Dutch. In this first round, the Catholic and imperial cause had triumphed.

The Second Phase, 1621–1630 When the truce between the Spaniards and the Dutch expired in 1621 and warfare resumed in Germany as well as in the Netherlands, the Protestants made no progress for ten years. A new imperial army was raised by Albrecht von Wallenstein, a minor Bohemian nobleman and remarkable opportunist who had become one of the richest men in the empire. By 1627 Wallenstein's army had begun to conquer the northern region of the empire, the last major center of Protestant strength. To emphasize his supremacy, Ferdinand issued the Edict of Restitution in 1629, ordering the restoration to Catholics of all the territories they had lost to Protestants since 1552.

But these Habsburg successes were more apparent than real, because it was only the extreme disorganization of the empire that permitted a mercenary captain like Wallenstein to achieve such immense military power. Once the princes realized the danger he posed to their independence, they united (Catholic as well as Protestant) against the Habsburgs, and in 1630 they forced the dismissal of Wallenstein by threatening to keep Ferdinand's son from the imperial succession. This concession proved fatal to the emperor's cause, for

Jan Asselyn
THE BATTLE OF LÜTZEN
Although it is not an accurate rendition of the scene, this painting of Gustavus Adolphus (the horseman in a brown coat with sword raised) shot by a gunman in red does give the flavor of seventeenth-century battle. Because of the chaos, the smoke, and the poor visibility that often obscured what was happening, Gustavus' escort did not notice when Gustavus was in fact hit by a musket shot that shattered his left arm and caused his horse to bolt. Further shots killed him, and not until hours after the battle was his seminaked body found, stripped of its finery.
Herzog Anton Ulrich-Museum, Braunschweig. Museum photo, B. P. Keiser

Sweden and France were preparing to unleash new aggressions against the Habsburgs, and Wallenstein was the one military leader who might have been able to resist the onslaught.

The Third Phase, 1630–1632   The year 1630 marked the beginning of a change in fortune for the Protestants and also a drift toward the purely political aim (of resisting the Habsburgs) that was coming to dominate the war. Although France's king was a Catholic, he was ready to join with Protestants against other Catholics so as to undermine Habsburg power. In 1631, the French allied with Gustavus Adolphus of Sweden, who, dismayed by Ferdinand's treatment of Protestants and fearing a Habsburg threat to Swedish lands around the Baltic Sea, had invaded the empire in 1630. The following year Gustavus destroyed an imperial army in a decisive battle that turned the tide against the Habsburgs.

Ferdinand hastily recalled Wallenstein, whose troops met the Swedes in battle at Lützen in 1632. Although Gustavus' soldiers won the day, he himself was killed, and his death saved the Habsburg Dynasty. Nothing, however, could restore Ferdinand's former position. The emperor was forced by the princes to turn against Wallenstein once more; a few months later Ferdinand had Wallenstein assassinated. The removal of the great general marked the end of an era, because Wallenstein was the last leader for more than two centuries who was capable of establishing unified authority in what is now Germany.

The Fourth Phase, 1632–1648 Gustavus' success opened the final phase of the war, as political ambitions—the quest of the empire's princes for independence and the struggle between the Habsburgs and their enemies—almost completely replaced religious aims. The Protestant princes began to raise new armies, and by 1635 Ferdinand had to make peace with them. In return for their promise of assistance in driving out the Swedes, Ferdinand agreed to suspend the Edict of Restitution and to grant amnesty to all but Frederick of the Palatinate and a few Bohemian rebels. Ferdinand was renouncing most of his ambitions, and it seemed that peace might return at last.

But the French could not let matters rest. In 1635 they finally declared war on Ferdinand. For the next thirteen years, the French and Swedes rained unmitigated disaster on Germany. Peace negotiations began in 1641, but not until 1648 did the combatants sign the treaties of Westphalia. Even thereafter the war between France and Spain, pursued mainly in the Spanish Netherlands, continued for another eleven years; and hostilities around the Baltic among Sweden, Denmark, Poland, and Russia, which had started in 1611, did not end until 1661.

The Effect of War The wars and their effects (such as the diseases spread by armies) killed off more than a third of Germany's population. The conflict caused serious economic dislocation because a number of princes—already in serious financial straits—sharply debased their coinage. Their actions worsened the continent-wide trade depression that had begun around 1620 and had brought the great sixteenth-century boom to an end, causing the first drop in prices since 1500. Few contemporaries perceived the connection between war and economic trouble, but nobody could ignore the drain on men and resources, the crisis in international relations, or the widespread destruction caused by the conflict.

The Peace of Westphalia

By the 1630s it was becoming apparent that the fighting was getting out of hand and that it would not be easy to bring the conflicts to an end. There had never been such widespread or devastating warfare, and many diplomats felt that the settlement had to be of far greater scope than any negotiated before. And they were right. When at last the treaties were signed in 1648, after seven years of negotiation in the German province of Westphalia, a landmark in international relations was passed—remarkable not only because it brought an anarchic situation under control but because it created a new system for dealing with wars.

The most important innovation was the gathering at the peace conference of all the participants in the Thirty Years' War, rather than the usual practice of bringing only two or three belligerents together. The presence of delegations from 109 interested parties

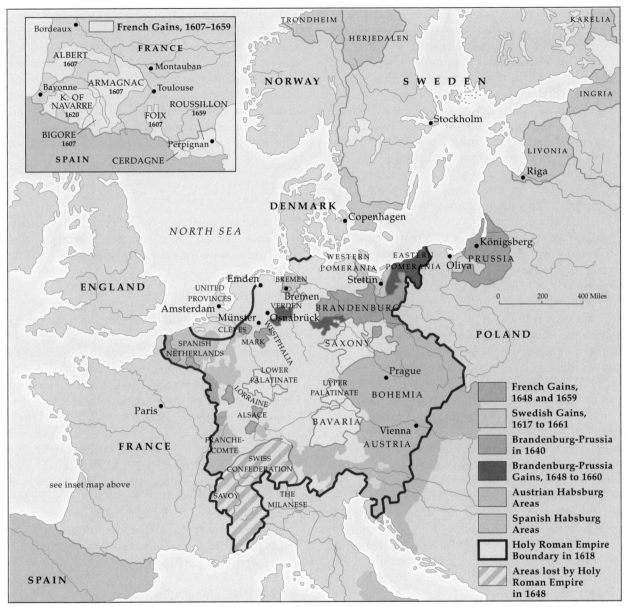

MAP 15.3 TERRITORIAL CHANGES, 1648–1661
This map shows the territorial changes that took place after the Thirty Years' War. The treaties of Westphalia (1648) and the Pyrenees (1659) arranged the principal transfers, but the settlements in the Baltic were not confirmed until the treaties of Copenhagen, Oliva (both 1660), and Kardis (1661). Who were the main winners and losers in the territorial changes of this period?

◆ For an online version, go to www.mhhe.com/chambers9 > chapter 15 > book maps

made possible, for the first time in European history, a series of all-embracing treaties that dealt with nearly every major international issue at one stroke. Visible at the meetings was the emergence of a state system. These independent states recognized that they were creating a mechanism for controlling their relations with one another. Although some fighting continued, the Peace of Westphalia in 1648 became the first comprehensive rearrangement of the map of Europe in modern times.

Peace Terms   The principal beneficiaries were France and Sweden, the chief aggressors during the last decade of the war. France gained the provinces of Alsace and Lorraine, and Sweden obtained extensive territories in the Holy Roman Empire. The main loser was the House of Habsburg, since both the United Provinces and the Swiss Confederation were recognized as independent states, and the German princes, who agreed not to join an alliance against the emperor, were otherwise given almost complete independence.

The princes' autonomy was formally established in 1657, when they elected as emperor Leopold I, the head of the House of Habsburg, in return for two promises. First, Leopold would give no help to his cousins, the rulers of Spain; and second, the empire would be a state of princes, in which each ruler would be free from imperial interference. This freedom permitted the rise of Brandenburg-Prussia and the growth of absolutism—the belief that the political authority of the ruler was unlimited—within the major principalities. Moreover, the Habsburgs' capitulation prepared the way for their reorientation toward the east along the Danube River—the beginnings of the Austro-Hungarian Empire.

The Effects of Westphalia For more than a century, the settlement reached at Westphalia was regarded as the basis for all international negotiations. Even major new accords, such as the one that ended yet another series of wars in 1713, were seen mainly as adjustments of the decisions of 1648. In practice, of course, multinational conferences were no more effective than brief, limited negotiations in reducing tensions among states. Wars continued to break out, and armies grew in size and skill. But diplomats did believe that international affairs were under better control and that the chaos of the Thirty Years' War had been replaced by something more stable and more clearly defined.

This confidence was reinforced as it became clear after 1648 that armies were trying to improve discipline and avoid the excesses of the previous thirty years. As religious passions waned, combat became less vicious and the treatment of civilians became more orderly. On battlefields, better discipline reduced the casualty rate from one death per three soldiers in the 1630s to one death in seven, or even one in twenty, during the early 1700s. The aims of war also changed significantly.

Changed International Relations The most obvious differences after the Peace of Westphalia were that France replaced Spain as the continent's dominant power and that northern countries—especially England and the Netherlands, where growth in population and in commerce resumed more quickly than elsewhere—took over Europe's economic leadership. But behind this outward shift a more fundamental transformation was taking place. What had become apparent in the later stages of the Thirty Years' War was that Europe's states were prepared to fight only for economic, territorial, or political advantages. Dynastic aims were still important, but supranational goals like religious causes could no longer determine a state's foreign policy.

The Thirty Years' War was the last major international conflict in Europe in which two religious camps organized their forces as blocs. After 1648 such connections gave way to purely national interests; it is no surprise that the papacy denounced the peace vehemently. For this shift marked the decisive stage of a process that had been under way since the Late Middle Ages: the emergence of the state as the basic unit and object of loyalty in Western civilization. That it had taken a major crisis, a descent into international anarchy, to bring about so momentous a change is an indication of how profoundly the upheavals of the mid-seventeenth century, this age of crisis, affected European history.

THE MILITARY REVOLUTION

The constant warfare of the sixteenth and seventeenth centuries brought about dramatic changes in the ways that battles were fought and armies were organized.

Weapons and Tactics

The Use of Gunpowder Though it had been known since the 1330s, gunpowder became central to warfare only around 1500. The result was the creation of a new type of industry, cannon and gun manufacture, and also a transformation of tactics. Individual castles could no longer be defended against explosives; even towns had to build heavy and elaborate fortifications if they were to resist the new firepower. Sieges became expensive, complex operations whose purpose was to bring explosives right up to a town wall so that it could be blown up. This process required an intricate system of trenches, because walls were built in star shapes so as to multiply angles of fire and make any approach dangerous. Although they became increasingly costly, sieges remained essential to the strategy of warfare until the eighteenth century.

New Tactics In open battles, the effects of gunpowder were equally expensive. The new tactics that appeared around 1500, perfected by the Spaniards, relied on massed ranks of infantry, organized in huge squares, that made the traditional cavalry charge obsolete. Interspersed with the gunners were soldiers carrying pikes. They fended off horses or opposing infantry while the men with guns tried to mow the enemy down. The squares with the best discipline usually won, and for more than a century after the reign of Ferdinand of Aragon, the Spaniards had the best army in Europe. Each square had about three thousand troops, and to maintain enough squares to fight all of Spain's battles required an army numbering approximately forty thousand. The cost of keeping that many men clothed, fed, and housed, let alone equipped and paid, was enormous. But worse was to come: New tactics emerged in the early seventeenth century that required even more soldiers.

Anonymous
WAFFENHANDLUNG, ENGRAVING AFTER JACQUES DE GHEYN
The expansion of armies and the professionalization of war
in the seventeenth century were reflected in the founding of
military academies and in the growing acceptance of the
notion that warfare was a science. There was now a market
for published manuals, especially if they had illustrations
like this one, which shows how a pikeman was supposed to
crouch and hold his weapons (stabilizing his pike against his
foot) when facing a cavalry charge.
Deutsches Historisches Museum, Berlin, Germany

Since nobody could outdo the Spaniards at their own
methods, a different approach was developed by their
rivals. The first advance was made by Maurice of Nassau, in the Dutch revolt against Spain. He relied not on
sheer weight and power but on flexibility and mobility.
Then Sweden's Gustavus Adolphus, one of the geniuses of the history of warfare, found a way to achieve
mobility on the field without losing power. His main
invention was the salvo: Instead of having his muske-
teers fire one row at a time, like the Spaniards, he had
them all fire at once. What he lost in continuity of shot
he gained in a fearsome blast that, if properly timed,
could shatter enemy ranks. Huge, slow-moving squares
were simply no match for smaller, faster units that rid-
dled them with well-coordinated salvos.

The Organization and Support of Armies

These tactical changes brought about steady increases
in the size of armies, because the more units there
were, the better they could be placed on the battlefield.
Although the Spanish army hardly grew between 1560
and 1640, remaining at 40,000 to 60,000 men, the

Swedes had 150,000 by 1632; and at the end of the century, Louis XIV considered a force of 400,000 essential
to maintain his dominant position in Europe.

This growth had far-reaching consequences. One
was the need for **conscription,** which Gustavus introduced in the late 1620s. At least half his army consisted of his own subjects, who were easier to control
than foreign mercenaries. Because it also made sense
not to disband such huge forces each autumn, when
the campaigning season ended, most armies were kept
permanently ready. To strengthen discipline, new
mechanisms were developed: drilling, combat training,
uniforms, and the various officer ranks we still have.
And the need to maintain so many soldiers the year
round caused a rapid expansion of supporting administrative personnel. Taxation mushroomed. All levels of
society felt the impact, but especially the lower classes,
who paid the bulk of the taxes and provided most of the
recruits.

The Life of the Soldier

Some soldiers genuinely wanted to join up. They had
heard stories of adventure, booty, and comradeship, and
they were tempted by free food and clothing. But many
"volunteers" did not want to go, for they had also heard
of the hardship and danger. Unfortunately for them, recruiting officers had quotas, and villages had to provide
the numbers. Community pressure, bribery, enlistment
of drunken men, and even outright kidnapping helped
fill the ranks.

Joining an army did not necessarily mean cutting
oneself off from friends or family. Men from a particular area enlisted together and, in some cases, wives and
even children came along. There were dozens of jobs to
do aside from fighting, because soldiers needed cooks,
launderers, peddlers, and other tradespeople. An army
in the field often needed five people for every soldier.
Few barracks were built, and therefore, unless they
were on the march or out in the open on a battlefield,
troops were housed (or billeted) with ordinary citizens.
Since soldiers almost never received their wages on
time—delays could be as long as a year or more—they
rarely could pay for their food and housing. Local civilians, therefore, had to supply their needs or risk the
thievery that was universal. It was no wonder that the
approach of an army was a terrifying event.

Discomforts of Military Life Military life was not
easy. Soldiers suffered constant discomfort. A garrison
might be able to settle into a town in reasonable conditions for a long stretch, but if it was besieged, it became
hungry, fearful, and vulnerable. Days spent on the
march could be grim, exhausting, and uncertain; even
in camps soldiers were often filthy and wet. Real danger

Sebastian Vrancx
A MILITARY CAMP
Vrancx was himself a soldier, and the many military scenes he painted during the Thirty Years' War give us a sense of the life of the soldier during the long months when there were no campaigns or battles. Conditions could be grim, but there were many hours during which a soldier could simply nap, chat, or play dice.
Hamburg/Hamburger Kunsthalle/The Bridgeman Art Library

was not common, though it was intense during battles and occasionally during sieges. Even a simple wound could be fatal, because medical care was generally appalling. Despite traditional recreations—drink, gambling, and the brawls common among soldiers—the attractions of army service were limited; most military men had few regrets when they returned to civilian life.

REVOLUTION IN ENGLAND

In the 1640s and 1650s the growing burdens of war and taxation, and the mounting assertiveness of governments, sparked upheavals throughout Europe that were the equivalent in domestic politics of the crisis in international relations. In country after country, people rose up in vain attempts to restore the individual and regional autonomies that were being eroded by power-

ful central governments. Only in England, however, did the revolt become a revolution—an attempt to overturn the social and political system and create a new structure for society.

Pressures for Change

The Gentry   The central figures in the drama were the gentry, a social group immediately below the nobles at the head of society. They ranged from people considered great in a parish or other small locality to courtiers considered great throughout the land. Although in Elizabeth's reign there were never more than sixty nobles, the gentry numbered close to twenty thousand. Most of the gentry were doing well economically, profiting from agricultural holdings and crown offices. A number also became involved in industrial activity, and hundreds invested in new overseas trading and colonial ventures. The gentry's participation in commerce made them unique among the landed classes of Europe, whose members were traditionally contemptuous of business affairs, and it testified to the enterprise and vigor of England's social leaders. Long important in local administration, they flocked to the House of Commons to express their views on public matters. Their ambitions eventually posed a serious threat to the monarchy, especially when linked with the effects of rapid economic change.

Economic Advance   In Elizabeth's reign, thanks to a general boom in trade, England's merchants, aided by leading courtiers, had begun to transform the country's economy. They opened commercial links throughout Europe and parts of Asia and promoted significant industrial development at home. Mining and manufacture developed rapidly, and shipbuilding became a major industry. The production of coal increased fourteen-fold between 1540 and 1680, creating fortunes and an expertise in industrial techniques that took England far ahead of its neighbors.

The economic vigor and growth that ensued gave the classes that benefited most—gentry and merchants—a cohesion and a sense of purpose that made it dangerous to oppose them when they felt their rights infringed. They were coming to see themselves as leaders of the nation, almost alongside the nobility. They wanted respect for their wishes, and they bitterly resented the economic interference and political high-handedness of Elizabeth's successors.

The Puritans   Heightening this unease was the sympathy that many of the gentry felt toward a small but vociferous group of religious reformers, the **Puritans.** Puritans believed that the Protestant Anglican Church established by Elizabeth was still too close to Roman Catholicism, and they wanted further reductions in ritual and hierarchy. Elizabeth refused, and although she tried to avoid a confrontation, in the last years of her reign she had to silence the most outspoken of her critics. As a result, the Puritans became a disgruntled minority. By the 1630s, when the government tried to repress religious dissent more vigorously, many people in England, non-Puritan as well as Puritan, felt that the monarchy was leading the country astray and was ignoring the wishes of its subjects. Leading parliamentarians in particular soon came to believe that major changes were needed to restore good government in England.

Parliament and the Law

The place where the gentry made their views known was Parliament, the nation's supreme legislative body. Three-quarters of the House of Commons consisted of gentry. They were better educated than ever before, and nearly half of them had legal training. Since the Commons had to approve all taxation, the gentry had the leverage to pursue their grievances.

The monarchy was still the dominant force in the country when Elizabeth died in 1603, but Parliament's demand to be heard was gathering momentum. Although the queen had been careful with money, in the last twenty years of her reign her resources had been overtaxed by war with Spain and an economic depression. Thus, she bequeathed to her successor, Scotland's James Stuart, a huge debt—£400,000, the equal of a year's royal revenue; his struggle to pay it off gave the Commons the means to seek changes in royal policy.

James I's Difficulties   Trouble began during the reign of James I (r. 1603–1625), who had a far more exalted view of his own powers than Elizabeth and who did not hesitate to tell his subjects that he considered his authority almost unlimited. In response, gentry opposed to royal policies dominated parliamentary proceedings, and they engaged in a running battle with the king. They blocked the union of England with Scotland that James sought. They drew up an "Apology" explaining his mistakes and his ignorance, as a Scotsman, of English traditions. They forced two of his ministers to resign in disgrace. And they wrung repeated concessions from him, including the unprecedented right for Parliament to discuss foreign policy.

Conflict over the Law   The Commons used the law to justify their resistance to royal power. The basic legal system of the country was the common law—justice administered on the basis of precedents and parliamentary statutes and relying on the opinions of juries. This system stood in contrast to Roman law, prevalent on the Continent, where royal edicts could make law and decisions were reached by judges without juries. Such practices existed in England only in a few royal courts of law, such as Star Chamber, which, because it was directly under the crown, came to be seen as an instrument of repression.

The common lawyers, whose leaders were also prominent in the Commons, resented the growing business of the royal courts and attacked them in Parliament. Both James and his successor were accused of pressuring judges, particularly after they won a series of famous cases involving a subject's right to criticize the monarch. Thus, the crown could be portrayed as disregarding not only the desires of the people but the law itself. The king still had broad powers, but when he exercised them contrary to Parliament's wishes, his actions seemed to many to be taking on the appearance of tyranny.

Rising Antagonisms

The confrontation between Parliament and king grew worse during the 1620s, especially in the reign of James's son, Charles I (r. 1625–1649). At the Parliament of 1628–1629, the open challenge to the crown reached a climax in the Petition of Right, which has become a landmark in constitutional history. The petition demanded an end to imprisonment without cause shown, to taxation without the consent of Parliament, to martial law in peacetime, and to the billeting of troops among civilians. Charles agreed, in the hope of gaining much-needed subsidies, but then broke his word. To many, this betrayal seemed to threaten Parliament's essential role in government alongside the king. Seeking to end discussion of these issues in the Commons, Charles ordered Parliament dissolved.

Resentful subjects were clearly on the brink of openly defying their king. Puritans, common lawyers, and disenchanted country gentry had taken over the House of Commons; Charles avoided further trouble only by refusing to call another session of Parliament. This he managed to do for eleven years, all the while increasing the repression of Puritanism and using extraordinary measures (such as reviving crown rights to special taxes that had not been demanded for a long time) to raise revenues that did not require parliamentary consent. But in 1639, the Calvinist Scots took up arms rather than accept the Anglican prayer book, and the parliamentarians had their chance. To pay for an army to fight the Scots, Charles had to turn to Parliament, which demanded that he first redress its grievances. When he resisted, civil war followed.

Civil War

By the summer of 1640, the Scots occupied most of northern England, and Charles, after quarrelling with and dismissing one assembly, was forced to summon a new Parliament. This sat for thirteen years, earning the appropriate name of the Long Parliament.

In its first year, the House of Commons abolished the royal courts, such as Star Chamber, and made mandatory the writ of habeas corpus (which prevented imprisonment without cause shown); it declared taxation without parliamentary consent illegal; and it ruled that Parliament had to meet at least once every three years. Meanwhile, the Puritans in the Commons prepared to reform the church. Oliver Cromwell, one of their leaders, demanded abolition of the Anglican Book of Common Prayer and strongly attacked the authority and very existence of bishops. The climactic vote came the next year, when the Commons passed a Grand Remonstrance, which outlined for the king all the legislation they had passed and asked that bishops be deprived of votes in the House of Lords.

The Two Sides   This demand was the prelude to a more revolutionary Puritan assault on the structure of the Church, but in fact the Grand Remonstrance passed by only eleven votes. A moderate group was detaching itself from the Puritans, and it was to become the nucleus of a royalist party. The nation's chief grievances had been redressed, and there was no longer a uniform desire for change. Still, Charles misjudged the situation and tried to arrest five leaders of the Commons, supposedly for plotting treason with the Scots. But Parliament resisted, and the citizens of London, openly hostile to Charles, sheltered the five. England now began to split in two. By late 1642 both the royalists and the antiroyalists had assembled armies, and the Civil War was under way.

What made so many people overcome their habitual loyalty to the monarchy? We know that the royalists in Parliament were considerably younger than their opponents, which suggests that it was long experience with the Stuarts and nostalgia for Elizabeth that created revolutionaries. Another clear divide was regional. The south and east of England were primarily antiroyalist, while the north and west were mostly royalist. These divisions indicated that the more cosmopolitan areas, closer to the Continent and also centers of Puritanism, were largely on Parliament's side. The decision was often a personal matter: A prominent family and its locality chose one side because its rival, a nearby family, had chosen the other. The Puritans were certainly antiroyalist, but they were a minority in the country and influential in the House of Commons only because they were so vocal and determined. Like all revolutions, this one was animated by a small group of radicals (in this case, Puritans) who alone kept the momentum going.

Independents and Presbyterians   As the fighting began, a group among the Puritans known as Independents urged that the Anglican Church be replaced by a congregational system in which each local congregation, free of all central authority, would decide its own form of worship. The most important leader of the Independents in Parliament was Oliver Cromwell. Opposed to them, but also considered Puritans, were the Presbyterians, who wanted to establish a strictly organized Calvinist system, like the one in Scotland in which local congregations were subject to centralized authority. Since both the Scots, whose alliance was vital in the war, and a majority of the Puritans in the Commons were Presbyterians, Cromwell agreed to give way, but only for the moment. The two sides also quarreled over the goals of the war. The Independents were in general more determined to force Charles into total submission, and eventually they had their way.

As the fighting continued, Cromwell persuaded the Commons to allow him to reorganize the antiroyalist troops. His New Model Army—whipped to fervor by

sermons, prayers, and the singing of psalms—became unbeatable. At Naseby in 1645, it won a major victory, and a year later Charles surrendered. The next two years were chaotic. The Presbyterians and Independents quarreled over what to do with the king, and finally civil war resumed. This time the Presbyterians and Scots backed Charles against the Independents. But even with this alliance the royalists were no match for the New Model Army; Cromwell soon defeated his opponents and captured the king.

The King's Fate At the same time, in 1647, the Independents abolished the House of Lords and removed all Presbyterians from the House of Commons. This "Rump" Parliament tried to negotiate with Charles but discovered that he continued to plot a return to power. With Cromwell's approval, the Commons decided that their monarch, untrustworthy and a troublemaker, would have to die. A trial of dubious legality was held, and though many of the participants refused to sign the death warrant, the "holy, anointed" king was executed by his subjects in January 1649, to the horror of all Europe and most of England.

England under Cromwell

Oliver Cromwell was now master of England. The republic established after Charles's execution was officially ruled by the Rump Parliament, but a Council of State led by Cromwell controlled policy with the backing of the army. And they had to contend with a ferment of political and social ideas. One group, known as the Levellers, demanded the vote for nearly all adult males and parliamentary elections every other year. The men of property among the Puritans, notably Cromwell himself, were disturbed by the egalitarianism of these proposals and insisted that only men with an "interest" in England—that is, land—should be qualified to vote.

Radical Ideas Even more radical were the Diggers, a communistic sect that sought to implement the spirit of primitive Christianity by abolishing personal property; the Society of Friends, which stressed personal inspiration as the source of faith and all action; and the Fifth Monarchists, a messianic group who believed that the "saints"—themselves—should rule because the Day of Judgment was at hand. People of great ability, such as the famous poet John Milton, contributed to the fantastic flood of pamphlets and suggestions for reform that poured forth in these years, and their ideas inspired future revolutionaries. But at the time, they merely put Cromwell on the defensive, forcing him to maintain control at all costs.

Cromwell's Aims Cromwell himself fought for two overriding causes: religious freedom (except for the Anglican and Catholic churches) and constitutional government. But he achieved neither, and he grew increasingly unhappy at the Rump Parliament's refusal to enact reforms. He dissolved the assembly in 1653 (the final end of the Long Parliament), and during the remaining five

OLIVER CROMWELL'S AIMS

When Parliament in late 1656 offered to make Oliver Cromwell the king of England as a way of restoring political stability, he hesitated before replying. When he finally came to Parliament with his response on April 13, 1657, he turned down the offer of a crown and explained in a long speech—from which a passage follows—why he felt it would be wrong to reestablish a monarchy in England.

"I do think you ought to attend to the settling of the peace and liberties of this Nation. Otherwise the Nation will fall in pieces. And in that, so far as I can, I am ready to serve not as a King, but as a Constable. For truly I have, before God, often thought that I could not tell what my business was, save comparing myself to a good Constable set to keep the peace of the parish. And truly this hath been my content and satisfaction in the troubles I have undergone . . . I was a person who, from my first employment, was suddenly lifted up from lesser trusts to greater. . . . The Providence of God hath laid aside this Title of King; and that not by sudden humor, but by issue of ten or twelve years Civil War, wherein much blood hath been shed. I will not dispute the justice of it when it was done. But God in His severity hath eradicated a whole Family, and thrust them out of the land. And God hath seemed providential not only in striking at the family but at the Name [of king]. It is blotted out. God blasted the very Title. I will not seek to set up that which Providence hath destroyed, and laid in the dust: I would not build Jericho again."

From Thomas Carlyle (ed.), *Oliver Cromwell's Letters and Speeches*, Vol. 3, London, 1908, pp. 230, 231, and 235.

years of his life he tried desperately to lay down a new constitutional structure for his government.

Cromwell was driven by noble aspirations, but in the end he had to rule by military dictatorship. From 1653 on he was called lord protector and ruled through eleven major generals, each responsible for a different district of England and supported by a tax on the estates of royalists. To quell dissent, he banned newspapers; to prevent disorder, he took such measures as enlisting innkeepers as government spies. Cromwell was always a reluctant revolutionary; he hated power and sought only limited ends. Some revolutionaries, like Lenin, have a good idea of where they would like to be carried by events; others, like Cromwell, move painfully, hesitantly, and uncertainly to the extremes they finally reach. It was because he sought England's benefit so urgently and because he considered the nation too precious to abandon to irreligion or tyranny that Cromwell remained determinedly in command to the end of his life.

The End of the Revolution Gradually, more traditional political forms reappeared. The Parliament of 1656 offered Cromwell the crown, and, though he refused, he took the title of "His Highness" and ensured that the succession would go to his son. Cromwell was monarch in all but name, yet only his presence ensured stability (see "Oliver Cromwell's Aims," above). After he died, his quiet, retiring son Richard proved no match for the scheming generals of the army, who created political turmoil. To bring an end to the uncertainty, General George Monck, the commander of a well-disciplined force in Scotland, marched south in 1660, assumed control, and invited the son of Charles I, Charles II, to return from exile and restore the monarchy.

Results of the Revolution Only the actions taken during the first months of the Long Parliament—the abolition of royal courts, the prohibition of taxation without parliamentary consent, and the establishment of the writ of habeas corpus—persisted beyond the revolution. Otherwise, everything seemed much the same as before: Bishops and lords were reinstated, religious dissent was again repressed, and Parliament was called and dissolved by the monarch. But the tone and balance of political relations had changed for good.

Henceforth, the gentry could no longer be denied a decisive voice in politics. In essence, this had been their revolution, and they had succeeded. When in the 1680s a king again tried to impose his wishes on the country without reference to Parliament, there was no need for another major upheaval. A quiet, bloodless coup reaffirmed the new role of the gentry and Parliament. The crisis of authority that had arisen from a long period of growing unease and open conflict had been resolved, and the English could settle into a system of rule that with only gradual modification remained in force for some two centuries.

Anonymous
THE SEINE FROM THE PONT NEUF, CA. 1635
Henry IV of France, celebrated in the equestrian statue overlooking the Seine that stands in Paris to this day, saw the physical reshaping of his capital as part of the effort to restore order after decades of civil war. He laid out the first squares in any European city, and under the shadow of his palace, the Louvre, he built the Pont Neuf (on the right)—the first open bridge (without houses on it) across the Seine.
Giraudon/Art Resource, NY

REVOLTS IN FRANCE AND SPAIN

The fact that political upheaval took place not only in England but in much of Europe in the 1640s and 1650s is the main reason that historians have come to speak of a "general crisis" during this period. Political institutions and political authority were being challenged in many countries, and although only England went through a revolution, the disruptions and conflicts were also significant in the two other major states of the age, France and Spain.

The France of Henry IV

In the 1590s Henry IV resumed the strengthening of royal power, which had been interrupted by the civil wars that had begun in the 1560s. He mollified the traditional landed aristocracy, known as the nobility of the sword, with places on his Council of Affairs and with large financial settlements. The principal bureaucrats, known as the nobility of the robe, controlled the country's administration, and Henry made sure to turn their interests to his benefit. Because all crown offices had to be bought, he used the system both to raise revenues and to guarantee the loyalty of the bureaucrats. He not only accelerated the sales of offices but also invented a

new device, an annual fee known as the *paulette,* which ensured that an officeholder's job would remain in his family when he died. This increased royal profits and also reduced the flow of newcomers, thus strengthening the commitment of existing officeholders to the crown.

By 1610 Henry had imposed his will throughout France, and he was secure enough to plan an invasion of the Holy Roman Empire. Although he was assassinated before he could join his army, and the invasion was called off, his heritage, especially in economic affairs, long outlived him. France's rich agriculture may have had one unfortunate effect—successful merchants abandoned commerce as soon as they could afford to move to the country and buy a title of nobility (and thus gain exemption from taxes)—but it did ensure a solid basis for the French economy. Indeed, agriculture suffered little during the civil wars, though the violence and the rising taxes did cause uprisings of peasants (the main victims of the tax system) almost every year from the 1590s to the 1670s.

Mercantilism   By restoring political stability, Henry ended the worst economic disruptions, but his main legacy was the notion that his increasingly powerful government was responsible for the health of the country's economy. This view was justified by a theory

RICHELIEU ON DIPLOMACY

The following passages are taken from a collection of the writings of Cardinal Richelieu that was put together after his death and published in 1688 under the title Political Testament. *The book is presented as a work of advice to the king and summarizes what Richelieu learned of politics and diplomacy as one of Europe's leading statesmen during the Thirty Years' War.*

"One cannot imagine how many advantages States gain from continued negotiations, if conducted wisely, unless one has experienced it oneself. I admit I did not realize this truth for five or six years after first being employed in the management of policy. But I am now so sure of it that I say boldly that to negotiate everywhere without cease, openly and secretly, even though one makes no immediate gains and future gains seem unlikely, is absolutely necessary for the good of the State. . . . He who negotiates all the time will find at last the right moment to achieve his aims, and even if he does not find it, at least it is true that he can lose nothing, and that through his negotiations he knows what is happening in the world, which is of no small consequence for the good of the State. . . . Important negotia-tions must not be interrupted for a moment. . . . One must not be disheartened by an unfortunate turn of events, because sometimes it happens that what is undertaken with good reason is achieved with little good fortune. . . . It is difficult to fight often and always win. . . . It is often because negotiations are so innocent that one can gain great advantages from them without ever faring badly. . . . In matters of State one must find an advantage in everything; that which can be useful must never be neglected."

From Louis Andrè (ed.), *Testament Politique* (Editions Robert Laffont, 1947), pp. 347–348 and 352; translated by T. K. Rabb.

developed mainly in France: **mercantilism,** which became an essential ingredient of absolutism. Mercantilism was more a set of attitudes than a systematic economic theory. Its basic premise—an erroneous one—was that the world contained a fixed amount of wealth and that each nation could enrich itself only at the expense of others. To some thinkers, this theory meant hoarding bullion (gold and silver); to others, it required a favorable balance of trade—more exports than imports. All mercantilists, however, agreed that state regulation of economic affairs was necessary for the welfare of a country. Only a strong, centralized government could encourage native industries, control production, set quality standards, allocate resources, establish tariffs, and take other measures to promote prosperity and improve trade. Thus, mercantilism was as much about politics as economics and fit perfectly with Henry's restoration of royal power. In line with their advocacy of activist policies, the mercantilists also approved of war. Even economic advance was linked to warfare in this violent age.

Louis XIII

Unrest reappeared when Henry's death left the throne to his nine-year-old son, Louis XIII (r. 1610–1643). The widowed queen, Marie de Medici, served as regent and soon faced revolts by Calvinists and disgruntled nobles. In the face of these troubles, Marie summoned the Es-tates General in 1614. This was their last meeting for 175 years, until the eve of the French Revolution; and the weakness they displayed, as various groups within the Estates fought one another over plans for political reform, demonstrated that the monarchy was the only institution that could unite the nation. The session revealed the impotence of those who opposed royal policies, and Marie brought criticism to an end by declaring her son to be of age and the regency dissolved. In this absolutist state, further protest could be defined as treason.

Richelieu For a decade, the monarchy lacked energetic direction; but in 1624, one of Marie's favorites, Armand du Plessis de Richelieu, a churchman who rose to be a cardinal through her favor, became chief minister and took control of the government. Over the next eighteen years, this ambitious and determined leader resumed Henry IV's assertion of royal authority (see "Richelieu on Diplomacy," above).

The monarchy had to manage a number of vested interests as it concentrated its power, and Richelieu's achievement was that he kept them under control. The strongest was the bureaucracy, whose ranks had been swollen by the sale of offices. Richelieu always paid close attention to the views of the bureaucrats, and one reason he had such influence over the king was that he acted as the head and representative of this army of royal servants. He also reduced the independence of traditional nobles by giving them positions in the regime as diplomats, soldiers, and officials without significant administrative responsibility. Finally, he took on the Huguenots in a military campaign. After he defeated them, he abolished most of the guarantees in the Edict of Nantes and ended the Huguenots' political independence.

Royal Administration   Under Richelieu the sale of offices broke all bounds: By 1633 it accounted for approximately one-half of royal revenues. Ten years later more than three-quarters of the crown's direct taxation was needed to pay the salaries of the officeholders. It was a vicious circle, and the only solution was to increase the taxes on the lower classes. As this financial burden grew, Richelieu had to improve the government's control over the realm to obtain the revenue he needed. He increased the power of the **intendants,** the government's chief agents in the localities, and established them (instead of the nobles) as the principal representatives of the monarchy in each province of France. Unlike the nobles, the *intendants* depended entirely on royal favor for their position; consequently, they enthusiastically recruited for the army, arranged billeting, supervised the raising of taxes, and enforced the king's decrees. They soon came to be hated figures, both because of the rising taxes and because they threatened the power of the nobles. The result was a succession of peasant uprisings, often led by local notables who resented the rise of the *intendants* and of royal power.

Political and Social Crisis

France's foreign wars made the discontent worse, and it was clear that eventually the opponents of the central government would reassert themselves. But the centralization of power by the crown had been so successful that when trouble erupted, in a series of revolts known as the *Fronde* (or "sling," the simple weapon of the rebels), there was no serious effort to reshape the social order or the political system. The principal actors in the Fronde came from the upper levels of society: nobles, townsmen, and members of the regional courts and legislatures known as parlements. Only rarely were these groups joined by peasants, who may have been resentful of taxes and other government demands and vulnerable to starvation when harvests failed, but the Fronde never raised issues that connected with the peasants' uprisings. These focused on issues like food scarcities, which often brought women into prominent roles, especially since soldiers were reluctant to shoot them. But without noble support, such disorders remained fairly low-scale; they never reached the level of disruption that was to overtake France in the Revolution.

Mazarin   The death of Louis XIII in 1643, followed by a regency because Louis XIV was only five years old, offered an opportunity to those who wanted to reverse the rise of absolutism. Louis XIII's widow, Anne of Austria, took over the government and placed all the power in the hands of an Italian, Cardinal Giulio Mazarin. He used his position to amass a huge fortune, and he was therefore a perfect target for the anger caused by the encroachment of central government on local authority.

Early in 1648 Mazarin sought to gain a respite from the monarch's perennial financial trouble by withholding payment of the salaries of some royal officials for four years. In response, the members of various institutions in Paris, including the Parlement, drew up a charter of demands. They wanted the office of *intendant* abolished, no new offices created, power to approve taxes, and enactment of a habeas corpus law.

The Fronde   Mazarin reacted by arresting the Paris Parlement's leaders, thus sparking a popular rebellion in the city that forced him and the royal family to flee from the capital—an experience the young Louis XIV never forgot. In 1649 Mazarin promised to redress the *parlementaires'* grievances, and he was allowed to return to Paris. But the trouble was far from over; during that summer, uprisings spread throughout France, particularly among peasants and in the old Huguenot stronghold, the southwest.

The next three years were marked by political chaos, mainly as a result of intrigues and shifting alliances among the nobility. As it became clear that the perpetual unrest was producing no results, Mazarin was able to take advantage of disillusionment among nobles and *parlementaires* to reassert the position of the monarchy. He used military force and threats of force to subdue Paris and most of the rebels in the countryside, and he brought the regency to an end by declaring the fourteen-year-old Louis of age in 1652. Although the nobles were not finally subdued until the following year, and peasants continued their occasional regional uprisings for many years to come, the crown now established its authority as the basis for order in the realm. As surely as England, France had surmounted its crisis and found a stable solution for long-standing conflicts.

Sources of Discontent in Spain

For Spain the crisis that swept much of Europe in the mid-seventeenth century—with revolt in England and France and war in the empire—meant the end of the country's international power. Yet the difficulties the monarchy faced had their roots in the sixteenth century. Philip II had already found it difficult to hold his sprawling empire together despite his elaborate bureaucracy. Obsessively suspicious, he maintained close

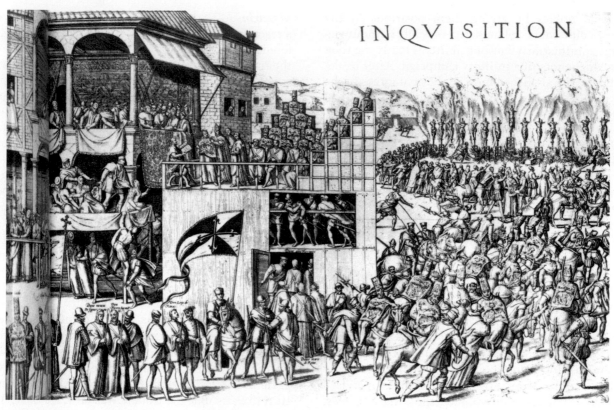

INQVISITION

Anonymous
ENGRAVING OF THE SPANISH INQUISITION, 1560
The burning of heretics was a major public event in sixteenth-century Spain. Aimed mainly at people who practiced Judaism or Islam secretly and in a few cases at Protestants, the Inquisition's investigations usually led to imprisonment or lesser punishments. The occasional executions of those who determinedly refused to accept Catholic teachings, even after torture, were carried out by secular authorities, and they attracted huge crowds.
Bibliothèque Nationale de France, Paris

control over all administrative decisions, and government action was, therefore, agonizingly slow. Moreover, the bureaucracy was run by Castilian nobles, who were resented as outsiders in other regions of the empire. And the standing army, though essential to royal power, was a terrible financial drain.

Philip did gain wide admiration in Spain for his devoutness. His commitment to religion undoubtedly promoted political cohesion, but the economic strains caused by relentless religious warfare eventually undermined Spanish power.

Economic Difficulties Spain was a rich country in Philip's reign, but the most profitable activities were monopolized by limited groups. Because royal policy valued convenience above social benefit, the city of Seville (dominated by foreign bankers) received a monopoly over shipping to and from the New World; other lucrative pursuits, such as wool and wine production, were also controlled by a small coterie of insiders. The

only important economic activities that involved large numbers of Spaniards were shipping and the prosperous Mediterranean trade, centered in Barcelona, which brought wealth to much of Catalonia. Thus, the influx of silver into Spain was not profitably invested within the country. Drastically overextended in foreign commitments, Philip had to declare himself bankrupt three times. For a while it seemed that the problems might ease because there was peace during the reign of Philip's son, Philip III (r. 1598–1621). But in fact, Philip III's government was incompetent and corrupt, capable neither of dealing with the serious consequences of the spending on war nor of broadening the country's exports beyond wool and wine. And when the flow of treasure from the New World began to dwindle after 1600, the crown was deprived of a major source of income that it was unable to replace (see "Imports of Treasure to Spain . . . ," p. 453). The decline was caused partly by a growing use of precious metals in the New World colonies but also by depletion of the mines.

IMPORTS OF TREASURE TO SPAIN FROM THE NEW WORLD, 1591–1660	
Decade	Total Value*
1591–1600	85,536,000
1601–1610	66,970,000
1611–1620	65,568,000
1621–1630	62,358,000
1631–1640	40,110,000
1641–1650	30,651,000
1651–1660	12,785,000

*In ducats.

Adapted from J. H. Elliott, *Imperial Spain, 1469–1716,* Edward Arnold, Hodder Neadling PLC Group, 1964, p. 175.

In the meantime, tax returns at home were shrinking. The most significant cause of this decrease was a series of severe plagues, which reduced the population of Castile and Aragon from 10 million in 1590 to 6 million in 1700. No other country in Europe suffered a demographic reversal of this proportion during the seventeenth century. In addition, sheep farming took over huge tracts of arable land, and Spain had to rely increasingly on imports of expensive foodstuffs to feed its people. When Spain resumed large-scale fighting against the Dutch and French under Philip IV (r. 1621–1665), the burdens became too much to bear. The effort to maintain the commitment to war despite totally inadequate finances was to bring the greatest state in Europe to its knees.

Revolt and Secession

The final crisis was brought about by the policies of Philip IV's chief minister, the count of Olivares. His aim was to unite the realm so that all the territories shared equally the burden of maintaining Spanish power. Although Castile would no longer dominate the government, it would also not have to provide the bulk of the taxes and army. Olivares' program was called the Union of Arms, and while it seemed eminently reasonable, it caused a series of revolts in the 1640s that split Spain apart.

The reason was that Castile's dominance had made the other provinces feel that local independence was being undermined by a centralized regime. They saw the Union of Arms, imposed by Olivares, as the last straw. Moreover, the plan appeared at a time when Spain's military and economic fortunes were in decline. France had declared war on the Habsburgs in 1635, the funds to support an army were becoming harder to raise, and in desperation Olivares pressed more vigorously for the Union of Arms. But all he accomplished was to provoke revolts against Castile in the 1640s by Catalonia, Portugal, Naples, and Sicily. By 1641 Catalonia and Portugal had declared themselves independent republics and placed themselves under French protection. Plots began to appear against Olivares, and Philip dismissed the one minister who had understood Spain's problems but who, in trying to solve them, had made them worse.

The Revolts The Catalonian rebellion continued for another eleven years, and it was thwarted in the end only because the peasants and town mobs transformed the resistance to the central government into an attack on the privileged and wealthy classes. When this happened, the Catalan nobility abandoned the cause and joined the government side. About the same time, the Fronde forced the withdrawal of French troops from Catalonia. When the last major holdout, Barcelona, fell to a royal army in 1652, the Catalan nobles could regain their rights and powers, and the revolt was over.

The Portuguese had no social upheaval; as a result, though not officially granted independence from Spain until 1668, they defended their autonomy easily and even invaded Castile in the 1640s. But the revolts that the people of Sicily and Naples directed at their Castilian rulers in 1647 took on social overtones. In Naples the unrest developed into a tremendous mob uprising led by a local fisherman. The poor turned against all representatives of government and wealth they could find, and chaos ensued until the leader of the revolt was killed. The violence in Sicily, the result of soaring taxes, was aimed primarily at government officials. But in both Naples and Sicily the government was able to reassert its authority by force within a few months.

Consequences The effect of this unrest was to end the Spanish government's international ambitions and, thus, the worst of its economic difficulties. Like England and France, Spain found a new way of life after its crisis: It became a stable second-level state, heavily agricultural, run by its nobility.

POLITICAL CHANGE IN AN AGE OF CRISIS

Although the level of violence was highest in England and Spain, almost all of Europe's countries experienced the political upheavals of this era of "general crisis." In some cases—for instance, Sweden—the conflict was minor and did little to disturb the peace of the land. But everywhere the basic issue—Who should hold political authority?—caused some degree of strife. And

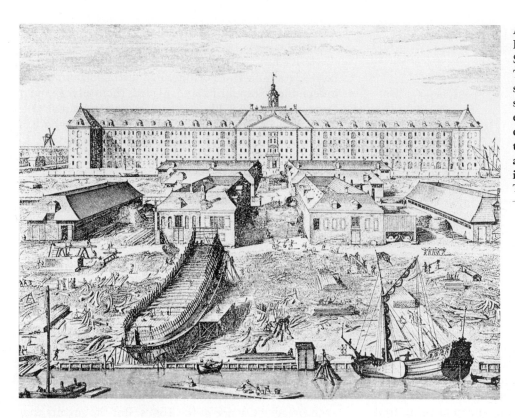

Anonymous
ENGRAVING OF A DUTCH
SHIPYARD
**The Dutch became the best
shipbuilders in Europe in the
seventeenth century; the
efficiency of their ships, which
could be manned by fewer sailors
than those of other countries, was
a major reason for their successes
in trade and commerce.**
The Granger Collection, New York

each state had to find its own solutions to the competing demands of governments and their subjects.

The United Provinces

The Dutch did not escape the struggles against the power of centralized governments that created an atmosphere of crisis in much of Europe during the middle decades of the seventeenth century. Despite the remarkable fluidity of their society, the Dutch, too, became embroiled in a confrontation between a ruling family seeking to extend its authority and citizens defending the autonomy of their local regions. The outcome determined the structure of their government for more than a century.

The United Provinces were unique in a number of ways. Other republics existed in Europe, but they were controlled by small oligarchies; the Dutch, who had a long tradition of a strong representative assembly, the Estates General, had created a nation in which many citizens participated in government through elected delegates. Although powerful merchants and a few aristocrats close to the House of Orange did create a small elite, the social differentiation was less than elsewhere in Europe. The resulting openness and homogeneity underlay the economic mastery and cultural brilliance of the United Provinces.

Commerce and Tolerance   The most striking accomplishment of the Dutch was their rise to supremacy in the world of commerce. Amsterdam displaced Antwerp as the Continent's financial capital and gained control of the trade of the world's richest markets. In addition, the Dutch rapidly emerged as the cheapest international shippers. As a result, by the middle of the seventeenth century they had become the chief carriers of European commerce.

The openness of Dutch society permitted the freest exchange of ideas of the time. The new state gave refuge to believers of all kinds, whether extreme Protestant radicals or Catholics who wore their faith lightly, and Amsterdam became the center of a brilliant Jewish community. This freedom attracted some of the greatest minds in Europe and fostered remarkable artistic creativity. The energy that produced this outpouring reflected the pride of a tiny nation that was winning its independence from Spain.

Two Political Parties   There was, however, a basic split within the United Provinces. The two most urbanized and commercial provinces, Holland and Zeeland, dominated the Estates General because they supplied a majority of its taxes. Their representatives formed a mercantile party, which advocated peace abroad so that their trade could flourish unhampered, government by the Estates General so that they could make their influence felt, and religious toleration so that their cities could attract enterprising people of all faiths. In opposition to this mercantile interest was the House of Orange: the descendants of William of Orange, who sought to establish their family's leadership of the Dutch. They were supported by the more rural provinces and stood for war because their authority and popularity derived from their command of the army, for centralized power to enhance the position of the family, and for the strict Calvinism that was upheld in the rural provinces.

The differences between the two factions led Maurice of Nassau to use religion as a pretext to execute his chief opponent, Jan van Oldenbarneveldt, the representative of the province of Holland, in 1618. Oldenbarneveldt was against war with Spain, and his removal left the House of Orange in control of the country. Maurice resumed the war in 1621, and for more than twenty years, his family remained in command, unassailable because it led the army in wartime. Not until 1648—when a new leader, William II, tried to prolong the fighting—did the mercantile party reassert itself by insisting on peace. As a result, the Dutch signed the Treaty of Westphalia, which recognized the independence of the United Provinces. It now seemed that Holland and Zeeland had gained the upper hand. But their struggle with the House of Orange continued (there was even a threat by Orange troops to besiege Amsterdam) until William II suddenly died in 1650, leaving as his successor a baby son, William III.

Jan De Witt   The mercantile interest now assumed full power, and Jan De Witt, the representative of the province of Holland, took over the government in 1653. De Witt's aims were to leave as much authority as possible in the hands of the provinces, particularly Holland; to weaken the executive and prevent a revival of the House of Orange; to pursue trading advantage; and to maintain peace so that the economic supremacy of the Dutch would not be endangered. For nearly twenty years he guided the country in its golden age. But in 1672 French armies overran the southern provinces, and De Witt lacked the military instinct to fight a dangerous enemy. The Dutch at once turned to the family that had led them to independence; a mob murdered De Witt; and the House of Orange, under William III, resumed the centralization that henceforth was to characterize the political structure of the United Provinces. The country had not experienced a midcentury upheaval as severe as those of its neighbors, but it had nevertheless been forced to endure unrest and violence before the form of its government was securely established.

Sweden

The Swedes, too, settled their political system in the mid-seventeenth century. In 1600 Sweden, a Lutheran country of a million people, was one of the backwaters of Europe. A feudal nobility dominated the countryside, a barter economy made money almost unknown, and both trade and towns were virtually nonexistent. Moreover, the country lacked a capital, central institutions, and government machinery. The royal administration consisted of the king and a few courtiers; other officials were appointed only to deal with specific problems as they arose.

Gustavus Adolphus (r. 1611–1632) transformed this situation. He won over the nobles by giving them dominant positions in a newly expanded bureaucracy, and he reorganized his army. Thus equipped both to govern and to fight, Gustavus embarked on a remarkable series of conquests abroad. By 1629 he had made Sweden the most powerful state in the Baltic area. He then entered the Thirty Years' War, advancing victoriously through the Holy Roman Empire until his death, in 1632, during the showdown battle with Wallenstein. Without their great general, the Swedes could do little more than hang on to their gains, but they were now a force to be reckoned with in international affairs.

Government and Economy　The highly efficient system of government established by Gustavus and his chief adviser, Axel Oxenstierna, was to be the envy of other countries until the twentieth century. At the heart of the system were five administrative departments, each led by a nobleman, with the most important—the Chancellery, for diplomacy and internal affairs—run by Oxenstierna. An administrative center emerged in Stockholm, and the new bureaucracy proved that it could run the nation, supply the army, and implement policy even during the last twelve years of Gustavus' reign, when the king himself was almost always abroad.

A major cause of Sweden's amazing rise was the development of the domestic economy, stimulated by the opening up of copper mines and the development of a major iron industry. The country's traditional tar and timber exports were also stepped up, and a fleet was built. By 1700 Stockholm had become an important trading and financial center, growing in the course of the century from fewer than five thousand to more than fifty thousand inhabitants.

The Nobles　The one source of tension amidst this remarkable progress was the position of the nobles. After Gustavus died, they openly challenged the monarchy for control of government and society. Between 1611 and 1652 they more than doubled the proportion of land they owned in Sweden, and much of this growth was at the expense of the crown, which granted away or sold lands to help the war effort abroad. Both peasants and townspeople viewed these developments with alarm, because the nobility usually pursued its own, rather than public, interests. The concern intensified when, in 1648, the nobles in neighboring Denmark took advantage of the death of a strong king to gain control of their government. Two years later the showdown came in Sweden.

Political Confrontation　The monarch now was Gustavus' daughter Christina, an able but erratic young queen who usually allowed Oxenstierna to run the government. For some time, she had hoped to abdicate her throne, become a Catholic, and leave Sweden—an ambition she fulfilled in 1654. She wanted her cousin Charles recognized as her successor, but the nobles threatened to create a republic if she abdicated. The queen, therefore, summoned the Riksdag, Sweden's usually weak representative assembly, in 1650; she encouraged the townspeople and peasants to raise their grievances and allowed them to attack the aristocracy. Soon these groups were demanding the return of nobles' lands to the crown, freedom of speech, and real power; under this pressure, the nobility gave way and recognized Charles X as successor to the throne.

The political upheaval of 1650 was short-lived. Once Christina had her way, she turned against the Riksdag and rejected the lower estates' demands. Only gradually did power shift away from the great nobles toward a broader elite of lesser nobles and bureaucrats, but the turning point in Sweden, as elsewhere, was during the crisis years of the mid-seventeenth century.

Eastern Europe and the Crisis

In Eastern Europe, too, long-term patterns became clear in this period. The limits of Ottoman rule were reconfirmed when an attack on Vienna failed in 1683. Although the Ottomans' control of the Balkans did not immediately waver, their government was increasingly beset by internal problems, and their retreat from Hungary was under way by 1700. Further north, Poland's weak central government lost all claim to real authority in 1648 when it proved unable to stop a group of nobles in the rich province of the Ukraine from switching allegiance from the king of Poland to the tsar in Moscow. And in Russia, following a period of disorder known as the Time of Troubles (1584–1613), the new Romanov **Dynasty** began consolidating its power. The nobility was won over; the last possibilities for escaping serfdom were closed; the legal system was codified; the church came under the tsar's control; and the revolts that erupted against these changes between 1648 and 1672—involving peasants and Cossacks (marauding horsemen, mainly from the South), and often looking like rural revolts in the West, especially France—were brutally suppressed. As elsewhere in Europe, long-standing conflicts between centralizing regimes and their opponents were resolved, and a new political system, supported by the government's military power, was established for centuries to come. Further east, the Ming Dynasty of China was overthrown by the new Ch'ing Dynasty in 1644, a shift that was also accompanied by peasant revolts. That parallel suggests that this was a time of upheaval throughout much of the world, possibly because of a cooling in climate that affected food crops. But everywhere the outcome was a return to stability: crisis there may have been, but the restoration of order was a worldwide phenomenon, too.

Summary

Because these struggles were so widespread, historians have called the midcentury period an age of "general crisis." In country after country, people tried to resist the growing ambitions of central governments. These confrontations reached crisis proportions in almost all cases during the 1640s and 1650s and then subsided at the very time that the anarchy of warfare and international relations was resolved by the Peace of Westphalia. As a result, the sense of settlement after 1660 contrasted sharply with the turmoil of the preceding decades. Moreover, the progression in politics from turbulence to calm had its analogs in the cultural and social developments of the sixteenth and seventeenth centuries.

QUESTIONS FOR FURTHER THOUGHT

1. Are the social benefits of warfare so minimal, compared to its destructive effects, that one can dismiss them as unimportant?

2. Why are there differences in the ways warfare changes domestic politics?

RECOMMENDED READING

Sources

Bodin, Jean. *On Sovereignty*. Julian H. Franklin (ed. and tr.). 1992. An abridgment of Bodin's *Six Books of the Republic*.

Kossmann, E. H., and A. E. Mellink. *Texts Concerning the Revolt of the Netherlands*. 1974. A collection of Spanish and Dutch documents that reveal the different political and religious goals of the two sides.

Studies

*Aston, Trevor (ed.). *Crisis in Europe, 1560–1660: Essays from Past and Present*. 1965. This is a collection of the essays in which the "general crisis" interpretation was initially put forward and discussed.

Braudel, Fernand. *The Mediterranean and the Mediterranean World in the Age of Philip II*. S. Reynolds (tr.). 2 vols. 1972 and 1973. A pioneering and far-ranging work of social history.

Coward, Barry. *The Cromwellian Protectorate*. 2002.

*Duplessis, Robert R. *Transitions to Capitalism in Early Modern Europe*. 1997.

*Elliott, J. H. *Richelieu and Olivares*. 1984. A comparative study of the two statesmen who dominated Europe in the 1620s and 1630s; also analyzes the changing nature of political authority.

*Hale, J. R. *War and Society in Renaissance Europe, 1450–1620*. 1985. A vivid account of what it meant to be a soldier.

Kishlansky, Mark A. *A Monarchy Transformed: Britain, 1603–1714*. 1997.

MacCaffrey, Wallace. *Elizabeth I*. 1994.

*Mattingly, Garrett. *The Armada*. 1959. This beautifully written book, which was a best seller when it first appeared, is a gripping account of a major international crisis.

Moote, A. Lloyd. *The Revolt of the Judges: The Parlement of Paris and the Fronde, 1643–1652*. 1971. The most detailed account of the causes of the Fronde and its failures.

Parker, Geoffrey. *The Army of Flanders and the Spanish Road, 1567–1659: The Logistics of Spanish Victory and Defeat in the Low Countries' Wars*. 2004.

———. *The Dutch Revolt*. 1977. This brief book gives a good introduction to the revolt of the Netherlands and the nature of Dutch society in the seventeenth century.

———. *The Thirty Years' War*. 1984. The most up-to-date history of the war.

Parker, Geoffrey, and Lesley M. Smith (eds.). *The General Crisis of the Seventeenth Century*. 1997.

Pierson, Peter. *Philip II of Spain*. 1975. A clear and lively biography of the dominant figure of the second half of the sixteenth century.

*Rabb, Theodore K. *The Struggle for Stability in Early Modern Europe*. 1975. An assessment of the "crisis" interpretation, including extensive bibliographic references.

Rogers, Clifford, J. *The Military Revolution Debate: Readings on the Military Transformation of Early Modern Europe*. 1995.

*Available in paperback.

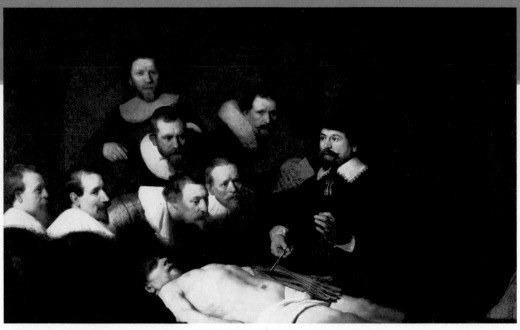

Rembrandt van Rijn
THE ANATOMY LESSON OF DR. NICOLAAS TULP, **1632**
**Among the many representations of the public anatomy lessons so popular in seventeenth-
century Holland, the most famous is one of Rembrandt's greatest paintings,** *The Anatomy Lesson
of Dr. Nicolaas Tulp.* **Here art reflects the new fascination with science.**
Mauritshuis, The Hague

Chapter Sixteen

CULTURE AND SOCIETY IN THE AGE OF THE SCIENTIFIC REVOLUTION

SCIENTIFIC ADVANCE FROM COPERNICUS TO NEWTON • THE EFFECTS OF THE DISCOVERIES • THE ARTS AND LITERATURE • SOCIAL PATTERNS AND POPULAR CULTURE

Of all the many changes of the sixteenth and seventeenth centuries, none had a more far-reaching impact than the scientific revolution. By creating a new way of understanding how nature worked—and by solving long-standing problems in physics, astronomy, and anatomy—the theorists and experimenters of this period gave Europeans a new sense of confidence and certainty. They also began to set their civilization apart from those of the rest of the world, where the outlook of the scientist did not take hold for centuries. Although the revolution began with disturbing questions, but few clear answers, about the physical world, it ended by offering a promise of knowledge and truth that was eagerly embraced by a society racked by decades of religious and political turmoil and uncertainty. Indeed, it is remarkable how closely intellectual and cultural patterns paralleled the progression from struggle and doubt to stable resolution that marked the political developments of these years. In the mid-seventeenth century, just as Europe's states were able to create more settled conditions following a major crisis, so in the realms of philosophy and the study of nature a long period of searching, anxiety, and dispute was resolved by scientists whose discoveries and self-assurance helped restore a sense of order in intellectual life. And in literature, the arts, and social relations, a time of insecurity and doubt also gave way to an atmosphere of confidence and calm.

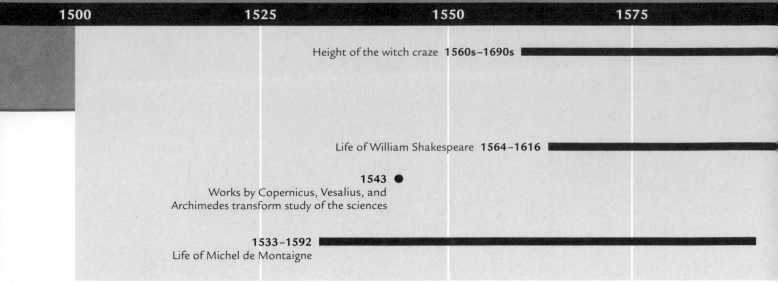

Height of the witch craze **1560s–1690s**

Life of William Shakespeare **1564–1616**

1543 ●
Works by Copernicus, Vesalius, and
Archimedes transform study of the sciences

1533–1592
Life of Michel de Montaigne

SCIENTIFIC ADVANCE FROM COPERNICUS TO NEWTON

Fundamental to the transformation of Europe in the seventeenth century were advances in the knowledge of how nature worked. At first the new discoveries added to the uncertainties of the age, but eventually the scientists were seen as models of orderly thought, who had at last solved ancient problems in convincing fashion.

Origins of the Scientific Revolution

The Importance of Antiquity   Until the sixteenth century, the study of nature in Europe was inspired by the ancient Greeks. Their work shaped subsequent research in three main fields: Aristotle in physics, Ptolemy in astronomy, and Galen in medicine. The most dramatic advances during the **scientific revolution** came in these fields, to some extent because it was becoming evident that the ancient theories could not account for new observations without highly complicated adjustments. For instance, Ptolemy's picture of the heavens, in which all motion was circular around a central earth, did not readily explain the peculiar motion that observers noticed in some planets, which at times seemed to be moving backward. Similarly, dissections often showed Galen's anatomical theories to be wrong.

Despite these problems, scientists (who in the sixteenth and seventeenth centuries were still known as "natural philosophers," or seekers of wisdom about nature) preferred making adjustments rather than beginning anew. And it is unlikely they would have abandoned their cherished theories if it had not been for other influences at work in this period. One such

stimulus to rethinking was the Humanists' rediscovery of a number of previously unknown ancient scientists, who had not always agreed with the theories of Aristotle or Ptolemy. A particularly important rediscovery was the work of Archimedes, whose writings on dynamics helped inspire new ideas in physics.

The Influence of "Magical" Beliefs   Another influence was a growing interest in what we now dismiss as "magic," but which at the time was regarded as a serious intellectual enterprise. There were various avenues of magical inquiry, many of which had been pursued in other civilizations, as well as Europe, for centuries. Alchemy was the belief that matter could be understood and transformed by mixing substances and using secret formulas. A famous sixteenth-century alchemist, Paracelsus, suggested that metals as well as plants might have medicinal properties, and he helped demonstrate that mercury (if carefully used) could cure syphilis. Another favorite study was astrology, which claimed that natural phenomena could be predicted if planetary movements were properly interpreted.

What linked these "magical" beliefs was the conviction that the world could be understood through simple, comprehensive keys to nature. The theories of Neoplatonism—an influential school of thought during the Renaissance, based on Plato's belief that truth lay in essential but hidden "forms"—supported this conviction, as did some of the mystical ideas that attracted attention at this time. One of the latter, derived from a system of Jewish thought known as *cabala*, suggested that the universe might be built around magical arrangements of numbers. The ancient Greek mathematician Pythagoras had also suggested that numerical patterns might connect all of nature, and his ideas now gained new attention. For all its irrational elements, it

1606–1669 Life of Rembrandt van Rijn

1607 Premier of Monteverdi's opera *Orfeo*

1633 Condemnation of Galileo by the Inquisition

1637 Descartes, *Discourse on Method*

1660 Founding of the Royal Society in London

1687 Newton, *Principia*

was precisely this interest in new and simple solutions for long-standing problems that made natural philosophers capable, for the first time, of discarding the honored theories they had inherited from antiquity, trying different ones, paying greater attention to mathematics, and eventually creating an intellectual revolution.

Observations, Experiments, and Instruments Two other influences deserve mention. The first was Europe's fascination with technological invention. The architects, navigators, engineers, and weapons experts of the Renaissance were important pioneers of a new reliance on measurement and observation that affected not only how domes were built or heavy cannons were moved but also how problems in physics were addressed. A second, and related, influence was the growing interest in experiment among anatomists. In particular, the medical school at the University of Padua became famous for its dissections and direct observations of nature; many leading figures in the scientific revolution were trained there.

It was not too surprising, therefore, that during the sixteenth and seventeenth centuries important new instruments were invented, which helped make scientific discovery possible: the telescope, the vacuum pump, the thermometer, the barometer, and the microscope. These instruments encouraged the development of a scientific approach that was entirely new in the seventeenth century: It did not go back to the ancients, to the practitioners of magic, or to the engineers. This approach rested on the belief that in order to make nature reveal its secrets, it had to be made to do things it did not do normally. What this meant was that one did not simply observe phenomena that occurred normally in nature—for instance, the way a stick seems to bend when it is placed in a glass of water—but created

Pieter Brueghel the Elder
THE ALCHEMIST
This down-to-earth portrayal, typical of Brueghel's art, shows the alchemist as an undisciplined figure. He is surrounded by a chaos of instruments and half-finished experiments, and his helpers resemble witches. Like Brueghel, most people thought it unlikely that this disorganized figure would make a major contribution to the understanding of nature.
Pen and brown ink on paper, Kd Z 4399. Kupferstichkabinett, Staatliche Museen zu Berlin, Germany. Bildarchiv Preussischer Kulturbesitz/Art Resource, NY

461

conditions that were not normal. With the telescope, one saw secrets hidden to the naked eye; with the vacuum pump, one could understand the properties of air.

The Breakthroughs

Vesalius   The earliest scientific advances came in anatomy and astronomy, and by coincidence they were announced in two books published in 1543, which was also the year when the earliest printed edition of Archimedes appeared. The first book, *The Structure of the Human Body* by Andreas Vesalius (1514–1564), a member of the Padua faculty, pointed out errors in the work of Galen, the chief authority in medical practice for over a thousand years. Using dissections, Vesalius produced anatomical descriptions that opened a new era of careful observation and experimentation in studies of the body.

Copernicus   The second book, *On the Revolutions of the Heavenly Spheres* by Nicolaus Copernicus (1473–1543), a Polish cleric who had studied at Padua, had far greater consequences. A first-rate mathematician, Copernicus believed that the calculations of planetary movements under Ptolemy's system had grown too complex. In Ptolemaic astronomy, the planets and the sun, attached to transparent, crystalline spheres, revolved around the earth. All motion was circular, and irregularities were accounted for by **epicycles**—movement around small revolving spheres that were attached to the larger spheres. Influenced by Neoplatonic ideas, Copernicus believed that a simpler picture would reflect more accurately the true structure of the universe. In sound Neoplatonic fashion, he argued that the sun, as the most splendid of celestial bodies, ought rightfully to be at the center of an orderly and harmonious universe. The earth, no longer immobile, would thus circle the sun.

Copernicus' system was, in fact, scarcely simpler than Ptolemy's—the spheres and epicycles were just as complex—and he had no way of demonstrating the superiority of his theory. But he was such a fine mathematician that his successors found his calculations of planetary motions indispensable. His ideas thus became part of intellectual discussion, drawn on when Pope Gregory XIII decided to reform the calendar in 1582. The Julian calendar, in use since Roman times, counted century years as leap years, thus adding extra days that caused Easter—whose date is determined by the position of the sun—to drift farther and farther away from its normal occurrence in late March. The reform produced the Gregorian calendar, which we still use. Ten days were simply dropped: October 5, 1582, became October 15; and since then only one out of every four century years has been counted as a leap year (1900 had no February 29, but 2000 did). The need

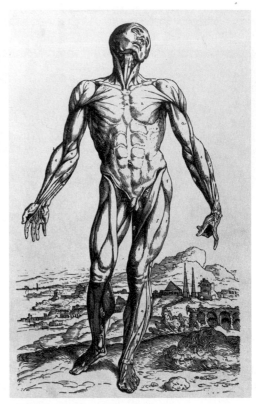

Titian (attrib.)
ENGRAVING ILLUSTRATING THE STRUCTURE OF THE HUMAN BODY BY ANDREAS VESALIUS, 1543
Almost as remarkable as the findings themselves were these illustrations of the results of Vesalius' dissections. Traditionally, professors of anatomy read from textbooks to their students while lowly barber-surgeons cut up a cadaver and displayed the parts being discussed. Vesalius did his dissections himself and thus could observe directly such structures as the musculature. Here his illustrator displays the muscles on a gesturing figure and places it in a stretch of countryside near Padua, where Vesalius taught.

for calendar reform had been one of the motives for Copernicus' studies, which thus proved useful even though his theories remained controversial.

Theories in Conflict   For more than half a century, the effect of *Revolutions* was growing uncertainty, as the scholarly community argued over the validity of the new ideas. The leading astronomer of the period, the Dane Tycho Brahe (1546–1601), produced the most remarkable observations of the heavens before the invention of the telescope by plotting the paths of the moon and planets every night for decades. But the only theory he could come up with was an uneasy compromise between the Ptolemaic and Copernican systems. There was similar indecision among anatomists, who admired Vesalius but were not ready to discard Galen.

Kepler and Galileo Address the Uncertainties

As late as 1600, it seemed that scientists were creating more problems than solutions. But then two brilliant discoverers—the German Johannes Kepler (1571–1630) and Galileo Galilei, an Italian professor of mathematics—made major advances on the work of Copernicus and helped resolve the uncertainties in the field of astronomy.

Kepler and the Laws of Planetary Motion Like Copernicus, Kepler believed that only the language of mathematics could describe the movements of the heavens. He was a famous astrologer and an advocate of magical theories, but he was also convinced that Copernicus was right. He threw himself into the task of confirming the sun-centered (heliocentric) theory, and by studying Brahe's observations, he discovered three laws of planetary motion (published in 1609 and 1619) that opened a new era in astronomy. Kepler was able to prove that the orbits of the planets are ellipses and that there is a regularity, based on their distance from the sun, which determines the movements of all planets. So revolutionary were these laws that few astronomers accepted them until Isaac Newton used them fifty years later as the basis for a new system of the heavens.

Galileo and a New Physics A contemporary of Kepler's, the Italian Galileo Galilei (1564–1642), made further advances when he became the first to perceive the connection between planetary motion and motion on earth. His studies revealed the importance to astronomy not only of observation and mathematics but also of physics. Moreover, Galileo's self-consciousness about technique, argument, and evidence marks him as one of the first investigators of nature to approach his work in essentially the same way as a modern scientist.

The study of motion inspired Galileo's most fundamental scientific contributions. When he began his investigations, the Aristotelian view that a body is naturally at rest and needs to be pushed constantly to keep moving dominated the study of dynamics. Galileo broke with this tradition, developing instead a new type of physical explanation that was perfected by Isaac Newton half a century later. Much of Galileo's work was based on observation. From watching how workers at the Arsenal in Venice used pulleys and other devices to lift huge weights, he gained insights into physics; adapting a Dutch lens maker's invention, he built a primitive telescope that was essential to his studies of the heavens; and his seemingly mundane experiments, such as swinging a pendulum or rolling balls down inclined planes, were crucial means of testing his theo-

CHRONOLOGY
The Scientific Revolution

1543	Publication of Copernicus' *On the Revolutions of the Heavenly Spheres*.
	Publication of Vesalius' *The Structure of the Human Body*.
	First printing of the work of Archimedes.
1582	Pope Gregory XIII reforms the calendar.
1609	Publication of Kepler's first two laws of planetary motion.
1610	Publication of Galileo's *Starry Messenger*.
1619	Publication of Kepler's third law of planetary motion.
1627	Publication of Bacon's *New Atlantis*.
1628	Publication of Harvey's *On the Motion of the Heart*.
1632	Publication of Galileo's *Dialogue on the Two Great World Systems*.
1633	Condemnation of Galileo by the Inquisition.
1637	Publication of Descartes' *Discourse on Method*.
1639	Pascal's theorem concerning conic sections.
1660	Founding of the Royal Society of London for Improving Natural Knowledge.
1666	Founding of the French Royal Academy of Sciences.
1687	Publication of Newton's *Mathematical Principles of Natural Philosophy*.

ries. Indeed, it was by moving from observations to abstraction that Galileo arrived at the first wholly new way of understanding motion since Aristotle: the principle of inertia.

This breakthrough could not have been made by observation alone, for the discovery of inertia depended on mathematical abstraction, the ability to imagine a situation that cannot be created experimentally: the motion of a perfectly smooth ball across a perfectly smooth plane, free of any outside forces, such as friction. Galileo's conclusion was that "any velocity once imparted to a moving body will be rigidly maintained as long as external causes of acceleration and retardation are removed. . . . If the velocity is uniform, it will not be diminished or slackened, much less destroyed." This insight overturned the Aristotelian view. Galileo had demonstrated that only mathematical language could describe the underlying principles of nature.

A New Astronomy Galileo's most celebrated work was in astronomy. He first became famous in 1610, when he published his discoveries, made with the telescope, that Jupiter has satellites and the moon has mountains. Both these revelations were further blows to traditional beliefs, which held that the earth is changing and imperfect while the heavens are immutable and unblemished. Now, however, it seemed that other planets had satellites, just like the earth, and that these satellites might have the same rough surface as the earth. This was startling enough, but Galileo also argued that the principles of terrestrial physics could be used to explain phenomena in the heavens. He calculated the height of the mountains on the moon by using the geometric techniques of surveyors, and he described the moon's secondary light—seen while it is a crescent—as a reflection of sunlight from the earth. Galileo was treating his own planet simply as one part of a uniform universe. Every physical law, he was saying, is equally applicable on earth and in the heavens, including the laws of motion. As early as 1597 Galileo had admitted that some of his discoveries in physics could be explained only if the earth were moving, and during the next thirty years he became the most famous advocate of Copernicanism in Europe (see "Galileo and Kepler on Copernicus," p. 465).

Galileo Galilei
THE MOON, 1610
This sketch of the moon's surface appeared in Galileo's *Starry Messenger* (1610). It shows what he had observed through the telescope and had interpreted as proof that the moon had a rugged surface because the lighted area within the dark section had to be mountains. These caught the light of the setting sun longer than surrounding lower terrain and revealed, for example, a large cavity in the lower center of the sketch.
New York Public Library

Galileo made a powerful case. Why, he asked, was it necessary to say that the entire universe revolved around the earth when all celestial motions could be explained by the rotation of a single planet, the earth? When academic and religious critics argued that we would feel the earth moving or pointed out that the Bible said Joshua made the sun stand still, he reacted with scorn. In response to religious objections, he asserted that "in discussions of physical problems we ought to begin not from the authority of scriptural passages, but from sense experience and necessary demonstrations."

Conflict with the Church For all the brilliance of his arguments, Galileo was now on dangerous ground. Although traditionally the Catholic Church had not concerned itself with investigations of nature, in the early seventeenth century the situation was changing. The Church was deep in the struggle with Protestantism, and it responded to the challenge to its authority by trying to control potentially questionable views. And Galileo's biting sarcasm toward other scientists antagonized Jesuit and Dominican astronomers. These two orders were the chief upholders of orthodoxy in the Church. They referred Galileo's views to the Inquisition and then guided the attack on Copernicanism by seeking to condemn the brilliant advocate who had made the theory famous throughout Europe.

The Book and the Trial In 1616 the Inquisition forbade Galileo, within certain limits, to teach the heretical doctrine that the earth moves. When one of his friends was elected pope in 1623, however, Galileo thought he would be safe in writing a major work on astronomy. The result was his *Dialogue on the Two Great World Systems*, published in 1632 (with the approval, probably accidental, of the Church). A marvelously witty, elegant book, the *Dialogue* is one of the few monuments in the history of science that the layperson can read with pleasure. And so it was intended. Galileo wrote it in Italian, not the Latin that had always been used for scholarly works, because he wanted to reach the widest possible audience.

In April 1633 he was brought before the Inquisition for having defied the order not to teach Copernicanism. In a trial that has caused controversy ever since, the aged astronomer, fearing excommunication, abjured the "errors and heresies" of believing that the earth moved. But he did not remain docile for the remainder of his life, though he was kept under house arrest and progressively lost his eyesight. Many of his letters ridiculed his opponents, and in 1638 he published (in tolerant Holland) his principal work on physics, the *Two New Sciences*.

GALILEO AND KEPLER ON COPERNICUS

In 1597 Kepler sent Galileo a copy of his New Astronomy, *which argued for the Copernican theory of the heavens, and asked the Italian for his opinion. The exchange of letters that followed, with Galileo cautious and Kepler urging him on, reflects an age when the new ideas were not yet proved and also gives a hint, in Kepler's last comments, of the troubles that lay ahead.*

Galileo to Kepler: "Like you, I accepted the Copernican position several years ago. I have written up many reasons on the subject, but have not dared until now to bring them into the open. I would dare publish my thoughts if there were many like you; but, since there are not, I shall forbear."

Kepler's Reply: "I could only have wished that you, who have so profound an insight, would choose another way. You advise us to retreat before the general ignorance and not to expose ourselves to the violent attacks of the mob of scholars. But after a tremendous task has been begun in our time, first by Copernicus and then by many very learned mathematicians, and when the assertion that the Earth moves can no longer be considered something new, would it not be much better to pull the wagon to its goal by our joint efforts, now that we have got it under way, and gradually, with powerful voices, to shout down the common herd? Be of good cheer, Galileo, and come out publicly! If I judge correctly, there are only a few of the distinguished mathematicians of Europe who would part company with us, so great is the power of truth. If Italy seems a less favorable place for your publication, perhaps Germany will allow us this freedom."

From Giorgio de Santillana, *The Crime of Galileo,* Chicago: University of Chicago Press, 1955, pp. 11, 14–15.

Galileo's Legacy   The condemnation of Galileo discouraged further scientific activity by his compatriots. Italy had been a leader of the new investigations, but now major further advances were made by the English, Dutch, and French. Yet this shift showed merely that the rise of science, once begun, could not be halted for long. By the late 1630s, no self-respecting astronomer could deny the correctness of the Copernican theory.

Assurance Spreads   The new studies of nature may have caused tremendous bewilderment at first, as scientists struggled with the ideas of pioneers like Copernicus and Vesalius. But in the end these investigations created a renewed sense of certainty about the physical world, which was to have a far-reaching influence. This was true not only in physics and astronomy but also in anatomy, where, in 1628, another genius of the scientific revolution, the English doctor William Harvey, revolutionized the understanding of the human body when he identified the function of the heart and proved that the blood circulates.

The Climax of the Scientific Revolution: Isaac Newton

The culmination of the scientific revolution was the work of Isaac Newton (1642–1727), who made decisive contributions to mathematics, physics, astronomy, and optics and brought to a climax the changes that had begun with Copernicus. He united physics and astronomy into a single system to explain all motion, he helped transform mathematics by developing the calculus, and he established some of the basic laws of modern physics.

Part of the explanation of his versatility lies in the workings of the scientific community at the time. Newton was a retiring man who nevertheless got into fierce arguments with prominent contemporaries, such as the learned German scholar and scientist Wilhelm von Leibniz, who was working on the calculus. If not for his active participation in meetings of scientists at the recently founded Royal Society of London (see p. 468), Newton might never have pursued his researches to their conclusion. He disliked the give-and-take of these discussions, but he felt forced, in order to prove that he had solved various problems, to prepare some of his most important papers for the Royal Society. Such institutions were now being established throughout Europe to promote the advance of science, and their creation indicates how far the scientific community had come since the days of Copernicus, who had worked largely in isolation.

The Principia   Newton's masterpiece, *The Mathematical Principles of Natural Philosophy* (1687)—usually referred to by the first word of its Latin title, the *Principia*—was the last widely influential book to be written in Latin, the traditional language of scholarship. Latin was still useful to Newton, who wanted as many experts as possible to read the book, which claimed that everything he said was proved by experiment or by mathematics.

The most dramatic of Newton's findings was the solution to the ancient problem of motion. Building on Galileo's advances and overturning Aristotle's theories once and for all, Newton defined his system in three laws: first, in the absence of force, motion continues in a straight line; second, the rate of change of the motion is determined by the forces acting on it (such as friction); and third, action and reaction between two bodies are equal and opposite. To arrive at these laws, he defined the concepts of mass, inertia, and force in relation to velocity and acceleration as we know them today.

Newton extended these principles to the entire universe by demonstrating that his laws govern the motions of the moon and planets too. Using the concept of gravity, he provided the explanation of the movement of objects in space that is the foundation for current space travel. There is a balance, he said, between the earth's pull on the moon and the forward motion of the satellite, which would continue in a straight line were it not for the earth's gravity. Consequently, the moon moves in an elliptical orbit in which neither gravity nor inertia gains control. The same pattern is followed by the planets around the sun (as Kepler had shown).

The Influence of Newton   The general philosophical implication of the uniformity that Newton described—that the world was stable and orderly—was as important as his specific discoveries in making him one of the idols of his own and the next centuries. The educated applauded Newton's achievements, and he was the first scientist to receive a knighthood in England. Only a few decades after the appearance of the *Principia*, the poet Alexander Pope summed up the public feeling:

> Nature and nature's law lay hid in night;
> God said, "Let Newton be!" and all was light.

So overpowering was Newton's stature that in physics and astronomy the remarkable advances of 150 years slowed down for more than half a century after the publication of the *Principia*. There was a general impression that somehow Newton had done it all, that no important problems remained. There were other reasons for the slowdown—changing patterns in education, an inevitable lessening of momentum—but none was so powerful as the reverence for Newton, who became the intellectual symbol of his own and succeeding ages.

THE EFFECTS OF THE DISCOVERIES

The scientists' discoveries about the physical universe made them famous. But it was the *way* they proved their case that made them so influential. The success of their reasoning encouraged a new level of confidence in human powers that helped end the doubts and uncertainties of the previous age.

A New Epistemology

Galileo had stressed that his discoveries rested on a way of thinking that had an independent value, and he refused to allow traditional considerations, such as common sense or theological teachings, to interfere with his conclusions. Scientists were now moving toward a new **epistemology**, a new theory of how to obtain and verify knowledge. They stressed experience, reason, and doubt; they rejected all unsubstantiated authority; and they developed a revolutionary way of determining what was a true description of physical reality.

Scientific Method   The process the scientists said they followed, after they had formulated a hypothesis, consisted of three parts: first, observations; second, a generalization induced from the observations; and third, tests of the generalization by experiments whose outcome could be predicted by the generalization. A generalization remained valid only as long as it was not contradicted by experiments specifically designed to test it. The scientist used no data except the results of strict observation—such as the time it took balls to roll down Galileo's inclined planes—and scientific reasoning uncovered the laws, principles, or patterns that emerged from the observations. Since measurement was the key to the data, the observations had a numerical, not a subjective, value. Thus, the language of science came to be mathematics.

In fact, scientists rarely reach conclusions in the exact way this idealized scheme suggests. Galileo's perfectly smooth balls and planes, for instance, did not exist, but Galileo understood the relevant physical theory so well that he knew what would happen if one rolled across the other, and he used this "experiment" to demonstrate the principle of inertia. In other words, experiments as well as hypotheses can occur in the mind; the essence of scientific method is a special way of looking at and understanding nature.

The Wider Influence of Scientific Thought

The principles of scientific inquiry received attention throughout the intellectual community only gradually; it took time for the power of the scientists' method to be recognized. If the new methods were to be accepted, their effectiveness would have to be demonstrated to more than a few specialists. This wider understanding was eventually achieved by midcentury, as much through the efforts of ardent propagandizers as through the writings of the great innovators themselves. Gradually, they convinced a broad, educated public that science, after first causing doubts by challenging ancient truths, now offered a promise of certainty that was not to be found anywhere else in an age of general crisis.

Bacon and Descartes

Bacon's Vision of Science   Although he was not an important scientist himself, Francis Bacon was the greatest of science's propagandists, and he inspired a whole generation with his vision of what it could accomplish for humanity. His description of an ideal society in the *New Atlantis*—published in 1627, the year after his death—is a vision of science as the savior of the human race. It predicts a time when those doing research at the highest levels will be regarded as the most important people in the state and will work on vast government-supported projects to gather all known facts about the physical universe. By a process of gradual **induction,** this information will lead to universal laws that, in turn, will enable people to improve their lot on earth. Bacon's view of research as a collective enterprise inspired a number of later scientists, and by the mid-seventeenth century, his ideas had entered the mainstream of European thought.

Descartes and the Principle of Doubt   The Frenchman René Descartes (1596–1650) made the first concentrated attempt to apply the new methods of science to theories of knowledge, and, in so doing, he laid the foundations for modern philosophy. The impulse behind his work was his realization that, for all the importance of observation and experiment, people can be deceived by their senses. In order to find some solid truth, therefore, he decided to apply to all knowledge the principle of doubt—the refusal to accept any authority without strict verification. He began with the assumption that he could know unquestionably only one thing: that he was doubting. This assumption allowed him to proceed to the observation "I think, therefore I am," because the act of doubting proved he was thinking, and thinking, in turn, demonstrated his existence.

From the proof of his own existence he derived a crucial statement: That whatever is clearly and distinctly thought must be true. This assertion in turn enabled him to construct a proof of God's existence. We cannot fail to realize that we are imperfect, he argued, and we must therefore have an idea of perfection

Frans Hals
PORTRAIT OF DESCARTES, **1649**
The increasingly common portraits of scientists in the seventeenth century testify to their growing fame. In this case, Descartes sat for one of the Netherlands' most renowned artists, and because the painting was copied in a number of engravings, his face became as well known as that of many kings and princes.
Erich Lessing/Art Resource, NY

against which we may be measured. If we have a clear idea of what perfection is, then it must exist; hence, there must be a God.

The Discourse on Method   Descartes' proof may have served primarily to show that the principle of doubt did not contradict religious belief, but it also reflected the emphasis on the power of the mind in his major work, *Discourse on the Method of Rightly Conducting the Reason and Seeking Truth in the Sciences* (1637). Thought is a pure and unmistakable guide, he said, and only by relying on its operations can people hope to advance their understanding of the world. Descartes developed this view into a fundamental proposition about the nature of the world—a proposition that philosophers have been wrestling with ever since. He stated that there is an essential divide between thought and extension (tangible objects) or, put another way, between spirit and matter. Bacon and Galileo had insisted that science, the study of nature, is separate from and unaffected by faith. But Descartes turned this distinction into a far-reaching principle, dividing not only science from faith but even the reality of the world from our perception of that reality. There is a difference, in other words, between a chair and how we think of it as a chair.

The Influence of Descartes Descartes' emphasis on the operations of the mind gave a new direction to epistemological discussions. A hypothesis gained credibility not so much from external proofs as from the logical tightness of the arguments used to support it. Descartes thus applied what he considered the methods of science to all of knowledge. Not only the phenomena of nature but all truth had to be investigated according to the methods of the scientist.

Descartes' contributions to scientific research were theoretical rather than experimental. In physics, he was the first to perceive the distinction between mass and weight; and in mathematics, he was the first to apply algebraic notations and methods to geometry, thus founding analytic geometry. Above all, his emphasis on the principle of doubt undermined forever traditional assumptions such as the belief in the hierarchical organization of the universe.

Pascal's Protest Against the New Science

At midcentury only one important voice still protested against the new science and, in particular, against the philosophy of Descartes. It belonged to a Frenchman, Blaise Pascal, a brilliant mathematician and experimenter. Pascal's investigations of probability in games of chance produced the theorem that still bears his name, and his research in conic sections helped lay the foundations for integral calculus. He also helped discover barometric pressure and invented a calculating machine. In his late twenties, however, Pascal became increasingly dissatisfied with scientific research, and he began to wonder whether his life was being properly spent. Moved by a growing concern with faith, Pascal had a mystical experience in November 1654 that made him resolve to devote his life to the salvation of his soul.

The Pensées During the few remaining years of his life, Pascal wrote a collection of reflections—some only a few words long, some many pages—that were gathered together after his death and published as the *Pensées* (or "Reflections"). These writings revealed not only the beliefs of a deeply religious man but also the anxieties of a scientist who feared the growing influ-

ence of science. He did not wish to put an end to research; he merely wanted people to realize that the truths uncovered by science were limited and not as important as the truths perceived by faith. As he put it in one of his more memorable *pensées*, "The heart has its reasons that reason cannot know."

Pascal's protest was unique, but the fact that it was put forward at all indicates how high the status of the scientist and his methods had risen by the 1650s. Just a quarter-century earlier, such a dramatic change in fortune would have been hard to predict. But now the new epistemology, after its initial disturbing assault on ancient views, was offering one of the few promises of certainty in an age of upheaval and general crisis. In intellectual matters as in politics, turmoil was gradually giving way to assurance.

Science Institutionalized

Many besides Bacon realized that scientific work should be a cooperative endeavor and that information should be exchanged among all its practitioners. A scientific society founded in Rome in 1603 made the first major effort to apply this view, and it was soon followed up in France, where in the early seventeenth century a friar named Marin Mersenne became the center of an international network of correspondents interested in scientific work. He also spread news by bringing scientists together for discussions and experiments. Contacts that were developed at these meetings led eventually to a more permanent and systematic organization of scientific activity.

The Royal Society In England, the first steps toward such organization were taken at Oxford during the Civil War in the 1640s, when the revolutionaries captured the city and replaced those at the university who taught traditional natural philosophy. A few of the newcomers formed what they called the Invisible College, a group that met to exchange information and discuss each other's work. The group included only one first-class scientist, the chemist Robert Boyle; but in 1660 he and eleven others formed an official organization, the Royal Society of London for Improving Natural Knowledge, with headquarters in the capital. In 1662 it was granted a charter by Charles II—the first sign of a link with political authority that not only boosted science but also indicated the growing presence of central governments in all areas of society.

The Royal Society's purposes were openly Baconian. Its aim for a few years—until everyone realized it was impossible—was to gather all knowledge about nature, particularly if it had practical uses. For a long time the members offered their services for the public good, helping in one instance to develop for the government

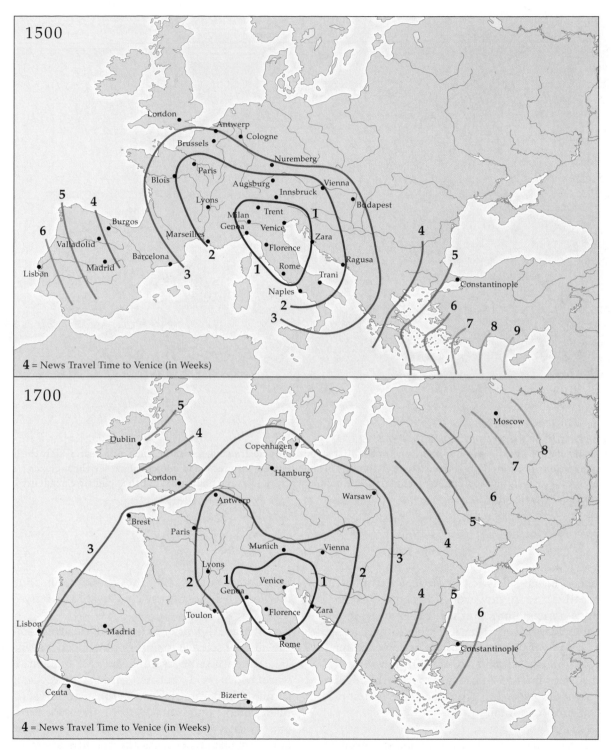

MAP 16.1 SPEED OF NEWS TRAVELING TO VENICE IN 1500 AND 1700
Although the dramatic advances in communications lay in the future, by 1700 improved roads and canals and more efficient shipping did bring about significant advances in the distance news could travel in two or three weeks. How much faster could news get from Madrid to Venice in 1700 than in 1500? What about from Constantinople to Venice? Why might communication across Western Europe have speeded up more than across Eastern Europe?

◆ For an online version, go to www.mhhe.com/chambers9 > chapter 16 > book maps

Charles-Nicolas Cochin
THE ACADÈMIE ROYALE DES SCIENCES, PARIS, ENGRAVING, **1698**
This celebration of the work done by one of the first scientific societies suggests the variety of research that these organizations promoted. In contrast to the students of theology, who merely read books (as we see through the arch on the right), the geographers, engineers, astronomers, physicists, and anatomists of the scientific academy examine the real world.
© British Museum, Department of Prints and Drawings ([C292] Neg # N/N R8-85)

the science of social statistics ("political arithmetic," as it was called). Soon, however, it became clear that the society's principal function was to serve as a headquarters and clearing center for research. Its secretaries maintained an enormous correspondence to encourage English and foreign scholars to send in news of their discoveries. And in 1665 the society began the regular publication of *Philosophical Transactions*, the first professional scientific journal.

Other Scientific Societies Imitators soon followed. In 1666 Louis XIV gave his blessing to the founding of a French Royal Academy of Sciences, and similar organizations were established in Naples and Berlin by 1700. Membership in these societies was limited and highly prized, a sign of the glamour that was beginning to attach itself to the new studies. By the 1660s there could be no doubt that science, secure in royal patronage, had become a model for all thought. Its practitioners were extravagantly admired, and throughout intellectual and high social circles, there was a scramble to apply its methods to almost every conceivable activity.

The Wider Appeal of Science Descartes had applied the ideas of science to philosophy in general; Bacon had said they must be useful. And the applications soon were widespread. Formal gardens were designed to show the order, harmony, and reason that science had made such prized qualities. Methods of fortification and warfare were affected by the new emphasis on accurate measurement. As the scientists' activities became more popular and fashionable, even aristocrats began to spend time playing at science. Herbariums and small observatories were added to country estates, and parties featured an evening of star gazing. Science also fascinated the general populace. Among the most eagerly anticipated occasions in seventeenth-century Holland was the public anatomy lesson. The body of a criminal would be brought to an enormous hall that was packed with students and a fascinated public. A famous surgeon would dissect the cadaver, announcing and displaying each organ as he removed it.

On the whole, the reverence for science and its methods did not develop from an understanding of its actual accomplishments or its potential consequences. Rather, it was caused by the fame of the spectacular discoveries that had offered new and convincing solutions to centuries-old problems in astronomy, physics, and anatomy. Here was a promise of certainty and order in a world that otherwise was bedeviled by conflict and doubt. As a result, the protests of Pascal could be ignored, and the new discipline could be given unblemished admiration. The entire world was coming to be viewed through the scientist's eyes—a striking achievement for a recently minor member of the intellectual community—and the qualities of regularity and harmony associated with science began to appear in the work of artists and writers.

THE ARTS AND LITERATURE

We have seen that in the mid-seventeenth century a more settled Europe emerged from the political turbulence and crisis of the late 1500s and early 1600s. And we have seen that the development of science followed a similar pattern—with decades of uncertainty as old truths were challenged, and then a new sense of assurance in the mid-seventeenth century. Not surprisingly, so too did the concerns of the arts and literature.

Unsettling Art

Mannerism   One response that was provoked by the upheavals of the sixteenth century was the attempt to escape reality, an effort that was echoed by some of the painters of the age, known as *Mannerists*. The Mannerists and their patrons reacted against the serenity and idealization of the High Renaissance by cultivating artificial and esoteric images of the world; they undermined perspective, distorted human figures, and devised unnatural colors and lighting to create startling effects.

El Greco   Mannerism was embodied in El Greco (1541–1614), a Greek who was trained in Italy and settled in Spain. His compelling and almost mystic canvases created an otherworldly alternative to the troubles of his time. El Greco's cool colors, eerie lighting, and elongated and often agonized human beings make him one of the most distinctive painters in the history of art (see p. 432). After 1600, though, painters increasingly rejected the Mannerists' flight from reality; eventually the arts, too, reflected the sense of settlement that descended over European civilization in the mid-seventeenth century.

Unsettling Writers

Michel de Montaigne   In the world of literature, the concerns of the age were most vividly expressed by the Frenchman Michel de Montaigne (1533–1592). Obsessed by the death he saw all around him and determined to overcome his fears, he retired in 1570 to his country home in order to "essay," or test, his innermost feelings by writing short pieces of prose even about subjects he did not fully comprehend. In the process he created a new literary form, the essay, that also helped shape the modern French language. But his chief influence was philosophical: He has inspired the search for self-knowledge ever since.

At first Montaigne's anxieties led him to radical doubt about the possibility of finding truth; known as **skepticism,** this preoccupation inspired the total uncertainty of his motto, "Que sais-je?" ("What do I know?"). Eventually, however, Montaigne struggled toward a more confident view, taking as his model the ancient saying "Know thyself." By looking into one's own person, one can find values that hold true at least for oneself, and these will reflect the values of all humanity. Montaigne came close to a morality without theology, because good and self-determination were more important to him than doctrine, and he saw everywhere religious people committing inhuman acts. Trying to be an angel is wrong, he said; being good is enough.

Montaigne was also one of the first writers to use non-Western models to criticize Europeans. He met a cannibal who had been brought to France, and he suggested that those who kill for food were more moral than those who kill for other purposes, such as religious beliefs.

Neostoicism   A more general approach to morality was a theory known as **Neostoicism,** inspired by the ancient Stoics' emphasis on self-knowledge and a calm acceptance of the world. The most influential of the Neostoics, a Dutch writer named Justus Lipsius, argued that public leaders ought to be guided by profound self-examination. Lipsius urged rulers to be restrained and self-disciplined, and he was much admired by the kings and royal ministers of the seventeenth century.

Cervantes   In Spain the disillusionment that accompanied the political and economic decline of Europe's most powerful state was perfectly captured by Miguel de Cervantes (1547–1616). Cervantes saw the wide gap between the hopes and the realities of his day—in religion, in social institutions, in human behavior—and made the dichotomy the basis of scathing social satire in his novel *Don Quixote.*

At one level, Cervantes was ridiculing the excessive chivalry of the Spanish nobility in his portrayal of a knight who was ready to tilt at windmills, though he obviously admired the sincerity of his well-meaning hero and sympathized with him as a perennial loser. On another level, the author brought to life the Europe of the time—the ordinary people and their hypocrisies and intolerances—with a liveliness rarely matched in literature. Cervantes avoided politics, but he was clearly directing many of his sharpest barbs at the brutality and disregard for human values that were characteristic of his fanatical times. And in England another towering figure was grappling with similar problems.

Shakespeare   For the English-speaking world, the most brilliant writer of this and all other periods was William Shakespeare (1564–1616), whose characters bring to life almost every conceivable mood: searing grief, airy romance, rousing nationalism, uproarious humor. Despite his modest education, his imagery shows a familiarity with subjects ranging from astronomy to seamanship, from alchemy to warfare. It is not surprising, therefore, that some have doubted that one man could have produced this amazing body of work. During most of his writing career, Shakespeare was involved with a theatrical company, where he often had to produce plays on short notice. He thus had the best of all possible tests—audience reactions—as he gained mastery of theatrical techniques.

Shakespeare's plays made timeless statements about human behavior: love, hatred, violence, sin. Of particular interest to the historian, however, is what he tells us about attitudes that belong especially to his own era. Again and again, legality and stability are shown as fundamental virtues amidst turbulent times. Shakespeare's expressions of patriotism are particularly intense; when in *Richard II* the king's uncle, John of Gaunt, lies dying, he pours out his love for his country in words that have moved the English ever since:

> This royal throne of kings, this scepter'd isle,
> This earth of majesty, this seat of Mars,
> This other Eden, demi-paradise, . . .
> This happy breed of men, this little world,
> This precious stone set in the silver sea, . . .
> This blessed plot, this earth,
> This realm, this England.
>
> *Richard II*, act 2, scene 1

As in so much of the art and writing of the time, instability is a central concern of Shakespeare's plays. His four most famous tragedies—*Hamlet, King Lear, Macbeth*, and *Othello*—end in disillusionment: The heroes are ruined by irresoluteness, pride, ambition, and jealousy. Shakespeare was exploring a theme that had absorbed playwrights since Euripides—the fatal flaws that destroy the great—and producing dramas of revenge that were popular in his day; but the plays also

demonstrate his deep understanding of human nature. Whatever one's hopes, one cannot forget human weakness, the inevitability of decay, and the constant threat of disaster. The contrast appears with compelling clarity in a speech delivered by Hamlet:

> What a piece of work is man! How noble in reason! how infinite in faculties! in form and moving how express and admirable! in action how like an angel! in apprehension how like a god! the beauty of the world, the paragon of animals! And yet to me what is this quintessence of dust? Man delights not me.
>
> *Hamlet*, act 2, scene 2

Despite such pessimism, despite the deep sense of human inadequacy, the basic impression Shakespeare gives is of immense vigor, of a restlessness and confidence that recall the many achievements of the sixteenth century. Yet a sense of decay is never far absent. Repeatedly, people seem utterly helpless, overtaken by events they cannot control. Nothing remains constant or dependable, and everything that seems solid or reassuring, be it the love of a daughter or the crown of England, is challenged. In this atmosphere of ceaseless change, where landmarks easily disappear, Shakespeare conveys the tensions of his time.

The Return of Assurance in the Arts

The Baroque   After 1600, the arts began to move toward the assurance and sense of settlement that was descending over other areas of European civilization. A new style, the **Baroque,** sought to drown the uneasiness of Mannerism in a blaze of grandeur. Passion, drama, mystery, and awe were the qualities of the Baroque: Every art form—from music to literature, from architecture to opera—had to involve, arouse, and uplift its audience.

The Baroque style was closely associated with the Counter-Reformation's emphasis on gorgeous display in Catholic ritual. The patronage of leading Church figures made Rome a magnet for the major painters of the period. Elsewhere, the Baroque flourished primarily at the leading Catholic courts of the seventeenth century, most notably the Habsburg courts in Madrid, Prague, and Brussels, and remained influential well into the eighteenth century in such Catholic areas as the Spanish Empire. Few styles have conveyed so strong a sense of grandeur, theatricality, and ornateness.

Caravaggio   The artist who first shaped the new aesthetic, Caravaggio (1571–1610), lived most of his life in Rome. Although he received commissions from high Church figures and spent time in a cardinal's household, he was equally at home among the beggars and petty criminals of Rome's dark back streets. These

Caravaggio
THE SUPPER AT EMMAUS, CA. **1597**
By choosing moments of high drama and using sharp contrasts of light, Caravaggio created an immediacy that came to be one of the hallmarks of Baroque painting. Here he shows the moment during the supper at Emmaus when his disciples suddenly recognized the resurrected Christ. The force of their emotions and their almost theatrical gestures convey the intensity of the moment, but many at the time objected to the craggy, tattered appearance of the disciples. These were not idealized figures, as was expected, but ordinary people at a humble table.
Reproduced by courtesy of the Trustees, © The National Gallery, London (NG172)

ordinary people served as Caravaggio's models, which shocked those who believed it inappropriate for such humble characters to represent the holy figures of biblical scenes. Yet the power of Caravaggio's paintings—their depiction of highly emotional moments, and the drama created by their sharp contrasts of light and dark—made his work much prized. He had to flee Rome after he killed someone in a brawl, but he left behind an outpouring of work that influenced an entire generation of painters.

Rubens   Among those who came to Rome to study Caravaggio's art was Peter Paul Rubens (1577–1640), the principal ornament of the brilliant Habsburg court at Brussels. His major themes typified the grandeur that came to be the hallmark of Baroque style: glorifi-

cations of great rulers and also of the ceremony and mystery of Catholicism. Rubens' secular paintings convey enormous strength; his religious works overwhelm the viewer with the majesty of the Church and excite the believer's piety by stressing the power of the faith.

Velázquez   Other artists glorified rulers through idealized portraiture. The greatest court painter of the age was Diego Velázquez (1599–1660). His portraits of members of the Spanish court depict rulers and their surroundings in the stately atmosphere appropriate to the theme. Yet occasionally Velázquez hinted at the weakness of an ineffective monarch in his rendering of the face, even though the basic purpose of his work was always to exalt royal power. And his celebration of a notable Habsburg victory, *The Surrender of Breda*,

Artemisia Gentileschi
JUDITH SLAYING HOLOFERNES, CA. 1620
Female artists were rare in the seventeenth century because they were not allowed to become apprentices. But Artemisia (1593–1652) was the daughter of a painter who happened to be a friend of Caravaggio, and she had the opportunity to become a gifted exponent of Baroque style. Known throughout Europe for her vivid portrayals of dramatic scenes (she painted the murder of Holofernes by the biblical heroine Judith at least five times), she practiced her chosen profession with considerable success, despite the trauma of being raped at age seventeen by a friend of her father's—an act of violence that may be reflected (and avenged) in this painting.
Uffizi, Florence, Italy. Scala/Art Resource, NY

Peter Paul Rubens
DESCENT FROM THE CROSS, 1612
This huge altarpiece was one of the first pictures Rubens painted upon returning to his native Antwerp after spending most of his twenties developing his art in Italy. The ambitious scale, the strong emotions, the vivid lighting, and the dramatic action showed the artist's commitment to the Baroque style that had recently evolved in Italy. The powerful impact of the altarpiece helped make him one of the most sought-after painters of the day.
Center panel. Scala/Art Resource, NY

Diego Velázquez
THE SURRENDER OF BREDA, 1635
The contrasting postures of victory and defeat are masterfully captured by Diego Velázquez in *The Surrender of Breda*. The Dutch soldiers droop their heads and lances, but the victorious Spaniards hardly show triumph, and the gesture of the victorious general, Ambrogio Spinola, is one of consolation and understanding.
Oroñoz

managed to suggest the sadness and emptiness as much as the glory of war.

Bernini   GianLorenzo Bernini (1598–1680) brought to sculpture and architecture the qualities that Rubens brought to painting, and like Rubens he was closely associated with the Counter-Reformation. Pope Urban VIII commissioned him in 1629 to complete both the inside and the outer setting of the basilica of St. Peter's in Rome. For the interior, Bernini designed a splendid papal throne that seems to float on clouds beneath a burst of sunlight. For the exterior, he created an enormous plaza, surrounded by a double colonnade, that is the largest such plaza in Europe. Similarly, his dramatic religious works reflect the desire of the Counter-

Reformation popes to electrify the faithful. The sensual and overpowering altarpiece dedicated to the Spanish mystic St. Teresa makes a direct appeal to the emotions of the beholder that is the epitome of the excitement and confidence of the Baroque.

New Dimensions in Music   The seventeenth century was significant, too, as a decisive time in the history of music. New instruments, notably in the keyboard and string families, enabled composers to create richer effects than had been possible before. Particularly in Italy, which in the sixteenth and seventeenth centuries was the chief center of new ideas in music, musicians began to explore the potential of a form that first emerged in these years: the opera. Drawing on the

GianLorenzo Bernini
ST. PETER'S SQUARE AND CHURCH, ROME
The magnificent circular double colonnade that Bernini created in front of St. Peter's is one of the triumphs of Baroque architecture. The church itself was already the largest in Christendom (markers in the floor still indicate how far other famous churches would reach if placed inside St. Peter's), and it was topped by the huge dome Michelangelo had designed. The vast enclosed space that Bernini built reinforced the grandeur of a church that was the pope's own.
Joachim Messerschmidt/Corbis Stock Market

resources of the theater, painting, architecture, music, and dance, an operatic production could achieve splendors that were beyond the reach of any one of these arts on its own. The form was perfectly attuned to the courtly culture of the age, to the love of display among the princes of Europe, and to the Baroque determination to overwhelm one's audience.

The dominant figure in seventeenth-century music was the Italian Claudio Monteverdi (1567–1643), one of the most innovative composers of all time. He has been called with some justification the creator of both the operatic form and the orchestra. His masterpiece, *Orfeo* (1607), was a tremendous success, and in the course of the next century operas gained in richness and complexity, attracting composers, as well as audiences, in ever-increasing numbers.

Stability and Restraint in the Arts

Classicism   **Classicism,** the other major style of the seventeenth century, attempted to recapture (though on a much larger scale than Renaissance imitations of antiquity) the aesthetic values and the strict forms that had been favored in ancient Greece and Rome. Like the Baroque, Classicism aimed for grandiose effects, but unlike the Baroque, it achieved them through restraint and discipline within a formal structure. The gradual rise of the Classical style in the seventeenth century echoed the trend toward stability that was taking place in other areas of intellectual life and in politics. In the arts, the age of striving and unrest was coming to an end.

Poussin   The epitome of disciplined expression and conscious imitation of Classical antiquity was Nicolas Poussin (1594–1665), a French artist who spent much of his career in Rome. Poussin was no less interested than his contemporaries in momentous and dramatic subjects, but the atmosphere is always more subdued than in the work of Velázquez or Rubens. The colors are muted, the figures are restrained, and the settings are serene. Peaceful landscapes, men and women in togas, and ruins of Classical buildings are features of his art.

The Dutch Style   In the United Provinces different forces were at work, and they led to a style that was much more intimate than the grandiose outpourings of a Rubens or a Velázquez. Two aspects of Dutch society, Protestantism and republicanism, had a particular influence on its painters. The Reformed Church frowned on religious art, which reduced the demand for paintings of biblical scenes. Religious works, therefore, tended to express personal faith. And the absence of a court meant that the chief patrons of art were sober merchants, who were far more interested in precise, dignified portraits than in ornate displays. The result,

Gian Lorenzo Bernini
THE ECSTASY OF ST. TERESA, **1652**
Bernini's sculpture is as dramatic an example of Baroque art as the paintings of Caravaggio. The moment that St. Teresa described in her autobiography at which she attained mystic ecstasy, as an angel repeatedly pierced her heart with a dart, became in Bernini's hands the centerpiece of a theatrical tableau. He placed the patrons who had commissioned the work on two walls of the chapel that houses this altarpiece, sitting in what seem to be boxes and looking at the stage on which the drama unfolds.
Scala/Art Resource, NY

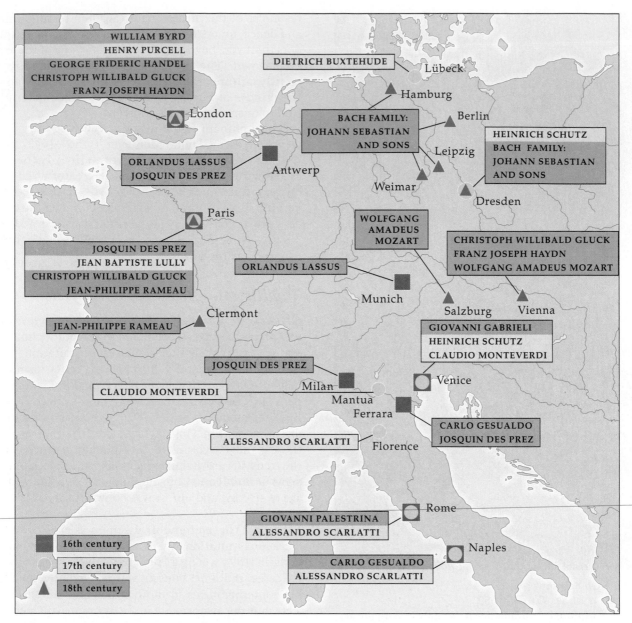

MAP 16.2 CENTERS OF MUSIC, 1500–1800
This map indicates the shifting centers of new ideas in music from Flanders and Italy in the sixteenth century, to Italy in the seventeenth, and on to Germany in the eighteenth. Where, outside of Germany, were other key centers of creativity in music in the eighteenth century?

◆ For an online version, go to www.mhhe.com/chambers9 > chapter 16 > book maps

notably in the profound and moving works of Rembrandt, was a compelling art whose beauty lies in its calmness and restraint.

Rembrandt Rembrandt van Rijn (1606–1669) explored an amazing range of themes, but he was particularly fascinated by human character, emotion, and self-revelation. Whether children or old people, simple servant girls or rich burghers, his subjects are presented without elaboration or idealization; always the person-

ality speaks for itself. Rembrandt's most remarkable achievement in portraiture—and one of the most moving series of canvases in the history of art—is his depiction of the changes in his own face over his lifetime. The brash youth turns into the confident, successful, middle-aged man, one of the most sought-after painters in Holland. But in his late thirties the sorrows mounted: He lost his beloved wife, and commissions began to diminish. Sadness fills the eyes in these pictures. The last portraits move from despair to a final,

Nicolas Poussin
The Inspiration of the Poet, CA. 1628
Whereas Baroque art emphasized emotion, the Classical style sought to embody reason. Poussin, the leading Classical artist of his time, believed that painting, like poetry, had to elevate the minds of its audience. The poet was thus a particularly apt subject for him—a noble and serious theme that could be presented as a scene from antiquity, with formal figures, muted colors, and ancient symbols like the laurel wreath. Poussin's views became the official doctrine of the academy of art founded in France with royal approval, and they influenced generations of painters.
Louvre, Paris, France. Scala/Art Resource, NY

quiet resignation as his sight slowly failed. Taken together, these paintings bear comparison with Montaigne's essays as monuments to the exploration of one's own spirit—a searching appraisal that brings all who see it to a deeper understanding of human nature.

Like the advocates of Classicism, Rembrandt in his restraint seems to anticipate the art of the next generation. After his death in 1669, serenity, calm, and elegance became the watchwords of European painting. An age of repose and grace was succeeding a time of upheaval as surely in the arts as in other spheres of life.

Rembrandt van Rijn
Self-Portrait with Palette, 1660
More than sixty self-portraits by Rembrandt have survived; though all are penetrating explorations of human character, those from his last years are especially moving. We see him here in his mid-fifties with the tools of his trade. Adapting Caravaggio's interest in light, he uses different shades of brown and the illumination of the face to create a somber and reflective mood. The very act of thinking is captured in this canvas, not to mention the full life that is etched in Rembrandt's wrinkles.
Louvre, Paris, France. Scala/Art Resource, NY

Classicism in Drama   By the middle of the seventeenth century, the formalism of the Classical style was also being extended to literature, especially drama. This change was most noticeable in France, but it soon moved through Western Europe, as leading critics insisted that new plays conform to the structure laid down by the ancients. In particular, they wanted the three Classical unities observed: unity of place, which required that all scenes take place without change of location; unity of time, which demanded that the events in the play occur within a twenty-four-hour period; and unity of action, which dictated simplicity and purity of plot.

Corneille   The work of Pierre Corneille (1606–1684), the dominant figure in the French theater during the midcentury years, reflects the rise of Classicism. His early plays were complex and involved, and even after he came into contact with the Classical tradition, he did not accept its rules easily. His masterpiece, *Le Cid* (1636), based on the legends of a medieval Spanish hero, technically observed the three unities, but only by compressing an entire tragic love affair, a military campaign, and many other events into one day. The play won immediate popular success, but the critics, urged on by the royal minister Cardinal Richelieu, who admired the regularity and order of Classical style, condemned Corneille for imperfect observance of the three unities. Thereafter, he adhered to the Classical forms, though he was never entirely at ease with their restraints.

Passion was not absent from the Classical play; the works of Jean Racine (1639–1699), the model Classical dramatist, generate some of the most intense emotion ever seen on the stage. But the exuberance of earlier drama was disappearing. Nobody summed up the values of Classicism better than Racine in his eulogy of Corneille:

> You know in what a condition the stage was when he began to write. . . . All the rules of art, and even those of decency and decorum, broken everywhere. . . . Corneille, after having for some time sought the right path and

struggled against the bad taste of his day, inspired by extraordinary genius and helped by the study of the ancients, at last brought reason upon the stage.

Paul Mesnard (ed.), *Oeuvres de J. Racine*, Vol. 4, 1886, p. 366, trans. T. K. Rabb.

This was exactly the progression—from turbulence to calm—that was apparent throughout European culture in this period.

SOCIAL PATTERNS AND POPULAR CULTURE

The new sense of orderliness, of upheaval subdued, was visible throughout European society in the last years of the seventeenth century. After decades of political and religious conflict, of expressions of uneasiness in philosophy, literature, and the arts, stability and confidence were on the rise. Similarly, the end of population decline, the restoration of social order, and the suppression of disruptive forces like witchcraft indicated that the tensions were easing at all levels of society.

Population Trends

The sixteenth-century rise in Europe's population was succeeded by a period of decline that in most areas lasted long after the political and intellectual upheavals subsided. The rise had been fragile, because throughout these centuries only one child in two reached adulthood. Each couple had to give birth to four children merely to replace themselves, and since they had to wait until they were financially independent to marry—usually in their mid-twenties—they rarely had the chance to produce a big family. Before improvements in nutrition in the nineteenth century, women could bear children only until their late thirties; on average, therefore, a woman had some twelve years in which to give birth to four children to maintain the population. Because lactation delayed ovulation, the

EUROPE'S POPULATION, 1600–1700, BY REGIONS			
Region	*1600**	*1700*	*Percentage Change*
Spain, Portugal, Italy	23.6	22.7	−4
France, Switzerland, Germany	35.0	36.2	+3
British Isles, Low Countries, Scandinavia	12.0	16.1	+34
Total	70.6	75.0	+6

*All figures are in millions.
From Jan de Vries, *The Economy of Europe in an Age of Crisis, 1600–1750*, Cambridge, 1976, p. 5.

mean interval between births was almost two and a half years, which meant that most couples were capable of raising only two children to adulthood. As soon as there was outside pressure—such as plague, famine, or war—population growth became impossible.

The worst of these outside pressures in the seventeenth century was the Thirty Years' War, which alone caused the death of more than 5 million people. It also helped plunge Europe into a debilitating economic depression, which, in turn, decreased the means of relieving the regular famines that afflicted all areas. Disasters like these were not easily absorbed, despite government efforts to distribute food and take other measures to combat natural calamities. Only when better times returned could population increase resume. Because England and the Netherlands led in economic recovery, they experienced a demographic revival long before their neighbors; indeed, the rise in their numbers, which began in the 1660s, accounted for most of the slight population increase the whole of Europe was able to achieve in this difficult century. By 1700, though, prosperity and population were again on the rise—both a reflection and a cause of Europe's newfound assurance and stability.

Social Status

The determinants of status in modern times—wealth, education, and family background—were viewed rather differently in the seventeenth century. Wealth was significant chiefly to merchants, education was important mainly among professionals, and background was vital primarily to the nobility. But in this period the significance of these three social indicators began to shift. Wealth became a more general source of status, as ever-larger numbers of successful merchants bought offices, lands, and titles that allowed them to enter the nobility. Education was also becoming more highly prized; throughout Europe attendance at institutions of higher learning soared after 1550, bringing to universities the sons of artisans as well as nobles. And although background was being scrutinized ever more defensively by old-line nobles, who regarded family lineage as the only criterion for acceptance into their ranks, their resistance to change was futile as the "new" aristocrats multiplied.

In general, it was assumed that everyone occupied a fixed place in the social hierarchy and that it was against the order of nature for someone to move to another level. The growing social importance of wealth and education, however, indicates that mobility was possible. Thanks to the expansion of bureaucracies, it became easier to move to new levels, either by winning favor at court or by buying an office.

Contradictions in the Status of Women   At each level of society, women were usually treated as subordinate by the legal system: In many countries, even the widows of aristocrats could not inherit their husbands' estates; an abbess could never become prominent in Church government; and the few women allowed to practice a trade were excluded from the leadership of their guild. Yet there were notable businesswomen and female artists, writers, and even scientists among the growing numbers of successful self-made people in this period. Widows often inherited their husbands' businesses and pursued thriving careers in their own right, from publishing to innkeeping. One of Caravaggio's most distinguished disciples was Artemisia Gentileschi; the Englishwoman Aphra Behn was a widely known playwright; and some of the leading patrons of intellectual life were the female aristocrats who ran literary circles, particularly in Paris. In fiction and drama, female characters often appeared as the equals of males, despite the legal restrictions of the time and the warnings against such equality in sermons and moral treatises.

Mobility and Crime

The Peasants' Plight   The remarkable economic advances of the sixteenth century helped change attitudes toward wealth, but they brought few benefits to the lower levels of society. Peasants throughout Europe were, in fact, entering a time of increasing difficulty at the end of the sixteenth century. Their taxes were rising rapidly, but the prices they got for the food they grew were stabilizing. Moreover, landowners were starting what has been called the "seigneurial reaction"—making additional demands on their tenants, raising rents, and squeezing as much as they could out of the lands they owned. The effects of famine and war were also more severe at this level of society. The only escapes were to cities or armies, both of which grew rapidly in the seventeenth century. Many of those who fled their villages, however, remained on the road, part of the huge bodies of vagrants and beggars who were a common sight throughout Europe.

A few of those who settled in a town or city improved their lot, but for the large majority, poverty in cities was even more miserable and hungry than poverty on the land. Few could become apprentices, and day laborers were poorly paid and usually out of work. As for military careers, armies were carriers of disease, frequently ill fed, and subject to constant hardship.

Crime and Punishment   For many, therefore, the only alternative to starvation was crime. One area of London in the seventeenth century was totally controlled by the underworld. It offered refuge to fugitives and was never entered by respectable citizens. Robbery and violence—committed equally by desperate men, women, and even children—were common in most cities. As a result, social events like dinners and outings, or visits to the theater, took place during the daytime because the streets were unsafe at night.

If caught, Europe's criminals were treated harshly. In an age before regular police forces, however, catching them was difficult. Crime was usually the responsibility of local authorities, who depended on part-time officials (known in England as constables) for law enforcement. Only in response to major outbreaks, such as a gang of robbers preying on travelers, would the authorities recruit a more substantial armed band (rather like a posse in the American West) to pursue criminals. If such efforts succeeded in bringing offenders to justice, the defendants found they had few rights, especially if they were poor, and punishments were severe. Torture was a common means of extracting confessions; various forms of maiming, such as chopping off a hand or an ear, were considered acceptable penalties; and repeated thefts could lead to execution. Society's hierarchical instincts were apparent even in civil disputes, where nobles were usually immune from prosecution and women often could not start a case. If a woman was raped, for example, she had to find a man to bring suit.

Change in the Villages and Cities

Loss of Village Cohesiveness Over three-quarters of Europe's population still lived in small village communities, but their structure was changing. In Eastern Europe, peasants were being reduced to serfdom; in the West—our principal concern—familiar relationships and institutions were changing.

The essence of the traditional village had been its isolation. Cut off from frequent contact with the world beyond its immediate region, it had been self-sufficient and closely knit. Everyone knew everyone else, and mutual help was vital for survival. There might be distinctions among villagers—some more prosperous, others less so—but the sense of cohesiveness was powerful. It extended even to the main "outsiders" in the village, the priest and the local lord. The priest was often indistinguishable from his parishioners: almost as poor and sometimes hardly more literate. He adapted to local customs and beliefs, frequently taking part in semipagan rituals so as to keep his authority with his flock. The lord could be exploitative and demanding; but he considered the village his livelihood, and he therefore kept in close touch with its affairs and did all he could to ensure its safety, orderliness, and well-being.

Forces of Change The main intrusions onto this scene were economic and demographic. As a result of the boom in agricultural prices during the sixteenth century, followed by the economic difficulties of the seventeenth, differences in the wealth of the villagers became more marked. The richer peasants began to set themselves apart from their poorer neighbors, and the feeling of village unity began to break down. These divisions were exacerbated by the rise in population during the sixteenth century—which strained resources and forced the less fortunate to leave in search of better opportunities in cities—and by the pressures of taxation, exploitation, plague, and famine during the more difficult times of the seventeenth century.

Another intrusion that undermined the traditional cohesion of the community was the increased presence of royal officials. For centuries, elected councils, drawn from every part of the population, had run village affairs throughout Europe. In the late seventeenth century, however, these councils began to disappear as outside forces—in some cases a nearby lord, but more often government officials—asserted their control over the localities. Tax gatherers and army recruiters were now familiar figures throughout Europe. Although they were often the target of peasant rebellions, they were also welcomed when, for example, they distributed food during a famine. Their long-term influence, however, was the creation of a new layer of outside authority in the village, which was another cause of the division and fragmentation that led many to flee to the city.

As these outside intrusions multiplied, the interests of the local lord, who traditionally had defended the village's autonomy and had offered help in times of need, also changed. Nobles were beginning to look more and more to royal courts and capital cities, rather than to their local holdings, for position and power. The natural corollary was the "seigneurial reaction," with lords treating the villages they dominated as sources of income and increasingly distancing themselves from the inhabitants. Their commitment to charitable works declined, and they tended more and more to leave the welfare of the local population to church or government officials.

City Life As village life changed, the inhabitants who felt forced to leave headed for the city—an impersonal place where, instead of joining a cohesive population, they found themselves part of a mingling of peoples. The growing cities needed ever wider regions to provide them with food and goods, and they attracted the many who could not make ends meet in the countryside. Long-distance communications became more common, especially as localities were linked into national market and trade networks, and in the cities the new immigrants met others from distant villages.

A city was a far more chaotic place than a rural community. Urban society in general was fragmentary and

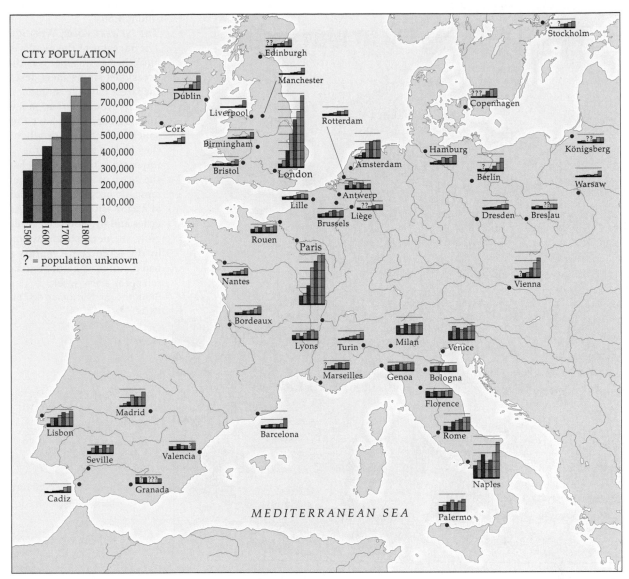

CITY POPULATION

900,000
800,000
700,000
600,000
500,000
400,000
300,000
200,000
100,000
0

1500 1600 1700 1800

? = population unknown

MAP 16.3 THE GROWTH OF CITIES, 1500–1800
In addition to the remarkable rise in the population of Europe's cities, particularly after 1550, this map reveals the northward shift in the distribution of the largest cities: in 1500, three of the four largest were in Italy; in 1700, only one. When did London overtake Paris as the largest city in Europe?
◆ For an online version, go to www.mhhe.com/chambers9 > chapter 16 > book maps

disorganized, even if an individual area, such as a parish, seemed distinct and cohesive—some parishes, for example, were associated with a single trade. A city's craft guilds gave structure to artisans and shopkeepers, regulating their lives and providing welfare, but less than half the population could join a guild. The rest did odd jobs or turned to crime. The chief attraction of cities was the wide variety of economic opportunity: for women, in such areas as selling goods and processing food; for men, in construction, on the docks, and in delivery services. But employment was unpredictable, and citizens did not have community support to fall back on in hard times as they did in the village. Even forms of recreation and enjoyment were different in the city.

Popular Culture in the City   One major difference between country and town was the level of literacy. Only in urban areas were there significant numbers of people who could read: It has been estimated that in cities perhaps a third of adult males were literate by 1700. Not only was reading necessary for commerce but it had been strongly encouraged by the Reformation, with its insistence that the faithful read the Bible for themselves.

Anonymous
THE NEWSVENDOR, WOODCUT
The ancestor of the regularly
published newspaper was the
occasional single sheet describing
the latest news or rumors.
Printers would produce a few
hundred copies and have them
sold by street vendors whenever
they had an event of some
importance to describe: a battle,
the death of a ruler, or some
fantastic occurrence like the birth
of a baby with two heads. As
cities and the potential readership
grew, the news sheets expanded;
by the seventeenth century they
had distinctive names and began
to appear every week.
Bibliothèque Nationale de France,
Paris

This stimulus ensured that literacy also rose among women, who increasingly became pupils at the growing number of schools in Europe (although they were still not admitted to universities). As many as 25 percent of the adult women in cities may have been able to read.

These changes had a notable effect on urban life. There was now a readership for newspapers, which became common by the mid-seventeenth century, as did the coffeehouses in which they were often read. Although newspaper stories were regularly inaccurate or untrue, and their writers (relying on informants at courts) could find themselves prosecuted for showing the authorities in a bad light, they were avidly consumed, and they made politics for the first time a subject of wide interest and discussion. Theater and opera also became popular entertainments, with women for the first time taking stage roles and obtaining performances for plays they had written. Sales of books surged, often because they had a popular audience, and they gave broad circulation to traditional favorites, such as travel stories and lives of saints, as well as to the latest ideas of science.

Belief in Magic and Rituals

Although in the countryside cultural patterns looked different—with lower literacy, simpler recreations, and more visible religiosity—there was one area of popular culture in which the outlook of the city and the village was remarkably similar: the belief in magic. The townspeople may have seemed more sophisticated, but the basic assumption they shared with their country cousins was that mysterious forces controlled nature and their own lives and that there was little they could do to ensure their own well-being. The world was full of spirits, and all one could do was encourage the good, defend oneself against the evil, and hope that the good would win. Nothing that happened—a calf dying, lightning striking a house—was accidental. Everything had a purpose. Any unusual event was an omen, part of a larger plan, or the action of some unseen force.

Charivari   To strengthen themselves against trouble, people used whatever help they could find. They organized special processions and holidays to celebrate good times such as harvests, to lament misfortunes, to complain about oppression, or to poke fun at scandalous behavior. These occasions, known as "rough music" in England and *charivari* in France, often used the theme of "the world turned upside down" to make their point. In the set pieces in a procession, a fool might be dressed up as a king, a woman might be shown beating her husband, or a tax collector might appear hanging from a tree. Whether ridiculing a dominating wife or lamenting the lack of bread, the community was expressing its solidarity in the face of difficulty or distasteful behavior through these rituals. They were a form of public opinion, enabling people to let off steam and express themselves.

The potential for violence was always present at such gatherings, especially when religious or social differences became entangled with other resentments. The viciousness of ordinary Protestants and Catholics toward one another revealed a frustration and aggressiveness that was not far below the surface. When food was scarce or new impositions had been ordered by their rulers, peasants and townspeople needed little excuse to show their anger openly. Women often took the

lead, not only because they had firsthand experience of the difficulty of feeding a family but also because troops were more reluctant to attack them.

Magical Remedies   Ordinary people also had other outlets for their frustrations. Recognizing their powerlessness in the face of outside forces, they resorted to their version of the magic that the literate were finding so fashionable at this very time. Whereas the sophisticated patronized astrologers, paying handsomely for horoscopes and advice about how to live their lives, the peasants and the poor consulted popular almanacs or sought out "cunning men" and wise women for secret spells, potions, and other remedies for their anxieties. Even religious ceremonies were thought of as being related to the rituals of the magical world, in which so-called white witches—the friendly kind—gave assistance when a ring was lost or when the butter would not form out of the milk.

Witches and Witch-Hunts   Misfortunes were never just plain bad luck; rather, there was intent behind everything that happened. Events were willed, and if they turned out badly, they must have been willed by the good witch's opposite, the evil witch. Such beliefs often led to cruel persecutions of innocent victims—usually helpless old women, able to do nothing but mutter curses when taunted by neighbors, and easy targets if someone had to be blamed for unfortunate happenings.

This quest for scapegoats naturally focused on the most vulnerable members of society, such as Jews or, in the case of witches, women. Accusations were often directed at a woman who was old and alone, with nobody to defend her. She was feared because she seemed to be an outsider or not sufficiently deferential to her supposed betters. It was believed that witches read strange books and knew magic spells, an indication of what many regarded as inappropriate and dangerous levels of literacy for a woman.

In the sixteenth and seventeenth centuries, the hunt for witches intensified to levels never previously reached. This period has been called the era of the "great witch craze," and for good reason. There were outbursts in every part of Europe, and tens of thousands of the accused were executed. Dozens of men, most of them clerics, made witch-hunting a full-time profession and persuaded civic and other government authorities to devote their resources to stamping out this threat to social and religious stability. Suspects were almost always tortured, and it is not too surprising that they usually "confessed" and implicated others as servants of the devil. The practices that were uncovered varied—in some areas witches were said to dance with the devil, in others to fly on broomsticks, in

Hans Baldung Grien
***WITCHES*, WOODCUT**
This woodcut by the German artist Grien shows the popular image of witches in early modern Europe. One carries a potion while flying on a goat. The others put together the ingredients for a magic potion in a jar inscribed with mystical symbols. The fact that witches were thought to be learned women who could understand magic was another reason they were feared by a Europe that expected women to be uneducated.

others to be possessed by evil spirits who could induce dreadful (and possibly psychosomatic) symptoms—but the punishment was usually the same: burning at the stake. And the hysteria was infectious. One accusation could trigger dozens more until entire regions were swept with fear and hatred.

Forces of Restraint

By the middle of the seventeenth century, the wave of assaults on witches was beginning to recede (see "A Witness Analyzes the Witch Craze," p. 487). Social and political leaders came to realize that the campaigns

A WITNESS ANALYZES THE WITCH CRAZE

Although for most Europeans around 1600 witchcraft was real—a religious problem caused by the devil—there were a few observers who were beginning to think more analytically about the reasons for the rapid spread of accusations. One such observer was a clergyman named Linden, who was attached to the cathedral of the great city of Trier in western Germany. His description of a witch-hunt in the Trier region ignored the standard religious explanations.

"Inasmuch as it was popularly believed that the continued sterility of many years was caused by witches, the whole area rose to exterminate the witches. This movement was promoted by many in office, who hoped to gain wealth from the persecution. And so special accusers, inquisitors, notaries, judges, and constables dragged to trial and torture human beings of both sexes and burned them in great numbers. Scarcely any of those who were accused escaped punishment. So far did the madness of the furious populace and the courts go in this thirst for blood and booty that there was scarcely anybody who was not smirched by some suspicion of this crime. Meanwhile, notaries, copyists and innkeepers grew rich. The executioner rode a fine horse, like a noble of the court, and dressed in gold and silver; his wife competed with noble dames in the richness of her array. A direr pestilence or a more ruthless invader could hardly have ravaged the territory than this inquisition and persecution without bounds. Many were the reasons for doubting that all were really guilty. At last, though the flames were still unsated, the people grew poor, rules were made and enforced restricting the fees and costs of examinations, and suddenly, as when in war funds fail, the zeal of the persecutors died out."

From George L. Burr (ed.), "The Witch Persecutions," *Translations and Reprints from the Original Sources of European History*, Vol. 3, Philadelphia: University of Pennsylvania, 1902, pp. 13–14.

against witches could endanger authority, especially when accusations were turned against the rich and privileged classes. Increasingly, therefore, cases were not brought to trial, and when they were, lawyers and doctors (who treated the subject less emotionally than the clergy) cast doubt on the validity of the testimony. Gradually, excesses were restrained and control was reestablished; by 1700 there was only a trickle of new incidents.

The decline in accusations of witchcraft reflected not only the more general quieting down of conflict and upheaval in the late seventeenth century but also the growing proportion of Europe's population that was living in cities. Here, less reliant on the luck of good weather, people could feel themselves more in control of their own fates. If there were unexpected fires, there were fire brigades; if a house burned down, there might even be insurance—a new protection for individuals that was spreading in the late 1600s. A process that has been called the "disenchantment" of the world—growing skepticism about spirits and mysterious forces, and greater self-reliance—was under way.

Religious Discipline   The churches played an important part in suppressing the traditional reliance on magic. In Catholic countries the Counter-Reformation produced better-educated priests who were trained to impose official doctrine instead of tolerating unusual local customs. Among Protestants, ministers were similarly well educated and denounced magical practices as idolatrous or superstitious. And both camps treated passion and enthusiasm with suspicion. Habits did not change overnight, but gradually ordinary people were being persuaded to abandon old fears and beliefs. There were still major scares in midcentury. An eclipse in 1654 prompted panic throughout Europe; comets still inspired prophecies of the end of the world; and in the 1660s a self-proclaimed messiah named Shabtai Zvi attracted a massive following among the Jews of Europe and the Middle East. Increasingly, though, such visions of doom or the end of time were becoming fringe beliefs, dismissed by authorities and most elements of society. Eclipses and comets now had scientific explanations, and the messiah came to be regarded as a spiritual, not an immediate, promise.

Summary

Even at the level of popular culture, therefore, Europeans had reason to feel, by the late seventeenth century, that a time of upheaval and uncertainty was over. A sense of confidence and orderliness was returning, and in intellectual circles the optimism seemed justified by the achievements of science. In fact, there arose a scholarly dispute around 1700, known as the "battle of the books," in which one side claimed, for the first time, that the "moderns" had outshone the "ancients." Using the scientists as their chief example, the advocates of the "moderns" argued—in a remarkable break with the reverence for the past that had dominated medieval and Renaissance culture—that advances in thought were possible and that one did not always have to accept the superiority of antiquity. Such self-confidence made it clear that, in the world of ideas as surely as in the world of politics, a period of turbulence had given way to an era of renewed assurance and stability.

QUESTIONS FOR FURTHER THOUGHT

1. Are there similarities in the creativity that marks the scientist and the artist?

2. Is it fair to ask whether popular beliefs and rituals do more harm than good?

RECOMMENDED READING

Sources

*Drake, Stillman (tr. and ed.). *Discoveries and Opinions of Galileo.* 1957. The complete texts of some of Galileo's most important works.

*Hall, Marie Boas (ed.). *Nature and Nature's Laws: Documents of the Scientific Revolution.* 1970. A good collection of documents by and about the pioneers of modern science.

Studies

Biagioli, Mario. *Galileo, Courtier: The Practice of Science in the Culture of Absolutism.* 1993. A fascinating study of the political forces at work in Galileo's career.

Braudel, Fernand. *Capitalism and Material Life, 1400–1800.* Miriam Kochan (tr.). 1973. A classic, pioneering study of the structure of daily life in early modern Europe.

*Burke, Peter. *Popular Culture in Early Modern Europe.* 1978. A lively introduction to the many forms of expression and belief among the ordinary people of Europe.

Fara, Patricia. *Newton: The Making of a Genius.* 2002.

*Gutmann, Myron P. *Toward the Modern Economy: Early Industry in Europe, 1500–1800.* 1988. A clear survey of recent work on economic development in this period.

*Ladurie, Emmanuel Le Roy. *The Peasants of Languedoc.* John Day (tr.). 1966. A brilliant evocation of peasant life in France in the sixteenth and seventeenth centuries.

*Levack, Brian P. *The Witch-Hunt in Early Modern Europe.* 1987. An excellent survey of the belief in witchcraft and its consequences.

Oppenheimer, Paul. *Rubens: A Portrait.* 2002.

Rabb, Theodore K. *Renaissance Lives.* 1993. Brief biographies of fifteen people, both famous and obscure, who lived just before and during this period.

*Shapin, S. *The Scientific Revolution.* 1996.

*Shearman, John. *Mannerism.* 1968. The best short introduction to a difficult artistic style.

*Thomas, Keith. *Religion and the Decline of Magic.* 1976. The most thorough account of popular culture yet published, this enormous book, while dealing mainly with England, treats at length such subjects as witchcraft, astrology, and ghosts in a most readable style.

Wiesner, Merry E. *Women and Gender in Early Modern Europe.* 1993.

*Available in paperback.

Nicolas de Largilliére
LOUIS XIV AND HIS FAMILY
Louis XIV (seated) is shown here in full regal splendor surrounded by three of his heirs. On his right is his eldest son, on his left is his eldest grandson, and, reaching out his hand, is his eldest great-grandson, held by his governess. All three of these heirs died before Louis, and thus they never became kings of France.

Chapter Seventeen

THE EMERGENCE OF THE EUROPEAN STATE SYSTEM

ABSOLUTISM IN FRANCE • OTHER PATTERNS OF ABSOLUTISM • ALTERNATIVES TO
ABSOLUTISM • THE INTERNATIONAL SYSTEM

The acceptance of strong central governments that emerged out of the crisis of the mid-seventeenth century was a victory not merely for kings but for an entire way of organizing society. As a result of huge increases in the scale of warfare and taxation, bureaucracies had mushroomed, and their presence was felt throughout Europe. Yet no central administration, however powerful, could function without the support of the nobles who ruled the countryside. Regional loyalties had dominated European society for centuries, and only a regime that drew on those loyalties could hope to maintain the support of its subjects. The political structures that developed during the century following the 1650s were, therefore, the work not only of ambitious princes but also of a nobility long accustomed to exercising authority and now prepared to find new ways of exerting its influence. To the leaders of society during the century following the crisis of the 1640s and 1650s, it was clear that state building and the imposition of their power on the rest of the world were now ever more central to rulers' ambitions, and required a common effort to establish stronger political, social, military, financial, and religious structures that would support effective government. The institutions and practices they created have remained essential to the modern state ever since.

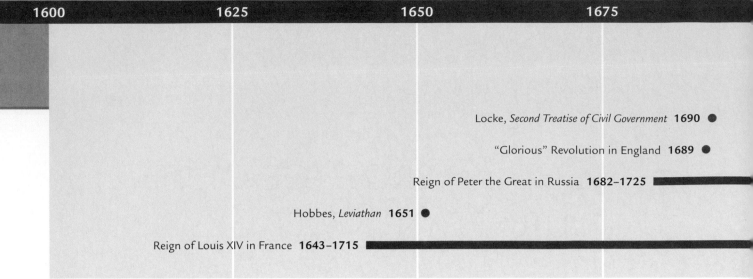

Locke, *Second Treatise of Civil Government* **1690** ●

"Glorious" Revolution in England **1689** ●

Reign of Peter the Great in Russia **1682–1725**

Hobbes, *Leviathan* **1651** ●

Reign of Louis XIV in France **1643–1715**

ABSOLUTISM IN FRANCE

One way of creating a strong, centralized state was the political system known as **absolutism:** the belief that power emanated from the monarch's unlimited authority. Absolutism was based on a theory known as the **divine right of kings,** derived from the fact that kings were anointed with holy oil at their coronations; it asserted that the monarch was God's representative on earth.

The Rule of Louis XIV

The most famous absolutist state was the Kingdom of France, which became the most powerful regime in Europe. Taken to an extreme, as it was by Louis XIV (1643–1715), absolutism justified unlimited power and treated treason as blasphemy. The leading advocate of the theory, Bishop Bossuet, called Louis God's lieutenant and argued that the Bible itself endorsed absolutism. In reality, the king worked in close partnership with the nobles to maintain order, and he often (though not always) felt obliged to defend their local authority as a reinforcement of his own power. Nevertheless, the very notion that the king not only was supreme but could assert his will with armies and bureaucracies of unprecedented size gave absolutism both an image and a reality that set it apart from previous systems of monarchical rule. Here at last was a force that could hold together and control the increasingly complex interactions of regions and interest groups that made up a state.

Versailles The setting in which a central government operated often reflected its power and its methods. Philip II in the late 1500s had created, at the Escorial outside Madrid, the first isolated palace that controlled a large realm. A hundred years later, Louis XIV created at Versailles, near Paris, a far more elaborate court as the center of an even larger and more intrusive bureaucracy than Philip's. The isolation of government and the exercise of vast personal power seemed to go hand in hand.

The king moved the court in the 1680s to Versailles, 12 miles from Paris, where, at a cost of half a year's royal income, he transformed a small chateau his father had built into the largest building in Europe. There, far from Parisian mobs, he enjoyed the splendor and the ceremonies, centered on himself, which exalted his majesty. His self-aggrandizing image as "Sun King" was symbolized by coins that showed the sun's rays falling first on Louis and only then, by reflection, onto his subjects. Every French nobleman of any significance spent time each year at Versailles, not only to maintain access to royal patronage and governmental affairs but also to demonstrate the wide support for Louis' system of rule. Historians have called this process the domestication of the aristocracy, as great lords who had once drawn their status from their lineage or lands came to regard service to the throne as the best route to power. But the benefits cut both ways. The king gained the services of influential administrators, and they gained privileges and rewards without the uncertainties that had accompanied their traditional resistance to central control.

Court Life The visible symbol of Louis' absolutism was Versailles. Here the leaders of France assembled, and around them swirled the most envied social circles of the time. From the court emanated the policies and directives that increasingly affected the lives of the king's subjects and also determined France's relations with other states.

492

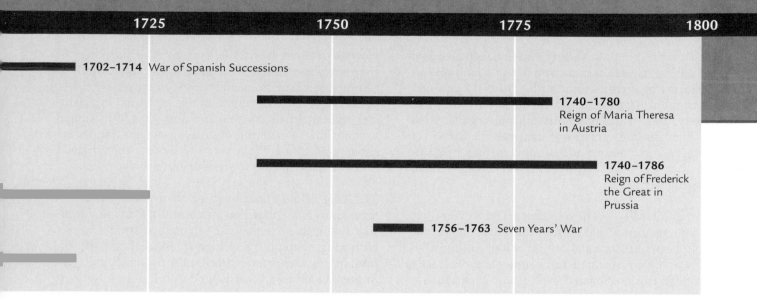

1725	1750	1775	1800

1702–1714 War of Spanish Successions

1740–1780
Reign of Maria Theresa
in Austria

1740–1786
Reign of Frederick
the Great in
Prussia

1756–1763 Seven Years' War

At Versailles, too, French culture was shaped by the king's patronage of those artists and writers who appealed to the royal taste. For serious drama and history, Louis turned to the playwright and writer Racine (1639–1699); for comedy, to the theatrical producer and playwright Molière (1622–1673); and for opera and the first performances of what we now call ballet, to the composer Lully (1632–1687). Moreover, all artistic expression, from poetry to painting, was regulated by royal academies that were founded in the 1600s;

PERSPECTIVE VIEW OF VERSAILLES FROM THE PLACE D'ARMES, 1698
This painting shows Versailles not long before Louis decided to move there; he was soon to begin an enormous expansion into the gardens at the back that more than doubled the size of the buildings. In this scene, the royal coach, with its entourage, is just about to enter the château.
Giraudon/Art Resource, NY

backed by the king's authority, these academies laid down rules for what was acceptable in such areas as verse forms or architectural style. Official taste was what counted. The dazzling displays at Versailles had to observe strict rules of dignity and gravity that were considered the only means of exalting the king. Yet everything was done on a scale and with a magnificence that no other European ruler could match, though many tried.

Paris and Versailles   The one alternative to Versailles as a center of society and culture was Paris, and indeed the split between court and capital was one of the divisions between government and people that eventually was to lead to the French Revolution. A particularly notable difference was in the role of women. Versailles was overwhelmingly a male society. Women achieved prominence only as royal mistresses in Louis' early years or as the creators of a rigidly pious atmosphere in his last years. They were also essential to the highly elaborate rituals of civility and manners that developed at Versailles. But they were allowed no independent initiative in social or cultural matters.

In Paris, by contrast, women established and dominated the gatherings known as **salons** that promoted easy conversation, a mixture of social backgrounds, and forms of expression—political discussion and ribald humor, for example—that were not acceptable at the staid and sober court. Yet the contrasts were not merely between the formal palace and the relaxed salon. Even before Louis moved to Versailles, he banned as improper one of Molière's comedies, *Tartuffe*, which mocked excessive religious devoutness. It took five years of reworking by Molière before Louis allowed the play to be performed (1669), and it then became a major hit in Paris, but it was never a favorite at court.

Government

Absolutism was more than a device to satisfy royal whims, for Louis was a gifted administrator and politician who used his power for state building. By creating and reorganizing government institutions, he strengthened his authority at home and increased his ascendancy over his neighbors. The longest-lasting result of his absolutism was that the French state won control over three crucial activities: the use of armed force, the formulation and execution of laws, and the collection and expenditure of revenue. These functions, in turn, depended on a centrally controlled bureaucracy responsive to royal orders and efficient enough to carry them out in distant provinces over the objections of local groups.

Nobody could suppress all vested interests and local loyalties, but the bureaucracy was supposed to be insulated from outside pressure by the absolute monarch's power to remove and transfer appointees. This independence was also promoted by training programs, improved administrative methods, and the use of experts wherever possible—both in the central bureaucracy and in provincial offices. Yet the system could not have functioned without the cooperation of local aristocrats, who were encouraged to use the power and income they derived from official positions to strengthen central authority.

The King's Dual Functions   At the head of this structure, Louis XIV carried off successfully a dual function that few monarchs had the talent to sustain: He was both king in council and king in court. Louis the administrator coexisted with Louis the courtier, who hunted, cultivated the arts, and indulged in huge banquets. Among his many imitators, however, the easier side of absolutism, court life, consumed an excessive share of a state's resources and became an end in itself. The effect was to give prestige to the leisure pursuits of the upper classes while sapping the energies of influential figures. Louis was one of the few who avoided sacrificing affairs of state to regal pomp.

Like court life, government policy under Louis XIV was tailored to the aim of state building. As he was to discover, the resources and powers at his disposal were not endless. But until the last years of his reign, they served his many purposes extremely well (see "Louis XIV on Kingship," p. 495). Moreover, Louis had superb support at the highest levels of his administration—ministers whose viewpoints differed but whose skills were carefully blended by their ruler.

Competing Ministers   Until the late 1680s the king's two leading advisers were Jean-Baptiste Colbert and the marquis of Louvois. Colbert was a financial wizard who regarded a mercantilist policy as the key to state building. He believed that the government should give priority to increasing France's wealth. As a result, he believed that the chief danger to the country's well-being was the United Provinces, Europe's great trader state, and that royal resources should be poured into the navy, manufacturing, and shipping. By contrast, Louvois, the son of a military administrator, consistently emphasized the army as the foundation of France's power. He believed that the country was threatened primarily by land—by the Holy Roman Empire on its flat, vulnerable northeast frontier—and thus that resources should be allocated to the army and to border fortifications.

Foreign Policy

Louis tried to balance these goals within his overall aims—to expand France's frontiers and to assert his superiority over other European states. Like the magnifi-

LOUIS XIV ON KINGSHIP

From time to time, Louis XIV put on paper brief accounts of his actions: For example, he wrote some brief memoirs in the late 1660s. These reflections about his role as king were intended as a guide for his son and indicate both his high view of kingship and the seriousness with which he approached his duties. The following are extracts from his memoirs and other writings.

"Homage is due to kings, and they do whatever they like. It certainly must be agreed that, however bad a prince may be, it is always a heinous crime for his subjects to rebel against him. He who gave men kings willed that they should be respected as His lieutenants, and reserved to Himself the right to question their conduct. It is His will that everyone who is born a subject should obey without qualification. This law, as clear as it is universal, was not made only for the sake of princes: it is also for the good of the people themselves. It is therefore the duty of kings to sustain by their own example the religion upon which they rely; and they must realize that, if their subjects see them plunged in vice or violence, they can hardly render to their person the respect due to their office, or recognize in them the living image of Him who is all-holy as well as almighty.

"It is a fine thing, a noble and enjoyable thing, to be a king. But it is not without its pains, its fatigues, and its troubles. One must work hard to reign. In working for the state, a king is working for himself. The good of the one is the glory of the other. When the state is prosperous, famous, and powerful, the king who is the cause of it is glorious; and he ought in consequence to have a larger share than others do of all that is most agreeable in life."

From J. M. Thompson, *Lectures on Foreign History, 1494–1789,* Oxford: Blackwell, 1956, pp. 172–174.

Antoine Watteau
FÊTE IN THE PARK, **1718**
The luxurious life of the nobility during the eighteenth century is captured in this scene of men and women in fine silks, enjoying a picnic in a lovely park setting.
Reproduced by Permission of the Trustees of the Wallace Collection, London

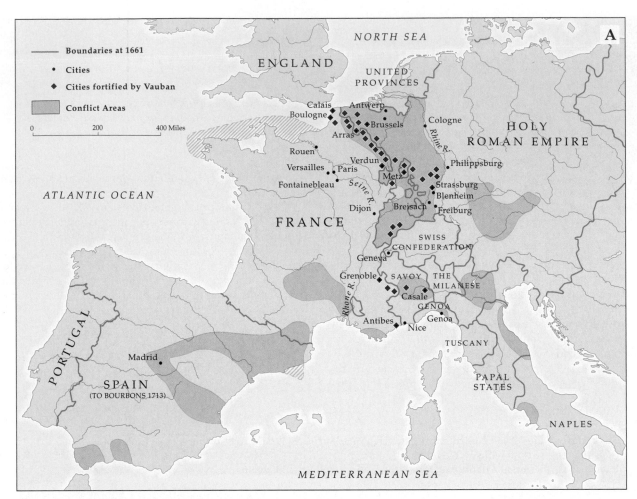

MAP 17.1A　THE WARS OF LOUIS XIV
Louis XIV's aggressive aims took his troops to many areas of Europe.
◆ For an online version, go to www.mhhe.com/chambers9 > chapter 17 > book maps

cence of his court, his power on the international scene served to demonstrate *la gloire* (the glory) of France. But his effort to expand that power prompted his neighbors to form coalitions and alliances of common defense, designed to keep him in check. From this response was to emerge the concept of a state system and the notion of a **balance of power** among the states of Europe.

In his early years Louis relied heavily on Colbert, who moved gradually toward war with the Dutch when he was unable to undermine their control of French maritime trade. But the war (1672–1678) was a failure, and so the pendulum swung toward Louvois' priorities. In the early 1680s Louis adopted the marquis's aims and claimed a succession of territories on France's northeast border. No one claim seemed large enough to provoke his neighbors to fight, especially

since the Holy Roman Emperor, Leopold I, was distracted by a resumption in 1682 of war with the Turks in the east. The result was that France was able to annex large segments of territory until, in 1686, a league of other European states was formed to restrain Louis' growing power (see maps 17.1A and 17.1B).

Louis versus Europe　The leaders of the league were William III of the United Provinces and Emperor Leopold. Leopold was prepared to join the struggle because his war with the Turks turned in his favor after 1683, when his troops broke a Turkish siege of Vienna. And six years later William became a far more formidable foe when he gained the English throne. In 1688 the league finally went to war to put an end to French expansion. When Louis began to lose the territories he had gained in the 1680s, he decided to seek peace and

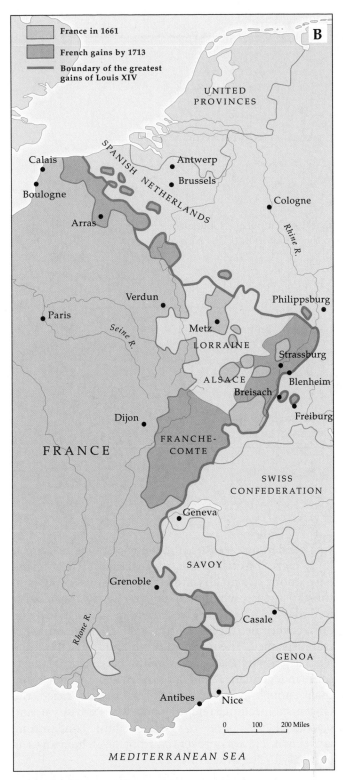

MAP 17.1B
THE WARS OF LOUIS XIV
The main conflict was on France's eastern border, where Louis made small but significant gains. Why was there so much conflict along this border?

◆ For an online version, go to www.mhhe.com/chambers9 > chapter 17 > book maps

remove Louvois from power in 1690, though the war did not end until 1697. But the respite did not last long. Four years later France became involved in a bitter war that brought famine, wretched poverty, and humiliation. This was a war to gain the Spanish throne for Louis' family, regardless of the devastating consequences of the fighting. This final, ruinous enterprise revealed both the new power of France and its limits. By launching an all-out attempt to establish his supremacy in Europe, Louis showed that he felt capable of taking on the whole of the continent; but by then he no longer had the economic and military base at home or the weak opposition abroad to ensure success.

Economic strains had begun to appear in the 1690s, when shattering famines throughout France reduced tax revenues and the size of the workforce, even as enemies began to unite abroad. Louis had the most formidable army in Europe—400,000 men by the end of his reign—but both William and Leopold believed he could be defeated by a combined assault, and they led the attack in the final showdown when the Habsburg king of Spain, Charles II, died without an heir in 1700.

The War of Spanish Succession There were various claimants to the Spanish throne, but Charles's choice was Philip, Louis XIV's grandson (see "The Spanish Succession, 1700," p. 498). Had Louis been willing to agree not to unite the thrones of France and Spain and to allow the Spanish empire to be opened (for the first time) to foreign traders, Charles's wish might have been respected. But Louis refused to compromise, and in 1701 William and Leopold created the so-called Grand Alliance, which declared war on France the following year. The French now had to fight virtually all of Europe in a war over the Spanish succession, not only at home but also overseas, in India, Canada, and the Caribbean.

Led by two brilliant generals—the Englishman John Churchill, duke of Marlborough, and the Austrian Prince Eugène—the Grand Alliance won a series of smashing victories. France's hardships were increased by a terrible famine in 1709. Although the criticism of his policies became fierce and dangerous rebellions erupted, the Sun King retained his hold over his subjects. Despite military disaster, he was able to keep his nation's borders intact and the Spanish throne for his grandson (though he had to give up the possibility of union with France and end the restrictions on trade in the Spanish empire) when peace treaties were signed at Utrecht in 1713 and 1714. When it was all over, Louis' great task of state building, both at home and abroad, had withstood the severest of tests: defeat on the battlefield.

THE SPANISH SUCCESSION, 1700

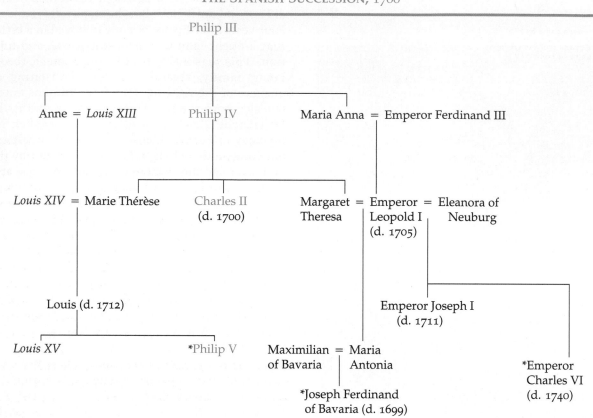

Note: Names in blue = kings of Spain; names in r ed = kings of France.

*People designated at various times as heirs of Charles II.

Domestic Policy

Control and Reform The assertion of royal supremacy at home was almost complete by the time Louis came to power, but he extended centralized control to religion and social institutions. Both the Protestant Huguenots and the Catholic Jansenists interfered with the religious uniformity that Louis considered essential in an absolutist state. As a result, pressures against these groups mounted steadily. In 1685 Louis revoked the Edict of Nantes, now almost a century old, which had granted Protestants limited toleration, and he forced France's 1 million Huguenots either to leave the country (four-fifths did) or to convert to Catholicism. This was a political rather than a religious step, taken to promote unity despite the economic consequences that followed the departure of a vigorous, productive, and entrepreneurial minority.

Jansenism was more elusive. It had far fewer followers, and it was a movement that emphasized spiritual values within Catholicism. But the very fact that it challenged the official Church emphasis on ritual and was condemned by Rome made it a source of unrest. Even more unsettling was its success in gaining support among the magistrate class—the royal officers in the parlements, who had to register all royal edicts before they became law. The Parlement of Paris was the only governmental institution that offered Louis any real resistance. The issues over which it caused trouble were usually religious, and the link between *parlementaire* independence and Jansenism gave Louis more than enough reason for displeasure. He razed the Jansenists' headquarters, the Abbey of Port-Royal, and persuaded the pope to issue a bull condemning Jansenism. He was prevented from implementing the bull only by his death in 1715.

The drive toward uniformity that prompted these actions was reflected in all of domestic policy. Louis kept in check what little protest arose in the parlements and either forbade or overruled their efforts to block his decrees; major uprisings by peasants in central France in the 1690s and 1700s were ruthlessly suppressed; Parisian publishers came under bureaucratic supervision; and the *intendants*, the government's chief provincial officers, were given increased authority, especially to supply the ever-growing money and recruitment needs of the army.

At the outset of his rule, Louis also used his power to improve France's economy. In these early years, under Colbert's ministry, major efforts were made to stimulate manufacturing, agriculture, and home and foreign trade. Some industries, notably those involving luxuries, like the silk production of Lyons, received considerable help and owed their prosperity to royal patronage. Colbert also tried, not entirely effectively, to reduce the crippling effects of France's countless internal tolls. These were usually nobles' perquisites, and they could multiply the cost of shipped goods. The government divided the country into a number of districts, within which shipments were to be toll-free, but the system never removed the worst abuses. Louis also hoped to boost foreign trade, at first by financing new overseas trading companies and later by founding new port cities as naval and commercial centers. He achieved notable success only in the West Indies, where sugar plantations became a source of great wealth.

The End of an Era

Louis' success in state building was remarkable, and France became the envy of Europe. Yet ever since the Sun King's reign, historians have recalled the famines and wars of his last years and have contrasted his glittering court with the misery of most French people. Taxes and rents rose remorselessly, and in many regions the hardships were made worse by significant declines in the population. Particularly after the famines of the 1690s and 1709, many contemporaries remarked on the dreadful condition of France's peasants.

The reign of Louis XIV can thus be regarded as the end of an era in the life of the lower classes. By pushing his need for resources to its limits, he inflicted a level of suffering that was not to recur, because governments increasingly came to realize that state building depended on the welfare and support of their people. In the eighteenth century, although there was still much suffering to come, the terrible subsistence crises, with their cycles of famine and plague, came to an end, largely because of official efforts to distribute food in starving areas and to isolate and suppress outbreaks of plague. Thus, although the hand of the central government was heavier in 1715 than a hundred years before, it was becoming more obviously a beneficent as well as a burdensome force. The Counter-Reformation Church, growing in strength since the Council of Trent, also had a more salutary influence as religious struggles died away, for it brought into local parishes better-educated and more dedicated priests who, as part of their new commitment to service, exerted themselves to calm the outbreaks of witchcraft and irrational fear that had swept the countryside for centuries. Despite the strains Louis had caused, therefore, his absolutist authority was now firmly in place and could ensure a dominant European role for a united and powerful France.

France after Louis XIV

The Sun King had created a model for absolutism in partnership with his nobility, but the traditional ambitions of the nobles reasserted themselves after he died in 1715, leaving a child as his heir. The duke of Orlèans, Louis XIV's nephew, who became regent until 1723, sought to restore the aristocrats' authority. He also gave the parlements political power and replaced royal bureaucrats with councils composed of leading members of the nobility. The councils were unable to govern effectively, but the parlements would never again surrender their power to veto royal legislation. They became a rallying point for those who opposed centralization and wished to limit the king's powers.

Finance was also a serious problem for the government, because of the debts left by Louis XIV's wars. A brilliant Scottish financier, John Law, suggested an answer: a government-sponsored central bank that would issue paper notes, expand credit, and encourage investment in a new trading company for the French colonies. By tying the bank to this company, the Company of the Occident, a venture that promised subscribers vast profits from the Louisiana territory in North America, Law set off an investment boom. But the public's greed soon pushed prices for the company's stock to insanely high levels. A bust was inevitable, and when it came, in 1720, the entire scheme of bank notes and credit collapsed.

Louis XV and Fleury   Political and financial problems were to plague France throughout the eighteenth century, until the leaders of the French Revolution sought radical ways to solve them in the 1790s. Yet the uncertainties of the regency did give way to a long period of stability after 1726, when Louis XV gave almost unlimited authority to his aging tutor and adviser, Cardinal Fleury. Cautious, dedicated to the monarchy, and surrounded by talented subordinates, Fleury made absolutism function quietly and effectively and enabled France to recover from the setbacks that had marked the end of Louis XIV's reign. Fleury's tenure coincided with abundant harvests, slowly rising population, and increased commercial activity.

Political Problems   Fleury contained the ambitions of the governing class, but when he died in 1743 at the age of 90, the pressures exploded. War hawks plunged

HISTORICAL ISSUES: TWO VIEWS OF LOUIS XIV

Implicit in any assessment of the reign of Louis XIV in France is a judgment about the nature of absolutism and the kind of government the continental European monarchies created in the late seventeenth and eighteenth centuries. From the perspective of Frenchman Albert Sorel, a historian of the French Revolution writing at the end of the nineteenth century, the Revolution had been necessary to save France from Louis' heritage. For the American John Rule, a historian who concerned himself primarily with the development of political institutions during the seventeenth century, the marks of Louis XIV's rule were caution, bureaucracy, and order.

Sorel: "The edifice of the state enjoyed incomparable brilliance and splendor, but it resembled a Gothic cathedral in which the height of the nave and the arches had been pushed beyond all reason, weakening the walls as they were raised ever higher. Louis XIV carried the principle of monarchy to its utmost limit, and abused it in all respects to the point of excess. He left the nation crushed by war, mutilated by banishments, and impatient of the yoke which it felt to be ruinous. Men were worn-out, the treasury empty, all relationships strained by the violence of tension, and in the immense framework of the state there remained no institution except the accidental appearance of genius. Things had reached a point where, if a great king did not appear, there would be a great revolution."

From Albert Sorel, *L'Europe et la rèvolution française*, 3rd ed., Vol. 1, Paris, 1893, p. 199, as translated in William F. Church (ed.), *The Greatness of Louis XIV: Myth or Reality?*, Boston: D. C. Heath, 1959, p. 63.

Rule: "As Louis XIV himself said of the tasks of kingship, they were at once great, noble, and delightful. Yet Louis' enjoyment of his craft was tempered by political prudence. At an early age he learned to listen attentively to his advisers, to speak when spoken to, to ponder evidence, to avoid confrontations, to dissemble, to wait. He believed that time and tact would conquer. Despite all the evidence provided him by his ministers and his servants, Louis often hesitated before making a decision; he brooded, and in some instances put off decisions altogether. As he grew older, the king tended to hide his person and his office. Even his officials seldom saw the king for more than a brief interview. And as decision-making became centralized in the hands of the ministers, [so] the municipalities, the judges, the local estates, the guilds and at times the peasantry contested royal encroachments on their rights. Yet to many in the kingdom, Louis represented a modern king, an agent of stability whose struggle was their struggle and whose goal was to contain the crises of the age."

From John C. Rule, "Louis XIV, *Roi-Bureaucrate*," in Rule (ed.), *Louis XIV and the Craft of Kingship*, Columbus: Ohio State University Press, 1969, pp. 91–92.

France into the first of several unsuccessful wars with its neighbors that strained French credit to the breaking point. At home royal authority also deteriorated. Having no one to replace Fleury as chief minister, Louis XV put his confidence in a succession of advisers, some capable, some mediocre. But he did not back them when attacks arose from court factions. Uninterested in government, he avoided confrontation, neglected affairs of state, and devoted himself instead to hunting and to court ceremony.

Although Louis XV provided weak leadership, France's difficulties were structural as well as personal. The main problems—special privileges and finance—posed almost impossible challenges. Governments that levy new taxes arbitrarily seem despotic, even if the need for them is clear and the distribution equitable. One of France's soundest taxes was the *vingtième*, or twentieth, which was supposed to tap the income of all

parts of French society roughly equally. But the nobility and clergy evaded most of the tax. Naturally, aggressive royal ministers wanted to remedy that situation. In the 1750s, for example, an effort was made to put teeth into the *vingtième's* bite on the clergy's huge wealth. But the effort failed. The clergy resisted furiously; and the parlements denounced the "despotism" of a crown that taxed its subjects arbitrarily. Thus, the privileged groups not only blocked reforms but also made the monarch's position more difficult by their opposition and rhetoric of liberty.

The Long Term Despite these special interests, the 1700s were a time of notable advance for Europe's most populous and wealthy state. France enjoyed remarkable expansion in population, in the rural economy, in commerce, and in empire building. No one knew at the time that the failures of reforming royal ministers in

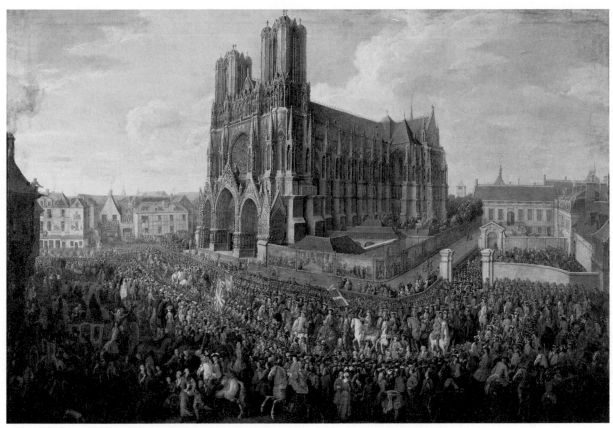

Pierre Denis Martin
PROCESSION AFTER LOUIS XV'S CORONATION AT RHEIMS, 26 OCTOBER 1722, CA. 1724
This magnificent scene, in front of the cathedral in which French kings traditionally were crowned, provides a sense of the throngs who came to celebrate the day in 1722 when Louis XV officially came of age and received his crown. Paintings depicting royal virtue were erected around the cathedral, and Louis himself (in red on a white horse just to the right of center) was preceded by a flag covered with his symbol, the fleur-de-lis. The other flags remind us that this event was an occasion for international pageantry.
Giraudon/Art Resource, NY

the mid-1700s foretold a stalemate that would help bring the old regime crashing down.

OTHER PATTERNS OF ABSOLUTISM

Four other monarchies pursued state building through absolutist regimes in this period, often in imitation of the French model. The governments they created in Vienna, Berlin, Madrid, and St. Petersburg differed in strengths and weaknesses, but all were attempts to centralize power around a formidable ruler.

The Habsburgs at Vienna

The closest imitation of Versailles was the court of the Habsburg Leopold I, the Holy Roman emperor (1658–1705). Heir to a reduced inheritance that gave him control over only Bohemia, Austria, and a small part of

Hungary, Leopold still maintained a splendid establishment. His plans for a new palace, Schönbrunn, that was supposed to outshine Versailles were modified only because of a lack of funds. And his promotion of the court as the center of all political and social life turned Vienna into what it had never been before: a city for nobles as well as small-time traders.

Nevertheless, Leopold did not display the pretensions of the Sun King. He was a younger son and had come to the throne only because of the death of his brother. Indecisive, retiring, and deeply religious, he had no fondness for the bravado Louis XIV enjoyed. He was a composer of some talent, and his patronage laid the foundation for the great musical culture that was to be one of Vienna's chief glories. But he did inherit considerable royal authority, which he sought to expand—though unlike Louis XIV he relied on a small group of leading nobles to devise policy and run his government.

Government Policy The Thirty Years' War that ended in 1648 had revealed that the elected head of the Holy Roman Empire could no longer control the princes who nominally owed him allegiance. In his own domains, however, he could maintain his control with the cooperation of his nobility. The Privy Council, which in effect ran Leopold's government, was filled largely with members of aristocratic families, and his chief advisers were always prominent nobles. To make policy, he consulted each of his ministers and then, even when all agreed, came to decisions with agonizing slowness.

Unlike the other courts of Europe, Schönbrunn did not favor only native-born aristocrats. The leader of Austria's armies during the Turks' siege of Vienna in 1683 was Charles, duke of Lorraine, whose duchy had been taken over by the French. His predecessor as field marshal had been an Italian, and his successor was to be one of the most brilliant soldiers of the age, Prince Eugène of Savoy. They became members of the Austrian nobility only when Leopold gave them titles within his own dominions, but they all fitted easily into the aristocratic circles that controlled the government and the army.

Eugène and Austria's Military Success Prince Eugène (1663–1736) was a spectacular symbol of the aristocracy's continuing dominance of politics and society. A member of one of Europe's most distinguished families, he had been raised in France but found himself passed over when Louis XIV awarded army commissions, perhaps because he had been intended for the Church. Yet he was determined to have a military career, and he volunteered to serve the Austrians in the war with the Turks that, following the siege of Vienna, was to expand Habsburg territory in the Balkans by the time peace was signed in 1699 (see map 17.2). Eugène's talents quickly became evident: He was field marshal of Austria's troops by the time he was 30. Over the next forty years, as intermittent war with the Turks continued, he became a decisive influence in Habsburg affairs. Though foreign-born, he was the minister primarily responsible for the transformation of Vienna's policies from defensive to aggressive.

Until the siege of Vienna by the Turks in 1683, Leopold's cautiousness kept Austria simply holding the line, both against Louis XIV and against the Turks. In the 1690s, however, at Eugène's urging, he tried a bolder course and in the process laid the foundations for a new Habsburg empire along the Danube River: Austria-Hungary. He helped create the coalition that defeated Louis in the 1700s, he intervened in Italy so that his landlocked domains could gain an outlet to the sea, and he began the long process of pushing the Turks

out of the Balkans. Although Leopold did not live to see the advance completed, by the time of Eugène's death, the Austrians' progress against the Turks had brought them within a hundred miles of the Black Sea.

The Power of the Nobility Yet the local power of the nobility tempered the centralization of Leopold's dominions. Unlike Louis XIV, who supported his nobles only if they worked for him, Leopold gave them influence in the government without first establishing control over all his lands. The nobles did not cause the Habsburgs as much trouble as they had during the Thirty Years' War, but Leopold had to limit his centralization outside Austria. Moreover, as Austrians came increasingly to dominate the court, the nobles of Hungary and Bohemia reacted by clinging stubbornly to their local rights. Thus, compared to France, Leopold's was an absolutism under which the nobility retained far more autonomous power.

The Hohenzollerns at Berlin

The one new power that emerged to prominence during the age of Louis XIV was Brandenburg-Prussia, and here again state building was made possible by a close alliance between a powerful ruler and his nobles. Frederick William of Hohenzollern (r. 1640–1688), known as the "great elector," ruled scattered territories that stretched seven hundred miles from Cleves, on the Rhine, to a part of Prussia on the Baltic. That so fragmented and disconnected a set of lands could be shaped into a major European power was a testimony to the political abilities of the Hohenzollerns. The process began when, taking advantage of the uncertainties that followed the Thirty Years' War, Frederick William made his territories the dominant principality in northern Germany and at the same time strengthened his power over his subjects.

Foreign Policy His first task was in foreign affairs, because when he became elector, the troops of the various states that were fighting the Thirty Years' War swarmed over his possessions. Frederick William realized that even a minor prince could emerge from these disasters in a good position if he had an army. With some military force at his disposal, he could become a useful ally for the big powers, who could then help him against his neighbors; while at home he would have the strength to crush his opponents.

By 1648 Frederick William had eight thousand troops, and he was backed by both the Dutch and the French in the Westphalia negotiations that year as a possible restraint on Sweden in northern Europe. With-

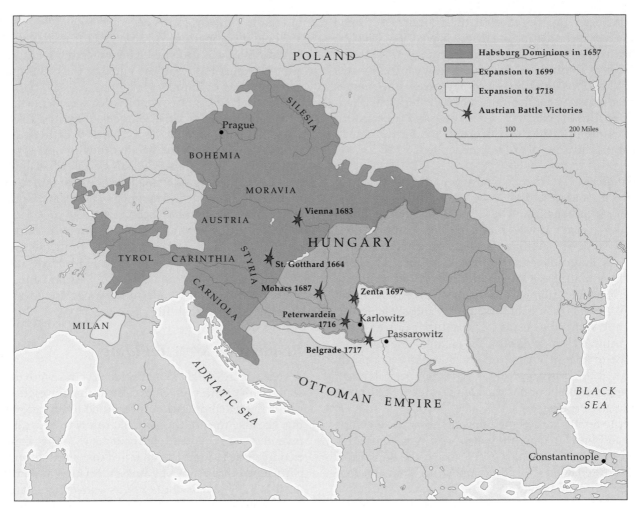

MAP 17.2 THE AUSTRIAN EMPIRE, 1657–1718
The steady advance of the Habsburgs into the Balkans was marked by a succession of victories; their gains were confirmed by treaties with the Turks at Karlowitz (1699) and Passarowitz (1718). **How much bigger were Habsburg dominions in 1718 than they were in 1657?**
◆ For an online version, go to www.mhhe.com/chambers9 > chapter 17 > book maps

out having done much to earn new territory, he did very well in the peace settlement, and he then took advantage of wars around the Baltic in the 1650s to confirm his gains by switching sides at crucial moments. In the process, his army grew to twenty-two thousand men, and he began to use it to impose his will on his own lands. The fact that the army was essential to Frederick William's success—at home and abroad—was to influence much of Prussia's and thus also Germany's subsequent history.

Domestic Policy   The role of the military in establishing the elector's supremacy was apparent throughout Brandenburg-Prussia's society. In 1653 the Diet of Brandenburg met for the last time, sealing its own fate by giving Frederick William the right to raise taxes without its consent. The War Chest, the office in charge of financing the army, took over the functions of a treasury department and collected government revenue even when the state was at peace. The implementation of policies in the localities was placed in the hands of war commissars—who originally were responsible for military recruitment, billeting, and supply but now became the principal agents of all government departments.

Apart from the representative assemblies, Frederick William faced real resistance only from the long-independent cities of his realm. Accustomed to going their own way because authority had been fragmented in the empire for centuries, and especially during the Thirty Years' War, city leaders were dismayed when the elector began to intervene in their affairs. Yet once again sheer intimidation overcame opposition. The last determined effort to dispute his authority arose in the rich city of Königsberg, which allied with the Estates General of Prussia to refuse to pay taxes. But this resistance was crushed in 1662, when Frederick William marched into the city with a few thousand troops. Similar pressure brought the towns of Cleves into submission after centuries of proud independence.

The Junkers   The main supporters and beneficiaries of the elector's state building were the Prussian nobles, known as **Junkers** (from the German for "young lord," *jung herr*). In fact, it was an alliance between the nobility and Frederick William that undermined the Diet, the cities, and the representative assemblies. The leading Junker families saw their best opportunities for the future in cooperation with the central government, and both in the representative assemblies and in the localities, they worked to establish absolutist power—that is, to remove all restraints on the elector. The most significant indicator of the Junkers' success was that by the end of the century, two tax rates had been devised, one for cities and one for the countryside, to the great advantage of the latter.

As the nobles staffed the upper levels of the elector's army and bureaucracy, they also won new prosperity for themselves. Particularly in Prussia, the support of the elector enabled them to reimpose serfdom and consolidate their land holdings into vast, highly profitable estates. This area was a major grain producer, and the Junkers maximized their profits by growing and distributing their produce themselves, thus eliminating middlemen. Efficiency became their hallmark, and their wealth was soon famous throughout the Holy Roman Empire. These Prussian entrepreneurs were probably the most successful group of European aristocrats in pursuing economic and political power.

Frederick III   Unlike Louis in France, Frederick William had little interest in court life. The Berlin court became the focus of society only under his son, Elector Frederick III, who ruled from 1688. The great elector had begun the development of his capital, Berlin, into a cultural center—he founded what was to become one of the finest libraries in the world, the Prussian State Library—but this was never among his prime concerns. His son, by contrast, had little interest in state building, but he did enjoy princely pomp and encouraged the arts with enthusiasm.

Frederick III lacked only one attribute of royalty: a crown. When Emperor Leopold I, who still had the right to confer titles in the empire, needed Prussia's troops during the War of the Spanish Succession, he gave Frederick, in return, the right to call himself "king in Prussia"; the title soon became "king of Prussia." At a splendid coronation in 1701, Elector Frederick III of Brandenburg was crowned King Frederick I, and thereafter his court felt itself the equal of the other monarchical centers of Europe.

Frederick determinedly promoted social and cultural glitter. He made his palace a focus of art and polite society that competed, he hoped, with Versailles. A construction program beautified Berlin with new churches and huge public buildings. He also established an Academy of Sciences and persuaded the most famous German scientist and philosopher of the day, Gottfried Wilhelm von Leibniz, to become its first president. All these activities obtained generous support from state revenues, as did the universities of Brandenburg and Prussia. By the end of his reign in 1713, Frederick had given his realm a throne, celebrated artistic and intellectual activity, and an elegant aristocracy at the head of social and political life.

Rivalry and State Building

Europe's increasingly self-confident states were in constant rivalry with their neighbors during the eighteenth century. The competition intensified their state building, because the conflicts forced rulers to expand their revenues, armies, and bureaucracies. The counterexample was Poland, which failed to centralize and was partitioned three times by Russia, Austria, and Prussia, until in 1795 it ceased to exist as a sovereign state. Political consolidation, by putting a premium on military and economic power, shaped both the map of modern Europe and the centralization of the major states.

The relationship between international rivalry and internal development is well illustrated by Prussia and Austria. In the mid-eighteenth century these two powers sought to dominate central Europe, and they launched reforms to wage their struggle more effectively. Their absolute rulers built their states by increasing the size of their armies, collecting larger revenues, and developing bureaucracies for the war effort. Whether the ruler was a modern pragmatist like Frederick II of Prussia or a pious traditionalist like Maria Theresa of Austria, both understood the demands of the state system.

The Prussia of Frederick William I

Prussia's Frederick William I (r. 1713–1740) relentlessly pursued a strengthened absolutism at home and Europe-wide influence abroad. Strikingly different from his refined father, this spartan ruler approached affairs of state as all business and little pleasure. He disdained court life, dismissed numerous courtiers, and cut the salaries of those who remained. Uncluttered by royal cere-

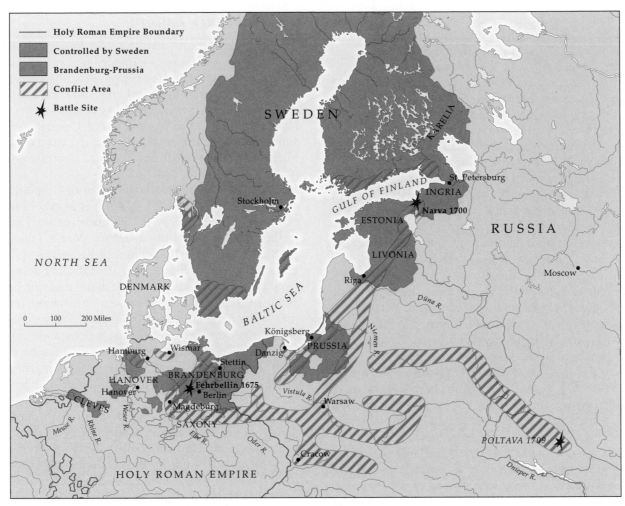

MAP 17.3 CONFLICT IN THE BALTIC AREA, 1660–1721
The fighting around the Baltic eventually destroyed Sweden's power in northern Europe; the new powers were to be
Brandenburg-Prussia and Russia. At what point did Sweden no longer dominate the Baltic?
◆ For an online version, go to www.mhhe.com/chambers9 > chapter 17 > book maps

monies, his days were strictly regulated as he attempted to supervise all government activities personally.

Emphasis on the Military   It has been said that Frederick William I organized his state to serve his military power. During his reign the army grew from 38,000 to 83,000, making it the fourth largest in Europe, behind France, Russia, and Austria. And all his soldiers had to undergo intensive drilling and wear standardized uniforms. Determined to build an effective force, he forbade his subjects to serve in foreign armies and compelled the sons of nobles to attend cadet schools to learn martial skills and attitudes. But Frederick William did not intend to die in battle. For all his involvement with military life, he avoided committing his army to battle and was able to pass it on intact to his son.

Centralization kept pace with the growth of the army. In 1723 the General Directory of Finance, War, and Do-mains took over all government functions except justice, education, and religion. A super-agency, it collected revenues and oversaw expenditures (mostly military) and local administration. Even education was seen merely as a way to encourage people to serve the state. Frederick made education compulsory for all children, ordering local communities to set up schools where there were none, though he never enforced these decrees. Uninterested in intellectual pursuits for their own sake, the king allowed the universities to decline; they did not fit his relentless vision of how to build his state.

Frederick the Great

Frederick William I's most notable triumph, perhaps, was the grooming of his successor. This was no mean task. Frederick II (r. 1740–1786) seemed opposite in temperament to his father and little inclined to follow in his footsteps. The father was a God-fearing German Protestant. The son disdained German culture and was a deist (see p. 558). Sentimental and artistically inclined, Frederick II was a composer of music who played the flute, wrote poetry, and greatly admired French culture. He even wrote philosophical treatises and corresponded with leading European intellectuals.

But the young prince was not exempt from the effort to draw all Prussians into the task of state building. On the contrary: His father forced him to work at all levels of the state apparatus so as to experience them directly, from shoveling hay on a royal farm to marching with the troops. The father trained his son for kingship, reshaping his personality, giving him a sense of duty, and toughening him for leadership. Despite Frederick's resistance, this hard apprenticeship succeeded.

Frederick's Absolutism

When he assumed the throne in 1740, Frederick II was prepared to lead Prussia in a ruthless struggle for power and territory. While his intellectual turn of mind caused him to agonize over moral issues and the nature of his role, he never flinched from exercising power. But he did try to justify absolutism at home and aggression abroad. He claimed undivided power for the ruler, not because the dynasty had a divine mission but because only absolute rule could bring results. The king, he said, was the first servant of the state, and in the long run an enlightened monarch might lead his people to a more rational and moral existence. Some of his objectives, such as religious toleration and judicial reform, he could reach at once, and by putting them into effect Frederick gained a reputation as an **"enlightened" absolutist.**

But these were minor matters. The paramount issue, security, provided the best justification for absolutism. Success here required Prussia to improve its vulnerable geographic position by acquiring more territory, stronger borders, and the power to face other European states as an equal. Until that was achieved, Frederick would not consider the domestic reforms that might disrupt the flow of taxes or men into the army, or provoke his nobility. The capture of territory was his most singular contribution to the rise of Prussia and what earned him his title of Frederick the Great. As it happened, a suitable task for his army presented itself in the year Frederick II came to the throne, 1748—an attack on the province of Silesia, which the Habsburgs controlled but were unable to defend. Prussia had no claim to the province; it was simply a wealthy neighboring domain that would expand Prussia's territory. Yet the conquest of Silesia brought to a new level the state building that the great elector had begun in 1648; the reaction also shaped state building in the Habsburg Empire.

The Habsburg Empire

The Habsburg Empire was like a dynastic holding company of diverse territories under one crown: Austria, Bohemia, Hungary, and other possessions such as the Austrian Netherlands, Lombardy, and Tuscany. The emperors hoped to integrate Austria, Bohemia, and Hungary into a Catholic, centralized, German-speaking super-state. But the traditional representative assemblies in these provinces resisted such centralization.

International Rivalry

In the reign of Leopold's successor, Charles VI (r. 1711–1740), yet another problem complicated the destiny of this multinational empire, for his only heir was his daughter, Maria Theresa. In 1713 Charles drafted a document known as the Pragmatic Sanction, declaring that all Habsburg dominions would pass intact to the eldest heir, male or female; and for the next twenty-five years he sought recognition of the Pragmatic Sanction from the European powers. By making all kinds of concessions and promises, he won this recognition on paper. But when he died in 1740, his daughter found that the commitments were worthless: The succession was challenged by force from several sides. Concentrating on diplomacy alone, Charles had neglected the work of state building, leaving an empty treasury, an inadequately trained army, and an ineffective bureaucracy.

In contrast to Austria, Prussia had a full treasury, a powerful army, and a confident ruler, Frederick II, who seized the Habsburg province of Silesia without qualm. His justification was simply **"reasons of state,"** combined with the Habsburgs' faltering fortunes. And Maria Theresa had her hands more than full, because the French declared war on her to support their ally Bavaria's claim to the Habsburg throne. Meanwhile, Spain hoped to win back control of Austria's Italian possessions. Worse yet, Maria Theresa faced a rebellion by the Czech nobles in Bohemia. Her position would probably have been hopeless if Hungary's Magyar nobles had followed suit. But Maria Theresa promised them autonomy within the Habsburg Empire, and they offered her the troops she needed to resist the invaders.

The War of Austrian Succession

In the War of Austrian Succession (1740–1748) that followed, Maria Theresa learned the elements of state building. With her Hungarian troops and with financial help from her one ally, Britain, she fought her opponents to a stalemate. Frederick's conquest of Silesia proved to be the only significant territorial change produced by the war. Even for England and France, who fought the war mainly in overseas colonies, it was a standoff. But Maria Theresa was now determined to recover Silesia

E. F. Cunningham
THE RETURN OF FREDERICK II FROM A MANEUVRE, 1787
**Were it not for the richly embroidered saddle cover and the fine white horse, Frederick the Great would be hard to
spot among his officers. Nor is there anything to indicate that the two men on the black and brown horses behind
him are his nephew and grandnephew. This sober evocation of a king as a professional soldier contrasts strikingly
with earlier glorifications (see painting, p. 419).**
Staatliche Museen Preussischer Kulturbesitz Nationalgalerie/BPK Berlin

and humiliate Prussia, and this required a determined
effort of state building.

Maria Theresa   The woman whose authority was established not by her father's negotiations but by force
of arms was a marked contrast to her archenemy, Frederick. The Prussian king was practical and irreligious;
Maria Theresa was moralistic and pious. Her personality and her ruling style were deceptively traditional,
however, for she was a shrewd innovator in the business of building and reasserting the power of her state.

Unlike Frederick, Maria Theresa had a strong regard
for her dynasty. In this respect, being a woman made no
difference to the policies or government of the empire.
She believed in the divine mission of the Habsburgs
and conscientiously attended to the practical needs of
her realm.

Reform in Church and State   It was because she put
the state's interests first that this most pious of
Catholic sovereigns—who disdained religious toleration
and loathed atheists—felt obliged to reform the Church.
Responding to waste and self-interest in her monasteries, she forbade the founding of new establishments.
She also abolished the clergy's exemptions from taxes,
something the French king found impossible to do.

A new bureaucratic apparatus was constructed on
the models of French and Prussian absolutism. In Vienna, reorganized central ministries recruited staffs of
experts. In the provinces, new agents were appointed
who were largely free of local interests, though some
concession did have to be made to the regional traditions of the Habsburg realm. The core domains (exclud-
ing Hungary and the Italian possessions) were
reorganized into ten provinces, each subdivided into

Martin van Meytens
MARIA THERESA AND HER FAMILY, **1750**
Although the setting is just as splendid, the portrayal of Maria Theresa with her husband and thirteen of her sixteen children suggests a domesticity that is absent from Louis XIV's family portrait of half a century before (see painting, p. 490).
Galleria Palatina, Palazzo Pitti, Florence, Italy. Scala/Art Resource, NY

districts directed by royal officials. With the help of these officials, the central government could wrest new taxes from the local diets. Meanwhile, Maria Theresa brought important nobles from all her domains to Vienna to participate in its social and administrative life. She also reformed the military, improving the training of troops and establishing academies to produce a more professional officer corps. Thus did international needs help shape domestic political reforms.

Habsburgs and Bourbons at Madrid

In Spain the Habsburgs had little success in state building either at home or abroad. The king who followed Philip IV, Charles II (r. 1665–1700), was a sickly man, incapable of having children; and the War of the Spanish Succession seriously reduced the inheritance he left. Both the southern Netherlands and most of Italy passed to the Austrian Habsburgs, and Spain's overseas possessions often paid little notice to the homeland.

The Spanish nobility was even more successful than the Austrian in turning absolutism to its advantage. In 1650 the crown had been able to recapture Catalonia's loyalty only by granting the province's aristocracy virtual autonomy, and this pattern recurred throughout Spain's territories. Parasitic, unproductive nobles controlled the regime, often for personal gain. The country fell into economic and cultural stagnation, subservient to a group of powerful families, with its former glory visible mainly in its strong navy.

Bourbon Spain   Yet Spain and its vast overseas possessions remained a force in eighteenth-century affairs. When the Bourbons gained the crown, following the War of Spanish Succession, they ended the traditional independence of Aragon, Catalonia, and Valencia and integrated these provinces into the kind of united Spain Olivares had sought eighty years earlier. They imported the position of *intendant* from France to administer the provinces, and although the nobles remained far more independent, the Bourbons did begin to impose uniform procedures on the country. In midcentury the ideas of enlightened absolutism that were visible elsewhere in Europe had their effect, largely because of a liberal reformer, Count Pedro de Campomanes. The most remarkable change concerned the religious order that had been identified with Spain since the days of its founder, Loyola: the Jesuits. They had become too powerful and too opposed to reform, and so they were expelled from Spanish territory in 1767.

In a sense, though, the Jesuits were to have their revenge. Spain's colonies in America were flourishing in the eighteenth century: Their trade with Europe was booming; they were attracting new settlers; and by 1800 they had over 14 million inhabitants. But they were still subject to the same absolutist control as the homeland. It was largely under the inspiration of disgruntled Jesuits that the idea of breaking free from Spain took hold in the empire, an idea that led to the independence movements of the 1800s.

Peter the Great at St. Petersburg

One of the reasons the new absolutist regimes of the late seventeenth and eighteenth centuries seemed so different from their predecessors was that many of them consciously created new settings for themselves. Versailles, Schönbrunn, and Berlin were all either new or totally transformed sites for royal courts. But only one of the autocrats of the period went so far as to build an entirely new capital: Tsar Peter I (the Great) of Russia (1682–1725), who named the new city St. Petersburg after his patron saint.

Peter's Fierce Absolutism   None of the state-building rulers of the period had Peter's terrifying energy or ruthless determination to exercise absolute control. He was only nine when he was chosen tsar, and in his early years, when his sister and his mother were the effective rulers, he witnessed ghastly massacres of members of his family and their associates by soldiers in Moscow. Like little Louis XIV, endangered by Paris mobs during the Fronde, Peter determined to leave his capital city. Soon after he assumed full powers in 1696, therefore, he shifted his court to St. Petersburg, despite thousands of deaths among the peasants who were forced to build the city in a cold and inhospitable swamp. Well over six feet tall—a giant by the standards of the time—Peter terrorized those around him, especially during his many drunken rages. His only son, Alexis, a weak and retiring figure, became the focus of opposition to the tsar, and Peter had him put in prison, where Alexis mysteriously died. Peter refused even to attend his funeral.

Western Models   Early in his reign, Peter suffered a humiliating military defeat at the hands of the Swedes. This merely confirmed his view that, in order to compete with Europe's powers, he had to bring to Russia some of the advances the Western nations had recently made. To observe these achievements firsthand, Peter traveled incognito through France, England, and the Netherlands in 1697 and 1698, paying special attention to economic, administrative, and military practices (such as the functioning of a Dutch shipyard). Many of his initiatives were to derive from this journey, including his importation of Western court rituals, his founding of an Academy of Sciences in 1725, and his encouragement of the first Russian newspaper.

Italian artists were brought to Russia, along with Scandinavian army officers, German engineers, and Dutch shipbuilders, not only to apply their skills but also to teach them to the Russians. St. Petersburg, the finest eighteenth-century city built in Classical style, is mainly the work of Italians. But gradually Russians

took over their own institutions—military academies produced native officers, for example—and by the end of Peter's reign they had little need of foreign experts.

Bureaucratization   In ruling Russia, Peter virtually ignored the Duma, the traditional advisory council, and concentrated instead on his bureaucracy. He carried out countless changes until he had created an administrative apparatus much larger than the one he had inherited. Here again he copied Western models—notably Prussia, where nobles ran the bureaucracy and the army, and Sweden, where a complex system of government departments had been created. Peter organized his administration into similar departments: Each had either a specialized function, such as finance, or responsibility for a geographic area, such as Siberia. The result was an elaborate but unified hierarchy of authority, rising from local agents of the government through provincial officials up to the staffs and governors of eleven large administrative units and finally to the leaders of the regime in the capital. Peter began the saturating bureaucratization that characterized Russia from that time on.

The Imposition of Social Order   The tsar's policies laid the foundations for a two-class society that persisted until the twentieth century. Previously, a number of ranks had existed within both the nobility and the peasantry, and a group in the middle was seen sometimes as the lowest nobles and sometimes as the highest peasants. Under Peter such mingling disappeared. All peasants were reduced to one level, subject to a new poll tax, military conscription, and forced public work, such as the building of St. Petersburg. Below them were serfs, whose numbers were increased by legislation restricting their movement. Peasants had a few advantages over serfs, such as the freedom to move, but their living conditions were often equally dreadful. Serfdom itself spread throughout all areas of Peter's dominions and became essential to his state building because, on royal lands as well as the estates of the nobles, serfs worked and ran the agricultural enterprise that was Russia's economic base.

At the same time, Peter created a single class of nobles by substituting status within the bureaucracy for status within the traditional hierarchy of titles. In 1722 he issued a table of bureaucratic ranks that gave everyone a place according to the office he held. Differentiations still existed, but they were no longer unbridgeable, as they had been when family was the decisive determinant of status. The result was a more controlled social order and greater uniformity than in France or Brandenburg-Prussia. The Russian aristocracy was the bureaucracy, and the bureaucracy the aristocracy.

The Subjugation of the Nobility   This was not a voluntary alliance between nobles and government, such as existed in the West; in return for his support and his total subjection of the peasantry, Peter required the nobles to provide officials for his bureaucracy and officers for his army. When he began the construction of St. Petersburg, he also demanded that the leading families build splendid mansions in his new capital. In effect, the tsar offered privilege and wealth in exchange for conscription into public service. Thus, there was hardly any sense of partnership between nobility and throne: The tsar often had to use coercion to ensure that his wishes were followed. On the other hand, Peter helped build up the nobles' fortunes and their control of the countryside. It has been estimated that by 1710 he had put under the supervision of great landowners more than forty thousand peasant and serf households that had formerly been under the crown. And he was liberal in conferring new titles—some of them, such as count and baron, copies of German examples.

Control of the Church   Peter's determination to stamp his authority on Russia was also apparent in his destruction of ecclesiastical independence. He accomplished this with one blow: He simply did not replace the patriarch of the Russian Church who died in 1700. Peter took over the monasteries and their vast income for his own purposes and appointed a procurator (at first an army officer) to supervise religious affairs. The Church was, in effect, made a branch of government.

Military Expansion   The purpose of all these radical changes was to assert the tsar's power both at home and abroad. Peter established a huge standing army, more than three hundred thousand strong by the 1720s, and imported the latest military techniques from the West. One of Peter's most cherished projects, the creation of a navy, had limited success, but there could be no doubt that he transformed Russia's capacity for war and its position among European states. He extended Russia's frontier to the south and west, and, at the battle of Poltava in 1709, reversed his early defeat by the Swedes. This victory began the dismantling of Sweden's empire, for it was followed by more than a decade of Russian advance into Estonia, Livonia, and Poland. The very vastness of his realm justified Peter's drive for absolute control, and by the time of his death he had made Russia the dominant power in the Baltic and a major influence in European affairs.

ALTERNATIVES TO ABSOLUTISM

The absolutist regimes offered one model of political and social organization, but an alternative model—equally committed to uniformity, order, and state building—was also created in the late seventeenth century: governments dominated by aristocrats or merchants. The contrast between the two was noted by contemporary political theorists, especially opponents of absolutism, who preferred **constitutionalism.** And yet the differences were often less sharp than the theorists suggested, mainly because the position of the aristocracy was similar throughout Europe.

Aristocracy in the United Provinces, Sweden, and Poland

In the Dutch republic, the succession of William III to the office of Stadholder in 1672 seemed to be a move toward absolutism. As he led the successful resistance to Louis XIV in war (1672–1678), he increasingly concentrated government in his own hands. Soon, however, the power of merchants and provincial leaders in the Estates General reasserted itself. William did not want to sign a peace treaty with Louis when the French invasion failed. He wanted instead to take the war into France and reinforce his own authority by keeping the position of commander in chief. But the Estates General, led by the province of Holland, ended the war.

A decade later William sought the English crown, but he did so only with the approval of the Estates General, and he had to leave separate the representative assemblies that governed the two countries. When William died without an heir, his policies were continued by his close friend Antonius Heinsius, who held the same position of grand pensionary of Holland that Jan de Witt had once occupied; but the government was in effect controlled by the Estates General. This representative assembly now had to preside over the decline of a great power. In finance and trade, the Dutch were gradually overtaken by the English, while in the war against Louis XIV, they had to support the crippling burden of maintaining a land force, only to hand over command to England.

Dutch Society   The aristocrats of the United Provinces differed from the usual European pattern. Instead of ancient families and bureaucratic dynasties, they boasted merchants and mayors. The prominent citizens of the leading cities were the backbone of the Dutch upper classes. Moreover, social distinctions were less prominent than in any other country of Europe. The elite was composed of hard-working financiers and traders, richer and more powerful but not essentially more privileged or leisured than those farther down the social ladder. The inequality described in much eighteenth-century political writing—the special place nobles had, often including some immunity from the law—was far less noticeable in the United Provinces. There was no glittering court, and although here as elsewhere a small group controlled the country, it did so for largely economic ends and in different style.

Sweden   The Swedes created yet another nonabsolutist model of state building. After a long struggle with the king, the nobles emerged as the country's dominant political force. During the reign of Charles XI (1660–1697), the monarchy was able to force the great lords to return to the state the huge tracts of land they

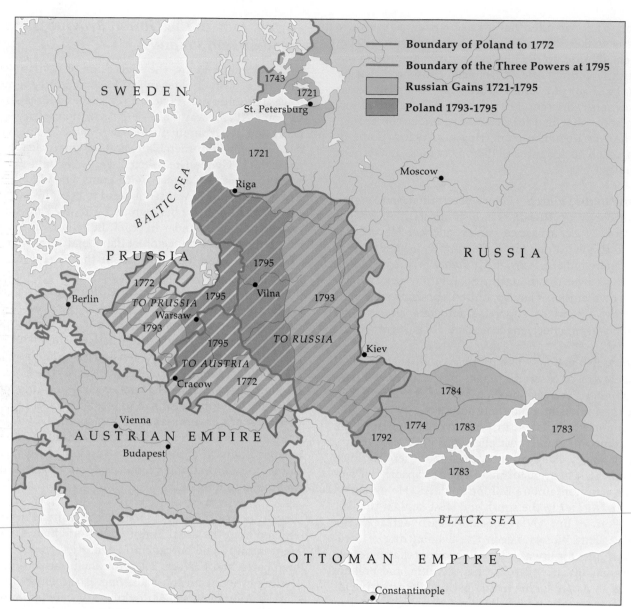

MAP 17.4 THE EXPANSION OF RUSSIA AND THE PARTITION OF POLAND
All three of the powers in Eastern Europe—Prussia, Russia, and Austria—gained territory from the dismemberment of Poland. Which country was the chief beneficiary of the partition? In addition to the territory it gained from Poland, where else was Russia expanding in the period 1721–1795?
◆ For an online version, go to www.mhhe.com/chambers9 > chapter 17 > book maps

had received as rewards for loyalty earlier in the century. Since Charles stayed out of Europe's wars, he was able to conserve his resources and avoid relying on the nobility as he strengthened the smoothly running bureaucracy he had inherited from Gustavus Adolphus.

His successor, Charles XII (r. 1697–1718), however, revived Sweden's tradition of military conquest. He won land from Peter the Great, but then made the fatal decision to invade Russia. Defeated at the battle of Poltava in 1709, Charles had to retreat and watch helplessly as the Swedish Empire was dismembered. By the

time he was killed in battle nine years later, his neighbors had begun to overrun his lands, and, in treaties signed from 1719 to 1721, Sweden reverted to roughly the territory it had had a century before.

Naturally, the nobles took advantage of Charles XII's frequent absences to reassert their authority. They ran Sweden's highly efficient government while he was campaigning and forced his successor, Queen Ulrika, to accept a constitution that gave the Riksdag effective control over the country. The new structure, modeled on England's political system, gave the nobility the role of the English gentry—leaders of society and the shapers of its politics. A splendid court arose, and Stockholm became one of the more elegant and cultured aristocratic centers in Europe.

Poland Warsaw fared less well. In fact, the strongest contrast to the French political and social model in the late seventeenth century was Poland. The sheer chaos and disunity that plagued Poland until it ceased to exist as a state in the late eighteenth century were the direct result of continued dominance by the old landed aristocracy, which blocked all attempts to centralize the government. There were highly capable kings in this period—notably John III, who achieved Europe-wide fame by relieving Vienna from the Turkish siege in 1683. These monarchs could quite easily gather an army to fight, and fight well, against Poland's many foes: Germans, Swedes, Russians, and Turks. But once a battle was over, the ruler could exercise no more than nominal leadership. Each king was elected by the assembly of nobles and had to agree not to interfere with the independence of the great lords, who were growing rich from serf labor on fertile lands. The crown had neither revenue nor bureaucracy to speak of, and so the country continued to resemble a feudal kingdom, where power remained in the localities.

The Triumph of the Gentry in England

The model for a nonabsolutist regime was England, even though King Charles II (r. 1660–1685) seemed to have powers similar to those of his ill-fated father, Charles I. He still summoned and dissolved Parliament, made all appointments in the bureaucracy, and signed every law. But he no longer had prerogative courts like Star Chamber, he could not arrest a member of Parliament, and he could not create a new seat in the Commons. Even two ancient prerogatives, the king's right to dispense with an act of Parliament for a specific individual or group and his right to suspend an act completely, proved empty when Charles II tried to exercise them. Nor could he raise money without Parliament; instead, he was given a fixed annual income, financed by a tax on beer.

The Gentry and Parliament The real control of the country's affairs had by this time passed to the group of substantial landowners known as the gentry. In a country of some 5 million people, perhaps fifteen to twenty thousand families were considered gentry—local leaders throughout England, despite having neither titles of nobility nor special privileges. Amounting to 2 percent of the population, they probably represented about the same proportion as the titled nobles in other states. Yet the gentry differed from these other nobles in that they

ENGRAVING FROM *THE WESTMINSTER MAGAZINE*, 1774
Political cartoons were standard fare in eighteenth-century newspapers and magazines. This one shows a weeping king of Poland and an angry Turk (who made no gains) after Poland was carved up in 1772 by Frederick the Great, the Austrian emperor, and the Russian empress. Louis XV sits by without helping his ally Poland, and all are urged on by the devil under the table.

had won the right to determine national policy through Parliament. Whereas nobles elsewhere depended on monarchs for power, the English revolution had made the gentry an independent force. Their authority was now hallowed by custom, upheld by law, and maintained by the House of Commons.

Not all the gentry took a continuing interest in affairs of state, and only a few of their number sat in the roughly five-hundred-member House of Commons. Even the Commons did not exercise a constant influence over the government; nevertheless, the ministers of the king had to be prominent representatives of the gentry, and they had to be able to win the support of a majority of the members of the Commons. Policy was still set by the king and his ministers, but the Commons had to be persuaded that the policies were correct; without parliamentary approval, a minister could not long survive.

The Succession Despite occasional conflicts, this structure worked relatively smoothly throughout Charles II's reign. But the gentry feared that Charles's brother, James, next in line for the succession and an open Catholic, might try to restore Catholicism in England. To prevent this, they attempted in 1680 to force Charles to exclude James from the throne. But in the end the traditional respect for legitimacy, combined with some shrewd maneuvering by Charles, ensured that there would be no tampering with the succession.

Soon, however, the reign of James II (r. 1685–1688) turned into a disaster. Elated by his acceptance as king, James rashly offered Catholics the very encouragement the gentry feared. This was a direct challenge to the gentry's newly won power, and in 1688 seven of their leaders, including members of England's most prominent families, invited the Protestant ruler of the United Provinces, William III, to invade and take over the throne. Though William landed with an army half the size of the king's, James, uncertain of his support, decided not to risk battle and fled to exile in France. Because the transfer of the monarchy was bloodless and confirmed the supremacy of Parliament, it came to be called the Glorious Revolution.

William and Mary The new king gained what little title he had to the crown through his wife, Mary (see the genealogical table below), and Parliament proclaimed the couple joint monarchs early in 1689. The Dutch ruler took the throne primarily to bring England into his relentless struggles against Louis XIV, and he willingly accepted a settlement that confirmed the essential role of Parliament in the government. A **Bill of Rights** determined the succession to the throne, defined Parliament's powers, and established basic civil rights. An Act of Toleration put an end to all religious persecution, though members of the official Church of England were still the only people allowed to vote, sit in Parliament, hold a government office, or attend a university. In 1694 a statute declared that Parliament had to meet and new elections had to be held at least once every three years.

Despite the restrictions on his authority, William exercised strong leadership. He guided England into an aggressive foreign policy, picked ministers favorable to his aims, and never let Parliament sit when he was out of the country to pursue the war or to oversee Dutch affairs. In his reign, too, the central government grew considerably, gaining new powers and positions, and

THE ENGLISH SUCCESSION FROM THE STUARTS TO THE HANOVERIANS

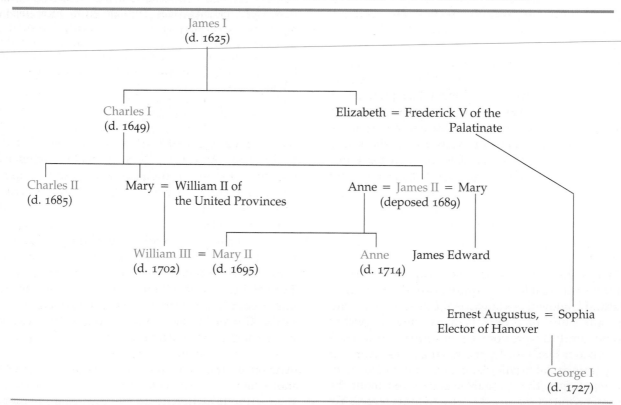

Note: Names in blue = monarchs of England.

thus new opportunities for political patronage. But unlike James, William recognized his limits. He tried to have the Bill of Rights reversed and a standing army established, but he gave up when these efforts provoked major opposition. By and large, therefore, the gentry were content to let the king rule as he saw fit, for they had shown by their intervention in 1688 that ultimately they controlled the country.

Politics and Prosperity

The political system in England now reflected the social system: A small elite controlled both the country's policy and its institutions. This group was far from united, however, as was apparent when a party system began to appear in Parliament during Charles II's reign. On one side was the **Whig** party, that opposed royal prerogatives and Catholicism and was largely responsible for the attempt to exclude James II from the throne. The rival **Tory** party stood for the independence and authority of the crown and favored a ceremonial and traditional Anglicanism.

Party Conflict   Because the Whigs had been the main advocates of the removal of James II, they controlled the government for most of William III's reign. They supported his war against Louis XIV (1689–1697), because France harbored both James and his followers (the romantic but ill-fated Jacobites, who kept trying to restore James's line to the throne). This was a fairly nonpartisan issue, but the Tories and Whigs still competed fiercely for voters. Because the qualification for voting—owning land worth forty shillings a year in rent—had become less restrictive as a result of inflation (which made forty shillings a fairly modest sum) and was not to be raised to a higher minimum until the late 1700s, England now had what would be its largest electorate before the 1860s. Almost 5 percent of the population (more than 15 percent of adult males) could vote, and although results were usually determined by powerful local magnates, fierce politicking was common. And in the election of 1700 there was a major upset: The Tories won by opposing renewal of war with Louis XIV, who had seemed restrained since the end of the previous war in 1697.

Within two years, however, and despite William's death in 1702, England was again at war with France, this time over the Spanish succession; and soon the Whigs were again in control of the government. The identification of the parties with their attitude toward war continued until 1710, when weariness over the fighting brought the Tories back into power. They persuaded Queen Anne, William's successor, to make peace with France at Utrecht in 1713; and they lost power only because they made the mistake of negotiating with the rebel Jacobites after Anne died in 1714 without an heir. Anne's successor was a German prince, the elector of Hanover, who founded the new Hanoverian Dynasty as George I (1714–1727). Since they firmly supported his succession, the Whigs regained control of the government when George came to the throne. They then entrenched themselves for almost a century.

The Sea and the Economy   At the same time, England was winning for itself unprecedented prosperity and laying the foundations of its world power. The English navy was the premier force on the sea, the decisive victor over France during the worldwide struggle of the early eighteenth century. Overseas, England founded new colonies and steadily expanded the empire. When England and Scotland joined into one kingdom in 1707, the union created a Great Britain ready to exercise a worldwide influence.

The economic advances were equally remarkable. A notable achievement was the establishment of the Bank of England in 1694. The bank gained permission to raise money from the public and then lend it to the government at a favorable 8 percent interest. Within 12 days its founders raised more than a million pounds, demonstrating not only the financial stability of England's government but also the commitment of the elite to the country's political structure. London was becoming the financial capital of the world, with her merchants gaining control of maritime trade from east Asia to North America. And the benefits of the boom also helped the lower levels of society.

English Society   With the possible exception of the Dutch, ordinary English people were better off than their equivalents elsewhere in Europe. Compared with the sixteenth century, there was little starvation. The system of poor relief may often have been inhumane in forcing the unfortunate to work in horrifying workhouses, but it did provide them with the shelter and food they had long lacked. It is true that thousands still found themselves unable to make a living in their home villages each year and were forced by poverty to take to the roads. And the many who ended up in London hardly improved their situation. The stream of immigrants was driving the capital's population toward half a million, and the city contained frightful slums and miserable crime-ridden sections. Even a terrible fire in London in 1666 did little to improve the appallingly crowded living conditions, because the city was rebuilt much as before, the only notable additions being a series of splendid churches. But the grimness should not be overdrawn.

After more than a century of inflation, the laborer could once again make a decent living, and artisans

William Hogarth
The Polling, **1754**
Despite the high reputation of the polling day as the central moment in the system of representative government, Hogarth's depiction of it in this scene suggests how corrupt and disheveled the process of voting was. The sick and the foolish are among the mob of voters; the central figure looks bewildered as he is told what to do; on the right a bloated official cannot decide whether a voter should be allowed to take his oath on the Bible with a wooden hand; and all ignore the distress of Britannia, the symbol of Britain, in her coach on the left.
By courtesy of the Trustees of Sir John Soane's Museum, London

were enjoying a growing demand for their work. Higher in the social scale, more men had a say in the political process than before, and more found opportunities for advancement in the rising economy—in trade overseas, in the bureaucracy, or in the expanding market for luxury goods. It has been estimated that in 1730 there were about sixty thousand adult males in what we would call the professions. England also had better roads than any other European country and a more impartial judicial system. Yet none of these gains could compare with those that the gentry made. In fact, many of the improvements, such as fair administration of justice, were indirect results of what the upper classes had won for themselves. The fruits of progress clearly belonged primarily to the gentry.

The Growth of Stability

Like the absolutist regimes, the British government in the 1700s was able to advance state building—to expand its authority and its international power. This was the work not so much of a monarch as of the "political nation": the landowners and leading townsmen who elected almost all the members of Parliament. Their control of the nation was visible in the distribution of the 558 seats in the House of Commons, which bore little relation to the size of constituencies. In 1793, for example, fifty-one English and Welsh boroughs, with fewer than fifteen hundred voters, elected one hundred members of Parliament, nearly a fifth of the Commons. Many districts were safely in the pocket

NEW GALLOWS AT THE OLD BAILEY, ENGRAVING
It was an indication of the severity of English criminal justice that the gallows erected near the chief court in London, the Old Bailey, in the mid-eighteenth century was specially constructed so that ten condemned criminals, both men and women, could be executed at once.
© British Museum

of a prominent local family; and elsewhere elections were often determined by bribery, influence, and intimidation. On the national level, loose party alignments pitted Whigs, who wanted a strong Parliament and usually preferred commercial to agricultural interests, against Tories, who tended to support the king and policies that favored large landholders. But the realities of politics were shaped by small factions within these larger groups, and alliances revolved around the control of patronage and office.

War and Taxes   As the financial and military needs and capabilities of the government expanded, Parliament now created a thoroughly bureaucratized state. Britain had always prided itself on having a smaller government and lower taxes than its neighbors, largely because, as an island, it had avoided the need for a standing army. All that now came to an end. Starting with the struggle against Louis XIV, wars required constant increases in resources, troops, and administrators. A steadily expanding navy had to be supported, as did an army that reached almost two hundred thousand men by the 1770s. Before the 1690s, public expenditures rarely amounted to 2 million a year; by the 1770s, they were almost 30 million, and most of that was

spent on the military. In this period, as a result, Britain's fiscal bureaucracy more than tripled in size. The recruiting officer became a regular sight, and so too did the treasury men who were imposing increasingly heavy tax burdens.

Unlike their counterparts on the Continent, however, the wealthier classes in Britain paid considerable taxes to support this state building, and they maintained more fluid relations with other classes. The landed gentry and the commercial class, in particular, were often linked by marriage and by financial or political associations. Even great aristocrats sometimes had close ties with the business leaders of London. The lower levels of society, however, found the barriers as high as they had ever been. For all of Britain's prosperity, the lower third of society remained poor and often desperate. As a result, despite a severe system of justice and frequent capital punishment, crime was endemic in both country and town. The eighteenth century was the heyday of that romantic but violent figure, the highwayman.

The Age of Walpole   The first two rulers of the Hanoverian Dynasty, George I (r. 1714–1727) and George II (r. 1727–1760), could not speak English fluently. The

Samuel Scott
THE BUILDING OF WESTMINSTER
BRIDGE, CA. 1742
The elegance, but not the squalor, of city life in the eighteenth century is suggested by this view of Westminster.
The Metropolitan Museum of Art, Purchase, Charles B. Curtis Fund and Joseph Pulitzer Bequest, 1944. (44.56) Photograph © 1993 The Metropolitan Museum of Art

language barrier and their concern for their German territory of Hanover left them often uninterested in British politics, and this helped Parliament grow in authority. Its dominant figure for over twenty years was Sir Robert Walpole, who rose to prominence because of his skillful handling of fiscal policy during the panic following the collapse of an overseas trading company in 1720. This crash, known as the South Sea Bubble, resembled the failure of John Law's similar scheme in France, but it had less effect on government finances. Thereafter, Walpole controlled British politics until 1742, mainly by dispensing patronage liberally and staying at peace.

Many historians have called Walpole the first prime minister, though the title was not official. He insisted that all ministers inform and consult with the House of Commons as well as with the king, and he continued to sit in Parliament in order to recruit support for his decisions. Not until the next century was it accepted that the Commons could force a minister to resign. But Walpole took a first step toward ministerial responsibility, and to the notion that the ministers as a body or "cabinet" had a common task, and he thus shaped the future structure of British government.

Commercial Interests In Great Britain as in France, the economic expansion of the eighteenth century increased the wealth and the social and political weight of the commercial and financial middle class. Although Londoners remained around 11 percent of the population, the proportion of the English who lived in other sizable towns doubled in the 1700s; and by 1800 some 30 percent of the country's inhabitants were urbanized. Walpole's policy of peace pleased the large landlords but angered this growing body of merchants and businesspeople, who feared the growth of French commerce and colonial settlements. They found their champion

in William Pitt, later earl of Chatham, the grandson of a man who had made a fortune in India. Eloquent, self-confident, and infused with a vision of Britain's imperial destiny, Pitt began his parliamentary career in 1738 by attacking the government's timid policies and demanding that France be driven from the seas. Though Walpole's policies continued even after his resignation in 1742, Pitt's moment finally came in 1758, when Britain became involved in a European war that was to confirm its importance in continental affairs (see pp. 523–524).

Contrasts in Political Thought

The intensive development of both absolutist and antiabsolutist forms in the seventeenth century stimulated an outpouring of ideas about the nature and purposes of government. Two Englishmen, in particular, developed theories about the basis of political authority that have been influential ever since.

Hobbes Thomas Hobbes, a brilliant scholar from a poor family who earned his livelihood as the tutor to aristocrats' sons, determined to use the strictly logical methods of the scientist to analyze political behavior. As a young man Hobbes was secretary to Francis Bacon, who doubtless gave him a taste for science. And the almost scientific reasoning is the essence of his masterpiece, *Leviathan* (1651), which began with a few premises about human nature from which Hobbes deduced major conclusions about political forms.

Leviathan Hobbes's premises, drawn from his observation of the strife-ridden Europe of the 1640s and 1650s, were stark and uncompromising. People, he asserted, are selfish and ambitious; consequently, unless

government that is totally free to do whatever it wishes is best equipped to keep the peace, and peace is always better than the previous turmoil. The power of Hobbes's logic, and the endorsement he seemed to give to absolutism, made his views enormously influential. But his approach also aroused hostility. Although later political theorists were deeply affected by his ideas, many of Hobbes's successors denounced him as godless, immoral, cynical, and unfeeling. It was dislike of his message, not weaknesses in his analysis, that made many people unwilling to accept his views.

Locke   John Locke, a quiet Oxford professor who admired Hobbes but sought to soften his conclusions, based his political analysis on a general theory of knowledge. Locke believed that at birth a person's mind is a *tabula rasa*, a clean slate; nothing, he said, is inborn or preordained. As human beings grow, they observe and experience the world. Once they have gathered enough data through their senses, their minds begin to work on the data. Then, with the help of reason, they perceive patterns, discovering the order and harmony that permeate the universe. Locke was convinced that this underlying order exists and that every person, regardless of individual experiences, must reach the same conclusions about its nature and structure.

When Locke turned his attention to political thought, he put into systematic form the views of the English gentry and other antiabsolutists throughout Europe. The *Second Treatise of Civil Government*, published in 1690, was deeply influenced by Hobbes. From his great predecessor, Locke took the notions that a state of nature is a state of war and that only a contract among the people can end the anarchy that precedes the establishment of civil society. But his conclusions were decidedly different.

Of Civil Government   Using the principles of his theory of knowledge, Locke asserted that, applying reason to politics, one can prove the inalienability of three rights of an individual: life, liberty, and property. Like Hobbes, he believed that there must be a sovereign power, but he argued that it has no power over these three natural rights of its subjects without their consent. And this consent—for taxes, for example—must come from a representative assembly of men of property, such as Parliament. The affirmation of property as one of the three natural rights (it became "the pursuit of happiness" in the more egalitarian American Declaration of Independence) is significant. Here Locke revealed himself as the voice of the gentry. Only those with a tangible stake in their country have a right to control its destiny, and that stake must be protected as surely as their life and liberty. The concept of liberty remained vague, but it was taken to imply the sorts of

PORTRAIT OF THOMAS HOBBES
This depiction of the famous philosopher shows him with a twinkle in the eye and a smile that might seem surprising, given the pessimism about human nature in his *Leviathan*.
Art Resource, NY

restrained, they fight a perpetual war with their fellows. The weak are more cunning and the strong more stupid. Given these unsavory characteristics, the **state of nature**—which precedes the existence of society—is a state of war, in which life is "solitary, poor, nasty, brutish, and short." Hobbes concluded that the only way to restrain this instinctive aggressiveness is to erect an absolute and sovereign power that will maintain peace. Everyone should submit to the sovereign because the alternative is the anarchy of the state of nature. The moment of submission is the moment of the birth of orderly society.

In a startling innovation, Hobbes suggested that the transition from nature to society is accomplished by a contract that is implicitly accepted by all who wish to end the chaos. The unprecedented feature of the contract is that it is not between ruler and ruled; it is binding only on the ruled. They agree among themselves to submit to the sovereign; the sovereign is thus not a party to the contract and is not limited in any way. A

LOCKE ON THE ORIGINS OF GOVERNMENT

The heart of John Locke's Second Treatise of Civil Government, *written in the mid-1680s before England's Glorious Revolution but published in 1690, is its optimism about human nature—as opposed to Hobbes's pessimism. In this passage Locke explains why, in his view, people create political systems.*

"If man in the state of nature be so free, if he be absolute lord of his own person and possessions, equal to the greatest, and subject to nobody, why will he part with his freedom, and subject himself to the dominion and control of any other power? To which it is obvious to answer, that though in the state of nature he hath such a right, yet the enjoyment of it is very uncertain, and constantly exposed to the invasions of others. This makes him willing to quit this condition, which, however free, is full of fears and continual dangers; and it is not without reason that he seeks out and is willing to join in society with others, who have a mind to unite, for the mutual preservation of their lives, liberties, and estates, which I call by the general name, property. The great and chief end, therefore, of men's putting themselves under government, is the preservation of their property.

"But though men when they enter into society give up the equality, liberty, and power they had in the state of nature into the hands of society; yet it being only with an intention in every one the better to preserve himself, his liberty, and property, the power of the society can never be supposed to extend further than the common good. And all this to be directed to no other end but the peace, safety, and public good of the people."

From John Locke, *The Second Treatise of Civil Government,* Thomas P. Peardon (ed.), Indianapolis: Bobbs-Merrill, 1952, chapter 9, pp. 70–73.

freedom, such as freedom from arbitrary arrest, that appeared in the English Bill of Rights. Hobbes allowed a person to protect only his or her life. Locke permitted the overthrow of the sovereign power if it infringed on the subjects' rights—a course the English followed with James II and the Americans with George III.

Locke's prime concern was to defend the individual against the state, a concern that has remained essential to liberal thought ever since (see "Locke on the Origins of Government," above). But it is important to realize that his emphasis on property served the elite better than the mass of society. With Locke to reassure them, the upper classes put their stamp on eighteenth-century European civilization.

THE INTERNATIONAL SYSTEM

While rulers built up their states by enlarging bureaucracies, strengthening governmental institutions, and expanding resources, they also had to consider how best to deal with their neighbors. In an age that emphasized reasoned and practical solutions to problems, there was hope that an orderly system could be devised for international relations. If the reality fell short of the ideal, there were nevertheless many who thought they were creating a more systematic and organized structure for diplomacy and warfare.

Diplomacy and Warfare

One obstacle to the creation of impersonal international relations was the continuing influence of traditional dynastic interests. Princes and their ministers tried to preserve a family's succession, and they arranged marriages to gain new titles or alliances. Part of the reason that those perennial rivals, Britain and France, remained at peace for nearly thirty years until 1740 was that the rulers in both countries felt insecure on their thrones and thus had personal motives for not wanting to risk aggressive foreign policies.

Gradually, however, dynastic interests gave way to policies based on a more impersonal conception of the state. Leaders like Frederick II of Prussia and William Pitt of Britain tried to shape their diplomacy to what they considered the needs of their states. "Reasons of state" centered on security, which could be guaranteed only by force. Thus, the search for defensible borders and the weakening of rivals became obvious goals. Eighteenth-century leaders believed that the end (security and prosperity) justified the means (the use of power). Chasing the impossible goal of complete invulnerability, leaders felt justified in using the crudest tactics in dealing with their neighbors.

"Balance of Power" and the Diplomatic System   If there was any broad, commonly accepted principle at work, it was that hegemony, or domination by one

Louis Nicolas Blarenberghe
THE BATTLE OF FONTENOY, **1745**
This panorama shows the English and Dutch assaulting the French position in a battle in present-day Belgium. The French lines form a huge semicircle from the distant town to the wood on the left. The main attacking force in the center, surrounded by gunfire, eventually retreated, and news of the victory was brought to Louis XV, in red on the right, by a horseman in blue who is doffing his hat.
Photo: Gérard Blot. Château de Versailles et de Trianon, Versailles, France. Réunion des Musées Nationaux/Art Resource, NY. Giraudon/Art Resource, NY

state, had to be resisted because it threatened international security. The concern aroused by Louis XIV's ambitions showed the principle at work, when those whom he sought to dominate joined together to frustrate his designs. The aim was to establish equilibrium in Europe by a balance of power, with no single state achieving hegemony.

The diplomats, guided by reasons of state and the balance of power, knew there were times when they had to spy and deceive. Yet diplomacy also could stabilize: In the eighteenth century it grew as a serious profession, paralleling the rationalization of the state itself. Foreign ministries were staffed with experts and clerks, who kept extensive archives, while the heads of the diplomatic machine, the ambassadors, were stationed in permanent embassies abroad. This routinized management of foreign relations helped foster a sense of collective identity among Europe's states despite their endless struggles. French was now the common language of diplomacy; by 1774 even a treaty between Turks and Russians was drafted in that language. And socially the diplomats were cosmopolitan aristocrats

who saw themselves as members of the same fraternity, even if the great powers dominated international agreements, usually at the expense of the smaller states. Resolving disputes by negotiation could be as amoral as war.

Armies and Navies

Despite the settlement of some conflicts by diplomacy, others led to war. Whereas Britain emphasized its navy, on the Continent the focus of bureaucratic innovation and monetary expenditure was the standing army, whose growth was striking. France set the pace. After 1680 the size of its forces never fell below 200,000. In Prussia the army increased in size from 39,000 to 200,000 men between 1713 and 1786. But the cost, technology, and tactics of armies and navies served to limit the devastation of eighteenth-century warfare. The expenses led rulers to conserve men, equipment, and ships carefully. Princes were quick to declare war but slow to commit armies or navies to battle. Casualties also became less numerous as discipline improved

ENGRAVING OF A MILITARY ACADEMY, FROM H. F. VON FLEMING, *VOLKOMMENE TEUTSCHE SOLDAT*, 1726
This scene, of young men studying fortifications and tactics in a German academy, would have been familiar to the sons of nobles throughout Europe who trained for a military career in the eighteenth century.

and the ferocity that had been caused by religious passions died away.

Tactics and Discipline   On land, the building and besieging of fortresses continued to preoccupy military planners, even though the impregnable defenses built by the French engineer Sebastian Vauban to protect France's northeastern border were simply bypassed by the English general Marlborough when he pursued the French army in the War of the Spanish Succession. The decisive encounter was still the battle between armies, where the majority of the troops—the infantry—used their training to maneuver and fire in carefully controlled line formations. The aim of strategy was not to annihilate but to nudge an opposing army into abandoning a position in the face of superior maneuvers. Improved organization also reduced brutality. Better supplied by a system of magazines and more tightly disciplined by constant drilling, troops were less likely to desert or plunder than they had been during the Thirty Years' War. At sea, the British achieved superi-

ority by maneuvering carefully controlled lines of ships and seeking to outnumber or outflank the enemy.

As these practices took hold, some encounters were fought as if they were taking place on a parade ground or in a naval strategy room. Pitched battles were increasingly avoided, for even important victories might be nullified if a winning army or navy returned to its home bases for the winter. And no victor ever demanded unconditional surrender; in almost all cases, a commander would hesitate to pursue a defeated company or squadron.

Officers   The officer corps were generally the preserve of Europe's nobility, though they also served as channels of upward social mobility for wealthy sons of middle-class families who purchased commissions. In either case, the officer ranks tended to be filled by men who lacked the professional training for effective leadership. The branches of service that showed the most progress were the artillery and the engineers, in which competent middle-class officers played an unusually large role.

MAP 17.5 PRUSSIA AND THE AUSTRIAN EMPIRE, 1721–1772
The steady territorial advances of Prussia had created a major power in northern and eastern Europe, alongside the Austrian Empire, by the time of the first partition of Poland in 1772. Which was the most extensive of Prussia's gains between 1721 and 1772?
◆ For an online version, go to www.mhhe.com/chambers9 > chapter 17 > book maps

Weak Alliances   A final limit on the scale of war in the eighteenth century was the inherent weakness of coalitions, which formed whenever a general war erupted. On paper these alliances looked formidable. On battlefields, however, they were hampered by primitive communications and lack of mobility even at the peak of cooperation. Moreover, the partnerships rarely lasted very long. The competitiveness of the state system bred distrust among allies as well as enemies.

The Seven Years' War

The pressures created by the competition of states and dynasties finally exploded in a major war, the Seven Years' War (1756–1763). Its roots lay in a realignment of diplomatic alliances prompted by Austria. Previously, the Bourbon-Habsburg rivalry had been the cornerstone of European diplomacy. But by the 1750s two other antago-

nisms had taken over: French competition with the British in the New World and Austria's vendetta against Prussia over Silesia. For Austria, the rivalry with Bourbon France was no longer important. Its position in the Holy Roman Empire depended now on humbling Prussia. French hostility toward Austria had also lessened, and thus Austria was free to lead a turnabout in alliances—a diplomatic revolution—so as to forge an anti-Prussian coalition with France and Russia. Russia was crucial. The pious Empress Elizabeth of Russia loathed Frederick II and saw him as an obstacle to Russian ambitions in Eastern Europe. Geographical vulnerability also made Prussia an inviting target, and so the stage was set for war.

Prussia tried to compensate for its vulnerability. But its countermoves only alienated the other powers. Frederick sought to stay out of the Anglo-French rivalry by coming to terms with both these states. He had been France's ally in the past, but he now sought a

MARIA THERESA IN A VEHEMENT MOOD

The animosities and ambitions that shaped international relations in the eighteenth century were exemplified by the Empress Maria Theresa. Her furious reaction to the event that destroyed Europe's old diplomatic system—England's signing of the Convention of Westminster with Maria Theresa's archenemy, Frederick the Great—suggests how deep were the feelings that brought about the midcentury conflagration. After learning the news and deciding (in response) to ally herself with France, she told the British ambassador on May 13, 1756, exactly where she stood.

"I have not abandoned the old system, but Great Britain has abandoned me and the system, by concluding the Prussian treaty, the first intelligence of which struck me like a fit of apoplexy. I and the king of Prussia are incompatible; and no consideration on earth will ever induce me to enter into any engagement to which he is a party. Why should you be surprised if, following your example in concluding a treaty with Prussia, I should now enter into an engagement with France?

"I am far from being French in my disposition, and do not deny that the court of Versailles has been my bitterest enemy; but I have little to fear from France, and I have no other recourse than to form such arrangements as will secure what remains to me. My principal aim is to secure my hereditary possessions. I have truly but two enemies whom I really dread, the king of Prussia and the Turks; and while I and Russia continue on the same good terms as now exist between us, we shall, I trust, be able to convince Europe, that we are in a condition to defend ourselves against those adversaries, however formidable."

From William Coxe, *History of the House of Austria*, Vol. 3, London: Bohn, 1847, pp. 363–364.

treaty with England, and in January 1756 the English, hoping to protect the royal territory of Hanover, signed a neutrality accord with Prussia, the Convention of Westminster. The French, who had not been informed of the negotiations in advance, saw the Convention as an insult, if not a betrayal: the act of an untrustworthy ally. France overreacted, turned against Prussia, and thus fell into Austria's design (see "Maria Theresa in a Vehement Mood," above). Russia too considered the Convention of Westminster a betrayal by its supposed ally England. English bribes and diplomacy were unable to keep Russia from actively joining Austria to plan Prussia's dismemberment.

The Course of War Fearing encirclement, Frederick gambled on a preventive war through Saxony in 1756. Although he conquered the duchy, his plan backfired, for it activated the coalition that he dreaded. Russia and France met their commitments to Austria, and the three began a combined offensive against Prussia. For a time Frederick's genius as a general brought him success. Skillful tactics and daring surprise movements brought some victories, but strategically the Prussian position was shaky. Frederick had to dash in all directions across his provinces to repel invading armies whose combined strength far exceeded his own. Disaster was avoided mainly because the Russian army returned east for winter quarters regardless of its gains, but even so, the Russians occupied Berlin.

On the verge of exhaustion, Prussia at best seemed to face a stalemate with a considerable loss of territory; at worst, the war would continue and bring about a total Prussian collapse. But the other powers were also war-weary, and Frederick's enemies were becoming increasingly distrustful of one another. In the end, Prussia was saved by one of those sudden changes of reign that could cause dramatic reversals of policy in Europe. In January 1762 Empress Elizabeth died and was replaced temporarily by Tsar Peter III, a passionate admirer of Frederick. He quickly pulled Russia out of the war and returned Frederick's conquered eastern domains of Prussia and Pomerania. In Britain, meanwhile, William Pitt was replaced by the more pacific earl of Bute, who brought about a reconciliation with France; both countries then ended their insistence on punishing Prussia. Austria's coalition collapsed.

Peace The terms of the Peace of Hubertusburg (1763), settling the continental phase of the Seven Years' War, were therefore surprisingly favorable to Prussia. Prussia returned Saxony to Austria but paid no compensation for the devastation of the duchy, and the Austrians recognized Silesia as Prussian. In short, the status quo was restored. Frederick could return to Berlin, his dominion preserved partly by his army but mainly by luck and the continuing fragility of international alliances.

Summary

If, amidst the state building of the eighteenth century, Europe's regimes were ready to sustain a major war even if it brought about few territorial changes, that was not simply because of the expansion of government and the disciplining of armies. It was also the result of remarkable economic advances and the availability of new resources that were flowing into Europe from the development of overseas empires. In politics, this was primarily an age of consolidation; in economics, it was a time of profound transformation.

QUESTIONS FOR FURTHER THOUGHT

1. Although Americans naturally prefer regimes that provide for representation and citizen participation in government, are there times when it is advantageous for a state to have an authoritarian or absolutist regime?

2. How important is the development of a capital city or a center of government in the process of state building?

RECOMMENDED READING

Sources

*Hobbes, Thomas. *Leviathan.* 1651. Any modern edition.

*Locke, John. *Second Treatise of Civil Government.* 1690. Any modern edition.

Luvvas, J. (ed.). *Frederick the Great on the Art of War.* 1966.

Studies

*Behrens, C. B. A. *Society, Government, and the Enlightenment: The Experience of Eighteenth-Century France and Prussia.* 1985.

Brewer, John. *The Sinews of Power: War, Money, and the English State, 1688–1783.* 1989. The work that demonstrated the importance of the military and the growth of bureaucracy in eighteenth-century England.

*Hatton, R. N. *Europe in the Age of Louis XIV.* 1969. A beautifully illustrated and vividly interpretive history of the period that Louis dominated.

*Holmes, Geoffrey. *The Making of a Great Power: Late Stuart and Early Georgian Britain, 1660–1722;* and *The Age of Oligarchy: Pre-industrial Britain, 1722–1783.* 1993. The best detailed survey.

Hughes, Lindsey. *Peter the Great: A Biography.* 2002.

Lossky, Andrew. *Louis XIV and the French Monarchy.* 1994.

Mettam, Roger. *Power and Faction in Louis XIV's France.* 1988. An analysis of government and power under absolutist rule.

Oresko, Robert, G. C. Gibbs, and H. M. Scott (eds.). *Royal and Republican Sovereignty in Early Modern Europe.* 1997.

*Plumb, J. H. *The Growth of Political Stability in England, 1675–1725.* 1969. A brief, lucid survey of the development of parliamentary democracy.

Raeff, Marc. *The Well-Ordered Police State: Social and Institutional Change through Law in the Germanies and Russia, 1600–1800.* 1983.

*Tuck, Richard. *Hobbes.* 1989. A clear introduction to Hobbes's thought.

Weigley, R. F. *The Age of Battles: The Quest for Decisive Warfare from Breitenfeld to Waterloo.* 1991. The best military history of the age.

*Available in paperback.

Philip van Dijk
BRISTOL DOCKS AND QUAY, CA. 1780
Commerce increased dramatically in the Atlantic ports of England and France as ships embarked for Africa, the Caribbean, North America, and Spanish America as well as other parts of Europe. Shown here, the port of Bristol in England.
Bristol City Museum and Art Gallery, UK/Bridgeman Art Library

THE WEALTH OF NATIONS

DEMOGRAPHIC AND ECONOMIC GROWTH • THE NEW SHAPE OF INDUSTRY •
INNOVATION AND TRADITION IN AGRICULTURE • EIGHTEENTH-CENTURY EMPIRES

In the early eighteenth century the great majority of Europe's people still lived directly off the land. With a few regional exceptions, the agrarian economy remained immobile: It seemed to have no capacity for dramatic growth. Technology, social arrangements, and management techniques offered little prospect of improvement in production. Several new developments, however, were about to touch off a remarkable surge of economic advance. The first sign, and a growing stimulus for this new situation, was the sustained growth of Europe's population. This depended in turn on an expanding and surer food supply. While changes in agrarian output on the Continent were modest but significant, in England innovations in the control and use of land dramatically increased food production and changed the very structure of rural society.

The exploitation of overseas colonies provided another critical stimulus for European economic growth. Colonial trade in slaves and in sugar, tobacco, and other raw materials radiated from port cities like London and Bristol in England and Bordeaux and Nantes in France. An infrastructure of supportive trades and processing facilities developed around these ports and fed trade networks for the reexport across Europe of finished colonial products. The colonies, in turn, offered new markets for goods manufactured in Europe, such as cotton fabrics. The Atlantic slave trade and plantation slavery in the New World underpinned most of this commerce.

In one small corner of the economy, the growing demand for cotton cloth at home and abroad touched off a quest among English textile merchants for changes in the organization and technology of production. Dramatic structural change in English cotton manufacturing heralded the remarkable economic transformation known as industrialization. By the early nineteenth century, fundamental changes in the methods of raising food and producing goods were under way in Britain and were spreading to the Continent. This chapter explores the character of economic development; the impediments to that process; the nature of eighteenth-century innovations in agriculture, manufacturing, and trade; and some of the social consequences of these economic transformations.

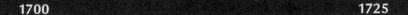

1700   1725

1730s ■■■■■
Sustained population growth begins in Europe;
slave trade monopolies broken

● **1694** Bank of England chartered

DEMOGRAPHIC AND ECONOMIC GROWTH

Perhaps the most basic, long-term historical variable is the movement of population. Historical demographers deal with the migrations of existing populations, from country to city, across national borders or even oceans. More fundamentally, they study the trends over time within populations and chart death rates, birthrates, and the growth or decline of population. Similarly, economic historians analyze macroeconomic trends in production and prices, which in turn can reinforce population growth or deter it. In this section we will consider certain trends in the demography and economy of eighteenth-century Europe, which combined to support economic growth.

A New Demographic Era

In the relationship between people and the land, between demography and agriculture, European life before the eighteenth century showed little change. Levels of population seemed to flow like the tides, in cyclical or wavelike patterns. Population might increase substantially over several generations, but eventually crop failures or the ravages of plague and other contagious diseases would drive the level of population down once again. In extreme cases, a lack of able-bodied workers led to the abandonment of land, and entire villages disappeared altogether. Such dramatic population losses had last occurred in seventeenth-century Germany, Poland, and Mediterranean Europe (the southern parts of Italy, Spain, and France).

For centuries Europe's population had been vulnerable to subsistence crises. Successions of poor harvests or crop failures might leave the population without adequate food and would drive up the price of grain and flour beyond what the poorest people could afford. If actual starvation did not carry them off, undernourishment made people more vulnerable than usual to disease. Such crises could also set off a chain of side effects, from unemployment to pessimism, that made people postpone marriage and childbearing. Thus, subsistence crises could drive down the birthrate as well as drive up the death rate, causing in combination a substantial loss in population.

Population Growth Although barely perceived by most Europeans at the time, a new era in Europe's demography began around 1730, and by 1800 Europe's population had grown by at least 50 percent. (Since the first censuses were not taken until the early nineteenth century, all population figures prior to that time are only estimates.) Europe's estimated population jumped from about 120 million to about 180 or 190 million. Europe had probably never before experienced so rapid and substantial an increase in the number of its people. Prussia and Sweden may have doubled their populations, while Spain's grew from 7.5 million to about 11.5 million. High growth rates in England and Wales raised the population there from an estimated 5 million people in 1700 to more than 9 million in 1801, the date of the first British census. The French, according to the best estimates, numbered about 19 million at the death of Louis XIV in 1715 and probably about 26 million in 1789. France was the most densely populated large nation in Europe in the late eighteenth century and, with the exception of the vast Russian Empire, the most populous state.

Europe's population growth of the eighteenth century continued and indeed accelerated during the nineteenth century, thus breaking once and for all the tidelike cycles and immobility of Europe's demography.

1750s Enclosure movement begins in England

● **1757** Battle of Plassey in Bengal

● **1763** Peace of Paris settles Great War for Empire

● **1776** Smith, *Wealth of Nations*; Watt develops steam engine

Arkwright opens Cromford cotton-spinning factory **1780s**

India Act begins the British raj **1784** ●

Radischev's exposé of Russian serfdom **1790** ●

Baptisms and Burials at Auneuil (1660–1790)

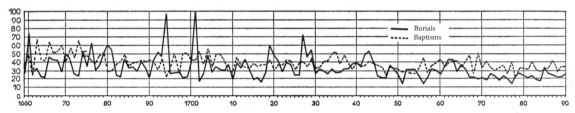

Baptisms and Burials at Saint-Lambert des Levées (1600–1790)

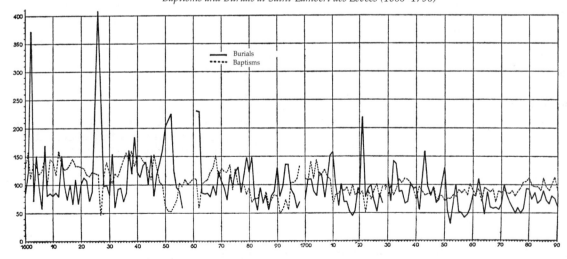

In these two French parishes, the seventeenth century came to a close with severe food shortages and sharp surges of mortality. In a more favorable economic climate, by contrast, the later eighteenth century brought an almost consistent annual surplus of births over deaths.

What caused this fundamental transformation in the underlying structure of European history?

Falling Death Rates There are two possible explanations for rapid population growth: a fall in death rates or a rise in birthrates. The consensus among historians is that a decline in mortality rates, rather than a rise in birthrates, accounts for most of the population growth in the eighteenth century, although England seems to have been an exception. Declines in the death rate did not occur because of improvements in medical science or hygiene, which became important factors in driving down mortality only in the later nineteenth century. Instead, Europe was beginning to enjoy a stabler and better food supply, perhaps owing to a mild improvement in average climate compared with that of the seventeenth century, which some historians regard as a "little ice age" of unusually cold and wet weather. The opening of new agricultural land in Poland, Hungary, and Russia helped increase Europe's food supplies, as did incremental advances in transportation networks and agrarian changes in England (to be discussed later in this chapter).

Europe's population remained extremely vulnerable to disease. Endemic diseases such as tuberculosis, typhoid, and malaria still ravaged the populations of many regions. Periodic epidemics of dysentery (which attacked the digestive system), influenza (lethal to the respiratory systems of the elderly), typhus (a lice-borne disease that flourished in the conditions of poverty), and smallpox (which assaulted rich and poor alike) continued to take their toll. But a better-nourished population could perhaps stand up to those assaults with greater success.

With the exception of England, birthrates in most regions of Europe do not seem to have increased in the eighteenth century. A high average age at marriage, with women typically well into their twenties and men in their mid to late twenties, served to check population growth. Since the birth of illegitimate children remained relatively rare, late marriages kept women from becoming pregnant during some of their most fecund years; they therefore had fewer babies altogether. In England, however, where greater geographic mobility and economic opportunities may have encouraged young couples to start families earlier, the average age at marriage came down and birthrates increased, helping to explain Britain's explosive population growth.

Profit Inflation: The Movement of Prices

The population grew in eighteenth-century Europe in tandem with an increasing pace and scale of economic activity. Europe's overall wealth expanded, though not steadily and consistently. While the economy experienced periods of fluctuation, of growth and decline, the long-term, or secular, trend was positive, compared with the stagnation and economic difficulty that prevailed (outside of England) during the "long seventeenth century," until roughly 1730. Scholars have made particularly rigorous studies of the economic cycles in France as revealed through the history of prices, and there is reason to believe that economies elsewhere in Europe behaved comparably to France's.

During the first decades of the eighteenth century, prices generally remained stable, perpetuating the long depression of the seventeenth century and no doubt reflecting the exhaustion of the European states from the War of the Spanish Succession. As with Europe's demographic growth, significant economic growth began around 1730 and lasted up until the peace settlements that followed the Napoleonic wars in 1815. Gradual inflation in prices dominated the era. Since French money was kept stable after 1726, the upward movement of prices must be attributed to other causes. Primarily, the rise in prices reflected the stimulus and pressures of a growing population in France and a growing demand for food, land, goods, and employment.

Gently rising prices and gradual, mild inflation usually stimulate the economy—unlike sharp spikes of inflation that create hard times. This nearly century-long cycle of "profit inflation" generated economic growth. There were, of course, periodic reversals or countercyclical trends. In France, for example, prosperity leveled off around 1770, ushering in two decades of falling profits, unemployment, and hard times.

The Impact of Inflation   Over the long term, the inflation did not affect all products, all sectors of the economy, or all segments of society equally. Prices in France between 1726 and 1789 increased by an average of about 65 percent. The cost of grains, the basic food for the poor, rose slightly more than the average and considerably more than other agricultural products, such as wine and meat. Rents rose sharply, suggesting a shortage of available land. Real wages, on the other hand, increased by a meager 22 percent in the same period, which points to a glut of workers competing for employment and to hard times for many wage earners.

These differentials had important social and economic effects. High rents in the countryside and low wages in the city took wealth from the poor and delivered it to the landlord and employer. Inflation helped drive many tenants from the soil, to the advantage of their better-off neighbors, who were eager to expand their holdings. In the city, inflation enabled merchants and manufacturers to sell goods for more and pay workers relatively less.

Protoindustrialization

Agriculture alone could not ensure economic growth in a heavily populated country like England, France, or the Netherlands. The excess of people to land in such countries meant that many rural people could not actually earn their livelihood in agriculture. One solution for needy families was domestic manufacturing. Traditionally, artisans in urban guilds manufactured the

In contrast to textile work, common artisanal trades such as shoemaking, tailoring, dressmaking, furniture making, and food services would continue to be conducted in small workshops down through the nineteenth century.
Bulloz/© Photo RMN/Art Resource, NY

cloth fabrics used by Europeans. But textiles could also be produced through the putting-out system, whereby merchants distributed raw materials like wool or flax to rural households. Men and women would spin the raw material into yarn on hand-powered spinning machines; rural weavers working on looms in their cottages would then weave the yarn into cloth.

Protoindustrialization is the name historians give to a type of economic development that occurred before the rise of the factory system in the late eighteenth century. In this phase, the volume of rural manufacturing increased under the putting-out system, as more rural families devoted more time to industrial work—primarily spinning, weaving, or finishing textiles. This trend was particularly noticeable in certain regions of the Netherlands, Belgium, the Rhineland, France, and England, where the towns remained sources of capital, materials, and marketing services but where merchants employed labor in the countryside.

Protoindustrialization had important economic, social, and demographic repercussions. Economically, it strengthened marketing networks, spurred capital accumulation that could be reinvested in production, generated additional revenue for needy rural families, and thereby increased their demand for products and services. Socially, it familiarized rural inhabitants with industrial processes and cash relationships. Demographically, it may have loosened restraints on marriages and births, which in turn might have led to increased migration into the cities and thus to urban growth. On the other hand, protoindustrialization did not lead to significant technological improvements or to marked advances in productivity.

THE NEW SHAPE OF INDUSTRY

While most economic activity continued in traditional fashion, dramatic change began during the late eighteenth century in a few corners of the English economy, especially in the manufacture of cotton cloth. Structural economic transformation hinged on increasing the productivity of labor, through two kinds of innovation: the development of more efficient tools and machines and the exploitation of new sources of energy to drive those machines. These innovations in turn led to a reorganization of labor in a new kind of site called the factory.

Such changes in production, however, did not arise out of thin air. They were rooted in a host of favorable preconditions in English society. The legal system regulating property rights, efficient financial institutions, market structures, growing consumer demand, even a new mode of economic analysis—the free-market doctrines of Adam Smith—provided a favorable environment for the innovations in textile manufacturing toward the end of the century. As such changes spread and visibly changed the landscape, critics would later describe them as an "industrial revolution." That term no doubt overstates the case—since it took decades for such changes to take hold more widely—but it is safe to say that the European economy would never be the same.

Toward a New Economic Order

In analyzing any economic system—traditional or modern, capitalist or socialist—economists distinguish between performance and structure. *Performance* is measured by output: the total, or gross, product and the amount produced per individual in the community. This per capita productivity is generally the best measure of an economy's performance. A distinctive feature of an industrial economy is its capacity for sustained growth in per capita production. *Structure* refers to all those characteristics of a society that support or affect performance. Economic, legal, and political institutions; tax policies; technology; demographic movements; even culture and ideology all make up the structure underlying the economy.

Industrialization required innovations in technology, which dramatically raised per capita productivity, but these innovations alone do not entirely explain the advent of industrialism. Social structure itself influences technological development in any age. To ask why dramatic change occurred in industry is thus to pose two deeper questions: What were the structural obstacles to technological innovation and entrepreneurship in traditional European society? And what changes in that society, from the late eighteenth century onward, promoted and rewarded innovation?

Impediments to Economic Innovation
One major obstacle to innovation was the small size of most European markets, which were cut off from one another by physical barriers, political frontiers, tariff walls, and different laws, moneys, and units of measurement. Small markets slowed the growth of specialized manufacture and limited the mobility of capital and labor. Similarly, the highly skewed distribution of wealth typical of many European communities distorted the structure of demand. In many countries, a narrow aristocracy absorbed most disposable income, and the economy organized itself largely to serve the wealthy few. Catering to the desires of the rich, the economy produced expensive luxury goods, often exquisite in quality and workmanship but always in relatively small quantities. Such small markets and skewed demand dampened the incentive to manufacture an abundance of relatively inexpensive goods.

Also crucial to the industrializing process was the question of property rights and privileges—whether they would encourage a high rate of return on innovation or impede it. In the towns, the guilds presented a major obstacle to economic innovation. Guild regulations, or government regulation of the economy enforced by the guilds, prescribed the techniques to be used in production and often dictated the terms and conditions under which goods could be sold, apprentices taken on, or workers hired. Out of simple self-interest, given their stake in existing arrangements, the guilds favored traditional technology and managerial techniques.

Governments, too, helped sustain these restrictive practices, principally by exploiting them for their own fiscal benefit. The French government, for example, collected substantial fees from guilds and could turn to them for loans as well. Governments also restricted economic activity by licensing monopoly companies with exclusive rights to trade in certain regions, such as the East Indies, or to manufacture certain products, such as fine porcelain. With ensured markets and profits, these companies were not likely to assume the risks of new ventures, and they blocked others from doing so. Cultural attitudes may also have discouraged entrepreneurial efforts. Many persons, particularly in the aristocratic classes, still regarded money made in trade or manufacture as somehow tainted. The highest aspiration of successful French business families seems often to have been the purchase of a noble title.

Adam Smith
Although these institutions and attitudes still marked European life in the eighteenth century, they were subject to ever sharper criticisms. From midcentury on, certain French social thinkers denounced guild control of production in the towns and economic privilege and monopoly in all forms. But the seminal work in this new school of economic thought was *An Inquiry into the Nature and Causes of the Wealth of Nations* (1776) by the Scottish philosopher Adam Smith. Smith argued that money in and of itself did not constitute wealth but was merely its marker. Wealth derived from the added value in manufactured items produced by the combination of invested capital

LAISSEZ-FAIRE IDEOLOGY

At the heart of Adam Smith's laissez-faire ideology was a belief that individual self-interest is the motor of economic progress, a notion epitomized in this selection by Smith's reference to the "invisible hand." By the same token, each region or country should pursue what it does best, an argument against protective tariffs for domestic industry.

"Every individual is continually exerting himself to find out the most advantageous employment for whatever capital he can command. . . . But it is only for the sake of profit that any man employs a capital in the support of industry; and he will always, therefore, endeavor to employ it in the support of that industry of which the produce is likely to be of the greatest value, or to exchange for the greatest quantity either of money or of other goods. . . . [In so doing] he generally neither intends to promote the public interest, nor knows how much he is promoting it. . . . he intends only his own security; and by directing that industry in such a manner as its produce may be of the greatest value, he intends only his own gain. [But] he is in this, as in many other cases, led by an invisible hand to promote an end which was not part of his intention. By pursuing his own interest he frequently promotes that of the society more effectually than when he really intends to promote it.

"What is the species of domestic industry which his capital can employ, and of which the produce is likely to be of the greatest value, every individual, it is evident, can, in his local situation, judge much better than any statesman or lawgiver can do for him. . . .

"To give the monopoly of the home market to the produce of domestic industry, in any particular art or manufacture, is in some measure to direct private people in what manner they ought to employ their capitals, and must, in almost all cases, be either a useless or hurtful regulation. If the produce of domestic can be brought there as cheaply as that of foreign industry, the regulation is evidently useless. If it cannot, it must generally be hurtful. . . . If a foreign country can supply us with a commodity cheaper than we ourselves can make it, better buy it from them with some part of the produce of our own industry."

A. Smith, *An Inquiry into the Nature and Causes of the Wealth of Nations,* 1776, book 4, ch. 2.

and labor. Smith believed that economic progress required that each individual be allowed to pursue his or her own self-interest freely, without restriction by guilds, the state, or tradition. He argued that on all levels of economic activity—from manufacturing to the flow of international trade—a natural division of labor should be encouraged. High tariffs, guild restrictions, and mercantilist restraints on free trade all artificially obstructed economic activity. Smith became a founding father of **laissez-faire** economic theory, meaning, in effect: Let individuals freely pursue their own economic interests. In the aggregate, free individual enterprise would create more wealth than any artificial regulation could encourage (see "Laissez-Faire Ideology," above).

Laissez-faire became a battle cry taken up by British businesspeople and factory owners in the early nineteenth century. Such arguments slowly affected policy. In 1786 France and Britain signed a free-trade treaty, lowering protective tariffs on imported textiles. Guilds were already growing weaker in most towns and were relatively powerless in towns of recent growth, like Manchester and Birmingham in England, where new industries such as cotton manufacturing escaped guild supervision altogether. This trend reached its culmination when the government of revolutionary France permanently dissolved all guilds and restrictive trade associations in 1791. Similarly, the British Parliament revoked the laws regulating apprenticeships in the 1790s. Legally and socially, the entrepreneur was winning greater freedom.

The Roots of Economic Transformation in England

Of all the nations of Europe, England was the first to develop a social structure that strongly supported innovation and economic growth. England's advantages were many, some of them deeply rooted in geography and history. This comparatively small realm contained an excellent balance of resources. The plain to the south and east, where traditional centers of English settlement concentrated, was fertile and productive. The uplands to the north and west possessed rich deposits of coal and iron, and their streams had powered flour mills since the Middle Ages.

Proximity to the sea was another natural advantage. No part of the island kingdom was distant from the coast. At a time when water transport offered the sole economical means for moving bulky commodities, the sea brought coal close to iron, raw materials close to factories, and products close to markets. Above all, the sea gave Britain's merchants access to the much wider world beyond their shores.

Efficiency of transport was critical in setting the size of markets. During the eighteenth century, Britain witnessed a boom in the building of canals and turnpikes by private individuals or syndicates. By 1815 the country possessed some 2,600 miles of canals linking rivers, ports, and other towns. In addition, few institutional obstructions to the movement of goods existed. United under a strong monarchy, Britain was free of internal tariff barriers, unlike prerevolutionary France, Germany, or Italy. Merchants everywhere counted in the same money, measured their goods by the same standards, and conducted their affairs under the protection of the common law. By contrast, in France differences in provincial legal codes and in weights and measures complicated and slowed exchange. As the writer Voltaire sarcastically remarked, the traveler crossing France by coach changed laws as frequently as horses.

The English probably had the highest standard of living in Europe and generated strong consumer demand for manufactured goods. English society was less stratified than that on the Continent, the aristocracy powerful but much smaller. Primogeniture (with the family's land going to the eldest son) was the rule among both the peers (the titled members of the House of Lords) and the country gentlemen or squires. Left without lands, younger sons had to seek careers in other walks of life, and some turned toward commerce. They frequently recruited capital for their ventures from their landed fathers and elder brothers. English religious dissenters, chiefly Calvinists and Quakers, formed another pool of potential entrepreneurs; denied careers in government because of their religion, many turned their energies to business enterprises.

British Financial Management A high rate of reinvestment is critical to industrialization; reinvestment, in turn, depends on the skillful management of money by both individuals and public institutions. Here again, Britain enjoyed advantages. Early industrial enterprises could rely on Britain's growing banking system to meet their capital needs. In the seventeenth century, the goldsmiths of London had assumed the functions of bankers. They accepted and guarded deposits, extended loans, transferred upon request credits from one account to another, and changed money. In the eighteenth century, banking services became available beyond London; the number of country banks rose from three hundred in 1780 to more than seven hundred by 1810. English businesspeople were familiar with banknotes and other forms of commercial papers,

and their confidence in paper facilitated the recruitment and flow of capital.

The founding of the Bank of England in 1694 marked an epoch in the history of European finance. The bank took responsibility for managing England's public debt, sold shares to the public, and faithfully met the interest payments due to the shareholders, with the help of government revenue (such as the customs duties efficiently collected on Britain's extensive foreign trade). When the government needed to borrow, it could turn to the Bank of England for assistance. This stability in government finances ensured a measure of stability for the entire money market and, most important, held down interest rates in both the public and private sectors. In general, since the Glorious Revolution of 1688, England's government had been sensitive to the interests of the business classes, who in turn had confidence in the government. Such close ties between money and power facilitated economic investment.

In contrast, France lacked a sound central bank, and extensive government borrowing drove up interest rates in the private sector as well. On balance, although limited capital and conservative management held back French business enterprises, they dampened but did not suppress the expansion of the economy. France remained a leader in producing wool and linen cloth as well as iron, but it seemed more inclined to produce luxury items or very cheap, low-quality goods. On the other hand, England (with its higher standard of living and strong domestic demand) seemed more adept at producing standardized products of reasonably good quality.

Cotton: The Beginning of Industrialization

The process of early industrialization in England was extremely complex and remains difficult to explain. What seems certain is that a strong demand for cheap goods was growing at home and abroad in the eighteenth century, and a small but important segment of the English community sensed this opportunity and responded to it.

Specifically, the market for cotton goods became the most propulsive force for change in industrial production. Thanks to slave labor in plantation colonies, the supply of raw cotton was rising dramatically. On the demand side, lightweight cotton goods were durable, washable, versatile, and cheaper than woolen or linen cloth. Cotton, therefore, had a bright future as an item of mass consumption. But traditional textile manufacturing centers in England (the regions of protoindustrialization such as East Anglia and the Yorkshire districts) could not satisfy the growing demand. The organization and technology of the putting-out system had reached its limits. For one thing, the merchant was

Richard Arkwright not only invented this power-driven machine to spin cotton yarn but also proved to be a highly successful entrepreneur with the factory he constructed at Cromford in the Lancashire region.
The Science Museum, London

The engineering firm of Bolton & Watt became famous for its steam engines, whose complex mechanisms of cams, gears, and levers could harness the power of steam to a variety of uses in industry and transportation.
The Science Museum, London

limited to the labor supply in his own district; the farther he went to find cottage workers, the longer it took and the more cumbersome it became to pass the materials back and forth. Second, he could not adequately control his workers. Clothiers were bedeviled with embezzlement of raw materials, poor workmanship, and lateness in finishing assigned work. English clothiers were therefore on the lookout for technological or organizational innovations to help them meet a growing demand for textiles.

Machines and Factories   Weavers could turn out large amounts of cloth thanks to the invention of the fly shuttle in the 1730s, which permitted the construction of larger and faster handlooms. But traditional methods of spinning the yarn caused a bottleneck in the production process. Responding to this problem, inventors built new kinds of spinning machines that could be grouped in large factories or mills. Richard Arkwright's water frame drew cotton fibers through rollers and twisted them into thread. Not simply an inventor but an entrepreneur (one who combined the various factors of production into a profitable enterprise), Arkwright initially housed his machines in a large factory sited

near a river so that his machines could be propelled by waterpower.

At around the same time, James Watt had been perfecting the technology of steam engines—machinery originally used to power suction pumps that would evacuate water from the pits of coal mines. The earliest steam engine had produced a simple up-and-down motion. Watt not only redesigned it to make it far more efficient and powerful but also developed a system of gears to harness the engine's energy into rotary motion that could drive other types of machines. In 1785 Arkwright became one of Watt's first customers when he switched from waterpower to steam engines as the means of driving the spinning machines in his new cotton factory at Cromford. With Arkwright (who became a millionaire) and Watt, the modern factory system was launched (see "Richard Arkwright's Achievement," p. 536).

Spinning factories, however, disrupted the equilibrium between spinning and weaving in the other direction: Yarn was now abundant, but hand-loom weavers could not keep up with the pace. This disequilibrium created a brief golden age for the weavers, but merchants were eager to break the new bottleneck. In 1784 Edmund Cartwright designed a power-driven loom. Small technical flaws and the violent opposition of hand-loom weavers retarded the widescale adoption of power looms until the early nineteenth century, but then both spinning and weaving were totally transformed. Power-driven machinery boosted the output of yarn and cloth astronomically, while merchants could assemble their workers in factories and scrutinize their every move to maximize production. In a factory, one

RICHARD ARKWRIGHT'S ACHIEVEMENT

This celebration of British industrialization, the factory system, and entrepreneurship begins by extolling Richard Arkwright's accomplishments in the 1780s.

"When the first water frames for spinning cotton were erected at Cromford, about sixty years ago, mankind were little aware of the mighty revolution which the new system of labour was destined by Providence to achieve, not only in the structure of British society, but in the fortunes of the world at large. Arkwright alone had the sagacity to discern, and the boldness to predict in glowing language, how vastly productive human industry would become, when no longer proportioned in its results to muscular effort, which is by its nature fitful and capricious, but when made to consist in the task of guiding the work of mechanical fingers and arms, regularly impelled with great velocity by some indefatigable physical power [such as a steam engine].

"The main difficulty did not lie so much in the invention of a proper self-acting mechanism for drawing out and twisting cotton into a continuous thread, as in the distribution of different members of the apparatus into one co-operative body . . . and above all, in training human beings to renounce their desultory habits of work, and to identify themselves with the unvarying regularity of the complex automaton. To devise and administer a successful code of factory discipline, suited to the necessities of factory diligence, was the Herculean enterprise, the noble achievement of Arkwright. . . . It required, in fact, a man of Napoleonic nerve and ambition to subdue the refractory tempers of work-people accustomed to irregular paroxysms of diligence, and to urge on his multifarious and intricate constructions in the face of prejudice, passion, and envy."

Andrew Ure, *The Philosophy of Manufactures*, 1835.

small boy could watch over two mechanized looms whose output was fifteen times greater than that of a skilled hand-loom weaver.

INNOVATION AND TRADITION IN AGRICULTURE

In England around 1700, an estimated 80 percent of the population lived directly from agriculture; a century later that proportion had fallen to approximately 40 percent. This shift of labor from agriculture would have been inconceivable had English farming not become far more productive during that period. English farmers introduced significant improvements in their methods of cultivation, including the techniques of convertible husbandry and the enclosure of large compact farms. These enabled English agriculture to supply the growing towns with food as well as excess labor and capital. On the Continent, however, whether bound to the land as serfs in Eastern Europe or legally free in the West, peasants generally clung to traditional agrarian ways. Time-worn survival strategies provided the best hope for security but also ensured a climate hostile to untested innovations.

Convertible Husbandry

A central problem in any agricultural system is that repeated harvests on the same land eventually rob the soil of its fertility. Since the Early Middle Ages, the usual method of restoring a field's fertility involved letting the land lie fallow for a season (that is, resting it by planting nothing) every second or third year. This fallowing allowed bacteria in the soil to take needed nitrogen from the air. A quicker and better method, heavy manuring, could not be used widely because most farmers were unable to support sufficient livestock to produce the manure. Feeding farm animals, particularly with fodder during the winter, was beyond the means of most peasants.

But fallowing was an extremely inefficient and wasteful method of restoring the soil's fertility. One key to improving agricultural productivity, therefore, lay in eliminating the fallow periods, which in turn required that more animals be raised to provide fertilizer. In a given year, instead of being taken out of cultivation, a field could be planted not with grain but with turnips or with nitrogen-fixing grasses that could supply fodder for livestock. The grazing livestock would in turn deposit abundant quantities of manure on those fields. Thus, by the end of that season the soil's fertility would be greater, and next year's grain crop was likely to produce a higher yield than if the field had simply been left fallow the year before.

One of the first British landlords to adopt this approach on a broad scale was Jethro Tull, an agriculturist and inventor. Tull's zeal in advocating new farming methods proved infectious. By the late eighteenth century, Norfolk, in the east of England, had achieved particular prominence for such techniques, known as convertible husbandry.

Livestock and people could range freely over the land in open-field villages after the crops were harvested. The regrouping of scattered parcels and the enclosure of those consolidated properties would put an end to an entire rural way of life.

Improving Landlords With convertible husbandry, innovative (or "improving") landlords never let their land lie fallow but always put it to some productive use. They also experimented with techniques designed to enhance the texture of the soil. If soil was normally too thin to retain water effectively, farmers added clays or marl to help bind the soil. In those regions in which the soil had the opposite problem of clumping too rigidly after rainfalls, they lightened the soil by adding chalk and lime to inhibit the clotting.

Eighteenth-century agrarian innovators also experimented with the selective breeding of animals. Some improved the quality of pigs, while others developed new breeds of sheep and dramatically increased the weight of marketed cattle. Soil management and livestock breeding did not depend on any high-tech knowledge or machinery but simply on a willingness to experiment in land management and to invest capital to achieve higher yields.

The Enclosure Movement in Britain

To make use of new agricultural methods, farmers had to be free to manage the land as they saw fit. This land management was all but impossible under the **open-field system** that had dominated the countryside in Europe since the Middle Ages. Under the open-field system, even the largest landlords usually held their property in numerous elongated strips that were mixed in with and open to the land of their neighbors. Owners of contiguous strips had to follow the same routines of cultivation. One farmer could not plant grasses to graze cattle when another was raising wheat or leaving the land fallow. The village as a whole determined what routines should be followed. The village also decided such matters as how many cattle each member could graze on common meadows and how much wood each could take from the forest. The open-field system froze the technology of cultivation at the levels of the Middle Ages.

Landowners who wished to form compact farms and apply new methods could do so only by enclosing their own properties. Both common law and cost considerations, however, worked against fencing the numerous narrow strips unless the property of the entire village could be rearranged, which required the agreement of all the community. Such voluntary **enclosures** were nearly impossible to organize. In England, however, there was an alternative: An act of Parliament, usually passed in response to a petition by large landowners, could order the enclosure of all agrarian property in a village even against the opposition of some of its inhabitants. Then large landowners could fence in their land and manage it at their discretion.

Enclosing properties in a village was expensive. The lands of the village had to be surveyed and redistributed, in compact blocks, among the members in proportion to their former holdings. But over the course of the eighteenth century, the high rents and returns that could be earned with the new farming methods made enclosures very desirable investments. Numerous acts authorizing enclosure in a village had been passed by Parliament in earlier periods, but a new wave of such acts began to mount around the middle of the eighteenth century. Parliament passed 156 individual acts of enclosure in the decade of the 1750s; from 1800 to 1810 it passed 906 acts. Cumulatively, the enclosure movement all but eradicated the traditional open-field village from the British countryside.

The Impact of Enclosure While enclosure was clearly rational from an economic standpoint, it brought much human misery in its wake. The redistribution of the land deprived the poor of their traditional rights to the village's common land (which was usually divided among the villagers as well) and often left them with tiny, unprofitable plots. Frequently, they were forced to sell their holdings to their richer neighbors and seek employment as laborers or urban workers. However, no

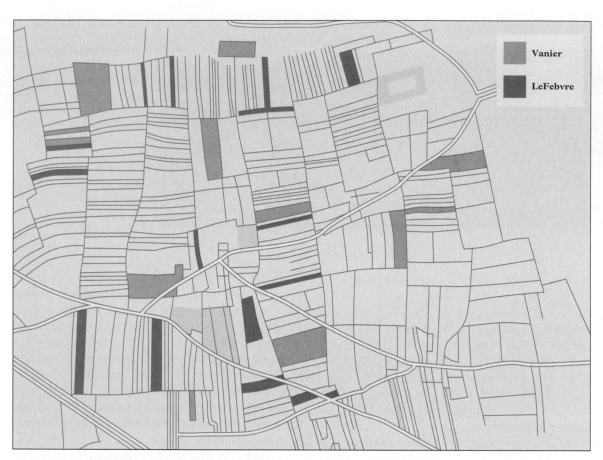

MAP 18.1 AN OPEN-FIELD VILLAGE IN FRANCE
The land in this northern French village, originally blocked out in large fields, was subsequently subdivided into small strips owned by individual landowners or peasants. What do you notice about the holdings of the two landowners Vanier and LeFebvre? What might have been the challenges to managing such holdings in an open-field system? How would consolidating and enclosing their properties affect the ability of these landowners to manage and cultivate the land? How would such changes affect peasants and other villagers who once had access to the open fields?
◆ For an online version, go to www.mhhe.com/chambers9 > chapter 18 > book maps

massive rural depopulation occurred in the wake of enclosures. For one thing, the actual work of fencing the fields required a good deal of labor, and some of the new husbandry techniques were also labor-intensive.

The enclosure movement transformed the English countryside physically and socially, giving it the appearance it retains today of large verdant fields, neatly defined by hedges and fences. Enclosures in Britain led to the domination of rural society by great landlords and their prosperous tenant farmers, who usually held their farms under long leases. Conversely, enclosures resulted in the near disappearance in England of the small peasant-type cultivators still typical of Western Europe. If enclosures did not abruptly push people to the towns, neither did they encourage growth in rural settlements. Enclosures were, therefore, a major factor in the steady shift of Britain's population from countryside to city and in the emergence of the first urban, industrial economy in the nineteenth century.

Serfs and Peasants on the Continent

On the Continent, peasants continued to work their small plots of land—whether owned or rented—in the village of their ancestors. In Eastern Europe, however, the peasants' status was still defined by a system of **serfdom** similar to that which prevailed in Western Europe during the Middle Ages.

Lords and Serfs in Eastern Europe In most of Central and Eastern Europe, nobles retained a near monopoly on the ownership of land and peasants remained serfs, their personal freedom severely limited by the lord's supervision. Serfs could not marry, move away, or enter a trade without their lord's permission. This personal servitude

In Poland and Russia rural lords had direct control over their serfs without intervention by the state. Their powers included the right to inflict corporal punishment.
Bettmann/Corbis

ensured that peasants would be available to provide the labor that the lord required. In return the peasants received access to plots of land (which they did not actually own) and perhaps some rudimentary capital, such as seed for their crops. Much of their time, however, was spent in providing unpaid labor on their lord's domain, the amount of labor service determined by custom rather than by law. Labor service often took up three days a week, and even more during harvest time. In Russia it was said that the peasants worked half the year for their master and only half for themselves (see "The Condition of the Serfs in Russia," p. 540).

The degree of exploitation in European serfdom naturally varied. In Russia, Poland, Hungary, and certain small German states, the status of the serf scarcely differed from that of a slave. Russian and Polish serfs were in effect chattels who could be sold or traded at their lords' discretion, independent of the land they lived on or their family ties. In Russia the state itself owned many peasants and could assign them to work in the mines and factories of the Ural Mountains. Russian and Polish lords could inflict severe corporal punishment on their serfs, up to forty lashes or six months in prison. Peasants had no right of appeal to the state against such punishments.

Serfdom was not as severe in Prussia or the Habsburg monarchy, and the state did assure peasants of certain basic legal rights. In theory, peasants could not be expelled from their plots so long as they paid all their dues and rendered all the services they owed, although in practice the lords could usually remove them if they wished to. Since it was increasingly profitable for the lords to farm large domains directly, many felt an incentive to oust peasants from their tenures or to increase peasant labor services beyond customary limits.

Lords and Peasants in Western Europe In Western Europe, by contrast, serfdom had waned. Most peasants were personally free and were free to buy land if they could afford it. Peasants were not necessarily secure or prosperous, however. There was not enough land to satisfy the needs of all peasant families, and lack of real independence was the rule. Moreover, most French, German, Spanish, and Italian peasants still lived under the authority of a local noble in a system called **seigneurialism.** The peasants owed these lords various dues and obligations on their land, even if the peasants otherwise owned it. Seigneurial fees and charges (for example, a proportion of the harvest, somewhere between 5 and 15 percent) could be a considerable source of income for the lord and an oppressive burden to the already hard-pressed peasant. In addition, the lords administered petty justice in both civil and criminal matters; enjoyed the exclusive privilege of hunting rights

THE CONDITION OF THE SERFS IN RUSSIA

For publishing this unprecedented critique of the miseries and injustices of serfdom, the author was imprisoned by Catherine II.

"A certain man left the capital, acquired a small village of one or two hundred souls [i.e., serfs], and determined to make his living by agriculture. . . . To this end he thought it the surest method to make his peasants resemble tools that have neither will nor impulse; and to a certain extent he actually made them like the soldiers of the present time who are commanded in a mass, who move to battle in a mass, and who count for nothing when acting singly. To attain this end he took away from his peasants the small allotment of plough land and the hay meadows which noblemen usually give them for their bare maintenance, as a recompense for all the forced labor which they demand from them. In a word, this nobleman forced all his peasants and their wives and children to work every day of the year for him. Lest they should starve, he doled out to them a definite quantity of bread. . . . If there was any real meat, it was only in Easter Week.

"These serfs also received clothing befitting their condition. . . . Naturally these serfs had no cows, horses, ewes, or rams. Their master did not withhold from these serfs the permission, but rather the means to have them. Whoever was a little better off and ate sparingly, kept a few chickens, which the master sometimes took for himself, paying for them as he pleased.

"In a short time he added to his two hundred souls another two hundred as victims of his greed, and proceeding with them just as with the first, he increased his holdings year after year, thus multiplying the number of those groaning in his fields. Now he counts them by the thousands and is praised as a famous agriculturalist.

"Barbarian! What good does it do the country that every year a few thousand more bushels of grain are grown, if those who produce it are valued on a par with the ox whose job it is to break the heavy furrow? Or do we think our citizens happy because our granaries are full and their stomachs empty?"

Alexander Radischev, *A Journey from St. Petersburg to Moscow*, 1790.

---

across the lands of the village, no matter who owned them; and profited from monopolies on food-processing operations such as flour mills, bread ovens, and wine presses.

Concerned as they were with securing their basic livelihood, few peasants worried about trying to increase productivity with new farming methods. Satisfied with time-tested methods of cultivation, they could not risk the hazards of novel techniques. Along with growing grain for their own consumption, peasant households had to meet several obligations as well: royal taxes, rents, seigneurial dues, the tithe to the local church, and interest payments on their debts. In short, most peasant households in Western Europe were extremely insecure and relied on custom and tradition as their surest guides.

Peasant Survival Strategies Every peasant household in Western Europe hoped to control enough land to ensure its subsistence and meet its obligations. Ideally, it would own this land. But most peasants did not own as much land as they needed and were obliged to rent additional plots or enter into sharecropping arrangements. Peasants therefore hated to see the consolidation of small plots into large farms, for this meant that the small plots that they might one day afford to buy or

lease were becoming scarcer. The lords and the most prosperous peasants, on the other hand, were interested in extending their holdings, just like the "improving" landlords across the English Channel.

When the land that small peasants owned and rented did not meet their needs, they employed other survival strategies. Peasants could hire out as laborers on larger farms or migrate for a few months to other regions to help with grain or wine harvests. They might practice a simple rural handicraft or weave cloth for merchants on the putting-out system. Some peasants engaged in illegal activities such as poaching game on restricted land or smuggling salt in avoidance of royal taxes. When all else failed, a destitute peasant family might be forced to take to the road as beggars.

The Family Economy In their precarious situation, peasants depended on strong family bonds. A peasant holding was a partnership between husband and wife, who usually waited until they had accumulated enough resources, including the bride's dowry, to establish their own household. Men looked for physical vigor and domestic skills in their prospective brides. ("When a girl knows how to knead and bake bread, she is fit to wed," went a French proverb.) In peasant households the wife's domain was inside the cottage,

Nicolas-Bernard Lépicié
COUR DE FERME
**While changes in agricultural
practices transformed the rural
population of England and
Russia, the small-holding
peasant remained the most
typical social type in France. In
the peasant "family economy,"
husband and wife each made
vital contributions to the
household's productivity.**
Musée du Louvre, Photo ©
R.M.N./Art Resource, NY

where she cooked, repaired clothing, and perhaps spent her evenings spinning yarn. Wives were also responsible for the small vegetable gardens or the precious hens and chickens that peasants maintained to raise cash for their obligations. The husband's work was outside: gathering fuel, caring for draft animals (if the family owned any), plowing the land, planting the fields, and nurturing the crops. But at harvest time everyone worked in the fields.

Peasants also drew strength from community solidarity. Many villages possessed common lands open to all residents. Poorer peasants could forage there for fuel and building materials, and could inexpensively graze whatever livestock they owned. Since villagers generally planted the same crops at the same times, after the harvest livestock was allowed to roam over the arable fields and graze on the stubble of the open fields, a practice known as vacant pasture. All in all, insecurity and the scarcity of land in continental villages made it risky and improbable that peasants would adopt innovative methods or agree to the division of common land.

The Limits of Agrarian Change on the Continent
Change, therefore, came more slowly to the continental countryside than it did to England. The Netherlands, the Paris basin and the northeast of France, the Rhineland in Germany, and the Po Valley of Italy experienced the most active development—all areas of dense settlement in which high food prices encouraged landlords with large farms to invest in agricultural improvements and to adopt innovative methods.

Like their English counterparts, innovating continental farmers waged a battle for managerial freedom, though the changes they sought were not as sweeping as the English enclosure movement. Most French villages worked the land under an open-field system in which peasants followed the same rhythms and routines of cultivation as their neighbors, with the village also determining the rights of its members on common lands. From the middle of the century on, the governing institutions of several provinces banned obligatory vacant pasture and allowed individual owners to enclose their land; some authorized the division of communal lands as well. But the French monarchy did not adopt enclosure as national policy, and after the 1760s provincial authorities proved reluctant to enforce enclosure ordinances against the vigorous opposition of peasants. Traces of the medieval village thus lasted longer in France and Western Europe than in England.

In France in 1789, on the eve of the Revolution, probably 35 percent of the land was owned by the peasants who worked it. In this regard, the French peasants were more favored than those of most other European countries. But this society of small peasant farms was vulnerable to population pressures and was threatened by sharp movements in prices—two major characteristics of eighteenth-century economic history, as we have seen.

In the regions close to the Mediterranean Sea, such as southern Italy, difficult geographical and climatic conditions—the often rugged terrain, thin soil, and dearth of summer rain—did not readily allow the introduction of new techniques either, although many peasants improved their income by planting market crops such as grapes for wine or olives for oil instead of grains for their own consumption. Still, most peasants continued to work their lands much as they had in the Late Middle Ages and for the same poor reward. Fertile areas near the Baltic Sea, such as east Prussia, benefited from the growing demand for grains in Western countries, but on the whole, Eastern Europe did not experience structural agrarian change until the next century.

EIGHTEENTH-CENTURY EMPIRES

The economic dynamism of the eighteenth century derived not simply from growing population and consumer demand, or from English innovations in agriculture and textile manufacturing. Europe's favorable position as a generator of wealth owed as much to its mercantile empires across the seas. Colonial trade became an engine of economic growth in Britain and France. Plantation economies in the Atlantic world, fueled by the West African slave trade, provided sugar, tobacco, and cotton for an ever-expanding consumer demand. In the East spices, fine cloths, tea, and luxury goods similarly enriched European merchants. But behind the merchants and trading companies stood the military and naval muscle of the British and French states. Their rivalry finally erupted in a "Great War for Empire"—the global dimension of the Seven Year's War on the Continent. Here British victories came not only in North America and the Caribbean, but also in South Asia, where they ousted the French from their foothold in India. This left the British free to extend their sway in the nineteenth century over India, which became "the jewel in the crown" of British imperial dominion.

Mercantile and Naval Competition

After 1715 a new era began in the saga of European colonial development. The three pioneers in overseas expansion had by now grown passive, content to defend domains already conquered. Portugal, whose dominion over Brazil was recognized at the Peace of Utrecht in 1715, retired from active contention. Likewise, the Dutch could scarcely compete for new footholds overseas and now protected their interests through cautious neutrality. Although Spain continued its efforts to exclude outsiders from trade with its vast empire in the New World, it did not pose much of a threat to others. The stage of active competition was left to the two other Atlantic powers, France and Britain.

The Decline of the Dutch

The case of Dutch decline is an instructive counterexample to the rise of French and British fortunes. In the seventeenth century the United Provinces, or Dutch Netherlands, had been Europe's greatest maritime power. But this federated state emerged from the wars of Louis XIV in a much weakened position. The country had survived intact, but it now suffered from demographic and political stagnation. The population of 2.5 million failed to rise much during the eighteenth century, thus setting the Dutch apart from their French and British rivals. As a federation of loosely joined provinces, whose seven provincial oligarchies rarely acted in concert, the Netherlands could barely ensure the common defense of the realm.

The Dutch economy suffered when French and English merchants sought to eliminate them as the middlemen of maritime commerce and when their industry failed to compete effectively. Heavy taxes on manufactured goods and the high wages demanded by Dutch artisans forced up the price of Dutch products. What kept the nation from slipping completely out of Europe's economic life was its financial institutions. Dutch merchants shifted their activity away from actual trading ventures into the safer, lucrative areas of credit and finance. Their country was the first to perfect the uses of paper currency, a stock market, and a central bank. Amsterdam's merchant-bankers loaned large amounts of money to private borrowers and foreign governments, as the Dutch became financial brokers instead of traders.

The British and French Commercial Empires

Great Britain, a nation that had barely been able to hold its own against the Dutch in the seventeenth century, now began its rise to domination of the seas. Its one serious competitor was France, the only state in Europe to maintain both a large army and a large navy. Their rivalry played itself out in four regions. The West Indies, where both France and Britain had colonized several sugar-producing islands, constituted the fulcrum of both empires. The West Indian plantation economy, in turn, depended on slave-producing West Africa. The third area of colonial expansion was the North American continent, where Britain's thirteen colonies became centers of settlement whereas New France remained primarily a trading area. Finally, both nations sponsored powerful companies for trade with India and other Asian lands. These companies were supposed to compete for markets without establishing colonies.

The two colonial systems had obvious differences and important similarities. French absolutism fostered a centralized structure of control for its colonies, with intendants and military governors ruling across the seas as they did in the provinces at home. Britain's North American colonies, by contrast, remained independent from each other and to a degree escaped direct control from the home government, although Crown and Parliament both claimed jurisdiction over them. British colonies each had a royal governor but also a local assembly of sorts, and most developed traditions of self-government. Nonetheless, the French and British faced similar problems and achieved generally similar results. Both applied mercantilist principles to the regulation of colonial trade, and both strengthened their navies to protect it.

Mercantilism Mercantilist doctrine supported the regulation of trade by the state in order to increase the state's power against its neighbors (see chapter 15). **Mercantilism** was not limited to the Atlantic colonial powers. Prussia was guided by mercantilism as much as were Britain and France, for all regarded the economic activities of their subjects as subordinate to the interests of the state.

Mercantilist theory advocated a favorable balance of trade as signified by a net inflow of gold and silver, and it assumed that a state's share of bullion could increase only at its neighbor's expense. (Adam Smith would attack this doctrine in 1776, as we have seen.) Colonies could promote a favorable balance of trade by producing valuable raw materials or staple crops for the parent country and by providing protected markets for the parent country's manufactured goods. Foreign states were to be excluded from these benefits as much as possible. By tariffs, elaborate regulations, bounties, or prohibitions, each government sought to channel trade between its colonies and itself. Spain, for example, restricted trade with its New World colonies exclusively to Spanish merchant vessels, although smugglers and pirates made a mockery of this policy.

Europe's governments sought to exploit overseas colonies for the benefit of the parent country and not simply for the profit of those who invested or settled abroad. But most of the parties to this commerce prospered. The large West Indian planters made fortunes, as did the most successful merchants, manufacturers, and shipowners at home who were involved in colonial trade. Illicit trade also brought rewards to colonial merchants; John Hancock took the risk of smuggling food supplies from Boston to French West Indian planters in exchange for handsome profits.

"Empire" generally meant "trade," but this seaborne commerce depended on naval power: Merchant ships had to be protected, trading rivals excluded, and regula-tions enforced. This reciprocal relationship between the expansion of trade and the deployment of naval forces added to the competitive nature of colonial expansion. Naval vessels needed stopping places for reprovisioning and refitting, which meant that ports had to be secured in strategic locations such as Africa, India, and the Caribbean and denied to rivals whenever possible.

The Profits of Global Commerce

The call of colonial markets invigorated European economic life. Colonial commerce provided new products, like sugar, and stimulated new consumer demand, which in turn created an impetus for manufacturing at home. It is estimated that the value of French commerce quadrupled during the eighteenth century. By the 1770s commerce with their colonies accounted for almost one-third of the total volume of both British and French foreign trade. The West Indies trade (mainly in sugar) bulked the largest, and its expansion was truly spectacular. The value of French imports from the West Indies increased more than tenfold between 1716 and 1788, from 16 million to 185 million livres.

The West Indies seemed to be ideal colonies. By virtue of their tropical climate and isolation from European society, which made slavery possible, the islands produced valuable crops difficult to raise elsewhere: tobacco, cotton, indigo, and especially sugar, a luxury that popular European taste soon turned into a necessity. Moreover, the islands could produce little else and therefore depended on exports from Europe. They could not raise an adequate supply of food animals or grain to feed the vast slave population, they could not cut enough lumber for building, and they certainly could not manufacture the luxury goods demanded by the planter class.

Triangular Trade Numerous variations of **triangular trade** (between the home country and two overseas

THE GROWTH OF ENGLAND'S FOREIGN TRADE IN THE EIGHTEENTH CENTURY

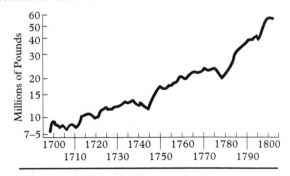

Three-year averages of combined imports and exports
Adapted from Phyllis Dean and W. A. Cole, *British Economic Growth, 1688–1959*, Cambridge University Press, 1964, p. 49.

MAGNITUDE OF THE SLAVE TRADE

The following figures represent the best current estimate of the number of persons removed from Africa and transported as slaves to the New World during the entire period of the Atlantic slave trade.

British Caribbean	1,665,000
British North America (to 1786)	275,000
United States (after 1786)	124,000
French Caribbean	1,600,000
Dutch Caribbean	500,000
Brazil	3,646,000
Spanish America	1,552,000

From Philip D. Curtain, *The Atlantic Slave Trade: A Census*, University of Wisconsin Press, 1969.

areas) revolved around the West Indies. One pattern began with a ship departing from a British port with a cargo of manufactured products—paper, knives, pots, blankets, and the like—destined for the shopkeepers of North America. Landing at Marblehead, Massachusetts, or Philadelphia, the ship might exchange its goods for New England fish oil, fish, beef, and timber. These products would then be transported to Jamaica or Barbados to be traded for sugar that would be turned over to British refineries many months later. Another variation might see a ship set out from Newport, Rhode Island (the chief slaving port in North America), with a cargo of New England rum. Landing in West Africa, the ship would acquire slaves in exchange for the rum and then sail to the Indies to sell the slaves for bills of exchange or for molasses, from which more rum could be distilled. French and British manufacturers in the port cities made fortunes by refining or finishing colonial products such as sugar, indigo, tobacco, and furs and reexporting them to other European markets. Colonial commerce was superimposed on a complex pattern of European trade in which the Atlantic states carried off the lion's share of the profits.

Slavery, the Foundation of Empire

Much of this dynamic global trade rested on slavery. Endless, backbreaking labor transformed a favorable climate and the investment of speculators into harvested plantation crops (see "A British Defense of Slavery and the Plantation Economy," p. 545). A publication of the chamber of commerce of Nantes, France's chief slaving port, publicly argued that without slavery there would be no French colonial commerce at all. At the height of the Atlantic slave traffic, about 88,000 blacks were removed from Africa annually—half in British ships, a quarter in French, and the rest in Dutch, Portuguese, Danish, and American ships (see

"Magnitude of the Slave Trade"). More than 600,000 slaves were imported into the island of Jamaica in the eighteenth century. The population of Saint-Domingue around 1790 comprised about half a million slaves, compared with 35,000 whites of all nationalities and 28,000 mulattoes and free blacks.

Trafficking in slaves was competitive and risky but highly profitable. The demand for slaves in the West Indies, Brazil, Venezuela, and the southern colonies of North America kept rising, pushing up prices. In both Britain and France, chartered companies holding exclusive rights from the Crown originally monopolized the slave trade. They did not actually colonize or conquer African territory but instead established forts, or "factories," on the West African coast for the coordination and defense of their slaving expeditions. Gradually, the monopolies were challenged by other merchants and investors who combined to launch their own ships on slaving voyages. The West Indian planters, who needed more slaves, welcomed all additional sources. The independent traders clustered in port cities like Bristol and Liverpool in England, and by the 1730s they had broken the monopoly on the slave trade.

The Ordeal of Enslavement   Europeans alone did not condemn black Africans to slavery. In this period, Europeans scarcely penetrated the interior of the continent; the forbidding topography and the resistance of the natives confined them to coastal areas. The actual enslavement took place in the interior at the hands of aggressive local groups whose chiefs became the intermediaries of this commerce. The competition among European traders for the slaves tended to drive up the prices that African middlemen could command in hardware, cloth, liquor, or guns. In response, some traders ventured into new areas in which the Africans might be more eager to come to terms. Increasing demand, rising prices, and competitiveness spread the slave trade and further blighted the future of West African society.

Many blacks failed to survive the process of enslavement at all. Some perished on the forced marches from the interior to the coast or on the nightmarish **Middle Passage** across the Atlantic, which has been compared to the transit in freight cars of Jewish prisoners to Nazi extermination camps in World War II. Because the risks of slaving ventures were high and the time lag between investment and return somewhere from one to two years, the traders sought to maximize their profits by jamming as many captives as possible onto the ships. Medium-sized ships carried as many as five hundred slaves on a voyage, all packed below deck in only enough space for each person to lie at full length pressed against neighboring bodies, and with only enough headroom to crawl, not to stand. Food and pro-

A BRITISH DEFENSE OF SLAVERY AND THE PLANTATION ECONOMY

"The most approved judges of the commercial interests of these Kingdoms have ever been of the opinion that our West Indies and African Trades are the most nationally beneficial of any we carry on. It is also allowed on all hands that the Trade to Africa is the branch which renders our American Colonies and Plantations so advantageous to Great Britain; that traffic only affording our plantations a constant supply of Negroe servants [slaves] for the culture of their lands in the produce of *sugars, tobacco, rice, rum, cotton, pimento,* and all others our plantations produce. So that the extensive employment of our shipping in, to, and from America, the great brood of seamen consequent thereupon, and the daily bread of the most considerable part of our British Manufacturers, are owing primarily to the labor of Negroes; who, as they were the first happy instrument of raising our Plantations, so their labor only can support and preserve them, and render them still more and more profitable to their Mother Kingdom.

"The Negroe Trade therefore, and the natural consequences resulting from it, may be justly esteemed an inexhaustible fund of Wealth and Naval Power to this Nation. And by the overplus of Negroes above what have served our own Plantations, we have drawn likewise no inconsiderable quantities of treasure from the Spaniards. . . . What renders the Negroe Trade still more estimable and important is that near nine tenths of those Negroes are paid for in Africa with British produce and manufactures only. We send no specie of bullion to pay for the products of Africa. . . . And it may be worth consideration, that while our Plantations depend only on planting by Negroes, they will neither depopulate our own Country, become independent of her Dominion, or any way interfere [i.e., compete] with the interests of the British Manufacturer, Merchant, or Landed Gentleman."

Malachy Postlethwayt, *The National and Private Advantages of the African Trade Considered,* London, 1746.

A European commercial settlement on the Guinea coast of Africa in the early 18th century. The four compounds belong to Portugal (left), France (centre), England (right) and Holland (right foreground). In the left foreground the French director (numbered 14) returns with his train of servants. (4)

An early eighteenth-century European commercial settlement on the west coast of Africa consisted of four national compounds: Portuguese, French, English, and Dutch.

visions were held to a minimum. The mortality rate that resulted from these conditions was a staggering 10 percent or more on average, and in extreme cases exceeded 50 percent (see diagram, p 546).

Agitation against slavery by Quakers and other reformers in Britain and France focused initially on the practices of the slave trade rather than on slavery itself. After the 1780s, participation in the Atlantic slave trade tapered off, and the supply of slaves was replenished mainly from children born to slaves already in the New World. A dismal chapter in Europe's relations with the outside world dwindled to an end, although

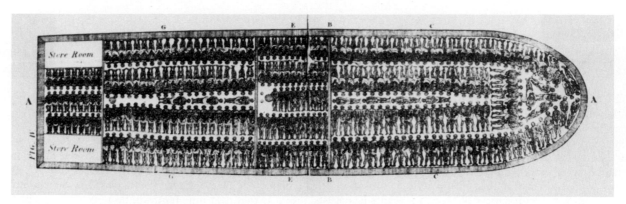

This diagram of "tight packing" below deck conveys the horror of the trans-Atlantic slaving voyages, known as the Middle Passage. The drawing was circulated by British antislavery reformers.
The Library of Congress

the final suppression of slaving voyages did not come for several more decades.

Mounting Colonial Conflicts

In the New World, the population of Britain's North American colonies reached about 1.5 million by mid-century. Some colonists pushed the frontier westward, while others clustered around the original settlements, a few of which—like Boston, New York, and Philadelphia—could now be called cities. The westward extension of the frontier and the growth of towns gave a vitality to the British colonial world that New France appeared to lack. Since there was little enthusiasm among the French for emigration to the Louisiana Territory or Canada, the French remained thinly spread in their vast dominions. Yet France's colonies were well organized and profitable.

As French fishermen and fur traders prospered in Canada, French soldiers established a series of strongholds to support them, including the bastion of Fort Louisbourg at the entrance to the Gulf of St. Lawrence and a string of forts near the Great Lakes (see map 18.2), which served as bridgeheads for French fur traders and as a security buffer for Quebec province. In Louisiana, at the other end of the continent, New Orleans guarded the terminus of the Mississippi River. On their side, the British established their first large military base in North America at Halifax, Nova Scotia, contesting French penetration of the fishing grounds and waterways of the St. Lawrence Gulf.

Conflict on the Frontier   The unsettled Ohio Valley was a second focus of colonial rivalry in North America. Pushing south from their Great Lakes trading forts and north from their posts on the Mississippi, the French began to assume control over that wilderness. A new string of forts formed pivots for potential French domination of the whole area between the Appalachian Mountains and the Mississippi—territory claimed and coveted by British subjects in the thirteen colonies. The threat grew that the French might completely cut off the westward expansion of these colonies. On their side, the French feared that British penetration of the Ohio Valley would lead to encroachments on their Canadian territory.

In jockeying for position, both sides sought the allegiance of the American Indians, and in this respect the French gradually gained the upper hand. Because they were traders only, not settlers, the French did not force the Native Americans from their traditional hunting grounds as the British had done repeatedly. Hence, the American Indians were willing to cooperate with the French in sealing off the Ohio Valley. A large land investment company, the Ohio Company of Virginia, faced ruin with that prospect, and in 1745 it attempted to break the French and Indian hold on the Ohio Valley by sending an expedition against Fort Duquesne. Led by a young militiaman named George Washington, the raid failed.

Contrary to a British tradition of letting settled colonies pay for themselves, the home government eventually shouldered the burden of colonial defense. An expedition of British army regulars was sent to do the job that the colonial militia could not accomplish. Limited skirmishes were about to give way to a full-scale war as each side began to reinforce its garrisons and naval squadrons. In May 1756, after several years of unofficial hostilities, Britain and France formally declared war.

The Great War for Empire

The pressures created by the competition of states, dynasties, and colonial empires in the eighteenth century exploded in midcentury in Europe's last large-scale war before the French Revolution. Its continental phase, known as the Seven Years' War, centered on the bitter

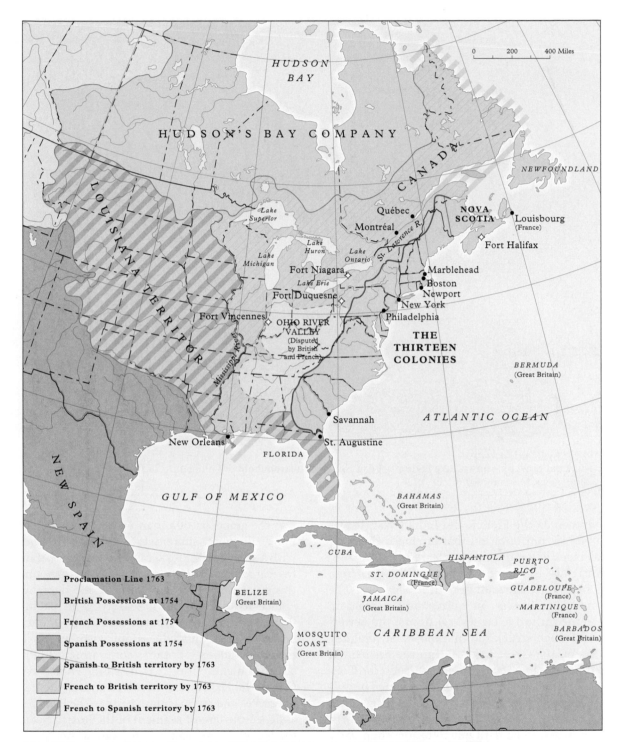

MAP 18.2 ANGLO-FRENCH RIVALRY IN NORTH AMERICA AND THE CARIBBEAN AS OF 1756
Notice the French and British possessions in North America in 1754. Is it clear from this map why the French and British struggled for control of the Ohio River Valley? Who appears to have had the advantage?
◆ For an online version, go to www.mhhe.com/chambers9 > chapter 18 > book maps

rivalry between Austria and Prussia, but enmeshed Russia, France, and Britain as well. As we saw in chapter 17, this protracted war ended in 1763 with a peace treaty that essentially restored the status quo. The

other phase of this midcentury conflagration revolved around Anglo-French competition for empire in North America, the West Indies, and India. Historians call it the Great War for Empire, and its North American

Britain's Glory, CA. 1758
British naval power is shown here laying siege to the French stronghold of Louisbourg in July 1758.
New Brunswick Museum, Saint John, N.B.

sector is known as the French and Indian War. It was this great global confrontation that produced the most striking changes when the smoke cleared.

The Great War for Empire was one of Britain's high moments in history, the stuff of patriotic legends. The conflict started, however, in quite another fashion. Jumping to the initiative on several fronts, the better-coordinated French struck the first blows. Several key British forts on the Great Lakes fell to the French. At the same time, Britain's expeditionary force to the Continent, fighting in alliance with Prussia, suffered humiliating defeats. Yet the French had disadvantages that would show in the long run. Spread so thinly in North America, they would be hard put to follow their early success in the French and Indian War. More important, France depended on naval support to reinforce, supply, and move its troops; unfortunately for France, a fairly even naval matchup in the 1740s had turned into clear British naval superiority by the 1750s. British ships of the line outnumbered French ships almost two to one.

Pitt's Strategy When William Pitt became Britain's prime minister in 1758, the tide was about to turn in the Great War for Empire. Pitt, later the Earl of Chatham,

was the grandson of a man who had made a fortune in India. Eloquent, supremely self-confident, and infused with a vision of Britain's imperial destiny, Pitt had begun his career in Parliament in 1738 by denouncing the timid policies of the government and demanding that France be driven from the seas. Now he had his chance to lead Britain in the battle against its archrival. Pitt brought single-mindedness and vigor to his task. Although he honored Britain's commitment to Prussia, he attached highest priority to defeating France in the colonial world. His strategy involved an immediate series of offensives and an imaginative use of the British navy. He assigned the largest segment of the British fleet to cover the French home fleet, and he waited.

The French hoped to invade the British Isles as the surest method of bringing the enemy to the peace table, and the French fleet was ordered to prepare the way. In 1759 major battles were joined between French squadrons from Brest and Toulon and the British ships assigned to cover them. The British decimated the French fleet in these naval battles and thus decided the fate of colonial empires. Henceforth, the British had an almost free hand at sea and could prevent France from deploying its superior military forces in the colonial world. Unable to transport men and supplies to its colonies, France could no longer reinforce its garrisons or repel amphibious landings by the British. In every theater of the war, French colonial possessions fell to the British, thanks to Britain's naval supremacy.

In the French and Indian War, for example, Britain's forces defeated France in the battle of Quebec in September 1759. Had the French been able to reinforce Montreal, which they still held, they could have launched a counterattack against Britain's overextended lines. But Pitt's successful naval strategy had made it impossible for the French to reinforce their overseas garrisons. By September 1760 this last outpost of French power in North America capitulated to the British, who had already ousted the French from the Ohio Valley and the Great Lakes area. In the West Indies the long duel between the two powers also turned into a rout. One by one Britain seized the French islands.

The Treaty of Paris   In the peace negotiations that followed (concluded by the **Treaty of Paris** in 1763), Britain did not insist on retaining all its conquests. A war-weary British government was prepared to return certain colonies to France in exchange for an end to the fighting. Since British West Indian planters feared competition from the inclusion of the French islands in the British trading system, the British government returned several of those sugar-producing islands. But France did surrender Canada, which Britain chose to retain, perhaps unwisely; the British occupation of Canada removed the threat of French power, which had helped keep the restive colonists of North America loyal to Britain. (On that front, France would soon have its revenge when it came to the aid of the rebellious thirteen colonies in the War for American Independence.) In the long run, a relatively minor matter in the Treaty of Paris, which excluded French troops from India, proved to be supremely important.

The British Foothold in India

A Decaying Empire   Like England and France in the Late Middle Ages or like fifteenth-century Italy, the Indian subcontinent was in a state of political disintegration by the eighteenth century. The decline of the once mighty Mughal Empire stemmed from ethnic strife, dynastic instability, and factionalism, greed, and incompetence in the ruling circles. As yet the decline had little to do with European incursions. In 1739, for example, it was a Persian army that fought its way to Delhi and sacked that ancient capital of the Mughal Empire.

Trading for the spices, tea, and textiles produced in India, British and French merchants had quietly pros-

pered on the fringes of the subcontinent. Britain administered its political and commercial interests in India through the London **East India Company**—a private corporation established in the seventeenth century to compete with the Dutch in the Far East. The company's commercial depots in India formed a tripod pattern at Bombay, Calcutta, and Madras. Initially, neither the English nor the French sought to establish colonies in India. They used small armed forces merely to defend their commercial interests and property and depended on the good will of the native *nawabs* (provincial governors), who encouraged European traders in order to fill their own coffers with tribute payments.

As their struggle for supremacy around the globe heated up, however, the French and British began to maneuver more aggressively by force and diplomacy among native groups in India, much as they were doing in the Ohio Valley and the Great Lakes regions of North America. While the French initially got the better of this game, taking Madras from the British briefly in the 1740s, the British were learning fast how to maximize their military and diplomatic assets to outmaneuver both the French and any natives who rose to challenge them. When the *nawab* of Bengal tilted toward the French in 1756 and decided to teach the British a lesson after they had fortified their positions without his permission, he set in motion a catastrophic change in the subcontinent's balance of power.

From Trade to Conquest   Young Robert Clive, who had sailed to India as a lowly and ill-paid clerk of the East India Company in the 1740s, was by now in charge of the nine hundred Europeans and fifteen hundred *sepoys*, or native soldiers, employed by the company. The company directed Clive to oust the French and to suppress any native opposition to British influence in the huge and populous province of Bengal. Clive faced an army of almost 50,000 men fielded by the *nawab*, but he subverted it by bribing a general who coveted the *nawab's* position for himself. After the decisive battle of Plassey (June 1757), as the body of the *nawab* floated downriver, Clive escorted his successor to the throne.

After Plassey the *nawabs* became figureheads. Real power lay in the East India Company's hands, in an arrangement known as "dual government." The East India Company exercised the most oppressive kind of domination in Bengal: unchecked power without responsibility. The company collected taxes, controlled trade, and increased its military control. Greedy company officials siphoned off much of the treasure into their own pockets. Men like Clive who had sailed to India poor later returned with fortunes to England, where they were known as "nabobs" (a sarcastic play on the term *nawab*).

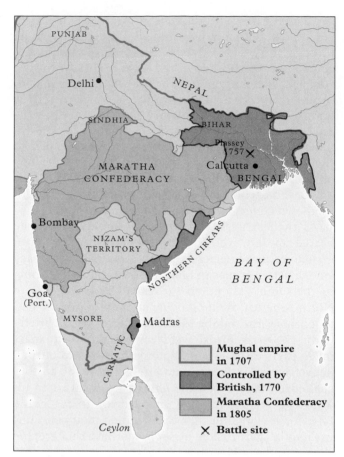

MAP 18.3 THE BEGINNINGS OF THE BRITISH RAJ IN INDIA
Britain's interests in India were initially commercial, with
the London East India Company's merchants setting up
depots to trade for such key Indian goods as spices, tea, and
textiles. Eventually, trade interest turned to conquest.
◆ For an online version, go to www.mhhe.com/chambers9 >
chapter 18 > book maps

Thomas Hickey
COLONEL KIRKPATRIC WITH ATTENDANTS
This painting depicts a British district officer in 1799 in
Madras, one of the regions of the Indian subcontinent in
which the British began to exercise control after they ousted
the French and defeated native forces that challenged them.
The official's main function was to supervise the collection
of taxes, which he did with the cooperation of local Indian
princes and merchants.
Courtesy of the National Gallery of Ireland

Britain thus won primacy in Bengal, the economic
heartland of India, by exploiting Indian rivalries in the
chaos of the tottering Mughal Empire, at first ruling indirectly through native puppets. A number of civil wars
made it easier for the British to dominate much of India. The company's muskets, cannons, and discipline
defeated the last serious attack mounted against it in
1764. In the process the British ousted the French from
any influence in the subcontinent, as agreed in the
Treaty of Paris. Thus, on the verge of losing one empire
in North America, the British were laying the foundations for another in South Asia.

When Parliament passed the India Act of 1784, the
British government effectively replaced the company as
the ultimate authority and named a new ruling official,
the governor-general of India. Ironically, the first to fill
that office was Lord Cornwallis, who had brought the
American War of Independence to a close by surrender-
ing to the rebels at Yorktown in 1781.

The British Raj To create a class loyal to British rule,
or **raj**, Cornwallis turned India's rural gentry into landlords by giving them title deeds. Traditionally, the gentry had collected rents from their peasants, but could
not remove them from the land. Now, as owners in the
new Western sense, they could evict the peasants and
do with the land whatever they wished. The governor-
general reserved the highest positions in the army and
civil bureaucracy for whites, however. In each district
he appointed two British magistrates, one combining
the functions of police superintendent and tax collector and the other responsible for administering justice.
They were assisted by a horde of Indian clerks, run-
ners, and translators. In addition the British monopolized the commerce in salt and opium. The salt
monopoly extracted money from the Indian population, while the opium was exported to China in exchange for Chinese tea to satisfy consumer demand
back in Britain.

Later in the nineteenth century, behind the British soldiers, tax collectors, and magistrates, came educators and reformers with a novel sense of mission. As one of them put it, "we hope to create a class of persons Indian in blood and color, but English in taste, in opinion, in morals and intellect." By the 1830s, in other words, the British were not simply extracting wealth or strategic advantage from India but considered India as their own dominion in which they were duty bound to impose their own values on the Indian people.

Summary

French and English merchants capitalized aggressively on the commercial opportunities afforded by overseas colonies, plantation economies, and slavery, but these traders required backing by their states in the form of naval power. The growth of the British and French empires thus reflected the dynamics of the competitive European state system. Those empires propelled the growth of a global maritime economy and thus became major factors in the economic dynamism of the eighteenth century. It is well to remember, however, that two totally disenfranchised groups supported the entire structure of state power and mercantile profit: the slaves in the colonies and the serfs, peasants, or agricultural laborers in Europe. Their toil produced the food supplies, staple commodities, and revenues that sustained the merchants, landowners, rulers, armies, and navies of the great powers. The economic future, however, lay not with plantation slavery, serfdom, or seigneurialism but with innovations in agriculture and industrial production that would yield sustained economic growth and whose roots in England we have sketched. Along with the intellectual and cultural transformations to be discussed in the next chapter, these agricultural and industrial innovations heralded the dawn of the modern era.

QUESTIONS FOR FURTHER THOUGHT

1. In what ways can demographic trends affect economic and social development?
2. How can one best understand the economic transformations observable in late eighteenth-century England? What particular advantages did English society have in fostering innovation?
3. What are the principal characteristics of a traditional peasant society? How significant were the differences between peasant society in Eastern and Western Europe, and what accounts for the differences?
4. How did the imperial rivalry of France and Britain play out across the globe in the eighteenth century?

RECOMMENDED READING

Sources

Forster, Robert, and Elborg Forster (eds.). *European Society in the Eighteenth Century.* 1969. A varied and suggestive anthology.

Radischev, Alexander. *A Journey from St. Petersburg to Moscow* [1790]. 1958. The first major exposé of the miseries of Russian serfdom.

*Smith, Adam. *An Inquiry into the Nature and Causes of the Wealth of Nations* [1776]. 1961. The seminal work in the liberal economic tradition.

*Young, Arthur. *Travels in France during the Years 1787, 1788, 1789.* 1972. A critical view of French agriculture by an English expert.

Studies

*Ashton, T. S. *The Industrial Revolution, 1760–1830.* 1968. A brief, classic account of early industrialization in Britain.

*Berg, Maxine. *The Age of Manufactures: Industry, Innovation, and Work in Britain, 1700–1820.* 1986. An important revisionist view, emphasizing the persistence of domestic and workshop manufacturing alongside the new factory system.

*Blum, Jerome. *The End of the Old Order in Rural Europe.* 1976. A valuable trove of information on rural conditions, particularly in the regions of serfdom.

Brewer, John, N. McKendrick, and J. H. Plumb. *Birth of a Consumer Society: The Commercialization of Eighteenth Century England.* 1982. A pioneering book on the development of consumer demand.

Chambers, J. D., and G. E. Mingay. *The Agricultural Revolution, 1750–1880.* 1966. A reliable overview and interpretation.

Craton, Michael. *Sinews of Empire: A Short History of British Slavery.* 1974. An excellent synthesis.

*Davis, David B. *The Problem of Slavery in Western Culture.* 1966. And *The Problem of Slavery in the Age of Revolutions.* 1975. A comparative history of Western attitudes toward slavery from ancient times to the nineteenth century.

*De Vries, Jan. *The Economy of Europe in an Age of Crisis, 1600–1750.* 1976. A reliable survey of the European economy before the industrial revolution.

*Flinn, M. W. *The European Demographic System, 1500–1820.* 1981. A concise overview of the historical demography of early modern Europe.

*Gutmann, Myron. *Toward the Modern Economy: Early Industry in Europe.* 1988. Another fine synthesis illustrating the complexity of the European economy.

Hufton, Olwen. *The Poor of Eighteenth-Century France.* 1974. A luminous study of the survival strategies of the indigent and of the institutions that aided or repressed them.

*Klein, Herbert S. *The Atlantic Slave Trade.* 1999. A wide-ranging comparative synthesis.

LeRoy Ladurie, Emmanuel. *The Ancien Regime: A History of France, 1610–1774.* 1996. A synthesis by a leading French social and cultural historian.

*Mathias, Peter. *The First Industrial Nation: An Economic History of Britain, 1700–1914.* 2d ed. 1976. A reliable survey combining quantitative and descriptive analysis.

North, Douglass C. *Structure and Change in Economic History.* 1981. Stresses the importance of supportive legal institutions in the coming of industrialism.

*Parry, J. H. *Trade and Dominion: The European Overseas Empires in the Eighteenth Century.* 1971. A panoramic overview.

Post, John D. *Food Shortage, Climatic Variability, and Epidemic Disease in Pre-industrial Europe: The Mortality Peak in the Early 1740s.* 1985.

Reiley, James. *International Government Finance and the Amsterdam Capital Market, 1740–1815.* 1980. The Dutch success in shifting from commerce to finance.

*Rothschild, Emma. *Economic Sentiments: Adam Smith, Condorcet and the Enlightenment.* 2001. A provocative study of the rise of political economy.

Sheridan, Richard. *Sugar and Slavery: An Economic History of the British West Indies, 1623–1755.* 1974.

*Uglow, Jennifer. *The Lunar Men: Five Friends Whose Curiosity Changed the World.* 2002. Lively study of the engineers, entrepreneurs, and scientists of the Lunar Society of Birmingham whose innovations in technology spurred industrialization.

*Valenze, Deborah. *The First Industrial Woman.* 1995. A rich synthesis on women workers before and during early industrialization in Britain.

*Woloch, Isser. *Eighteenth-Century Europe: Tradition and Progress, 1715–1789.* 1982.

*Wrigley, E. A. *Population and History.* 1969. A fascinating introduction to the field of historical demography.

*Available in paperback.

Pietro Longhi
THE GEOGRAPHY LESSON
This painting of *The Geography Lesson* evokes the interest in exotic places among Europe's educated elites, male and female, during the eighteenth centruy.

Chapter Nineteen

THE AGE OF ENLIGHTENMENT

THE ENLIGHTENMENT • EIGHTEENTH-CENTURY ELITE CULTURE • POPULAR CULTURE

Sharp breaks have been rare in Europe's intellectual and religious life—two of the defining themes in the Western experience—but we are about to witness one. During the eighteenth century, the great scientific and philosophical innovations of the previous century evolved into a naturalistic worldview divorced from religion. Scientific knowledge and religious skepticism, previously the concerns of an extremely narrow group of learned people, entered the consciousness of Europe's elites in a way that would have startled Descartes or Newton. Displacing the authority of religion with that of reason, the new outlook offered an optimistic vision of future progress in human affairs. Known as the Enlightenment, this movement formed the intellectual foundation for a new sense of modernity.

Never since pagan times, certainly not during the Renaissance, was religious belief so directly challenged. Many important eighteenth-century intellectuals no longer believed in Christianity and wished to reduce its influence in society. They argued that there was no divine standard of morality, no afterlife to divert humanity from worldly concerns. These writers developed a strong, sometimes arrogant, sense of their own capacity to ignore traditional authority and guide society toward change.

The evolution of cultural institutions and the media of the day gave these writers an increasingly wide forum. While aristocratic patronage and classical culture remained influential, a new kind of middle-class culture was developing alongside a much wider reading public and an expanding sphere of public discussion.

Yet, as we turn to consider the Enlightenment within the varied cultural environments of the eighteenth century, we should not exaggerate. Although they were critics of their society, most eighteenth-century intellectuals lived comfortably amid Europe's high culture. They had scant interest in or understanding of the vibrant popular culture around them. On the contrary, their growing belief in "public opinion" referred solely to the educated elites of the aristocracy and the middle classes.

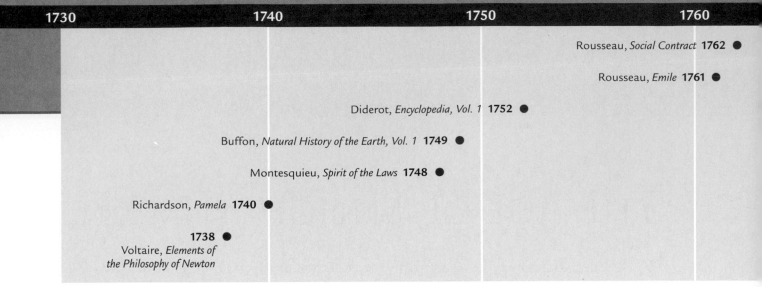

Rousseau, *Social Contract* **1762** ●

Rousseau, *Emile* **1761** ●

Diderot, *Encyclopedia, Vol. 1* **1752** ●

Buffon, *Natural History of the Earth, Vol. 1* **1749** ●

Montesquieu, *Spirit of the Laws* **1748** ●

Richardson, *Pamela* **1740** ●

1738 ●
Voltaire, *Elements of
the Philosophy of Newton*

THE ENLIGHTENMENT

Building on seventeenth-century science, skepticism in matters of religion, and a heightened appreciation for the culture of classical antiquity, eighteenth-century intellectuals approached their calling in a new spirit. They believed that human behavior and institutions could be studied rationally, like Newton's universe, and that their faults could be corrected. They saw themselves as participants in a movement—which they called the Enlightenment—that could make educated men and women more rational, tolerant, and virtuous. While the Enlightenment had creative adherents across the Western world, its capital was undoubtedly in Paris, where an ideology of progress and freedom gradually took shape. Renowned writers such as Voltaire, Diderot, and Rousseau produced a steady flow of remarkable works across a wide range of subjects, which governmental censorship could not suppress, try as it might.

The Broadening Reverberations of Science

It is hard to think of two men less revolutionary in temperament than the seventeenth century's René Descartes and Isaac Newton. Both were conservative on matters outside the confines of science, had relatively little concern for social institutions, remained practicing Christians, and wrote only for small learned audiences. Yet their legacy of insight into the world of nature produced in succeeding generations what has been described as "a permanent intellectual insurrection," which unfolded in a spirit undreamed of by either man.

The Popularization of Science While eighteenth-century scientists pondered the cosmologies of

Descartes and Newton, nonscientists in England and on the Continent applied the methodologies of Descartes, Newton, and the philosopher John Locke to other realms of human thought. They fused the notion of methodical doubt and naturalistic explanations of phenomena into a scientific or mathematical spirit, which at bottom simply meant confidence in reason and a skeptical attitude toward accepted dogmas. They attempted to popularize scientific method, with the aim of transforming the values of Western civilization. Writers translated the discoveries of scientists into clear and even amusing general reading. The literary talents of these enthusiasts helped make household words of Newton and Descartes among educated Europeans.

A more calculating and ambitious propagandist of the scientific spirit was the Frenchman François-Marie Arouet, who wrote under the pen name of Voltaire and is virtually synonymous with the Enlightenment. While his chief talents lay in literature and criticism, Voltaire also spent some time studying Newton's work. In 1738, in collaboration with his friend Madame du Châtelet, he published a widely read popularization called *Elements of the Philosophy of Newton.* However dry the study of physics, Voltaire argued, it frees the mind from dogma, and its experimental methods provide a model for the liberation of human thought. Moreover, Voltaire related Newton's achievement to the environment of a liberal England that also produced Francis Bacon and John Locke, the three of whom Voltaire adopted as his personal Trinity. In his *Philosophical Letters on the English* (1734)—a celebration of English toleration and an indirect attack on religious bigotry, censorship, and social snobbery in France—Voltaire had already noted the respect enjoyed in England by its writers and scientists.

Popularizations of scientific method stimulated public interest in science, as mathematicians, cartogra-

1764 Voltaire, *Philosophical Dictionary*

● **1772** Completion of Diderot's *Encyclopedia*

● **1774** Goethe, *Sorrows of Young Werther*; Habsburg School Ordinance

● **1778** Death of Voltaire

● **1781** Joseph II's Edict of Toleration

1780s Jacques-Louis David's neoclassical masterpieces

Wollstonecraft, *Vindication of the Rights of Woman* **1792** ●

French chemist Lavoisier conducts an experiment in his laboratory to study the composition of air during the process of respiration.
Bettmann/Corbis

phers, and astronomers made notable advances in their fields. But further scientific progress was far from automatic. In chemistry, for example, the traditions of alchemy persisted, and phenomena such as fire long escaped objective analysis. At the end of the century, however, a major breakthrough occurred when the Englishman Joseph Priestley isolated oxygen and the Frenchman Antoine Lavoisier analyzed the components of air and water and came close to explaining the process of combustion.

The vogue for science also had a dubious side, apparent, for example, in the great popularity of mesmerism. This pseudoscience of magnetic fields purported to offer its wealthy devotees relief from a variety of ailments by the use of special "electrical" baths and treatments. Although repeatedly condemned by the Academy of Sciences in Paris, mesmerism continued to attract educated followers.

Natural History The most widely followed scientific enterprise in the eighteenth century was **natural history,** the science of the earth's development—a combination of geology, zoology, and botany. This field of study was easy for the nonscientist to appreciate. Its foremost practitioner was G. L. Buffon, keeper of the French Botanical Gardens—a patronage position that allowed him to produce a multivolume *Natural History of the Earth* between 1749 and 1778. Drawing on a vast knowledge of phenomena such as fossils, Buffon went beyond previous attempts to classify the data of nature and provided both a description and a theory of the earth's development.

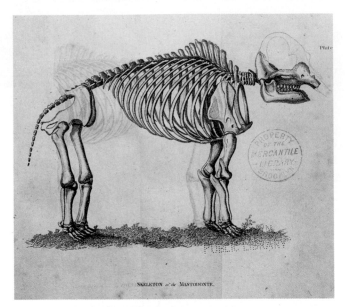

An image of a mastadon from the section on fossil remains in Buffon's *Natural History.*
Courtesy Brooklyn Public Library

Although he was a nonbeliever, Buffon did not explicitly attack religious versions of such events as the Creation; he simply ignored them, an omission of obvious significance to his readers. Similarly, while he did not specifically contend that human beings have evolved from beasts, he implied it. "It is possible," he wrote, "to descend by almost insensible degrees from the most perfect creature to the most formless matter." Buffon's earth did not derive from a singular act of divine creation that would explain the origins of human beings. The readers of his *Natural History* or its numerous popularizations in several languages thus encountered a universe that had developed through evolution.

Beyond Christianity

The erosion of biblical revelation as a source of authority is one hallmark of the Enlightenment. This shift derived some of its impetus from seventeenth-century scientists and liberal theologians who were themselves believing Christians but who opposed religious superstition or "enthusiasm," as they called it. They had hoped to accommodate religion to new philosophical standards and scientific formulations by eliminating the superstitious imagery that could make religion seem ridiculous and by treating the world of nature as a form of revelation in which God's majesty could be seen. The devil, for example, could be considered as a category of moral evil rather than as a specific horned creature with a pitchfork. They hoped to bolster the

Christian religion by deemphasizing miracles and focusing on reverence for the Creator and on the moral teachings of the Bible. Their approach did indeed help educated people adhere to Christianity during the eighteenth century. In the final analysis, however, this kind of thinking diminished the authority of religion in society.

Toleration   One current of thought that encouraged a more secular outlook was the idea of toleration, as propounded by the respected French critic Pierre Bayle. Consciously applying methodical doubt to subjects that Descartes had excluded from such treatment, Bayle's *Critical and Historical Dictionary* (1697) put the claims of religion to the test of critical reason. Certain Christian traditions emerged from this scrutiny as the equivalent of myth and fairy tale, and the history of Christianity appeared as a record of fanaticism and persecution. Bayle's chief target was Christianity's attempts to impose orthodoxy at any cost (for example, the Spanish Inquisition and Louis XIV's revocation of the Edict of Nantes and persecution of French Protestants). Though a devout Calvinist himself, Bayle advocated complete toleration, which would allow any person to practice any religion or none at all. An individual's moral behavior rather than his or her creed is what mattered, according to Bayle.

The most striking success of the eighteenth-century campaign for toleration came with the Edict of Toleration issued by the Habsburg emperor Joseph II on his ascendancy to the throne in 1781. For the first time, a Catholic Habsburg ruler recognized the right of Protestants and Jews in his realm to worship freely and to hold property and public office (see "Joseph II on Religious Toleration," p. 559). Joseph also tried to reduce the influence of the Catholic Church by ordering the dissolution of numerous monasteries on the grounds that they were useless and corrupt. Part of their confiscated wealth was used to support the medical school at the University of Vienna.

Deism   Voltaire became the Enlightenment's most vigorous antireligious polemicist. This prolific writer was one of the century's most brilliant literary stylists, historians, and poets. Those talents alone would have ensured his fame. But Voltaire was also a dedicated antagonist of Christianity. For tactical reasons, much of his attack against *l'infame* ("the infamous thing"), as he called Christianity, targeted such practices as monasticism or the behavior of priests. His ultimate target, though, was Christianity itself, which, he declared, "every sensible man, every honorable man must hold in horror."

Voltaire's masterpiece, a best seller called *The Philosophical Dictionary* (1764), had to be published

JOSEPH II ON RELIGIOUS TOLERATION

Between 1765 and 1781 Joseph II was joint ruler of the Habsburg Empire with his pious mother, Empress Maria Theresa. Joseph advocated a utilitarian approach to religious toleration (Document 1) but made little headway against Maria Theresa's traditional insistence that the state must actively combat religious dissent. Soon after Maria Theresa's death, Joseph promulgated a series of decrees on religion, including a landmark Toleration Edict for Protestants (Document 2) and even a special, if somewhat less sweeping, edict of toleration for the Jews of his domains.

1. LETTER TO MARIA THERESA, JULY 1777

"The word toleration has caused misunderstanding. . . . God preserve me from thinking it a matter of indifference whether the citizens turn Protestant or remain Catholics. . . . I would give all I possess if all the Protestants of your States would go over to Catholicism. The word *toleration* as I understand it, means only that I would employ any persons, without distinction of religion, in purely temporal matters, allow them to own property, practice trades, be citizens if they were qualified and if this would be of advantage to the State and its industry. . . . The undisturbed practice of their religion makes them far better subjects and causes them to avoid irreligion, which is a far greater danger to our Catholics."

2. TOLERATION EDICT OF OCTOBER 1781

"We have found Ourselves moved to grant to the adherents of the Lutheran and Calvinist religions, and also to the non Uniat Greek religion, everywhere, the appropriate private practice of their faith. . . . The Catholic religion alone shall continue to enjoy the prerogative of the public practice of its faith. . . . Non-Catholics are in future admitted under dispensation to buy houses and real property, to acquire municipal domicile and practice as master craftsmen, to take up academic appointments and posts in the public service, and are not to be required to take the oath in any form contrary to their religious tenets. . . . In all choices or appointments to official posts . . . difference of religion is to be disregarded."

From C. A. Macartney (ed.), *The Habsburg and Hohenzollern Dynasties in the 17th and 18th Centuries*, HarperCollins, 1970, pp. 151, 155–157.

---

anonymously and was burned by the authorities in Switzerland, France, and the Netherlands. Modeled after Bayle's dictionary, it was far more blunt. Of theology, he wrote, "We find man's insanity in all its plenitude." Organized religion is not simply false but pernicious, he argued. Voltaire believed that religious superstition inevitably bred fanaticism and predictably resulted in bloody episodes like the Saint Bartholomew's Day Massacre.

Voltaire hoped that educated Europeans would abandon Christianity in favor of **deism,** a belief that recognized God as the Creator but held that the world, once created, functions according to natural laws without interference by God. Humanity thus lives essentially on its own in an ordered universe, without hope or fear of divine intervention and without the threat of damnation or the hope of eternal salvation. For deists, religion should be a matter of private contemplation rather than public worship and mythic creeds. Although certain figures in the Enlightenment went beyond deism to a philosophical atheism, which rejected any concept of God as unprovable, Voltaire's mild deism remained a characteristic view of eighteenth-century writers. At bottom,

however, this form of spirituality was essentially secular. Broad-minded clergy could accept many of the arguments of eighteenth-century science and philosophy, but they could not accept deism.

The Philosophes

Science and secularism became the rallying points of a group of French intellectuals known as the **philosophes.** Their traditionalist opponents employed this term to mock the group's pretensions, but the philosophes themselves used that label with pride. They saw themselves as a vanguard, the men who raised the Enlightenment to the status of a self-conscious movement. The leaders of this influential coterie of writers were Voltaire and Denis Diderot. Its ranks included mathematicians Jean d'Alembert and the Marquis de Condorcet, the magistrate Baron de Montesquieu, the government official Jacques Turgot, and the atheist philosopher Baron d'Holbach. Thus, the French philosophes came from both the aristocracy and the middle class. Outside of France their kinship extended to a group of brilliant Scottish philosophers, including David Hume and Adam Smith; to the German

In 1745 the Habsburg monarchy expelled an estimated seventy thousand Jews from Prague to appease anti-Semitic sentiment.

playwright Gotthold Lessing and the philosopher Immanuel Kant; to the Italian economist and penal reformer the Marquis of Beccaria; and to such founders of the American Philosophical Society as Benjamin Franklin and Thomas Jefferson.

Intellectual Freedom   The philosophes shared above all else a critical spirit, the desire to reexamine the assumptions and institutions of their societies and expose them to the tests of reason, experience, and utility. Today this might sound banal, but it was not so at a time when almost everywhere religion permeated society. Asserting the primacy of reason meant turning away from faith, the essence of religion. It meant a decisive break with the Christian worldview, which placed religious doctrine at the center of society's values. The philosophes invoked the paganism of ancient Greece and Rome, where the spirit of rational inquiry prevailed among educated people. They ridiculed the Middle Ages as the "Dark Ages" and contrasted the religious spirit of that era to their own sense of liberation and modernity. In *The Decline and Fall of the Roman Empire* (1776–1788), the historian Edward Gibbon declared that Christianity had eclipsed a Roman civilization that had sought to live according to reason rather than myths.

The inspiration of antiquity was matched by the stimulus of modern science and philosophy. The philosophes laid claim to Newton, who made the universe intelligible without the aid of revelation, and Locke, who uncovered the workings of the human mind. From Locke they went on to argue that human

personality is malleable: Its nature is not fixed, let alone corrupted by original sin. People are, therefore, ultimately responsible to themselves for what they do with their lives. Existing arrangements are no more nor less sacred than experience has proved them to be. As the humanists had several centuries before, the philosophes placed human beings at the center of thought. Unlike most humanists, however, philosophes placed thought in the service of change and launched a noisy public movement.

Persecution and Triumph   Philosophes appeared clamorous to their contemporaries because they had to battle entrenched authority. Religious traditionalists and the apparatus of censorship in almost all countries threatened the intellectual freedom demanded by the philosophes. They often had to publish their works clandestinely and anonymously. Sometimes they were pressured into withholding manuscripts from publication altogether or into making humiliating public apologies for controversial books. Even with such caution, almost all philosophes saw some of their publications confiscated and burned. A few were forced into exile or sent to jail: Voltaire spent several decades across the French border in Switzerland, and Voltaire and Diderot both spent time in prison. Although the notoriety produced by these persecutions stimulated the sale of their works, the anxiety took its toll.

By the 1770s, however, the philosophes had survived their running war with the authorities. Some of them lived to see their ideas widely accepted and their works acclaimed. In 1778, the last year of his life, Voltaire

WHAT IS ENLIGHTENMENT?

The most concise formulation of the Enlightenment's spirit is conveyed in an essay of the 1780s by the German philosopher Immanuel Kant. As Kant makes clear, intellectual freedom and the role of public opinion refer not so much to the average person in the street as to the educated classes—serious writers (whom he calls "scholars") and their public. Note that in drawing the distinction between the public realm (where freedom is vital) and the private realm (where obedience is rightly expected), Kant reverses the labels that we would likely assign to the two realms today.

"Enlightenment is man's emergence from his self-imposed nonage. Nonage is the inability to use one's own understanding without another's guidance. This nonage is self-imposed if its cause lies not in lack of understanding but in indecision and lack of courage to use one's own mind without another's guidance. Dare to know. (*Sapere aude*). 'Have the courage to use your own understanding,' is therefore the motto of the Enlightenment.

"Laziness and cowardice are the reasons why such a large part of mankind gladly remain minors all their lives, long after nature has freed them from external guidance. They are the reasons why it is so easy for others to set themselves up as guardians. It is so comfortable to be a minor. If I have a book that thinks for me, a pastor who acts as my conscience, then I have no need to exert myself. . . .

"This enlightenment requires nothing but freedom: freedom to make public use of one's reason in all matters. . . . On the other hand, the private use of reason may frequently be narrowly restricted without especially hindering the progress of enlightenment. By 'public use of reason' I mean that use which man, as a scholar, makes of it before the reading public. I call 'private use' that use which a man makes of his reason in a civic post that has been entrusted to him . . . and where arguing is not permitted: one must obey. . . . Thus it would be very unfortunate if an officer on duty and under orders from his superiors should want to criticize the appropriateness or utility of his orders. He must obey. But as a scholar he could not rightfully be prevented from taking notice of the mistakes in the military service and from submitting his views to his public for its judgement."

returned triumphantly to Paris. When he attended a performance of one of his plays at the national theater, the audience greeted him with tumultuous enthusiasm. Even if the philosophes had contributed little else to the Western experience, their struggle for freedom of expression would merit them a significant place in its history.

Pioneering in the Social Sciences   But the philosophes achieved far more. In their scholarly and polemical writings, they investigated a wide range of subjects and pioneered in several new disciplines. Some philosophes—Voltaire, for example—were path-breaking historians. Moving beyond traditional chronicles of battles and rulers' biographies, they studied culture, social institutions, and government structures in an effort to understand past societies as well as describe major events. Practically inventing the notion of social science, they investigated the theoretical foundations of social organization (sociology) and the workings of the human mind (psychology). On a more practical level, they proposed fundamental reforms in such areas as the penal system and education.

The philosophes embedded their study of social science in questions of morality and the study of ethics. Enlightenment ethics were generally utilitarian. Such philosophers as David Hume tried to define good and evil in pragmatic terms; they argued that social utility should become the standard for public morality. This approach to moral philosophy in turn raised the question of whether any human values were absolute and eternal. Among the philosophers who grappled with this challenge, Kant tried to harmonize the notion of absolute moral values with practical reason.

Political Liberty   The most influential work of social science produced by the Enlightenment was probably *The Spirit of the Laws* (1748) by the French magistrate Montesquieu. The book offered a comparative study of governments and societies. On the one hand, Montesquieu introduced the perspective of relativism: He tried to analyze the institutions of government in relation to the special customs, climate, religion, and commerce of various countries. He thus argued that no single, ideal model of government existed. On the other hand, he deeply admired his own idealized version of the British system of government; he thereby implied that all societies could learn from the British about liberty.

Montesquieu's sections on liberty won a wide readership in Europe and in America, where the book was influential among the drafters of the U.S. Constitution.

An English engraving entitled "Voltaire's Staircase" suggests how the great writer stood at the center of Europe's literary and intellectual life. The fifth figure from the right at the top, Voltaire is bidding good-bye to d'Alembert, coeditor of the *Encyclopedia*.
Bettmann/Corbis

Political liberty, said Montesquieu, requires checks on those who hold power in a state, whether that power is exercised by a king, an aristocracy, or the people. Liberty can thrive only with a balance of powers, preferably by the separation of the executive, the legislative, and the judicial branches of government. Montesquieu ascribed a central role to aristocracies as checks on royal despotism. Indeed, many eighteenth-century writers on politics considered strong privileged groups, independent from both the crown and the people, as the only effective bulwarks against tyranny. To put it another way, Montesquieu's followers thought that the price for a society free from despotism was privilege for some of its members.

Liberal Economics French and British thinkers of the Enlightenment transformed economic theory with attacks against mercantilism and government regulation. We noted in chapter 18 Adam Smith's critique of artificial restraints on individual economic initiative. In France, the Physiocrats similarly argued that economic progress depended on freeing agriculture and trade from restrictions. Since in their view (unlike Adam Smith's) land was the only real source of wealth, they also called for reforms in the tax structure, with a uniform and equitable land tax. In opposition to a traditional popular insistence on government intervention to maintain supplies of grain and flour at fair prices, the Physiocrats advocated freedom for the grain trade to operate according to the dictates of supply and demand. The incentive of higher prices would encourage growers to expand productivity, they believed, and in this way the grain shortages that plagued Europe could eventually be eliminated, although at the cost of temporary hardship for most consumers.

Diderot and the Encyclopedia

The Enlightenment thus produced not only a new intellectual spirit but also a wide range of critical writings on various subjects. In addition, the French philosophes collectively generated a single work that exemplified their notion of how knowledge could be useful: Diderot's *Encyclopédie* (*Encyclopedia*).

Within a few years of arriving in Paris as a young man, Denis Diderot had published novels, plays, treatises on mathematics and moral philosophy, and critical essays on religion. His most original writings examined the role of passion in human personality and in any system of values derived from an understanding of human nature. Specifically, Diderot affirmed the role of sexuality, arguing against artificial taboos and repression. As an advocate of what was sometimes called "the natural man," Diderot belies the charge leveled against the philosophes that they overemphasized reason to the neglect of feeling.

Diderot's unusual boldness in getting his works published brought him a considerable reputation but also some real trouble. Two of his books were condemned by the authorities as contrary to religion, the state, and morals. In 1749 he spent one hundred days in prison and was released only after making a humiliating apology. At about that time, Diderot was approached by a publisher to translate a British encyclopedic reference work into French. After a number of false starts, he persuaded the publisher to sponsor instead an entirely new and more comprehensive work that would reflect the interests of the philosophes.

The Encyclopedia The *Encyclopedia, or Classified Dictionary of the Sciences, Arts, and Occupations*, an inventory of all fields of knowledge from the most theoretical to the most mundane, constituted an arsenal of critical concepts. As the preface stated: "Our Encyclopedia is a work that could only be carried out in a

Diderot's *Encyclopedia* focused much of its attention on technology. Illustrations of mechanical processes, such as the one shown here for making plate glass, filled eleven folio volumes.

philosophic century. . . . All things must be examined without sparing anyone's sensibilities. . . . The arts and sciences must regain their freedom." The ultimate purpose of the *Encyclopedia*, wrote its editors, was "to change the general way of thinking." Written in this spirit by an array of talented collaborators, the expensive twenty-eight-volume *Encyclopedia* (1752–1772) fulfilled the fondest hopes of its editors and four thousand initial subscribers.

In such a work, religion could scarcely be ignored, but neither could it be openly attacked. Instead, the editors treated religion with artful satire or else relegated it to a philosophical or historical plane. Demystified and subordinated, religion was probed and questioned like any other subject, much to the discomfort of learned but orthodox critics.

Science stood at the core of the *Encyclopedia*, but the editors emphasized the technological or practical side of science with numerous articles and plates illustrating machines, tools, and manufacturing processes. They praised the roles of mechanics, engineers, and artisans in society and stressed the benefits of efficient production in the advance of civilization. Such emphasis implied that technology and artisanal skills constituted valuable realms of knowledge comparable to theoretical sciences such as physics and mathematics.

On economic topics the encyclopedists tended to echo the Physiocratic crusade against restrictions on trade and agriculture. On questions of government, the authors generally endorsed absolute monarchy, provided it was reasonably efficient and just. The major political concerns of the editors were civil rights, freedom of expression, and the rule of law.

The Encyclopedia's Impact   In retrospect, after the French Revolution, the *Encyclopedia* does not seem very revolutionary. Yet in the context of the times, it assuredly was. The revolution that Diderot sought was intellectual. As he wrote in a letter to a friend, the encyclopedists were promoting "a revolution in the minds of men to free them from prejudice." Judging by the reaction of religious and government authorities, they were eminently successful. "Up till now," commented one French bishop, "hell has vomited its venom drop by drop." Now, he concluded, it could be found assembled between the *Encyclopedia's* covers.

After allowing the first three volumes to appear, the French government banned the *Encyclopedia* in 1759 and revoked the bookseller's license to issue the remaining volumes. As the attorney general of France put it: "There is a project formed, a society organized to propagate materialism, to destroy religion, to inspire a spirit of independence, and to nourish the corruption of morals." Most of the *Encyclopedia's* contributors prudently withdrew from the project, but Diderot went underground and continued the herculean task until the subscribers received every promised volume, including eleven magnificent folios of illustrations. By the time these appeared, the persecutions had receded. Indeed, the *Encyclopedia* was reprinted in cheaper editions (both legal and pirated) that sold out rapidly, earning fortunes for their publishers. This turn of events ensured the status of Diderot's project as the landmark of its age.

Jean-Jacques Rousseau

Arguably the most original and influential eighteenth-century thinker, Jean-Jacques Rousseau stood close to but self-consciously outside the coterie of the philosophes, for Rousseau provided in his life and writing a critique not only of the status quo but of the

Enlightenment itself. Obsessed with the issue of moral freedom, Rousseau found society far more oppressive than most philosophes would admit, and he considered the philosophes themselves to be part of the problem.

Young Rousseau won instant fame when he submitted a prize-winning essay in a contest sponsored by a provincial academy on the topic, "Has the restoration of the arts and sciences had a purifying effect upon morals?" Unlike most respondents, Rousseau answered that it had not. He argued that the lustrous cultural and scientific achievements of recent decades were producing pretension, conformity, and useless luxury. Most scientific pursuits, he wrote, "are the effect of idleness which generate idleness in their turn." The system of rewards in the arts produces "a servile and deceptive conformity . . . the dissolution of morals . . . and the corruption of taste." Against the decadence of high culture, he advocated a return "to the simplicity which prevailed in earliest times"—manly physical pastimes, self-reliance, independent citizens instead of fawning courtiers.

Rousseau's Moral Vision　Rousseau had no wish to return to a state of nature, a condition of anarchy in which force ruled and people were slaves of appetite. But the basis of morality, he argued, was conscience, not reason. "Virtue, sublime science of simple minds: are not your principles graven on every heart?" This became one of his basic themes in two popular works of fiction, *Julie, or the New Héloise* (1761), and *Emile, or Treatise on Education* (1762).

In the first novel, Julie is educated in virtue by her tutor St. Preux but allows herself to fall in love with and be seduced by him. In the second half of the novel, Julie breaks away from St. Preux and marries Monsieur de Wolmar, her father's wealthy friend. She maintains a distant friendship with her old lover and rears her children in exemplary fashion, overseeing their education. In the end she overcomes her past moral lapse and sacrifices her own life to save one of her children. Wolmar then brings in the chastened St. Preux to continue the children's education. This tale of love, virtue, and motherhood won an adoring audience of male and female readers who identified with the characters, shed tears over their moral dilemmas, and applauded Rousseau for this superb lesson in the new sensibility.

Emile recounts the story of a young boy raised to be a moral adult by a tutor who emphasized experience over book learning and who considered education a matter of individual self-development. This new kind of man of course required a comparably sensitive wife, attuned to practical matters and without vain aristocratic pretenses. Sophie, the girl in question, received a very different type of education, however, one concerned with virtue but far more limited in its scope. Rousseau depicted men and women liberating themselves from stultifying traditional values, yet in the new relation-

Nicolas Henri Jeaurat de Bertry
Allegory of the Revolution with a Portrait Medallion of J. J. Rousseau
The French revolutionaries acclaimed both Voltaire and Rousseau and transferred their remains to a new Pantheon. But Rousseau was the man considered by many French people to be the Revolution's spiritual father, as suggested by his position in this allegorical painting of 1793, filled with the new symbolism of liberty and equality.
Musée de la Ville de Paris, Musée Carnavalet, Paris, France. Giraudon/Art Resource, NY

ships he portrayed in these novels, women held a decidedly subordinate position. Their virtues were to be exclusively domestic in character, while the men would be prepared for public roles—a distinction that deeply troubled feminist thinkers in the future (see "Mary Wollstonecraft on the Education of Women," p. 565).

The Rebel as Cultural Hero　Rousseau himself was by no means a saint. His personal weaknesses—including the illegitimate child that he fathered and abandoned—doubtless contributed to his preoccupation with morality and conscience. Nonetheless, his rebellious life as well as his writings greatly impressed the generation of readers and writers coming of age in the 1770s and 1780s. Not only did he quarrel with the repressive authorities of Church and state—who repeatedly

MARY WOLLSTONECRAFT ON THE EDUCATION OF WOMEN

The sharpest challenge to Rousseau's widely shared attitude toward women came only in 1792, with the publication of Mary Wollstonecraft's A Vindication of the Rights of Woman. *Inspired by the French Revolution's doctrine of natural rights, this spirited writer deplored the fact that society kept women (in her words) frivolous, artificial, weak, and in a perpetual state of childhood. While men praised women for their beauty and grace, they hypocritically condemned them for a concern with vanity, fashion, and trivial matters, yet refused to treat them as rational human beings who could contribute to society as much as men. Her book emphasized the need for educational reform that would allow women to develop agile bodies and strong minds. Along the way Wollstonecraft took particular aim at Rousseau's* Emile.

"The conduct and manners of women, in fact, evidently prove that their minds are not in a healthy state; for, like the flowers which are planted in too rich a soil, strength and usefulness are sacrificed to beauty. . . . One cause of this barren blooming I attribute to a false system of education, gathered from the books written on this subject by men who, considering females rather as women than human creatures, have been more anxious to make them alluring mistresses than affectionate wives and rational mothers. The understanding of the sex has been so bubbled by this specious homage, that the civilized women of the present century, with a few exceptions, are only anxious to inspire love, when they ought to cherish a nobler ambition, and by their abilities and virtues exact respect.

"[T]he most perfect education, in my opinion, is such an exercise of the understanding as is best calculated to strengthen the body and form the heart. Or, in other words, to enable the individual to attain such habits of virtue as will render it independent. In fact, it is a farce to call any being virtuous whose virtues do not result from the exercise of its own reason. This was Rousseau's opinion respecting men: I extend it to women, and confidently assert that they have been drawn out of their sphere by false refinement, and not by an endeavor to acquire masculine qualities. Still the regal homage which they receive is so intoxicating, that till the manners of the times are changed, and formed on more reasonable principles, it may be impossible to convince them that the illegitimate power, which they obtain by degrading themselves, is a curse, and that they must return to nature and equality."

From Sandra M. Gilbert and Susan Gubar (eds.), *The Norton Anthology of Literature by Women: The Tradition in English*, W. W. Norton Co, 1985.

---

banned his books—but he also attacked the pretensions of his fellow philosophes, whom he considered arrogant, cynical, and lacking in spirituality.

By the 1770s the commanding figures of the Enlightenment, such as Voltaire and Diderot, had won their battles and had become masters of the most prestigious academies and channels of patronage. In a sense, they had themselves become the establishment. For younger writers frustrated by the existing distribution of influence and patronage, Rousseau became the inspiration.

Rousseau's Concept of Freedom   What proved to be Rousseau's most enduring work, *The Social Contract*, published in 1762, became famous only after the French Revolution dramatized the issues that the book had raised. (The Revolution, it could be said, did more for the book than Rousseau did for the Revolution, which he neither prophesied nor advocated.) *The Social Contract* was not meant as a blueprint for revolution but rather as an ideal standard against which readers might measure their own society. Rousseau did not expect that this standard could be achieved in practice, since existing states were too large and complex to allow the kind of participation that he considered essential.

For Rousseau, a government distinct from the individuals over whom it claims to exercise authority has no validity. Rousseau denied the almost universal idea that some people are meant to govern and others to obey. In the ideal polity, Rousseau said, individuals have a role in making the law to which they submit. By obeying it, they are thus obeying themselves as well as their fellow citizens. For this reason, they are free from arbitrary power. To found such an ideal society, each citizen would have to take part in creating a social contract laying out the society's ground rules. By doing so, these citizens would establish themselves as "the sovereign." This sovereign—the people—then creates a government that will carry on the day-to-day business of applying the laws.

Rousseau was not advocating simple majority rule but rather a quest for consensus as to the best interests of all citizens. Even if it *appears* contrary to the welfare of some or even many citizens, Rousseau believed, the best interest of the community must be every individual's best interest as well, since that individual is a member of the community. Rousseau called this difficult concept the **"general will."** Deferring to the general will means that an individual ultimately must do what

ROUSSEAU'S CONCEPT OF THE GENERAL WILL

"The essence of the social compact reduces itself to the following terms: Each of us puts his person and all his power in common under the supreme direction of the general will, and, in our collective capacity, we receive each member as an indivisible part of the whole. . . .

"In fact, each individual, as a man, may have a particular will contrary or dissimilar to the general will which he has as a citizen. His particular interest may speak to him quite differently from the common interest: his absolute and naturally independent existence may make him look upon what he owes to the common cause as a gratuitous contribution, the loss of which will do less harm to others than the payment of it is burdensome to himself. . . . He may wish to enjoy the rights of citizenship without being ready to fulfill the duties of a subject. The continuance of

such an injustice could not but prove the undoing of the body politic.

"In order then that the social compact may not be an empty formula, it tacitly includes the undertaking, which alone can give force to the rest, that whoever refuses to obey the general will shall be compelled to do so by the whole body. This means nothing less than that he will be forced to be free; for this is the condition which, by giving each citizen to his country, secures him against all personal dependence. In this lies the key to the working of the political machine."

From Jean-Jacques Rousseau, *The Social Contract*, Book 1, David Campbell Publishers.

---

one *ought*, not simply what one *wants*. This commitment derives from conscience, which must do battle within the individual against passion, appetite, and mere self-interest. Under the social contract, to use Rousseau's most striking phrase, the individual "will be forced to be free" (see "Rousseau's Concept of the General Will," above). Thus, for Rousseau, individual freedom depends on a political framework involving consent and participation as well as subordination of individual self-interest to the commonweal. More than any of the philosophes, Rousseau argued that individual freedom depends on the arrangements governing the collectivity.

EIGHTEENTH-CENTURY ELITE CULTURE

The Enlightenment was merely one dimension of Europe's vibrant cultural life in the eighteenth century. An explosive increase in publishing activity, legal and underground, served diverse audiences. New cultural forums and institutions, such as salons and freemasons lodges, combined with new media to create a **"public sphere"** for the uninhibited exchange of ideas. Meanwhile, the realm of literature saw remarkable innovation, including the rise of the novel. Royal courts and aristocracies still dominated most activity in music and the fine arts through their patronage, but here too the presence of a growing middle-class audience made itself felt and offered new opportunities of recognition for composers and artists.

Cosmopolitan High Culture

As the expansive, cosmopolitan aspects of European high culture are described here, it must be remembered that the mass of Europe's peasants and workers remained virtually untouched by these developments, insulated within their local environments and traditions. But the educated and wealthy, the numerically small and influential elites, enjoyed a sense of belonging to a common European civilization. French was the international language of this culture; even King Frederick II of Prussia favored French over German. Whatever the effects of Frederick's attitude might have been—the German dramatist Lessing, for one, considered it a deplorable cultural prejudice—the widespread knowledge of French meant that ideas and literature could circulate easily past language barriers.

The Appeal of Travel   Europeans sharpened their sense of common identity through travel literature and by their appetite for visiting foreign places. Although transportation was slow and uncomfortable, many embarked on a "grand tour," whose highlights included visits to Europe's large cities (such as London, Paris, Rome, and Vienna) and to the ruins of antiquity—to the glories of the modern and the ancient worlds.

Kings, princes, and municipal authorities were embellishing their towns with plazas, public gardens, theaters, and opera houses. Toward the end of the century, amenities such as street lighting and public transportation began to appear in a few cities, with London leading the way. From the private sector came two notable additions to the urban scene: the coffeehouse and the storefront window display. Coffeehouses, where customers

Anicet Charles G. Lemonnier
READING OF VOLTAIRE'S TRAGEDY "L'ORPHELIN DE LA CHINE" AT THE SALON OF MADAME GEOFFRIN, **1755**
This 1814 painting of Mme. Geoffrin's Salon in 1755 reflects the artist Lemonnier's imagination rather than historical reality. His canvas depicts an assemblage of all the major philosophes and their patrons that never actually took place. Yet it does accurately convey the social atmosphere and serious purpose of the Parisian salons. At the center is a bust of Voltaire, who lived in exile at the time.
Giraudon/Art Resource, NY

could chat or read, and enticing shop windows, which added to the pleasures of city walking (and stimulated consumer demand), enhanced the rhythms of urban life for tourists and residents alike. When a man is tired of London, Samuel Johnson remarked, he is tired of life.

Travelers on tour invariably passed from the attractions of bustling city life to the silent monuments of antiquity. As the philosophes recalled the virtues of pagan philosophers like Cicero, interest grew in surviving examples of Greek and Roman architecture and sculpture. Many would have agreed with the German art historian Johann Winckelmann that Greek sculpture was the most worthy standard of aesthetic beauty in all the world.

The Republic of Letters   Among writers, intellectuals, and scientists, the sense of a cosmopolitan European culture devolved into the concept of a "republic of letters." The phrase, introduced by sixteenth-century French humanists, was popularized by Pierre Bayle (noted earlier as a proponent of religious toleration), who published a critical journal that he called *News of the Republic of Letters.* The title implied that the realm of culture and

ideas stretched across Europe's political borders. In one sense, it was an exclusive republic, limited to the educated; but it was also an open society to which people of talent could belong regardless of their social origins.

Aside from the medium of the printed word, the republic of letters was organized around the salons and the academies. Both institutions encouraged social interchange by bringing together socially prominent men and women with talented writers. The philosophes themselves exemplified this social mixture, for their "family" was composed in almost equal measures of nobles (Montesquieu, Holbach, Condorcet) and commoners (Voltaire, Diderot, d'Alembert). Voltaire, while insisting that he was as good as any aristocrat, had no desire to topple the aristocracy from its position; rather, he sought amalgamation. As d'Alembert put it, talent on the one hand and birth and eminence on the other both deserve recognition.

The Salons and Masonic Lodges   Usually organized and led by women of wealthy bourgeois or noble families, the **salons** sought to bring together important writers with the influential persons they needed for favors and patronage. The salon of Madame Tencin, for example, helped launch Montesquieu's *Spirit of the Laws* in the 1740s, while the salon of Madame du Deffand in the 1760s became a forum in which the philosophes could test their ideas (see figure, p. 567). The salons also helped to enlarge the audience and contacts of the philosophes by introducing them to a flow of foreign visitors, ranging from German princes to Benjamin Franklin. Private newsletters kept interested foreigners and provincials abreast of activities in the Parisian salons when they could not attend personally, but salons also operated in Vienna, London, and Berlin.

The salons placed a premium on elegant conversation and wit. The women who ran them insisted that intellectuals make their ideas lucid and comprehensible, which increased the likelihood that their thought and writings would have some impact. The salons were also a forum in which men learned to take women seriously, and they constituted a unique cultural space for women between the domestic and public spheres. But the salons' emphasis on style over substance led Rousseau to denounce them as artificial rituals that prevented the display of genuine feeling and sincerity.

Throughout Europe, freemasonry was another important form of cultural sociability that often crossed the lines of class and (less commonly) of gender. Operating in an aura of secretiveness and symbolism, the masonic lodges fostered a curious mixture of spirituality and rationalism. Originating as clubs or fraternities dedicated to humane values, they attracted a wide range of educated nobles, commoners, and liberal clergy, while some lodges accepted women as well. But toward the end of the century, freemasonry was torn by sectarian controversies, and its influence seemed to be diminishing.

The Learned Academies As important for the dissemination of ideas in the eighteenth century as the salons were the learned academies. These ranged from the Lunar Society in Birmingham, a forum for innovative British industrialists and engineers, to state-sponsored academies in almost every capital of Southern and Central Europe, which served as conduits for advanced scientific and philosophical ideas coming from Western Europe. In France, moreover, academies were established in more than thirty provincial cities, most of which became strongholds of advanced thinking outside the capital.

These provincial academies were founded after the death of Louis XIV in 1715, as if in testimony to the liberating effect of his demise. Most began as literary institutes, concerned with upholding the purity of literary style. A few academies adhered to such goals well into midcentury, but most gradually shifted their interests from literary matters to scientific and practical questions in such areas as commerce, agriculture, and local administration. They became offshoots, so to speak, of the *Encyclopedia's* spirit. Indeed, when a Jesuit launched an attack against the *Encyclopedia* in the Lyons Academy, many members threatened to resign unless he retracted his remarks.

By the 1770s the essay contests sponsored by the provincial academies and the papers published by their members had turned to such topics as population growth, capital punishment and penology, education, poverty and welfare, the grain trade, the guilds, and the origins of sovereignty. A parallel shift in membership occurred. The local academies began as privileged corporations, dominated by the nobility of the region. Associate membership was extended to commoners from the ranks of civil servants, doctors, and professionals. Gradually, the distinction between regular and associate participants crumbled. The academies admitted more commoners to full membership, and a fragile social fusion took place.

Publishing and Reading

The eighteenth century saw a notable rise in publishing geared to several kinds of readers. Traveling circulating libraries originated in England around 1740 and opened untapped markets for reading material; by the end of the century almost one thousand traveling libraries had been established. "Booksellers," or publishers—the intermediary between author and reader—combined the functions of a modern editor, printer, salesperson, and (if need be) smuggler. Their judgment and marketing techniques helped create as well as fill the demand for books, since they conceived and financed a variety of works. The *Encyclopedia* originated as a bookseller's project; so, too, did such enduring masterpieces as Samuel Johnson's *Dictionary*, a monumental lexicon that helped purify and standardize the English language. Booksellers commissioned talented stylists to write popular versions of serious scientific, historical, and philosophical works. Recognizing a specialized demand among women readers, they increased the output of fictional romances and fashion magazines and also began to publish more fiction and poetry by women.

Journals and Newspapers The eighteenth century saw a proliferation of periodicals. In England, which pioneered in this domain, the number of periodicals increased from 25 to 158 between 1700 and 1780. In one successful model, Addison and Steele's *Spectator* (1711), each issue consisted of a single essay that sought in elegant but clear prose to raise the reader's standards of morality and taste. Their goal was "to enliven Morality with Wit, and to temper Wit with Morality. . . . To bring Philosophy . . . to dwell in clubs and assemblies, at tea-tables and coffeehouses." Eliza

A

DICTIONARY

OF THE

ENGLISH LANGUAGE:

IN WHICH

The WORDS are deduced from their ORIGINALS,

AND

ILLUSTRATED in their DIFFERENT SIGNIFICATIONS

BY

EXAMPLES from the best WRITERS.

TO WHICH ARE PREFIXED,

A HISTORY of the LANGUAGE,

AND

AN ENGLISH GRAMMAR.

BY SAMUEL JOHNSON, A. M.

IN TWO VOLUMES.

VOL. I.

Cum tabulis animum censoris sumet honesti :
Audebit quaecunque parum splendoris habebunt,
Et sine pondere erunt, et honore indigna ferentur,
Verba movere loco; quamvis invita recedant,
Et versentur adhuc intra penetralia Vestae :
Obscurata diu populo bonus eruet, atque
Proferet in lucem speciosa vocabula rerum,
Quae priscis memorata Catonibus atque Cethegis,
Nunc situs informis premit et deserta vetustas.   HOR.

—

LONDON

Printed by W. STRAHAN,

For J. and P. KNAPTON ; T. and T. LONGMAN ; C. HITCH and L. HAWES ;
A. MILLAR· and R. and J. DODSLEY.

MDCCLV.

The title page of Samuel Johnson's pioneering *Dictionary of the English Language* (1755 edition), one of the masterpieces of eighteenth-century literature.
The Mary Evans Picture Library

Haywood adapted this format in her journal, *The Female Spectator* (1744–1756), in which she advocated improvement in the treatment of women and greater "opportunities of enlarging our minds." Another type of journal published extracts and summaries of books and covered current events and entertainment; one such journal, the *Gentleman's Magazine*, reached the impressive circulation of fifteen thousand in 1740. More learned periodicals specialized in book reviews and serious articles on science and philosophy.

Most important for the future of reading habits in Europe was the daily newspaper, which originated in England. Papers like the *London Chronicle* at first pro-vided family entertainment and then took on classified advertisements (thereby spurring consumerism and the notion of fashion). English newspapers of course published news of current events, but only after strenuous battles for permission from a reluctant government did they win the right to report directly on parliamentary debates. In France, a handful of major Parisian newspapers enjoyed privileged monopolies in exchange for full compliance with government censorship. This arrangement severely restricted their ability to discuss government and politics, although other periodicals published outside France's borders helped satisfy the demand for such coverage in France.

"Bad Books"   The demand for books and the dynamism of the publishing industry created new employment opportunities for men and women. Although the number of would-be writers swelled, relatively few could achieve financial independence without patronage. Many remained poverty-stricken and frustrated.

Publishers thus could hire legions of otherwise unemployed writers to turn out the kinds of books for which they sensed a great demand: potboilers, romances, salacious pamphlets, and gossip sheets, which pandered to low tastes. Paid for quantity and speed rather than quality, these hack writers led a precarious, humiliating existence. Booksellers and desperate writers saw money to be made in sensational pamphlets assailing the character of notorious aristocrats; in partisan pamphlets attacking a particular faction in court politics; and in pornography. Sometimes they combined character assassination and pornography in pamphlets dwelling on the alleged perversions of rulers or courtiers. For all its wild exaggeration, such material helped "desacralize" monarchy and created a vivid image of a decadent aristocracy.

To satisfy the public's demand for gossip, character assassination, and pornography in violation of laws regulating the book trade in France, publishers located just across the French border marketed such books and pamphlets clandestinely. They smuggled this material into France, along with banned books by writers like Voltaire and Rousseau, using networks of couriers and distributors. In their sales lists of what they called Philosophic Books, the clandestine publishers lumped together banned books by serious writers along with such illicit publications as *The Scandalous Chronicles, The Private Life of Louis XV,* and *Venus in the Cloister* (a pornographic account of the alleged perversions of the clergy). The police made the same judgment. In attempting to stop the flow of "bad books," they scarcely distinguished between a banned work by Voltaire assaulting religious bigotry and a libelous pamphlet depicting the queen as a corrupt pervert.

Literature, Music, and Art

Unlike the artistic style of the seventeenth century, generally classified as baroque, the artistic style of the eighteenth century cannot be given a single stylistic label. The nature of the audience and the sources of support for writers and composers also varied considerably. But several trends proved to be of lasting importance: the rise of the novel in England, the birth of Romantic poetry, the development of the symphony in Austria, and the changing social context of French painting late in the century.

The Rise of the Novel   The modern novel had its strongest development in England, where writers and booksellers cultivated a growing middle-class reading public. The acknowledged pioneer of this new genre was Samuel Richardson. With a series of letters telling the story, Richardson's *Pamela, or Virtue Rewarded* (1740) recounted the trials and tribulations of an honest if somewhat hypocritical servant girl. Pamela's sexual virtue is repeatedly challenged but never conquered by her wealthy employer, Mr. B., who finally agrees to marry her. An instant success, this melodrama broke from the standard forms and heroic subjects of most narrative fiction. Richardson dealt with recognizable types of people.

Pamela's apparent hypocrisy, however, prompted a playwright and lawyer named Henry Fielding to pen a short satire called *Shamela,* which he followed with his own novel *Joseph Andrews.* Here comedy and adventure replaced melodrama; Fielding prefaced *Joseph Andrews* with a manifesto claiming that the novel was to be "a comic epic in prose." Fielding realized the full potential of his bold experimentation with literary forms in *Tom Jones* (1749), a colorful, robust, comic panorama of English society featuring a gallery of brilliantly developed characters and vivid depictions of varied social environments.

The novel was thus emerging as a form of fiction that told its story and treated the development of personality in a realistic social context. It seemed to mirror its times better than other forms of fiction. Like the dramas that filled the stage in the second half of the century, most novels focused on family life and everyday problems of love, marriage, and social relations. Novelists could use broad comedy, or they could be totally serious; they could experiment endlessly with forms and techniques and could deal with a wide range of social settings.

In *Evelina, or A Young Lady's Entrance into the World* (1778), the writer Fanny Burney used the flexibility of the novel to give a woman's perspective on eighteenth-century English social life. In the form of letters, like *Pamela* and Rousseau's *Julie, Evelina* traces a provincial girl's adventures in London as she discovers her true father and finds a suitable husband. While falling back on conventional melodrama, in which marriage is the only happy ending for a young woman, Burney also uses social satire to suggest how society restricts, and even endangers, an independent woman's life. If Burney was ambivalent about the possibilities for female independence in the social world, her own writing, together with that of other women writers of the period, demonstrated the opportunities for female artistic achievement.

The Birth of Romantic Poetry   During most of this century of innovation in prose fiction, poetry retained its traditional qualities. Still the most prized form of literary expression, poetry followed unchanging rules on what made good literature. Each poetic form had its particular essence and rules, but in all types of poems diction was supposed to be elegant and the sentiments refined. Poets were expected to transform the raw materials of emotion into delicate language and references that only the highly educated could appreciate. In this neoclassical tradition, art was meant to echo eternal standards of truth and beauty. Poets were not permitted to unburden their souls or hold forth on their own experiences. The audience for poetry was the narrowest segment of the reading public—"the wealthy few," in the phrase of William Wordsworth, who criticized eighteenth-century poets for pandering exclusively to that group.

By the end of the century, however, the restraints of **Neoclassicism** finally provoked rebellion in the ranks of English and German poets. Men like Friedrich von Schiller and Wordsworth defiantly raised the celebration of individual feeling and inner passion to the level of a creed, which came to be known as **Romanticism.** These young poets generally prized Rousseau's writings, seeing the Genevan rebel as someone who had forged a personal idiom of expression and who valued inner feeling, moral passion, and the wonders of nature. Hoping to appeal to a much broader audience, these poets decisively changed the nature of poetic composition and made this literary form, like the novel, a flexible vehicle of artistic expression.

Goethe   The writer who came to embody the new ambitions of poets, novelists, and dramatists was Johann von Goethe, whose long life (1749–1832) spanned the beginnings and the high point of the Romantic movement. A friend of Schiller and many of the German writers and philosophers of the day, he soon came to tower over all of them. Goethe first inspired a literary movement known as *Sturm und Drang* (Storm and Stress), which emphasized strong artistic emotions and gave early intimations of the Romantic temperament. The best-known work of Sturm und Drang was Goethe's *The Sorrows of Young Werther* (1774), a novel about a young man driven to despair and suicide by an impossible love.

Courted by many of the princes and monarchs of Germany, Goethe soon joined the circle of the duke who ruled the small city-state of Weimar, where he remained for the rest of his life. There flowed from his pen an astonishing stream of works—lyrical love poetry, powerful dramas, art and literary criticism, translations, philosophic reflections, an account of his travels in Italy, and studies of optics, botany, anatomy, and mathematics. Even though he held official posts in the duke's court, Goethe's literary output never flagged. His masterpiece, *Faust,* occupied him for nearly fifty years and revealed the progress of his art. The first part (published in 1808) imbued with romantic longing the story of a

man who yearns to master all of knowledge and who makes a pact with the devil to achieve his goal. But the second part (1831) emphasized the determination that came to be Goethe's credo. The final lines are:

> He only earns his freedom and existence
> Who daily conquers them anew.

What had begun in the youthful exuberance and energy of Romanticism ended in an almost classical mood of discipline. No wonder that Goethe seemed to his contemporaries to be the last "universal man," the embodiment of conflicting cultural values and Western civilization's struggle to resolve them.

The Symphony   For Europe's elites, music offered the supreme form of entertainment, and the development of the symphony in music paralleled the rise of the novel in literature. For much of the century, composers still served under royal, ecclesiastical, or aristocratic patronage. They were bound by rigid formulas of composition and by prevailing tastes tyrannically insistent on conventions. Most listeners wanted little more than pleasant melodies in familiar forms; instrumental music was often commissioned as background fare for balls or other social occasions.

The heartland of Europe's music tradition shifted during the eighteenth century from Italy and France to Austria. Here a trio of geniuses transformed the routines of eighteenth-century composition into original and enduring masterpieces. True, the early symphonies of Franz Joseph Haydn and young Wolfgang Amadeus Mozart were conventional exercises. As light and tuneful as its audience could wish, their early music had little emotional impact. By the end of their careers, however, these two composers had altered the symphonic form from three to four movements, had achieved extraordinary harmonic virtuosity, and had brought a deep if restrained emotionalism to their music. Haydn and Mozart had changed the symphony radically from the elegant trifles of earlier years.

Beethoven   Ludwig van Beethoven consummated this development and ensured that the symphony, like the novel and Romantic poetry, would be an adaptable vehicle for the expression of creative genius. In each of his nine symphonies, as well as in his five piano concertos, Beethoven progressively modified the standard formulas, enlarged the orchestra, and wrote movements of increasing intricacy. His last symphony burst the bonds of the form altogether. Beethoven introduced a large chorus singing one of Schiller's odes to conclude his *Ninth Symphony* (1824), making it a celebration in music of freedom and human kinship. Laden with passion, the music is nevertheless recognizable as an advanced form of the classical symphony. Thus, it provides a bridge between the music of two periods:

Jean-Baptiste Greuze
THE FATHER'S CURSE, **1777**
Instead of the aristocrats or classical figures that most artists chose for their subjects, Jean-Baptiste Greuze painted ordinary French people. His portraits and dramatic scenes (such as *The Father's Curse*) seemed to echo Rousseau's call for honest, "natural" feeling.
Louvre, Paris, France. Giraudon/ Arts Resource, NY

Élisabeth Vigée-Le Brun
MARIE ANTOINETTE WITH A ROSE
One of the leading French portrait painters, and the most successful female artist of the era anywhere, was Élisabeth Vigée-Le Brun, who enjoyed the patronage of Queen Marie Antoinette. Shown here is one of several portraits that she painted of the French queen.
Giraudon/Art Resource, NY

eighteenth-century classicism and nineteenth-century Romanticism.

Aristocratic and court patronage remained the surest foundation for a career in music during the eighteenth century. Haydn, for example, worked with mutual satisfaction as the court composer for one prince from 1761 to 1790. At the end of his long life, however, Haydn moved out on his own, having won enough international recognition to sign a lucrative contract with a London music publisher who underwrote performances of his last twelve symphonies. In contrast, Mozart had an unhappy experience trying to earn his living by composing. After a few miserable years as court composer for the Archbishop of Salzburg, Mozart escaped to Vienna but could not find a permanent employer. He was obliged to eke out an inadequate living by teaching, filling private commissions, and giving public concerts. Beethoven did much better at freeing himself from dependence on a single patron through individual commissions and public concerts.

The Social Context of Art   Unlike the situation in literature and music, there were no notable innovations in the field of painting during most of the eighteenth century. With the exception of the Frenchman Jacques-

Jacques-Louis David
THE OATH OF THE HORATII
The greatest innovation in French painting came in reaction to the artificiality of the rococo style and subject matter, with a return to favor of "noble simplicity and calm grandeur." This Neoclassical style found its supreme expression in the work of Jacques-Louis David. Such history paintings as *The Oath of the Horatii* evoked the ideal of civic virtue in ancient Greek and Roman civilization.
Louvre, Paris, France. Erich Lessing/ Art Resource, NY

Louis David, eighteenth-century painters were overshadowed by their predecessors. Neoclassicism remained a popular style in the late eighteenth century, with its themes inspired by antiquity and its timeless conceptions of form and beauty, comparable to the rules of Neoclassical poetry.

The social context of painting, however, was changing. Most commissions and patronage still depended on aristocrats and princes, but the public was beginning to claim a role as the judge of talent in the visual arts. Public opinion found its voice in a new breed of art critics, unaffiliated with official sources of patronage, who reached their new audience through the press in the second half of the century. The Royal Academy of Art in France created the opening for this new voice by sponsoring an annual public exhibition, or "salon," starting in 1737. People could view the canvases chosen by the Academy for these exhibitions and could reach their own judgments about the painters.

David and Greuze   David, a brilliant painter in the Neoclassical style, won the greatest renown in this arena of public opinion during the 1780s. He skillfully celebrated the values of the ancient world in such historical paintings as *The Oath of the Horatii* (see figure, above), *The Death of Socrates*, and *Brutus*. Discarding many of the standard conventions for history painting (and thereby drawing criticism from the Academy), David overwhelmed the public with his vivid imagery and the emotional force of his compositions. His paint-

ings of the 1780s unmistakably conveyed a yearning for civic virtue and patriotism that had yet to find its political outlet in France. Not surprisingly, David became the most engaged and triumphant painter of the French Revolution.

In an entirely different vein, a few eighteenth-century artists chose more mundane and "realistic" subjects or themes for their canvases, parallel in some respects to what novelists and playwrights were doing. Jean-Baptiste Greuze, for example, made a hit in the Parisian exhibitions of the 1770s with his sentimentalized paintings of ordinary people in family settings caught in a dramatic situation, such as the death of a father or the banishment of a disobedient son. William Hogarth, a superb London engraver who worked through the medium of prints and book illustrations, went further down the social pyramid with his remarkable scenes of life among the working classes and the poor.

POPULAR CULTURE

While the cultural world of aristocratic and middle-class elites has been extensively studied, the culture of artisans, peasants, and the urban poor remains more dimly known. In those sectors of society, culture primarily meant recreation, and it was essentially public and collective. Despite traditions of elementary schooling in certain regions and the spread of literacy among some groups, literacy rates remained generally low. Popular

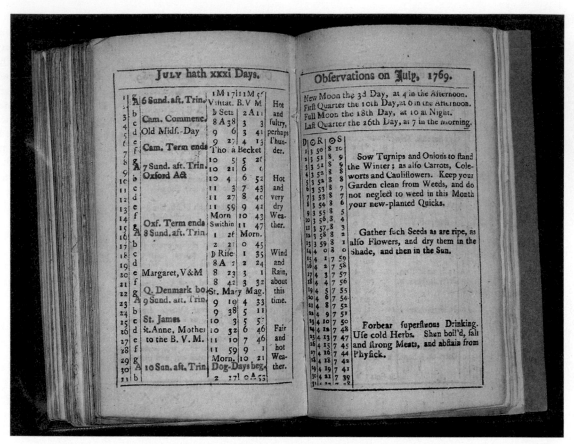

A page from an English almanac of 1769 on the month of July includes saints' days, information about likely weather patterns, and advice about agricultural matters and health care.
New York Public Library, Astor, Lenox, and Tilden Foundations

culture did have its written forms, but these were less prevalent than the oral traditions embodied in songs, folktales, and proverbs. Despite the rare firsthand traces of popular culture in the historical record, it is possible to suggest the rich variety of sociability and recreational practice among working people in traditional society.

Popular Literature

Far removed from the markets for Voltaire and the *Gentleman's Magazine* existed a distinct world of popular literature—the reading matter consumed by journeymen and peasants, the poor and the almost poor, those who could barely read and those who could not read at all. From the seventeenth through the early nineteenth century, publishers produced for this audience small booklets written anonymously, printed on cheap paper, costing only a few pennies, and sold by itinerant peddlers who knew the tastes of their customers. Presumably the booklets were often read aloud by those who could read to those who could not.

This popular literature took three major forms. Religious material included devotional tracts, saints' lives, catechisms, manuals of penitence, and Bible stories, all written simply and generously laced with miracles. Readers who were preoccupied with fears of death and damnation sought reassurance in these works that a virtuous life would end in salvation. Almanacs constituted a second type of popular literature, which appealed to the readers' concern for getting along in this life. Almanacs discussed things like the kinds of potions to take for illnesses, and featured astrology—how to read the stars and other signs for clues about the future. The third type of popular literature provided entertainment: tales and fables, burlesques and crude satires, mixtures of fiction and history in which miraculous events frequently helped bring the story to a satisfactory conclusion.

Although useful information may have trickled down through these booklets, most of them were escapist. The religiosity and supernatural events of popular literature separate it from the growing rationalism and secularism of elite culture. Moreover, it could be argued that by ignoring such problems as food shortages, high taxes, and material insecurity, popular writings fostered submissiveness, a fatalistic acceptance of

Most eighteenth-century elementary school teachers used the extremely inefficient individual method of instruction, in which pupils read to the teacher from whatever book they happened to bring from home, while the other pupils occupied themselves as best they could.
Tallandier, Bibliothèque des Arts Décoratifs, Paris. Editions

a dismal status quo. Glimpsing the content of this popular literature helps us understand why Voltaire had no hope of extending his ideas on religion to the masses.

Oral Tradition Oral tradition encompassed folktales told at the fireside on long winter nights, songs passed on from generation to generation, and sayings that embodied the conventional wisdom of the people.

Themes touching on hunger, sex, or oppression were more likely to turn up in songs or oral tales than in booklets. Songs and tales expressed the joyful bawdiness of ordinary men and women but also the ever-present hardships and dangers of daily life: the endless drudgery of work in the fields, the gnawing ache of an empty stomach, the cruelty of parental neglect or mean stepparents, the desperation of beggars on the road. The most fantastic tales evoked a threatening world in which strangers might turn out to be princes or good fairies but might just as well turn into wolves or witches. Oral tradition also celebrated the shrewdness and cunning of ordinary people struggling for survival, in the spirit of the saying: "Better a knave than a fool."

Literacy and Primary Schooling

The wars of religion had spurred the spread of literacy and elementary schooling in Europe. Protestantism explicitly promoted literacy so that Christians could read their Bibles directly; strongly Protestant societies such as Scotland, Switzerland, and Sweden had unusually high rates of literacy by the eighteenth century. The Catholic Church, as well, believed that the spread of lit-

eracy would serve its cause in the battle against heresy. While teaching reading, Catholic schoolmasters could provide religious instruction and could socialize children into the beliefs and behavior of a Catholic way of life.

A unique study of literacy in France carried out in the late nineteenth century, based on signatures versus *X*s on parish marriage registers all across the country, indicates a national literacy rate (meaning the ability to read) in 1686 of about 21 percent, which reached 37 percent a century later. These national averages, however, conceal striking regional and social disparities. The south of France had much lower rates than the north/northeast, and rural literacy rates lagged significantly behind those of the towns. While agricultural laborers rarely could read, urban artisans were generally literate. The widest gap of all separated men from women, the rates in 1786 being 47 and 27 percent, respectively. Similarly, estimates for England suggest a male literacy rate of slightly under 60 percent and a female rate of about 40 percent.

Primary Education Schooling was not intended to transform society or lift the mass of people out of the situations into which they were born. On the contrary, it was supposed to maintain the social order and reinforce the family in promoting piety and decent behavior among the young. Many among the elites (including Voltaire) were skeptical about the value of education for peasants and laborers. Might it not confuse them, or make it more difficult for them to accept the drudgery to which they seemed destined? Peasant or laboring parents might well have shared such skepticism about educating their young. Education could seem a waste of time when their children could be contributing to the family's livelihood; they might especially begrudge spending the money on tuition that most elementary schooling required.

A village usually hired a schoolmaster in consultation with the pastor or priest; schools usually straddled community and church, since the schoolmaster often served as the pastor's aide. Except in towns that had charitable endowments to support schooling, the parents, the village, or some combination of the two paid the schoolmaster, and for that reason numerous villages did without any schooling. Even a modest tuition could deter impoverished parents from hiring a master, enrolling their children, or keeping them in school for a sufficient time. Since schoolmasters taught reading first and writing separately and later, many pupils, especially girls, were not kept in school long enough to learn how to write anything but their names. Schooling, in other words, was largely demand-driven, the product of a community's level of wealth and interest.

Schooling in Central Europe

While England and France left primary schooling entirely to the chance of local initiative, the Habsburg monarchy seriously promoted primary education and thereby became the first Catholic realm to do so. The Habsburg General School Ordinance of 1774 authorized state subsidies, in combination with local funds, for the support of a school in almost every parish. Attendance was supposed to be compulsory, though the state had no way to enforce it. The state also intended to train future teachers at institutions called normal schools. A similar two-pronged strategy was adopted in Prussia under Frederick II at about the same time, although little was done to implement it.

In Prussia, as in most of Europe, schoolmasters remained barely competent and poorly paid. Frederick II indeed had a limiting vision of popular education: "It is enough for the country people to learn only a little reading and writing. . . . Instruction must be planned so that they receive only what is most essential for them but which is designed to keep them in the villages and not influence them to leave." As elsewhere in Europe, the goals of elementary schooling were to inculcate religion and morality, propagate the virtues of hard work, and promote deference to one's superiors.

Sociability and Recreation

If the educated elites had their salons, masonic lodges, and learned academies, the common people also formed organized cultural groups. Many artisans, for example, belonged to secret societies that combined fraternal and trade-union functions. Young unmarried artisans frequently traveled the country, stopping periodically to work with comrades in other towns in order to hone their skills. Artisans also relied on their associations for camaraderie and ritual celebrations. Married artisans often joined religious confraternities, which honored a patron saint and ensured a dignified funeral when they died, or mutual aid societies to which they contributed small monthly dues to pay for assistance if illness or accident should strike.

Taverns and Festivals

Corresponding to the coffeehouses of the urban middle classes were the taverns in working-class neighborhoods. These noisy, crowded places catered to a poor clientele, especially on Sunday and on Monday, which workingmen often took as a day off, honoring (as they put it) "Saint Monday." The urban common people were first beginning to consume wine in the eighteenth century, still something of a luxury except in its cheapest watered form. In England gin was the poor person's drink, cheap and plentiful until the government levied a hefty excise tax after realizing that too many people were drinking themselves into disability and death—a concern depicted in Hogarth's etchings, p. 577.

More commonly, drinking was not done in morbid fashion but as part of a healthy and vibrant outdoor life. Popular pastimes followed a calendar of holidays that provided occasions for group merrymaking, eating, drinking, dressing-up, contests, and games. Local festivals were particularly comfortable settings for single young men and women to meet each other. The highlight of a country year usually came in early autumn after the summer harvest was in, when most villages held a public feast that lasted several days. In Catholic countries similar festivities were often linked with church rituals. Popular observances included the commemoration of local patron saints, pilgrimages to holy places, and the period of Carnival before Lent. More generally, a growing "commercialization of leisure" in the eighteenth century supported new spectator sports, such as horse racing and boxing matches.

In early modern Europe, gentlefolk and commoners had been accustomed to mixing in recreational and religious settings: fairs and markets, sporting events, village or town festivals, Carnival in Catholic countries. But in the eighteenth century, as aristocrats and bourgeois alike became more concerned with good manners and refinement, these elite groups began to distance themselves from the bawdy and vulgar behavior of ordinary people. With growing intolerance, they censured popular recreational culture in the hope of "reforming" the people into a more sober and orderly lifestyle. Social status was based on birth or wealth, but cultural taste was becoming its behavioral marker.

William Hogarth

GIN LANE AND *BEER STREET*

In his *Gin Lane* etching of 1750, Hogarth depicted the results of excessive gin drinking by the English common people as death, apathy, and moral decay. A cheerful companion piece called *Beer Street*, however, suggested that drinking in moderation was an acceptable practice.

Hogarth, *Gin Lane.* The Metropolitan Museum of Art, Harris Brisbane Dick Fund, 1932. Photography © 2002 The Metropolitan Museum of Art, New York.

Hogarth, *Beer Street.* The Metropolitan Museum of Art, Harris Brisbane Dick Fund, 1932. [32.35 (123)]. Photograph © 2002 The Metropolitan Museum of Art, New York.

Summary

The philosophes, celebrated members of Europe's cultural establishment by the 1770s, hoped that their society would gradually reform itself under their inspiration. Although these writers criticized their society, they were not its subverters. Distrustful of the uneducated masses and afraid of popular emotion, superstition, and disorder, the philosophes were anything but democrats. Nonetheless, the Enlightenment challenged basic traditional values of European society: from Voltaire's polemics against Christianity through the sober social science of Diderot's *Encyclopedia* to the impassioned writings of Rousseau. Along with a flood of "bad books"—the pornography and scandal sheets of the clandestine publishers—booksellers, writers, and journalists disseminated critical ideas among Europe's educated men and women. The philosophes challenged the automatic respect for convention and authority, promoted the habit of independent reflection, and implanted the conviction that the reform of institutions was both necessary and possible. They promoted a climate that put the status quo on the defensive and in which revolution—when provoked under particular circumstances—would not be unthinkable.

QUESTIONS FOR FURTHER THOUGHT

1. What were the core values of the Enlightenment and how would you assess their strengths and weaknesses? What might have produced a backlash against Enlightenment values in subsequent periods? How might one defend them today?
2. How does the music, painting, and literature of the eighteenth century compare to the high culture of earlier periods you have studied, such as the Renaissance or the seventeenth century? Has the social or political context of cultural life changed? Were there comparable changes in the realm of popular culture?
3. What do you make of Jean-Jacques Rousseau?

RECOMMENDED READING

Sources

Gay, Peter (ed.). *The Enlightenment: A Comprehensive Anthology.* 1973.

Gendzier, Stephen (ed.). *Denis Diderot: The Encyclopedia: Selections.* 1967.

*Jacob, Margaret C. *The Enlightenment: A Brief History with Documents.* 2001.

Mohl, Mary R., and Helene Koon (eds.). *The Female Spectator: English Women Writers Before 1800.* 1977.

Vigée-Le Brun, Marie-Louise . . . Élisabeth. *Memoirs.* S. Evans (ed.). 1989. Memoirs of the most notable female painter in eighteenth-century France.

Studies

*Brewer, John. *The Pleasures of the Imagination: English Culture in the Eighteenth Century.* 1997. A lively, panoramic survey of the production and consumption of high culture in all its forms.

Bruford, W. H. *Germany in the Eighteenth Century: The Social Background of the Literary Revival.* 1952. A useful survey.

Buchan, James. *Crowded with Genius: The Scottish Enlightenment: Edinburgh's Moment of the Mind.* 2003. A popular history of the remarkable circle of Scottish philosophes, including Adam Smith and David Hume.

Capp, Bernard. *English Almanacs, 1500–1800: Astrology and the Popular Press.* 1979. A probing study of the most important genre of popular literature.

*Chartier, Roger. *The Cultural Origins of the French Revolution.* 1991. A synthesis of recent research on publishing, the public sphere, and the emergence of new political attitudes.

Cranston, Maurice. *Jean-Jacques, The Noble Savage,* and *The Solitary Self.* 1982, 1991, and 1995. A three-volume study of the life and work of Rousseau, critical but sympathetic.

*Crow, Thomas. *Painters and Public Life in Eighteenth-Century Paris.* 1985. A pioneering work on the development of a public sphere of critical discourse about art.

*Darnton, Robert. *The Forbidden Best Sellers of Pre-Revolutionary France.* 1995. A pathbreaking work on the circulation, content, and impact of banned books.

*Gay, Peter. *The Enlightenment: An Interpretation.* 2 vols. 1966 and 1969. A masterly, full-bodied exposition of Enlightenment thought.

*Goodman, Dena. *The Republic of Letters: A Cultural History of the French Enlightenment.* 1994. Focuses on the salons and the roles of women in cultural and intellectual life.

*Isherwood, Robert. *Farce and Fantasy: Popular Entertainment in Eighteenth-Century Paris.* 1986. A cultural and institutional history of fairs and popular theater.

Malcolmson, R. W. *Popular Recreations in English Society, 1700–1850.* 1973. A good survey of a neglected subject.

May, Gita. *Elisabeth Vigée-Le Brun: The Odyssey of an Artist in an Age of Revolution.* 2005. The public and private life of the period's most prominent female painter.

*Maza, Sarah. *Private Lives and Public Affairs: The Causes Célèbres of Pre-Revolutionary France.* 1993. An original analysis of scandals and lawsuits that raised social consciousness in the later eighteenth century.

McClellan, James. *Science Reorganized: Scientific Societies in the Eighteenth Century.* 1985.

Melton, James Van Horn. *Absolutism and the Eighteenth-Century Origins of Compulsory Schooling in Prussia and Austria.* 1988.

———. *The Rise of the Public in Enlightenment Europe.* 2001. An excellent comparative survey of the developing "public sphere" in Europe.

Palmer, Robert R. *Catholics and Unbelievers in Eighteenth-Century France.* 1939. The response of Catholic intellectuals to the century's philosophic thought.

Porter, Roy, and Mikulas Teich (eds.). *The Enlightenment in National Context.* 1981. A comprehensive geographic overview.

*Roche, Daniel. *France in the Enlightenment.* 1998. A masterly synthesis, especially on the Enlightenment and French society.

*Spencer, Samia (ed.). *French Women and the Age of Enlightenment.* 1984. A pioneering collection of essays on a variety of literary and historical themes.

Venturi, Franco. *Italy and the Enlightenment.* 1972. Essays on important Italian philosophes by a leading historian.

*Watt, Ian. *The Rise of the Novel: Studies of Defoe, Richardson, and Fielding.* 1957. The view from England.

Wilson, Arthur. *Diderot.* 1972. An exhaustive, reliable biography of the consummate French philosophe.

*Available in paperback.

Jean Duplessis-Bertaux
STORMING OF THE TUILERIES, COURS DU CAROUSSEL, AUGUST 10, 1792
The armed assault on the Tuileries Palace of August 10, 1792, brought an end to the monarchy and led directly to the founding of the first French Republic.
Giraudon/Art Resource, NY

Chapter Twenty

THE FRENCH REVOLUTION

REFORM AND POLITICAL CRISIS • 1789: THE FRENCH REVOLUTION •
THE RECONSTRUCTION OF FRANCE • THE SECOND REVOLUTION

Well into the eighteenth century, the long-standing social structures and political institutions of Europe were securely entrenched. Most monarchs still claimed to hold their authority directly from God. In cooperation with their aristocracies, they presided over realms composed of distinct orders of citizens, or *estates* as they were sometimes known. Each order had its particular rights, privileges, and obligations. But pressures for change were building during the century. In France, the force of public opinion grew increasingly potent by the 1780s. A financial or political crisis that could normally be managed by the monarchy threatened to snowball in this new environment. Such vulnerability was less evident in Austria, Prussia, and Russia, however, where strong monarchs instituted reforms to streamline their governments. Similarly, in Britain the political system proved resilient despite explosions of discontent at home and across the Atlantic.

Unquestionably, then, the French Revolution constituted the pivotal event of European history in the late eighteenth century. From its outbreak in 1789, the Revolution transformed the nature of sovereignty and law in France. Under its impetus, civic and social institutions were renewed, from local government and schooling to family relations and assistance for the poor. Soon its ideals of liberty, equality, and fraternity resonated across the borders of other European states, especially after war broke out in 1792 and French armies took the offensive.

The French Revolution's innovations defined the foundations of a liberal society and polity. Both at home and abroad, however, the new regime faced formidable opposition, and its struggle for survival propelled it in unanticipated directions. Some unforeseen turns, such as democracy and republicanism, became precedents for the future even if they soon aborted. Other developments, such as the Reign of Terror, seemed to nullify the original liberal values of 1789. The bloody struggles of the Revolution thus cast a shadow over this transformative event as they dramatized the brutal dilemma of means versus ends.

Civil Constitution of the Clergy **1790** ●

Peasant revolts and August 4 decree **July–August 1789** ●

Storming of the Bastille **July 1789** ●

Estates General become National Assembly **June 1789** ●

Failed Assembly of Notables in France **1787** ●

1780s
Joseph II's authoritarian reforms in Habsburg Empire
● **1776** American Declaration of Independence

REFORM AND POLITICAL CRISIS

To put the French Revolution into perspective, it helps to compare political tensions and conflicts elsewhere in Europe. Strong monarchs with reputations for being "enlightened" reigned in Prussia, Austria, Spain, and even Russia. Their stature seemingly contrasts with the mediocrity of Louis XV and Louis XVI, who ruled in France. Yet the former did not get far in reforming their realms or granting rights and freedom to their subjects. The limits of "enlightened absolutism," therefore, should be kept in mind when considering the crisis that confronted France. Meanwhile, in Britain energetic movements for political reform ran into determined opposition. This rigidity had a particular impact across the Atlantic, where Britain's thirteen colonies in North America were driven to rebellion and a revolutionary war for independence.

Enlightened Absolutism in Central and Eastern Europe

During the late nineteenth century, German historians invented the concept of enlightened absolutism to describe the Prussian and Habsburg monarchies of the eighteenth century. Critical of the ineptitude and weakness of French monarchs in that period, these historians argued that the strength of an enlightened ruler had been the surest basis for progress in early modern Europe. A king who ruled in his subjects' interest, they implied, avoided violent conflicts like those of the French Revolution. Earlier strong monarchs, such as Philip II of Spain and France's Louis XIV (who had once declared: "I am the state"), had been irresponsible; in contrast, these German historians argued, Frederick II of Prussia symbolized the enlightened phase of absolutism with his comment that the ruler is the "first servant of the state."

Previous chapters, however, have demonstrated that monarchs dealt with the same fundamental issues during all stages of absolutism. They always strove to assert their authority over their subjects and to maximize the power of their state in relation to other realms, principally by means of territorial expansion. Any notion that Enlightenment thinking caused monarchs to abandon these efforts is misleading. Still, several eighteenth-century monarchs did initiate reforms and did modify their styles of ruling in order to appear more modern or enlightened. Frederick II of Prussia and Catherine II of Russia, for example, lavished praise on Voltaire and Diderot, and those philosophes returned the compliment. These rulers may simply have been engaging in public relations. Yet the fact that they seemed supportive of such writers suggests that absolutism had indeed adopted a new image.

Catherine the Great (r. 1762–1796) played this game to its limit. In 1767 she announced a new experiment in the direction of representative government—a policy hailed as a landmark by her philosophe admirers, who were too remote from St. Petersburg to see its insincerity. Catherine convened a Legislative Commission, a body of delegates from various strata of Russian society who were invited to present grievances, propose reforms, and then debate the proposals. In the end, however, she sent the delegates home under the pretext of having to turn her attention to a war with Turkey. Little came of the Legislative Commission except some good publicity for Catherine. In fact, she later promulgated a Charter of the Nobility, which, instead of limiting the nobility's privileges, strengthened their corporate status and increased their control over their serfs in exchange for their loyalty to the throne.

● **April 1792** French war against Austria and Prussia

● **August 1792** French monarchy overthrown

● **January 1793** Execution of Louis XVI

● **March 1793** Vendée rebellion begins

● **June 1793** Purge of the Girondins

● **August 1793** *Levée en masse*

● **September–October 1793** Jacobin dictatorship and Reign of Terror begin

● **July 1794** Fall of Robespierre

Conceptions of Enlightened Rule in Germany   In justification of absolute monarchy, eighteenth-century German writers depicted the state as a machine and the ruler as its mainspring. Progress came from sound administration, through an enlightened monarch and well-trained officials. In keeping with this notion, German universities began to train government bureaucrats, and professors offered courses in the science of public finance and administration called *cameralism.*

The orders for the bureaucracy came from the monarchs, who were expected to dedicate themselves to the welfare of their subjects in return for their subjects' obedience. The framework for this command-obedience chain was to be a coherent body of public law, fairly administered by state officials. According to its advocates, this system would produce the rule of law, without the need for a written constitution or a representative parliament. The ruler and his or her officials, following their sense of public responsibility and rational analysis, would ensure the citizens' rights and well-being.

Joseph II and the Limits of Absolutism

Joseph II, coruler of the Habsburg Empire with his mother, Maria Theresa, from 1765 and sole ruler in the 1780s, vigorously promoted reform from above. Unlike Frederick or Catherine, he did not openly identify with the philosophes, and he maintained his own Catholic faith. But Joseph proved to be the most innovative of the century's major rulers as well as one of its most autocratic personalities. It was a problematic combination.

Sound rule for Emperor Joseph involved far more than the customary administrative and financial reform necessary for survival in the competitive state system. With startling boldness he implemented several reforms long advocated by Enlightenment thinkers: freedom of expression, religious toleration, greater state control over the Catholic Church, and legal reform. A new criminal code, for example, reduced the use of the death penalty, ended judicial torture, and allowed for no class differences in the application of the laws. By greatly reducing royal censorship, Joseph made it possible for Vienna to become a major center of literary activity. And we have already noted Joseph's remarkable Edicts of Religious Toleration for Protestants and for Jews. But Joseph's religious policies did not stop there. To make the Catholic Church serve its parishioners better, Joseph forced the clergy to modernize its rituals and services. Most of his Catholic subjects, however, preferred their traditional ways to Joseph's streamlined brand of Catholicism. These "reforms" proved extremely unpopular.

Agrarian Reform   Joseph's most ambitious policies aimed to transform the economic and social position of the peasants. Elsewhere, agrarian reform was generally the weak side of enlightened absolutism, since Frederick II and Catherine II did little to improve the lot of the peasants or serfs in their realms. Joseph, however, set out to eradicate serfdom and to convert Habsburg peasants into free individuals in command of their persons and of the land they cultivated.

By royal decree, Joseph abolished personal servitude and gave peasants the right to move, marry, and enter any trade they wished. He then promulgated laws to secure peasants' control over the land they worked. Finally and most remarkably, he sought to limit the financial obligations of peasant tenants to their lords and to the state. All land was to be surveyed and subject to a uniform tax. Twelve percent of the land's annual yield would go to the state and a maximum of 18 percent would go to the lord. This tax replaced

Joseph II, shown here visiting a peasant's field, actually promulgated his momentous agrarian reform edicts without any significant consultation with the peasants before or after the fact.
Austrian Press & Information Service

previous seigneurial obligations in which peasants owed service to their lord that could consume more than one hundred days of labor a year.

Joseph ordered these reforms in an authoritarian fashion, with little consultation and no consent from any quarter. Predictably, these reforms provoked fierce opposition among the landowning nobles. But they also perplexed most peasants, who already distrusted the government because of its arbitrary religious policies. Joseph made no effort to build support among the peasants by carefully explaining the reforms, let alone by modifying their details after getting feedback from the grass roots.

His arbitrary manner, however, was not incidental. Joseph acknowledged no other way of doing things, no limitation on his own sovereignty. In reaction to the opposition that his reforms aroused, he moved to suppress dissent in the firmest possible way. Not only did he restore censorship in his last years, but he elevated the police department to the status of an imperial ministry and gave it unprecedented powers. By the time he died, in 1790, Joseph was a disillusioned man. His realm resembled a police state, and his successors quickly restored serfdom.

Upheavals in the British Empire

An aggressive monarch, George III, helped ignite political unrest in Great Britain. He was intent on advancing royal authority, but rather than bypass Parliament altogether, he simply tried, as Whig ministers had before him, to control its members through patronage and influence. The Whig aristocrats saw this operation as a threat to their own traditional power. Not only did they oppose the king and his ministers in Parliament, but they enlisted the support of citizens' groups outside of Parliament as well. These organizations were calling for political reform, including representation in Parliament proportionate to population, stricter laws against political corruption, and greater freedom of the press.

"Wilkes and Liberty"   John Wilkes, a member of Parliament and a journalist, became the center of this rising storm. Wilkes viciously attacked the king's prime minister, and by implication the king himself, over the terms of the Treaty of Paris, which ended the Seven Years' War in 1763. The government arrested him for seditious libel on a general warrant. When the courts quashed the indictment, the government then accused Wilkes of having authored a libelous pornographic poem, and this time he fled to France to avoid prison. He stayed in France for four years; but in 1768, still under indictment, he returned to stand once more for Parliament. Three times he was reelected, and three times the House of Commons refused to seat him. With the ardent support of radicals and to the acclaim of crowds in London, who marched to the chant of "Wilkes and Liberty," Wilkes finally took his seat in 1774.

Agitation for parliamentary reform drew support primarily from shopkeepers, artisans, and property owners, who had the franchise in a few districts but were denied it in most others. Thus, even without a right to vote, English citizens could engage in politics and mobilize the power of public opinion, in this case by rallying to Wilkes. Most radicals called only for political reform, not for the overthrow of the British political system. They retained a measure of respect for the nation's political traditions, which ideally guaranteed the rights of "freeborn Englishmen."

The committee that drafted the American Declaration of Independence included John Adams, Thomas Jefferson, and Benjamin Franklin, all shown here standing at the desk.
The Library of Congress

Rebellion in America   Great Britain did face revolutionary action in the thirteen North American colonies. George III and his prime minister, Lord North, attempted to force the colonies to pay the costs, past and present, of their own defense. The policy would have meant an increase in taxes and a centralization of authority in the governance of the British Empire. Colonial landowners, merchants, and artisans of the eastern seaboard organized petitions and boycotts in opposition to the proposed fiscal and constitutional changes.

The resistance in North America differed fundamentally from comparable movements in Europe. American political leaders did not appeal to a body of privileges that the actions of the monarchy were allegedly violating. Instead, they appealed to traditional rights supposedly enjoyed by all British subjects, regardless of status, and to theories of popular sovereignty and natural rights advanced by John Locke and other English libertarian writers. When conciliation and compromise with the British government failed,

the American Declaration of Independence in 1776 gave eloquent expression to those concepts. The lack of a rigid system of estates and hereditary privileges in American society, the fluid boundaries that separated the social strata, and the traditions of local government in the colonies—from town meetings in New England to the elected legislatures that had advised colonial governors—blunted the kinds of conflicts between aristocrats and commoners that derailed incipient revolutionary movements in Ireland, Belgium, and the Dutch Netherlands.

These differences help to explain the unique character of the American rebellion, which was simultaneously a war for independence and a political revolution. The theories that supported the rebellion, and the continuing alliance between social strata, made it the most democratic revolution of the eighteenth century before 1789. The American Revolution created the first state governments, and ultimately a national government, in which the exercise of power was grounded not on royal sovereignty or traditional privilege but on the participation and consent of male citizens (apart from the numerous black slaves, whose status did not change). Even more important as a historical precedent, perhaps, it was the first successful rebellion by overseas colonies against their European masters.

1789: THE FRENCH REVOLUTION

Although the rebellion in America stirred sympathy and interest across the Atlantic, it seemed remote from the realities of Europe. The French Revolution of 1789 proved to be the turning point in European history. Its sheer radicalism, creativity, and claims of universalism made it unique. Its ultimate slogan—"Liberty, Equality, Fraternity"—expressed social and civic ideals that became the foundations of modern Western civilization. In the name of individual liberty, French revolutionaries swept away the institutionalized constraints of the old regime: seigneurial charges upon the land, tax privileges, guild monopolies on commerce, and even (in 1794) black slavery overseas. The revolutionaries held that legitimate governments required written constitutions, elections, and powerful legislatures. They demanded equality before the law for all persons and uniformity of institutions for all regions of the country, denying the claims to special treatment of privileged groups, provinces, towns, or religions. The term *fraternity* expressed a different kind of revolutionary goal. Rousseauist in inspiration, it meant that all citizens, regardless of social class, or region, shared a common fate in society and that the nation's well-being could override the interests of individual citizens.

Origins of the Revolution

Those who made the Revolution believed they were rising against despotic government, in which citizens had no voice, and against inequality and privilege. Yet the government of France at that time was no more tyrannical or unjust than it had been in the past. On the contrary, a process of modest reform had been under way for several decades. What, then, set off the revolutionary upheaval? What had failed in France's long-standing political system?

An easy answer would be to point to the incompetence of King Louis XVI (r. 1774–1792) and his queen, Marie Antoinette. Louis was good-natured but weak and indecisive, a man of limited intelligence who lacked self-confidence and who preferred hunting deer to supervising the business of government. By no stretch of the imagination was he an enlightened absolutist. Worse yet, his young queen, a Habsburg

princess, was frivolous, meddlesome, and tactless. But even the most capable French ruler could not have escaped challenge and unrest in the 1780s.

The Cultural Climate In eighteenth-century France, as we have seen, intellectual ferment preceded political revolt. For decades the philosophes had questioned accepted political and religious beliefs. They undermined confidence that traditional ways were the best ways. But the philosophes harbored deep-seated fears of the uneducated masses and did not question the notion that educated and propertied elites should rule society; they wished only that the elites should be more enlightened and more open to new ideas. Indeed, the Enlightenment had become respectable by the 1770s, a kind of intellectual establishment. Rousseau damned that establishment and wrote of the need for simplicity, sincerity, and virtue, but the word *revolution* never flowed from his pen either.

More subversive perhaps than the writings of Enlightenment intellectuals were several sensational lawsuits centered on the scandalous doings of high aristocrats. The melodramatic legal briefs published by the lawyers in such cases were eagerly snatched up by the reading public along with prohibited "bad books"—the clandestine gossip sheets, libels, exposés, and pornography—discussed earlier. All this material—indirectly, at least—portrayed the French aristocracy as decadent and the monarchy as a ridiculous despotism. Royal officials and philosophes alike regarded the authors of this material as "the excrement of literature," as Voltaire put it. And writers forced to earn their living by turning out such stuff were no doubt embittered at being stuck on the bottom rung in the world of letters. Their resentment would explode once the Revolution began in 1789, and many became radical journalists either for or against the new regime. In itself, however, the "literary underground" of the old regime did not advocate, foresee, or directly cause the Revolution.

Class Conflict? Did the structure of French society, then, provoke the Revolution? Karl Marx, and the many historians inspired by him, certainly believed so. Marx saw the French Revolution as the necessary break marking the transition from the aristocratic feudalism of the Middle Ages to the era of middle-class capitalism. In this view, the French bourgeoisie, or middle classes, had been gaining in wealth during the eighteenth century and resented the privileges of the nobility, which created obstacles to their ambition. Though they framed their ideology in universal terms in 1789, the middle classes led the Revolution in order to change the political and social systems in their own interests.

Three decades of research have rendered this theory of the Revolution's origins untenable. Whether a sizable and coherent capitalist middle class actually existed in eighteenth-century France is questionable. In any case, the leaders of the Revolution in 1789 were lawyers, administrators, and liberal nobles, and rarely merchants or industrialists. Moreover, the barrier between the nobility of the Second Estate and the wealthy and educated members of the Third Estate was porous, the lines of social division frequently (though not always) blurred. Many members of the middle class identified themselves on official documents as "living nobly," as substantial property owners who did not work for a living. Conversely, wealthy nobles often invested in mining, overseas trade, and finance—activities usually associated with the middle classes. Even more important, the gap between the nobility and the middle classes was nothing compared with the gulf that separated both from the working people of town and country. In this revisionist historiography, the bourgeoisie did not make the Revolution so much as the Revolution made the bourgeoisie (see "On the Origins of the French Revolution," p. 588).

Yet numerous disruptive pressures were at work in French society. A growing population left large numbers of young people in town and country struggling to attain a stable place in society. New images and attitudes rippled through the media of the day, despite the state's efforts to censor material it deemed subversive. The nobility, long since banished by Louis XIV from an independent role in government, chafed at its exclusion, although it continued to enjoy a near monopoly on positions in the officer corps. The prosperous middle classes too aspired to a more active role in government. The monarchy struggled to contain these forces within the established social and political systems. Until the 1780s it succeeded, but then its troubles began in earnest.

Fiscal Crisis and Political Deadlock

When he took the throne in 1774, Louis XVI tried to conciliate elite opinion by recalling the parlements, or sovereign law courts, that his grandfather had banished in 1770 for opposing his policies. This concession to France's traditional "unwritten constitution" did not suffice to smooth the new sovereign's road. Louis' new controller-general of finances, Jacques Turgot, encountered a storm of opposition from privileged groups to the reforms he proposed.

The Failure of Reform   Turgot, an ally of the philosophes and an experienced administrator, hoped to encourage economic growth by a policy of nonintervention, or *laissez-faire*, that would give free play to economic markets and allow individuals maximum freedom to pursue their own economic interests. He proposed to remove all restrictions on commerce in grain and to abolish the guilds. In addition, he tried to cut down on expenses at court and to replace the obligation of peasants to work on the royal roads (the *corvée*) with a small new tax on all landholders. Privately, he also considered establishing elected advisory assemblies of landowners to assist in local administration. Vested interests, however, viewed Turgot as a dangerous innovator. When agitation against him mounted in the king's court at Versailles and in the Paris parlement, Louis took the easy way out and dismissed his contentious minister. With Turgot went perhaps the last hope for significant reform in France under royal leadership.

Deficit Financing   The king then turned to Jacques Necker, a banker from Geneva who had a reputation for financial wizardry. Necker had a shrewd sense of public relations. To finance the heavy costs of France's aid to the rebellious British colonies in North America, Necker avoided new taxes and instead floated a series of large loans at exorbitant interest rates as high as 10 percent.

By the 1780s royal finances hovered in a state of permanent crisis. Direct taxes on land, borne mainly by the peasants, were extremely high but were levied inequitably. The great variations in taxation from province to province and the numerous exemptions for privileged groups were regarded by those who benefited from them as traditional liberties. Any attempt to revoke these privileges therefore appeared to be tyrannical. Meanwhile, indirect taxes on commercial activity (customs duties, excise or sales taxes, and royal monopolies on salt and tobacco) hit regressively at consumers, especially in the towns. At the same time, the cycle of borrowing—the alternative to increased taxes—had reached its limits. New loans would only raise the huge interest payments already being paid out. By the 1780s those payments accounted for about half the royal budget and created additional budget deficits each year.

Calonne and the Assembly of Notables   When the king's new controller-general, Charles Calonne, pieced all this information together in 1787, he warned that, contrary to Necker's rosy projections, the monarchy was facing outright bankruptcy. Though no way had yet been found to win public confidence and forge a consensus for fiscal reform, the monarchy could no longer rely on old expedients. Calonne accordingly proposed to establish a new tax, called the *territorial subvention*, to be levied on the yield of all landed property without exemptions. At the same time, he proposed

HISTORICAL ISSUES: ON THE ORIGINS OF THE FRENCH REVOLUTION

A long-held view of the French Revolution's origins attributed the starring role to the middle class, "the rising bourgeoisie." Liberal historians of the nineteenth century regarded the middle class as the carrier of liberal ideals—individual freedom, civil equality, representative government—that finally came to fruition in the French Revolution. Marxists considered the triumph of capitalism to be the pivotal issue in modern history and linked it to the political ascendancy of the middle class in the French Revolution. In a sense, both versions of this "social interpretation" of the French Revolution read its causes back from its results. In his classic synthesis of 1939 embodying the social interpretation, for example, Georges Lefebvre begins with these observations:

"The ultimate cause of the French Revolution of 1789 goes deep into the history of France and of the western world. At the end of the eighteenth century the social structure of France was aristocratic. It showed the traces of having originated at a time when land was almost the only form of wealth, and when the possessors of land were the masters of those who needed it to work and to live. It is true that in the course of age-old struggles the king had been able gradually to deprive the lords of their political powers and subject nobles and clergy to his authority. But he had left them the first place in the social hierarchy.

"Meanwhile the growth of commerce and industry had created, step by step, a new form of wealth, mobile or commercial wealth, and a new class, called in France the bourgeoisie. . . . In the eighteenth century commerce, in-

dustry and finance occupied an increasingly important place in the national economy. It was the bourgeoisie that rescued the royal treasury in moments of crisis. . . . The role of the nobility had correspondingly declined; and the clergy, as the ideal which it proclaimed lost prestige, found its authority growing weaker. These groups preserved the highest rank in the legal structure of the country, but in reality economic power, personal abilities and confidence in the future had passed largely to the bourgeoisie. Such a discrepancy never lasts forever. The Revolution of 1789 restored the harmony between fact and law."

From Georges Lefebvre, *The Coming of the French Revolution*, R. R. Palmer (trans.), Princeton University Press, 1989.

Since the 1950s, revisionist historians have challenged this "social interpretation" of the French Revolution. In his synthesis, William Doyle summarizes some of their research and arguments.

"Money, not privilege, was the key to pre-revolutionary society in France. Wealth transcended all social barriers and bound great nobles and upper bourgeois together into an upper class unified by money. . . . Eighteenth-century capitalism was far from a bourgeois monopoly. One of its basic features was the heavy involvement of nobles. . . . [On the other hand,] the wealth of all social groups in pre-revolutionary France was overwhelmingly non-capitalist in nature. Capitalism had not become the dominant mode of production in the French economy before 1789. . . . there was between most of the nobility and the proprietary sectors of the middle class, a continuity of investment forms and socioeconomic values that made them, economically, a single group.

"If the nobility and the bourgeoisie had so much in common, why did they become such implacable enemies in 1789? [Since] the Revolution could not be explained in economic terms as a clash of opposed interests. . . . it was time to revert to a political explanation of the Revolution's outbreak. The radical reforms of 1789 were products of a political crisis, and not the outcome of long-maturing social and economic trends. [As historian George Taylor concluded:] 'It was essentially a political revolution with social consequences and not a social revolution with political consequences.' "

From William Doyle, *Origins of the French Revolution*, Oxford University Press, 1988.

to convene *provincial assemblies* elected by large landowners to advise royal officials on the collection and allocation of revenues.

Certain that the parlements would reject this scheme, Calonne convinced the king to convene an Assembly of Notables, comprising about 150 influential men, mainly but not exclusively from the aristocracy, who might more easily be persuaded to support the re-

forms. To Calonne's shock, the Assembly of Notables refused to endorse the proposed decrees. Instead, they denounced the lavish spending of the court and insisted on auditing the monarchy's financial accounts. Moreover, when the government now submitted Calonne's proposals to the parlement, it not only rejected them but demanded that Louis convene the **Estates General,** a body representing the clergy, nobility, and Third

Estate, which had not met since 1614. Louis responded by sending the members of the parlements into exile. But a huge outcry in Paris and in the provinces against this arbitrary act forced the king to back down: After all, the whole purpose of Calonne's proposals had been to build public confidence in the government.

Facing bankruptcy and unable to float new loans in this atmosphere, the king recalled the parlements, reappointed Necker, and agreed to convene the Estates General in May 1789. In the opinion of the English writer Arthur Young, who was visiting France, the kingdom was "on the verge of a revolution, but one likely to add to the scale of the nobility and clergy." The aristocracy's determined opposition was putting an end to absolutism in France. But it was not clear what would take its place.

From the Estates General to the National Assembly

The calling of the Estates General in 1789 created extraordinary excitement across the land. The king invited his subjects to express their opinions about this great event, and thousands did so in pamphlet form. Here the "patriot," or liberal, ideology first took shape. Self-styled patriots came from the ranks of the nobility and clergy as well as from the middle classes; they opposed traditionalists, whom they labeled as "aristocrats." Their top priority was the method of voting to be used in the Estates General. While the king accorded the Third Estate twice as many delegates as the two higher orders, he refused to promise that the deputies would all vote together (by head) rather than separately in three chambers (by order). Voting by order would mean that the two upper chambers would outweigh the Third Estate no matter how many deputies it had. Patriots had hoped that the lines dividing the nobility from the middle class would crumble in a common effort by France's elites at reform. Instead, it appeared as if the Estates General might sharpen the lines of separation between the orders.

The Critique of Privilege   It did not matter that the nobility had led the fight against absolutism. Even if they endorsed new constitutional checks on absolutism and accepted equality in the allocation of taxes, nobles would still hold vastly disproportionate powers if the Estates General voted by order. In the most influential pamphlet about the Estates General, Emmanuel Sieyès posed the question, "What is the Third Estate?" and answered flatly, "Everything." "And what has it been until now in the political order?" he asked. Answer: "Nothing." The nobility, he claimed, monopolized all the lucrative positions in society while doing little of its productive work. In the manifestos of Sieyès

THE AWAKENING OF THE THIRD ESTATE
Thousands of pamphlets discussed the calling of the Estates General in 1789, but the grievances of the Third Estate translated most readily into vivid imagery and caricature.
Roger-Viollet/Bibliothèque Nationale de France, Paris

and other patriots, the enemy was no longer simply absolutism but privilege as well.

Unlike reformers in England or the American revolutionaries of 1776, the French patriots did not simply claim that the king had violated historic traditions of liberty. Rather, they contemplated a complete break with a discredited past. As a basis for reform, they would substitute reason for tradition. It is this frame of mind that made the French Revolution so radical.

Cahiers and Elections   For the moment, however, patriot spokesmen stood far in advance of opinion at the grass roots. The king had invited all citizens to meet in their local parishes to elect delegates to district electoral assemblies and to draft grievance petitions (**cahiers**) setting forth their views. The great majority of rural cahiers were highly traditional in tone and complained only of particular local ills or high taxes, expressing confidence that the king would redress them. Only a few cahiers from cities like Paris invoked concepts of natural rights and popular sovereignty or demanded that France must have a written constitution, that sovereignty belonged to the nation, or that feudalism and regional privileges should be abolished. It is impossible, in other words, to read in the cahiers the future course of the Revolution. Still, these gatherings of citizens promoted reflection on France's problems and encouraged expectations for change. They thereby raised the nation's political consciousness.

So too did the local elections, whose royal ground rules were remarkably democratic. Virtually every

When the king opened the meeting of the Estates General, the deputies for each estate were directed to sit in three separate sections of the hall.
Bulloz/© Photo RMN/Art Resource, NY

adult male taxpayer was eligible to vote for electors, who, in turn, met in district assemblies to choose representatives of the Third Estate to the Estates General. The electoral assemblies were a kind of political seminar, where articulate local leaders emerged to be sent by their fellow citizens as deputies to Versailles. Most of these deputies were lawyers or officials, without a single peasant or artisan among them. In the elections for the First Estate, meanwhile, parish priests rather than Church notables formed a majority of the deputies. And in the elections for the Second Estate, about one-third of the deputies could be described as liberal nobles or patriots, the rest traditionalists.

Deadlock and Revolution   Popular expectation that the monarchy would provide leadership in reform proved to be ill-founded. When the deputies to the Estates General met on May 5, Necker and Louis XVI spoke to them only in generalities and left unsettled whether the estates would vote by order or by head. The upper two estates proceeded to organize their own chambers, but the deputies of the Third Estate balked. Vainly inviting the others to join them, the Third Estate took a decisive revolutionary step on June 17 by proclaiming that it formed a "National Assembly." A few days later more than a third of the deputies from

the clergy joined them. The king, on the other hand, decided to cast his lot with the nobility and locked the Third Estate out of its meeting hall until he could present his own program. But the deputies moved to an indoor tennis court and swore that they would not separate until they had given France a constitution.

The king ignored this act of defiance and addressed the delegates of all three orders on June 23. He promised equality in taxation, civil liberties, and regular meetings of the Estates General at which, however, voting would be by order. France would be provided with a constitution, he pledged, "but the ancient distinction of the three orders will be conserved in its entirety." He then ordered the three estates to retire to their individual meeting halls, but the Third Estate refused to move. "The assembled nation cannot receive orders," declared its spokesman. Startled by the determination of the patriots, the king backed down. For the time being, he recognized the National Assembly and ordered deputies from all three estates to join it.

Thus, the French Revolution began as a nonviolent, "legal" revolution. By their own will, delegates elected by France's three estates to represent their own districts to the king became instead the representatives of the entire nation. As such, they claimed to be the sovereign power in France—a claim that the king now

Jacques-Louis David
OATH OF THE TENNIS COURT, THE 20TH OF JUNE, 1789
Jacques-Louis David's depiction of the Tennis Court Oath, one of the great historical paintings, captures the deputies' sense of idealism and purpose.
Giraudon/Art Resource, NY

seemed powerless to contest. In fact, however, he was merely biding his time until he could deploy his army to subdue the capital and overwhelm the deputies at Versailles. The king ordered twenty thousand royal troops into the Paris region, due to arrive sometime in July.

The Convergence of Revolutions

The political struggle at Versailles was not occurring in isolation. The mass of French citizens, politically aroused by elections to the Estates General, was also mobilizing over subsistence issues. The winter and spring of 1788–1789 had brought severe economic difficulties, as crop failures and grain shortages almost doubled the price of flour and bread on which the population depended for subsistence. Unemployed vagrants filled the roads, angry consumers stormed grain convoys and marketplaces, and relations between town and country grew tense. Economic anxieties merged with rage over the obstructive behavior of aristocrats in Versailles. Parisians believed that food shortages and royal troops would be used to intimidate the people

into submission. They feared an "aristocratic plot" against the National Assembly and the patriot cause.

The Fall of the Bastille   When the king dismissed Necker on July 11, Parisians correctly assumed that a counterrevolution was about to begin. They prepared to resist, and most of the king's military units pulled back in the face of determined crowds. On July 14 Parisian crowds searching for weapons and ammunition laid siege to the **Bastille,** an old fortress that had once served as a royal prison and in which gunpowder was stored. The small garrison resisted, and a fierce firefight erupted. Although the troops soon capitulated, dozens of citizens were hit, providing the first martyrs of the Revolution, and the infuriated crowd massacred several soldiers as they left the fortress. Meanwhile, patriot electors ousted royal officials of the Paris city government, replaced them with a revolutionary municipality, and organized a citizens' militia to patrol the city. Similar municipal revolutions occurred in twenty-six of the thirty largest French cities, thus ensuring that the defiance in the capital would not be an isolated act.

THE STORMING OF THE BASTILLE
The fall of the Bastille was understood at the time to be a great turning point in history, and July 14 eventually became the French national holiday. Numerous prints and paintings evoke the daunting qualities of the fortress, the determination of the besieging crowd, and the valor of individuals in that crowd.
Bulloz/© Photo RMN/Art Resource, NY

The Parisian insurrection of July 14 not only saved the National Assembly but altered the Revolution's course by giving it a far more popular dimension. Again the king capitulated. He traveled to Paris on July 17 and, to please the people, donned a ribbon bearing three colors: white for the monarchy and blue and red for the capital. This *tricolor* would become the emblem of the new regime.

Peasant Revolts and the August 4 Decree These events did not pacify the anxious and hungry people of the countryside. Peasants had numerous and long-standing grievances. Population growth and the parceling of holdings reduced the margin of subsistence for many families, while the purchase of land by rich townspeople further shrank their opportunities for economic advancement. Seigneurial dues and church tithes weighed heavily on many peasants. Now, in addition, suspicions were rampant that nobles were

hoarding grain in order to stymie the patriotic cause. In July peasants in several regions sacked the houses of the nobles and burned the documents that recorded their seigneurial obligations.

This peasant insurgency blended into a vast movement known to historians as "the Great Fear." Rumors abounded that the vagrants who swarmed through the countryside were actually "brigands" in the pay of nobles, who were marching on villages to destroy the new harvest and cow the peasants into submission. The fear was baseless, but it stirred up the peasants' hatred and suspicion of the nobles, prompted armed mobilizations in hundreds of villages, and set off new attacks on manor houses.

Peasant revolts worried the deputies of the National Assembly, but they decided to appease the peasants rather than simply denounce their violence. On the night of August 4, therefore, certain deputies of the nobility and clergy dramatically renounced their ancient privileges. This action set the stage for the Assembly to decree "the abolition of feudalism" as well as the end of the church tithe, the sale of royal offices, regional tax privileges, and social privilege of all kinds. Later, it is true, the Assembly clarified the August 4 decree to ensure that property rights were maintained. While personal servitudes such as hunting rights, manorial justice, and labor services were suppressed outright, the Assembly decreed that most seigneurial dues would end only after the peasants had paid compensation to their lords. Peasants resented this onerous requirement, and most simply refused to pay the dues; pressure built until all seigneurial dues were finally abolished without compensation by a more radical government in 1793.

THE RECONSTRUCTION OF FRANCE

The summer of 1789 had seen a remarkable sequence of unprecedented events. A bloodless, juridical revolution from above (engineered by the patriot deputies to the Estates General) combined with popular mobilization from below in town and country made the French Revolution seem irresistible. After the clearing operations of August 4, the National Assembly set out not simply to enact reforms but to reconstruct French institutions on entirely new principles. With sovereignty wrested from the king and vested in the people's deputies, no aspect of France's social or political system was immune to scrutiny, not even slavery in the colonies. First, the Assembly adopted a set of general principles known as the Declaration of the Rights of Man and Citizen. Then it proceeded to draft a constitution, settle the question of voting rights (where the issue of women's citizenship first came up), reorganize the structures of public life, and determine the future of the Catholic clergy. None of this occurred without intense disagreement, especially over the religious issue and the role of the king. Moreover, Austria and Prussia eventually decided on armed intervention against revolutionary France. In 1792 war broke out, which led directly to the fall of the monarchy and to a new, violent turn in the Revolution.

The Declaration of the Rights of Man and Citizen

By sweeping away the old web of privileges, the August 4 decree permitted the Assembly to construct a new regime. Since it would take months to draft a constitution, the Assembly drew up a Declaration of the Rights of Man and Citizen to indicate its intentions (see "Two Views of the Rights of Man," p. 594). The Declaration was the death certificate of the old regime and a rally-

ing point for the future. It affirmed individual liberties but also set forth the basic obligation of citizenship: obedience to legitimate law. The Declaration enumerated **natural rights,** such as freedom of expression and freedom of religious conscience, but (unlike the America Bill of Rights) stipulated that even these rights could be circumscribed by law. It proclaimed the sovereignty of the nation and sketched the basic criteria for a legitimate government, such as representation and the separation of powers. The Declaration's concept of natural rights meant that the new regime would be based on the principles of reason rather than history or tradition.

In his *Reflections on the Revolution in France*, published in 1790, the Anglo-Irish statesman Edmund Burke condemned this attitude, as well as the violence of 1789. In this influential counterrevolutionary tract, Burke argued that France had passed from despotism to anarchy in the name of misguided, abstract principles. Burke distrusted the simplicity of reason that the Assembly celebrated. In his view, the complexity of traditional institutions served the public interest. Burke attacked the belief in natural rights that guided the revolutionaries; something was natural, he believed, only if it resulted from long historical development and habit. Trying to wipe the slate of history clean was a grievous error, he wrote, since society "is a contract between the dead, the living, and the unborn." Society's main right, in Burke's view, was the right to be well-governed by its rulers. Naturally this argument did not go unchallenged, even in England. Mary Wollstonecraft countered with *A Vindication of the Rights of Man*, followed shortly by her seminal *Vindication of the Rights of Woman*, while Thomas Paine published *The Rights of Man* in 1792 to refute Burke.

The New Constitution

Representative Government   From 1789 to 1791, the National Assembly acted as a Constituent Assembly to produce a constitution for France. While proclaiming equal civil rights for all French citizens, it effectively transferred political power from the monarchy and the privileged estates to the body of propertied citizens; in 1790 nobles lost their titles and became indistinguishable from other citizens. The new constitution created a limited monarchy with a clear separation of powers. Sovereignty effectively resided in the representatives of the people, a single-house legislature to be elected by a system of indirect voting. The king was to name and dismiss his ministers, but he was given only a suspensive or delaying veto over legislation; if a bill passed the Assembly in three successive years, it would become law even without royal approval.

TWO VIEWS OF THE RIGHTS OF MAN

The radical theoretical and practical implications of French revolutionary ideology are suggested in a comparison of two essentially contemporaneous documents. The Prussian General Code, a codification initiated by Frederick the Great and issued in its final form in 1791 after his death, reinforced the traditional prerogatives of the nobility under an umbrella of public law. The French National Assembly's Declaration of the Rights of Man and Citizen (1789) established the principle of civil equality alongside the doctrines of national sovereignty, representation, and the rule of law. While the Prussian General Code exemplifies the old order against which French revolutionary ideology took aim, the Declaration became a foundational document of the liberal tradition.

EXCERPTS FROM THE PRUSSIAN GENERAL CODE, 1791

- This general code contains the provisions by which the rights and obligations of inhabitants of the state, so far as they are not determined by particular laws, are to be judged.
- The rights of a man arise from his birth, from his estate, and from actions and arrangements with which the laws have associated a certain determinate effect.
- The general rights of man are grounded on the natural liberty to seek and further his own welfare, without injury to the rights of another.
- Persons to whom, by their birth, destination or principal occupation, equal rights are ascribed in civil society, make up together an *estate* of the state.
- The nobility, as the first estate in the state, most especially bears the obligation, by its distinctive destination, to maintain the defense of the state. . . .
- The nobleman has an especial right to places of honor in the state for which he has made himself fit.
- Only the nobleman has the right to possess noble property.
- Persons of the burgher [middle-class] estate cannot own noble property except by permission of the sovereign.
- Noblemen shall normally engage in no burgher livelihood or occupation.

From R. R. Palmer (trans.), *The Age of Democratic Revolution*, Princeton University Press, 1959, pp. 510–511.

EXCERPTS FROM THE FRENCH DECLARATION OF THE RIGHTS OF MAN AND CITIZEN, 1789

1. Men are born and remain free and equal in rights. Social distinctions may be based only on common utility.
3. The principle of all sovereignty rests essentially in the nation. No body and no individual may exercise authority which does not emanate expressly from the nation.
4. Liberty consists in the ability to do whatever does not harm another; hence the exercise of the natural rights of each man has no limits except those which assure to other members of society the enjoyment of the same rights. These limits can only be determined by law.
6. Law is the expression of the general will. All citizens have the right to take part, in person or by their representatives, in its formation. It must be the same for all whether it protects or penalizes. All citizens being equal in its eyes are equally admissible to all public dignities, offices and employments, according to their capacity, and with no other distinction than that of their virtues and talents.
13. For maintenance of public forces and for expenses of administration common taxation is necessary. It should be apportioned equally among all citizens according to their capacity to pay.
14. All citizens have the right, by themselves or through their representatives, to have demonstrated to them the necessity of public taxes, to consent to them freely, to follow the use made of the proceeds, and to determine the shares to be paid, the means of assessment and collection and the duration.

Under the French Constitution of 1791, every adult male of settled domicile who satisfied minimal tax-paying requirements (roughly two-thirds of all adult males) gained the right to vote, with a higher qualification needed to serve as an elector. Although it favored the propertied, France's new political system was vastly more democratic than Britain's. Still, the National Assembly considered the vote to be a civic function rather than a natural right. "Those who contribute nothing to the public establishment should have no direct influence on government," declared Sieyès. In the same frame of mind the Assembly excluded all women from voting.

Women in the Revolution That the Assembly even debated political rights for women testifies to the potential universalism of the Revolution's principles. A brief but spirited drive for women's suffrage advanced through pamphlets, petitions, and deputations to the Assembly—most notably the "Declaration of the Rights of Women" (1791) drafted by the playwright Olympe de Gouges. But the notion of gender difference

In October 1789 Parisian women were furious over the high cost of bread and suspicious of the king and queen. In concert with the National Guard, they set out on an armed march to confront the royal couple in Versailles. To appease the menacing crowd, Louis XVI agreed to return to Paris and to cooperate with revolutionary authorities.
Giraudon/Art Resource, NY

and separate spheres, popularized by Rousseau, easily prevailed. The great majority of deputies believed women to be too emotional. Too easily influenced to be independent, they must be excluded from the new public sphere—the more so because of the deputies' belief that elite women had used their sexual powers nefariously behind the scenes during the old regime to influence public policy. Now public life would be virtuous and transparent, uninfluenced by feminine wiles. Instead, women would devote themselves to their crucial nurturing and maternal roles in the domestic sphere.

This type of discourse has prompted some feminist scholars to claim that the revolutionary public sphere "was constructed not merely without women but against them." Balanced against this argument, however, is an offsetting consideration. Male revolutionaries may have distrusted women, and some were overt misogynists, yet their own ideology and political culture created unprecedented public space for women. True, women could not vote or hold office, but otherwise *citoyennes* had extensive opportunity for political participation. Women actively engaged in local conflicts over the Assembly's religious policy (discussed later in this chapter). In the towns they agitated over

food prices, and in October 1789 Parisian women led a mass demonstration to Versailles that forcibly returned the king and queen to Paris. Combining traditional concerns over food scarcities with antiaristocratic revolutionary ideology, women frequently goaded authorities like the national guard into action.

In unprecedented numbers women also took up the pen to publish pamphlets and journals. Their physical presence in public spaces was even more important. Women helped fill the galleries of the Assembly, of the Paris Jacobin Club, and later of the Revolutionary Tribunal—shouting approval or disapproval and in general monitoring their officials. In at least sixty towns women formed auxiliaries to the local Jacobin club, where they read newspapers, debated political issues, and participated in revolutionary festivals.

Nor did Rousseauian antifeminism prevent the revolutionaries from enacting dramatic advances in the civil status of women. Legislation between 1789 and 1794 created a more equitable family life by curbing paternal powers over children, lowering the age of majority, and equalizing the status of husbands and wives in regard to property. Viewing marriage as a contract between a free man and a free woman, the revolutionaries

MAP 20.1 REDIVIDING THE NATION'S TERRITORY IN 1789
The old regime provinces (left) were replaced by revolutionary departments (right). What advantages did this change bring for the French state?
◆ For an online version, go to www.mhhe.com/chambers9 > chapter 20 > book maps

provided the right of divorce to either spouse should the marriage go sour. A remarkably egalitarian inheritance law stipulated that daughters as well as sons were entitled to an equal share of a family's estate. Finally, in the domain of education—central to the feminist vision of Mary Wollstonecraft that the French Revolution had crystalized—an unprecedented system of universal and free primary schooling in 1794 extended to girls as well as boys and provided for state-salaried teachers of both sexes.

Race and Slavery As the Assembly excluded women from voting citizenship without much debate, other groups posed challenges on how to apply "the rights of man" to French society. In eastern France, where most of France's forty thousand Jews resided amid discrimination, public opinion scorned them as an alien race not entitled to citizenship. Eventually, however, the Assembly rejected that argument and extended civil and political equality to Jews. A similar debate raged over the status of the free Negroes and mulattoes in France's Caribbean colonies. White planters, in alliance with the merchants who traded with the islands, were intent on preserving slavery and demanded local control over the islands' racial policy as their best defense. The planters argued that they could not maintain slavery, which was manifestly based on race, unless free people of color were disenfranchised.

When the Assembly accepted this view, the mulattoes rebelled. But their abortive uprising had the unintended consequence of helping ignite a slave rebellion. Led by Toussaint-L'Ouverture, the blacks turned violently on their white masters and proclaimed the independence of the colony, which became known as Haiti. In 1794 the French revolutionary government abolished slavery in all French colonies. (For further discussion see "The Fight for Liberty and Equality in Saint-Domingue," p. 598.)

Unifying the Nation Within France the Assembly obliterated the political identities of the country's historic provinces and instead divided the nation's territory into eighty-three departments of roughly equal size (see map 20.1). Unlike the old provinces, each new department was to have exactly the same institutions. The departments were, in turn, subdivided into districts, cantons, and communes (the common designation for a village or town). On the one hand, this administrative transformation promoted local autonomy: The citizens of each department, district, and commune elected their own local officials, and in that sense political power was decentralized. On the other hand, these local governments were subordinated to the national legislature in Paris and became instruments for promoting national integration and uniformity.

The new administrative map also created the boundaries for a new judicial system. Sweeping away the parlements and law courts of the old regime, the revolutionaries established a justice of the peace in each canton, a civil court in each district, and a criminal court in each department. The judges on all tribunals were to be elected. The Assembly rejected the use of juries in civil cases but decreed that felonies would be tried by juries; also, criminal defendants for the first time gained the right to counsel. In civil law, the Assembly encouraged arbitration and mediation to avoid the time-consuming and expensive processes of formal litigation. In general, the revolutionaries hoped to make the administration of justice faster and more accessible.

Economic Individualism   The Assembly's clearing operations extended to economic institutions as well. Guided by the dogmas of laissez-faire theory and by its uncompromising hostility to privileged corporations, the Assembly sought to open up economic life to individual initiative, much as Turgot had attempted in the 1770s. Besides dismantling internal tariffs and chartered trading monopolies, it abolished merchants' and artisans' guilds and proclaimed the right of every citizen to enter any trade and conduct it freely. The government would no longer concern itself with regulating wages or the quality of goods. The Assembly also insisted that workers bargain in the economic marketplace as individuals, and it therefore banned workers' associations and strikes. The precepts of economic individualism extended to the countryside as well. At least in theory, peasants and landlords were free to cultivate their fields as they saw fit, regardless of traditional collective practices. In fact, those deep-rooted communal restraints proved to be extremely resistant to change.

The Revolution and the Church

To address the state's financial problems, the National Assembly acted in a way that the monarchy had never dared contemplate. Under revolutionary ideology, the French Catholic Church could no longer exist as an independent corporation—as a separate estate within the state. The Assembly, therefore, nationalized Church property (about 10 percent of the land in France), placing it "at the disposition of the nation," and made the state responsible for the upkeep of the Church. It then issued paper notes called **assignats,** which were backed by the value of these "national lands." The property was to be sold by auction at the district capitals to the highest bidders. This plan favored the bourgeois and rich peasants with ready capital and made it difficult for needy peasants to acquire the land, though some pooled their resources to do so.

The sale of Church lands and the issuance of assignats had several consequences. In the short run, they eliminated the need for new borrowing. Second, the hundreds of thousands of purchasers gained a strong vested interest in the Revolution, since a successful counterrevolution was likely to reclaim their properties for the Church. Finally, after war broke out with an Austrian-Prussian coalition in 1792, the government made the assignats a national currency and printed a volume of assignats way beyond their underlying value in land, thereby touching off severe inflation and new political turmoil.

Religious Schism   The issue of Church reform produced the Revolution's first and most fateful crisis. The Assembly intended to rid the Church of inequities that enriched the aristocratic prelates of the old regime. Many Catholics looked forward to such healthy changes that might bring the clergy closer to the people. In the **Civil Constitution of the Clergy** (1790), the Assembly reduced the number of bishops from 130 to 83 and reshaped diocesan boundaries to conform exactly with those of the new departments. Bishops and parish priests were to be chosen by the electoral assemblies in the departments and districts and were to be paid according to a uniform salary scale that favored those currently at the lower end. Like all other public officials, the clergy was to take an oath of loyalty to the constitution.

The clergy generally opposed the Civil Constitution because it had been dictated to them by the National Assembly; they argued that such questions as the selection of bishops and priests should be negotiated either with the Pope or with a National Church Council. But the Assembly asserted that it had the sovereign power to order such reforms, since they affected temporal rather than spiritual matters. In November 1790 the Assembly demanded that all clergy take the loyalty oath forthwith; those who refused would lose their positions and be pensioned off. In all of France only seven bishops and about 54 percent of the parish clergy swore the oath; but in the west of France only 15 percent of the priests complied. A schism tore through French Catholicism, since the laity had to take a position as well: Should parishioners remain loyal to their priests who had refused to take the oath (the nonjuring, or refractory, clergy) and thus be at odds with the state? Or should they accept the unfamiliar "constitutional clergy" designated by the districts to replace their own priests?

The Assembly's effort to impose reform in defiance of religious sensibilities and Church autonomy was a grave tactical error. The oath crisis polarized the nation. It seemed to link the Revolution with impiety and the Church with counterrevolution. In local

Global Moment

THE FIGHT FOR LIBERTY AND EQUALITY IN SAINT-DOMINGUE

The French colony Saint-Domingue shared the Caribbean island of Hispaniola with Spain's colony, Santo Domingo (today's Dominican Republic). The crown jewel of France's colonial empire, Saint-Domingue was responsible for about two-fifths of its overseas trade. Worked by about 500,000 slaves from Africa, its 8,000 plantations produced half of all the sugar consumed in continental Europe and the Americas. In the decade before the French Revolution, 30,000 to 40,000 new slaves had to be imported from Africa annually, to compensate for the loss of life from the brutal regimen of slavery on the plantations.

Forty thousand white people (including planters, tradesmen, and soldiers) inhabited this colony alongside the 500,000 black slaves and 30,000 free people of color—freed slaves and their descendants, who often intermarried with whites. Many of these free coloreds managed or possessed estates and slaves of their own. By the 1789s, however, the colony's white authorities were subjecting free people of color to stringent racial laws barring them from the professions and positions in the armed forces, and restricting them to wearing certain types of dress.

The outbreak of the French Revolution in 1789 had a profoundly unsettling effect on the island. While the revolutionaries fought for the principles of liberty, equality, and fraternity in Europe, the members of the National Assembly rebuffed similar demands from delegates of Saint-Domingue's people of color. Racial laws, the Assembly insisted, were a local matter for white planters and merchants, and revolutionary principles did not apply across the color line. In their view, plantation slavery contributed to French economic prosperity, and the maintenance of slavery depended on white supremacy. The Assembly gave in to pressure from the white colonial lobby in the belief that this alone would keep Saint-Domingue under French control.

Thwarted in Paris, the free colored people attempted to achieved liberation by force of arms, which the colony's whites, rich and poor alike, repelled. Neither side realized that a restive slave population was about to seize the initiative itself. In November 1791 thousands of slaves in the north of the colony rose up, setting fire to over a thousand plantations and massacring hundreds of whites. Still, as the free people of color and whites continued their own battle, each side began to recruit slaves as their foot soldiers. Finally, in April 1792 a more liberal Legislature in Paris granted members of the free colored community full French citizenship. Furious at this decision, royalist planters (who soon heard that the king himself had been overthrown) were ready to break free of France, its new Republic, and its new emissary to Saint-Domingue, a man named L.-F. Sonthonax. The son of a French planter, Sonthonax had risen through the ranks of the French Revolution. His main supporters on the island were the free people of color.

To complicate matters, in 1793 Britain and Spain declared war on France, and each sent military forces to wrest Saint-Domingue from the French. Sonthonax now had another fight on his hands. In return for their service as French soldiers, he freed many slaves, and in August 1793 he proclaimed the abolition of slavery in Saint-Domingue. This move then spurred abolitionist sentiment in the National Convention. In an historic decree of February 1794 it abolished slavery in all French colonies—a radical expansion of democratic ideals with enormous implications for the rest of the Atlantic world.

But the story does not end there. If the decrees of the Convention and its commissioner abolished slavery in Saint-Domingue, only the rebellion of the island's slaves and their continued fight for freedom under a forceful leader made emancipation permanent. That leader, Toussaint (1743–1803), was born on the island into slavery and served as a coachman on the Bréda sugar plantation until he was freed sometime in the 1770s. A man with great military aptitude, in 1793 he

Rebellious slaves in pitched battle with French soldiers on Saint-Domingue.
Bettmann/Corbis

joined the Spanish forces and earned the nickname *L'Ouverture* ("the opening") because "he could make an opening anywhere" in the French defenses. But in 1794 he changed sides, organized a new army for the French out of freed slaves, and led his troops into battles that eventually pushed out the Spanish and the British forces. By the time the British left in 1798, Toussaint had eliminated other political rivals to emerge as the supreme authority in the colony. Supporting emancipation, Toussaint proclaimed: "I want liberty and equality to reign in Saint-Domingue." To keep the economy and his army afloat, however, Toussaint reinstated the plantation system of cultivation, and used his army to impose forced labor and corporal punishment. In the constitution he promulgated in 1801, he made himself governor for life with the right to choose his successor.

By that time things had changed dramatically in France as well. Napoleon Bonaparte sought to regain full control of the colony. Toussaint L'Ouverture led the fight against the invading French army, but one of his own generals, J.-J. Dessalines, betrayed him. In June 1802 the first black leader in the Western world was handed over to French troops and sent to France, where he soon died in prison. Around that time news arrived that Bonaparte intended to restore slavery. Large numbers of former slaves and free coloreds joined the remnants of Toussaint's army, now led by Dessalines, who exhorted his troops to "burn houses, cut off heads"— brutality that the French returned in kind. Decimated by fever, however, and unable to receive reinforcements or supplies because of an English naval blockade, the remaining French force withdrew in 1804, and Dessalines declared full independence from France. To symbolize this dramatic break, he renamed his country Haiti, a term used on the island before the French had arrived.

continued

"I have given the French cannibals blood for blood," Dessalines declared; "I have avenged America."

The repercussions of the Haitian revolution spread throughout the Americas. The loss of life and property in the Haitian upheaval encouraged plantation societies elsewhere to reinforce their grip on slave labor. Cuba, Brazil, and the Southern United States tightened their slave and race codes, making it more difficult to free slaves and restricting free people of color. Napoleonic France restored slavery in Guadeloupe, another French colony in the Caribbean. Scorned or ignored by other governments and commercial interests, Haiti became an isolated backwater until the twentieth century.

But the Haitian slave rebellion also stimulated antislavery movements. Abolitionists in Britain and the United States argued that unless their governments moved toward gradual emancipation, similar violence would occur in British colonies and the American South. A reenergized British antislavery movement finally convinced Parliament to abolish the African slave trade in 1807. In the United States, New York and New Jersey passed emancipation laws, although similar legislation had failed in those states in the 1780s.

Despite the bitterness and bloodshed, the events in Haiti shook the rationale for slavery in the Atlantic world. The National Convention's pioneering decree of 1794 established emancipation as a legitimate goal of any democratic society. (It was France's democratic Second Republic of 1848 that definitively abolished slavery in all French colonies.) More fundamentally the Haitian revolution demonstrated the fervent desire of black slaves for freedom. Haiti's independence became irrefutable proof that slavery was not a natural condition for blacks; already in 1791, news of the uprising inspired Jamaican slave songs, and whites throughout the West Indies and North America noticed a growing insolence among the black population. In subsequent insurrections in Havana and Charleston, black militants tried to imitate the actions of Toussaint L'Ouverture and other leaders of the revolt. Haiti provided millions of blacks with a sense of identity apart from that of slave, and a ray of inspiration for their own liberation.

communities, refractory clergy began to preach against the entire Revolution. Local officials fought back by arresting them and demanding repressive laws. Civil strife rocked hundreds of communities.

Counterrevolution, Radicalism, and War

The King's Flight   Opposition to the Revolution had actually begun much earlier. After July 14 some of the king's relatives had left the country in disgust, thus becoming the first émigrés, or political exiles, of the Revolution. During the next three years, thousands of nobles, including two-thirds of the royal army's officer corps, joined the emigration. Across the Rhine River in Coblenz, émigrés formed an army that threatened to overthrow the new regime at the first opportunity. The king himself publicly submitted to the Revolution, but privately he smoldered in resentment. Finally, in June 1791, Louis and his family fled in secret from Paris, hoping to cross the Belgian frontier and enlist the aid of Austria. But Louis was stopped at the French village of Varennes and was forcibly returned to Paris.

Moderates hoped that this aborted escape would finally end the king's opposition to the Revolution. The Assembly, after all, needed his cooperation to make its constitutional monarchy viable. It did not wish to open the door to a republic or to further unrest. Radicals such as the journalist Jean-Paul Marat, on the other hand, had long thundered against the treachery of the king and the émigrés and against the Assembly itself for not acting vigorously against aristocrats and counterrevolutionaries. But the Assembly was determined to maintain the status quo and adopted the fiction that the king had been kidnapped. The Assembly reaffirmed the king's place in the new regime, but Louis' treasonous flight to Varennes ensured that radical agitation would continue.

The Outbreak of War   When the newly elected Legislative Assembly convened on October 1, 1791, the questions of counterrevolution at home and the prospect of war abroad dominated its stormy sessions. Both the right and the left saw advantages to be gained in a war between France and Austria. The king and his court hoped that a military defeat would discredit the new regime and restore full power to the monarchy. Most members of the **Jacobin Club**—the leading radical political club in Paris—wanted war to strike down the foreign supporters of the émigrés along with domestic counterrevolutionaries.

When Francis II ascended the throne of the Habsburg monarchy in March 1792, the stage was set for war. Unlike his father, Leopold, who had rejected intervention in France's affairs, Francis fell under the influence of émigrés and bellicose advisers. He was determined to assist the French queen, his aunt, and he also expected to make territorial gains. With both sides thus eager for battle, France went to war in April 1792 against a coalition of Austria, Prussia, and the émigrés.

Each camp expected rapid victory, but both were deceived. The French offensive quickly faltered, and invading armies soon crossed France's borders. The Legislative Assembly ordered the arrest of refractory clergy and called for a special corps of twenty thousand national guardsmen to protect Paris. Louis vetoed both measures and held to his decisions in spite of demonstrations against them in the capital. For all practical purposes, these vetoes were his last acts as king. The legislature also called for one hundred thousand volunteers to bolster the French army and defend the homeland.

The Fall of the Monarchy   As Prussian forces began a drive toward Paris, their commander, the Duke of Brunswick, rashly threatened to level the city if it resisted or if it harmed the royal family. When Louis XVI published this Brunswick Manifesto, it seemed proof that he was in league with the enemy. Far from intimidating the revolutionaries, the threat drove them forward. Since a divided Legislative Assembly refused to act decisively in the face of royal obstructionism, Parisian militants, spurred on by the Jacobin Club, organized an insurrection.

On August 10, 1792, a crowd of armed Parisians stormed the royal palace at the Tuileries, literally driving the king from the throne. The Assembly then had no choice but to declare Louis XVI suspended. That night more than half the Assembly's members themselves fled Paris, making it clear that the Assembly too had lost its legitimacy. The deputies who remained ordered elections for a National Convention to decide the king's fate, to draft a republican constitution, and to govern France during the current emergency. What the events of 1789 in Versailles and Paris had begun, the insurrection of August 10, 1792,

completed. The old regime in France had truly been destroyed.

THE SECOND REVOLUTION

By 1792—just three years after the fall of the Bastille—the Revolution had profoundly altered the foundations of government and society in France. The National Assembly introduced constitutional government, legislative representation, and a degree of local self-government. It repudiated absolutism, as well as aristocratic and group privilege; established civil equality and uniform institutions across the country; freed peasants from much of the seigneurial system and religious minorities from persecution. Yet the Revolution was far from over, for these changes had been won only against intense opposition, and the old order was far from vanquished. European monarchs and aristocrats encouraged refractory priests, émigrés, and royalists in France to resist.

The patriots, threatened in 1792 by military defeat and counterrevolution, were themselves divided. Some became radicalized, while others grew alienated from the Revolution's increasingly radical course. But each increment of opposition stiffened the resolve of the Revolution's strongest partisans. The dominant Jacobins forged an alliance with Parisian militants known as the ***sans-culottes*** (literally, men who wore trousers rather than fashionable knee breeches). Together they propelled France into a second revolution: a democratic republic that espoused a broadening notion of equality. At the same time, however, the Jacobin government instituted an improvised revolutionary dictatorship and a reign of terror against "the enemies of the people." Thus, the second revolution was distorted, as the ideals of equality became confused with the impulse to repress any opposition by the most drastic means.

The National Convention

The insurrection of August 10, 1792, created a vacuum of authority until the election of a National Convention was completed. A revolutionary Paris Commune, or city government, became one power center, but that bastion of radicalism could not control events even within its own domain. As thousands of volunteers left for the battlefront, Parisians nervously eyed the capital's jails, which overflowed with political prisoners and common criminals. Radical journalists like Marat saw these prisoners as a counterrevolutionary striking force and feared a plot to open the prisons. A growing sense of alarm finally exploded early in September. For three days groups of Parisians invaded the

Beset by invasion jitters and fearing a plot to force open the capital's overcrowded jails, mobs of Parisians invaded the prisons and over the course of three days in September 1792 slaughtered more than two thousand prisoners.
Bulloz/© Photo RMN/Art Resource, NY

prisons, set up "popular tribunals," and slaughtered more than two thousand prisoners. No official dared intervene to stop the carnage, known since as the September massacres.

The sense of panic eased, however, with the success of the French armies. Bolstered by units of volunteers, the army finally halted the invaders at the Battle of Valmy on September 20. Two months later it defeated the allies at Jemappes in the Austrian Netherlands, which the French now occupied. Meanwhile, the Convention convened and promptly declared France a republic.

Settling Louis XVI's fate proved to be extremely contentious. While the deputies unanimously found the former king guilty of treason, they divided sharply over the question of his punishment. Some argued for clemency, while others insisted that his execution was a necessary symbolic gesture as well as a fitting punishment for his betrayal. Finally, by a vote of 387 to 334, the Convention sentenced Louis to death and voted down efforts to reprieve this sentence or delay it for a popular referendum. On January 21, 1793, Louis was guillotined, put to death like an ordinary citizen. The deputies to the Convention had become regicides

(king killers) and would make no compromise with counterrevolution.

Factional Conflict From the Convention's opening day, two bitterly hostile groups of deputies vied for leadership and almost immobilized it with their rancorous conflict. One group became known as the *Girondins,* since several of its spokesmen were elected as deputies from the Gironde department. The Girondins were fiery orators and ambitious politicians who advocated provincial liberty and laissez-faire economics. They reacted hostilely to the growing radicalism of Paris and broke with or were expelled by the Jacobin Club, to which some had originally belonged. Meanwhile Parisian electors chose as their deputies leading members of the Jacobin Club, such as Danton, Robespierre, and Marat. The Parisian deputation to the Convention became the nucleus of a group known as the *Mountain,* so-called because it occupied the upper benches of the Convention's hall. The Mountain attracted the more militant provincial deputies and attacked the Girondins as treacherous compromisers unwilling to adopt bold measures in the face of crisis. The Girondins, in turn, denounced the Mountain as

After the National Convention concluded its trial of former King Louis XVI and voted to impose the death penalty without reprieve, "Louis Capet" was guillotined and the leaders of the Republic became regicides, king killers.
Bulloz/© Photo RMN/Art Resource, NY

would-be tyrants and captives of Parisian radicalism and held them responsible for the September prison massacres.

Several hundred deputies stood between these two factions. These centrists (known as the *Plain*) were committed to the Revolution but were uncertain which path to follow. The Plain detested popular agitation, but they were reluctant to turn against the sans-culottes.

The Revolutionary Crisis

By the spring of 1793 the National Convention faced a perilous convergence of invasion, civil war, and economic crises that demanded imaginative responses. Austria and Prussia had mounted a new offensive in 1793, their alliance strengthened by the addition of Spain, Piedmont, and Britain. Between March and September, military reversals occurred on every front. The Convention reacted by introducing a military draft, which in turn touched off a rebellion in western France by peasants and rural weavers, who had long resented the patriot middle class in the towns for monopolizing local political power and for persecuting their priests. In the isolated towns of the Vendée re-

gion, south of the Loire River, the rebels attacked the Republic's supporters. Priests and nobles offered leadership to the insurgents, who first organized into guerrilla bands and finally into a "Catholic and Royalist Army." The Vendée rebels briefly occupied several towns, massacred local patriots, and even threatened the port of Nantes, where British troops could have landed.

Meanwhile, economic troubles were provoking the Parisian sans-culottes. By early 1793 the Revolution's paper money, the assignat, had declined to 50 percent of its face value. Inflation was compounded by a poor harvest, food shortages, hoarding, and profiteering. Municipal authorities fixed the price of bread but could not always secure adequate supplies. Under these conditions the government could not even supply its armies.

The Purge of the Girondins   Spokesmen for the sans-culottes demanded that the Convention purge the Girondins and adopt a program of "public safety," including price controls for basic commodities, execution of hoarders and speculators, and forced requisitions of grain. Behind these demands lay the threat of armed

MAP 20.2 CONFLICTS IN REVOLUTIONARY FRANCE
According to this map, what were three types of conflicts challenging revolutionary France?
◆ For an online version, go to www.mhhe.com/chambers9 > chapter 20 > book maps

insurrection. This pressure from the sans-culottes aided the Mountain in their struggle against the Girondins, but it could easily have degenerated into anarchy. In a sense, all elements of the revolutionary crisis hinged on one problem: the lack of an effective government that would not simply respond to popular pressures but would organize and master them. When the sans-culottes mounted a massive armed demonstration for a purge of the Girondins on June 2, centrist deputies reluctantly agreed to go along. The Convention expelled twenty-three Girondin deputies, who were subsequently tried and executed for treason.

Factionalism in the Convention reflected conflict in the provinces. Moderate republicans in several cities struggled with local Jacobin radicals and sympathized with the Girondin deputies in their campaign against the Parisian sans-culottes. In the south, local Jacobins lost control of Marseilles, Bordeaux, and Lyons to their rivals, who then repudiated the Convention. As in the Vendée revolt, royalists soon took over the resistance in Lyons, France's second largest city. This act was an intolerable challenge to the Convention. Labeling the anti-Jacobin rebels in Lyons and elsewhere as "federal-

ists," the Convention dispatched armed forces to suppress them (see map 20.2). In the eyes of the Jacobins, to defy the Convention's authority was to betray France itself.

The Jacobin Dictatorship

Popular radicalism in Paris had helped bring the Mountain to power in the Convention. The question now was: Which side of this coalition between the Mountain and the sans-culottes would dominate the other? The sans-culottes seemed to believe that the sovereign people could dictate their will to the Convention. Popular agitation peaked on September 5, when a mass demonstration in Paris demanded new policies to ensure food supplies. To give force to the law, urged the sans-culottes, "Let terror be placed on the order of the day." The Convention responded with the Law of the Maximum, which imposed general price controls, and with the Law of Suspects, which empowered local revolutionary committees to imprison citizens whose loyalty they suspected.

Revolutionary Government   In June the triumphant Mountain had drafted a new democratic constitution for the French Republic and had submitted it to an unprecedented referendum, in which almost 2 million citizens had overwhelmingly voted yes. But the Convention formally laid the constitution aside and proclaimed the government "revolutionary until the peace." Elections, local self-government, and guarantees of individual liberty were to be suspended until the Republic had defeated its enemies within and without. The Convention placed responsibility for military, economic, and political policy, as well as control over local officials, in the hands of a twelve-man **Committee of Public Safety.** Spontaneous popular action was about to give way to revolutionary centralization.

Maximilien Robespierre emerged as the Committee's leading personality and tactician. An austere bachelor in his mid-thirties, Robespierre had been a provincial lawyer before the Revolution. As a deputy to the National Assembly he had ardently advocated greater democracy. His main political forum was the Paris Jacobin Club, which by 1793 he more or less dominated. In the Convention, Robespierre was inflexible and self-righteous in his dedication to the Revolution. He sought to appease the sans-culottes but also to control them, for he placed the Revolution's survival above any one viewpoint (see "Robespierre's Justification of the Terror," p. 606).

Local political clubs (numbering more than five thousand by 1794) formed crucial links in the chain of

Jules Benoit-Levy
BATTLE OF CHOLET OR THE SUICIDE OF GENERAL MOULININ, 1794
Bitter fighting in the Vendée between counterrevolutionaries and republicans caused a profound split in the loyalties of western France, which endured for at least the next hundred years. Each side cultivated its own memories of the event and honored its own martyrs.
Musée d'Art et d'Histoire, Cholet, France. Giraudon/Art Resource, NY

The Paris Jacobin Club began as a caucus for a group of liberal deputies to the National Assembly. During the Convention it became a bastion of democratic deputies and middle-class Parisian radicals while continuing to serve as a "mother club" for affiliated clubs in the provinces.
Bibliothèque Nationale, Paris, France. Giraudon/Art Resource, NY

ROBESPIERRE'S JUSTIFICATION OF THE TERROR

"If the spring of popular government in time of peace is virtue, the springs of popular government in revolution are at once *virtue and terror:* virtue, without which terror is fatal; terror, without which virtue is powerless. Terror is nothing other than justice, prompt, severe, inflexible; it is therefore an emanation of virtue. . . . It is a consequence of the general principle of democracy applied to our country's most urgent needs.

"It has been said that terror is the principle of despotic government. Does your government therefore resemble despotism? Yes, as the sword that gleams in the hands of the heroes of liberty resembles that with which the henchmen of tyranny are armed. Let the despot govern his brutalized subjects by terror; he is right, as a despot. Subdue by terror the enemies of liberty, and you will be right, as founders of the Republic. The government of the revolution is liberty's despotism against tyranny. Is force made only to protect crime?

"Society owes protection only to peaceable citizens; the only citizens in the Republic are the republicans. For it,

the royalists, the conspirators are only strangers or, rather, enemies. This terrible war waged by liberty against tyranny—is it not indivisible? Are the enemies within not the allies of the enemies without? The assassins who tear our country apart, the intriguers who buy the consciences that hold the people's mandate; the traitors who sell them; the mercenary pamphleteers hired to dishonor the people's cause, to kill public virtue, to stir up the fire of civil discord, and to prepare political counterrevolution—are all those men less guilty or less dangerous than the tyrants [abroad] whom they serve?

"We try to control revolutions with the quibbles of the courtroom; we treat conspiracies against the Republic like lawsuits between individuals. Tyranny kills, and liberty argues."

From Robespierre's speech to the Convention on "The Moral and Political Principles of Domestic Policy," February 1794.

revolutionary government. The clubs nominated citizens for posts on local revolutionary institutions, exercised surveillance over those officials, and served as "arsenals of public opinion." The clubs fostered the egalitarian ideals of the second revolution and supported the war effort. They also saw it as their civic duty to denounce fellow citizens for unpatriotic behavior and thereby sowed fear and recrimination across the land.

The Jacobins tolerated no serious dissent. The government's demand for unity during the emergency nullified the right to freedom of expression. Among those to fall were a group of ultrarevolutionaries led by Jacques-René Hébert, a leading radical journalist and Paris official. The extremists were accused of a plot against the Republic and were guillotined. In reality, Hébert had questioned what he deemed the Convention's leniency toward "enemies of the people." Next came the so-called indulgents. Headed by Georges-Jacques Danton, a leading member of the Jacobin Club, they publicly argued for a relaxation of rigorous measures. For this dissent they were indicted on trumped-up charges of treason and were sentenced to death by the revolutionary tribunal. This succession of purges, which started with the Girondins and later ended with Robespierre himself, suggested, as one victim put it, that "revolutions devour their own children."

The Reign of Terror   Most of those devoured by the French Revolution, however, were not its own children but a variety of armed rebels, counterrevolutionaries, and unfortunate citizens swept into the vortex of war and internal strife. As an official policy, the Reign of Terror sought to organize repression so as to avoid anarchic violence like the September massacres. It reflected a state of mind that saw threats and plots everywhere (some real, most imagined). The laws of the Terror struck most directly at the people perceived to be enemies of the Revolution: Refractory priests and émigrés, for instance, were banned from the Republic upon pain of death. But the Law of Suspects also led to the incarceration of as many as 300,000 ordinary citizens for their opinions, past behavior, or social status.

The Terror produced its own atrocities: the brutal drowning of imprisoned priests at Nantes; the execution of thousands of noncombatants during the military campaigns of the Vendée; and the summary executions of about two thousand citizens of Lyons, more than two-thirds of them from the wealthy classes. ("Lyons has made war against liberty," declared the Convention, "thus Lyons no longer exists.") But except in the two zones of intense civil war—western France and the area of "federalist" rebellion in the south (see map 20.2)—the Terror struck by examples, not by mass executions.

Antoine Jean Gros
PORTRAIT OF BONAPARTE AS FIRST CONSUL
**Napoleon Bonaparte as First Consul, at the height of his
popularity, painted by his admirer J.-B. Gros.**
Bulloz/© Photo RMN/Art Resource, NY

CHRONOLOGY
Napoleon's Ascendancy in France

Nov. 1799	Coup d'etat of 18 Brumaire.
Dec. 1799	Bonaparte becomes First Consul.
Feb. 1800	Inauguration of prefectorial system.
July 1801	Concordat with the Church.
May 1802	Legion of Honor founded.
Aug. 1802	Bonaparte becomes Life Consul.
March 1804	Promulgation of Civil Code.
May 1804	Napoleon becomes emperor.
Aug. 1807	Suppression of the Tribunate.
March 1808	Organization of the Imperial Nobility.

curtailed the free and familiar exercise of Catholicism. These policies provoked wide resentment among the mass of citizens whose commitment to Catholicism remained intact throughout the Revolution.

Though not a believer himself, Napoleon judged that major concessions to Catholic sentiment were in order, provided that the Church remained under the control of the state. In 1801 he negotiated a **Concordat,** or agreement, with Pope Pius VII. It stipulated that Catholicism was the "preferred" religion of France but protected religious freedom for non-Catholics. The Church was again free to operate in full public view and to restore the refractory priests. Primary education would espouse Catholic values and use Catholic texts, as it had before the Revolution, and clerical salaries would be paid by the state. Though nominated by the ruler, bishops would again be consecrated by the pope. But as a major concession to the Revolution, the Concordat stipulated that land confiscated from the Church and sold during the Revolution would be retained by its purchasers. On the other hand, the government dropped the ten-day week and restored the Gregorian calendar.

The balance of church-state relations tilted firmly in the state's favor, for Napoleon intended to use the clergy as a major prop of his regime. The pulpit and the primary school became instruments of social control, to be used, as a new catechism stated, "to bind the religious conscience of the people to the august person of the Emperor." As Napoleon put it, the clergy would be his "moral prefects." Devout Catholics came to resent this subordination of the Church. Eventually Pope Pius renounced the Concordat, to which Napoleon responded by removing the pontiff to France and placing him under house arrest.

The Era of the Notables

With civil equality established and feudalism abolished, Napoleon believed that the Revolution was complete. It remained to encourage an orderly hierarchical society to counteract what he regarded as the excessive individualism of revolutionary social policy. Napoleon intended to reassert the authority of the state, the elites, and, in family life, the father.

In the absence of electoral politics, Napoleon used the state's appointive powers to confer status on prominent local individuals, or **notables,** thus associating

FAMILY AND GENDER ROLES UNDER THE NAPOLEONIC CIVIL CODE

"Art. 148. The son who has not attained the full age of 25 years, the daughter who has not attained the full age of 21 years, cannot contract marriage without the consent of their father and mother; in case of disagreement, the consent of the father is sufficient.

"Art. 212. Married persons owe to each other fidelity, succor, assistance.

"Art. 213. The husband owes protection to his wife, the wife obedience to her husband.

"Art. 214. The wife is obliged to live with her husband, and to follow him to every place where he may judge it convenient to reside: the husband is obliged to receive her, and to furnish her with everything necessary for the wants of life, according to his means and station.

"Art. 215. The wife cannot plead [in court] in her own name, without the authority of her husband, even though she should be a public trader . . . or separate in property.

"Art. 217. A wife . . . cannot give, alienate, pledge, or acquire by free or chargeable title, without the concurrence of her husband in the act, or his consent in writing.

"Art. 219. If the husband refuses to authorize his wife to pass an act, the wife may cause her husband to be cited directly before the court of first instance . . . which may give or refuse its authority, after the husband shall have been heard, or duly summoned.

"Art. 229. The husband may demand a divorce on the ground of his wife's adultery.

"Art. 230. The wife may demand divorce on the ground of adultery in her husband, when he shall have brought his concubine into their common residence.

"Art. 231. The married parties may reciprocally demand divorce for outrageous conduct, ill-usage, or grievous injuries, exercised by one of them towards the other."

---

them with his regime. These local dignitaries were usually chosen from among the largest taxpayers: prosperous landowners, former nobles, businessmen, and professionals. Those who served the regime with distinction were honored by induction into the Legion of Honor, nine-tenths of whose members were military men. "It is with trinkets that mankind is governed," Napoleon once said. Legion of Honor awards and appointments to prestigious but powerless local bodies were precisely such trinkets.

Napoleon offered more tangible rewards to the country's leading bankers when he chartered a national bank that enjoyed the credit power derived from official ties to the state. In education, Napoleon created elite secondary schools, or *lycées*, to train future government officials, engineers, and officers. The *lycées* embodied the concept of careers open to talent and became part of a highly centralized French academic system called the *University*, which survived into the twentieth century.

The Civil Code Napoleon's most important legacy was a civil code regulating social relations and property rights. Baptized the Napoleonic Code, it was in some measure a revolutionary law code that progressives throughout Europe embraced. Wherever it was implemented, the **Civil Code** swept away feudal property relations and gave legal sanction to modern contractual notions of property. The code established the right to choose one's occupation, to receive equal treatment under the law, and to enjoy religious freedom. At the same time, it allowed employers to dominate their

workers by prohibiting strikes and trade unions. Nor did the code match property rights with popular rights like the right to subsistence.

Revolutionary legislation had emancipated women and children by establishing their civil rights. Napoleon undid most of this by restoring the father's absolute authority in the family. "A wife owes obedience to her husband," said the code, which proceeded to deprive wives of property and juridical rights established during the 1790s. The code curtailed the right to divorce, while establishing a kind of double standard in the dissolution of a marriage (see "Family and Gender Roles under the Napoleonic Civil Code," above). The code also expanded the husband's options in disposing of his estate, although each child was still guaranteed a portion.

The prefectorial system of local government, the Civil Code, the Concordat, the University, the Legion of Honor, and the local bodies of notables all proved to be durable institutions. They fulfilled Napoleon's desire to create a series of "granite masses" on which to reconstruct French society. His admirers emphasized that these institutions contributed to social stability as skillful compromises between revolutionary liberalism and an older belief in hierarchy and central authority. Detractors point out that these institutions were class oriented and excessively patriarchal. Moreover, they fostered overcentralized, rigid structures that might have sapped the vitality of French institutions in succeeding generations. Whatever their merits or defects, these institutions took root, unlike Napoleon's attempt to dominate all of Europe.

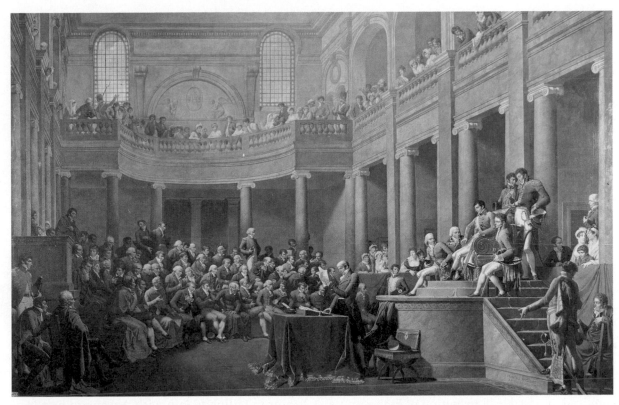

Nicolas Andre Monsiau
Deputies from the Cisalpine Republic of Italy proclaim Napoleon Bonaparte their president in 1802.
Chateaux de Versailles et de Trianon, Versailles, France. Erich Lessing/Art Resource, NY

NAPOLEONIC HEGEMONY IN EUROPE

After helping to give France a new government, Bonaparte turned to do battle against the second anti-French coalition in northern Italy. The outcome of his campaign against Austria would either solidify or destroy his regime. Within a few years, in the arena of international relations his ambitions lost all semblance of restraint. Bonaparte evolved from a winning general of the Republic to an imperial conqueror. After defeating his continental opponents on the battlefield in a series of ever more murderous campaigns, he still faced an implacable enemy in Britain. Unable to invade Britain, he resorted to economic warfare and blockade, but Britain withstood that assault as well. Meanwhile, the raw militarism of Napoleon's rule became evident in the relentless expansion of military conscription within the empire.

Military Supremacy and the Reorganization of Europe

Bonaparte's strategy in 1800 called for a repeat of the 1797 campaign: He would strike through Italy while the Army of the Rhine pushed eastward against Vienna. Following French victories at Marengo in Lombardy and in Germany, Austria sued for peace. The Treaty of Lunéville (February 1801) essentially restored France to the position it had held after Bonaparte's triumphs in Italy in 1797.

In Britain a war-weary government now stood alone against France and decided to negotiate. The Treaty of Amiens (March 1802) ended hostilities and reshuffled territorial holdings outside Europe, such as the Cape Colony in South Africa, which passed from the Dutch to the British. But this truce proved precarious since it did not settle the future of French influence in Europe or of commercial relations between the two great powers. Napoleon abided by the letter of the treaty but soon violated its spirit. Britain and Austria alike were dismayed by further expansion of French influence in Italy and Switzerland. Most important, perhaps, France seemed determined to exclude British trade rather than restore normal commercial relations. Historians agree that the Treaty of Amiens failed to keep the peace because neither side was ready to abandon its century-long struggle for predominance.

The Third Coalition   A third anti-French coalition soon took shape, a replay of its predecessors. France ostensibly fought to preserve the new regime at home and

Nicholas Pocock
NELSON'S FLAGSHIPS AT ANCHOR,
1807
Admiral Nelson's heavily armed
three-decker ship of the line,
which inflicted devastation on
the French fleet at Trafalgar.
National Maritime Museum,
Greenwich, London

its sister republics abroad. The coalition's objectives included the restoration of the Netherlands and Italy to "independence," the limitation of French influence elsewhere, and, if possible, a reduction of France to its prerevolutionary borders. Like most such alliances, the coalition would be dismembered piecemeal.

French hopes of settling the issue directly by invading Britain proved impossible once again. At the Battle of Trafalgar (October 1805), Admiral Nelson's fleet crushed the combined naval forces of France and its ally Spain. Nelson, an innovative tactician who broke rule-book procedures on the high seas just as French generals did on land, died of his wounds in the battle but ensured the security of the British Isles for the remainder of the Napoleonic era.

Napoleon, meanwhile, had turned against the Austro-Russian forces. Moving 200,000 French soldiers with unprecedented speed across the Continent, he took his enemies by surprise and won a dazzling succession of victories. After occupying Vienna he proceeded against the coalition's main army in December. Feigning weakness and retreat at the moment of battle, he drew his numerically superior opponents into an exposed position, crushed the center of their lines, and inflicted a decisive defeat. This Battle of Austerlitz was Napoleon's most brilliant tactical achievement, and it forced the Habsburgs to the peace table. The resulting Treaty of Pressburg (December 1805), extremely harsh and humiliating for Austria, imposed a large indemnity and required the Habsburgs to cede their Venetian provinces.

France and Germany By now the French sphere of influence had increased dramatically to include most of southern Germany, which Napoleon reorganized into the Confederation of the Rhine, a client realm of France (see map 21.2). France had kept Prussia neutral during the war with Austria by skillful diplomacy. Only after Austria made peace did Prussia recognize its error in failing to join with Austria to halt Napoleon. Belatedly, Prussia mobilized its famous but antiquated army; it was rewarded with stinging defeats by France in a number of encounters culminating in the Battle of Jena (October 1806). With the collapse of Prussian military power, the conquerors settled in Berlin and watched the prestige of the Prussian ruling class crumble. Napoleon was now master of northern Germany as well as the south. For a while it appeared that he might obliterate Prussia entirely, but he restored its sovereignty—after amputating part of its territory and imposing a crushing indemnity.

Napoleon was free to reorganize central Europe as he pleased. After formally proclaiming the end of the Holy Roman Empire in 1806, he liquidated numerous small German states and merged them into two new ones: the Kingdom of Westphalia, with his brother Jérôme on the throne, and the Grand Duchy of Berg, to be ruled by his brother-in-law Joachim Murat. His ally Saxony became a full-scale kingdom, while a new duchy of Warsaw was carved out of Prussian Poland. This "restoration" of Poland had propaganda value; it made the emperor appear as a champion of Polish aspirations, compared to the rulers of Prussia, Russia, and Austria, who had dismembered Poland in a series of partitions between 1772 and 1795. Moreover, Napoleon could now enlist a Polish army and use Polish territory as a base of operations against his remaining continental foe, Russia.

France and Russia In February 1807 Napoleon confronted the colossus of the east in the Battle of Eylau; the resulting carnage was horrifying but inconclusive.

Charles Meynier
THE DAY AFTER THE BATTLE OF EYLAU, 9 FEBRUARY 1807
Napoleon amidst the carnage on the battlefield of Eylau, the bloodiest engagement to date of the revolutionary-Napoleonic era, where the French and Russians fought each other to a stalemate in 1807.
Versailles, France. Giraudon/Art Resource, NY

When spring came, only a dramatic victory could preserve his conquests in central Europe and vindicate the extraordinary commitments of the past two years. The Battle of Friedland in June was a French victory that demoralized Russia's Tsar Alexander I and persuaded him to negotiate.

Meeting at Tilsit, the two rulers buried their differences and agreed, in effect, to partition Europe into eastern and western spheres of influence. Each would support the other's conquests and mediate in behalf of the other's interests. The Treaty of Tilsit (July 1807) sanctioned new annexations of territory directly into France and the reorganization of other conquered countries. The creation of new satellite kingdoms became the vehicle for Napoleon's domination of Europe. Like the French Republic, the sister republics became kingdoms between 1805 and 1807. And it happened that Napoleon had a large family of brothers ready to wear those new royal crowns.

The distorted shape of Napoleonic Europe is apparent on maps dating from 1808 to 1810 (see map 21.2). His chief satellites included the Kingdom of Holland, with brother Louis on the throne; the Kingdom of Italy, with Napoleon himself as king and his stepson Eugène de Beauharnais as viceroy; the Confederation of the Rhine, including brother Jérôme's Kingdom of Westphalia; the Kingdom of Naples, covering southern Italy, with brother Joseph the ruler until Napoleon transferred him to Spain and installed his brother-in-law Murat; and the Duchy of Warsaw. Belgium, the Rhineland, Tuscany, Piedmont, Genoa, and the Illyrian provinces had been annexed to France. Switzerland did not become a kingdom, but the Helvetic Republic (as it was now called) received a new constitution dictated by France. In 1810, after yet another war with Austria, a marriage was arranged between the house of Bonaparte and the house of Habsburg. Having divorced Joséphine de Beauharnais, Napoleon married princess Marie Louise, daughter of Francis II, who bore him a male heir the following year.

Naval War with Britain

For a time it seemed that Britain alone stood between Napoleon and his dream of hegemony over Europe. Since Britain was invulnerable to invasion, Napoleon hoped to destroy its influence by means of economic warfare. Unable to blockade British ports directly, he could try to close off the Continent: keep Britain from its markets, stop its exports, and thus ruin its trade and credit. Napoleon reasoned that if Britain had nowhere to sell its manufactured goods, no gold would come into the country and bankruptcy would eventually ensue. Meanwhile, overproduction would cause unemployment and labor unrest, which would turn the

MAP 21.2 EUROPE AROUND 1810
Note the extent of the French Empire as well as its satellite territories and allies. Was it plausible that the Napoleonic Empire could sustain its military power from Madrid to Warsaw?
◆ For an online version, go to www.mhhe.com/chambers9 > chapter 21 > book maps

British people against their government and force the latter to make peace with France. At the same time, French advantages in continental markets would increase with the elimination of British competition.

The Continental System Napoleon therefore launched his **Continental System** to prohibit British trade with all French allies. Even neutral ships were banned from European ports if they carried goods coming from the British Isles. Britain responded in 1807 with the Orders in Council, which in effect reversed the blockade: It *required* all neutral ships to stop at British ports to procure trading licenses and pay tariffs. In other words, the British insisted on regulating all trade between neutral states and European ports. Ships that failed to obey would be stopped on the high seas and captured. In an angry response, Napoleon, in turn, threatened to seize any neutral ship that obeyed the Orders in Council by stopping at British ports.

Thus, a total naval war between France and Britain enveloped all neutral nations. Indeed, neutral immunity virtually disappeared, since every ship was obliged to violate one system or the other and thus run afoul of naval patrols or privateers. While the British captured only about forty French ships a year after 1807 (for few were left afloat), they seized almost three thousand neutral vessels a year, including many from the United States.

Jean-Auguste-Dominique Ingres
NAPOLEON ON HIS IMPERIAL THRONE, **1806**
Emperor Napoleon I on his imperial throne in 1806, by the great portrait painter Ingres. Note the dramatic contrast in appearance with the young, intense military hero of the Republic in David's portrait at the beginning of this chapter.
Musée des Beaux-Arts, Rennes, France. Erich Lessing/Art Resource, NY

CHRONOLOGY
Napoleon and Europe

June 1800	Battle of Marengo and defeat of the Second Coalition.
Feb. 1801	Treaty of Lunéville with Austria.
March 1802	Treaty of Amiens with Britain.
Sept. 1802	Annexation of Piedmont.
1805–1806	Third Coalition forms.
Oct. 1805	Battle of Trafalgar and defeat of French fleet.
Dec. 1805	Battle of Austerlitz; defeat of Austria.
1806	Battle of Jena and humiliation of Prussia.
1807	Battles of Eylau and Friedland; stalemate with Russia.
July 1807	Treaty of Tilsit with Russia. Consolidation of satellite kingdoms.
1807	Launching of Continental System against British trade.
Feb. 1808	Invasion of Spain.
July 1809	Battle of Wagram; Austria defeated again.
April 1810	Napoleon weds princess Marie Louise of Austria.
Dec. 1810	Annexation of Holland.
July 1812	Invasion of Russia.
Oct. 1812	Retreat and destruction of Grand Army.
Oct. 1813	Battle of Leipzig and formation of Fourth Coalition.
March 1814	Battle of France and Napoleon's abdication.

The Continental System did hurt British trade. British gold reserves dwindled, and 1811 saw widespread unemployment and rioting. France was affected, in turn, by Britain's counterblockade, which cut it off from certain raw materials necessary for industrial production. But the satellite states, as economic vassals of France, suffered the most. In Amsterdam, for example, shipping volume declined from 1,350 ships entering the port in 1806 to 310 in 1809, and commercial revenues dropped calamitously. Out of loyalty to the people whom he ruled, Holland's King Louis Bonaparte tolerated smuggling. But this action so infuriated Napoleon that he ousted his brother from the throne and annexed the Kingdom of Holland directly to France. Smuggling

was, in fact, the weak link in the system, for it created holes in Napoleon's wall of economic sanctions that constantly needed plugging. This problem drove the emperor to ever more drastic actions.

The Napoleonic Conscription Machine

One key to Napoleon's unrestrained ambitions in Europe was the creation of an efficient administrative state in France and its annexed territories with the ability to continuously replenish the ranks of the imperial army.

The National Convention's mass levy of August 1793 had drafted all able-bodied unmarried men between the ages of eighteen and twenty-five. But this unprecedented mobilization had been meant as a one-time-only emergency measure, a temporary "requisition." There was no implication that subsequent cohorts of young men would face conscription into the army as part of their civic obligations. When the war resumed in 1798, however, the Directory passed a conscription law that made successive "classes" of young men (that is, those born in a particular year) subject to a military draft should the need arise. The Directory immediately implemented this law and called up three classes, but local officials reported massive draft evasion in most of the departments. Many French youths found the prospect of military service repugnant. From this shaky foundation, however, the Napoleonic regime developed a remarkably successful conscription system.

The Rules of the Game   After much trial and error with the details, timetables, and mechanisms, the system began to operate efficiently within a few years. The government assigned an annual quota of conscripts for each department. Using parish birth registers, the mayor of every community compiled a list of men reaching the age of nineteen that year. These youths were then led by their mayor to the cantonal seat on a specified day for a draft lottery. Panels of doctors at the departmental capitals later verified or rejected claims for medical exemptions. In all, about a third of French youths legally avoided military service because they were physically unfit—too short, lame, or suffering from poor eyesight, chronic diseases, or other infirmities.

In the draft lottery, youths picked numbers out of a box; marriage could no longer be used as an exemption, for obvious reasons. Those with high numbers were spared (for the time being), while those who drew low numbers filled the local induction quota. Two means of avoiding service remained: The wealthy could purchase a replacement, and the poor could flee. True, the regime had a bad conscience about allowing draftees to hire replacements, because the practice made its rhetoric about the duties of citizenship sound hollow. But to placate wealthy notables and peasants with large holdings (who were sometimes desperate to keep their sons on the farm), the government permitted the hiring of a replacement under strict guidelines that made it difficult and expensive but not impossible. The proportion of replacements was somewhere between 5 and 10 percent of all draftees.

Draft Evasion   For Napoleon's prefects, conscription levies were always the top priority among their duties, and draft evasion was the number one problem. Dogged persistence, bureaucratic routine, and various forms of coercion gradually overcame this chronic resistance. From time to time, columns of troops swept through areas in which evasion and desertion were most common and arrested culprits by the hundreds. But draft evaders

Royalist caricatures often depicted Napoleon as an ogre whose conscription machine devoured the nation's young men.
Bibliothèque Nationale de France, Paris

usually hid out in remote places—mountains, forests, marshes—so coercion had to be directed against their families as well. Heavy fines assessed against the parents did little good, since most were too poor to pay anything. A better tactic was to billet troops in the draft evaders' homes; if their families could not afford to feed the troops, then the community's wealthy taxpayers were required to do so. All these actions created pressure on the youths to turn themselves in. By 1811 the regime had broken the habit of draft evasion, and conscription was grudgingly becoming accepted as a disagreeable civic obligation, much like taxes. Just as draft calls began to rise sharply, draft evasion fell dramatically.

Napoleon had begun by drafting 60,000 Frenchmen annually, but by 1810 the annual quotas had risen steadily to 120,000, and they continued to climb. Moreover, in 1810 the emperor ordered the first of many "supplementary levies," calling up men from earlier classes who had drawn high lottery numbers. In January 1813, to look ahead, Napoleon replenished his armies by calling up the class of 1814 a year early and by making repeated supplementary calls on earlier classes.

Resistance to Napoleon

By 1808, with every major European power except Britain vanquished on the battlefield, Napoleon felt that nothing stood in his way. Since Spain and, later, Russia seemed unable or unwilling to stop smuggling from Britain, thus thwarting his strategy of economic warfare, the emperor decided to deal with each by force of arms. His calculations proved utterly mistaken, and in both places he ultimately suffered disastrous defeats. More generally, Napoleon's intrusion into Italy, Germany, Spain, and Russia set in motion various responses and movements of resistance. French expansion sparked new forms of nationalism in some quarters, but also liberalism and reaction. Finally, all his opponents coalesced, defeated Napoleon on the battlefield, and drove him from his throne.

The "Spanish Ulcer"

Spain and France shared a common interest in weakening British power in Europe and the colonial world. But the alliance they formed after making peace with each other in 1795 brought only troubles for Spain, including the loss of its Louisiana Territory in America and (at the Battle of Trafalgar) most of its naval fleet. The Spanish royal household, meanwhile, was mired in scandal. Prime Minister Manuel de Godoy, once a lover of the queen, was a corrupt opportunist and extremely unpopular with the people. Crown Prince Ferdinand despised Godoy and

Godoy's protectors, the king and queen, while Ferdinand's parents actively returned their son's hostility.

Napoleon looked on at this farce with irritation. At the zenith of his power, he concluded that he must reorganize Spain himself to bring it solidly into the Continental System. As a pretext for military intervention, he set in motion a plan to invade Portugal, supposedly to partition it with Spain. Once the French army was well inside Spain, however, Napoleon intended to impose his own political solution to Spain's instability.

Napoleon brought the squabbling king and prince to France, where he threatened and bribed one and then the other into abdicating. The emperor then gathered a group of handpicked Spanish notables who followed Napoleon's scenario by petitioning him to provide a new sovereign, preferably his brother Joseph. Joseph was duly proclaimed king of Spain. With 100,000 French troops already positioned around Madrid, Joseph prepared to assume his new throne, eager to rule under a liberal constitution and to believe his brother's statement that "all the better Spanish people are on your side." As he took up the crown, however, an unanticipated drama erupted.

Popular Resistance   Faced with military occupation, the disappearance of their royal family, and the crowning of a Frenchman, the Spanish people rose in rebellion. It began on May 2, 1808, when an angry crowd in Madrid rioted against French troops, who responded with firing squads and brutal reprisals. This bloody incident, known as the Dos de Mayo and captured in

Francisco Goya
THE THIRD OF MAY, **1808**
**The great Spanish artist Francisco Goya memorably captured the brutality of French reprisals against the citizens
of Madrid who dared to rebel against the Napoleonic occupation on May 2, 1808.**
Painted in 1814. Museo del Prado, Madrid, Spain. Erich Lessing/Art Resource, NY

Francisco de Goya
THE DISASTERS OF WAR: POPULACHO
**In a relentlessly bleak series of drawings collectively entitled *The Horrors of War,* Goya went on to record the savagery and
atrocities committed by both sides of the struggle in Spain.**
The Norton Simon Art Foundation, Pasadena, CA

SPANISH LIBERALS DRAFT A CONSTITUTION, 1812

"The general and extraordinary Cortes of the Spanish nation, duly organized . . . in order duly to discharge the lofty objective of furthering the glory, prosperity and welfare of the Nation as a whole, decrees the following political Constitution to assure the well-being and upright administration of the State.

"Art. 1: The Spanish Nation is the union of all Spaniards from both hemispheres.

"Art. 3: Sovereignty resides primarily in the Nation and because of this the right to establish the fundamental laws belongs to it exclusively.

"Art. 4: The Nation is obligated to preserve and protect with wise and just laws civil liberty, property and the other legitimate rights of all the individuals belonging to it.

"Art. 12: The religion of the Spanish Nation is and always will be the Catholic, Apostolic, Roman and only true faith. The Nation protects it with wise and just laws and prohibits the exercise of any other.

"Art. 14: The Government of the Spanish Nation is an hereditary limited Monarchy.

"Art. 15: The power to make laws resides in the Cortes with the King.

"Art. 16: The power to enforce laws resides in the King.

"Art. 27: The Cortes is the union of all the deputies that represent the Nation, named by the citizens.

"Art. 34: To elect deputies to the Cortes, electoral meetings will be held in the parish, the district, and the province.

"Art. 59: The electoral meetings on the district level will be made up of the electors chosen at the parish level who will convene at the seat of every district in order to name the electors who will then converge on the provincial capital to elect the deputies to the Cortes.

"Art. 338: The Cortes will annually establish or confirm all taxes, be they direct or indirect, general, provincial or municipal. . . .

"Art. 339: Taxes will be apportioned among all Spaniards in proportion to their abilities [to pay], without exception to any privilege."

From *Political Constitution of the Spanish Monarchy*, proclaimed in Cádiz, March 19, 1812, James B. Tueller (tr.).

Goya's famous paintings, has remained a source of Spanish national pride, for it touched off a sustained uprising against the French. Local notables created committees, or *juntas*, to organize resistance and to coordinate campaigns by regular Spanish troops. These troops were generally ineffective against the French, but they did produce one early victory: A half-starved French army was cut off and forced to surrender at Bailén in July 1808. This defeat broke the aura of Napoleonic invincibility.

The British saw a great opportunity to attack Napoleon in concert with the rebellious Spanish people. Landing an army in Portugal, the British bore the brunt of anti-French military operations in Spain. In what they called the Peninsular War, a grueling war of attrition, their forces drove the French out of Portugal. After five years of fighting and many reversals, they pushed the French back across the Pyrénées in November 1813. The British commander, the Duke of Wellington, grasped the French predicament when he said: "The more ground the French hold down in Spain, the weaker they will be at any given point."

About 30,000 Spanish **guerilla** fighters helped wear down the French and forced the occupiers to struggle for survival in hostile country. The guerillas drew French forces from the main battlefields, inflicted casualties, impeded the French access to food, and punished Spanish collaborators. Their harassment kept the invaders in a constant state of anxiety, which led the French to adopt harsh measures in reprisal. But these "pacification" tactics only escalated the war's brutality and further enraged the Spanish people.

Together, the Spanish regulars, the guerillas, and the British expeditionary force kept a massive French army of up to 300,000 men pinned down in Spain. Napoleon referred to the war as his "Spanish ulcer," an open sore that would not heal. Though he held the rebel fighters in contempt, other Europeans were inspired by their example of armed resistance to France.

The Spanish Liberals The war, however, proved a disaster for Spanish liberals. Torn between loyalty to Joseph, who would have liked to be a liberal ruler, and nationalist rebels, liberals faced a difficult dilemma. Those who collaborated with Joseph hoped to spare the people from a brutal war and to institute reform from above in the tradition of Spanish enlightened absolutism. But they found that Joseph could not rule independently; Napoleon gave the orders in Spain and relied on his generals to implement them. The liberals who joined the rebellion organized a provisional government by reviving the ancient Spanish parliament, or Cortes, in the southern town of Cádiz. Like the French National Assembly of 1789, the Cortes of Cádiz drafted a liberal constitution in 1812 (see "Spanish Liberals Draft a Constitution, 1812," above), which pleased the

British and was therefore tolerated for the time being by the juntas.

In reality, most nationalist rebels despised the liberals. They were fighting for the Catholic Church, the Spanish monarchy, and the old way of life. When in 1814 Wellington finally drove the French out of Spain and former crown prince Ferdinand VII took the throne, the joy of the Cádiz liberals quickly evaporated. As a royalist mob sacked the Cortes building, Ferdinand tore up the constitution of 1812, reinstated absolutism, restored the monasteries and the Inquisition, revived censorship, and arrested the leading liberals. Nationalist reactionaries emerged as the victors of the Spanish rebellion.

Independence in Spanish America   The Creoles, descendants of Spanish settlers who were born in the New World, also profited from the upheaval in Spain. Spain had been cut off from its vast empire of American colonies in 1805, when the British navy won control of the Atlantic after the Battle of Trafalgar. In 1807 a British force attacked Buenos Aires in Spain's viceroyalty of the Río de la Plata (now Argentina). The Argentines—who raised excellent cattle on the *pampas*, or grassy plains—were eager to trade their beef and hides for British goods, but Spain's rigid mercantilism had always prevented such beneficial commerce. The Argentines welcomed the prospect of free trade, but not the prospect of British conquest. With Spain unable to defend them, the Creoles organized their own militia and drove off the British, pushed aside the Spanish viceroy, and took power into their own hands. The subsequent upheaval in Spain led the Argentines to declare their independence. After Ferdinand regained the Spanish throne in 1814, he sent an army to reclaim the colony, but the Argentines, under General José de San Martín, drove it off, and Argentina made good on its claim to full independence.

Rebellion spread throughout Spanish America, led above all by Simón Bolívar, revered in the hemisphere as "The Liberator." After Napoleon removed the king of Spain in 1808, the Creoles in Spain's viceroyalty of New Granada (encompassing modern-day Venezuela, Colombia, and Ecuador) elected a congress, which declared independence from Spain. An arduous, protracted war with the Spanish garrisons followed, and by 1816 Spain had regained control of the region.

Bolívar resumed the struggle and gradually wore down the Spanish forces; in one campaign his army marched six hundred miles from the torrid Venezuelan lowlands over the snow-capped Andes Mountains to Colombia. Finally in 1819 the Spanish conceded defeat. Bolívar's dream of one unified, conservative republic of Gran Colombia soon disintegrated under regional pres-

MAP 21.3 SOUTH AMERICA AFTER INDEPENDENCE
◆ For an online version, go to www.mhhe.com/chambers9 > chapter 21 > book maps

sures into several independent states, but not before Bolívar launched one final military campaign and liberated Peru, Spain's remaining colony in South America (see map 21.3).

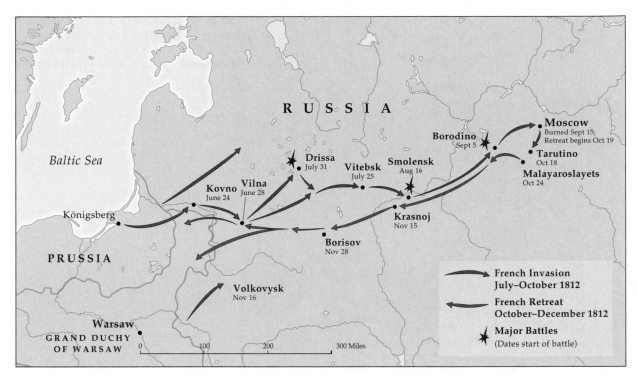

MAP 21.4 THE RUSSIAN CAMPAIGN OF 1812
◆ For an online version, go to www.mhhe.com/chambers9 > chapter 21 > book maps

The Russian Debacle

Napoleon did not yet realize in 1811 that his entanglement in Spain would drain French military power and encourage resistance in Central Europe. On the contrary, never were the emperor's schemes more grandiose. Surveying the crumbling state system of Europe, he imagined that it could be replaced with a vast empire, ruled from Paris and based on the Napoleonic Code. He mistakenly believed that the era of the balance of power among Europe's states was over and that nationalist sentiments need not constrain his actions.

Russia now loomed as the main obstacle to Napoleon's imperial reorganization and domination of Europe. Russia, a restive ally with ambitions of its own in Eastern Europe, resented the restrictions on its trade under the Continental System. British diplomats, anti-Napoleonic exiles such as Baron Stein of Prussia, and nationalist reactionaries at court all pressured the tsar to resist Napoleon. Russian court liberals, more concerned with domestic reforms, hoped on the contrary that Alexander would maintain peace with France, but by 1812 their influence on the tsar had waned. For his part, Napoleon wanted to enforce the Continental System and humble Russia. As he bluntly put it: "Let Alexander defeat the Persians, but don't let him meddle in the affairs of Europe."

Napoleon prepared for his most momentous military campaign. His objective was to annihilate Russia's army or, at the least, to conquer Moscow and chase the army to the point of disarray. To this end he marshaled a "Grand Army" of almost 600,000 men (half of them French, the remainder from his satellite states and allies) and moved them steadily by forced marches across Central Europe into Russia. The Russians responded by retreating in orderly fashion and avoiding a fight. Many Russian nobles abandoned their estates and burned their crops to the ground, leaving the Grand Army to operate far from its supply bases in territory stripped of food. At Borodino the Russians finally made a stand and sustained a frightful 45,000 casualties, but the remaining Russian troops managed to withdraw in order. Napoleon lost 35,000 men in that battle, but far more men and horses were dying from hunger, thirst, fatigue, and disease in the march across Russia's unending, barren territory. The greatly depleted ranks of the Grand Army staggered into Moscow on September 14, 1812, but the Russian army was still intact and far from demoralized.

The Destruction of the Grand Army   In fact, the condition of Moscow demoralized the French. They found the city deserted and bereft of badly needed supplies. The next night Moscow was mysteriously set ablaze, causing such extensive damage as to make it unfit to be the Grand Army's winter quarters. Realistic advisers warned the emperor that his situation was dangerous, while others told him what he wished to hear—that

Just as Goya's drawings captured the unique ferocity of the Spanish campaign, this illustration evokes the particular agonies of climate and logistics in the Russian debacle.
Photo Archive, Nationalbibliothek Austria

Russian resistance was crumbling. For weeks Napoleon hesitated. Logistically it was imperative that the French begin to retreat immediately, but that would constitute a political defeat. Only on October 19 did Napoleon finally order a retreat, but the order came too late.

The delay forced an utterly unrealistic pace on the bedraggled army as it headed west. Supplies were gone, medical care for the thousands of wounded nonexistent, horses lacking. Food shortages compelled foraging parties to sweep far from the main body of troops, where these men often fell prey to Russian guerillas. And there was the weather—Russia's bitter cold and deep snow, in which no commander would wish to find himself leading a retreat of several hundred miles, laden with wounded and loot but without food, fuel, horses, or proper clothing. Napoleon's poor planning, the harsh weather, and the operation of Russian guerilla bands made the long retreat a nightmare of suffering for the Grand Army. No more than 100,000 troops survived the ordeal. Worse yet, the Prussian contingent took the occasion to desert Napoleon, opening the possibility of mass defections and the formation of a new anti-Napoleonic coalition.

German Resistance and the Last Coalition

Napoleon was evidently impervious to the horror around him. On the sleigh ride out of Russia, he was al-ready planning how to raise new armies and set things aright. Other European statesmen, however, were ready to capitalize on Napoleon's defeat in Russia and demolish his empire once and for all. Provocative calls for a national uprising in various German states to throw off the tyrant's yoke reinforced the efforts of diplomats like Prussia's Baron Stein and Austria's Klemens von Metternich to revive the anti-Napoleonic coalition.

Reform from Above in Prussia In Prussia after the defeat of 1806, the government had introduced reforms intended to improve the quality of the bureaucracy by offering nonnobles more access to high positions and by reducing some of the nobility's privileges. The monarchy hoped thereby to salvage the position of the nobility and the authority of the state. Prussian military reformers adopted new methods of recruitment to build up a trained reserve force that could be rapidly mobilized, along with a corps of reserve officers to take command of these units. Prussia, in other words, hoped to achieve French-style efficiency and military mobilization without resorting to new concepts of citizenship, constitutions, legislatures, or the abolition of seigneurialism. On the level of propaganda and the symbolic gesture, writers in Prussia and other German states called for a popular war of liberation under the slogan "With God for King and Fatherland."

Against this background of Prussian military preparation and growing nationalist sentiment, the diplomats maneuvered and waited. Finally, in March 1813, King Frederick William III of Prussia signed a treaty with Russia to form an offensive coalition against Napoleon. A great struggle for Germany ensued between the Russo-Prussian forces and Napoleon and his allies. Austria continued to claim neutrality and offered to mediate the dispute, but at a meeting in Prague, Napoleon rejected an offer of peace in exchange for restoring all French conquests since 1802.

In August, as Napoleon learned of new defeats in Spain, Habsburg Emperor Francis finally declared war on his son-in-law. Napoleon called up underage and overage conscripts and was able to field one last army, but his major southern German ally, Bavaria, finally changed sides. A great battle raged around Leipzig for three days in October, and when the smoke cleared, Napoleon was in full retreat. German states were free from Napoleon's domination, but Prussia's rulers were also free from the need to concede further reforms in the political and social order.

The Fall of Napoleon   In the belief that he could rely on his conscription machine, Napoleon had rebuffed offers by the allies to negotiate peace in 1813. In fact, however, he reached the end of the line in November 1813 with a desperate call for 300,000 more men to defend France against the allies. Difficulties were inevitable, wrote one prefect, "when the number of men required exceeds the number available." Another reported: "There is scarcely a family that is not oppressed by conscription." Alongside sizable contingents of Italians, Germans, and other foreigners from the annexed territories and satellite states, nearly 2.5 million Frenchmen had been drafted by Napoleon. At least 1 million of those conscripts never returned.

With Napoleon driven back into France, British troops reinforced the coalition to ensure that it would not disintegrate once Central Europe had been liberated. The coalition offered final terms to the emperor: He could retain his throne, but France would be reduced to her "normal frontiers." (The precise meaning of this term was left purposely vague.) Napoleon, still hoping for a dramatic reversal, chose to fight, and with some reluctance the allies invaded France. Napoleon led the remnants of his army skillfully but to no avail. The French had lost confidence in him, conscription had reached its limits, and no popular spirit of resistance to invasion developed as it had in 1792. Paris fell in March 1814. The price of this defeat was unconditional surrender and the emperor's abdication. Napoleon was transported to the island of Elba, between Corsica and Italy, over which he was granted sovereignty. After twenty-two years of exile, the Bourbon Dynasty returned to France.

The Napoleonic Legend

For Napoleon, imperial authority—originating with him in France and radiating throughout Europe—represented the principle of rational progress. In his view, the old notion of balance of power among European states merely served as an excuse for the British to pursue their selfish interests. While paying lip service to the notion of Italian, Spanish, and Polish nationhood, Napoleon generally scorned patriotic opposition to his domination as an outmoded, reactionary sentiment—exemplified by the "barbaric" guerillas in Spain fighting for king and religion. Modern-minded Europeans, he believed, would see beyond historic, parochial traditions to the prospect of a new European order. Indeed, Napoleon's credibility with some reformers in Europe was considerable. The Bavarian prime minister, for instance, justified his collaboration with France in 1810 in these words: "The spirit of the new age is one of mobility, destruction, creativity. . . . The wars against France offer the [unfortunate] possibility of bringing back old constitutions, privileges, and property relations."

During his final exile, however, Napoleon came to recognize that nationalism was not necessarily reactionary—as one could plainly see in the nationalistic but liberal Cortes of Cádiz of 1812. Progressive thinking and nationalist aspirations could coexist. From exile Napoleon rewrote his life story to portray his career as a series of defensive wars against selfish adversaries (especially Britain) and as a battle in behalf of the nations of Europe against reactionary dynasties. In this way, Napoleon brilliantly (if falsely) put himself on the side of the future.

These memoirs and recollections from exile formed the basis of the Napoleonic legend, as potent a force historically, perhaps, as the reality of the Napoleonic experience. The image they projected emphasized how General Bonaparte had consolidated what was best about the French Revolution while pacifying a bitterly divided nation and saving it from chaos. They cast the imperial experience in a deceptively positive light, glossed over the tyranny and unending military slaughter, and aligned Napoleon with reason, efficiency, and modernity (see "Napoleon Justifies Himself in 1815," p. 638).

The Napoleonic legend also evoked a sense of grandeur and glory that moved ordinary people in years to come. Napoleon's dynamism and energy became his ultimate inspirational legacy to succeeding generations. In this way, the Napoleonic legend fed on the Romantic movement in literature and the arts. Many young romantics (including the poet William Wordsworth and

NAPOLEON JUSTIFIES HIMSELF IN 1815

"I have cleansed the Revolution, ennobled the common people, and restored the authority of kings. I have stirred all men to competition, I have rewarded merit wherever I found it, I have pushed back the boundaries of greatness. Is there any point on which I could be attacked and on which a historian could not take up my defense? My despotism? He can prove that dictatorship was absolutely necessary. Will it be said that I restricted freedom? He will be able to prove that license, anarchy, and general disorder were still on our doorstep. Shall I be accused of having loved war too much? He will show that I was always on the defensive. That I wanted to set up a universal monarchy? He will explain that it was merely the fortuitous result of circumstances and that I was led to it step by step by our very enemies. My ambition? Ah, no doubt he will find that I had ambition, a great deal of it—but the grandest and noblest perhaps, that ever was: the ambition of establishing and consecrating at last the kingdom of reason and the full exercise, the complete enjoyment, of all human capabilities!"

From B. Las Cases (ed.), *Mémorial de Sainte-Hélène*.

the composer Ludwig van Beethoven) saw in the French Revolution a release of creativity and a liberation of the individual spirit. Napoleon's tyranny eventually alienated most such creative people. But the Napoleonic legend, by emphasizing the bold creativity of his career, meshed nicely with the sense of individual possibility that the romantics cultivated. Napoleon's retrospective justifications of his reign may not be convincing, but one can only marvel at the irrepressible audacity of the man.

Summary

In the confrontations between Napoleon and his European adversaries, France still embodied the specter of revolution. Even if the revolutionary legacy in France amounted by that time to little more than Napoleon's contempt for the inefficiency and outmoded institutions of the old regime, France after Brumaire remained a powerful challenge to the status quo. Napoleon intended to abolish feudalism, institute centralized administrations, and implant the French Civil Code in all of France's satellite states. But by 1808 his extravagant international ambitions relied on increasingly tyrannical and militaristic measures. These in turn provoked a range of responses, including nationalist rebellions. Britain and Russia, then Prussia and Austria, joined forces once more to bring the Napoleonic Empire down, to restore the balance of power in Europe, and to reinstall the Bourbons in France. But the clock could not really be set back from Europe's experience of revolution and Napoleonic transformation. The era of modern political and social conflicts had begun.

QUESTIONS FOR FURTHER THOUGHT

1. Apart from Jesus, more books have probably been written about Napoleon than any other historical figure. What accounts for this enduring fascination? Compare Napoleon to dominant leaders of the past whom you have studied (e.g., Alexander the Great, Caesar, Philip II, and Louis XIV).

2. Was Napoleon a revolutionary? Did he consolidate or betray the French Revolution?

3. Using the boxed excerpt in which Napoleon justifies his conduct as a starting point, what is *your* assessment of his reign?

Recommended Reading
(See also chapter 20)

Sources

De Caulaincourt, Armand. *With Napoleon in Russia.* 1935. A remarkable account of the diplomacy and warfare of the 1812 debacle by a man at Napoleon's side.

Herold, J. C. (ed.). *The Mind of Napoleon.* 1961.

Thompson, J. M. (ed.). *Napoleon Self-Revealed.* 1934.

*Walter, Jakob. *The Diary of a Napoleonic Foot Soldier.* M. Raeff (ed.). 1991. A vivid and appalling account of the Russian campaign.

Studies

*Bergeron, Louis. *France under Napoleon.* 1981. A fresh and insightful evaluation of the Napoleonic settlement in France.

*Broers, Michael. *Europe under Napoleon, 1799–1815.* 1996. An incisive and up-to-date synthesis on French expansion in Europe.

Chandler, David. *Napoleon's Marshals.* 1986. By a leading expert on Napoleonic military history.

*Connelley, Owen. *Blundering to Glory: Napoleon's Military Campaigns.* 1988. An irreverent but incisive account of Napoleon's military leadership.

———. *Napoleon's Satellite Kingdoms.* 1965. A study of the states conquered by France and ruled by the Bonaparte family.

*Dwyer, Philip (ed.). *Napoleon and Europe.* 2001. A well-focused yet wide-ranging collection of essays with a comprehensive bibliography.

*Ellis, Geoffrey. *Napoleon.* 1997. A concise profile of the era.

Elting, John. *Swords around a Throne: Napoleon's Grande Armee.* 1988. An eminently readable military history.

*Englund, Steven. *Napoleon: A Political Life.* 2004. The most recent, and perhaps the best, one-volume biography in English.

Esdaile, Charles. *Fighting Napoleon: Guerrillas, Bandits, and Adventurers in Spain, 1808–1814.* 2004.

Forrest, Alan. *Conscripts and Deserters: The Army and French Society during the Revolution and Empire.*

1988. A study of popular resistance to revolutionary and Napoleonic conscription.

Gates, David. *The Spanish Ulcer: A History of the Peninsular War.* 1986. On the Spanish rebellion, the French response, and Wellington's expeditionary force.

*Geyl, Pieter. *Napoleon, For and Against.* 1949. Napoleon and the historians, as reviewed by a Dutch scholar with no illusions.

Hazareesingh, Sudhir. *The Legend of Napoleon.* 2004. A lively and suggestive study of an elusive subject.

*Lynch, John. *The Spanish American Revolutions, 1808–1826.* 1986. A comprehensive account of the independence movements in Spanish America and their aftermath.

Lyons, Martyn. *France under the Directory.* 1975. A brief topical survey of the Revolution's later, unheroic phase.

*———. *Napoleon Bonaparte and the Legacy of the French Revolution.* 1994. A good recent textbook.

Marcus, G. J. *A Naval History of England, II: The Age of Nelson.* 1971. The standard history of British naval supremacy.

Palmer, Robert R. *The World of the French Revolution.* 1971. Emphasizes the interplay of French power and revolutionary movements outside of France.

Rothenberg, Gunther. *The Art of Warfare in the Age of Napoleon.* 1978. A good analysis of strategy and tactics.

*Sheehan, James. *German History, 1770–1866.* 1989. An outstanding overview of this and other periods in German history.

*Sutherland, D. M. G. *France, 1789–1815: Revolution and Counter-revolution.* 1985. A fine general history of France in this period.

Tulard, Jean. *Napoleon: The Myth of the Savior.* 1984. A synthesis by the leading French expert on Napoleon.

*Woloch, Isser. *Napoleon and His Collaborators: The Making of a Dictatorship.* 2001.

Woolf, Stuart. *A History of Italy, 1700–1860.* 1979. An authoritative general history, with fine chapters on this period.

*Available in paperback.

Glossary

absolutism Political doctrine that the monarch is the source of all authority and government in a kingdom.

Academy Quarter of Athens in which Plato established a school.

Aeneid Epic poem by Roman poet Virgil about the founding of Rome.

agora Central market of a polis.

Allah Islamic term for God that derives from the Arabic word *al ilah*, meaning "The God."

Amon-Re "Hidden"; an unseen, universal god of Egypt.

Anabaptists Individuals who, pointing out that the Bible nowhere mentions infant baptism, argued that the sacrament was effective only if the believer understood what was happening and that therefore adults ought to be rebaptized. Opponents argued that infant baptism was necessary so that a baby would not be denied salvation if it died young.

anarchists Radical activists who called for the abolition of the state, sometimes by violent means.

anti-Semitism Anti-Jewish sentiment used to reinforce conservative, antiliberal and nationalist politics.

appeasement The policy by antiwar governments in Britain and France to placate Nazi Germany. Culminated in the Munich conference giving Germany control of Czechoslovakia in 1938; encouraged further German aggression.

apprenticeship Method by which young candidates, or apprentices, studied a particular trade under a master of that skill before admittance into the guild.

Areopagus Rock in central Athens that gave its name to a powerful governing council.

Arianism Heresy based on the teaching of Arius, an Alexandrian priest, which denied that Jesus was coequal with God the Father.

assignats Paper money issued by the French revolutionary governments, whose value was backed by nationalized church lands.

aton Disk of the sun, worshiped by Akhnaton, an Egyptian pharaoh.

Augustus "Most honored"; name conferred on the first emperor of Rome.

balance of power The belief that no one state should be permitted a dominant role in international affairs, and that alliances among their neighbors ought to restrain ambitious rulers.

Baroque Ornate style of art, music, literature, and architecture that emerged in the seventeenth century, characterized by an emphasis on grandeur, power, drama, and rich color.

Bastille A fortress prison seized on July 14, 1789, by Parisians looking for munitions to repulse the royal army; the event symbolized the Revolution's popular support.

Beguines Pious laywomen who lived in communities outside of convents.

Beowulf Anglo-Saxon epic that illustrates the weakness of tribal kingship.

Bill of Rights Document (usually only in a constitutional system) listing the protections from government oppression enjoyed by individual citizens.

billeting Providing board and lodging for troops by making ordinary citizens house and feed soldiers in their homes.

biometry The application of statistical methods to the analysis of biology and medicine.

Bismarck, Otto von The chief minister of Prussia's king, he masterminded the unification of Germany through military aggression and nationalist appeals.

Black Death Great plague of the fourteenth century that spread throughout Europe and resulted in huge loss of human life.

blitzkrieg "Lightning war"; German military tactic in which enemies were overrun with lightning speed using tanks and air power; led to the quick defeat of Poland in 1939 and France in 1940.

Bolsheviks "Majority faction"; the Leninist wing of the Russian Marxist party; after 1917, the Communist party.

broadsides Brief pamphlets or leaflets, often satiric, making sharp comments about a major issue of the day.

Brumaire The coup d'état in 1799 that overthrew the Directory and led to the dictatorship of Napoleon Bonaparte.

cahiers Grievance petitions written by local electoral assemblies, to be presented to the king by the deputies attending the Estates General in France.

Caliph In the Middle Ages, he was the religious and civil ruler of the Muslim empires, as in the Abbasid Caliphate.

Carolingian minuscule New form of formal, literary writing that used capital letters for the beginning of sentences and lowercase letters for the text.

cartel An informal association of manufacturers or suppliers who maintain prices at a high level and set production limits to control market demand.

Central Powers Name given to the coalition including Germany, Austria-Hungary, Turkey (the Ottoman Empire), and Bulgaria in World War I.

Chartism A mass working-class movement in Britain between 1837 and 1848 that derived its name from the People's Charter, a document calling for universal male suffrage, frequent elections by secret ballot, and other democratic reforms.

chivalry A new code of behavior that refined the manners of knights and nobles and adapted them to life in a noble household.

Cistercians Monastic order founded in 1098; they emphasized the emotional devotion to Christ's and Mary's humility.

Civil Code (Napoleonic Code) A grand codification of French law under Napoleon, which preserved certain gains of the Revolution such as legal equality and the abolition of seigneurial property, while clarifying contract and family law.

Civil Constitution of the Clergy The French Revolution's 1790 reform of the Catholic Church under which priests and bishops were elected by the laity, and parishes and dioceses were redrawn; created opposition to the Revolution and a schism within French Catholicism.

Classicism A movement in the arts that seeks to recapture the style and the subjects associated with ancient Greece and Rome.

Colonial Mandate Designation for the former colonial possessions of Germany and the Ottoman Empire, which the League of Nations placed under the control of the various Allied nations after World War I.

colonus In the Roman Empire, a free man who was settled as a worker on the land of another.

comitatus A Germanic warrior band organized under the leadership of an established chief.

Committee of Public Safety A committee of deputies to the National Convention that set political and military strategy and formed the hub of the revolutionary dictatorship of 1793–1794.

common law Laws that applied to the entire kingdom and were thus distinct from local customs, especially associated with England.

commune In medieval and Renaissance Europe, a self-governing association created by townsmen and headed by elected officials.

Concert of Europe A loose agreement by the major European powers to act together to maintain the conservative order in Europe and repress liberal and nationalistic uprisings after 1815.

Conciliar Movement Advocates of the authority of General Councils, rather than the papacy, in the Roman Church, especially active in the 1400s.

Concordat (of 1801) The religious settlement with Pope Pius VII that made Catholicism the "preferred" religion in France but protected religious freedom for non-Catholics.

confraternity A voluntary association of people; in earlier times, usually associations of laymen who wanted to intensify their religious piety.

Congress of Vienna An international congress that met from 1814 to 1815 to set peace terms for continental Europe after the Napoleonic Wars; notable for its creation of a European balance of power and the restoration of old dynasties.

conquistador A Spanish minor nobleman who led his country's expeditions of conquest into Central and South America in the sixteenth century.

conscription Policy of requiring all males of a certain age to sign up for a nation's army.

Constitutionalism The political doctrine that authority in a state depends on consent by the governed, or at least by the leaders of the society.

consuls Supreme magistrates in the Roman Republic, always holding office in pairs.

Continental System Economic sanctions established by Napoleon under which all ships carrying British goods or trading with Britain, even those from neutral countries, were banned from European ports and subject to seizure.

Corn Laws British grain tariffs seen as benefiting the landed gentry at the expense of higher bread prices for urban consumers; an opposition movement by middle-class reformers led to the repeal of nearly all duties in 1846.

Cortes The legislatures of the Spanish kingdoms—Aragon, Castile, and Navarre—which were made up of representatives of the Church, the aristocracy, and towns.

Counter-Reformation Refers to those who see the Catholic revival of the sixteenth century as a response to the Reformation. Those who consider it a natural development within the Church refer to the revival as the Catholic Reformation.

courtly love The polite relations between men and women.

crusades In the eleventh through thirteenth centuries, a series of armed expeditions of Christians to the East to overturn Islamic rule of the Holy Land.

Cubism Art form pioneered by Pablo Picasso and Georges Braque in the early twentieth century that rejected the artistic conventions of three-dimensional perspective and naturalistic representation for a flat, two-dimensional perspective and an abstract style.

Cuneiform System of writing by pressing wedge (Lat. *cuneus*) into clay.

curia regis An assembly of men who advised the king and acted as his principal court.

curiales Councilors in the Roman Empire.

curia Town council in the Roman Empire; later means royal court and central directing body of the Roman Catholic Church.

Cyrillic alphabet Developed by Cyril, a Slavonic script based on Greek letters.

danse macabre "Dance of death"; popular artist motif that depicted people from all different walks of life dancing with a skeleton as a foretaste of their deaths.

decolonization The gradual postwar withdrawal of European nations from colonial empires and the rise of national self-determination in former colonies; initiated a new era of global politics that intersected with the Cold War.

deism Belief in the existence of a supreme being but arising from reason rather than revelation.

Delian League Alliance of Greek states headed by Athens; became the Athenian Empire.

demesne land Land, worked by serfs, that the lord held for his own crops and profit.

demographic transition A pattern of declining birth rate accompanied by a more rapidly falling mortality rate that is characteristic of modern societies.

dialectic The art of analyzing logical relationships among propositions in a dialogue or discourse. Later, a philosophical term for Hegel, who applies the term simultaneously to both world history and ideas. It describes the development from one stage of consciousness to a superior one through a dynamic process of the fusion of contradictions into a higher truth.

dictator In the Roman Republic, a supreme officer whose term was limited to six months; this limit was broken by Sulla and Julius Caesar.

Diet The legislature of the Holy Roman Empire and many German states, bringing together representatives of princes, cities, and the Church.

Directory The centrist republican regime in France between 1795 and 1799; characterized by a weak executive, political polarization, and instability.

Divine Comedy Written by Dante, a medieval poem of personal spiritual exploration.

divine right of kings The belief that a monarch's powers derived directly from God, and thus that treason was a kind of blasphemy.

Doctrine of Petrine Succession The traditional Catholic (and medieval) view that Jesus himself endowed the apostle Peter with supreme responsibility for his church.

doctrine of survivals A term first employed by the anthropologist Edward Tyler (1832–1917) to refer to vertigial cultural phenomena from the past that continue to survive even though they have lost their utility.

Dorian Greeks Last wave of Greeks to immigrate, speaking the Doric dialect.

dynasty A family, usually of rulers, that maintains its authority from generation to generation.

East India Co. (British) A corporation that initially traded with native groups in India but eventually exercised an oppressive colonial dominance over Indian affairs.

enclosure The act of consolidating and fencing in land used in open-field agriculture or village common land.

Entente Powers Name of the members of the Triple Entente of 1907—Britain, France, and Russia—which expanded during World War I to include Belgium, Serbia, Greece, Italy, Romania, the Soviet Union, and the United States.

entrepreneur A person who organizes and assumes risk in a business venture in hopes of making a profit.

Epicureans Followers of the philosopher Epicurus who taught that everything is made of atoms (*a-toma* in Greek) and recommended a quiet life free of powerful emotional attachments.

epicycles In traditional astronomy, small circular orbits, revolving around the main circular orbit, that planets follow as they move through the sky.

epistemology Theory of how one obtains and verifies knowledge or truth.

equestrians Originally the Roman cavalry; became the business class of Rome.

Estates In a number of countries in Europe, representative assemblies that were composed of three houses of representatives: the clergy, the nobility, and townsmen.

Estates General An assembly convened by Louis XVI in 1789 that represented the clergy, the nobility, and the Third Estate; once used to win support for royal policy, it had not met since 1614.

ethnic cleansing A coordinated assault to drive members of a specific ethnicity out of a particular region.

Eucharist Also known as communion; Christian sacrament offered during a religious service in which consecrated bread and wine are consumed in celebration of the Lord's Last Supper.

eugenics The study of the improvement of the human race through selective breeding to eradicate less desirable traits in society. An extrapolation from the work of Charles Darwin, it was popularized by his cousin Francis Galton (1821–1911), in the nineteenth century.

Eurocommunism An alternative program for Western Europeans who disagreed with Soviet policies (particularly the invasion of Czechoslovakia) in Eastern Europe.

evolution The process by which species develop through the natural selection of traits best adapted to the environment.

existentialism A twentieth-century philosophy asserting that individuals are responsible for their own values and meanings in an indifferent universe.

famine Period of severe food scarcity due to too much or too little rainfall.

fascism A philosophy or system of government that advocates a dictatorship of the extreme right together with an ideology of belligerent nationalism.

fealty An oath, often accompanying the oath of homage, in which the vassal swears to uphold his homage.

feudalism An economic, political, and social organization of medieval Europe. Land was held by vassals from more powerful overlords in exchange for military and other services.

fief Land given to a vassal from his lord in exchange for specified terms of service; sometimes called benefice.

"Final Solution" Based on Nazi theories of racial inferiority, the systematic extermination of Jews in German-occupied Europe in massacres and death camps like Auschwitz from 1941 to 1945. Also known as the Holocaust or the Shoah.

Five-Year Plans Plans for the rapid, massive industrialization of the nation under the direction of the state initiated by the Soviet Union in the late 1920s.

forms In the thought of Plato, perfect models of all things; any object we see in life is only an imperfect imitation of the object's form (in Greek, *idea*, meaning something that can be seen).

Franco-Prussian War The conflict from 1870 to 1871 that led to the unification of Germany and (indirectly) to the creation of the French Third Republic; signaled the rise of Germany as a military power.

Frankfurt Parliament The assembly elected in 1848 to unify the various states of Germany under a new liberal constitution and a single monarch; it was dissolved in 1849 when Prussia spurned its projects.

Freikorps German postwar paramilitary groups, consisting mainly of war veterans, employed by both the new republican government and especially by far-right political movements such as the Nazis; literally "volunteer troops."

"general will" Rousseau's idealized concept of popular consensus, under which individual interests are subordinated to the public good.

gentry Owners of significant country estates in England, forming a distinct social group immediately below the nobility.

glasnost A Soviet policy under Mikhail Gorbachev permitting a more open discussion of political and social issues and freer dissemination of news and information.

Golden Horde The capital of a division of the Mongol Empire at Sarai, on the lower Volga River.

Gothic Style of Western European architecture and art that developed in the twelfth century; the style is characterized by vaulting and pointed arches.

Great Schism Major split of the Church in the period of 1378–1417, in which two, and later three, popes fought over the rule of the Church.

Greek Orthodox Church Modern term for the Eastern Orthodox Church, whose main departure from Catholicism is their belief that, in the Holy Trinity, the Holy Spirit proceeds only from the father.

guerillas In Spain during the Napoleonic occupation, groups of irregular fighters who harassed French troops, restricted access to supplies, and punished collaborators; a pioneering model for modern guerrilla warfare.

guilds Associations formed by merchants and master artisans to defend and promote their interests and to regulate the quality of the goods they produced and sold.

Hanseatic League Association of northern European trading cities that by the fourteenth century had imposed a monopoly over cities trading in the Baltic and North Seas.

heavy-wheeled plow A heavy, powerful plow that cut more deeply into the ground, forming furrows that drained excess water. It permitted cultivation of heavier river valley soils.

Hellenistic Age In Greek history, the period 323–330 B.C.

helots Publicly owned slaves in Sparta.

heresy Any belief contrary to church dogma; from Greek *hairesis*, "choice."

hieroglyphs "Sacred carvings"; Egyptian style of writing using pictures.

hijra Muhammad's migration from Mecca to Medina in 622; it marks the beginning of the Islamic calendar.

homage An oath of allegiance sworn by a vassal to his lord.

home front In the new time of total war during World War I, civilians—mostly women and men ineligible for military duty—remaining at home assumed a primary role in the national economy; their continued efforts were held up as indispensable to the war being fought on the military front.

Homo erectus "Erect human being"; predecessor of the modern human species *Homo sapiens.*

Humanism An intellectual movement of the Renaissance that emphasized the importance of having the ability to read, understand, and appreciate the writings of the ancient world.

Hundred Years' War War between France and England fought in the fourteenth and fifteenth centuries. Allegedly sparked by a dispute over French royal succession.

Hussites Followers of Hus, the Bohemian priest whose practices attempted to reduce the distinction between priest and worshippers.

iconoclasm In the Byzantine Empire, a rejection of religious icons or pictures of Jesus, Mary, and the saints that led to the destruction of a number of these religious images.

imperium Power of command held by Roman officers.

Impressionists A group of artists who conveyed subjective experiences by capturing the effects of light and color on canvas.

induction Starting with observation, the logical process by which one moves to general principles.

indulgences Grants to sinners by the Roman Catholic Church that reduce time for their souls in purgatory before they can ascend to heaven.

Inquisition A special papal court instituted by Pope Gregory IX for the purpose of rooting out heresy.

intendants French officials who ruled the country's provinces as direct representatives of the king.

Investiture Controversy Conflict between the German emperor and the pope over who had the authority to appoint bishops and "invest" them with their spiritual symbols of office, the ring and the staff.

Islam Strong monotheistic religion founded by Muhammad.

itinerant justices English justices who traveled and heard both criminal and civil pleas. In both cases, they relied on the testimony of a jury.

iurisprudentes* or *iurisconsulti Jurists or advisers in the Roman legal system whose opinions shaped laws.

ius civile "Civil law," or law relating to Roman citizens.

ius gentium "Law of the nations"; Roman law as applied to noncitizens or to all cultures.

Jacobin Club An influential political club whose leaders propelled the French Revolution toward a democratic republic and supported the use of severe repression against the Revolution's enemies.

Jacquerie French peasant revolt in 1358.

jingoism Attitude of extreme and belligerent patriotism often used to gain popular support for war and other political causes.

Julio-Claudians Dynasty of related rulers from 27 B.C. to A.D. 68 in Rome.

July Monarchy The liberal constitutional monarchy established in France from 1830 to 1848, in which the House of Orléans replaced the Bourbons; its modest reforms benefited most the wealthy middle class.

June Days An uprising in Paris in 1848 by radicals and workers that was brutally suppressed by government forces of France's new republic; the event symbolized the conflict between liberal democracy and working-class militancy.

Junkers Prussian aristocrats whose large estates and tradition of military and bureaucratic service ensured their dominance within the Prussian state.

justification by faith A central tenet of Luther's theology: belief that one is saved through the grace of God rather than good deeds.

Justinian's Code Known as the *Corpus Iuris Civilis,* this was the codification of Roman law undertaken by the Byzantine Emperor Justinian in 528.

Keynesian economics Economic theories and programs ascribed to John M. Keynes and his followers. Keynes argued against a totally laissez-faire economy, urging governments to minimize the effects of boom-and-bust economic cycles by manipulating interest rates and employment (through public works projects).

Koran The Muslim holy book that contains the prophecies Allah revealed to Muhammad; it was written between 651 and 652.

kyrios Greek, roughly "master"—for example, head of a family; used for Christian God.

laissez-faire The theory in which individual self-interest and free markets, rather than state regulation or guild protection, stimulate economic progress.

"last decree" *Senatus consultum ultimum,* "final resolution of the Senate"; an instruction to a consul to "see that the state suffers no harm"; a declaration of martial law, first used in 121 B.C. in Rome.

latifundia Large plantations in the Roman world, worked mainly by slaves.

League of Nations International organization created in the wake of the end of World War I and located in Geneva; the forerunner to the modern-day United Nations.

legion Main unit of the Roman army, in principle 6,000 men.

levée en masse A military draft by the French National Convention in August 1793 of unmarried men between the ages of eighteen and twenty-five that recruited about 300,000 new soldiers.

Linear B Script used on Crete, as well as in Greece, to write the early form of Greek.

Lollards Followers of Wycliffe, a vocal dissenter of the church's leadership. This group became an underground rural movement.

Lyceum School established by Aristotle, meeting in and taking its name from a grove in Athens.

Maastricht Treaty Changed the name of the European Community (EC) to the European Union (EU) in 1992. It also enlarged the powers of its parliament and called for a coordinated foreign policy and a common European currency by 1999.

maat Egyptian concept of right order.

Magna Carta "The Great Charter"; English royal charter of liberties granted by King John in 1215. Intended to settle disputes over the rights and privileges of England's nobility.

Magyars The Hungarian-speaking population of the Hapsburg Empire who began to push for Hungary's independence in the 1840s.

Mannerism Art style that emerged in the sixteenth century in response to the serenity and idealization of the High Renaissance. Mannerism is characterized by distorted, esoteric imagery and a sense of artificiality.

manor An estate held by the lord that included land, the people on the land, and a village, usually with a mill. A fief might contain a number of manors or sometimes just part of one.

manorialism An agricultural, legal, and social organization of land, including a nucleated village, large fields for agriculture, and serfs to work the land.

Marxism The political philosophy of Karl Marx, based on the premise that economic conditions determine the nature of society. Marxists advocate the overthrow of capitalism, which they believe will lead to the establishment of a classless society.

memsahib A term of respect used by Indians to address female social superiors. Used in the nineteenth century to refer to British women in colonial India, the term came to connote the blatant ethnocentrism and spoiled behavior associated with these women.

mendicant Orders of religious men, followers of Sts. Dominic and Francis of Assisi, who preached among the poor townsmen and lived a life of begging.

mercantilism The belief that the amount of wealth in the world was fixed, and that a nation should try to gain as much as it could at the expense of other nations, either by accumulating more gold or, in a more sophisticated version, by improving its balance of trade— that is, by exporting more than it imported. This doctrine led to some governmental regulation of commerce in a number of countries in the seventeenth and eighteenth centuries.

Mesopotamia "Land between the [Tigris and Euphrates] rivers," home of early civilizations.

Messiah In Hebrew, *mashiah:* one anointed by God to rule; title given by Christians to Jesus.

metropole Term used to describe European countries in the context of the dominant economic and cultural relationships they had with their colonies.

Middle Passage The harsh voyage of slaving ships from Africa to the Americas during which an average of 10 percent of the slaves perished.

Minoan Name for civilization on Crete, derived from legendary King Minos.

monasticism Practice of withdrawing from daily life to devote oneself to prayer in isolated communities.

Muslims Those who submit to the will of Allah. In Western Europe, often referred to as Saracens.

nationalism A social and political outlook insisting that the state should embody a national community united by some or all of the following: history, ethnicity, religion, common culture, and language.

nationalization State takeover of privately owned businesses; used in fascist Italy and the Soviet Union, but also in postwar Britain and France, to promote greater economic efficiency and social justice.

natural history The science of the earth's development accomplished through the study of geology, zoology, and botany.

natural rights Liberties that should be common to all people by virtue of their nature as human beings; one basis for the French Declaration of the Rights of Man and Citizen of 1789.

natural selection A central feature of Charles Darwin's (1809–1882) theory of evolution that suggests that only organisms best adapted to their environment survive and transmit their genes to succeeding generations, whereas those less adapted are eliminated.

Nazism The body of political and economic doctrines put into effect by the National Socialist German Workers' party in the Third German Reich. A fascist form of government based on state control of all industry, predominance of groups assumed to be racially superior, and supremacy of the Führer.

Neoclassicism A style of art and poetry inspired by themes from antiquity and its conceptions of form and beauty.

Neolithic Age New Stone Age; date of beginning of agriculture, about 11,000 B.C.

Neoplatonism Influential school of thought during the Renaissance, based on Plato's belief that truth lay in essential but hidden forms.

Neostoicism A sixteenth- and seventeenth-century school of philosophy dedicated to the revival of moral values, such as calmness, self-discipline, and steadfastness, first advanced by the Stoics in ancient Greece and Rome.

New Economic Policy (NEP) Lenin's compromise on economic and social policy for the USSR during the 1920s.

New World Name given to the Americas by sixteenth-century explorers and settlers.

Nicene Creed Declaration made at Nicaea in 325 that Jesus was coeternal with God.

Nominalists Individuals who subscribed to a school of thought in medieval Europe that rejected abstractions as the subject matter of philosophy and focused instead on one's experience of individual, distinct beings and objects.

North Atlantic Treaty Organization (NATO) Created in 1949 to coordinate military forces from the United States, Canada, and ten Western European nations in response to perceived Soviet threats in Europe.

notables Locally prominent and wealthy individuals whose support for Napoleon and subsequent French governments was encouraged by state recognition and honors.

novus homo A "new man"; in Roman politics, a man elected consul with no ancestor who had held this office.

October Manifesto Declaration by the tsar of Russia in 1905 that provided Russia with a written constitution and guaranteed freedom of speech and assembly.

oligarchy The rule of a state by a small number, often the Wealthy citizens.

open-field system The division of agricultural land on a manor into three large fields. The lord held land for his direct profit in these, and his serfs also had strips of land in all three fields. The land farmed by each individual was therefore mixed in with, and open to, neighboring plots. The medieval system lasted long after serfdom ended in England and France.

oral tradition Tales, songs, and adages passed on orally that were the core of traditional popular culture.

Osiris Egyptian god of fertility.

ostracism Procedure in ancient Athens by which men could be banished from the city; voting was done by scratching names on *ostraka* (potsherds).

Ottoman Empire Powerful and much feared empire of the Ottoman Turks, whose holdings stretched across the Middle East and Europe; began as a small state in the fourteenth century but soon took over Asia Minor and surrounded Byzantine territory, resulting in the fall of Constantinople in 1453.

Paleolithic Age Old Stone Age; age of stone tools, ending about 11,000 B.C.

papal bulls Papal letters, closed with a lead seal, or *bulla.*

papal *curia* The central bureaucracy of the pope; it served as the central financial and judicial administration and selected the new pope.

parlements The chief law courts in the regions of France; the members, who owned their offices, claimed the right to approve royal legislation for their regions, and sometimes clashed with the king.

Parliament English legislature, consisting of a House of Lords whose members were nobles and bishops, and a House of Commons whose members were elected gentry and townsmen.

patricians Upper class, a small minority, in Rome; the status was heredity.

perestroika A policy of economic and governmental reform instituted by Mikhail Gorbachev in the Soviet Union during the mid-1980s.

pharaoh Title of Egyptian kings from the New Kingdom onward.

Pharisees Jewish sect that believed in resurrection and accepted non-Jewish converts.

Philippics Orations by the Athenian politician, Demosthenes, attacking King Philip II of Macedonia; used also to refer to speeches of Cicero against Mark Antony.

philosophes A group of French intellectuals who used rational inquiry to advocate intellectual and religious freedom and a variety of practical reforms.

plebeians The great mass of Roman citizens; they were not blocked from holding office.

polis Especially in classical Greece, a city that was also an independent state, not sharing citizenship with any other state.

Politburo The principal policy-making and executive committee of the Russian Communist party.

postmodernism A later twentieth-century approach to the arts stressing relativism and multiple interpretations.

predestination The belief that God has preordained whether a person will be saved or damned, and nothing can be done to reverse this fate.

prefect The chief administrator in each French department appointed by the central government; a hallmark of centralization established by Napoleon but lasting into the twentieth century.

Principate The Roman Empire from Augustus down to Diocletian, so named from the republican term *princeps,* roughly "first citizen."

protoindustrialization Heavy concentrations of pre-factory manufacturing, in which urban merchants employed rural households to produce goods, especially textiles.

psychoanalysis A method of analyzing psychic phenomena and treating emotional disorders that involves treatment sessions during which the patient is encouraged to talk freely about personal experiences and especially about early childhood and dreams.

public sphere Forums outside the royal court, such as newspapers, salons, and academies, in which the educated public could participate in debate on the issues of the day.

Puritans Devout Protestants who believed in a stern moral code and rejected all hints of Catholic ritual or organization.

raj British rule in India, which had spread through most of the subcontinent by the mid-nineteenth century.

realism The depiction of ordinary, everyday subjects in art and literature as part of a broader social commentary; a reaction against the themes and styles typical of Romanticism or of academic painting.

reasons of state Often known by its French name, *raison d'état*, the doctrine that, especially in foreign affairs, a state is bound by no restraint when pursuing its interests.

Reformation The period of major change and variance in the fundamental beliefs of Christianity. The demands of the faithful varied and intensified throughout Western Europe, making it difficult for the Roman Catholic Church alone to accommodate all of them.

relativity Einstein's theory that all aspects of the physical universe must be defined in relative terms.

Renaissance Rebirth of classical culture that occurred in Italy after 1350.

Restorations Attempts by the powers in Europe to restore the dynasties and monarchical institutions (including the Bourbons in France) disrupted by the revolutionary and Napoleonic upheavals.

risorgimento A term meaning "resurgence," used to describe the liberal nationalist movement that led to the unification of Italy by 1870.

Roman Catholic "Universal" church; Christian church headed by a pope.

Romanesque Style of Western European architecture and art developed after 1000; the style is characterized by rounded arches, massive walls, and relatively simple ornamentation.

Romanticism An artistic movement that rejected classical aesthetic forms and norms, and which emphasized personal experience, emotion, or spirituality.

sacrament Means by which God distributes grace. Luther retained only baptism and the Eucharist.

Sadducees Conservative Jewish sect that did not believe in angels or resurrection because such teachings were not found in the five books of the Old Testament, known as the Pentateuch.

sagas Adventure stories told in prose that cover the Viking period to about 1000, when Iceland converted to Christianity.

Saint-Simonians A nineteenth-century movement that called for the reorganization of society by scientists and industrialists to achieve planned progress and prosperity.

salons Social gatherings, usually organized by elite women, that sought to promote discussion of Enlightenment ideas.

sans-culottes Parisian militants, mainly artisans and shopkeepers, who called for repression of counter-revolutionaries, price controls, and direct democracy; helped bring the Jacobins to power in 1793.

satyr play Comic, often vulgar, play performed after an ancient Greek tragedy.

Schlieffen Plan In World War I, the German military plan specifying how the army would fight a two-front war: Germany would invade Belgium and the Netherlands on its way to France, score a quick defeat in the west, and then concentrate its forces against Russia in the east.

Scholasticism A form of argument, or dialectic, developed in the Middle Ages, particularly with Abelard and Thomas Aquinas.

Scientific Revolution The succession of discoveries and the transformation of the investigation of nature that was brought about in the fields of astronomy, physics, and anatomy during the sixteenth and seventeenth centuries.

Second Empire The reign of Napoleon III in France from 1852 to 1870; while authoritarian in nature, the regime fostered popular support through social programs and nationalist sentiment.

second front In World War II, the establishment of an Allied front in Western Europe to match the Russians battling the Nazis in the East; after several delays, the Allies launched the second front with the Normandy invasion in June 1944.

seigneurialism A system prevalent in Western Europe by which peasants owed various fees and dues to the local lord even if the peasants owned their land.

serf or villein Peasant who was personally free, but bound to the lord of a manor and worked the land on the manor.

serfdom A feudal system of agricultural exploitation in which peasants were bound to their lord's estate and owed him forced labor.

sexagesimal System of mathematics based on the number 60.

sexual selection The theory that the traits that increase an organism's (typically male's) success in mating and transmitting its genes are selected and perpetuated. Differs from natural selection, which focuses only on traits that influence survival.

shell shock New psychological diagnosis applied to those soldiers exhibiting signs of psychic distress during the First World War, thought to be caused by the near-constant shelling experienced in the trenches.

sister republics States and territories that fell under French control during the Directory and were reconstituted as republics in collaboration with native revolutionaries.

Skepticism Philosophy that questions whether human beings can ever achieve certain knowledge.

Slavophiles Russian intellectuals who opposed Westernization and saw Russia's unique institutions and culture as superior; some supported autocracy but also favored emancipation of the serfs.

social Darwinism The application of Darwin's scientific theory of evolution to society, often in the service of reactionary and even racist ideas.

social welfare State-run programs for social security, education, medical care, and family benefits.

Sophists Teachers of rhetoric in classical Greece, especially in Athens.

Stalingrad The place where Russians fought ferociously, street by street, to halt the German advance in 1942; marked the turning point of the war on the Eastern front.

state of nature Description in political theory of the condition of humanity before the creation of governments.

steam engine A machine patented in 1782 that converted steam into mechanical energy; provided a cheap and flexible source of power critical for early industrialization.

Stoics Followers, in Greece and Rome, of thought of Zeno, who taught that the wise man leads a life of moderation, unmoved by joy or grief, and stands by his duty according to natural law.

strategic bombing A military doctrine of aerial bombardment of populated and industrial areas; intended to destroy morale and the industrial capacity to fight. Initiated by the Germans on Britain, but most fully used by the British and U.S. air forces.

Sturm und Drang A literary and artistic movement in Germany that emphasized strong artistic emotion; a precursor of the Romantic movement.

subinfeudation The grant of a fief by a vassal to a subordinate who becomes his vassal.

Sunni-Shiite schism Division within the Islamic religion over who should rule after Mohammad's death.

syndicalism A movement in which worker's organizations attempted to destroy bourgeois capitalism and gain control of industry by general strikes.

Talmud General body of Jewish tradition.

tariff A duty or custom fee imposed on imports, often to protect local agriculture or industry from competition.

Tetrarchy Rule of four co-emperors of Rome under Diocletian.

Thermidorian reaction The period between the fall of Robespierre and the establishment of the Directory during which the Convention dismantled the Terror and attacked egalitarian politics.

thermodynamics The study of the relationships between heat and other forms of energy; becomes one of the bases of nineteenth-century physics.

three-field system Agricultural system in which two-thirds of the land was cultivated on a rotating basis; it replaced the two-field system and resulted in increased productivity.

Tory English political party committed to a strong monarch and a strong Anglican Church.

total war Unprecedented type of warfare in which all segments of society, civilians and soldiers, men and women, were mobilized in the hope of ensuring victory.

totalitarianism A twentieth-century form of authoritarian government using force, technology, and bureaucracy to effect rule by a single party and controlling most aspects of the lives of the population.

tragedy The supreme dramatic form in ancient Greece, usually treating a mythological theme and leading to catastrophe for some of the characters.

transubstantiation Belief that bread and wine are transformed into the body and blood of Christ during the Eucharist.

Treaty of Paris (1763) Peace treaty ending the British and French war for empire in which France surrendered Canada to the British and lost its foothold in India.

Treaty of Tordesillas Signed in 1494, the treaty confirmed the pope's division of the world between the Portuguese and Spanish for exploration and conquest. Under its terms, a line was drawn some 1,200 miles west of the Cape Verde Islands, with Portugal granted all lands to the west and Spain granted all lands to the east.

trench warfare Static, defensive type of combat seen mostly on the Western front of World War I, where a war of attrition was fought in a complex system of underground trenches and supply lines.

triangular trade A complex pattern of colonial commerce between the home country (Britain or France) and its colonies in which refined or manufactured goods were exchanged for raw materials or slaves from West Africa.

tribunes Ten Roman plebeians, elected to protect the common people; some of them became powerful political activists.

triremes Greek warship, powered by three banks of oars.

triumvirate "Body of three men," a term applied to two such cabals in the Roman Republic.

trivium and quadrivium School curriculum that became the standard program of study in universities. The trivium comprised the verbal arts (grammar, rhetoric, and logic), while the quadrivium comprised the mathematical arts (arithmetic, astronomy, geometry, and music).

troubadour A writer of vernacular romantic lyrics or tales who enjoyed the patronage of nobles around Europe in the twelfth through fifteenth centuries.

tsar Title adopted by the Russian king; the term was the Slavic equivalent of the Latin term *caesar*.

tyrant In ancient Greek states, a powerful man who ruled in a polis without legal sanction, not necessarily a cruel despot.

ultraroyalists French reactionaries who not only supported divine-right monarchy but called for the return of lands taken from the émigrés during the Revolution.

usury Interest of profit on a loan; it was prohibited by the Church.

Utilitarianism British reform movement that believed that society should be based on "the greatest happiness for the greatest number," and that sound governments could make such calculations.

utopian Having to do with an ideal society, as presented in Sir Thomas More's book *Utopia*, which means "nowhere" in Greek.

vassal A free warrior who places himself under a lord, accepting the terms of loyal service, fighting in times of war, and counseling in times of peace.

Vatican II Vatican council called by Pope John XXIII in 1962. Vatican II made the leadership of the Church more international, directed attention to the concerns of developing nations, and ordered that Masses be conducted in the vernacular instead of Latin.

Vulgate The Latin translation of the Bible in the fourth century, identified with St. Jerome, which became the medieval Church's standard text and was deemed holy in the sixteenth century.

war guilt clause Article 231 of the Treaty of Versailles, specifying that Germany alone was responsible for causing the First World War.

Warsaw Pact The Russian response to NATO; an international military organization established in 1955 that included the Soviet Union and Eastern European communist states.

Weimar Republic Left-liberal German government established after the war, named for the city where German politicians formed the republic; instituted universal suffrage, and wrote a new democratic constitution.

Wergeld Literally, "man-payment"; in Germanic tribes, as a means to prevent feuds, payments given in compensation for crimes committed; the amount of compensation depended on the social rank of the individual.

Whig English political party committed to a strong Parliament and religious toleration.

Yalta Conference In February 1945, the meeting between Roosevelt, Churchill, and Stalin to set the postwar order in Europe. The conference agreed on the creation of the United Nations but was unable to counter future Soviet dominance in Eastern Europe.

Zeus Sky god; the chief god in Greek myth.

ziggurat Terraced tower built of baked brick in Mesopotamia.

Zollverein A customs union established by Prussia among most states in the German Confederation that allowed for free movement of goods; promoted the economic unification of Germany.

Text Credits

Chapter 11

Page 309 From C. Warren Hollister, et al., *Medieval Europe: A Short Sourcebook*, 1992. Reprinted by permission of The McGraw-Hill Companies, Inc. **Page 317** From "Did Women Have a Renaissance?" by Joan Kelly from Renate Bridenthal, Claudia Koonz, and Susan Stuard, *Becoming Visible: Women in European History*, 2nd ed. Copyright © 1987 by Houghton Mifflin Company. Adapted with permission. **Page 325** From G.G. Coulton and Eileen Power (eds.), *The Trial of Jeanne d' Arc*, W. P. Barrett (trans.), Routledge, 1931. Reprinted by permission of Taylor & Francis Books. **Page 332** From Richard Knolles in John J. Saunders (ed.), *The Muslim World on the Eve of Europe's Expansion*, Prentice-Hall, 1966, adapted by Theodore K. Rabb.

Chapter 12

Page 340 Petrarch, *Epistolae Familiares*, 24.8. Passages selected and translated by Theodore K. Rabb. **Page 350** From D. S. Chambers (ed.), *Patrons and Artists in the Italian Renaissance*, London: Macmillan, 1970, pp. 128–130 and 147–148. Reprinted by permission. **Page 362** From Matthew Spinka (ed.), *The Letters of John Hus*, Manchester: University Press, 1972, pp. 195–197.

Chapter 13

Page 371 Adapted from Lucien Febvre and Henri-Jean Martin, *The Coming of the Book: The Impact of Printing 1450–1800*, David Gerald (tr.), London, NLB, 1976, pp. 178–179, 184–185. Reprinted by permission. **Page 375** Translation from the Latin by Theodore K. Rabb of Luther's preface to the 1545 edition of his writings, in Otto Scheel (ed.), *Dokumente zu Luthers Entwicklung*, Tübingen: Mohr, 1929, pp. 191–192. **Page 389** From E. Allison Peers, *The Life of Teresa of Jesus*, London: Sheed & Ward, 1944; New York: Doubleday, 1960, pp. 258–260, 273–274. Reprinted by permission.

Chapter 14

Page 397 Adapted from J. H. Elliott, *Imperial Spain, 1469–1716*, New York, 1964, p. 175. **Page 404** From S. E. Morison, *Admiral of the Ocean Sea: A Life of Christopher Columbus*, Boston: Little, Brown, 1942, pp. 670–671. **Page 404** From Kirkpatrick Sale, *The Conquest of Paradise: Christopher Columbus and the Columbian Legacy*, New York: Knopf, 1990, pp. 209–210, 362.

Chapter 15

Page 450 From Louis André (ed.), *Testament politique* (Editions Robert Laffont, 1947), pp. 347–348 and 352; translated by Theodore K. Rabb. **Page 453** Adapted from J. H. Elliott, *Imperial Spain, 1469–1716*, Edward Arnold, The Hodder Neadling PLC Group, 1964, p. 175.

Chapter 16

Page 465 From Giorgio de Santillana, "Galileo and Kepler on Copernicus", from *The Crime of Galileo*, Chicago: University of Chicago Press, 1955, pp. 11 and 14–15. Reprinted by permission of the University of Chicago Press. **Page 480** From Jan de Vries, *The Economy of Europe in an Age of Crisis, 1600–1750*, Cambridge University Press, 1976, p. 5. Reprinted by permission.

Chapter 17

Page 495 From J. M. Thompson, *Lectures on Foreign History, 1494–1789*, Oxford: Blackwell, 1956, pp. 172–174. **Page 500** From Albert Sorel, *L'Europe et la révolution française*, 3rd ed., vol. 1, Paris, 1893, p. 199, as translated in William F. Church, *The Greatness of Loius XIV: Myth or Reality?* Copyright © 1959 by D.C. Heath and Company. Used with permission. **Page 500** From John C. Rule, "Louis XIV, Roi-Bureaucrate," in Rule (ed.), *Louis XIV and the Craft of Kingship*, Columbus: Ohio State University Press, 1969, pp. 91–92. Reprinted by permission. **Page 520** From John Locke, *The Second Treatise of Civil Government*, Thomas P. Peardon (ed.), Indianapolis: Bobbs-Merrill, 1952, chapter 9, pp. 70–73.

Chapter 18

Page 543 Adapted from Phyllis Dean and W. A. Cole, *British Economic Growth, 1688–1959*, Cambridge University Press, 1964, p. 49. Reprinted by permission. **Page 544** From Philip D. Curtin, *The Atlantic Slave Trade*. © 1969. Reprinted by permission of The University of Wisconsin Press.

Chapter 19

Page 559 From C. A. Macartney (ed.), *The Habsburg and Hohenzollern Dynasties in the 17th and 18th Centuries*, pp. 151 and 155–157. Copyright © 1970 by C. A. Macartney. Reprinted by permission of HarperCollins Publishers. **Page 565** From Sandra M. Gilbert and Susan Gubar (eds.), *The Norton Anthology of Literature by Women: The Tradition in English*, W. W. Norton Co., 1985. Reprinted by permission. **Page 566** From Jean-Jacques Rousseau, *The Social Contract*, Book 1, David Campbell Publishers. Reprinted by permission.

Chapter 20

Page 588 Georges Lefebvre, *The Coming of the French Revolution*. © 1947 Princeton University Press, 1975 renewed PUP. Reprinted by permission of Princeton University Press. **Page 588** From William Doyle, *Origins of the French Revolution*, 1988. Reprinted by permission of Oxford University Press. **Page 594** R. R. Palmer, *The Age of Democratic*

Chapter 21
Page 633 From *Political Constitution of the Spanish Monarchy*, proclaimed in Cadiz, March 19, 1812, (trans. James B. Tueller).
Page 638 From B. Las Cases (ed.), *Mémorial de Sainte-Hélène.*

Volume B Index